How I Tried to Be a Good Person.

Ulli Lust

FANTAGRAPHICS BOOKS

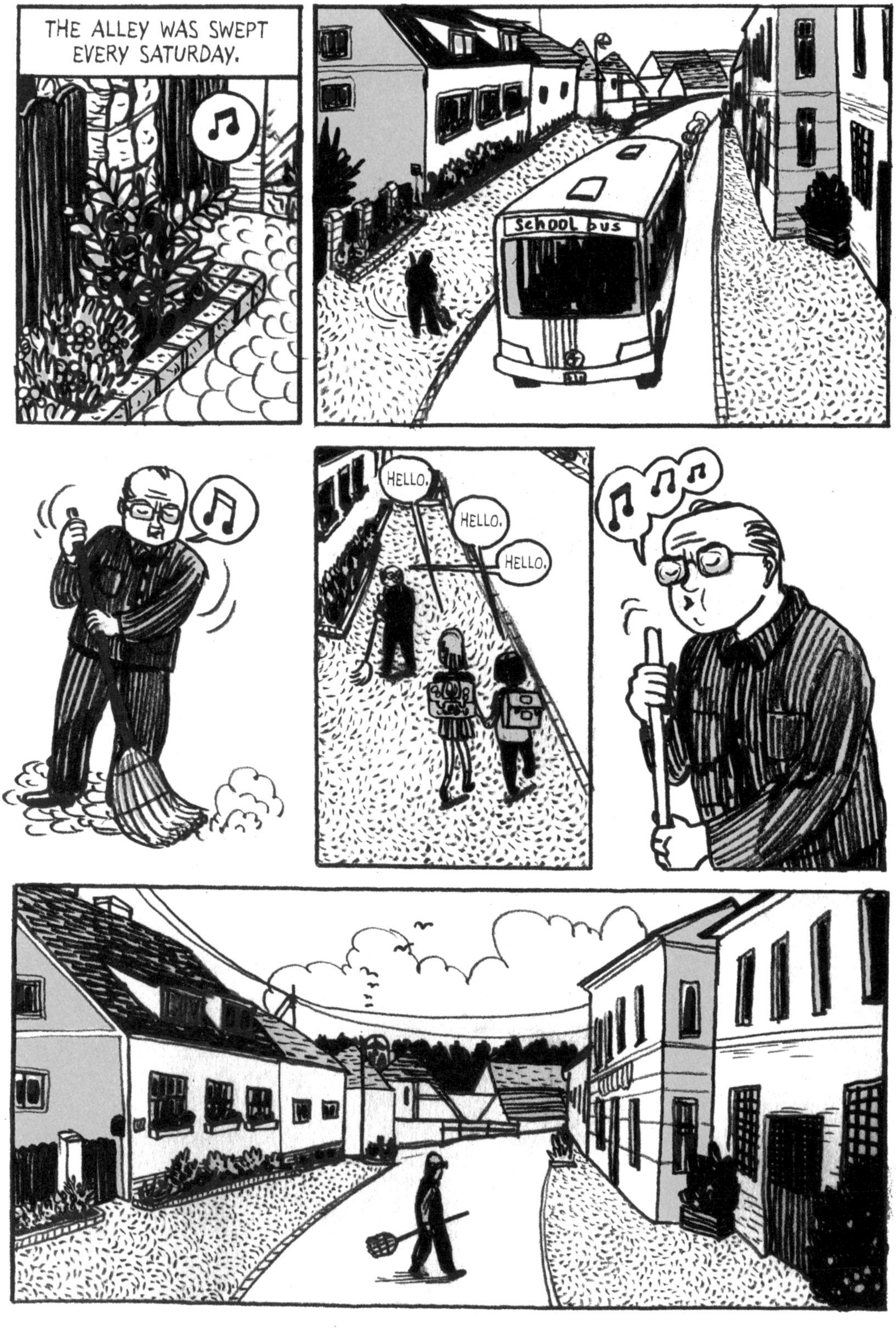
THE ALLEY WAS SWEPT EVERY SATURDAY.
SCHOOL BUS
HELLO.
HELLO.
HELLO.

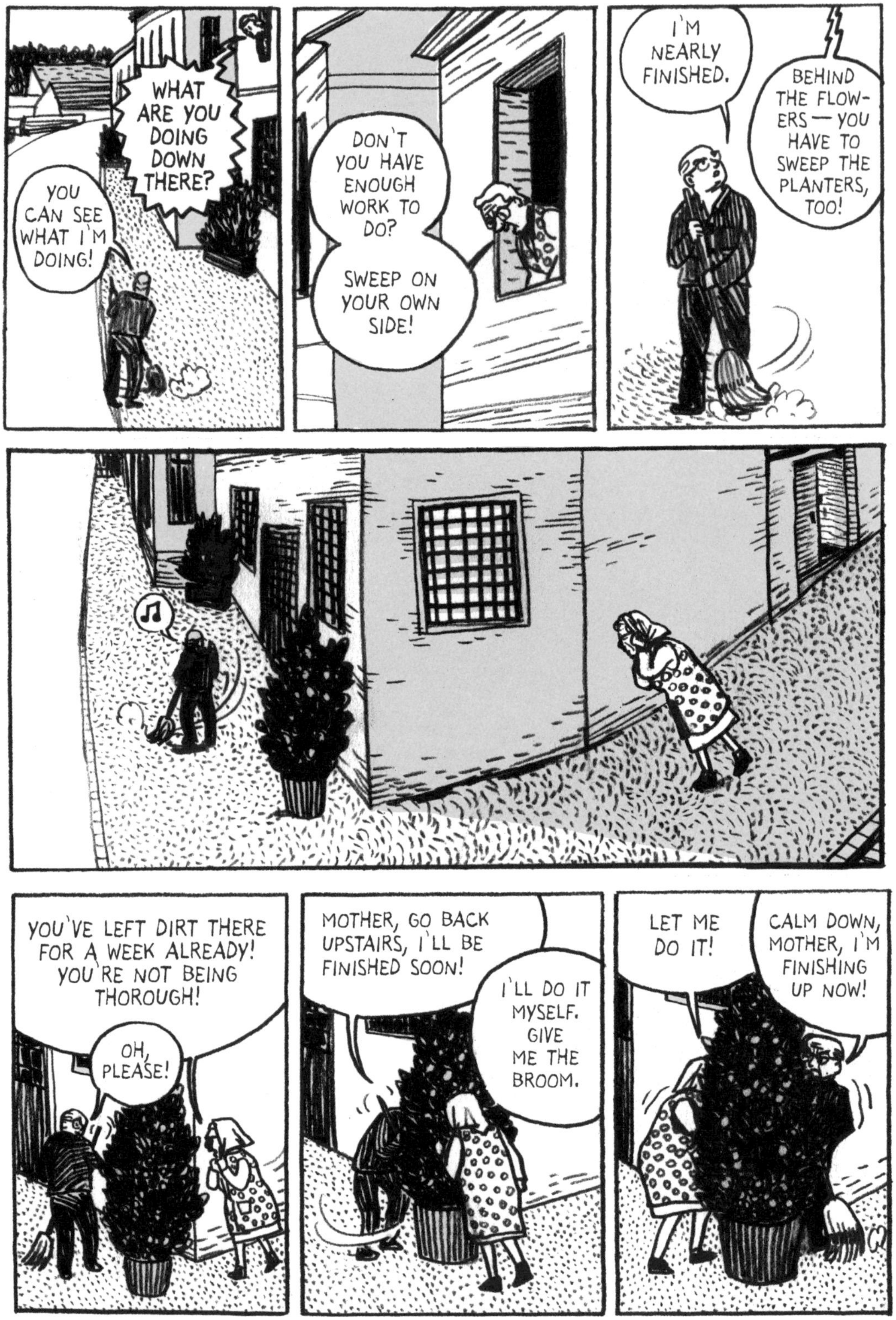
WHAT ARE YOU DOING DOWN THERE?
YOU CAN SEE WHAT I'M DOING!
DON'T YOU HAVE ENOUGH WORK TO DO?
SWEEP ON YOUR OWN SIDE!
I'M NEARLY FINISHED.
BEHIND THE FLOWERS — YOU HAVE TO SWEEP THE PLANTERS, TOO!
YOU'VE LEFT DIRT THERE FOR A WEEK ALREADY! YOU'RE NOT BEING THOROUGH!
OH, PLEASE!
MOTHER, GO BACK UPSTAIRS, I'LL BE FINISHED SOON!
I'LL DO IT MYSELF. GIVE ME THE BROOM.
LET ME DO IT!
CALM DOWN, MOTHER, I'M FINISHING UP NOW!

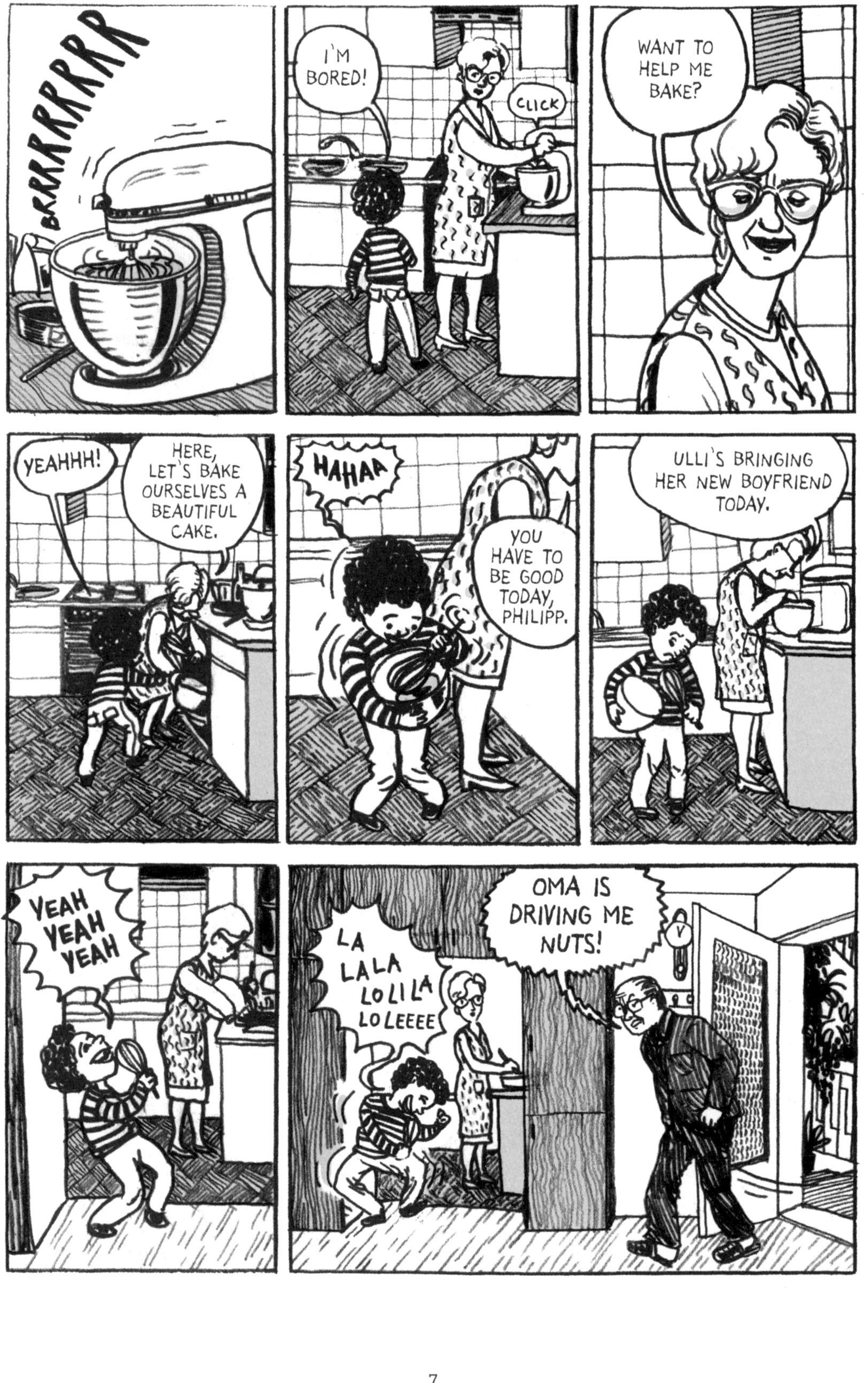
BRRRRRRRRRRR
I'M BORED!
CLICK
WANT TO HELP ME BAKE?
YEAHHH!
HERE, LET'S BAKE OURSELVES A BEAUTIFUL CAKE.
HAHAA
YOU HAVE TO BE GOOD TODAY, PHILIPP.
ULLI'S BRINGING HER NEW BOYFRIEND TODAY.
YEAH YEAH YEAH
LA LALA LOLILA LOLEEEE
OMA IS DRIVING ME NUTS!

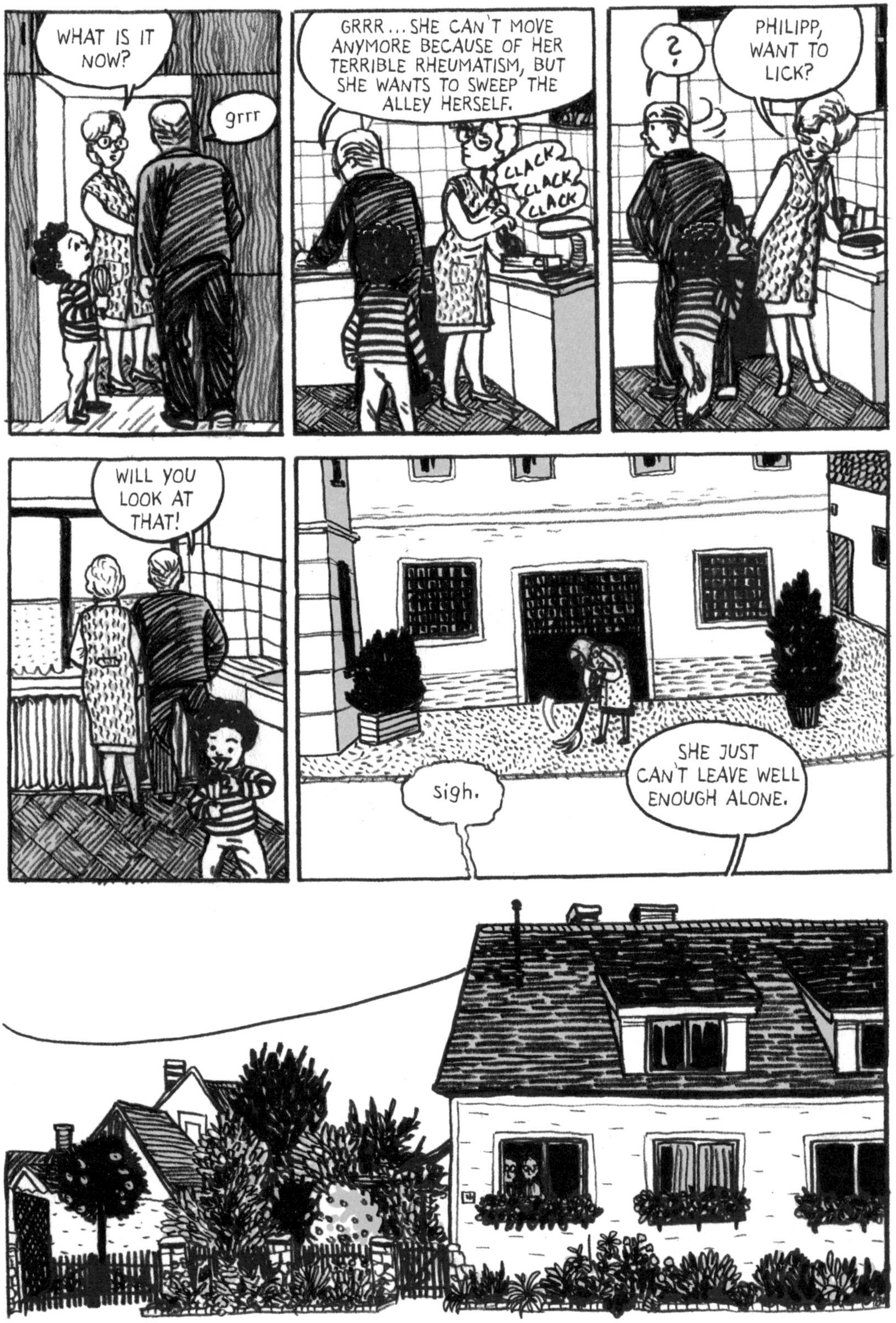
WHAT IS IT NOW?
grrr
GRRR... SHE CAN'T MOVE ANYMORE BECAUSE OF HER TERRIBLE RHEUMATISM, BUT SHE WANTS TO SWEEP THE ALLEY HERSELF.
CLACK CLACK CLACK
?
PHILIPP, WANT TO LICK?
WILL YOU LOOK AT THAT!
sigh.
SHE JUST CAN'T LEAVE WELL ENOUGH ALONE.

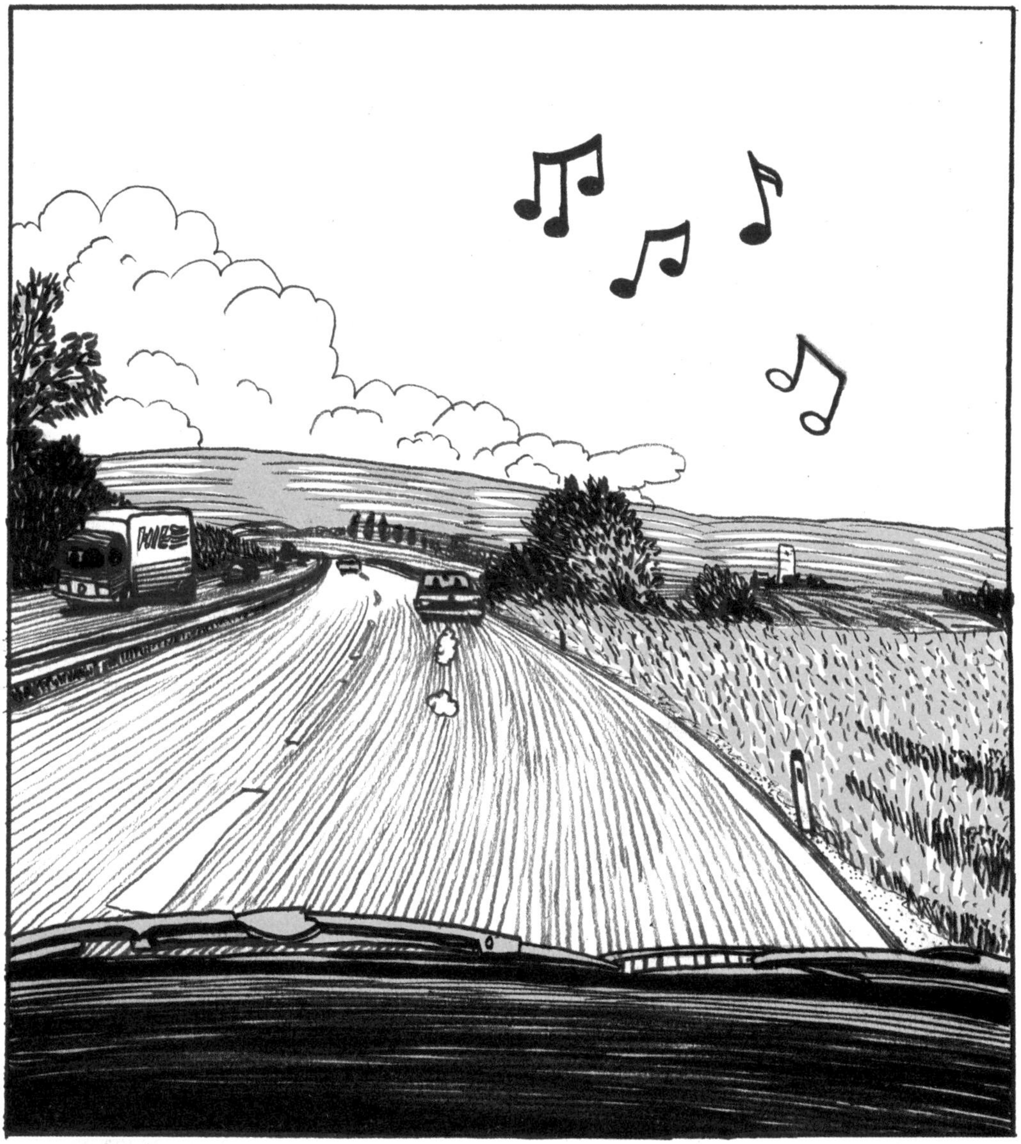

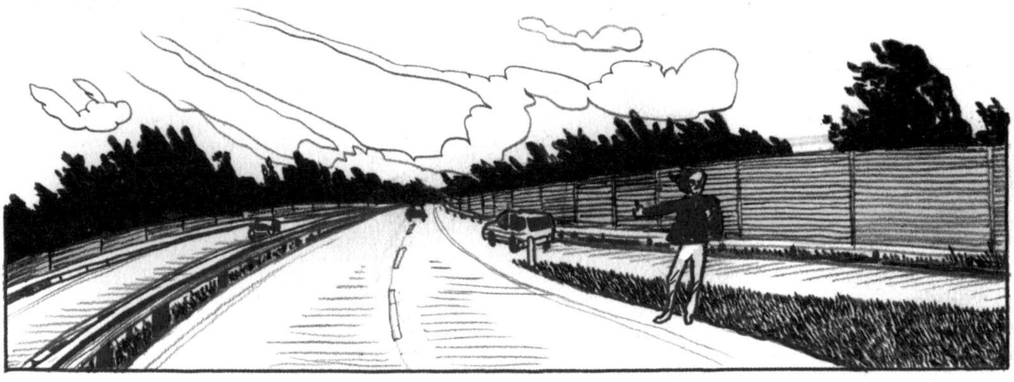

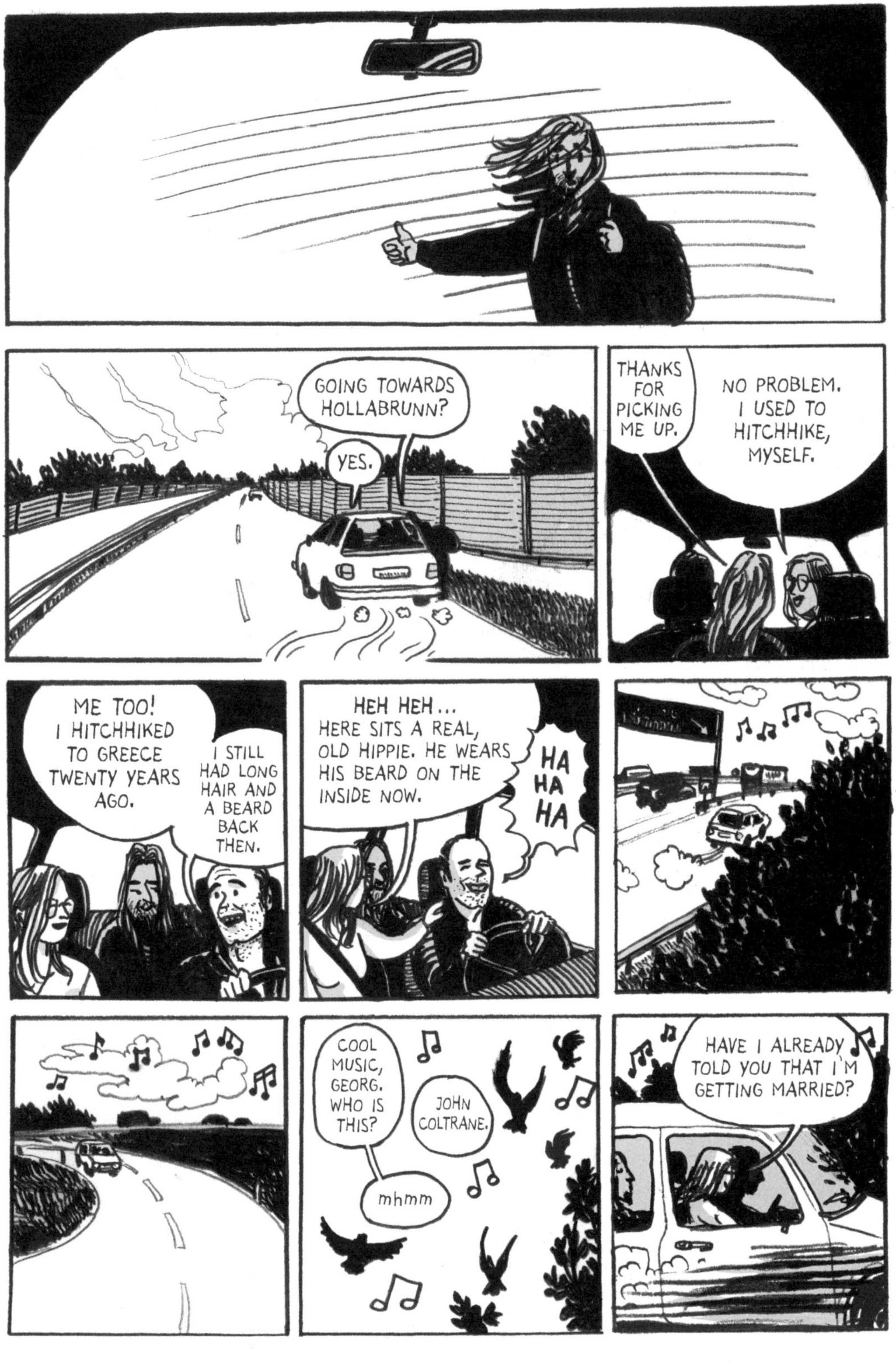
GOING TOWARDS HOLLABRUNN?
YES.
THANKS FOR PICKING ME UP.
NO PROBLEM. I USED TO HITCHHIKE, MYSELF.
ME TOO! I HITCHHIKED TO GREECE TWENTY YEARS AGO.
I STILL HAD LONG HAIR AND A BEARD BACK THEN.
HEH HEH... HERE SITS A REAL, OLD HIPPIE. HE WEARS HIS BEARD ON THE INSIDE NOW.
HA HA HA
COOL MUSIC, GEORG. WHO IS THIS?
JOHN COLTRANE.
mhmm
HAVE I ALREADY TOLD YOU THAT I'M GETTING MARRIED?

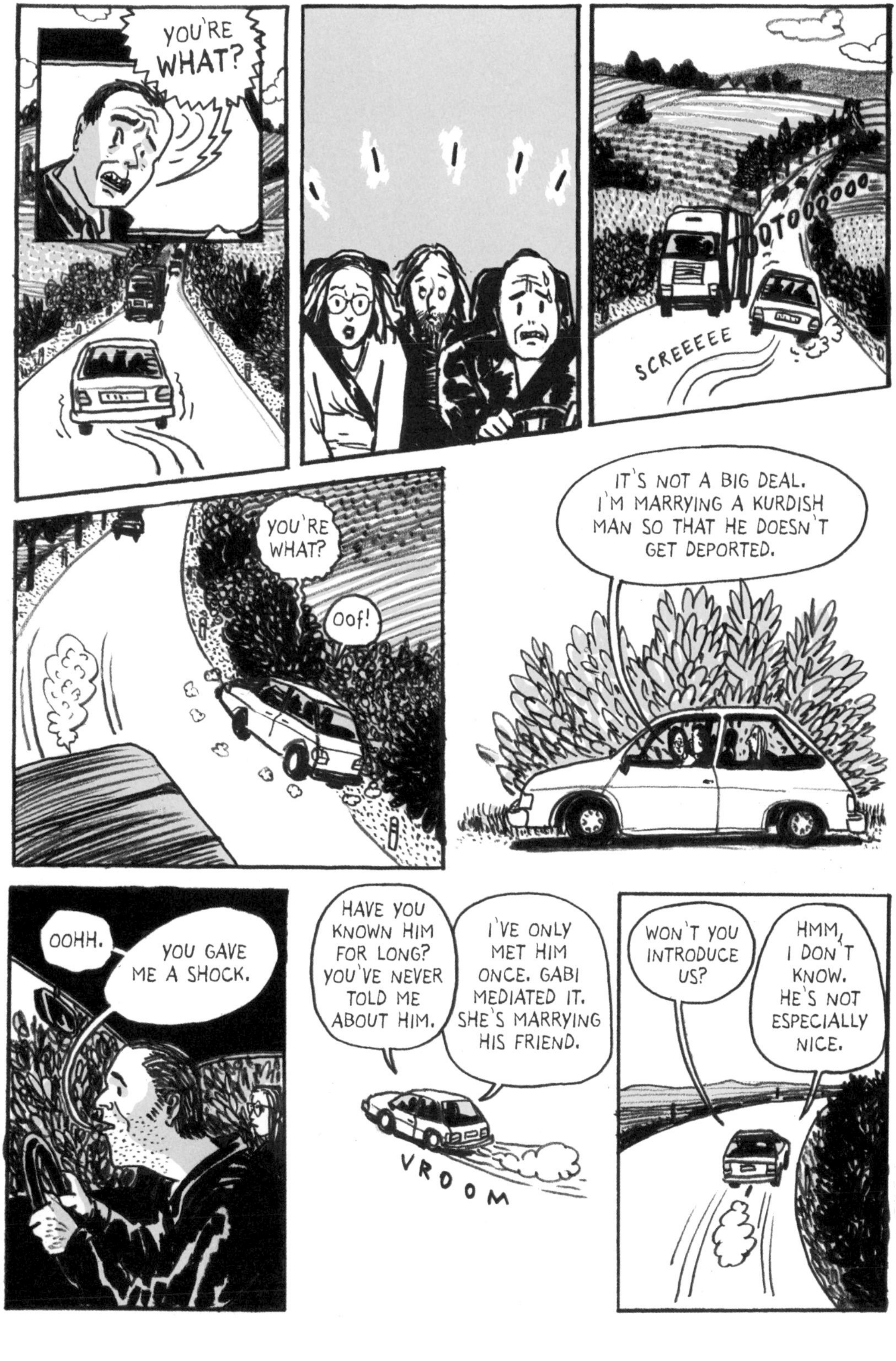
YOU'RE WHAT?
SCREEEEE
TOOOOOOOOO
YOU'RE WHAT?
Oof!
IT'S NOT A BIG DEAL. I'M MARRYING A KURDISH MAN SO THAT HE DOESN'T GET DEPORTED.
OOHH.
YOU GAVE ME A SHOCK.
HAVE YOU KNOWN HIM FOR LONG? YOU'VE NEVER TOLD ME ABOUT HIM.
I'VE ONLY MET HIM ONCE. GABI MEDIATED IT. SHE'S MARRYING HIS FRIEND.
VROOM
WON'T YOU INTRODUCE US?
HMM, I DON'T KNOW. HE'S NOT ESPECIALLY NICE.

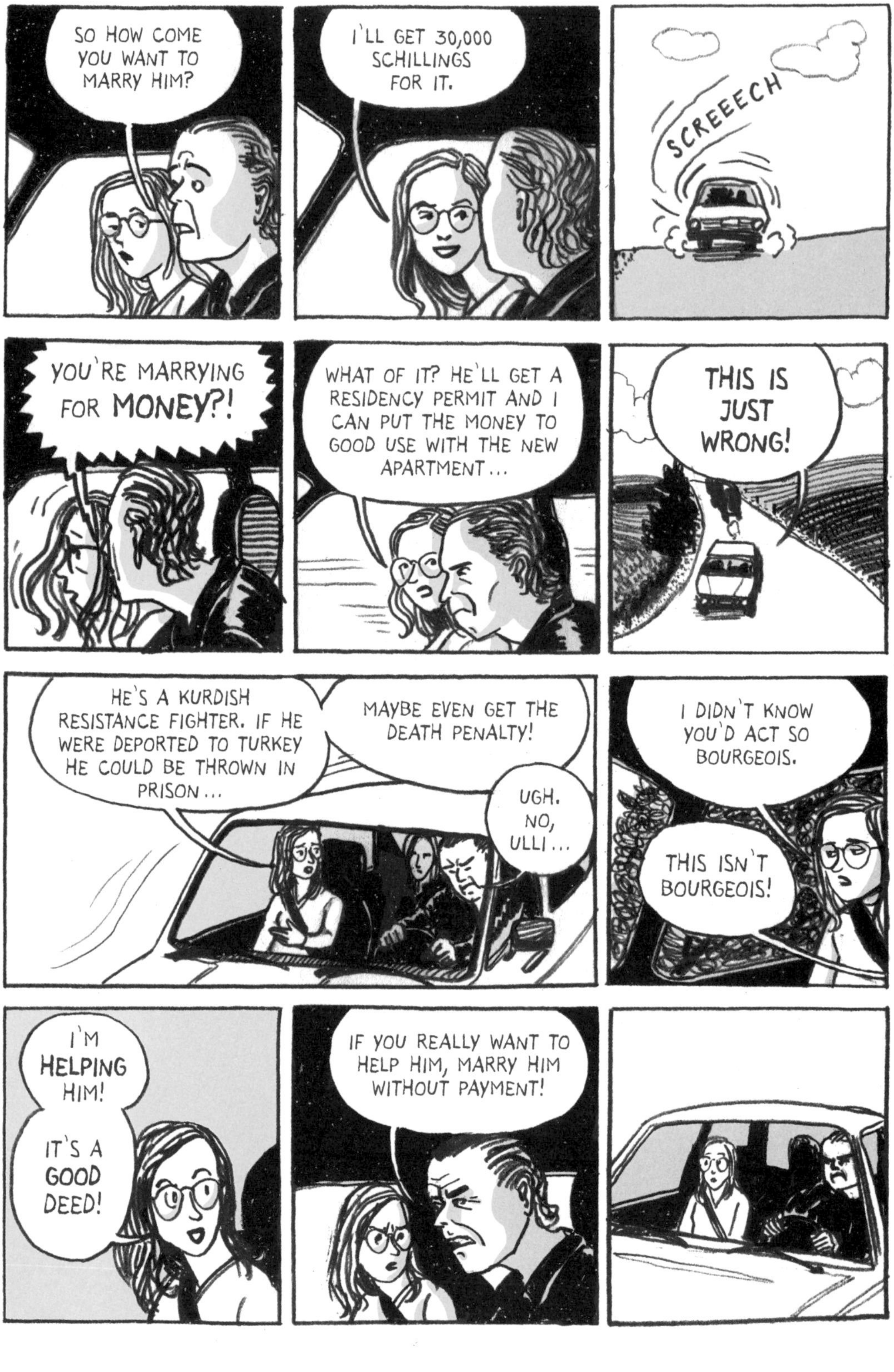
SO HOW COME YOU WANT TO MARRY HIM?
I'LL GET 30,000 SCHILLINGS FOR IT.
SCREEECH
YOU'RE MARRYING FOR **MONEY?!**
WHAT OF IT? HE'LL GET A RESIDENCY PERMIT AND I CAN PUT THE MONEY TO GOOD USE WITH THE NEW APARTMENT...
THIS IS JUST WRONG!
HE'S A KURDISH RESISTANCE FIGHTER. IF HE WERE DEPORTED TO TURKEY HE COULD BE THROWN IN PRISON...
MAYBE EVEN GET THE DEATH PENALTY!
UGH. NO, ULLI...
I DIDN'T KNOW YOU'D ACT SO BOURGEOIS.
THIS ISN'T BOURGEOIS!
I'M **HELPING** HIM!
IT'S A **GOOD** DEED!
IF YOU REALLY WANT TO HELP HIM, MARRY HIM WITHOUT PAYMENT!

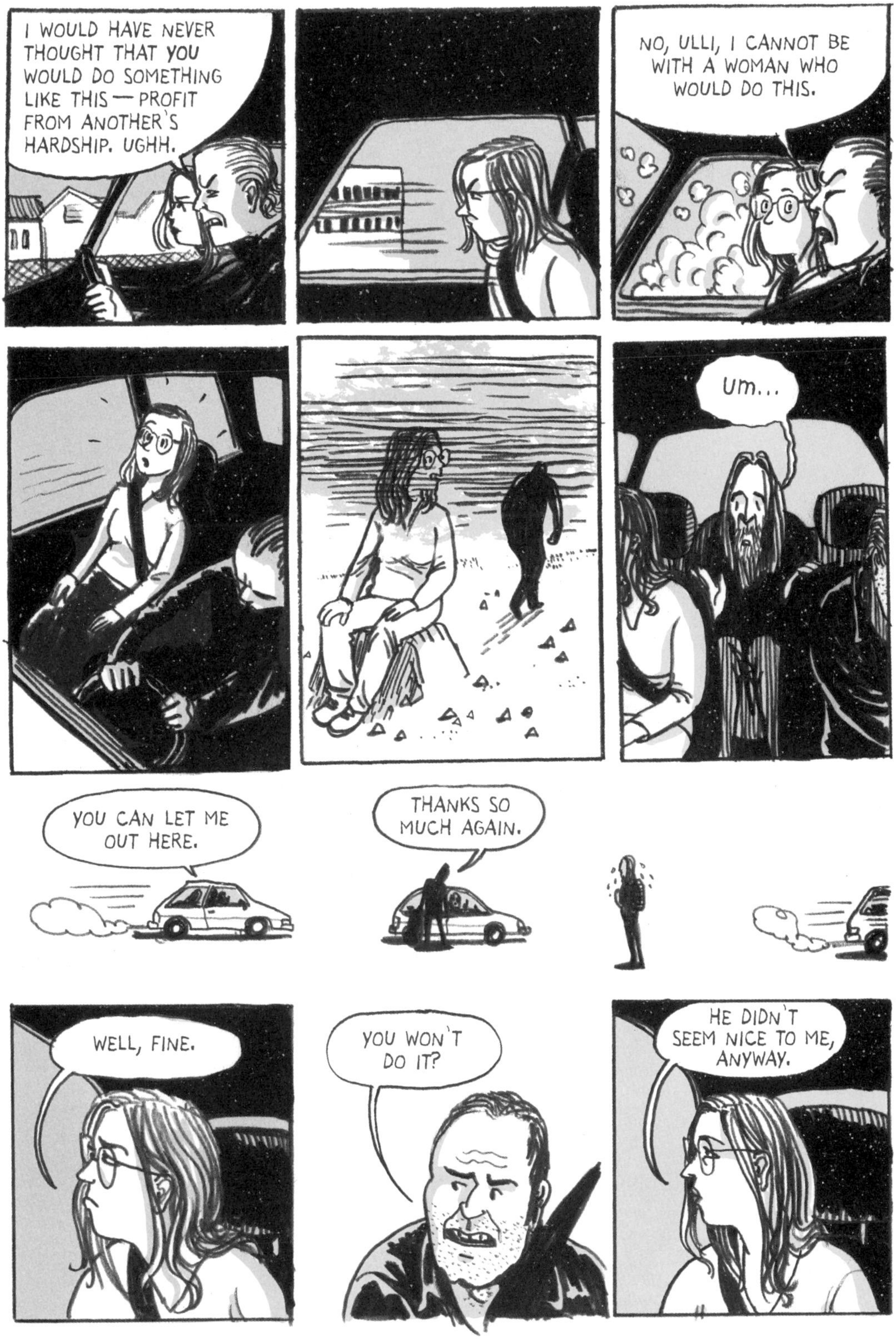
I WOULD HAVE NEVER THOUGHT THAT YOU WOULD DO SOMETHING LIKE THIS — PROFIT FROM ANOTHER'S HARDSHIP. UGHH.
NO, ULLI, I CANNOT BE WITH A WOMAN WHO WOULD DO THIS.
Um...
YOU CAN LET ME OUT HERE.
THANKS SO MUCH AGAIN.
WELL, FINE.
YOU WON'T DO IT?
HE DIDN'T SEEM NICE TO ME, ANYWAY.

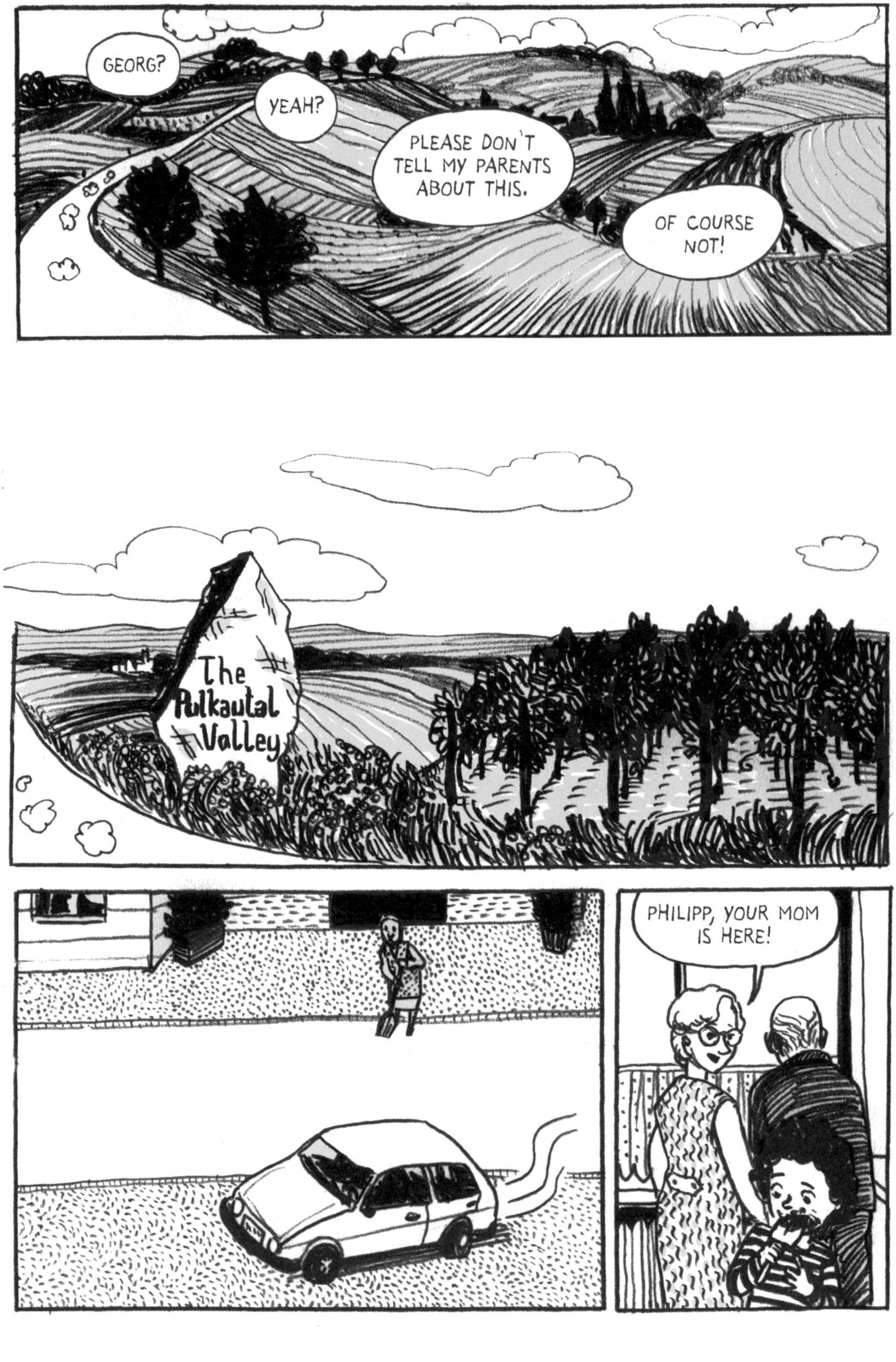
GEORG?
YEAH?
PLEASE DON'T TELL MY PARENTS ABOUT THIS.
OF COURSE NOT!
The Pulkautal Valley
PHILIPP, YOUR MOM IS HERE!

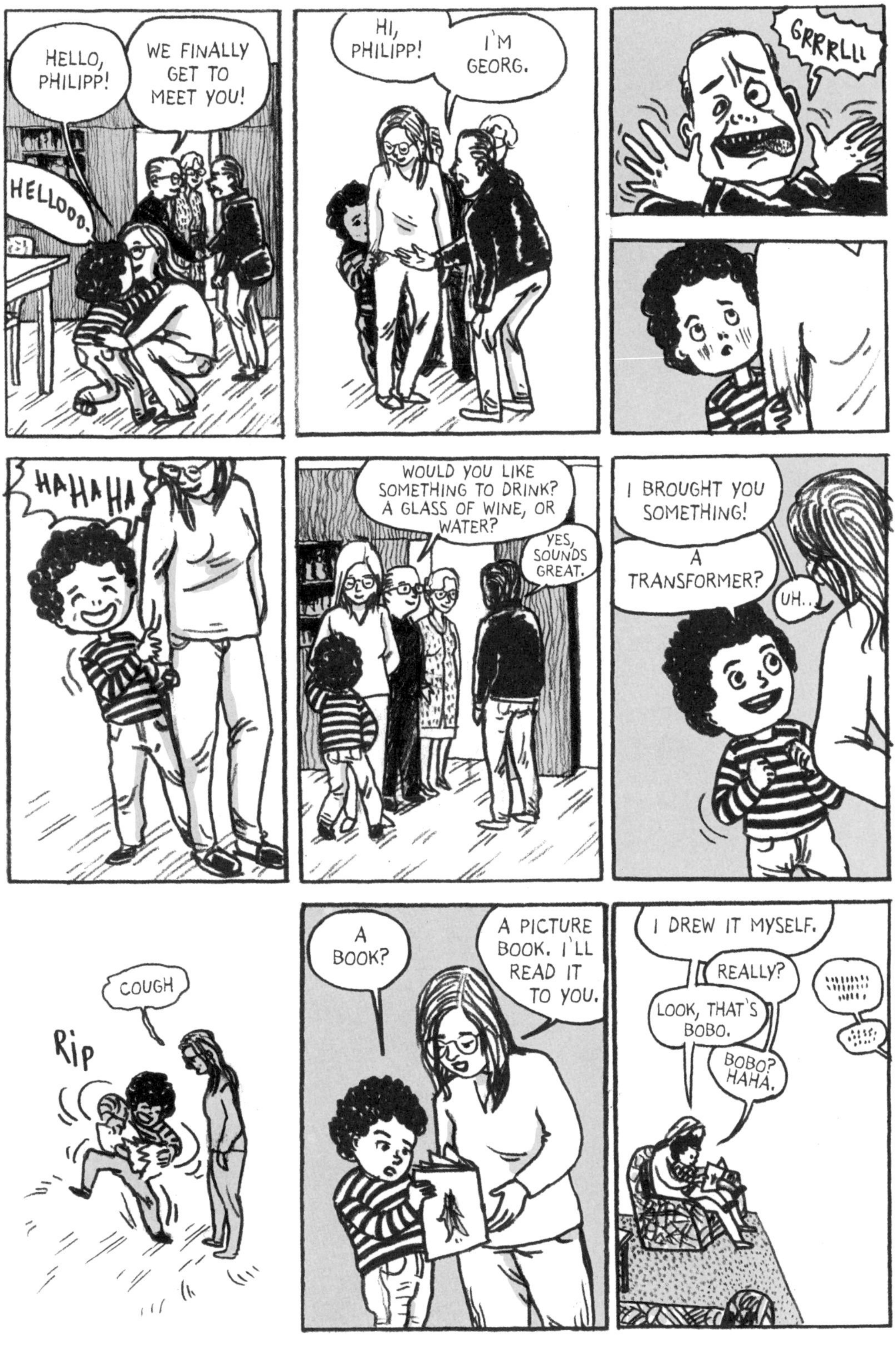
HELLO, PHILIPP!
WE FINALLY GET TO MEET YOU!
HELLOOO.
HI, PHILIPP!
I'M GEORG.
GRRRLLL
HAHAHA
WOULD YOU LIKE SOMETHING TO DRINK? A GLASS OF WINE, OR WATER?
YES, SOUNDS GREAT.
I BROUGHT YOU SOMETHING!
A TRANSFORMER?
UH...
COUGH
Rip
A BOOK?
A PICTURE BOOK. I'LL READ IT TO YOU.
I DREW IT MYSELF.
REALLY?
LOOK, THAT'S BOBO.
BOBO? HAHA.

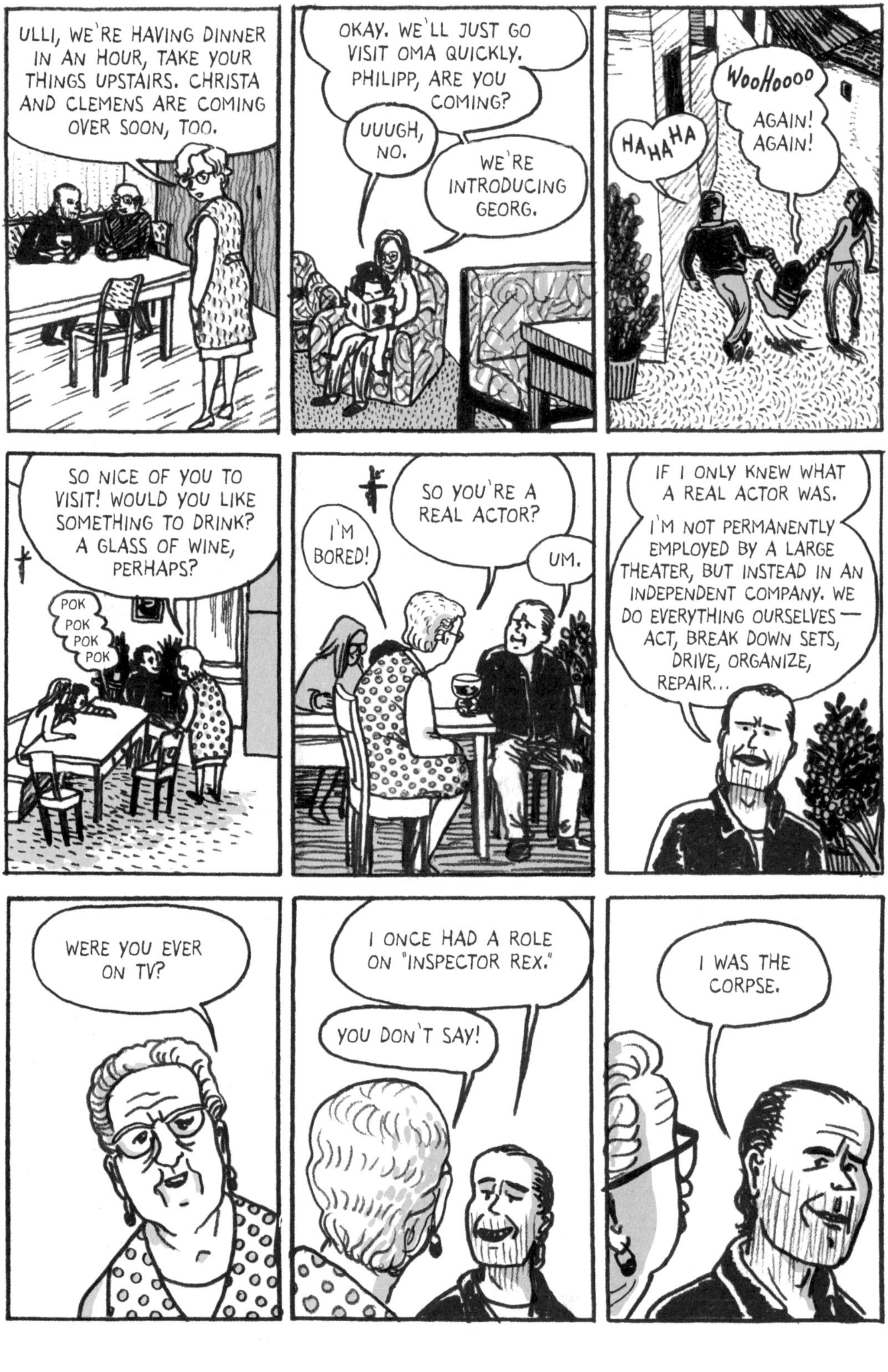
ULLI, WE'RE HAVING DINNER IN AN HOUR, TAKE YOUR THINGS UPSTAIRS. CHRISTA AND CLEMENS ARE COMING OVER SOON, TOO.
OKAY. WE'LL JUST GO VISIT OMA QUICKLY. PHILIPP, ARE YOU COMING?
UUUGH, NO.
WE'RE INTRODUCING GEORG.
HAHAHA
WooHoooo
AGAIN! AGAIN!
SO NICE OF YOU TO VISIT! WOULD YOU LIKE SOMETHING TO DRINK? A GLASS OF WINE, PERHAPS?
POK POK POK POK
SO YOU'RE A REAL ACTOR?
I'M BORED!
UM.
IF I ONLY KNEW WHAT A REAL ACTOR WAS.
I'M NOT PERMANENTLY EMPLOYED BY A LARGE THEATER, BUT INSTEAD IN AN INDEPENDENT COMPANY. WE DO EVERYTHING OURSELVES — ACT, BREAK DOWN SETS, DRIVE, ORGANIZE, REPAIR...
WERE YOU EVER ON TV?
I ONCE HAD A ROLE ON "INSPECTOR REX."
YOU DON'T SAY!
I WAS THE CORPSE.

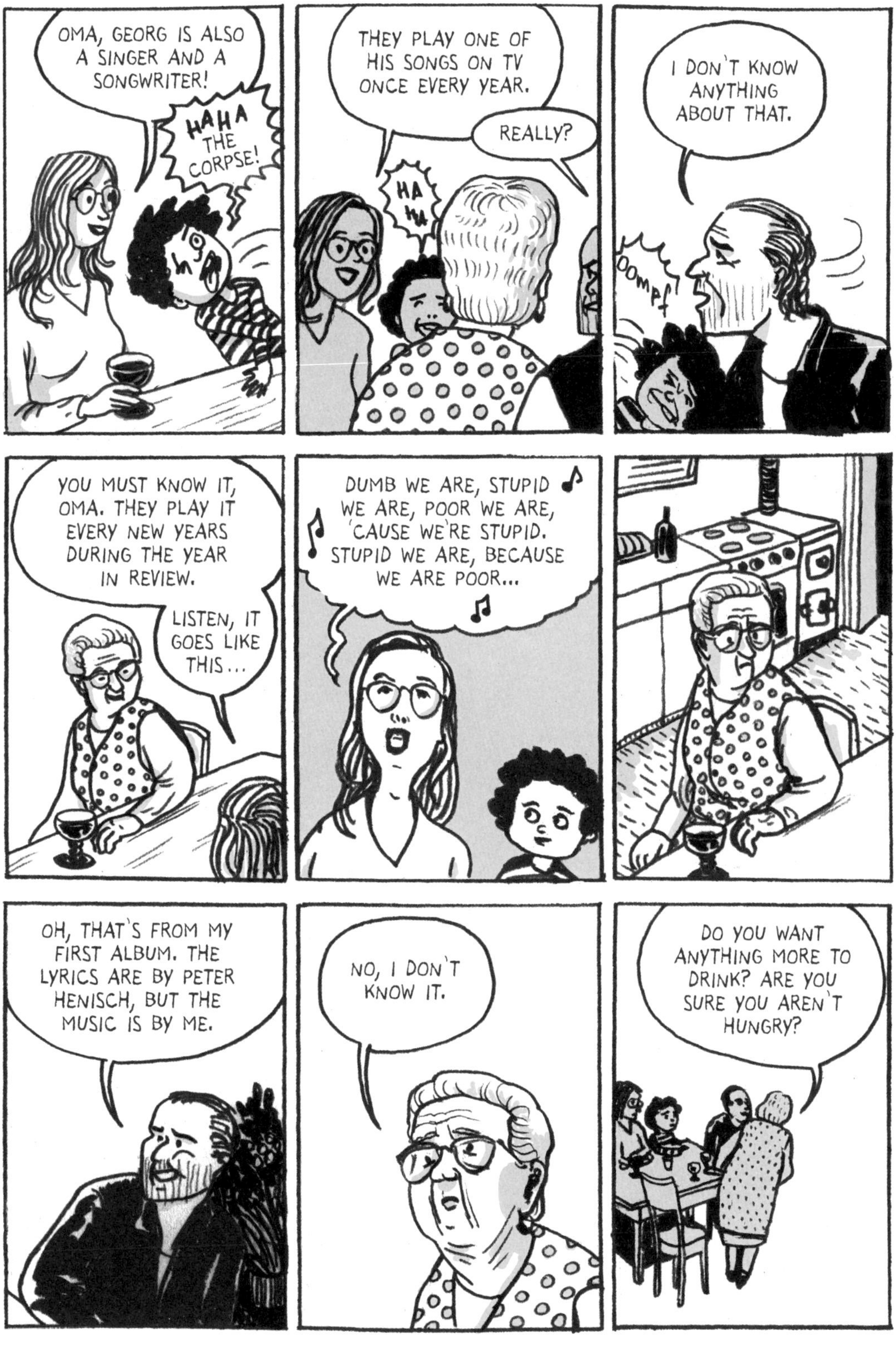
OMA, GEORG IS ALSO A SINGER AND A SONGWRITER!
HAHA THE CORPSE!
THEY PLAY ONE OF HIS SONGS ON TV ONCE EVERY YEAR.
REALLY?
HA HA
I DON'T KNOW ANYTHING ABOUT THAT.
OOMPf
YOU MUST KNOW IT, OMA. THEY PLAY IT EVERY NEW YEARS DURING THE YEAR IN REVIEW.
LISTEN, IT GOES LIKE THIS...
DUMB WE ARE, STUPID WE ARE, POOR WE ARE, 'CAUSE WE'RE STUPID. STUPID WE ARE, BECAUSE WE ARE POOR...
OH, THAT'S FROM MY FIRST ALBUM. THE LYRICS ARE BY PETER HENISCH, BUT THE MUSIC IS BY ME.
NO, I DON'T KNOW IT.
DO YOU WANT ANYTHING MORE TO DRINK? ARE YOU SURE YOU AREN'T HUNGRY?

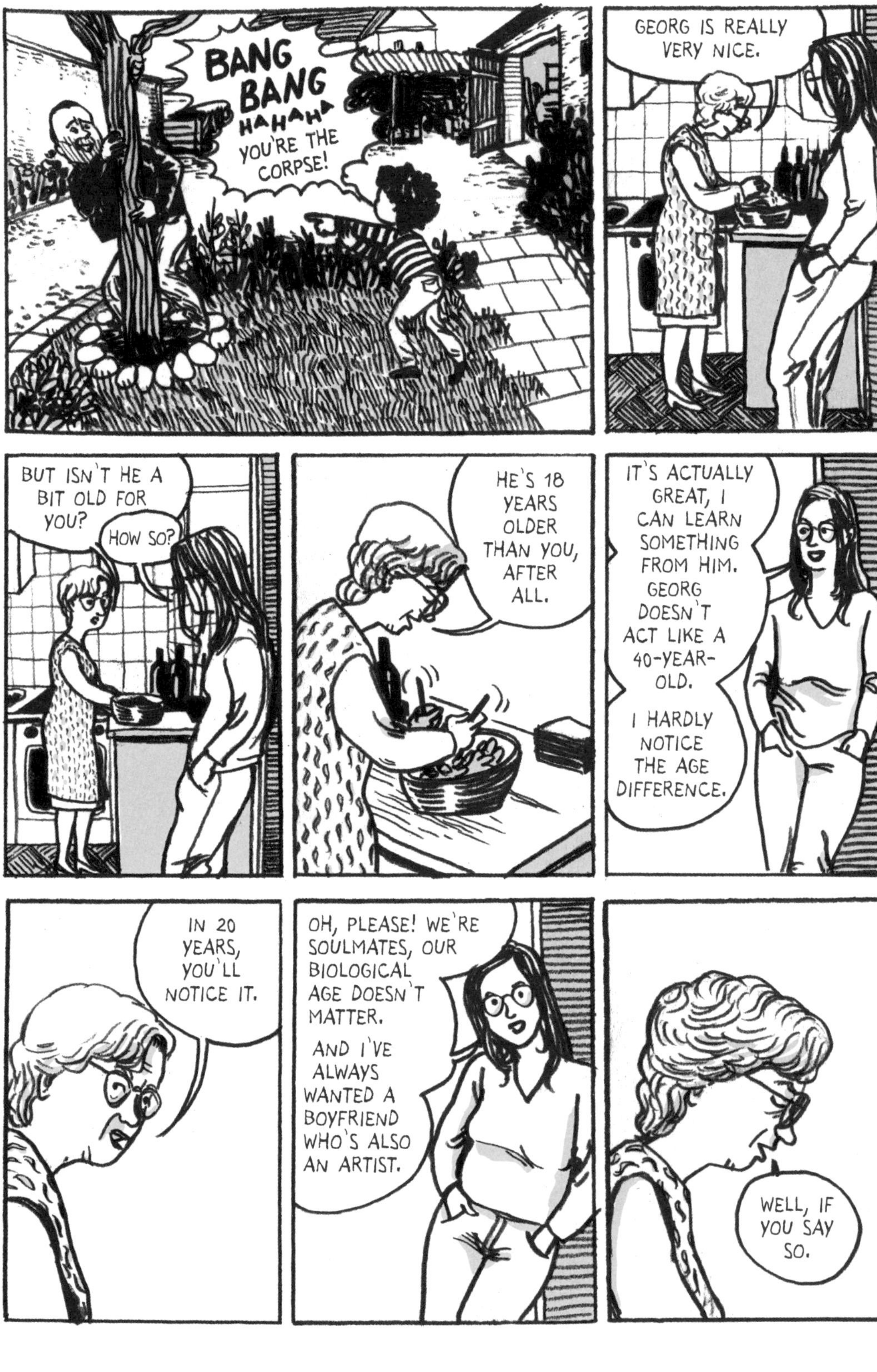
BANG
BANG
HAHAHA
YOU'RE THE CORPSE!
GEORG IS REALLY VERY NICE.
BUT ISN'T HE A BIT OLD FOR YOU?
HOW SO?
HE'S 18 YEARS OLDER THAN YOU, AFTER ALL.
IT'S ACTUALLY GREAT, I CAN LEARN SOMETHING FROM HIM. GEORG DOESN'T ACT LIKE A 40-YEAR-OLD.
I HARDLY NOTICE THE AGE DIFFERENCE.
IN 20 YEARS, YOU'LL NOTICE IT.
OH, PLEASE! WE'RE SOULMATES, OUR BIOLOGICAL AGE DOESN'T MATTER.
AND I'VE ALWAYS WANTED A BOYFRIEND WHO'S ALSO AN ARTIST.
WELL, IF YOU SAY SO.

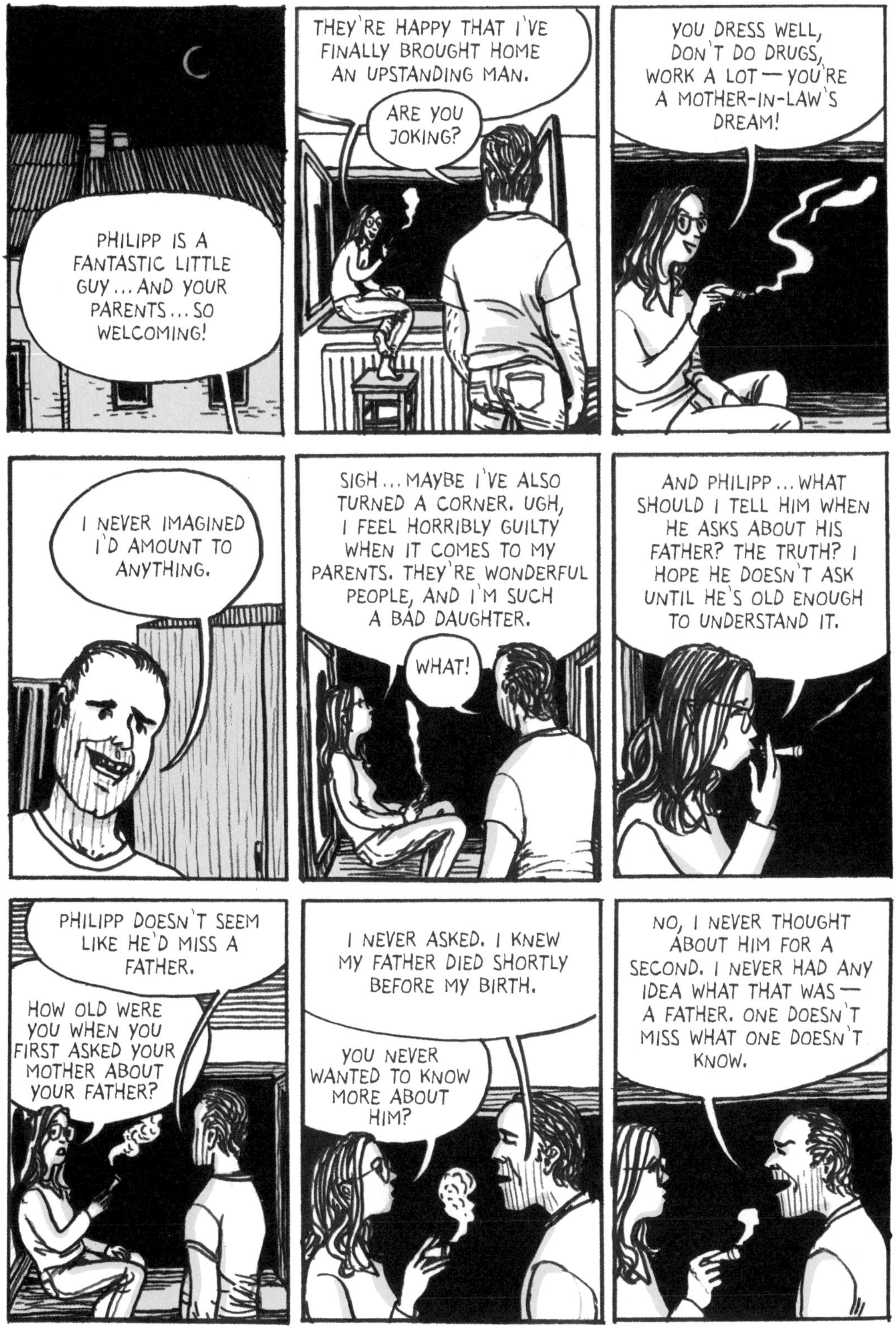
PHILIPP IS A FANTASTIC LITTLE GUY... AND YOUR PARENTS... SO WELCOMING!
THEY'RE HAPPY THAT I'VE FINALLY BROUGHT HOME AN UPSTANDING MAN.
ARE YOU JOKING?
YOU DRESS WELL, DON'T DO DRUGS, WORK A LOT—YOU'RE A MOTHER-IN-LAW'S DREAM!
I NEVER IMAGINED I'D AMOUNT TO ANYTHING.
SIGH... MAYBE I'VE ALSO TURNED A CORNER. UGH, I FEEL HORRIBLY GUILTY WHEN IT COMES TO MY PARENTS. THEY'RE WONDERFUL PEOPLE, AND I'M SUCH A BAD DAUGHTER.
WHAT!
AND PHILIPP... WHAT SHOULD I TELL HIM WHEN HE ASKS ABOUT HIS FATHER? THE TRUTH? I HOPE HE DOESN'T ASK UNTIL HE'S OLD ENOUGH TO UNDERSTAND IT.
PHILIPP DOESN'T SEEM LIKE HE'D MISS A FATHER.
HOW OLD WERE YOU WHEN YOU FIRST ASKED YOUR MOTHER ABOUT YOUR FATHER?
I NEVER ASKED. I KNEW MY FATHER DIED SHORTLY BEFORE MY BIRTH.
YOU NEVER WANTED TO KNOW MORE ABOUT HIM?
NO, I NEVER THOUGHT ABOUT HIM FOR A SECOND. I NEVER HAD ANY IDEA WHAT THAT WAS—A FATHER. ONE DOESN'T MISS WHAT ONE DOESN'T KNOW.

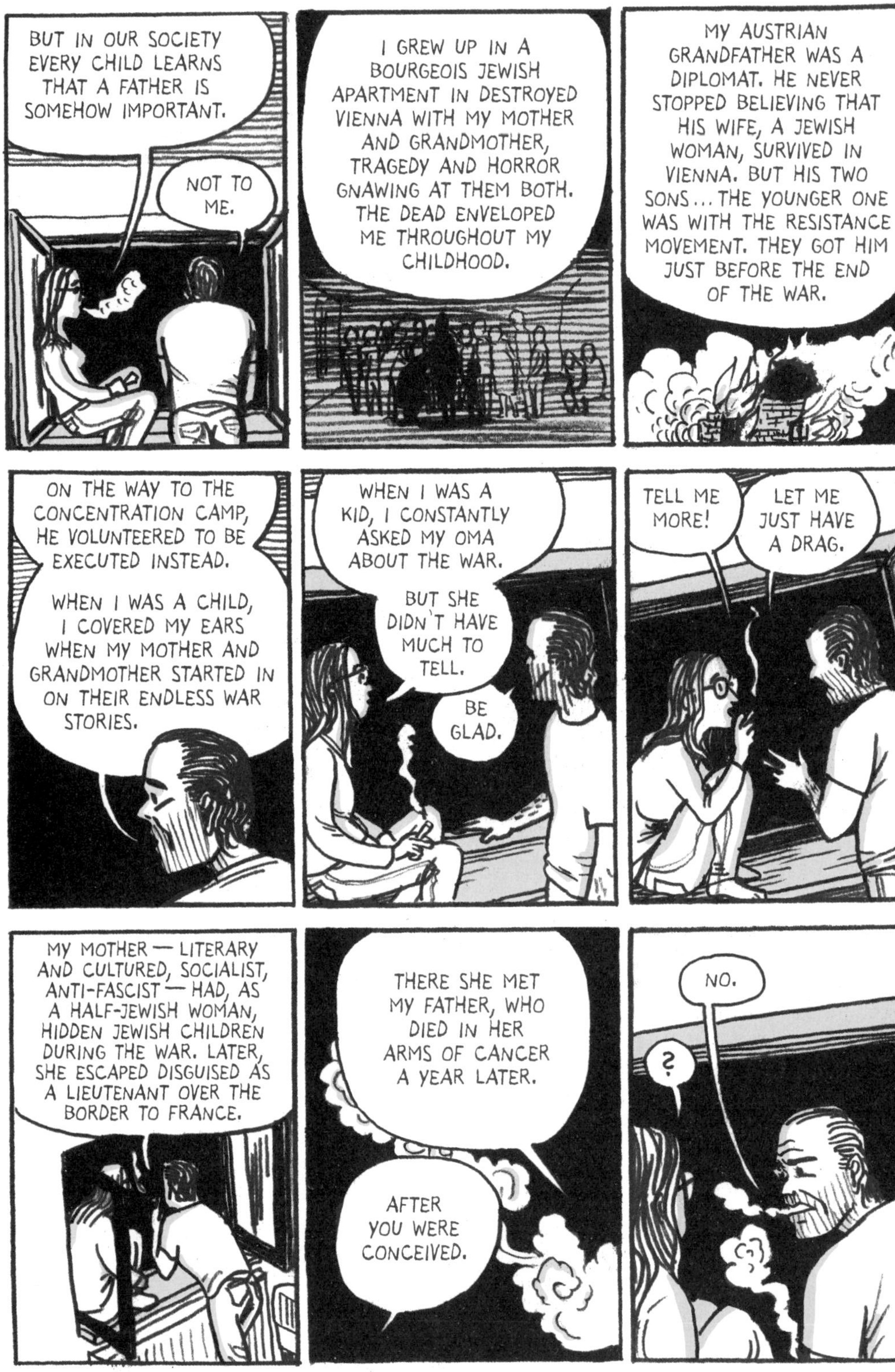
BUT IN OUR SOCIETY EVERY CHILD LEARNS THAT A FATHER IS SOMEHOW IMPORTANT.
NOT TO ME.
I GREW UP IN A BOURGEOIS JEWISH APARTMENT IN DESTROYED VIENNA WITH MY MOTHER AND GRANDMOTHER, TRAGEDY AND HORROR GNAWING AT THEM BOTH. THE DEAD ENVELOPED ME THROUGHOUT MY CHILDHOOD.
MY AUSTRIAN GRANDFATHER WAS A DIPLOMAT. HE NEVER STOPPED BELIEVING THAT HIS WIFE, A JEWISH WOMAN, SURVIVED IN VIENNA. BUT HIS TWO SONS... THE YOUNGER ONE WAS WITH THE RESISTANCE MOVEMENT. THEY GOT HIM JUST BEFORE THE END OF THE WAR.
ON THE WAY TO THE CONCENTRATION CAMP, HE VOLUNTEERED TO BE EXECUTED INSTEAD.
WHEN I WAS A CHILD, I COVERED MY EARS WHEN MY MOTHER AND GRANDMOTHER STARTED IN ON THEIR ENDLESS WAR STORIES.
WHEN I WAS A KID, I CONSTANTLY ASKED MY OMA ABOUT THE WAR.
BUT SHE DIDN'T HAVE MUCH TO TELL.
BE GLAD.
TELL ME MORE!
LET ME JUST HAVE A DRAG.
MY MOTHER — LITERARY AND CULTURED, SOCIALIST, ANTI-FASCIST — HAD, AS A HALF-JEWISH WOMAN, HIDDEN JEWISH CHILDREN DURING THE WAR. LATER, SHE ESCAPED DISGUISED AS A LIEUTENANT OVER THE BORDER TO FRANCE.
THERE SHE MET MY FATHER, WHO DIED IN HER ARMS OF CANCER A YEAR LATER.
AFTER YOU WERE CONCEIVED.
NO.
?

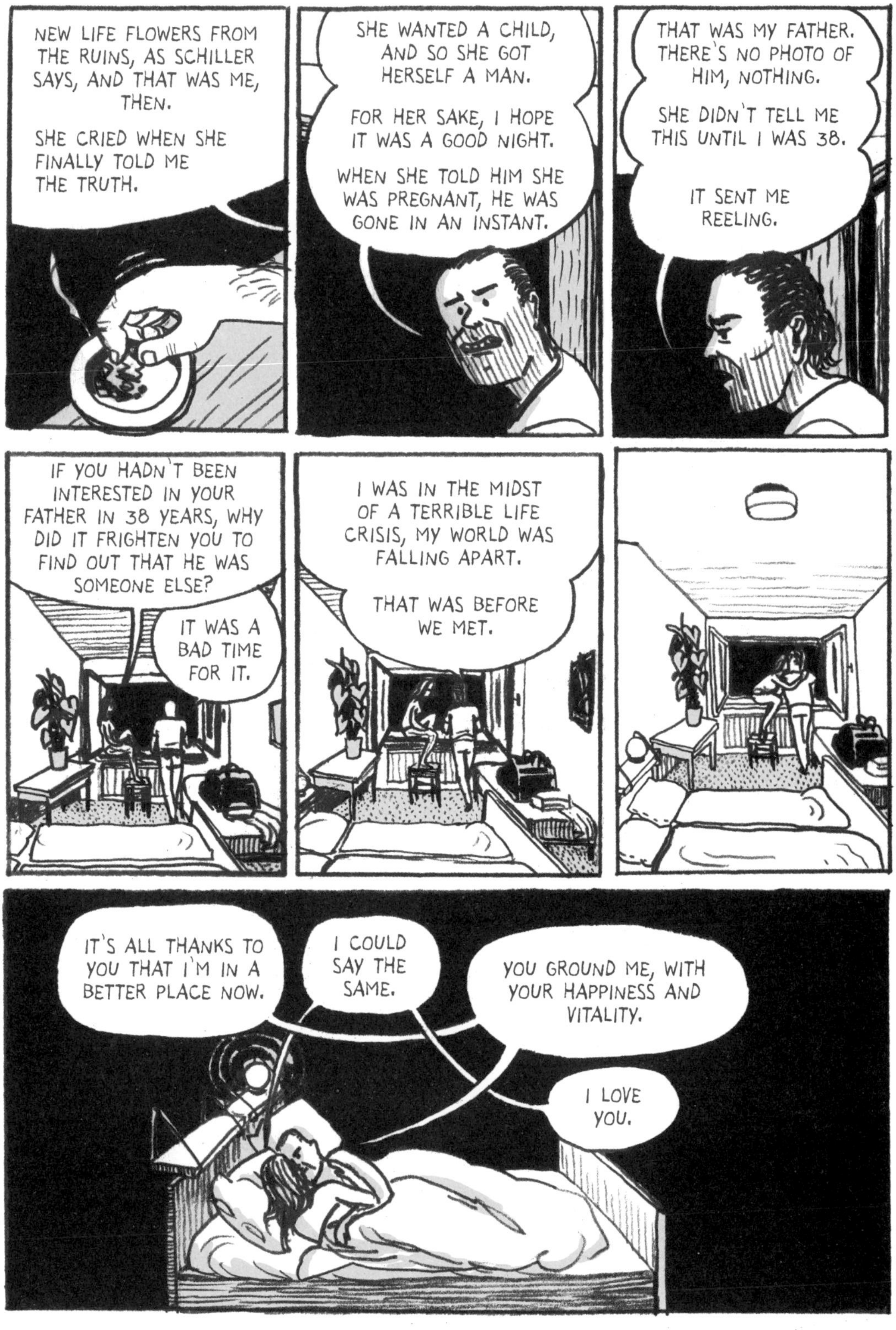
NEW LIFE FLOWERS FROM THE RUINS, AS SCHILLER SAYS, AND THAT WAS ME, THEN.
SHE CRIED WHEN SHE FINALLY TOLD ME THE TRUTH.
SHE WANTED A CHILD, AND SO SHE GOT HERSELF A MAN.
FOR HER SAKE, I HOPE IT WAS A GOOD NIGHT.
WHEN SHE TOLD HIM SHE WAS PREGNANT, HE WAS GONE IN AN INSTANT.
THAT WAS MY FATHER. THERE'S NO PHOTO OF HIM, NOTHING.
SHE DIDN'T TELL ME THIS UNTIL I WAS 38.
IT SENT ME REELING.
IF YOU HADN'T BEEN INTERESTED IN YOUR FATHER IN 38 YEARS, WHY DID IT FRIGHTEN YOU TO FIND OUT THAT HE WAS SOMEONE ELSE?
IT WAS A BAD TIME FOR IT.
I WAS IN THE MIDST OF A TERRIBLE LIFE CRISIS, MY WORLD WAS FALLING APART.
THAT WAS BEFORE WE MET.
IT'S ALL THANKS TO YOU THAT I'M IN A BETTER PLACE NOW.
I COULD SAY THE SAME.
YOU GROUND ME, WITH YOUR HAPPINESS AND VITALITY.
I LOVE YOU.

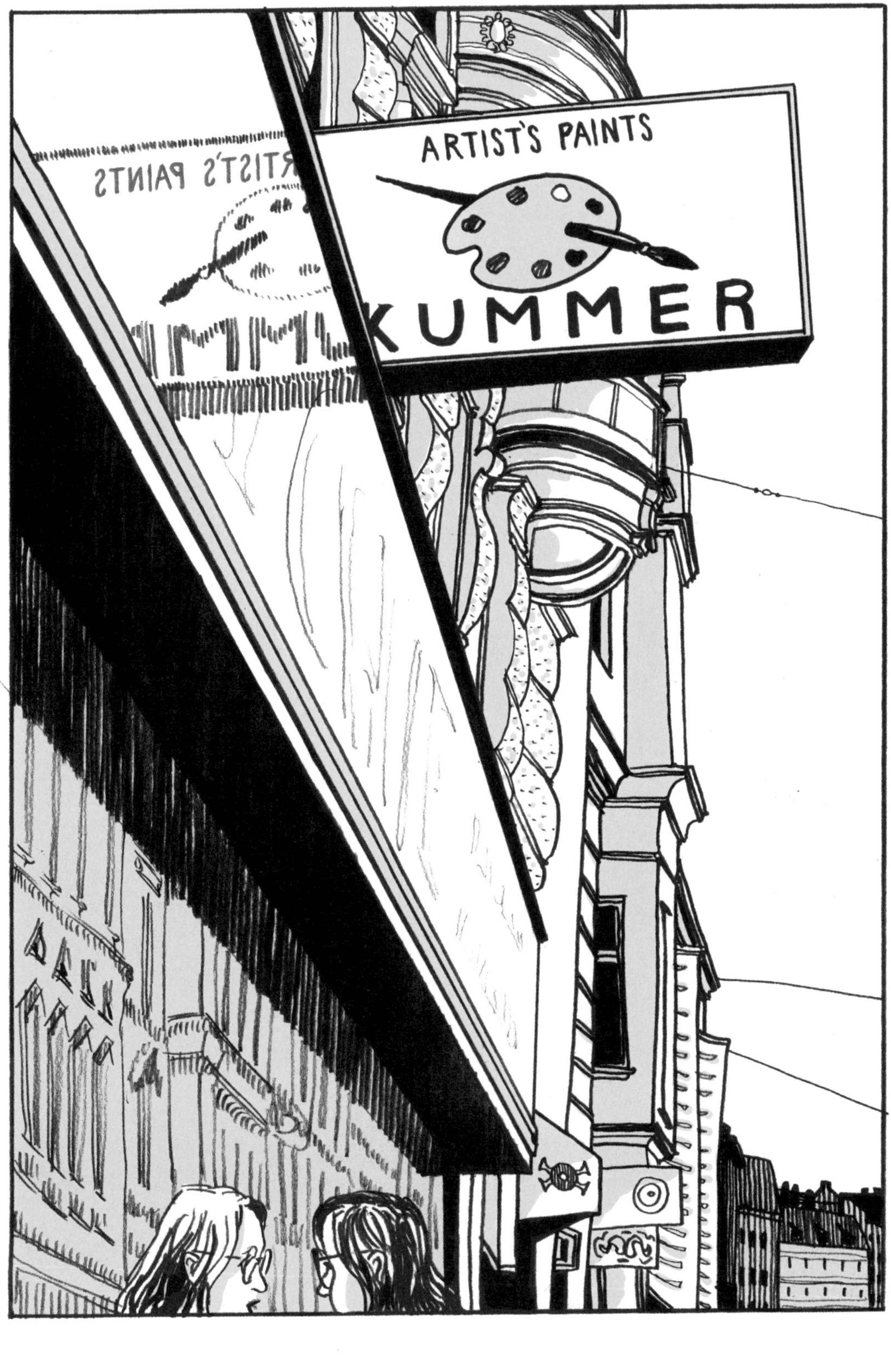
ARTIST'S PAINTS
KUMMER

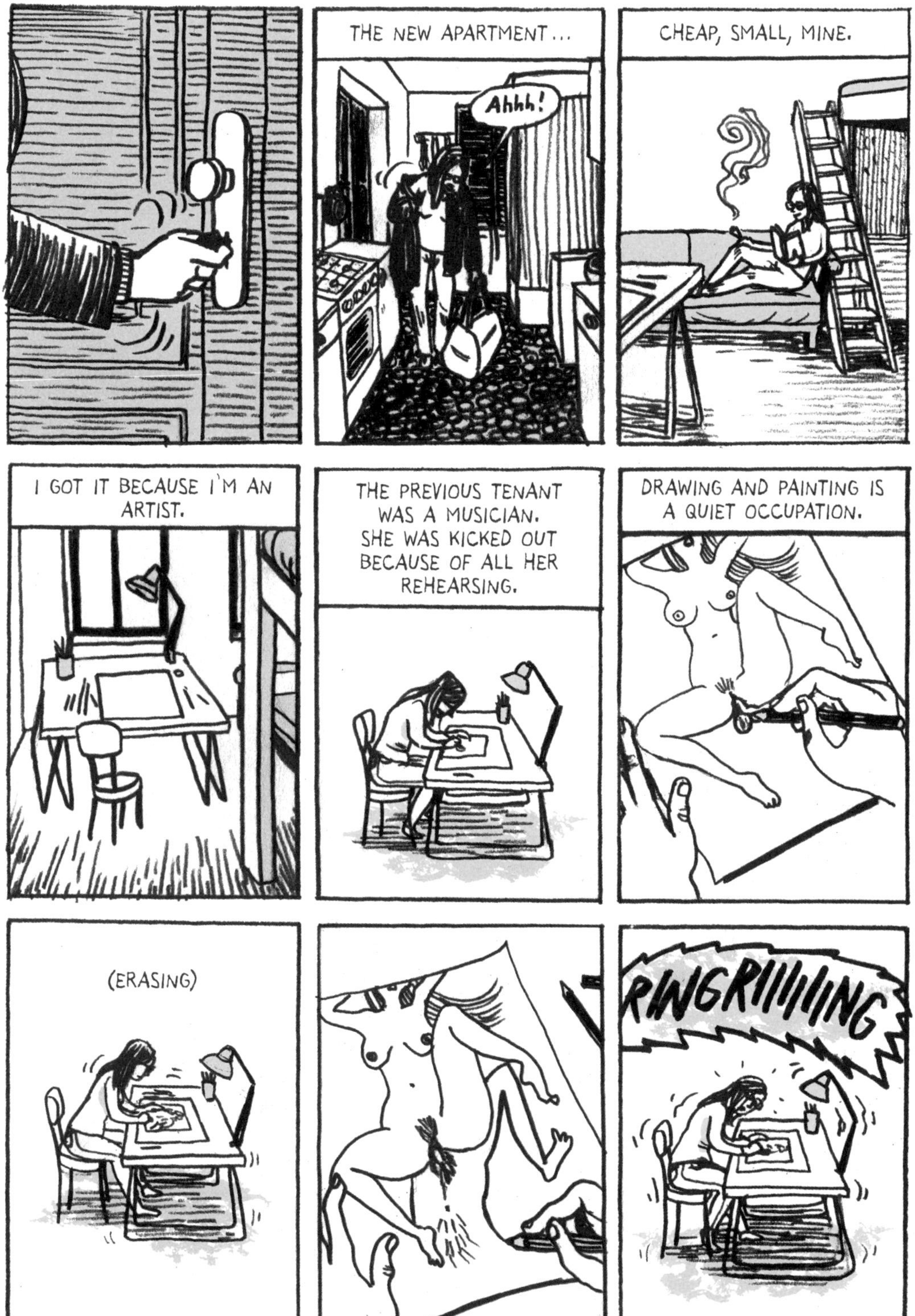

THE NEW APARTMENT...
Ahhh!
CHEAP, SMALL, MINE.
I GOT IT BECAUSE I'M AN ARTIST.
THE PREVIOUS TENANT WAS A MUSICIAN. SHE WAS KICKED OUT BECAUSE OF ALL HER REHEARSING.
DRAWING AND PAINTING IS A QUIET OCCUPATION.
(ERASING)
RINGRIIIIIING

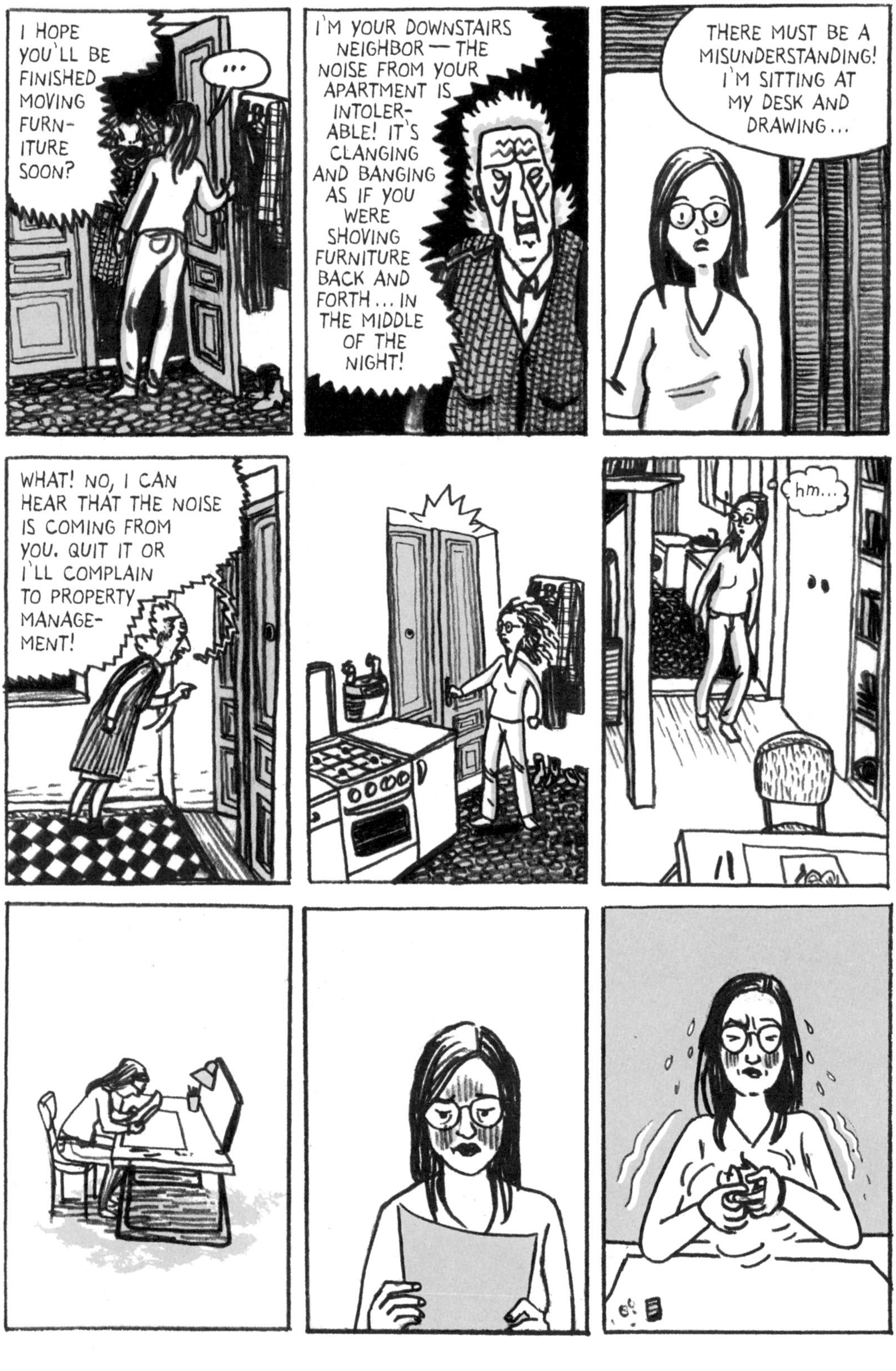
I HOPE YOU'LL BE FINISHED MOVING FURN-ITURE SOON?
...
I'M YOUR DOWNSTAIRS NEIGHBOR — THE NOISE FROM YOUR APARTMENT IS INTOLER-ABLE! IT'S CLANGING AND BANGING AS IF YOU WERE SHOVING FURNITURE BACK AND FORTH ... IN THE MIDDLE OF THE NIGHT!
THERE MUST BE A MISUNDERSTANDING! I'M SITTING AT MY DESK AND DRAWING ...
WHAT! NO, I CAN HEAR THAT THE NOISE IS COMING FROM YOU. QUIT IT OR I'LL COMPLAIN TO PROPERTY MANAGE-MENT!
hm...

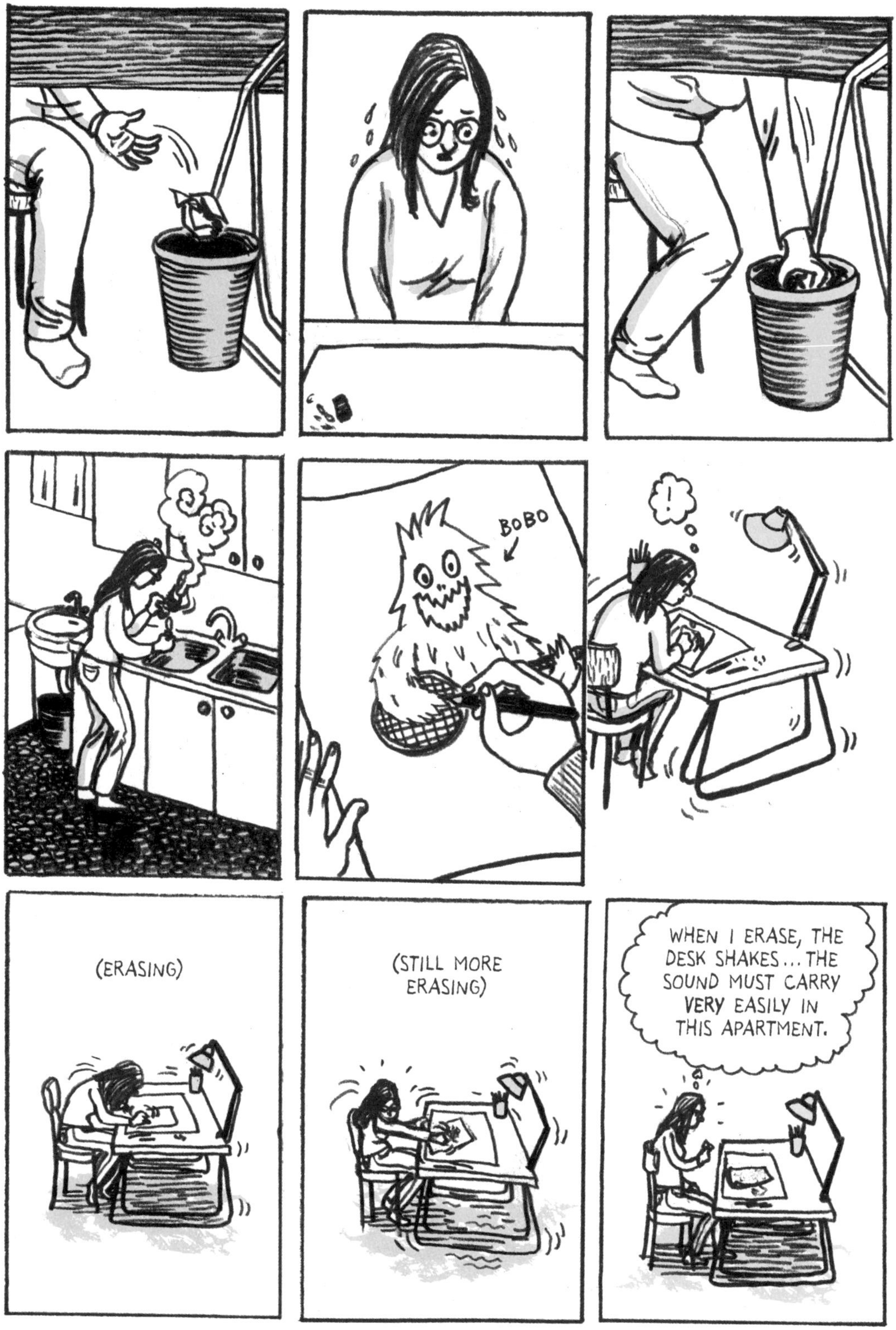
BOBO
!
(ERASING)
(STILL MORE ERASING)
WHEN I ERASE, THE DESK SHAKES... THE SOUND MUST CARRY VERY EASILY IN THIS APARTMENT.

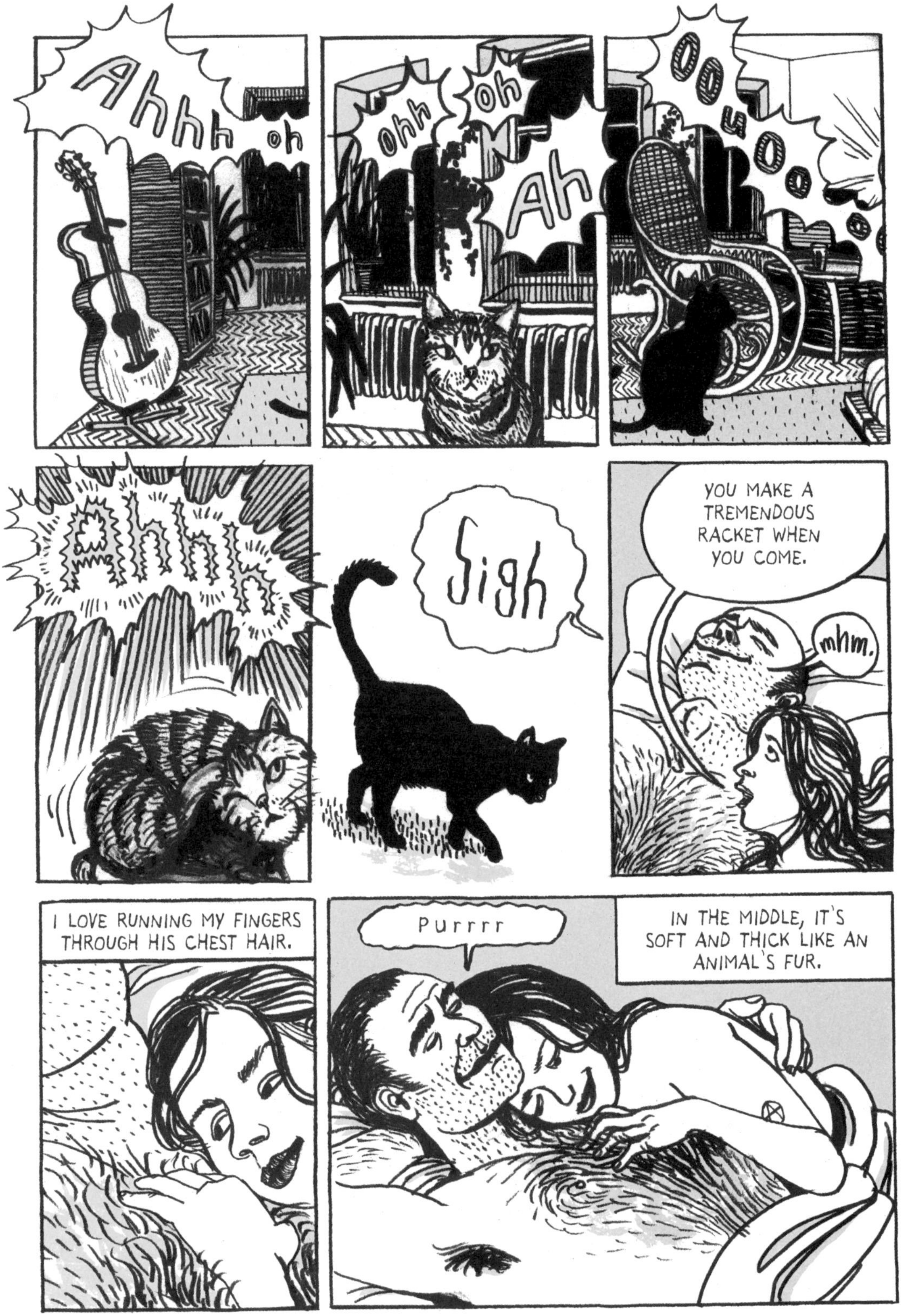

Ahhhh oh
ohh
oh
Ah
OOuOOooo
Ahhh
Sigh
YOU MAKE A TREMENDOUS RACKET WHEN YOU COME.
mhm.
I LOVE RUNNING MY FINGERS THROUGH HIS CHEST HAIR.
Purrrr
IN THE MIDDLE, IT'S SOFT AND THICK LIKE AN ANIMAL'S FUR.

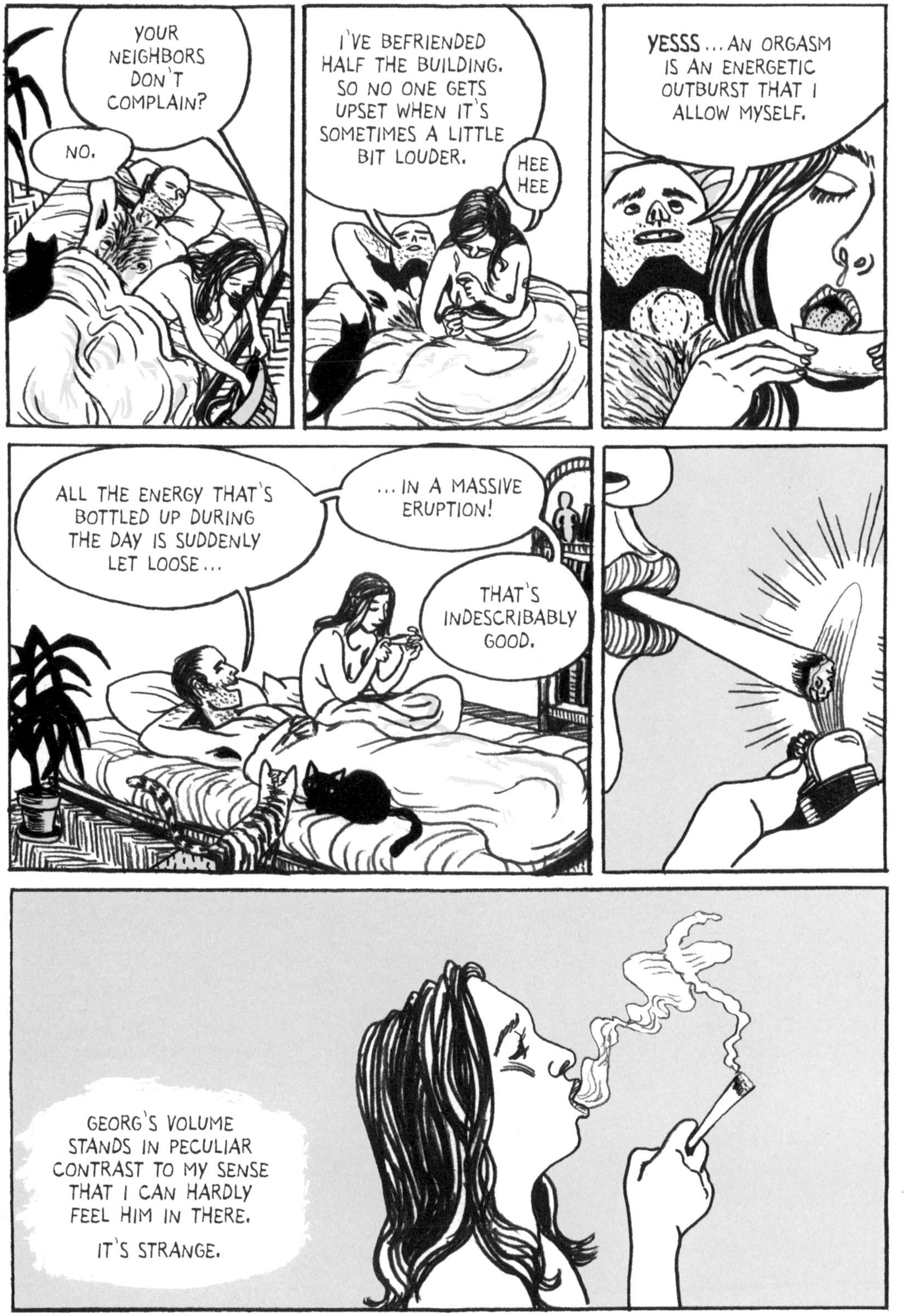
YOUR NEIGHBORS DON'T COMPLAIN?
NO.
I'VE BEFRIENDED HALF THE BUILDING. SO NO ONE GETS UPSET WHEN IT'S SOMETIMES A LITTLE BIT LOUDER.
HEE HEE
YESSS... AN ORGASM IS AN ENERGETIC OUTBURST THAT I ALLOW MYSELF.
ALL THE ENERGY THAT'S BOTTLED UP DURING THE DAY IS SUDDENLY LET LOOSE...
...IN A MASSIVE ERUPTION!
THAT'S INDESCRIBABLY GOOD.
GEORG'S VOLUME STANDS IN PECULIAR CONTRAST TO MY SENSE THAT I CAN HARDLY FEEL HIM IN THERE.
IT'S STRANGE.

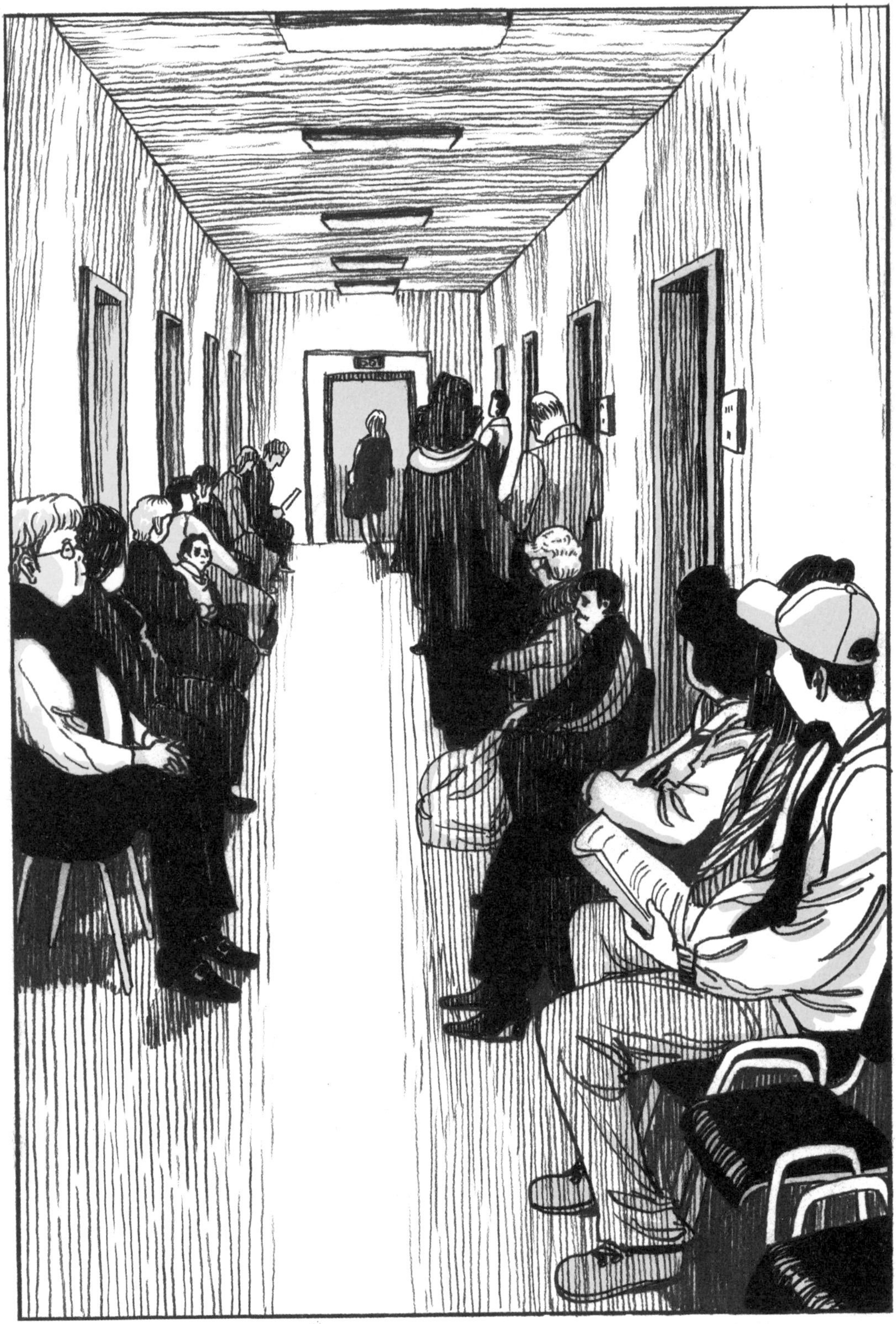

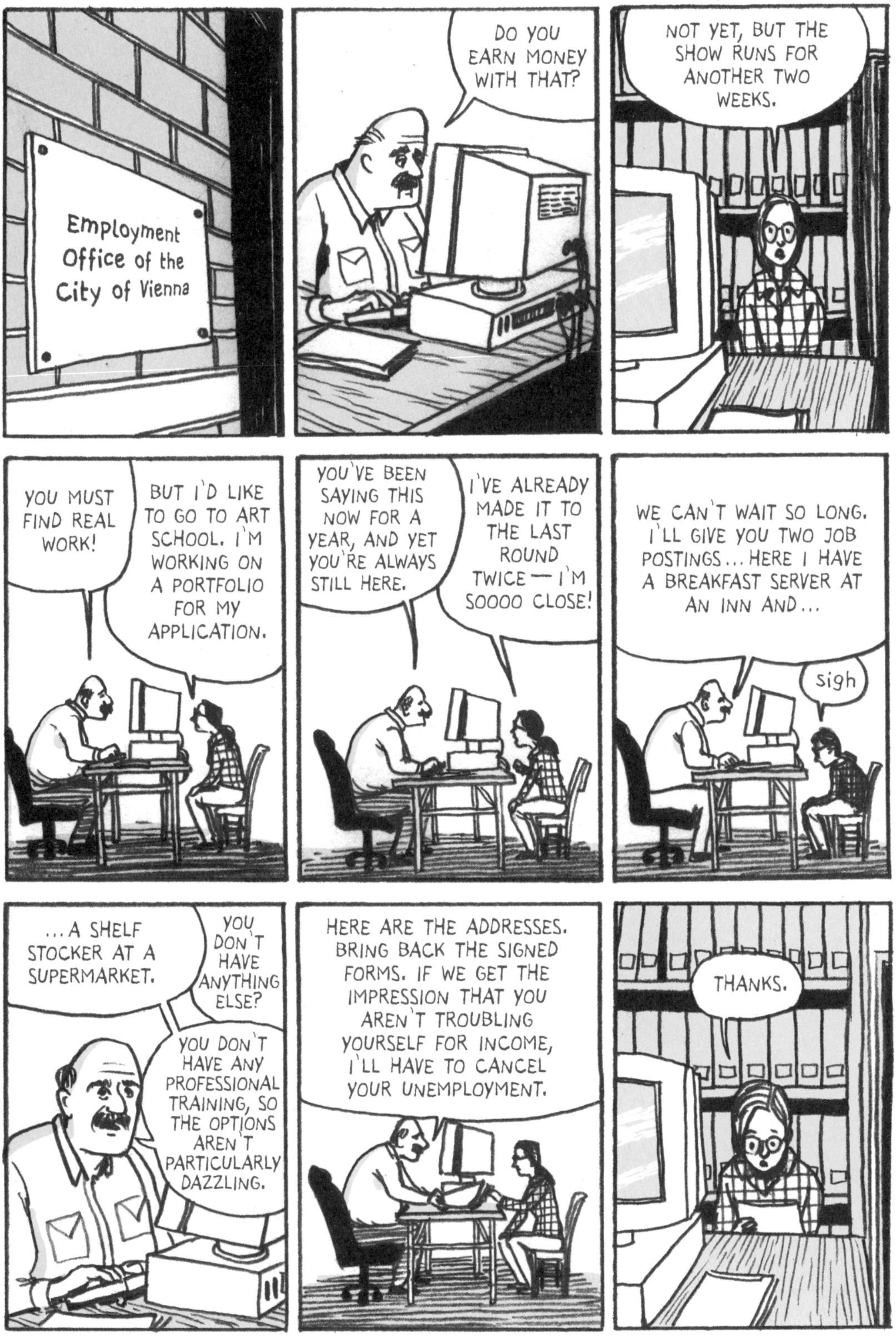
Employment Office of the City of Vienna
DO YOU EARN MONEY WITH THAT?
NOT YET, BUT THE SHOW RUNS FOR ANOTHER TWO WEEKS.
YOU MUST FIND REAL WORK!
BUT I'D LIKE TO GO TO ART SCHOOL. I'M WORKING ON A PORTFOLIO FOR MY APPLICATION.
YOU'VE BEEN SAYING THIS NOW FOR A YEAR, AND YET YOU'RE ALWAYS STILL HERE.
I'VE ALREADY MADE IT TO THE LAST ROUND TWICE — I'M SOOOO CLOSE!
WE CAN'T WAIT SO LONG. I'LL GIVE YOU TWO JOB POSTINGS... HERE I HAVE A BREAKFAST SERVER AT AN INN AND...
sigh
...A SHELF STOCKER AT A SUPERMARKET.
YOU DON'T HAVE ANYTHING ELSE?
YOU DON'T HAVE ANY PROFESSIONAL TRAINING, SO THE OPTIONS AREN'T PARTICULARLY DAZZLING.
HERE ARE THE ADDRESSES. BRING BACK THE SIGNED FORMS. IF WE GET THE IMPRESSION THAT YOU AREN'T TROUBLING YOURSELF FOR INCOME, I'LL HAVE TO CANCEL YOUR UNEMPLOYMENT.
THANKS.

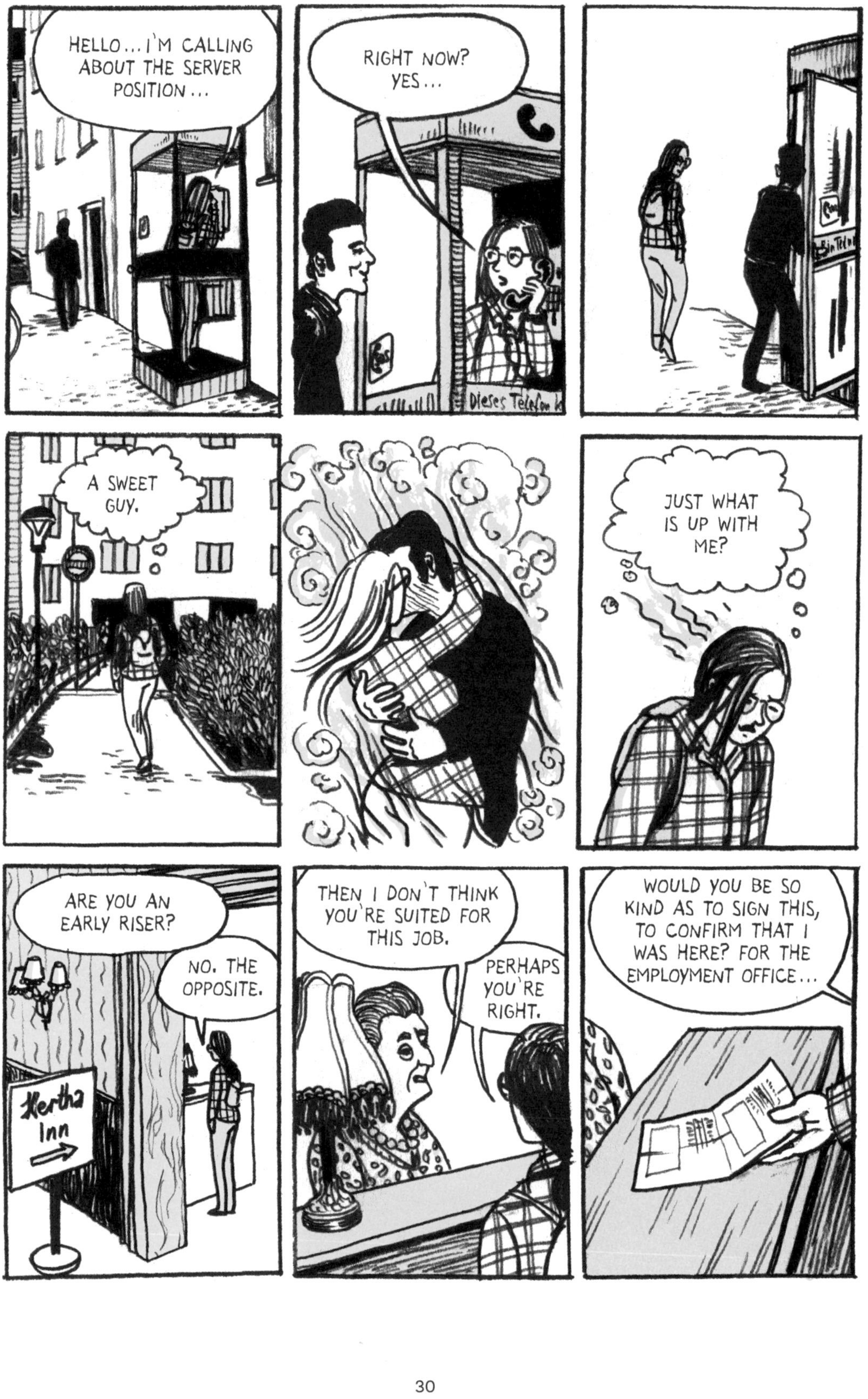
HELLO... I'M CALLING ABOUT THE SERVER POSITION...
RIGHT NOW? YES...
A SWEET GUY.
JUST WHAT IS UP WITH ME?
ARE YOU AN EARLY RISER?
NO. THE OPPOSITE.
Hertha Inn
THEN I DON'T THINK YOU'RE SUITED FOR THIS JOB.
PERHAPS YOU'RE RIGHT.
WOULD YOU BE SO KIND AS TO SIGN THIS, TO CONFIRM THAT I WAS HERE? FOR THE EMPLOYMENT OFFICE...

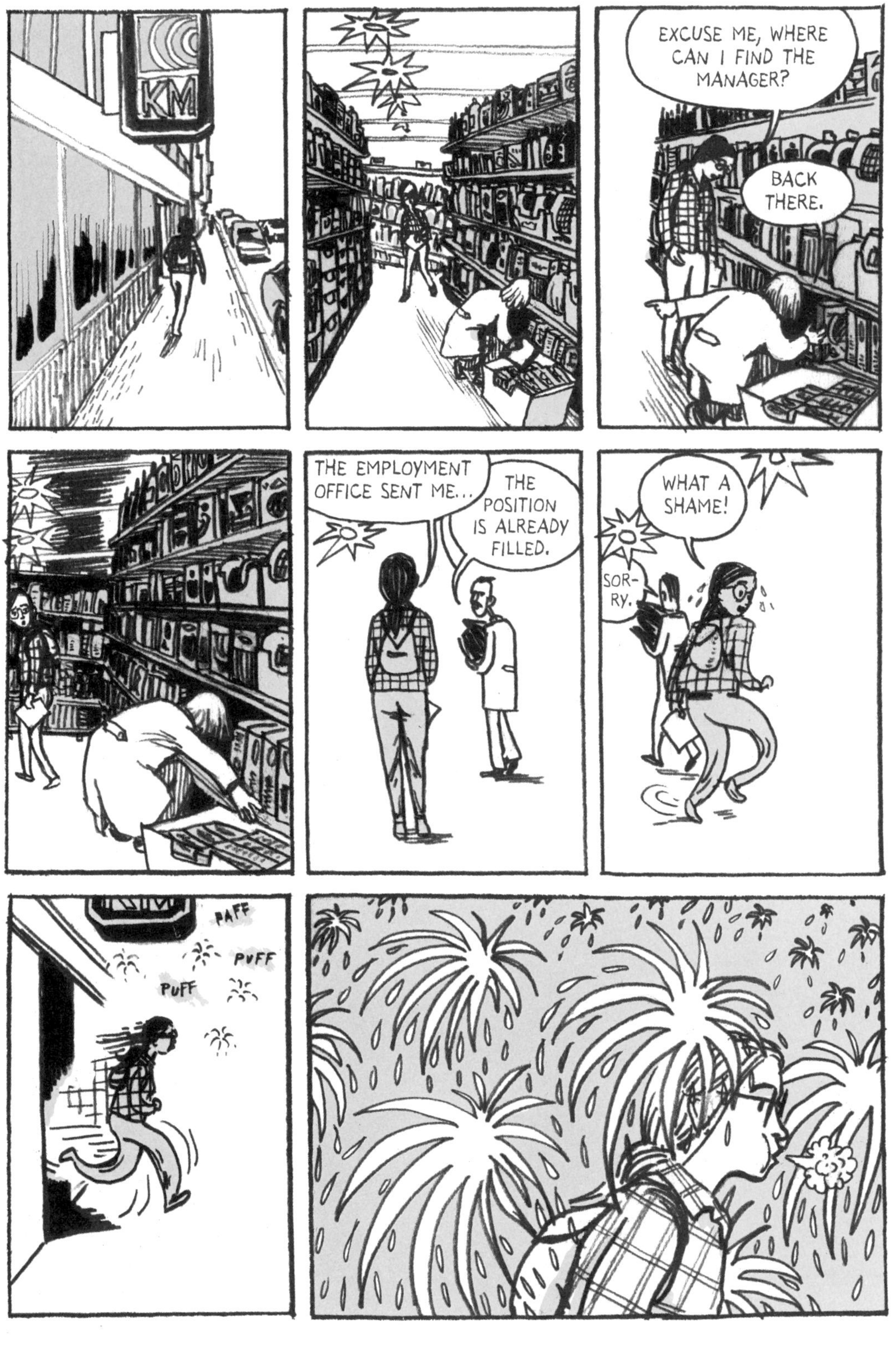

EXCUSE ME, WHERE CAN I FIND THE MANAGER?
BACK THERE.
THE EMPLOYMENT OFFICE SENT ME...
THE POSITION IS ALREADY FILLED.
WHAT A SHAME!
SOR-RY.
PAFF
PUFF
PUFF

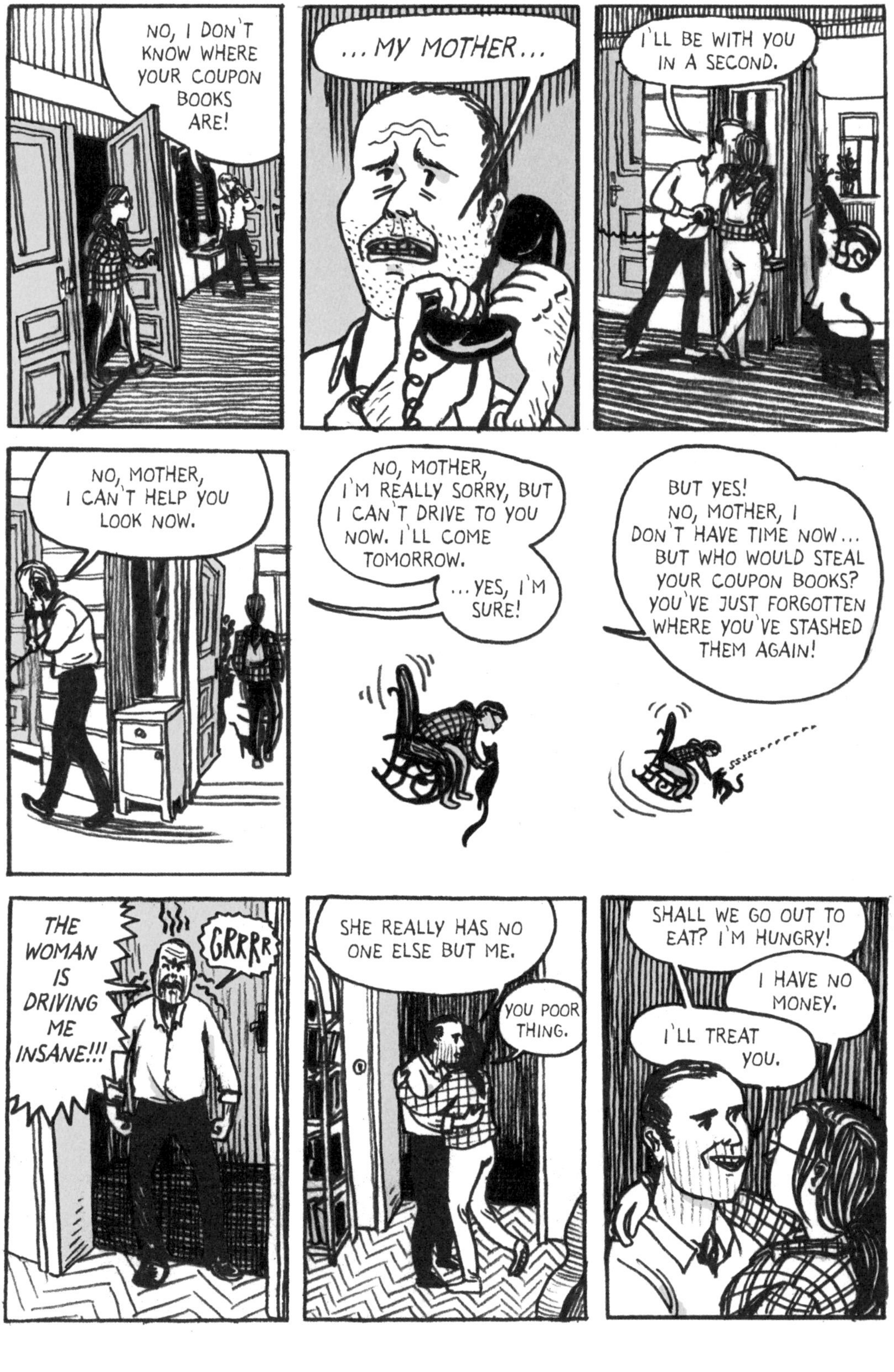
NO, I DON'T KNOW WHERE YOUR COUPON BOOKS ARE!
...MY MOTHER...
I'LL BE WITH YOU IN A SECOND.
NO, MOTHER, I CAN'T HELP YOU LOOK NOW.
NO, MOTHER, I'M REALLY SORRY, BUT I CAN'T DRIVE TO YOU NOW. I'LL COME TOMORROW.
...YES, I'M SURE!
BUT YES! NO, MOTHER, I DON'T HAVE TIME NOW... BUT WHO WOULD STEAL YOUR COUPON BOOKS? YOU'VE JUST FORGOTTEN WHERE YOU'VE STASHED THEM AGAIN!
THE WOMAN IS DRIVING ME INSANE!!!
GRRRR
SHE REALLY HAS NO ONE ELSE BUT ME.
YOU POOR THING.
SHALL WE GO OUT TO EAT? I'M HUNGRY!
I HAVE NO MONEY.
I'LL TREAT YOU.

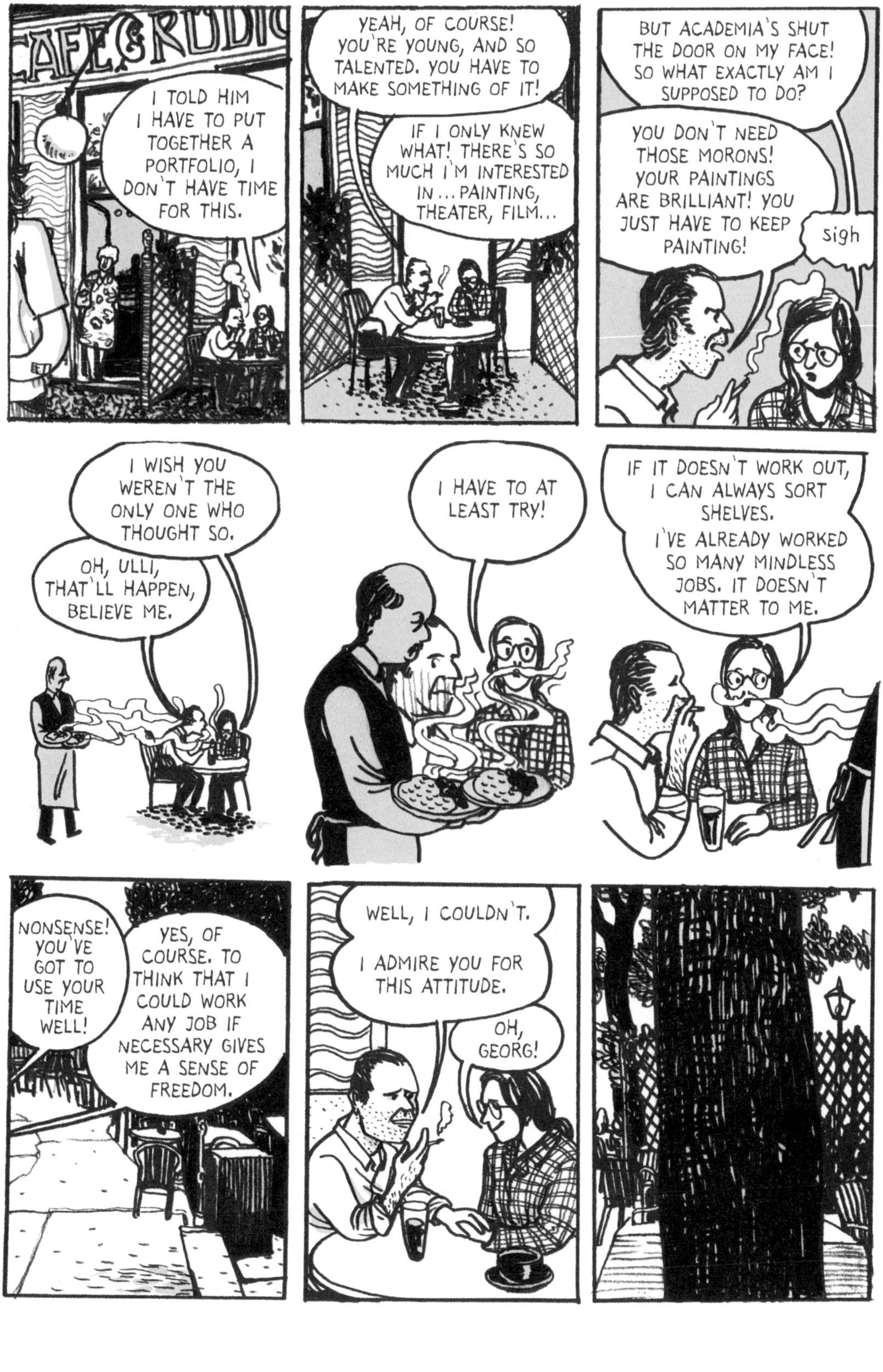
I TOLD HIM I HAVE TO PUT TOGETHER A PORTFOLIO, I DON'T HAVE TIME FOR THIS.
YEAH, OF COURSE! YOU'RE YOUNG, AND SO TALENTED. YOU HAVE TO MAKE SOMETHING OF IT!
IF I ONLY KNEW WHAT! THERE'S SO MUCH I'M INTERESTED IN... PAINTING, THEATER, FILM...
BUT ACADEMIA'S SHUT THE DOOR ON MY FACE! SO WHAT EXACTLY AM I SUPPOSED TO DO?
YOU DON'T NEED THOSE MORONS! YOUR PAINTINGS ARE BRILLIANT! YOU JUST HAVE TO KEEP PAINTING!
sigh
I WISH YOU WEREN'T THE ONLY ONE WHO THOUGHT SO.
OH, ULLI, THAT'LL HAPPEN, BELIEVE ME.
I HAVE TO AT LEAST TRY!
IF IT DOESN'T WORK OUT, I CAN ALWAYS SORT SHELVES.
I'VE ALREADY WORKED SO MANY MINDLESS JOBS. IT DOESN'T MATTER TO ME.
NONSENSE! YOU'VE GOT TO USE YOUR TIME WELL!
YES, OF COURSE. TO THINK THAT I COULD WORK ANY JOB IF NECESSARY GIVES ME A SENSE OF FREEDOM.
WELL, I COULDN'T.
I ADMIRE YOU FOR THIS ATTITUDE.
OH, GEORG!

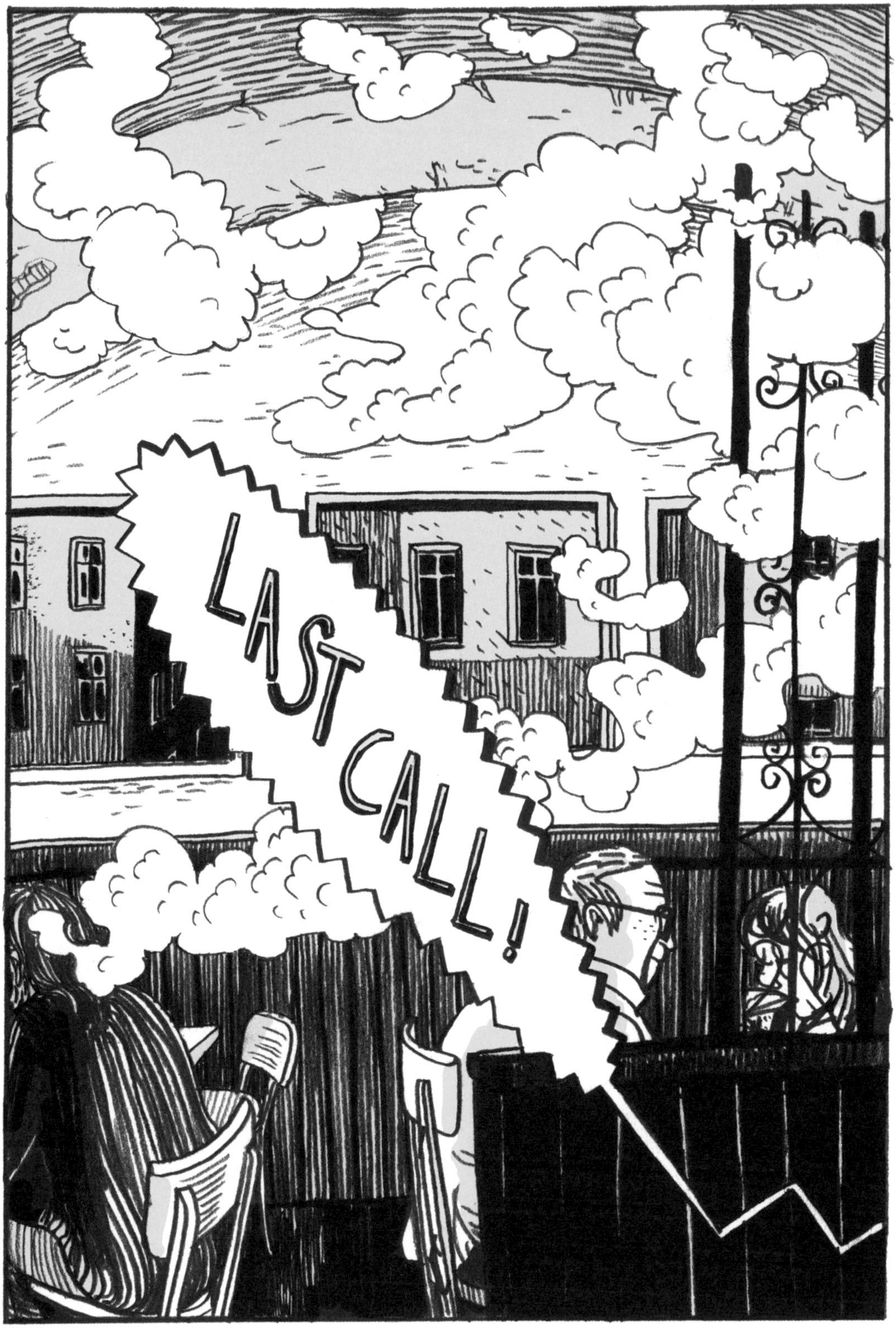
LAST CALL!

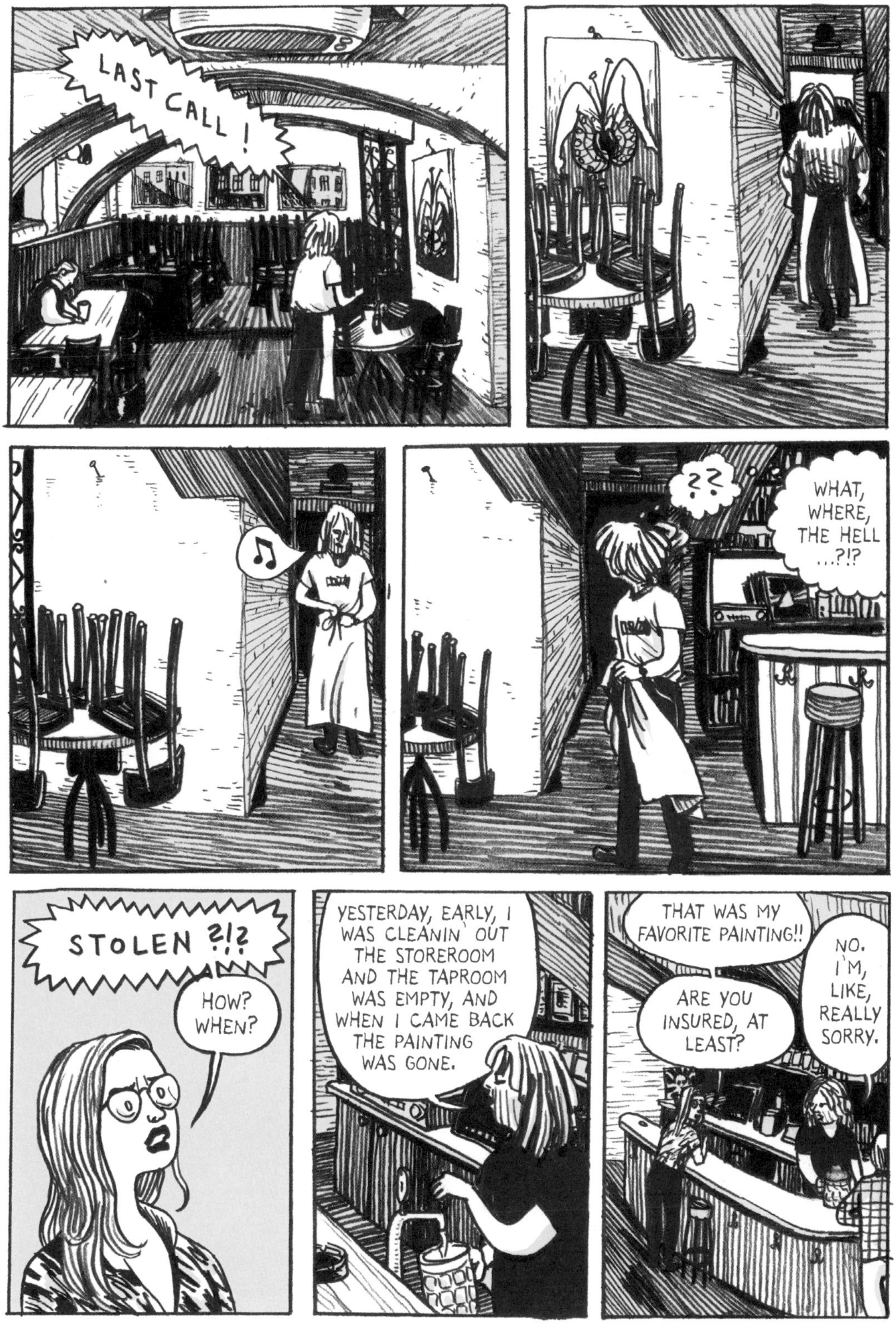
LAST CALL!
♫
WHAT, WHERE, THE HELL ...?!?
STOLEN ?!?
HOW? WHEN?
YESTERDAY, EARLY, I WAS CLEANIN' OUT THE STOREROOM AND THE TAPROOM WAS EMPTY, AND WHEN I CAME BACK THE PAINTING WAS GONE.
THAT WAS MY FAVORITE PAINTING!!
ARE YOU INSURED, AT LEAST?
NO. I'M, LIKE, REALLY SORRY.

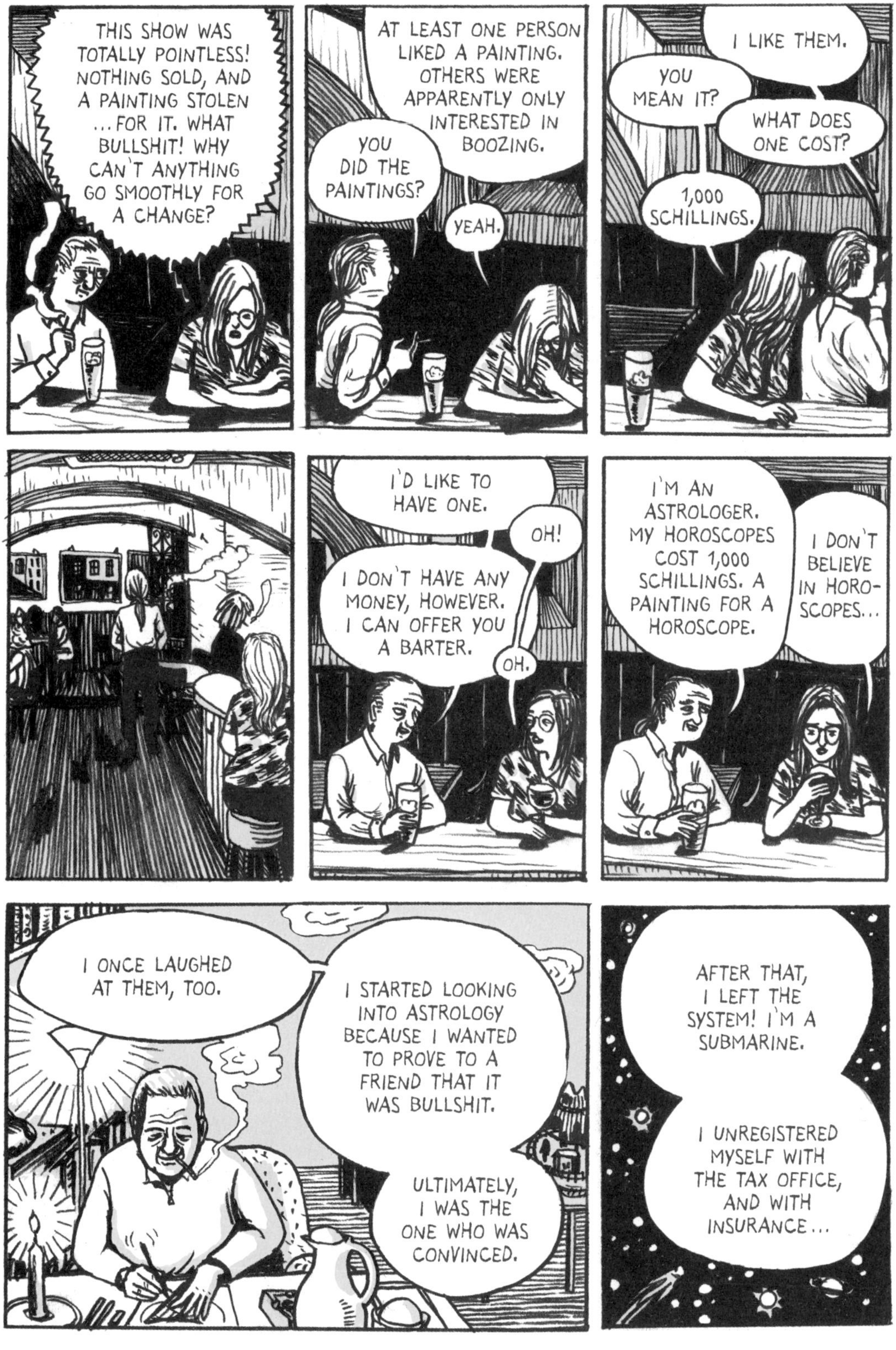
THIS SHOW WAS TOTALLY POINTLESS! NOTHING SOLD, AND A PAINTING STOLEN ...FOR IT. WHAT BULLSHIT! WHY CAN'T ANYTHING GO SMOOTHLY FOR A CHANGE?
AT LEAST ONE PERSON LIKED A PAINTING. OTHERS WERE APPARENTLY ONLY INTERESTED IN BOOZING.
YOU DID THE PAINTINGS?
YEAH.
I LIKE THEM.
YOU MEAN IT?
WHAT DOES ONE COST?
1,000 SCHILLINGS.
I'D LIKE TO HAVE ONE.
OH!
I DON'T HAVE ANY MONEY, HOWEVER. I CAN OFFER YOU A BARTER.
OH.
I'M AN ASTROLOGER. MY HOROSCOPES COST 1,000 SCHILLINGS. A PAINTING FOR A HOROSCOPE.
I DON'T BELIEVE IN HORO-SCOPES...
I ONCE LAUGHED AT THEM, TOO.
I STARTED LOOKING INTO ASTROLOGY BECAUSE I WANTED TO PROVE TO A FRIEND THAT IT WAS BULLSHIT.
ULTIMATELY, I WAS THE ONE WHO WAS CONVINCED.
AFTER THAT, I LEFT THE SYSTEM! I'M A SUBMARINE.
I UNREGISTERED MYSELF WITH THE TAX OFFICE, AND WITH INSURANCE...

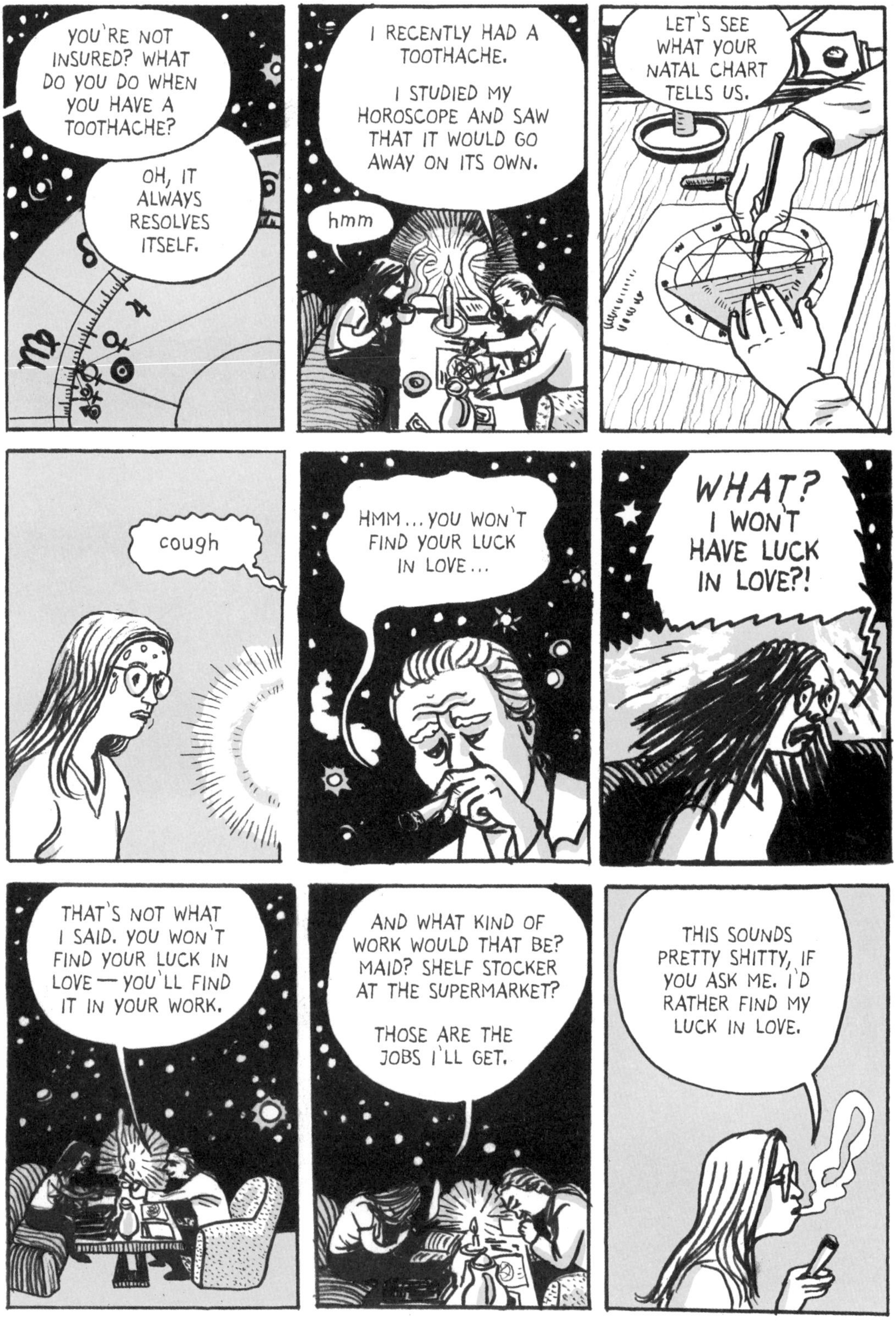
YOU'RE NOT INSURED? WHAT DO YOU DO WHEN YOU HAVE A TOOTHACHE?
OH, IT ALWAYS RESOLVES ITSELF.
I RECENTLY HAD A TOOTHACHE.
I STUDIED MY HOROSCOPE AND SAW THAT IT WOULD GO AWAY ON ITS OWN.
hmm
LET'S SEE WHAT YOUR NATAL CHART TELLS US.
cough
HMM... YOU WON'T FIND YOUR LUCK IN LOVE...
WHAT? I WON'T HAVE LUCK IN LOVE?!
THAT'S NOT WHAT I SAID. YOU WON'T FIND YOUR LUCK IN LOVE — YOU'LL FIND IT IN YOUR WORK.
AND WHAT KIND OF WORK WOULD THAT BE? MAID? SHELF STOCKER AT THE SUPERMARKET?
THOSE ARE THE JOBS I'LL GET.
THIS SOUNDS PRETTY SHITTY, IF YOU ASK ME. I'D RATHER FIND MY LUCK IN LOVE.

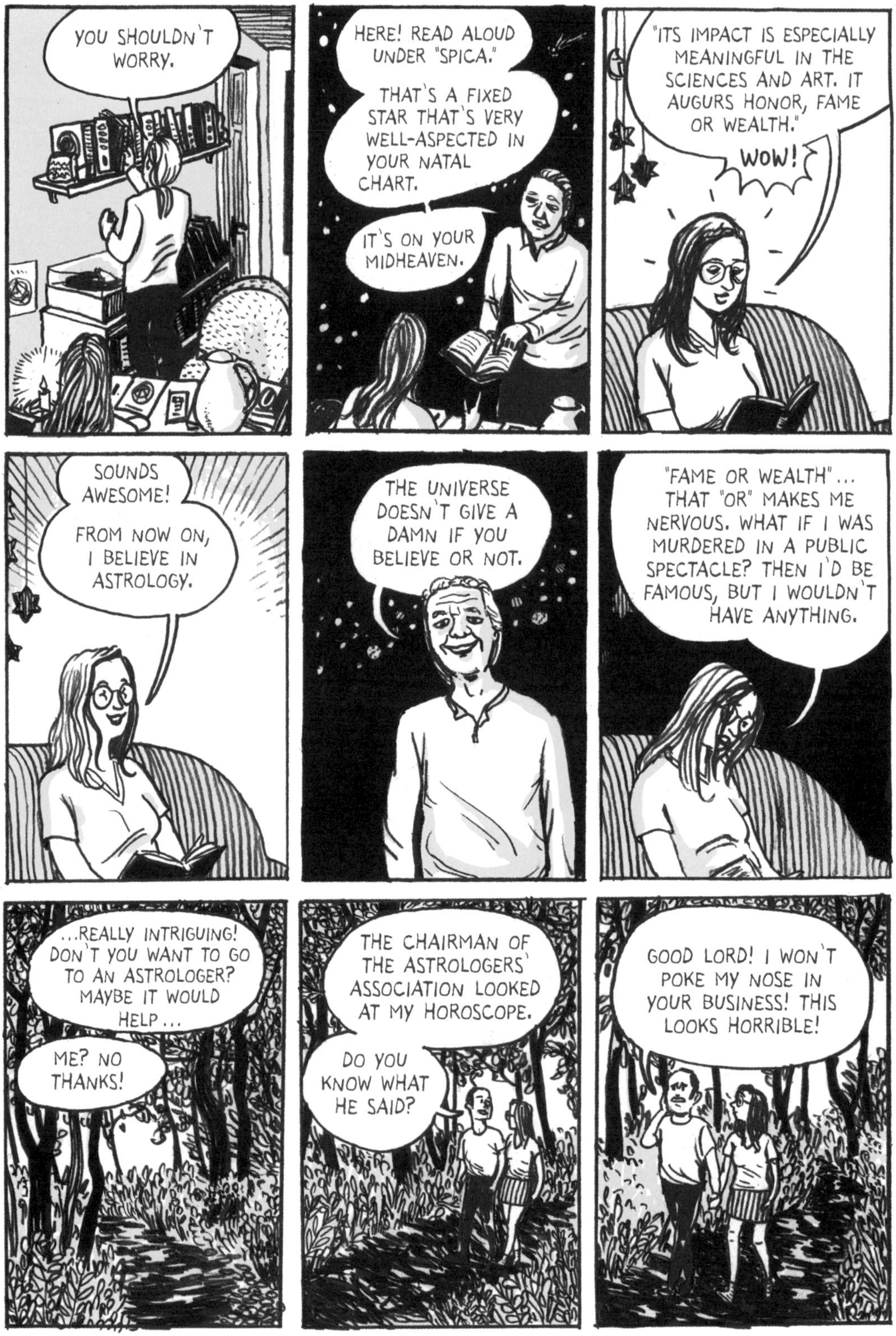
YOU SHOULDN'T WORRY.
HERE! READ ALOUD UNDER "SPICA."
THAT'S A FIXED STAR THAT'S VERY WELL-ASPECTED IN YOUR NATAL CHART.
IT'S ON YOUR MIDHEAVEN.
"ITS IMPACT IS ESPECIALLY MEANINGFUL IN THE SCIENCES AND ART. IT AUGURS HONOR, FAME OR WEALTH."
WOW!
SOUNDS AWESOME!
FROM NOW ON, I BELIEVE IN ASTROLOGY.
THE UNIVERSE DOESN'T GIVE A DAMN IF YOU BELIEVE OR NOT.
"FAME OR WEALTH"... THAT "OR" MAKES ME NERVOUS. WHAT IF I WAS MURDERED IN A PUBLIC SPECTACLE? THEN I'D BE FAMOUS, BUT I WOULDN'T HAVE ANYTHING.
...REALLY INTRIGUING! DON'T YOU WANT TO GO TO AN ASTROLOGER? MAYBE IT WOULD HELP...
ME? NO THANKS!
THE CHAIRMAN OF THE ASTROLOGERS' ASSOCIATION LOOKED AT MY HOROSCOPE.
DO YOU KNOW WHAT HE SAID?
GOOD LORD! I WON'T POKE MY NOSE IN YOUR BUSINESS! THIS LOOKS HORRIBLE!

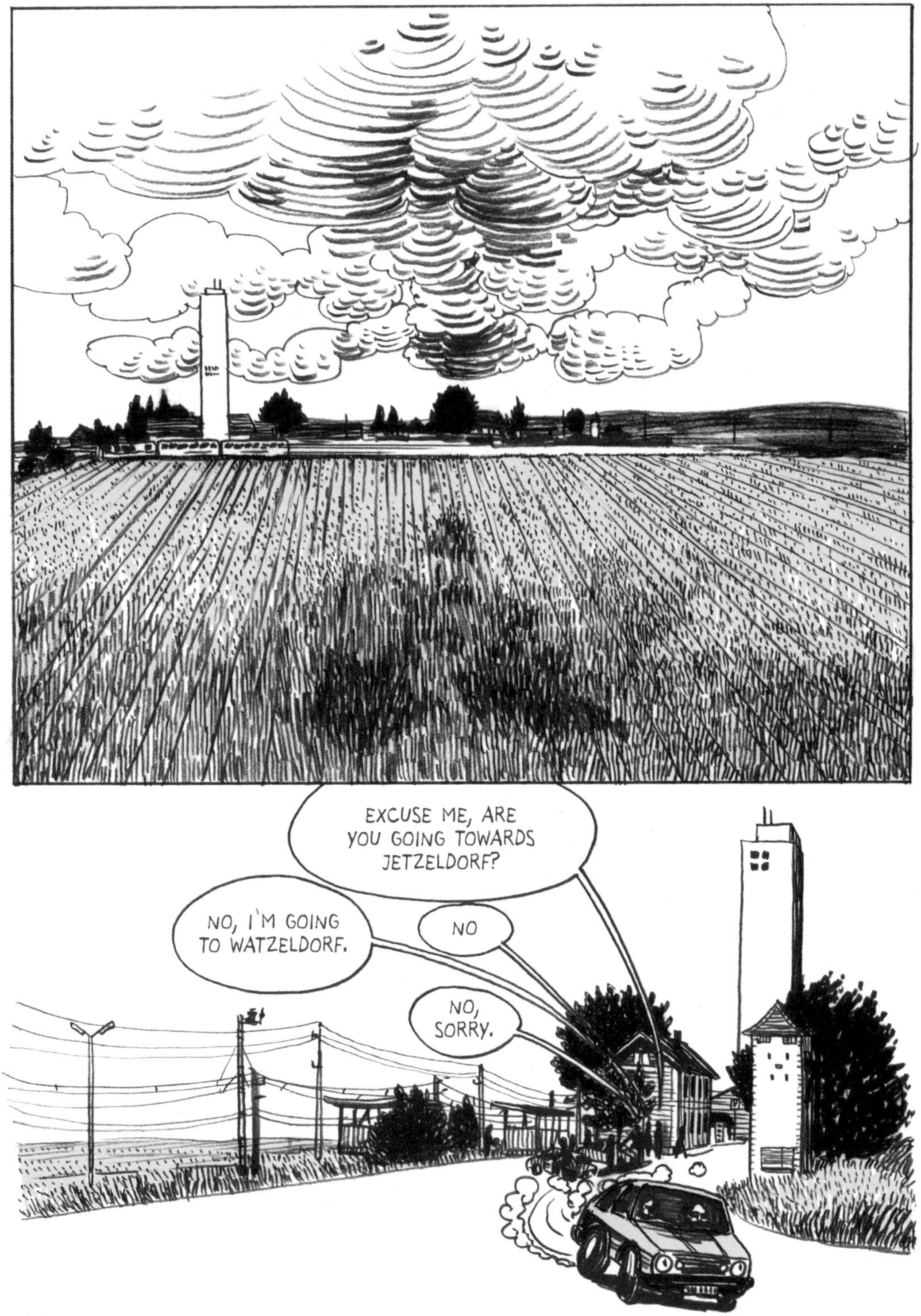
EXCUSE ME, ARE YOU GOING TOWARDS JETZELDORF?
NO, I'M GOING TO WATZELDORF.
NO
NO, SORRY.

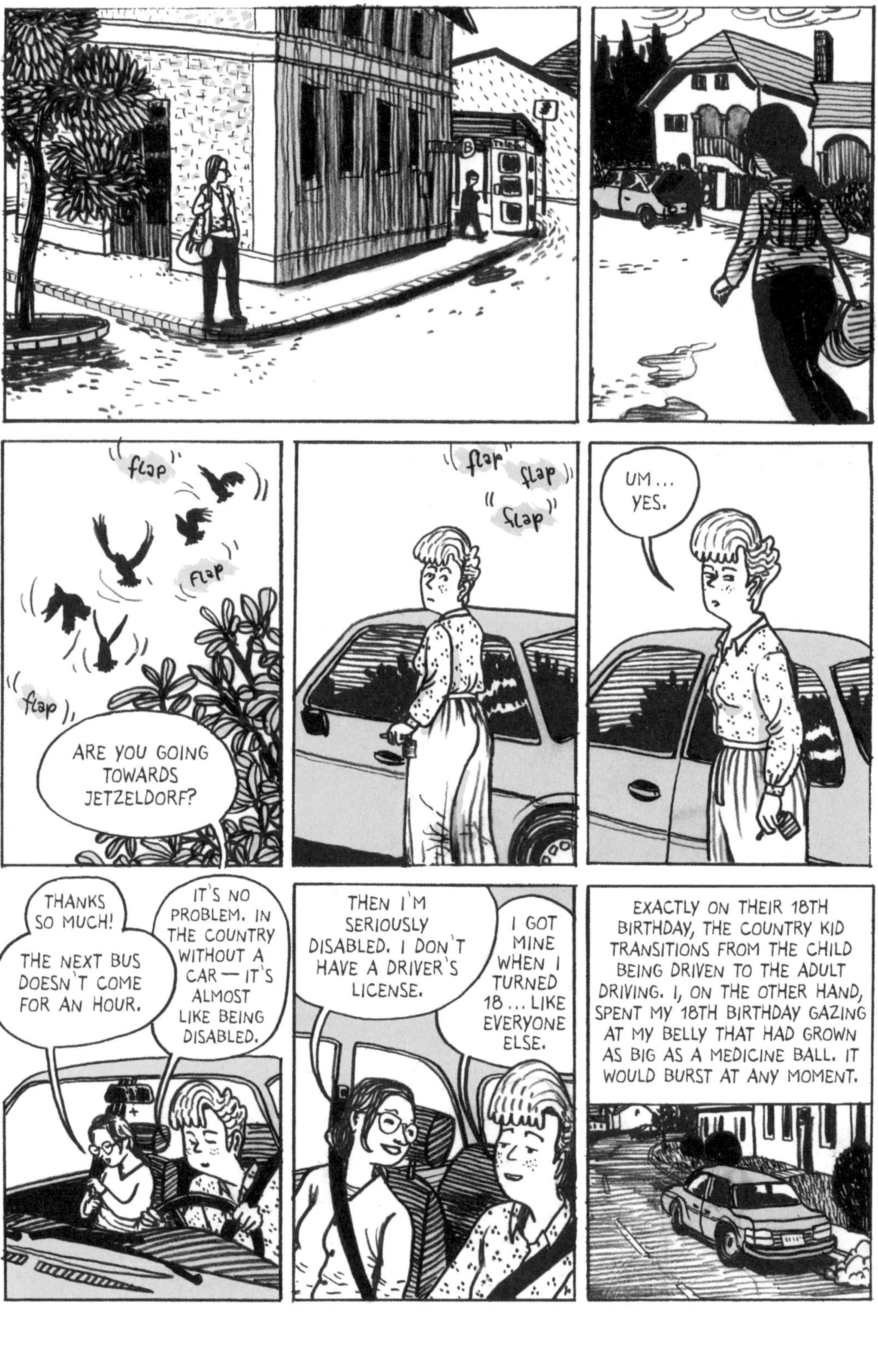
flap
flap
flap
ARE YOU GOING TOWARDS JETZELDORF?
flap
flap
flap
UM... YES.
THANKS SO MUCH!
THE NEXT BUS DOESN'T COME FOR AN HOUR.
IT'S NO PROBLEM. IN THE COUNTRY WITHOUT A CAR — IT'S ALMOST LIKE BEING DISABLED.
THEN I'M SERIOUSLY DISABLED. I DON'T HAVE A DRIVER'S LICENSE.
I GOT MINE WHEN I TURNED 18... LIKE EVERYONE ELSE.
EXACTLY ON THEIR 18TH BIRTHDAY, THE COUNTRY KID TRANSITIONS FROM THE CHILD BEING DRIVEN TO THE ADULT DRIVING. I, ON THE OTHER HAND, SPENT MY 18TH BIRTHDAY GAZING AT MY BELLY THAT HAD GROWN AS BIG AS A MEDICINE BALL. IT WOULD BURST AT ANY MOMENT.

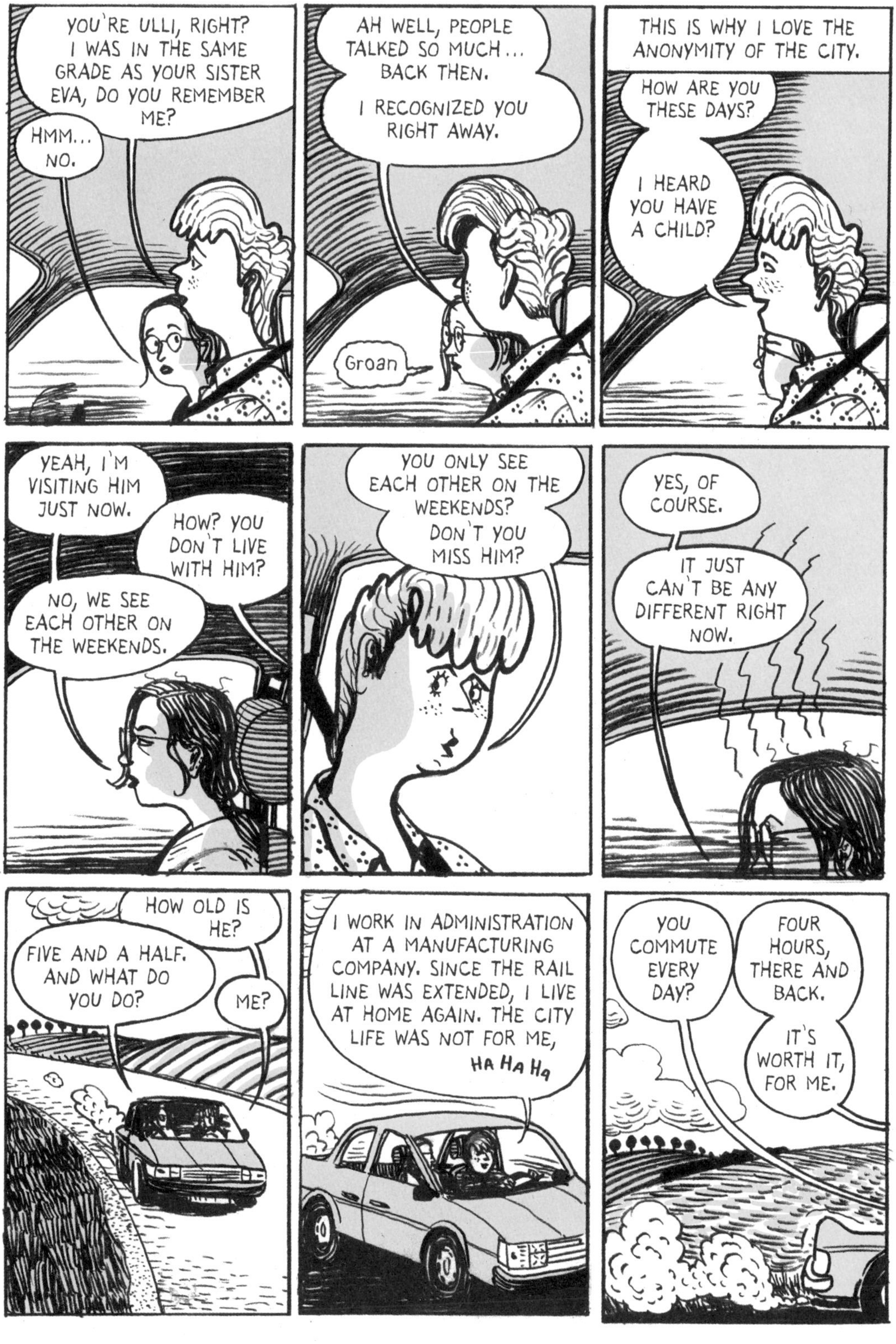

YOU'RE ULLI, RIGHT? I WAS IN THE SAME GRADE AS YOUR SISTER EVA, DO YOU REMEMBER ME?
HMM... NO.
AH WELL, PEOPLE TALKED SO MUCH... BACK THEN.
I RECOGNIZED YOU RIGHT AWAY.
Groan
THIS IS WHY I LOVE THE ANONYMITY OF THE CITY.
HOW ARE YOU THESE DAYS?
I HEARD YOU HAVE A CHILD?
YEAH, I'M VISITING HIM JUST NOW.
HOW? YOU DON'T LIVE WITH HIM?
NO, WE SEE EACH OTHER ON THE WEEKENDS.
YOU ONLY SEE EACH OTHER ON THE WEEKENDS?
DON'T YOU MISS HIM?
YES, OF COURSE.
IT JUST CAN'T BE ANY DIFFERENT RIGHT NOW.
HOW OLD IS HE?
FIVE AND A HALF. AND WHAT DO YOU DO?
ME?
I WORK IN ADMINISTRATION AT A MANUFACTURING COMPANY. SINCE THE RAIL LINE WAS EXTENDED, I LIVE AT HOME AGAIN. THE CITY LIFE WAS NOT FOR ME,
HA HA HA
YOU COMMUTE EVERY DAY?
FOUR HOURS, THERE AND BACK.
IT'S WORTH IT, FOR ME.

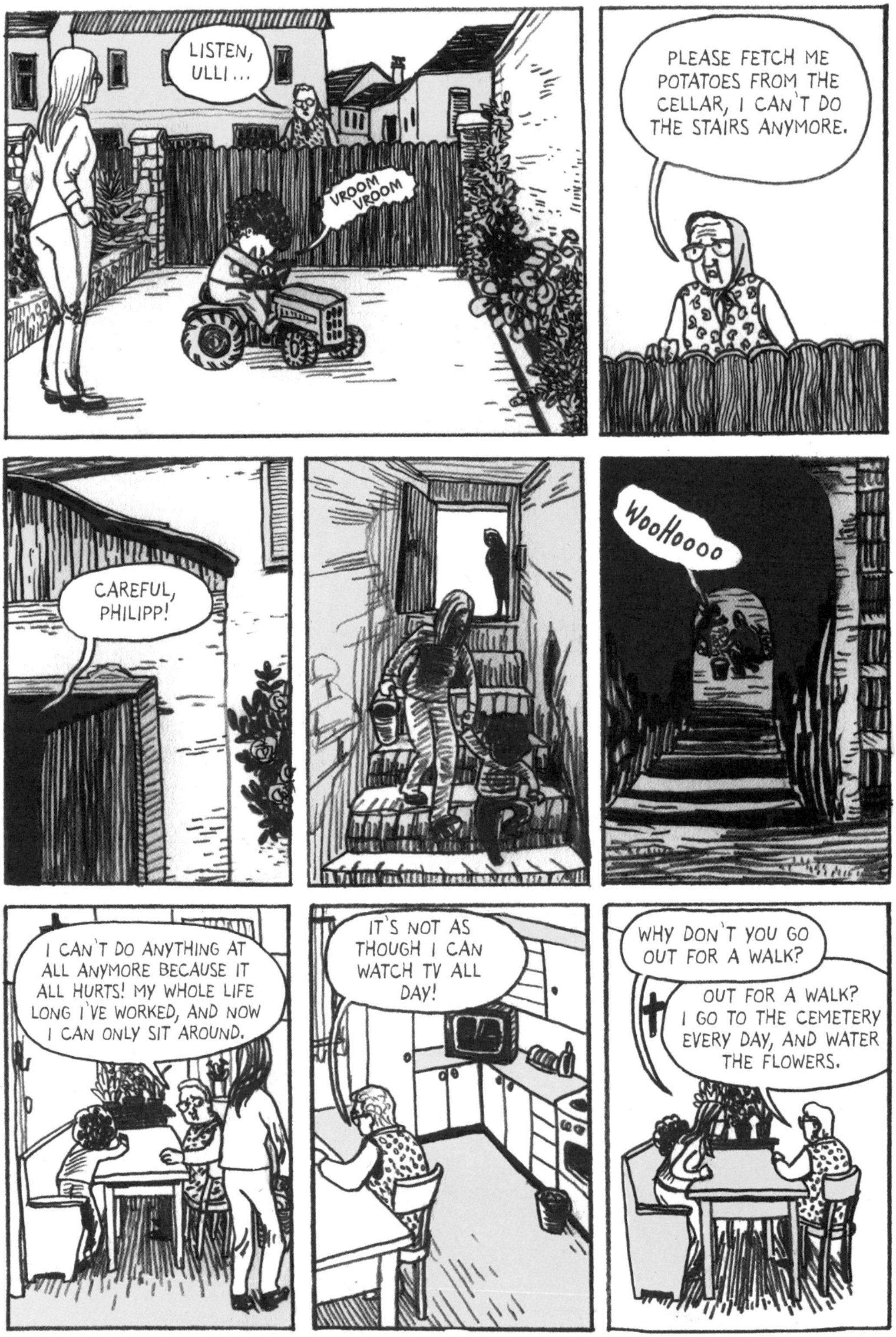
LISTEN, ULLI...
VROOM VROOM
PLEASE FETCH ME POTATOES FROM THE CELLAR, I CAN'T DO THE STAIRS ANYMORE.
CAREFUL, PHILIPP!
WooHoooo
I CAN'T DO ANYTHING AT ALL ANYMORE BECAUSE IT ALL HURTS! MY WHOLE LIFE LONG I'VE WORKED, AND NOW I CAN ONLY SIT AROUND.
IT'S NOT AS THOUGH I CAN WATCH TV ALL DAY!
WHY DON'T YOU GO OUT FOR A WALK?
OUT FOR A WALK? I GO TO THE CEMETERY EVERY DAY, AND WATER THE FLOWERS.

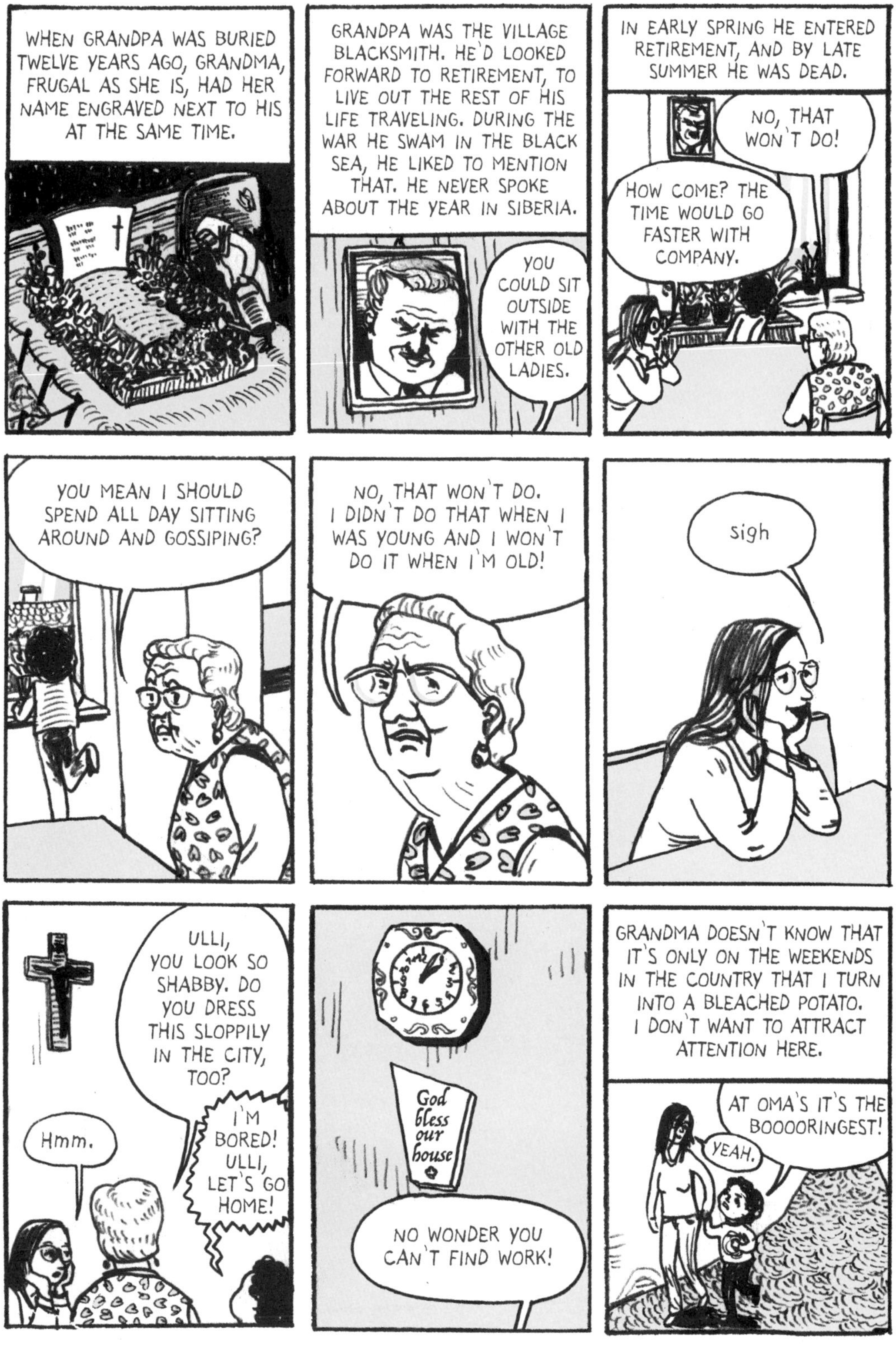
WHEN GRANDPA WAS BURIED TWELVE YEARS AGO, GRANDMA, FRUGAL AS SHE IS, HAD HER NAME ENGRAVED NEXT TO HIS AT THE SAME TIME.
GRANDPA WAS THE VILLAGE BLACKSMITH. HE'D LOOKED FORWARD TO RETIREMENT, TO LIVE OUT THE REST OF HIS LIFE TRAVELING. DURING THE WAR HE SWAM IN THE BLACK SEA, HE LIKED TO MENTION THAT. HE NEVER SPOKE ABOUT THE YEAR IN SIBERIA.
YOU COULD SIT OUTSIDE WITH THE OTHER OLD LADIES.
IN EARLY SPRING HE ENTERED RETIREMENT, AND BY LATE SUMMER HE WAS DEAD.
NO, THAT WON'T DO!
HOW COME? THE TIME WOULD GO FASTER WITH COMPANY.
YOU MEAN I SHOULD SPEND ALL DAY SITTING AROUND AND GOSSIPING?
NO, THAT WON'T DO. I DIDN'T DO THAT WHEN I WAS YOUNG AND I WON'T DO IT WHEN I'M OLD!
sigh
ULLI, YOU LOOK SO SHABBY. DO YOU DRESS THIS SLOPPILY IN THE CITY, TOO?
Hmm.
I'M BORED! ULLI, LET'S GO HOME!
God bless our house
NO WONDER YOU CAN'T FIND WORK!
GRANDMA DOESN'T KNOW THAT IT'S ONLY ON THE WEEKENDS IN THE COUNTRY THAT I TURN INTO A BLEACHED POTATO. I DON'T WANT TO ATTRACT ATTENTION HERE.
AT OMA'S IT'S THE BOOOORINGEST!
YEAH.

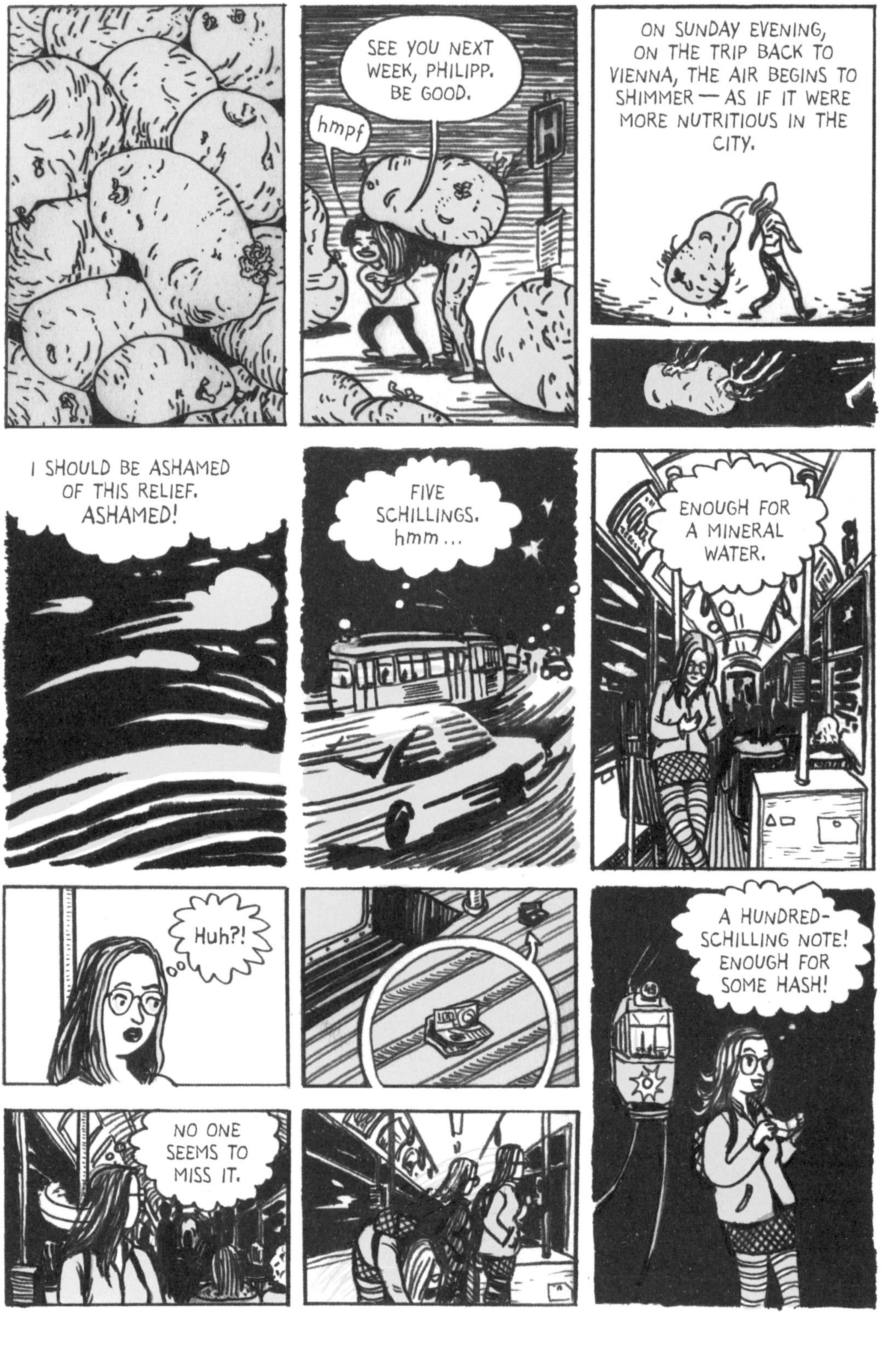

SEE YOU NEXT WEEK, PHILIPP. BE GOOD.
hmpf
ON SUNDAY EVENING, ON THE TRIP BACK TO VIENNA, THE AIR BEGINS TO SHIMMER — AS IF IT WERE MORE NUTRITIOUS IN THE CITY.
I SHOULD BE ASHAMED OF THIS RELIEF. ASHAMED!
FIVE SCHILLINGS. hmm...
ENOUGH FOR A MINERAL WATER.
Huh?!
A HUNDRED-SCHILLING NOTE! ENOUGH FOR SOME HASH!
NO ONE SEEMS TO MISS IT.

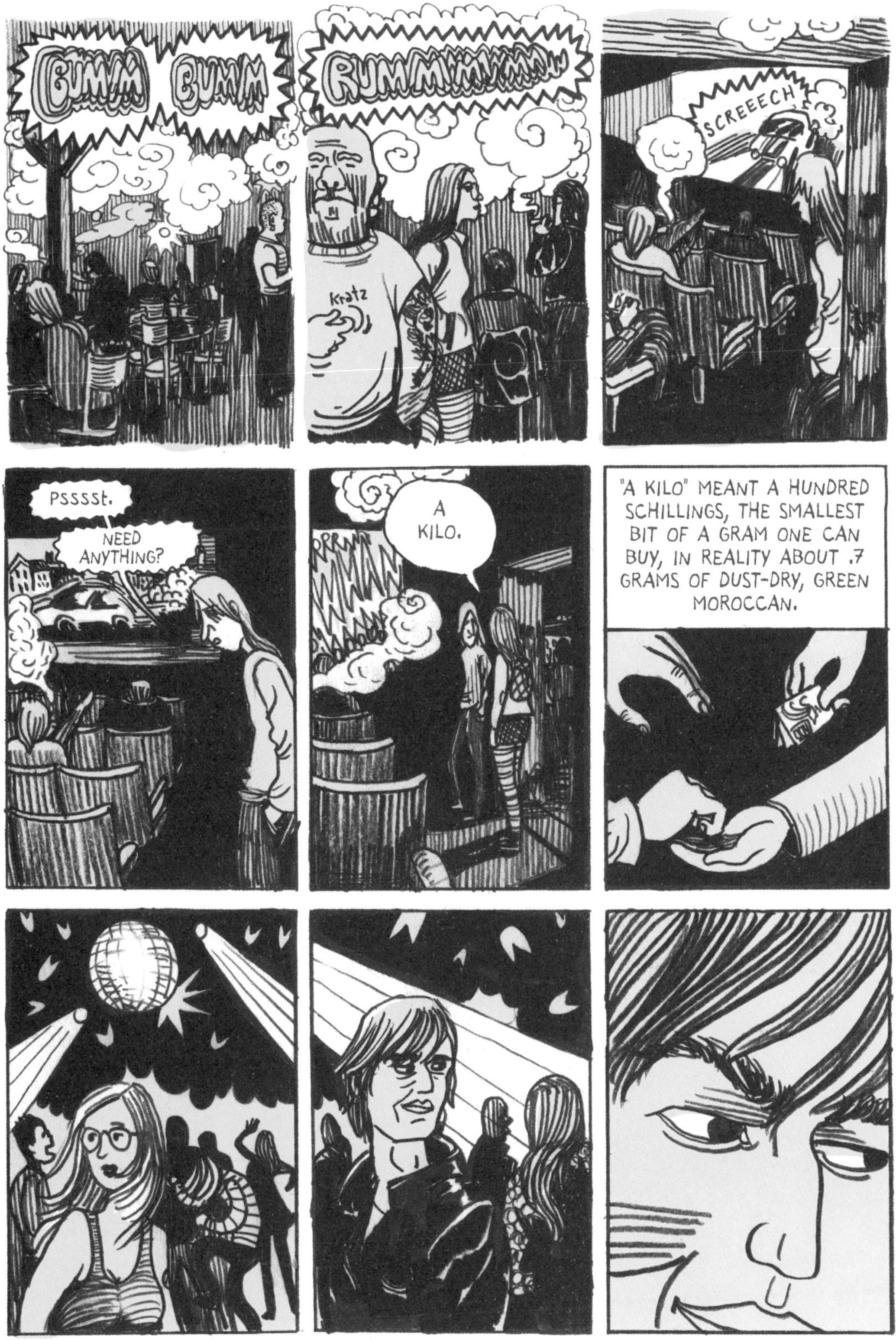
CUMM CUMM
RUMMMMMMM
Kratz
SCREEECH
PSSSSt.
NEED ANYTHING?
A KILO.
"A KILO" MEANT A HUNDRED SCHILLINGS, THE SMALLEST BIT OF A GRAM ONE CAN BUY, IN REALITY ABOUT .7 GRAMS OF DUST-DRY, GREEN MOROCCAN.

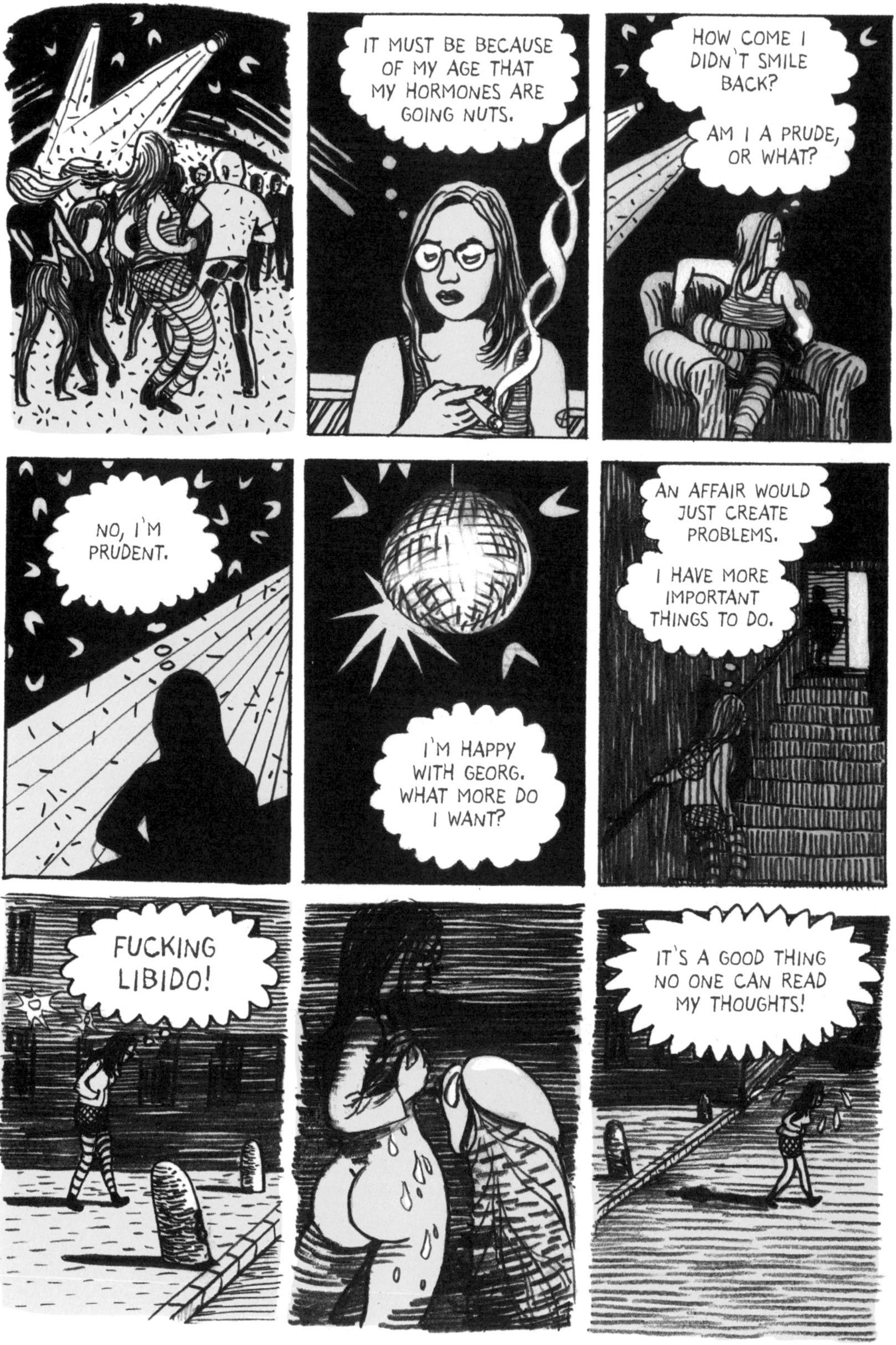
IT MUST BE BECAUSE OF MY AGE THAT MY HORMONES ARE GOING NUTS.
HOW COME I DIDN'T SMILE BACK?
AM I A PRUDE, OR WHAT?
NO, I'M PRUDENT.
I'M HAPPY WITH GEORG. WHAT MORE DO I WANT?
AN AFFAIR WOULD JUST CREATE PROBLEMS.
I HAVE MORE IMPORTANT THINGS TO DO.
FUCKING LIBIDO!
IT'S A GOOD THING NO ONE CAN READ MY THOUGHTS!

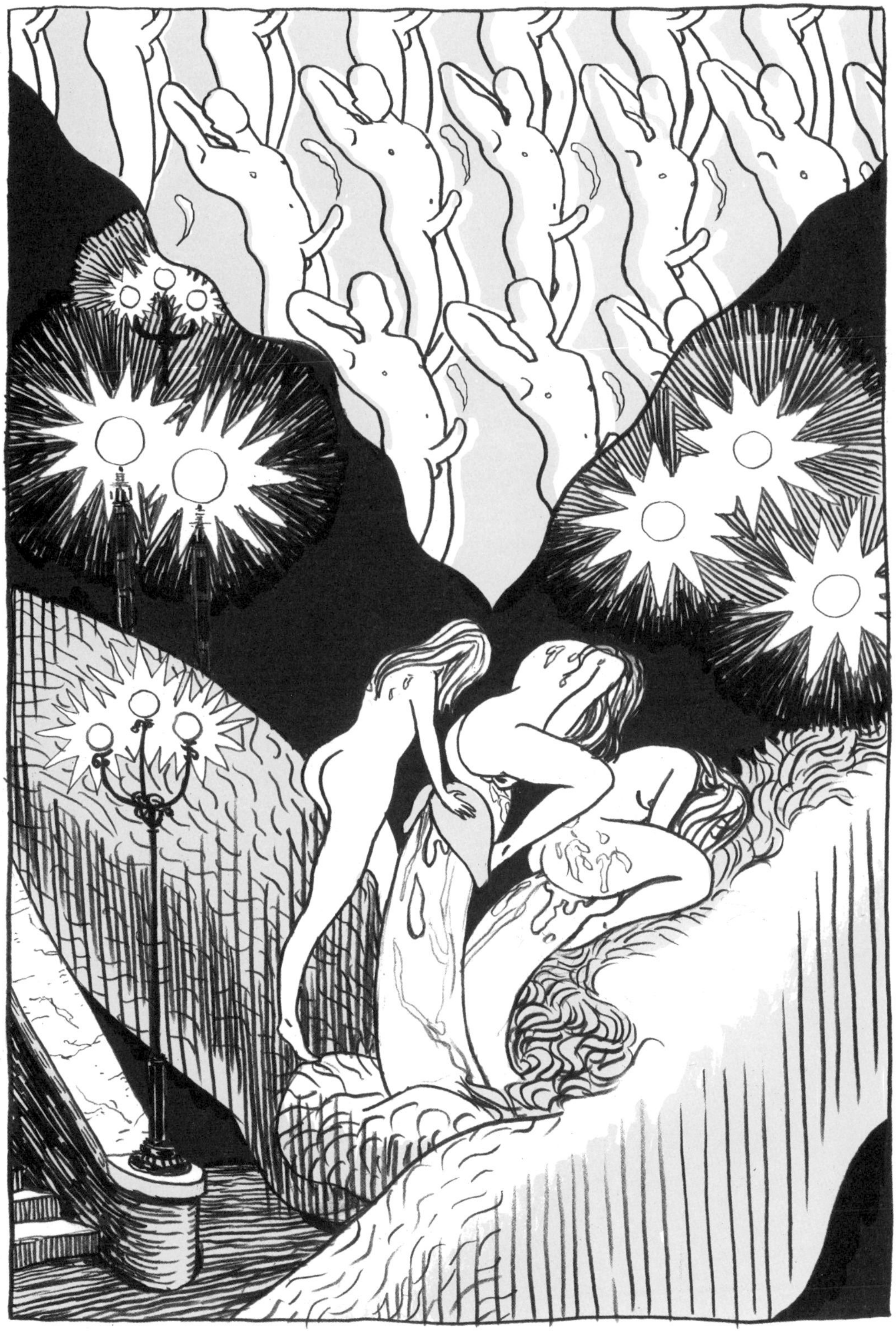

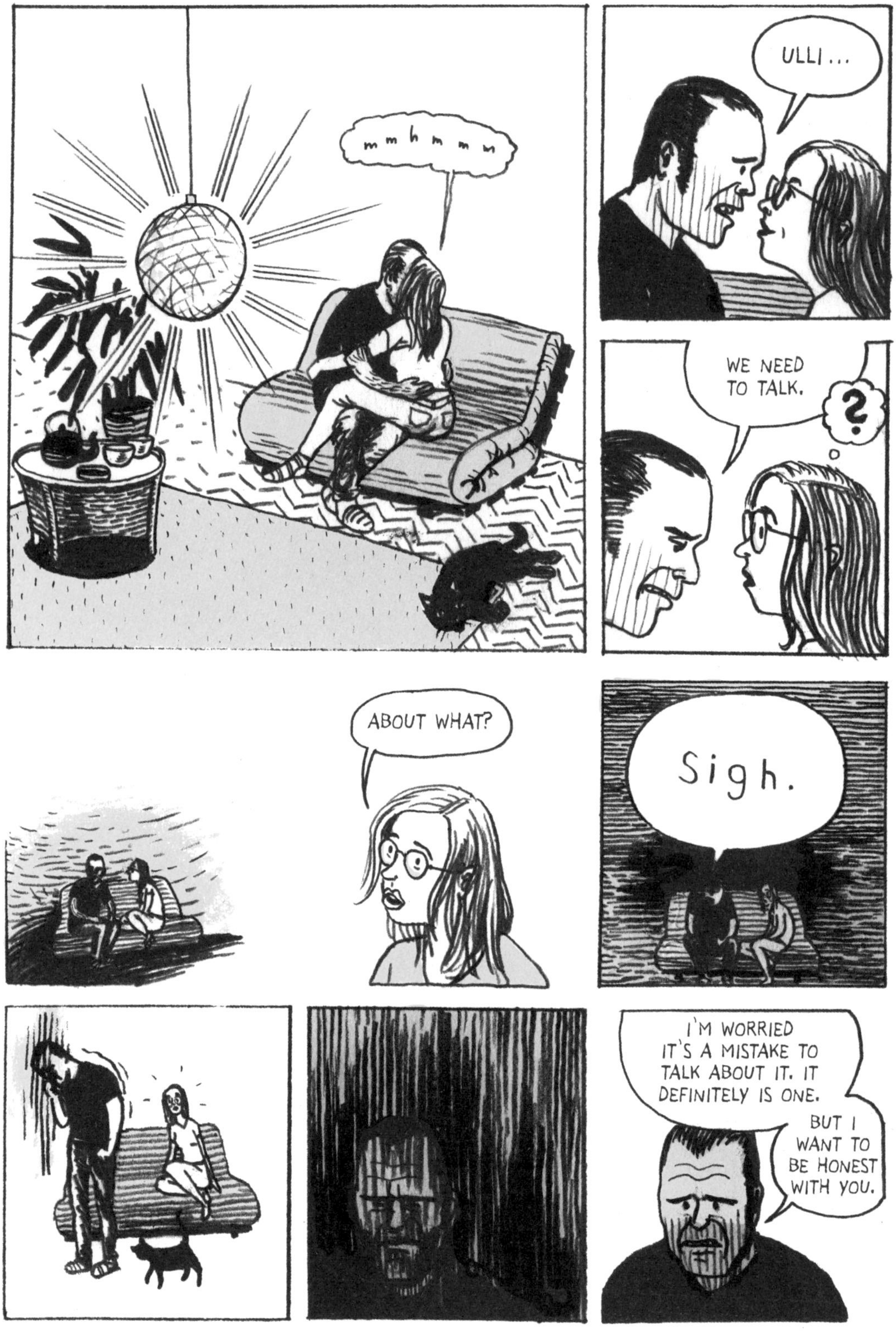
mmhmmm
ULLI...
WE NEED TO TALK.
?
ABOUT WHAT?
Sigh.
I'M WORRIED IT'S A MISTAKE TO TALK ABOUT IT. IT DEFINITELY IS ONE.
BUT I WANT TO BE HONEST WITH YOU.

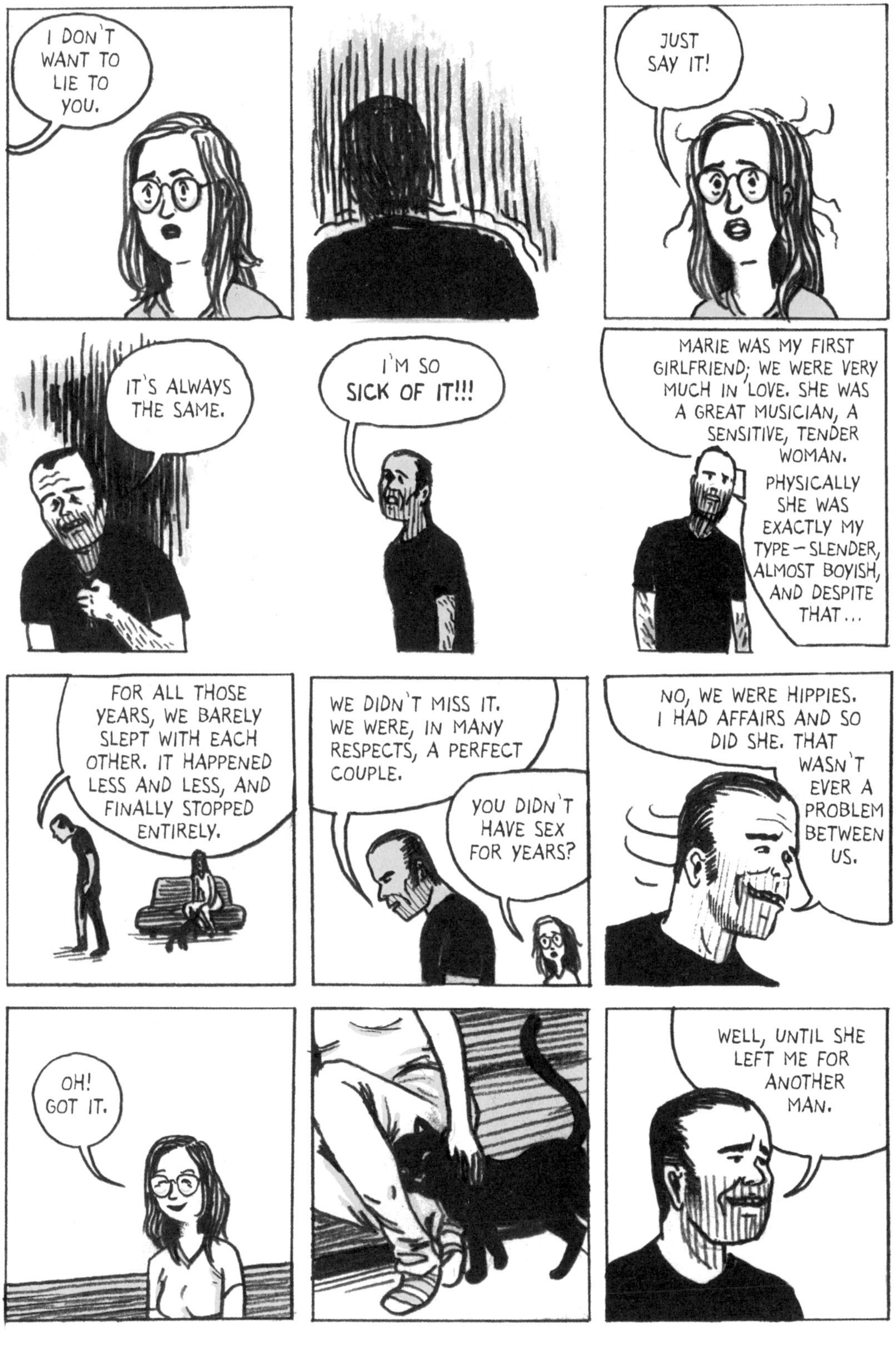
I DON'T WANT TO LIE TO YOU.
JUST SAY IT!
IT'S ALWAYS THE SAME.
I'M SO SICK OF IT!!!
MARIE WAS MY FIRST GIRLFRIEND; WE WERE VERY MUCH IN LOVE. SHE WAS A GREAT MUSICIAN, A SENSITIVE, TENDER WOMAN.
PHYSICALLY SHE WAS EXACTLY MY TYPE—SLENDER, ALMOST BOYISH, AND DESPITE THAT...
FOR ALL THOSE YEARS, WE BARELY SLEPT WITH EACH OTHER. IT HAPPENED LESS AND LESS, AND FINALLY STOPPED ENTIRELY.
WE DIDN'T MISS IT. WE WERE, IN MANY RESPECTS, A PERFECT COUPLE.
YOU DIDN'T HAVE SEX FOR YEARS?
NO, WE WERE HIPPIES. I HAD AFFAIRS AND SO DID SHE. THAT WASN'T EVER A PROBLEM BETWEEN US.
OH! GOT IT.
WELL, UNTIL SHE LEFT ME FOR ANOTHER MAN.

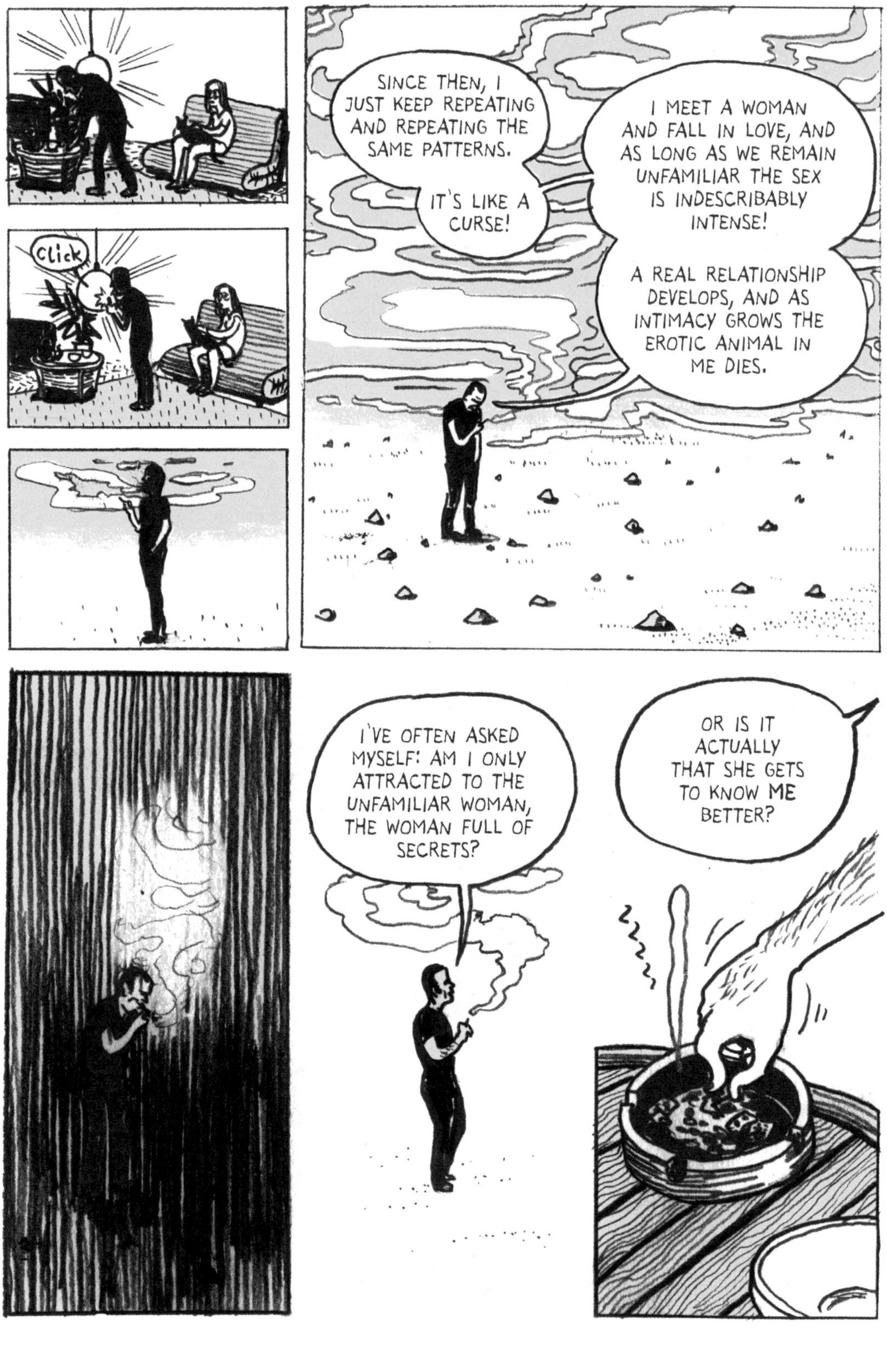

Click
SINCE THEN, I JUST KEEP REPEATING AND REPEATING THE SAME PATTERNS.
IT'S LIKE A CURSE!
I MEET A WOMAN AND FALL IN LOVE, AND AS LONG AS WE REMAIN UNFAMILIAR THE SEX IS INDESCRIBABLY INTENSE!
A REAL RELATIONSHIP DEVELOPS, AND AS INTIMACY GROWS THE EROTIC ANIMAL IN ME DIES.
I'VE OFTEN ASKED MYSELF: AM I ONLY ATTRACTED TO THE UNFAMILIAR WOMAN, THE WOMAN FULL OF SECRETS?
OR IS IT ACTUALLY THAT SHE GETS TO KNOW ME BETTER?

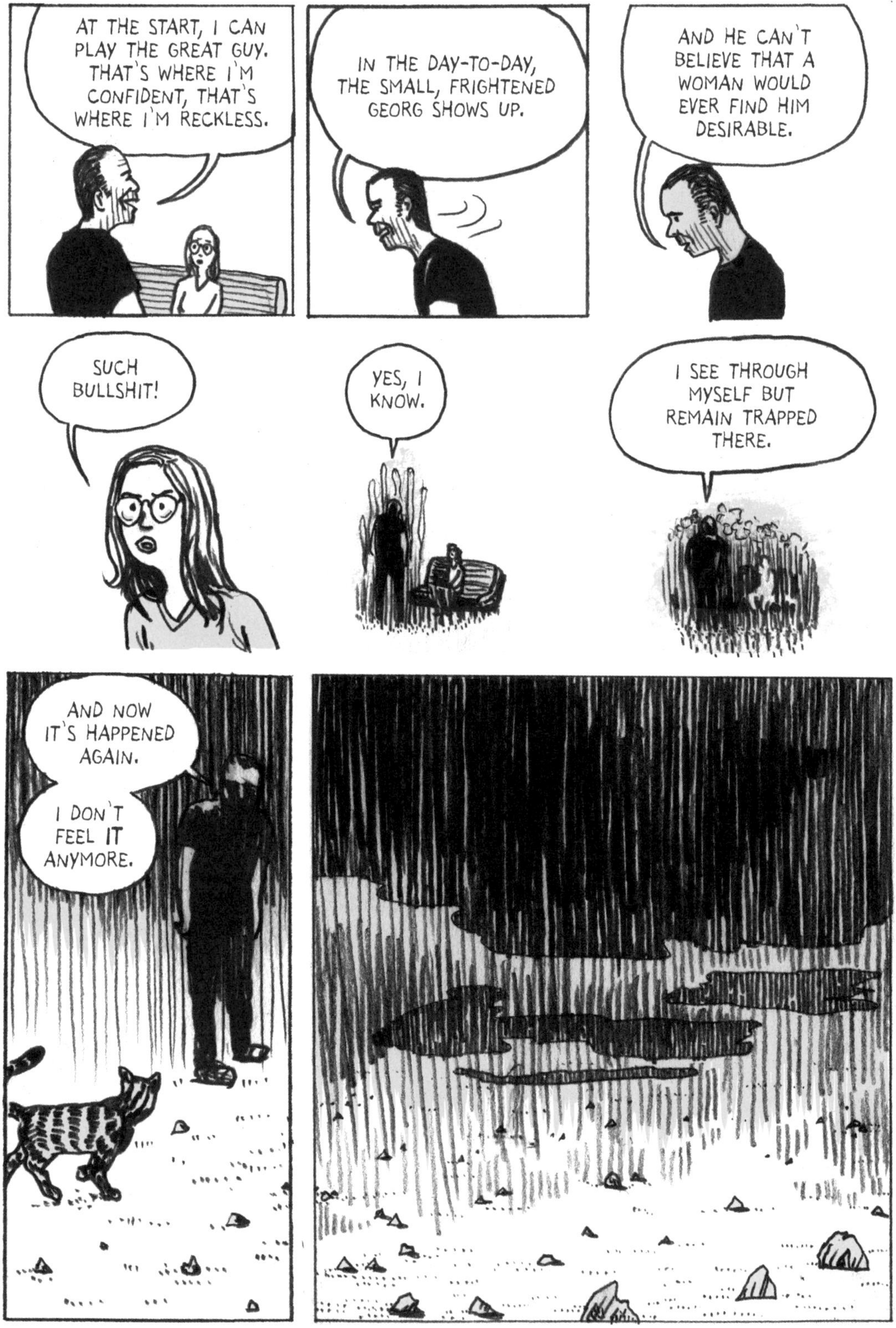
AT THE START, I CAN PLAY THE GREAT GUY. THAT'S WHERE I'M CONFIDENT, THAT'S WHERE I'M RECKLESS.
IN THE DAY-TO-DAY, THE SMALL, FRIGHTENED GEORG SHOWS UP.
AND HE CAN'T BELIEVE THAT A WOMAN WOULD EVER FIND HIM DESIRABLE.
SUCH BULLSHIT!
YES, I KNOW.
I SEE THROUGH MYSELF BUT REMAIN TRAPPED THERE.
AND NOW IT'S HAPPENED AGAIN.
I DON'T FEEL IT ANYMORE.

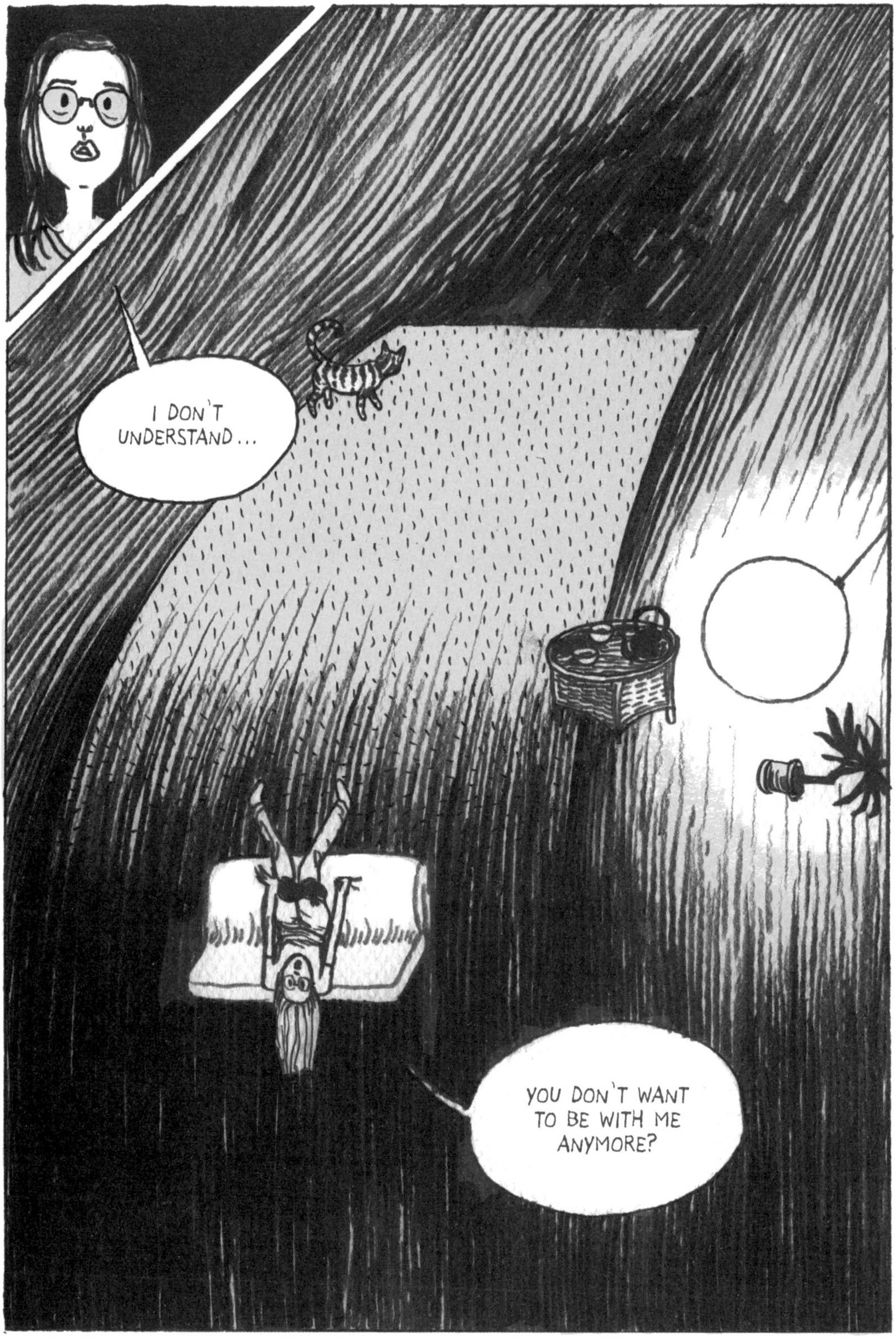
I DON'T UNDERSTAND...
YOU DON'T WANT TO BE WITH ME ANYMORE?

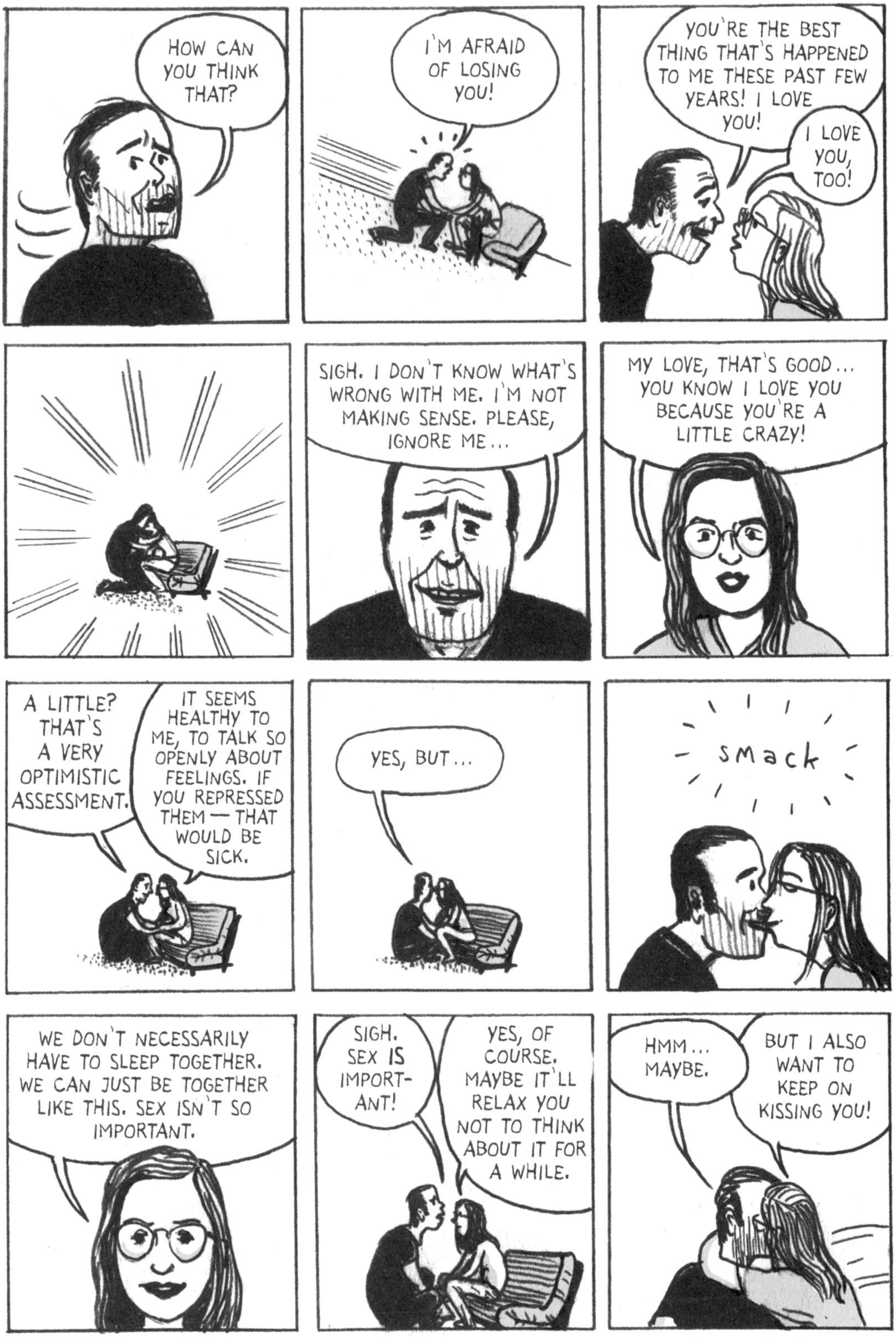
HOW CAN YOU THINK THAT?
I'M AFRAID OF LOSING YOU!
YOU'RE THE BEST THING THAT'S HAPPENED TO ME THESE PAST FEW YEARS! I LOVE YOU!
I LOVE YOU, TOO!
SIGH. I DON'T KNOW WHAT'S WRONG WITH ME. I'M NOT MAKING SENSE. PLEASE, IGNORE ME...
MY LOVE, THAT'S GOOD... YOU KNOW I LOVE YOU BECAUSE YOU'RE A LITTLE CRAZY!
A LITTLE? THAT'S A VERY OPTIMISTIC ASSESSMENT.
IT SEEMS HEALTHY TO ME, TO TALK SO OPENLY ABOUT FEELINGS. IF YOU REPRESSED THEM — THAT WOULD BE SICK.
YES, BUT...
smack
WE DON'T NECESSARILY HAVE TO SLEEP TOGETHER. WE CAN JUST BE TOGETHER LIKE THIS. SEX ISN'T SO IMPORTANT.
SIGH. SEX IS IMPORT-ANT!
YES, OF COURSE. MAYBE IT'LL RELAX YOU NOT TO THINK ABOUT IT FOR A WHILE.
HMM... MAYBE.
BUT I ALSO WANT TO KEEP ON KISSING YOU!

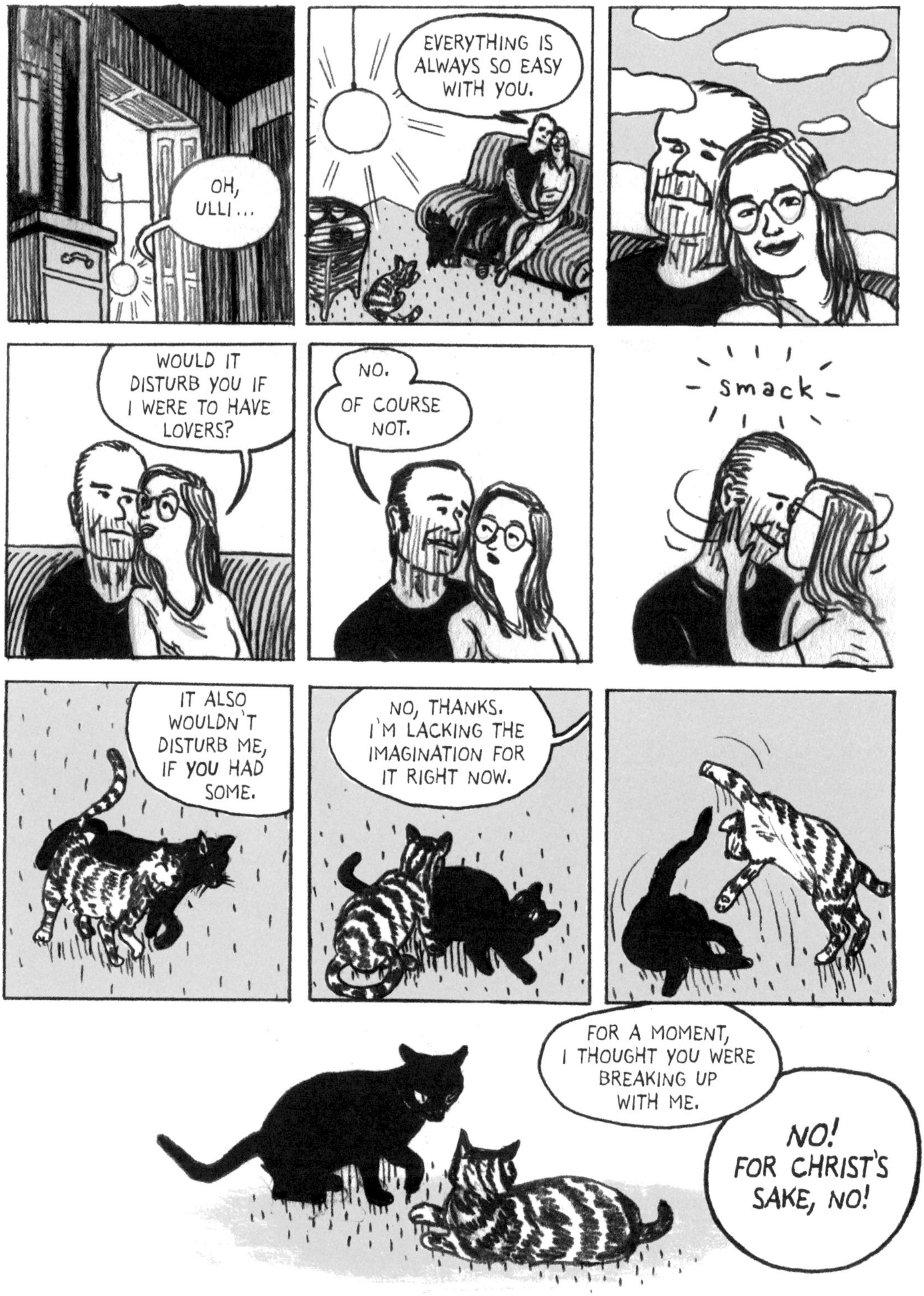
OH, ULLI...
EVERYTHING IS ALWAYS SO EASY WITH YOU.
WOULD IT DISTURB YOU IF I WERE TO HAVE LOVERS?
NO.
OF COURSE NOT.
smack
IT ALSO WOULDN'T DISTURB ME, IF YOU HAD SOME.
NO, THANKS. I'M LACKING THE IMAGINATION FOR IT RIGHT NOW.
FOR A MOMENT, I THOUGHT YOU WERE BREAKING UP WITH ME.
NO! FOR CHRIST'S SAKE, NO!

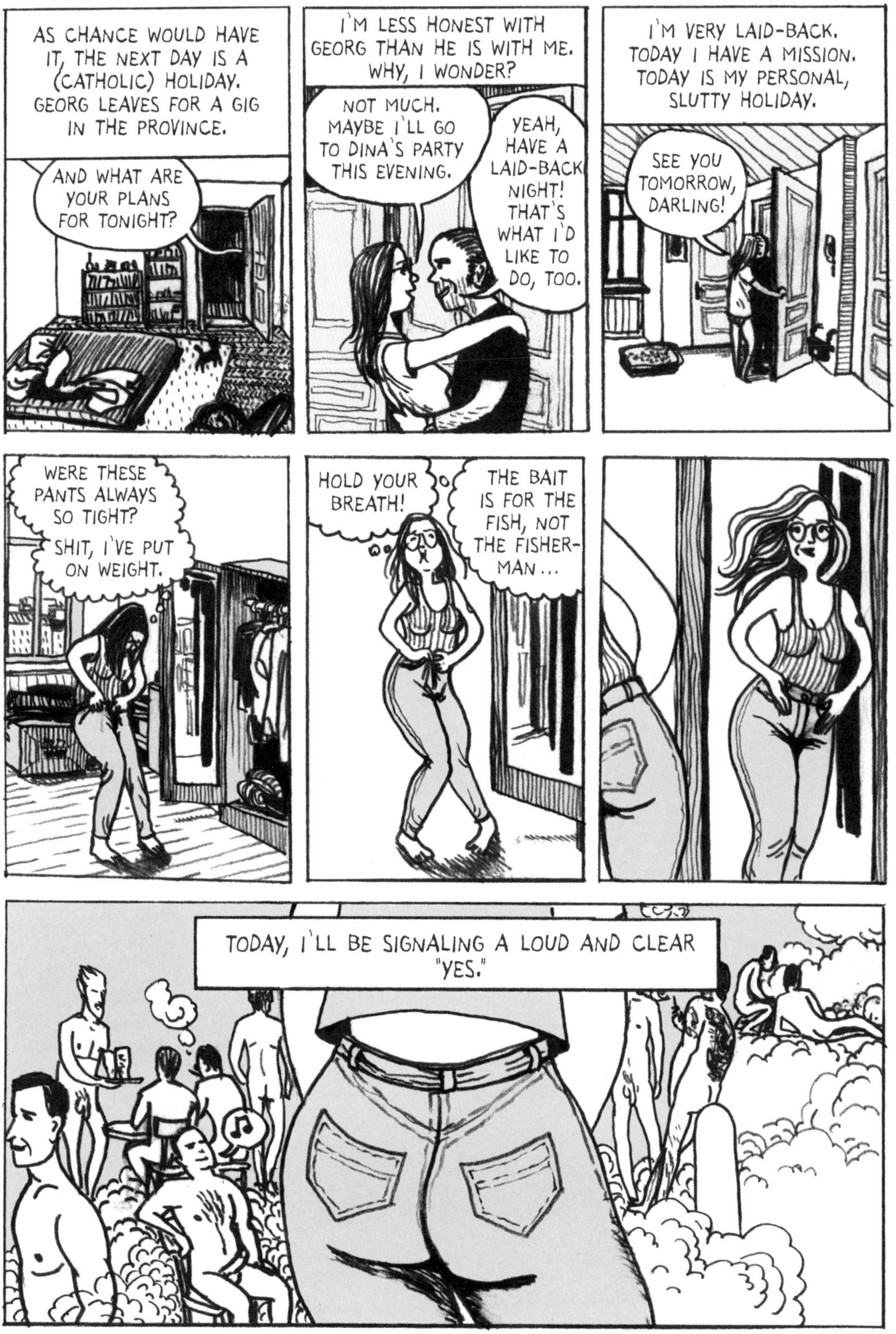
AS CHANCE WOULD HAVE IT, THE NEXT DAY IS A (CATHOLIC) HOLIDAY. GEORG LEAVES FOR A GIG IN THE PROVINCE.
AND WHAT ARE YOUR PLANS FOR TONIGHT?
I'M LESS HONEST WITH GEORG THAN HE IS WITH ME. WHY, I WONDER?
NOT MUCH. MAYBE I'LL GO TO DINA'S PARTY THIS EVENING.
YEAH, HAVE A LAID-BACK NIGHT! THAT'S WHAT I'D LIKE TO DO, TOO.
I'M VERY LAID-BACK. TODAY I HAVE A MISSION. TODAY IS MY PERSONAL, SLUTTY HOLIDAY.
SEE YOU TOMORROW, DARLING!
WERE THESE PANTS ALWAYS SO TIGHT?
SHIT, I'VE PUT ON WEIGHT.
HOLD YOUR BREATH!
THE BAIT IS FOR THE FISH, NOT THE FISHER-MAN...
TODAY, I'LL BE SIGNALING A LOUD AND CLEAR "YES."

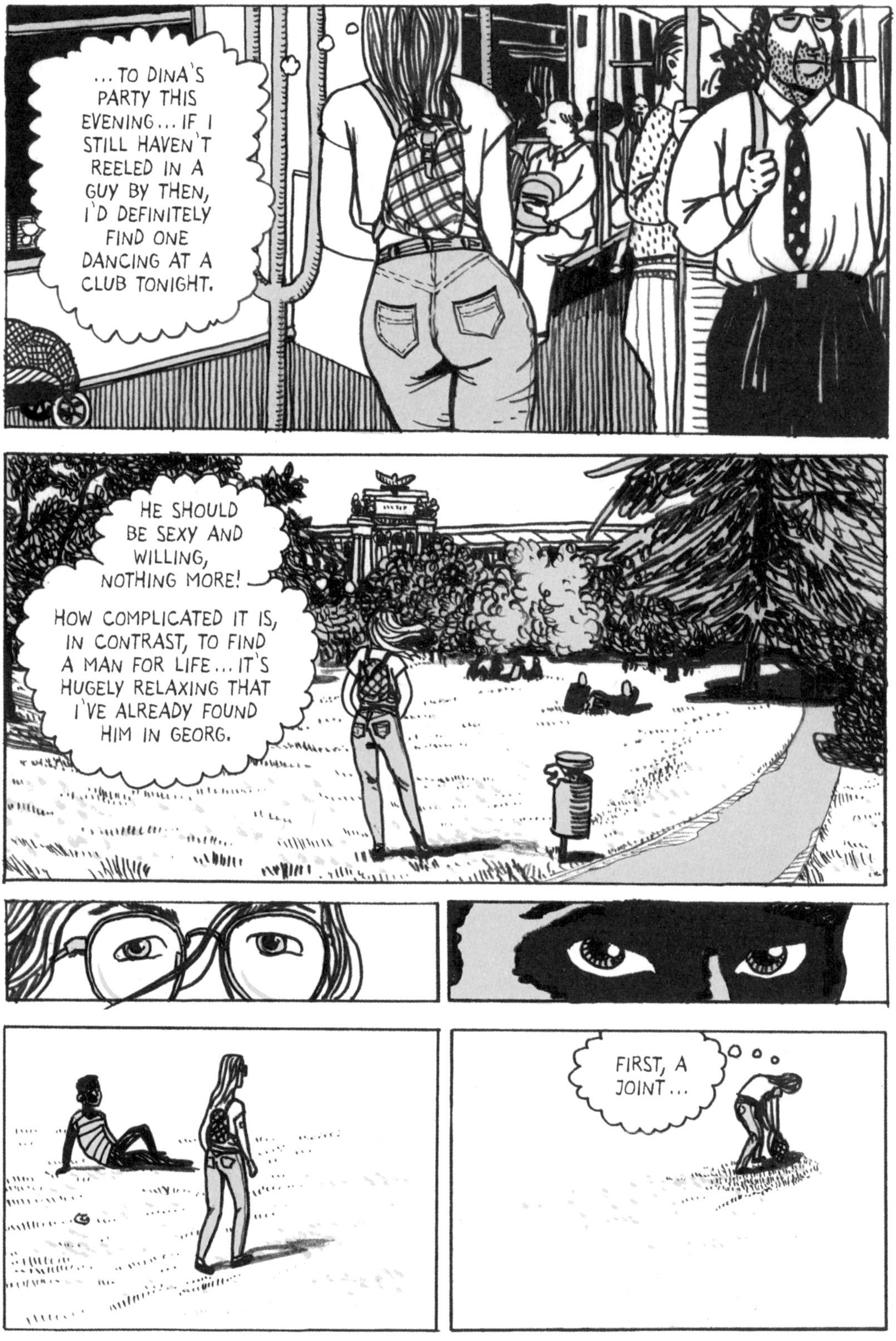
...TO DINA'S PARTY THIS EVENING... IF I STILL HAVEN'T REELED IN A GUY BY THEN, I'D DEFINITELY FIND ONE DANCING AT A CLUB TONIGHT.
HE SHOULD BE SEXY AND WILLING, NOTHING MORE!
HOW COMPLICATED IT IS, IN CONTRAST, TO FIND A MAN FOR LIFE... IT'S HUGELY RELAXING THAT I'VE ALREADY FOUND HIM IN GEORG.
FIRST, A JOINT...

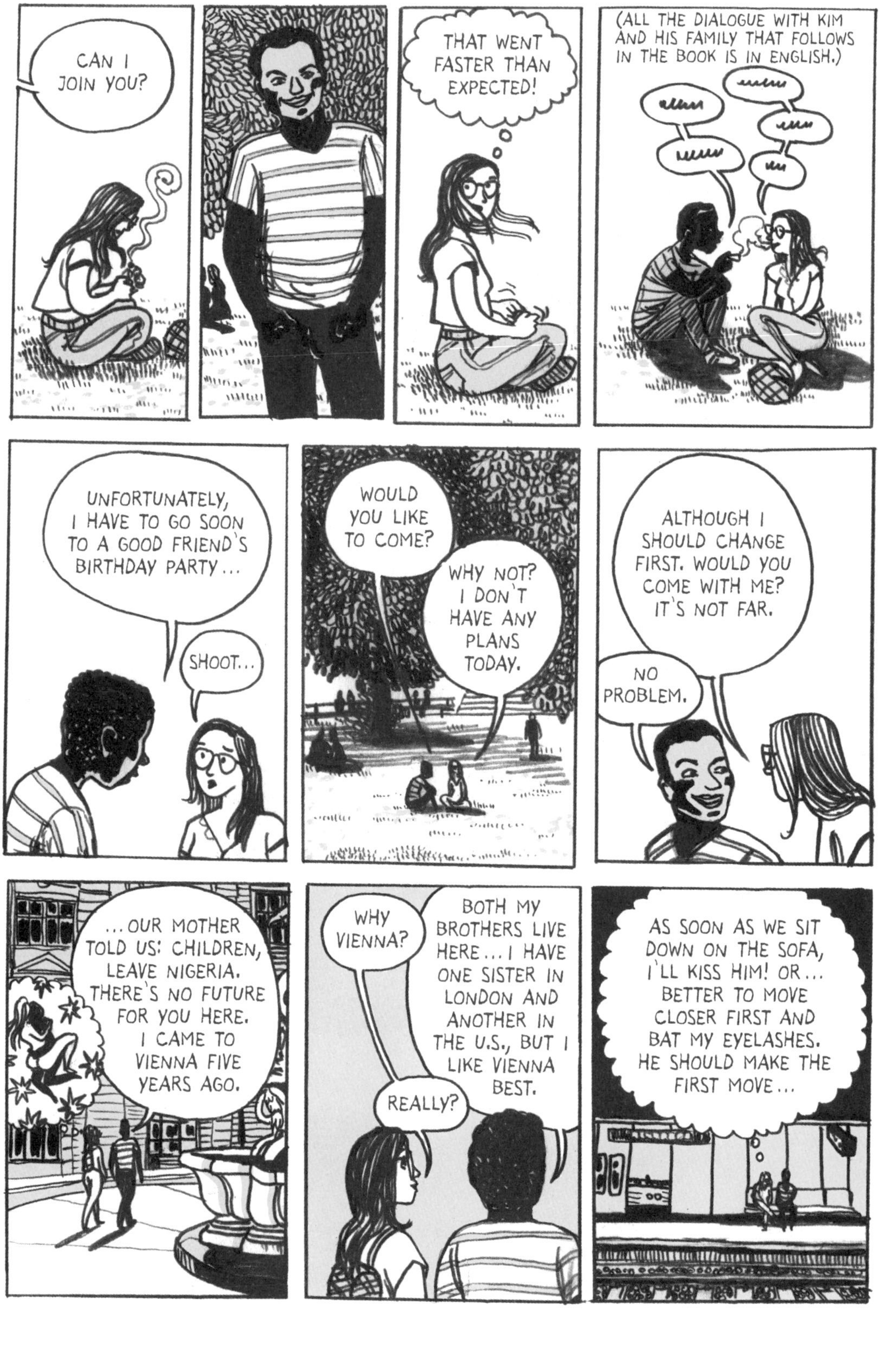
CAN I JOIN YOU?
THAT WENT FASTER THAN EXPECTED!
(ALL THE DIALOGUE WITH KIM AND HIS FAMILY THAT FOLLOWS IN THE BOOK IS IN ENGLISH.)
UNFORTUNATELY, I HAVE TO GO SOON TO A GOOD FRIEND'S BIRTHDAY PARTY...
SHOOT...
WOULD YOU LIKE TO COME?
WHY NOT? I DON'T HAVE ANY PLANS TODAY.
ALTHOUGH I SHOULD CHANGE FIRST. WOULD YOU COME WITH ME? IT'S NOT FAR.
NO PROBLEM.
...OUR MOTHER TOLD US: CHILDREN, LEAVE NIGERIA. THERE'S NO FUTURE FOR YOU HERE. I CAME TO VIENNA FIVE YEARS AGO.
WHY VIENNA?
BOTH MY BROTHERS LIVE HERE... I HAVE ONE SISTER IN LONDON AND ANOTHER IN THE U.S., BUT I LIKE VIENNA BEST.
REALLY?
AS SOON AS WE SIT DOWN ON THE SOFA, I'LL KISS HIM! OR... BETTER TO MOVE CLOSER FIRST AND BAT MY EYELASHES. HE SHOULD MAKE THE FIRST MOVE...

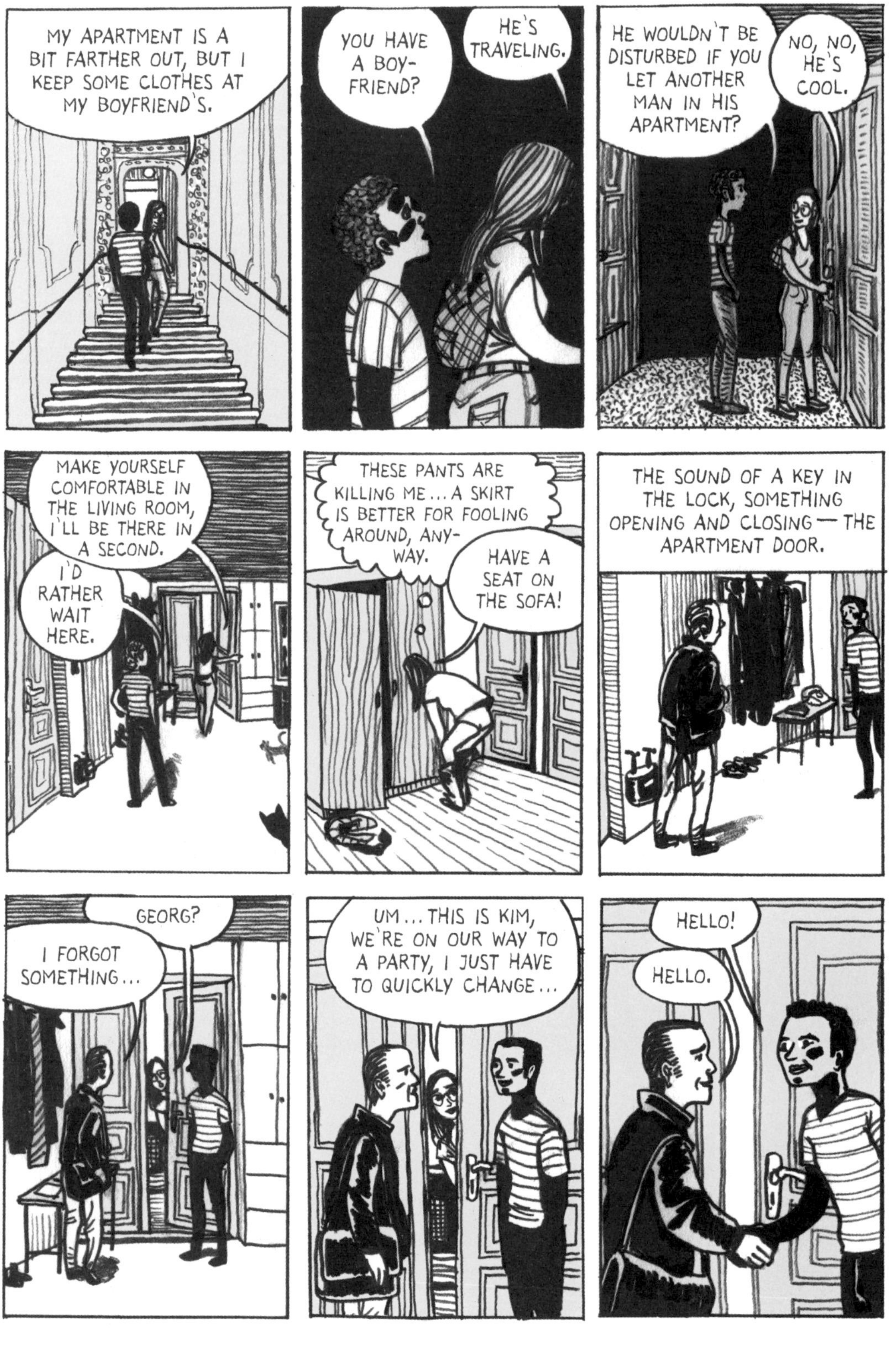
MY APARTMENT IS A BIT FARTHER OUT, BUT I KEEP SOME CLOTHES AT MY BOYFRIEND'S.
YOU HAVE A BOY-FRIEND?
HE'S TRAVELING.
HE WOULDN'T BE DISTURBED IF YOU LET ANOTHER MAN IN HIS APARTMENT?
NO, NO, HE'S COOL.
MAKE YOURSELF COMFORTABLE IN THE LIVING ROOM, I'LL BE THERE IN A SECOND.
I'D RATHER WAIT HERE.
THESE PANTS ARE KILLING ME... A SKIRT IS BETTER FOR FOOLING AROUND, ANY-WAY.
HAVE A SEAT ON THE SOFA!
THE SOUND OF A KEY IN THE LOCK, SOMETHING OPENING AND CLOSING — THE APARTMENT DOOR.
GEORG?
I FORGOT SOMETHING...
UM... THIS IS KIM, WE'RE ON OUR WAY TO A PARTY, I JUST HAVE TO QUICKLY CHANGE...
HELLO!
HELLO.

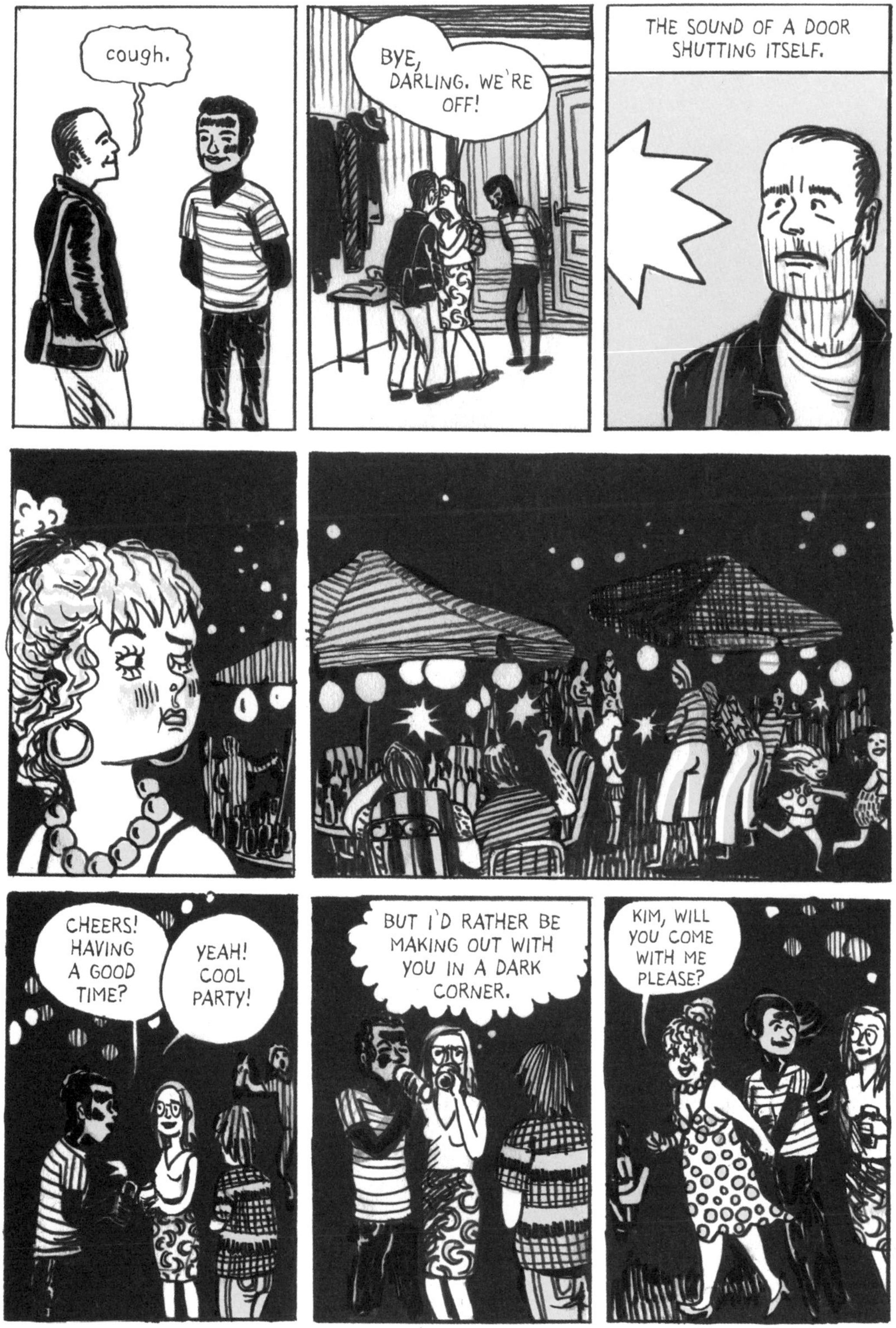
cough.
BYE, DARLING. WE'RE OFF!
THE SOUND OF A DOOR SHUTTING ITSELF.
CHEERS! HAVING A GOOD TIME?
YEAH! COOL PARTY!
BUT I'D RATHER BE MAKING OUT WITH YOU IN A DARK CORNER.
KIM, WILL YOU COME WITH ME PLEASE?

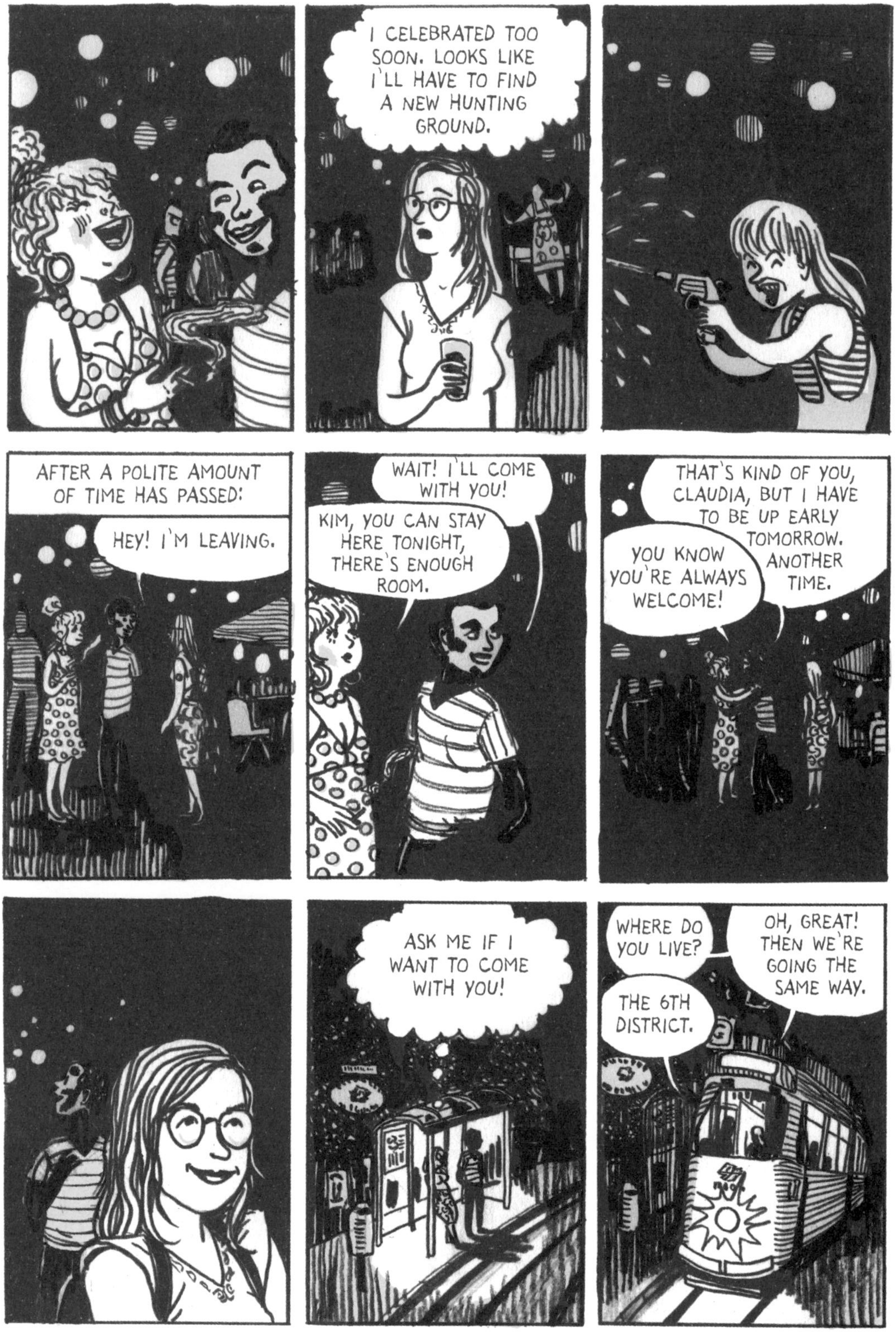
I CELEBRATED TOO SOON. LOOKS LIKE I'LL HAVE TO FIND A NEW HUNTING GROUND.
AFTER A POLITE AMOUNT OF TIME HAS PASSED:
HEY! I'M LEAVING.
WAIT! I'LL COME WITH YOU!
KIM, YOU CAN STAY HERE TONIGHT, THERE'S ENOUGH ROOM.
THAT'S KIND OF YOU, CLAUDIA, BUT I HAVE TO BE UP EARLY TOMORROW. ANOTHER TIME.
YOU KNOW YOU'RE ALWAYS WELCOME!
ASK ME IF I WANT TO COME WITH YOU!
WHERE DO YOU LIVE?
THE 6TH DISTRICT.
OH, GREAT! THEN WE'RE GOING THE SAME WAY.

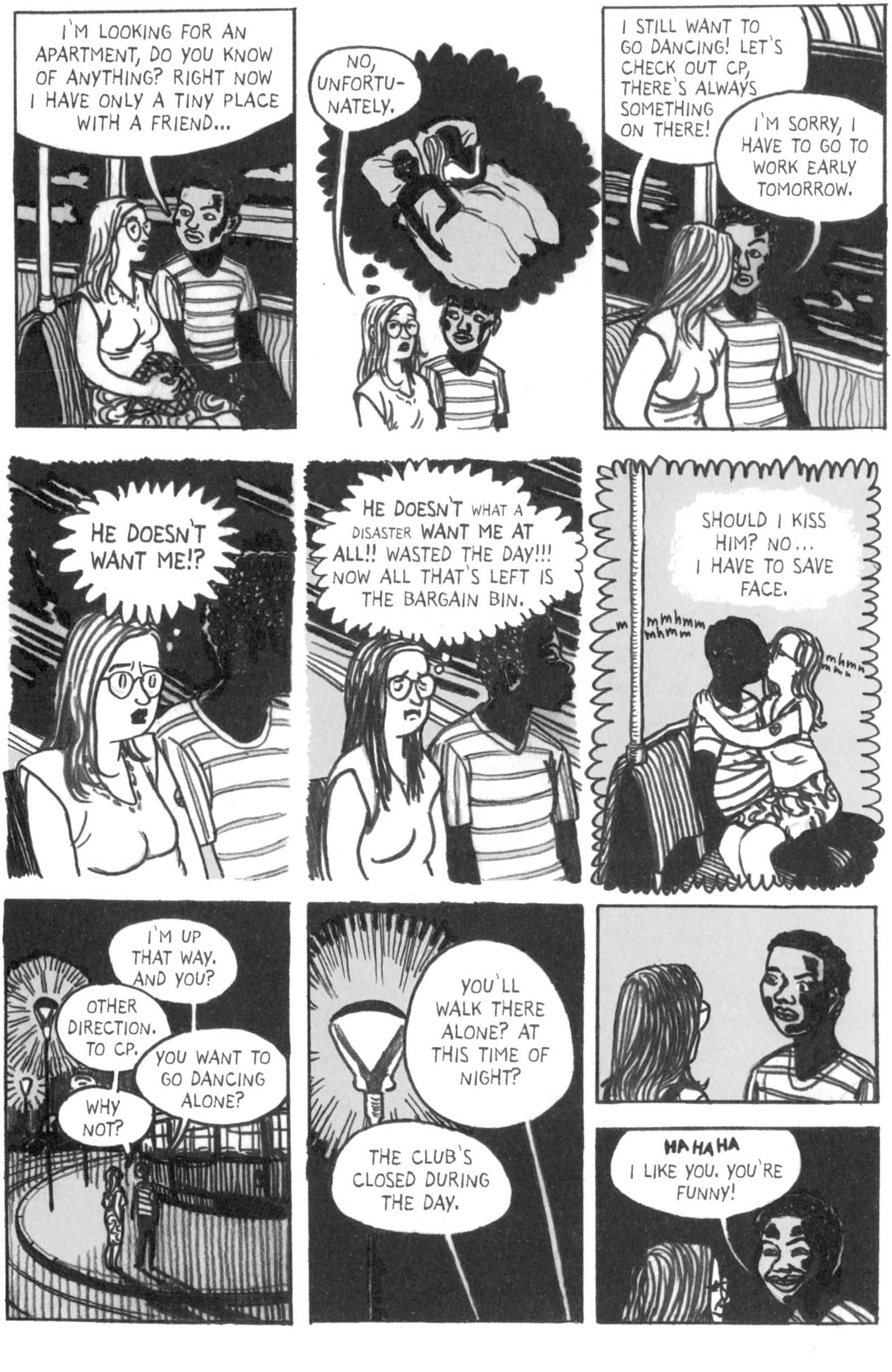
I'M LOOKING FOR AN APARTMENT, DO YOU KNOW OF ANYTHING? RIGHT NOW I HAVE ONLY A TINY PLACE WITH A FRIEND...
NO, UNFORTUNATELY.
I STILL WANT TO GO DANCING! LET'S CHECK OUT CP, THERE'S ALWAYS SOMETHING ON THERE!
I'M SORRY, I HAVE TO GO TO WORK EARLY TOMORROW.
HE DOESN'T WANT ME!?
HE DOESN'T WHAT A DISASTER WANT ME AT ALL!! WASTED THE DAY!!! NOW ALL THAT'S LEFT IS THE BARGAIN BIN.
SHOULD I KISS HIM? NO... I HAVE TO SAVE FACE.
mmhmm mhmm
mhmm
I'M UP THAT WAY. AND YOU?
OTHER DIRECTION. TO CP.
YOU WANT TO GO DANCING ALONE?
WHY NOT?
YOU'LL WALK THERE ALONE? AT THIS TIME OF NIGHT?
THE CLUB'S CLOSED DURING THE DAY.
HAHAHA
I LIKE YOU. YOU'RE FUNNY!

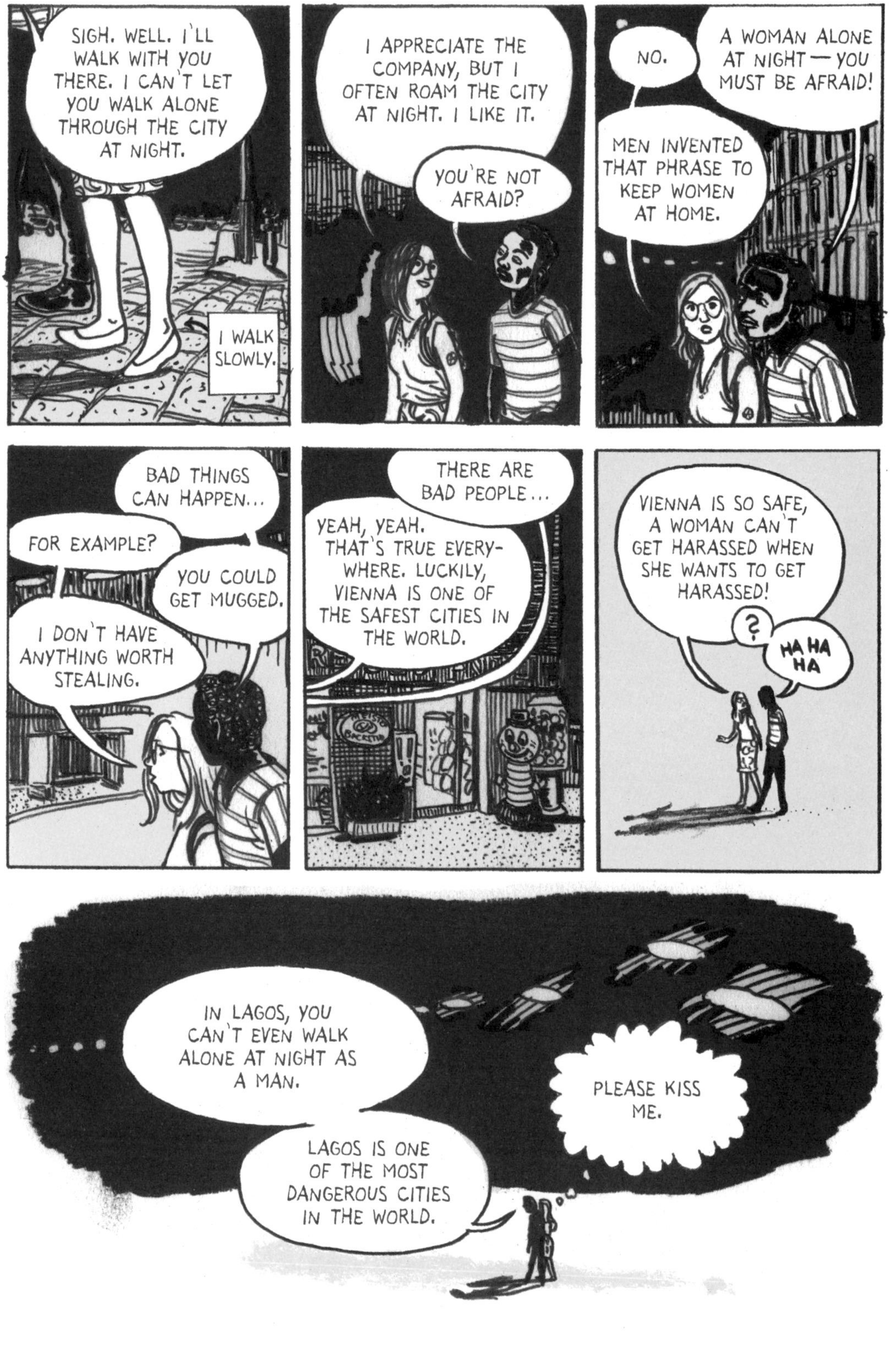
SIGH. WELL. I'LL WALK WITH YOU THERE. I CAN'T LET YOU WALK ALONE THROUGH THE CITY AT NIGHT.
I WALK SLOWLY.
I APPRECIATE THE COMPANY, BUT I OFTEN ROAM THE CITY AT NIGHT. I LIKE IT.
YOU'RE NOT AFRAID?
A WOMAN ALONE AT NIGHT — YOU MUST BE AFRAID!
NO.
MEN INVENTED THAT PHRASE TO KEEP WOMEN AT HOME.
BAD THINGS CAN HAPPEN...
FOR EXAMPLE?
YOU COULD GET MUGGED.
I DON'T HAVE ANYTHING WORTH STEALING.
THERE ARE BAD PEOPLE...
YEAH, YEAH. THAT'S TRUE EVERY-WHERE. LUCKILY, VIENNA IS ONE OF THE SAFEST CITIES IN THE WORLD.
VIENNA IS SO SAFE, A WOMAN CAN'T GET HARASSED WHEN SHE WANTS TO GET HARASSED!
?
HA HA HA
IN LAGOS, YOU CAN'T EVEN WALK ALONE AT NIGHT AS A MAN.
PLEASE KISS ME.
LAGOS IS ONE OF THE MOST DANGEROUS CITIES IN THE WORLD.

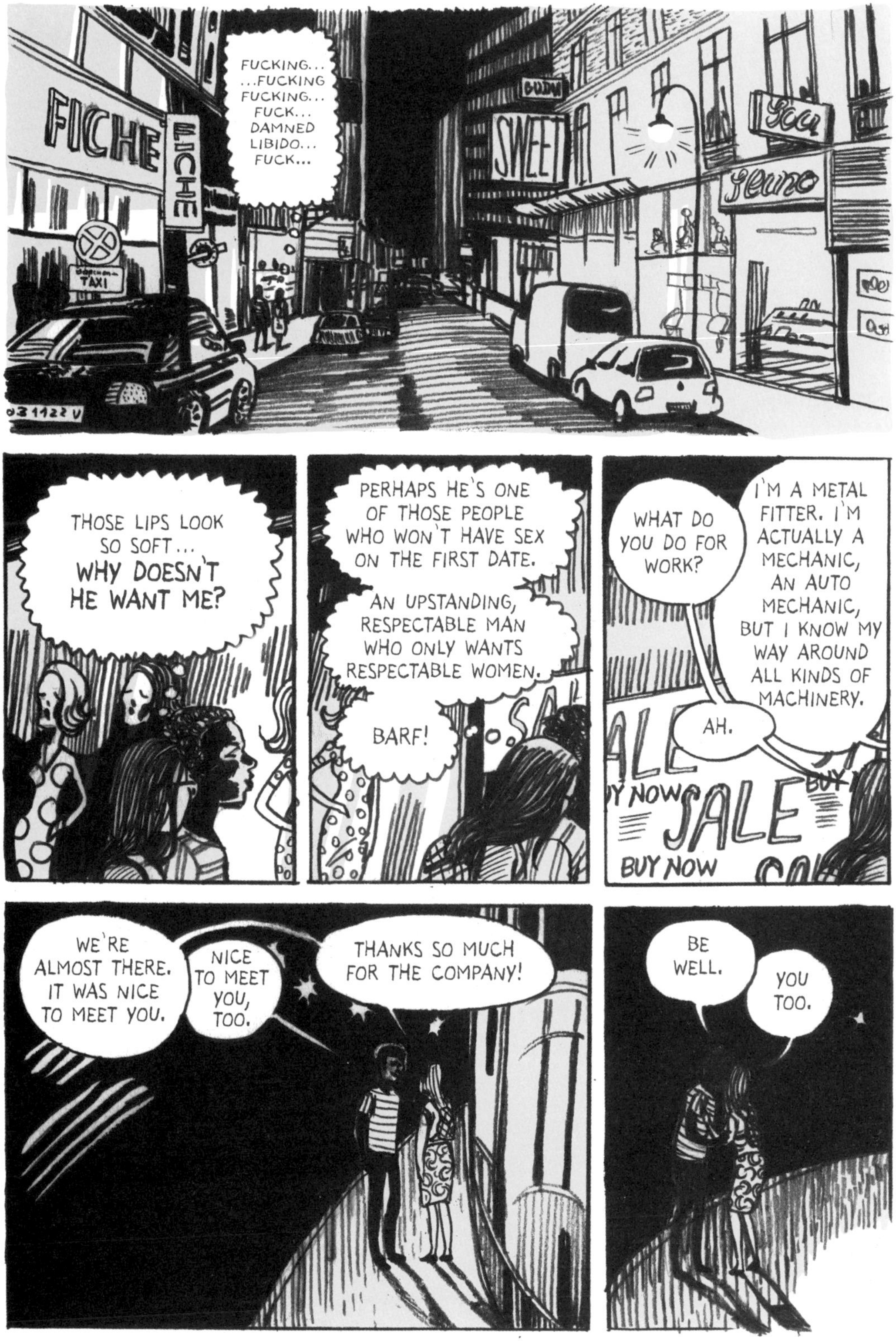
FICHE
FICHE
TAXI
SWEET
FUCKING... ...FUCKING FUCKING... FUCK... DAMNED LIBIDO... FUCK...
THOSE LIPS LOOK SO SOFT... WHY DOESN'T HE WANT ME?
PERHAPS HE'S ONE OF THOSE PEOPLE WHO WON'T HAVE SEX ON THE FIRST DATE.
AN UPSTANDING, RESPECTABLE MAN WHO ONLY WANTS RESPECTABLE WOMEN.
BARF!
WHAT DO YOU DO FOR WORK?
I'M A METAL FITTER. I'M ACTUALLY A MECHANIC, AN AUTO MECHANIC, BUT I KNOW MY WAY AROUND ALL KINDS OF MACHINERY.
AH.
SALE
BUY NOW
WE'RE ALMOST THERE. IT WAS NICE TO MEET YOU.
NICE TO MEET YOU, TOO.
THANKS SO MUCH FOR THE COMPANY!
BE WELL.
YOU TOO.

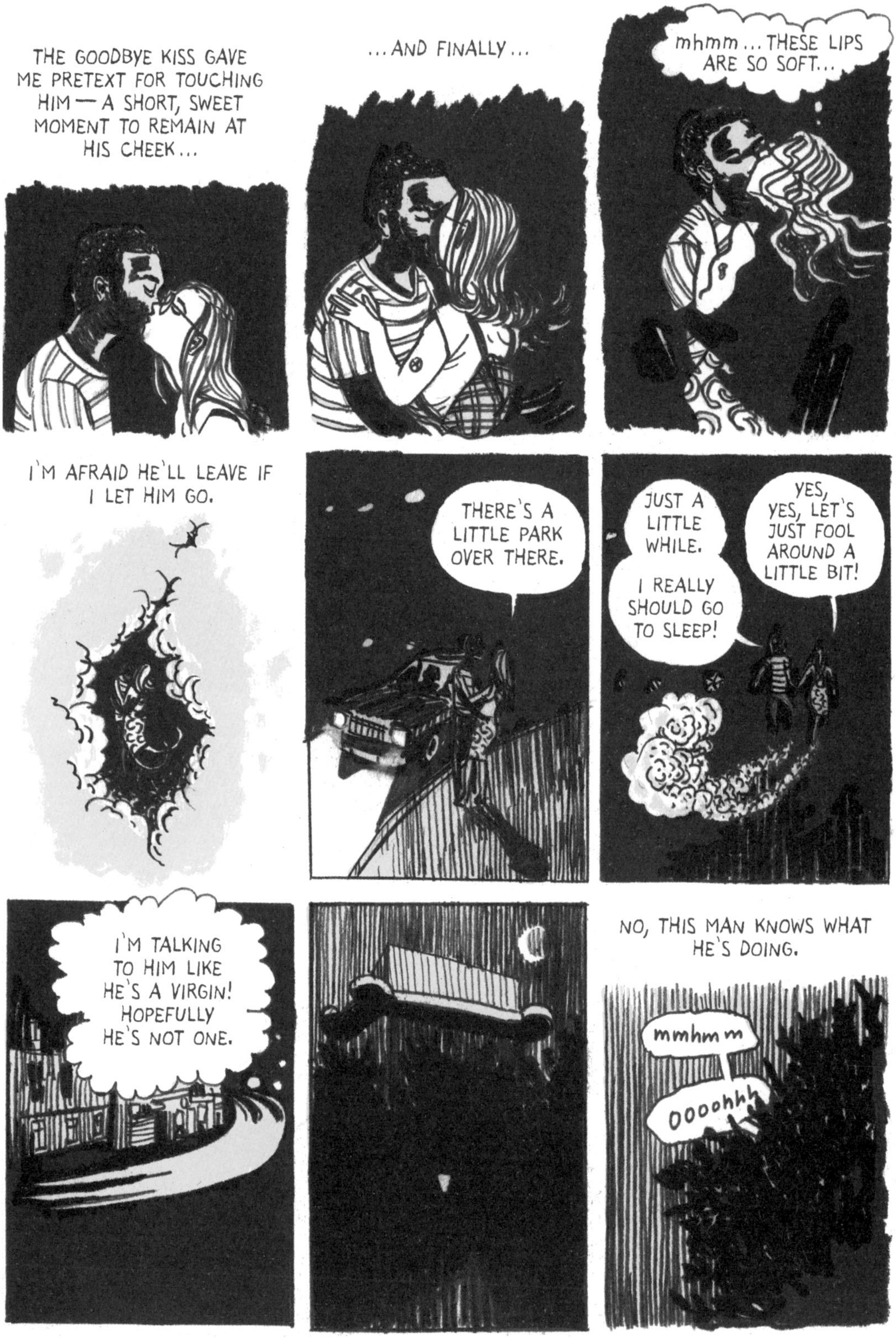
THE GOODBYE KISS GAVE ME PRETEXT FOR TOUCHING HIM — A SHORT, SWEET MOMENT TO REMAIN AT HIS CHEEK...
...AND FINALLY...
mhmm... THESE LIPS ARE SO SOFT...
I'M AFRAID HE'LL LEAVE IF I LET HIM GO.
THERE'S A LITTLE PARK OVER THERE.
JUST A LITTLE WHILE.
I REALLY SHOULD GO TO SLEEP!
YES, YES, LET'S JUST FOOL AROUND A LITTLE BIT!
I'M TALKING TO HIM LIKE HE'S A VIRGIN! HOPEFULLY HE'S NOT ONE.
NO, THIS MAN KNOWS WHAT HE'S DOING.
mmhmm
Ooooohhh

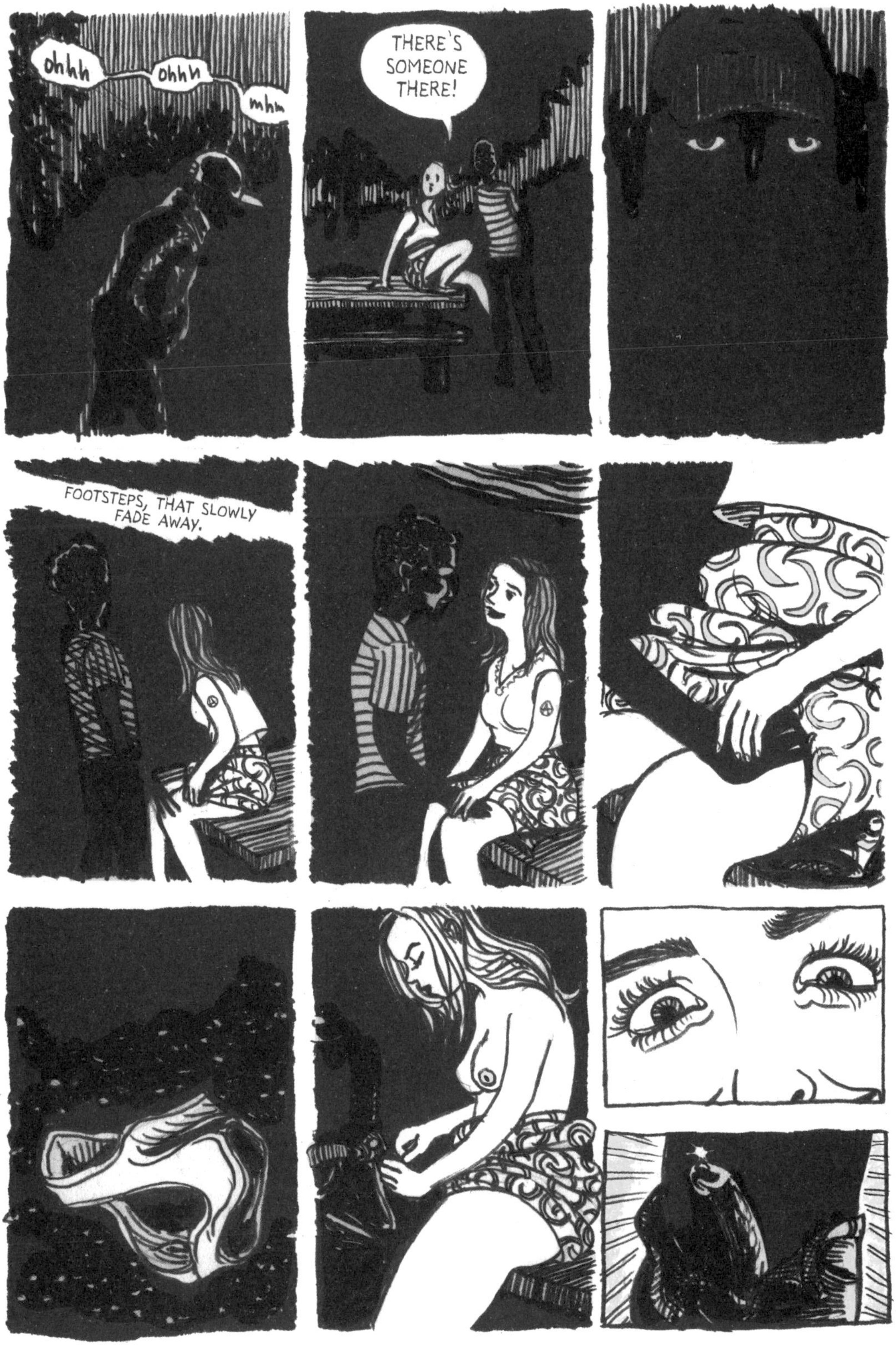
ohhh
ohhh
mhm
THERE'S SOMEONE THERE!
FOOTSTEPS, THAT SLOWLY FADE AWAY.

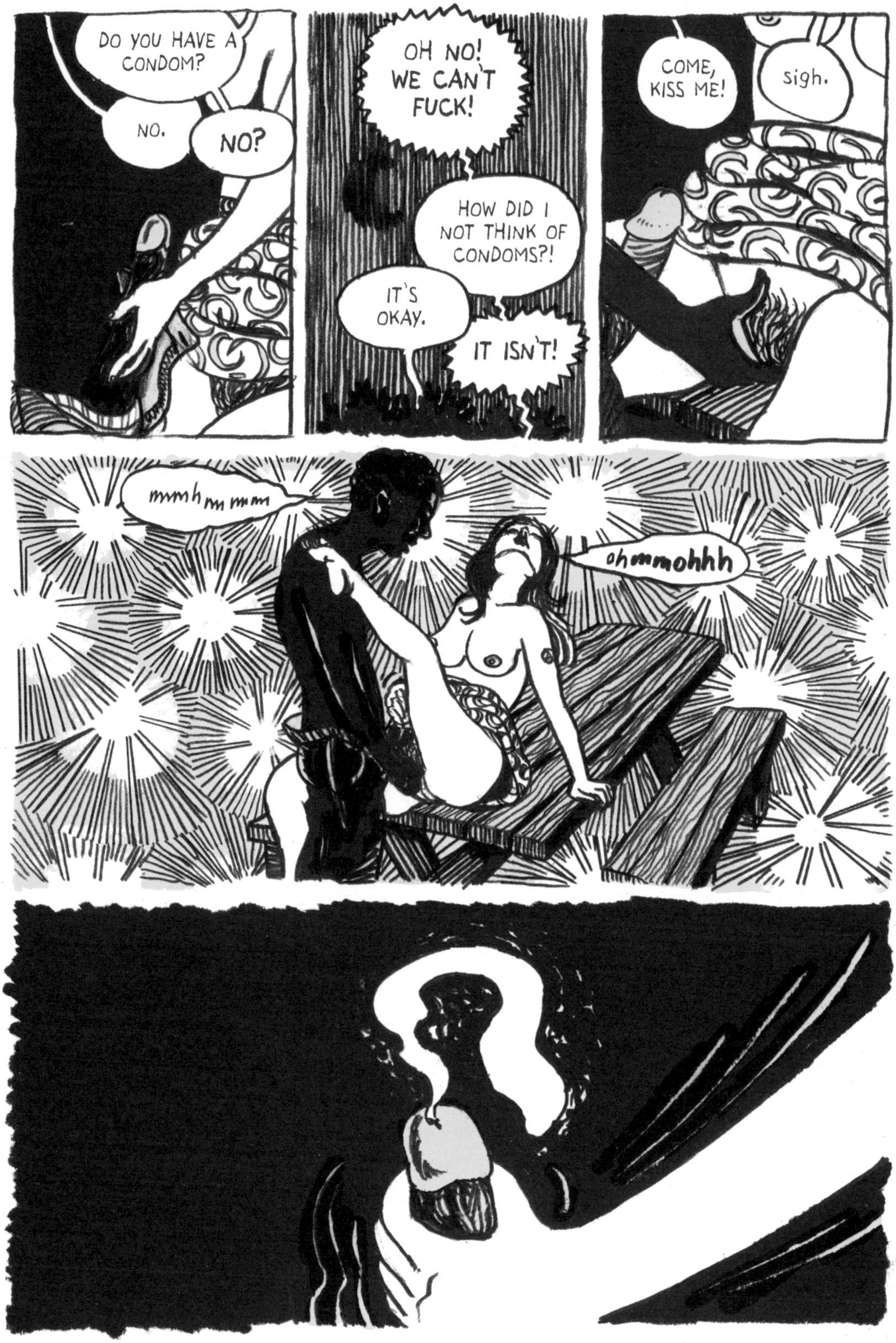
DO YOU HAVE A CONDOM?
NO.
NO?
OH NO! WE CAN'T FUCK!
HOW DID I NOT THINK OF CONDOMS?!
IT'S OKAY.
IT ISN'T!
COME, KISS ME!
sigh.
mmhmmmmm
ohmmohhh

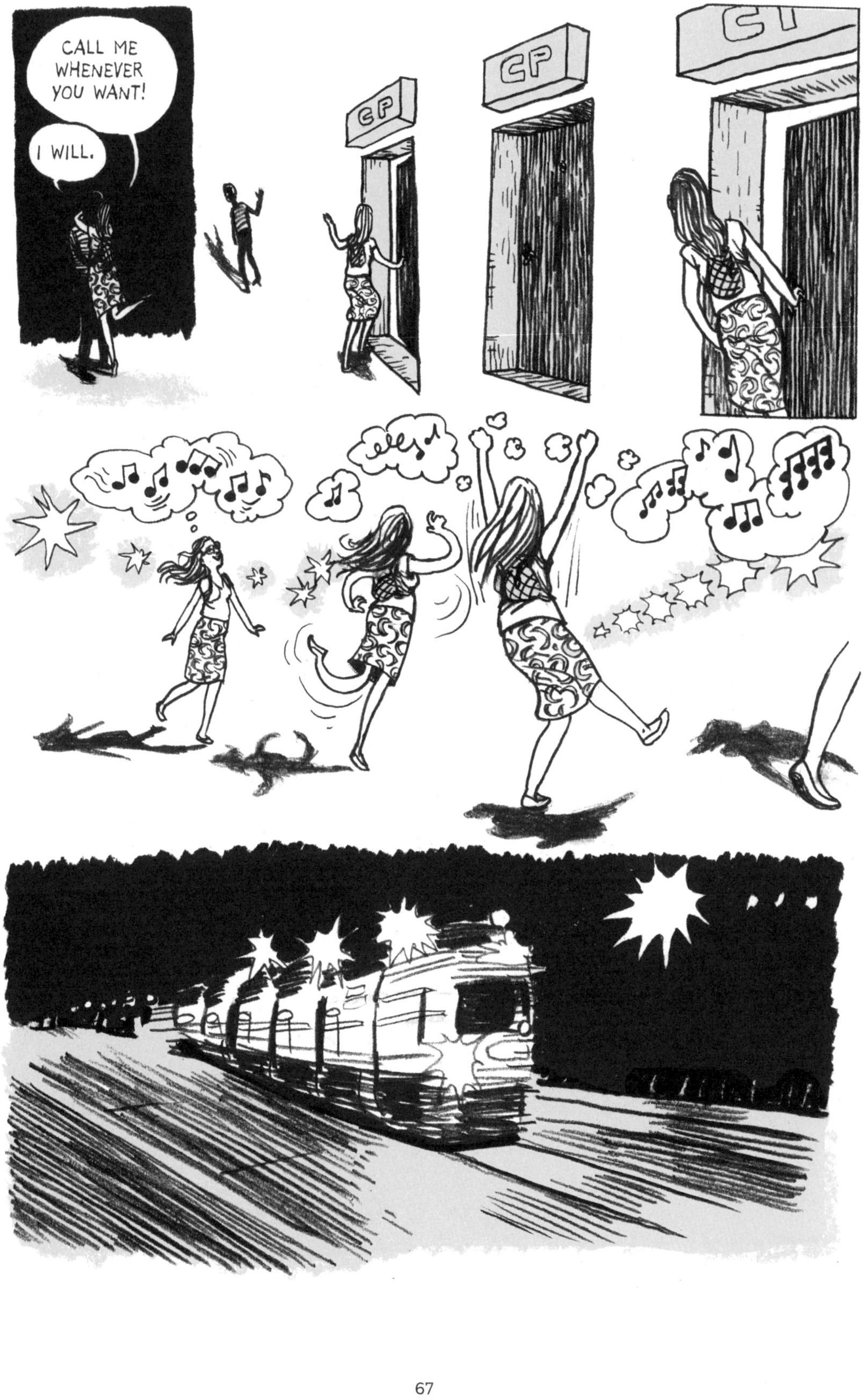
CALL ME WHENEVER YOU WANT!
I WILL.
CP
CP

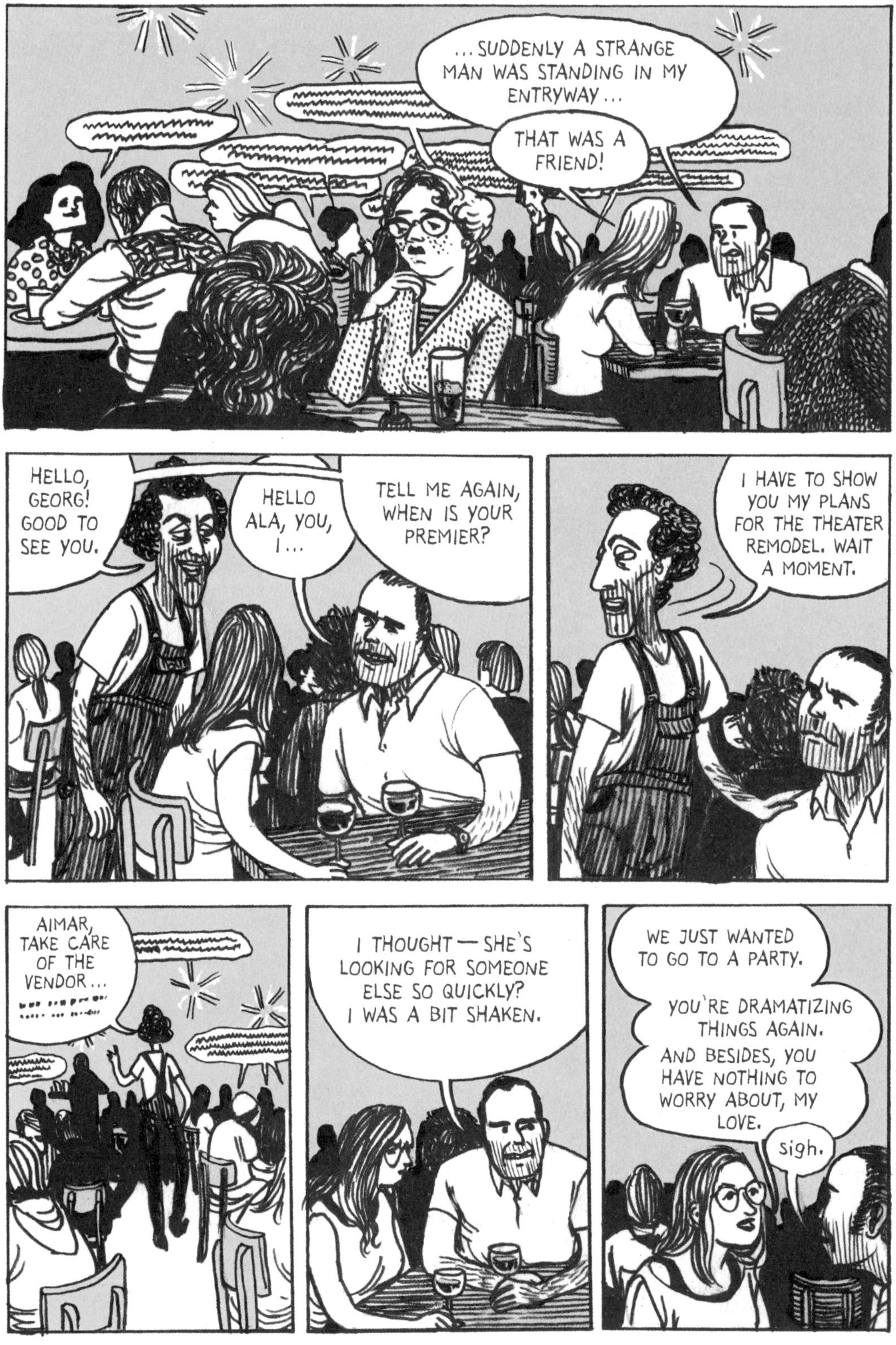
...SUDDENLY A STRANGE MAN WAS STANDING IN MY ENTRYWAY...
THAT WAS A FRIEND!
HELLO, GEORG! GOOD TO SEE YOU.
HELLO ALA, YOU, I...
TELL ME AGAIN, WHEN IS YOUR PREMIER?
I HAVE TO SHOW YOU MY PLANS FOR THE THEATER REMODEL. WAIT A MOMENT.
AIMAR, TAKE CARE OF THE VENDOR...
I THOUGHT — SHE'S LOOKING FOR SOMEONE ELSE SO QUICKLY? I WAS A BIT SHAKEN.
WE JUST WANTED TO GO TO A PARTY.
YOU'RE DRAMATIZING THINGS AGAIN.
AND BESIDES, YOU HAVE NOTHING TO WORRY ABOUT, MY LOVE.
sigh.

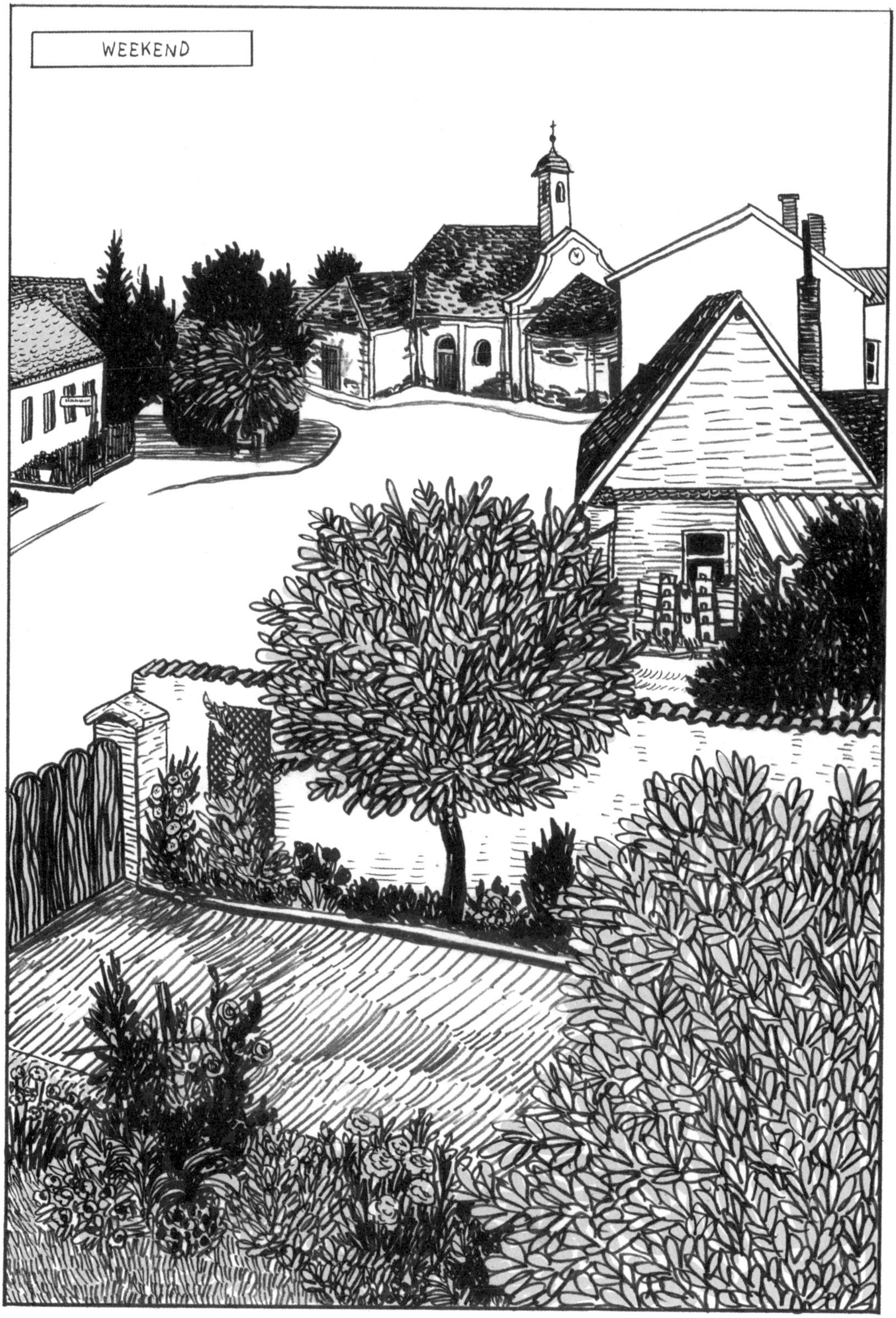
WEEKEND

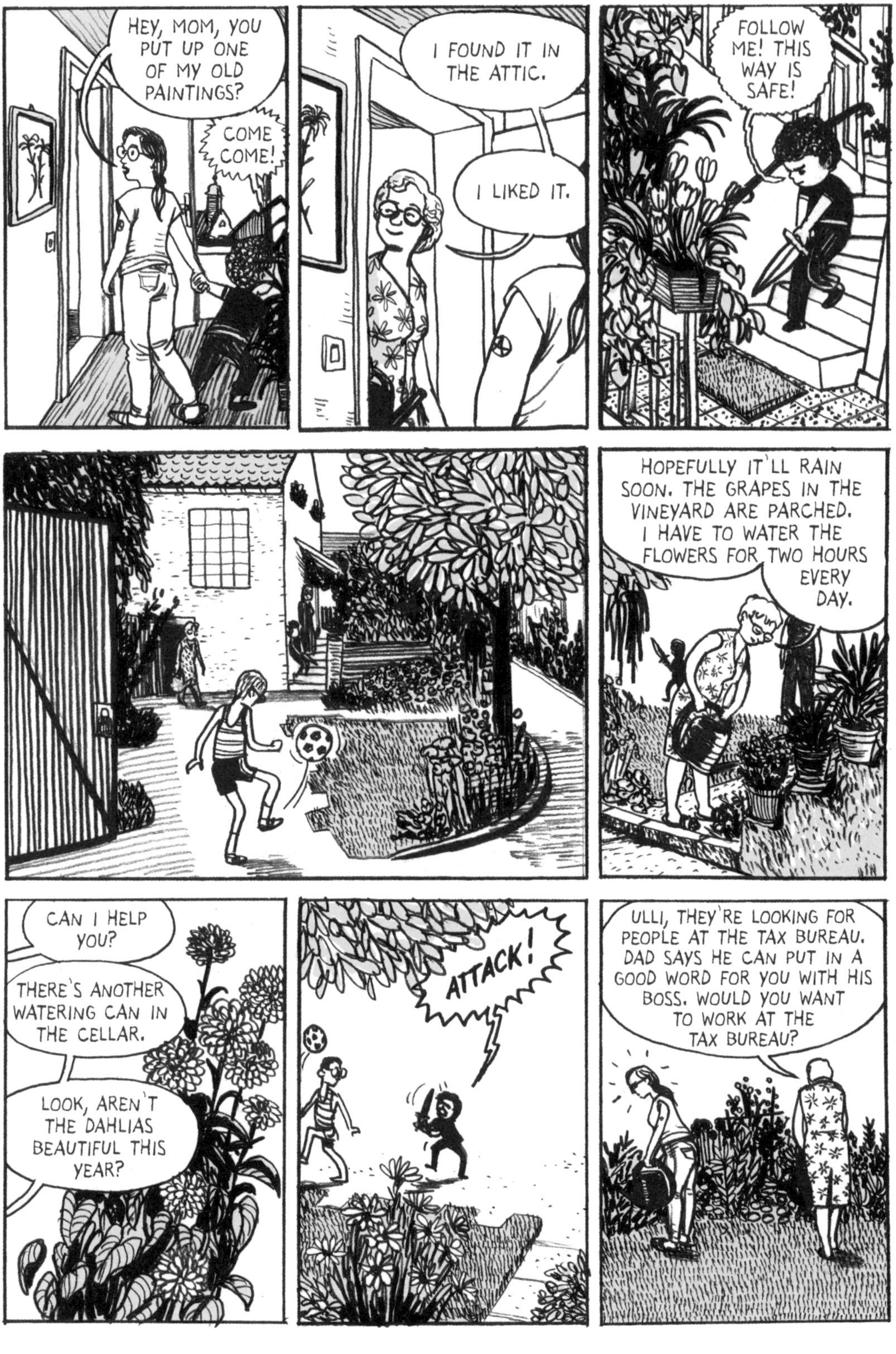
HEY, MOM, YOU PUT UP ONE OF MY OLD PAINTINGS?
COME COME!
I FOUND IT IN THE ATTIC.
I LIKED IT.
FOLLOW ME! THIS WAY IS SAFE!
HOPEFULLY IT'LL RAIN SOON. THE GRAPES IN THE VINEYARD ARE PARCHED. I HAVE TO WATER THE FLOWERS FOR TWO HOURS EVERY DAY.
CAN I HELP YOU?
THERE'S ANOTHER WATERING CAN IN THE CELLAR.
LOOK, AREN'T THE DAHLIAS BEAUTIFUL THIS YEAR?
ATTACK!
ULLI, THEY'RE LOOKING FOR PEOPLE AT THE TAX BUREAU. DAD SAYS HE CAN PUT IN A GOOD WORD FOR YOU WITH HIS BOSS. WOULD YOU WANT TO WORK AT THE TAX BUREAU?

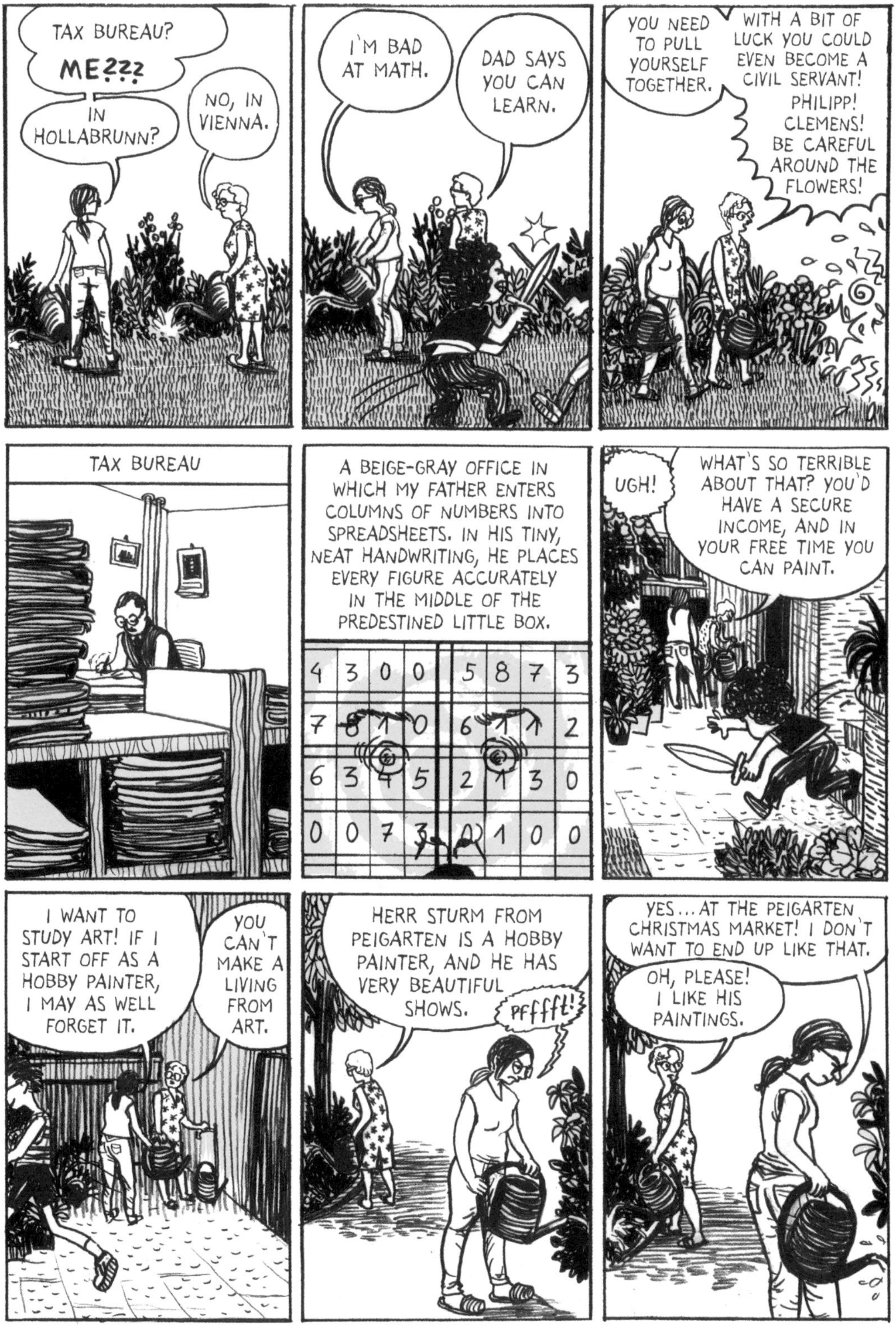
TAX BUREAU? ME??? IN HOLLABRUNN?
NO, IN VIENNA.
I'M BAD AT MATH.
DAD SAYS YOU CAN LEARN.
YOU NEED TO PULL YOURSELF TOGETHER.
WITH A BIT OF LUCK YOU COULD EVEN BECOME A CIVIL SERVANT! PHILIPP! CLEMENS! BE CAREFUL AROUND THE FLOWERS!
TAX BUREAU
A BEIGE-GRAY OFFICE IN WHICH MY FATHER ENTERS COLUMNS OF NUMBERS INTO SPREADSHEETS. IN HIS TINY, NEAT HANDWRITING, HE PLACES EVERY FIGURE ACCURATELY IN THE MIDDLE OF THE PREDESTINED LITTLE BOX.
UGH!
WHAT'S SO TERRIBLE ABOUT THAT? YOU'D HAVE A SECURE INCOME, AND IN YOUR FREE TIME YOU CAN PAINT.
I WANT TO STUDY ART! IF I START OFF AS A HOBBY PAINTER, I MAY AS WELL FORGET IT.
YOU CAN'T MAKE A LIVING FROM ART.
HERR STURM FROM PEIGARTEN IS A HOBBY PAINTER, AND HE HAS VERY BEAUTIFUL SHOWS.
PFFFFT!
YES... AT THE PEIGARTEN CHRISTMAS MARKET! I DON'T WANT TO END UP LIKE THAT.
OH, PLEASE! I LIKE HIS PAINTINGS.

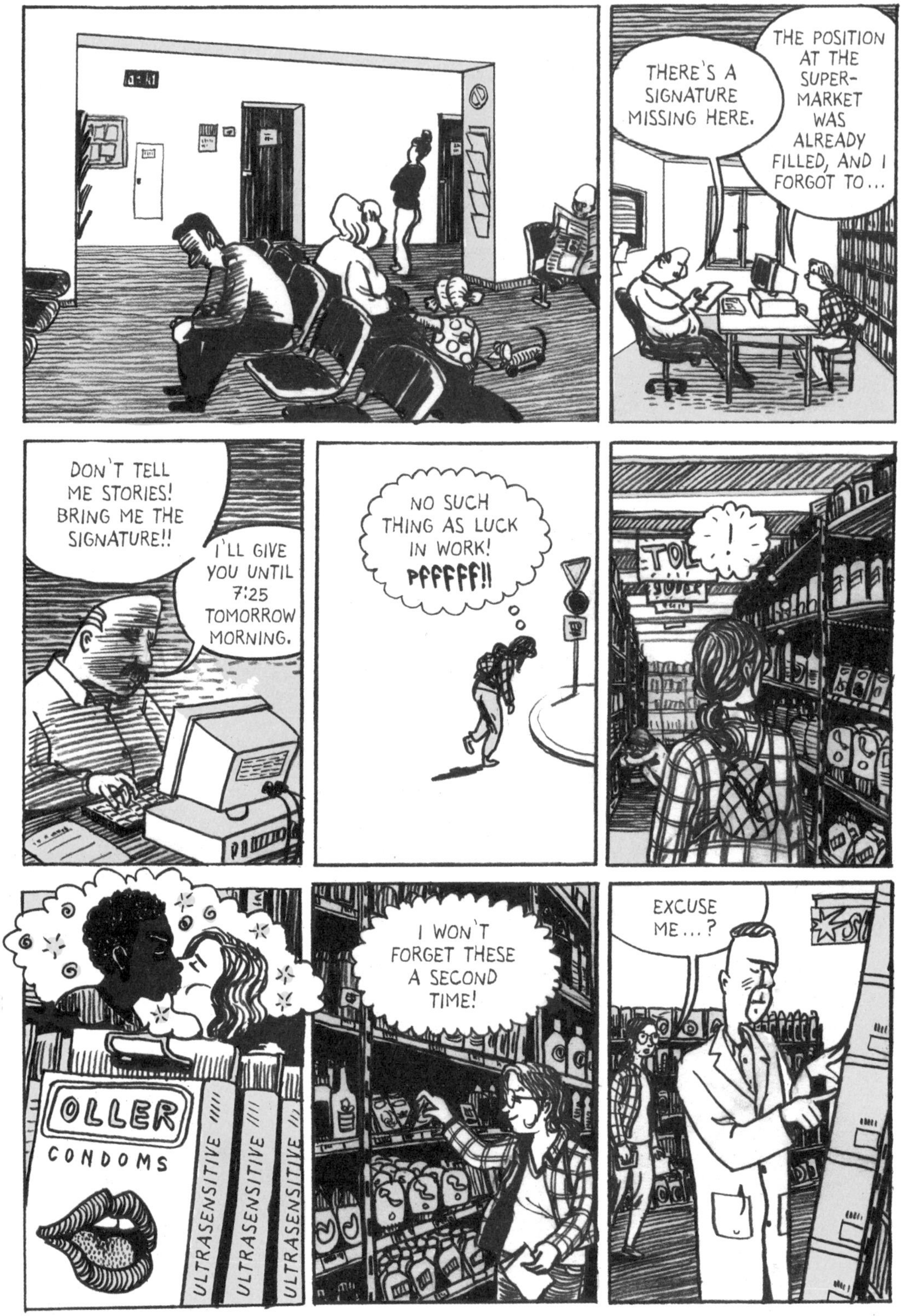
THERE'S A SIGNATURE MISSING HERE.
THE POSITION AT THE SUPER-MARKET WAS ALREADY FILLED, AND I FORGOT TO...
DON'T TELL ME STORIES! BRING ME THE SIGNATURE!!
I'LL GIVE YOU UNTIL 7:25 TOMORROW MORNING.
NO SUCH THING AS LUCK IN WORK! PFFFFF!!
OLLER
CONDOMS
ULTRASENSITIVE
ULTRASENSITIVE
ULTRASENSITIVE
I WON'T FORGET THESE A SECOND TIME!
EXCUSE ME...?

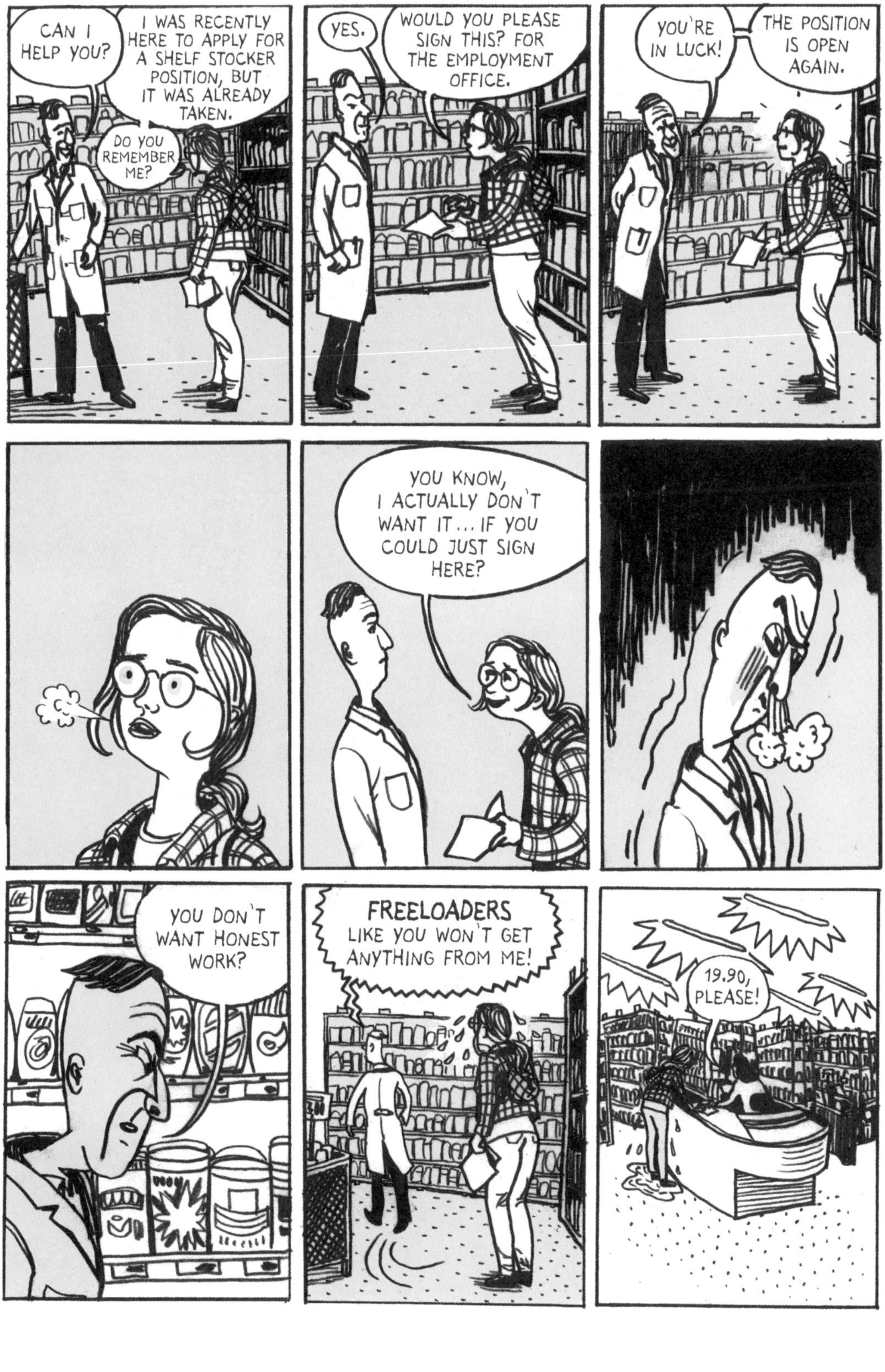
CAN I HELP YOU?
I WAS RECENTLY HERE TO APPLY FOR A SHELF STOCKER POSITION, BUT IT WAS ALREADY TAKEN.
DO YOU REMEMBER ME?
YES.
WOULD YOU PLEASE SIGN THIS? FOR THE EMPLOYMENT OFFICE.
YOU'RE IN LUCK!
THE POSITION IS OPEN AGAIN.
YOU KNOW, I ACTUALLY DON'T WANT IT... IF YOU COULD JUST SIGN HERE?
YOU DON'T WANT HONEST WORK?
FREELOADERS LIKE YOU WON'T GET ANYTHING FROM ME!
19.90, PLEASE!

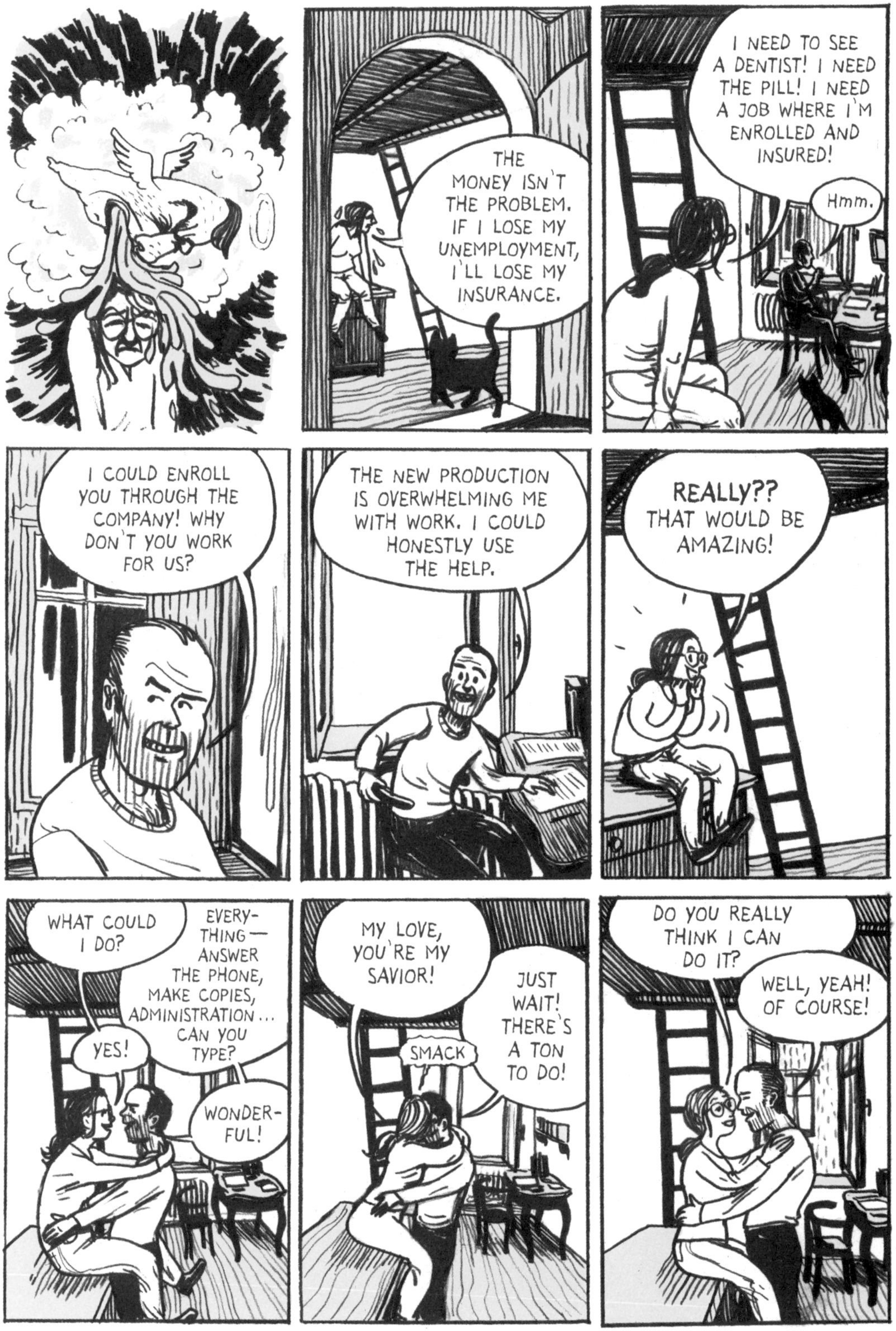
THE MONEY ISN'T THE PROBLEM. IF I LOSE MY UNEMPLOYMENT, I'LL LOSE MY INSURANCE.
I NEED TO SEE A DENTIST! I NEED THE PILL! I NEED A JOB WHERE I'M ENROLLED AND INSURED!
Hmm.
I COULD ENROLL YOU THROUGH THE COMPANY! WHY DON'T YOU WORK FOR US?
THE NEW PRODUCTION IS OVERWHELMING ME WITH WORK. I COULD HONESTLY USE THE HELP.
REALLY?? THAT WOULD BE AMAZING!
WHAT COULD I DO?
EVERYTHING— ANSWER THE PHONE, MAKE COPIES, ADMINISTRATION... CAN YOU TYPE?
YES!
WONDERFUL!
MY LOVE, YOU'RE MY SAVIOR!
SMACK
JUST WAIT! THERE'S A TON TO DO!
DO YOU REALLY THINK I CAN DO IT?
WELL, YEAH! OF COURSE!

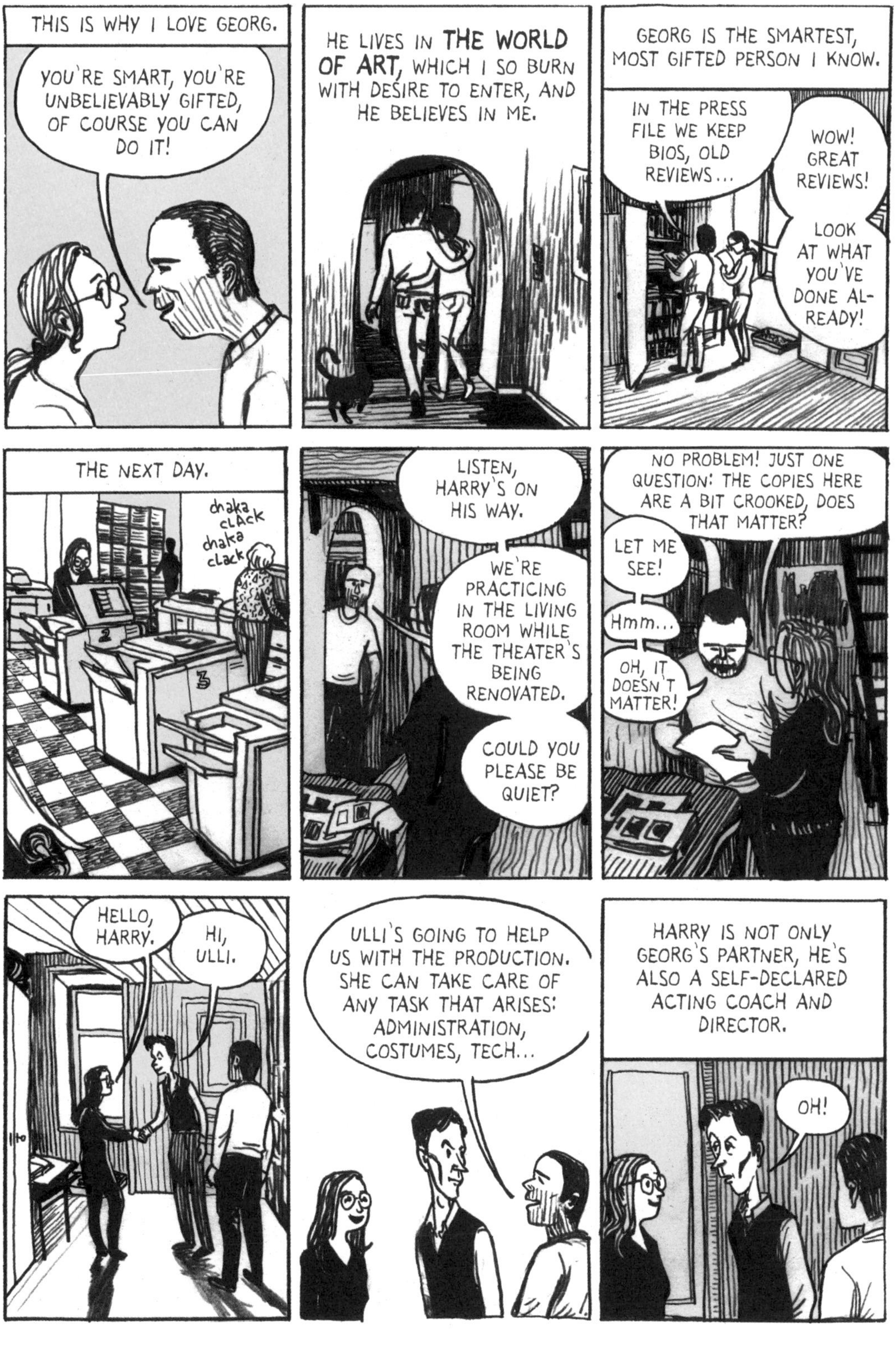

THIS IS WHY I LOVE GEORG.
YOU'RE SMART, YOU'RE UNBELIEVABLY GIFTED, OF COURSE YOU CAN DO IT!
HE LIVES IN THE WORLD OF ART, WHICH I SO BURN WITH DESIRE TO ENTER, AND HE BELIEVES IN ME.
GEORG IS THE SMARTEST, MOST GIFTED PERSON I KNOW.
IN THE PRESS FILE WE KEEP BIOS, OLD REVIEWS...
WOW! GREAT REVIEWS!
LOOK AT WHAT YOU'VE DONE AL-READY!
THE NEXT DAY.
chaka clack chaka clack
LISTEN, HARRY'S ON HIS WAY.
WE'RE PRACTICING IN THE LIVING ROOM WHILE THE THEATER'S BEING RENOVATED.
COULD YOU PLEASE BE QUIET?
NO PROBLEM! JUST ONE QUESTION: THE COPIES HERE ARE A BIT CROOKED, DOES THAT MATTER?
LET ME SEE!
Hmm...
OH, IT DOESN'T MATTER!
HELLO, HARRY.
HI, ULLI.
ULLI'S GOING TO HELP US WITH THE PRODUCTION. SHE CAN TAKE CARE OF ANY TASK THAT ARISES: ADMINISTRATION, COSTUMES, TECH...
HARRY IS NOT ONLY GEORG'S PARTNER, HE'S ALSO A SELF-DECLARED ACTING COACH AND DIRECTOR.
OH!

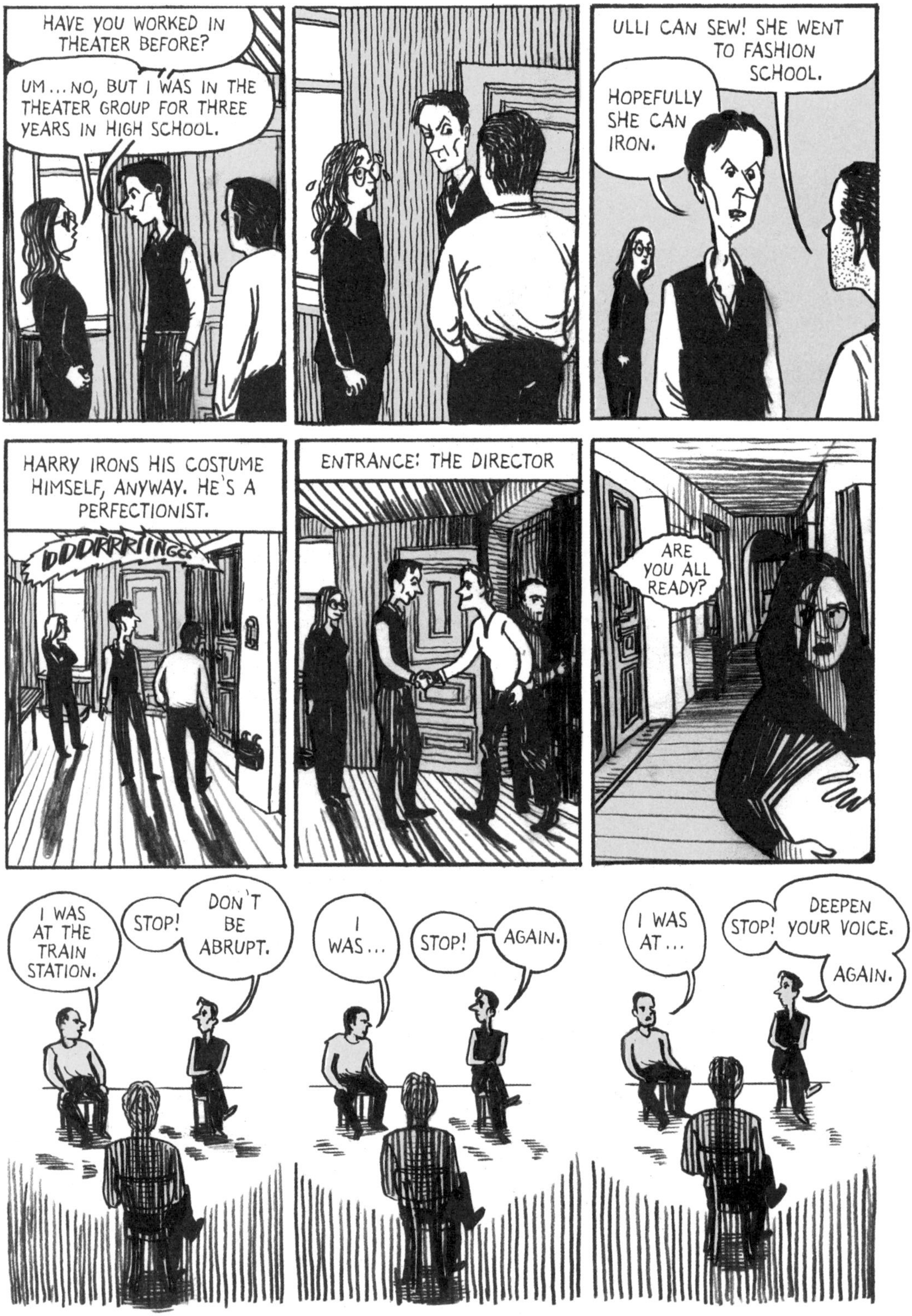
HAVE YOU WORKED IN THEATER BEFORE?
UM... NO, BUT I WAS IN THE THEATER GROUP FOR THREE YEARS IN HIGH SCHOOL.
ULLI CAN SEW! SHE WENT TO FASHION SCHOOL.
HOPEFULLY SHE CAN IRON.
HARRY IRONS HIS COSTUME HIMSELF, ANYWAY. HE'S A PERFECTIONIST.
DDDRRRIING
ENTRANCE: THE DIRECTOR
ARE YOU ALL READY?
I WAS AT THE TRAIN STATION.
STOP!
DON'T BE ABRUPT.
I WAS...
STOP!
AGAIN.
I WAS AT...
STOP!
DEEPEN YOUR VOICE.
AGAIN.

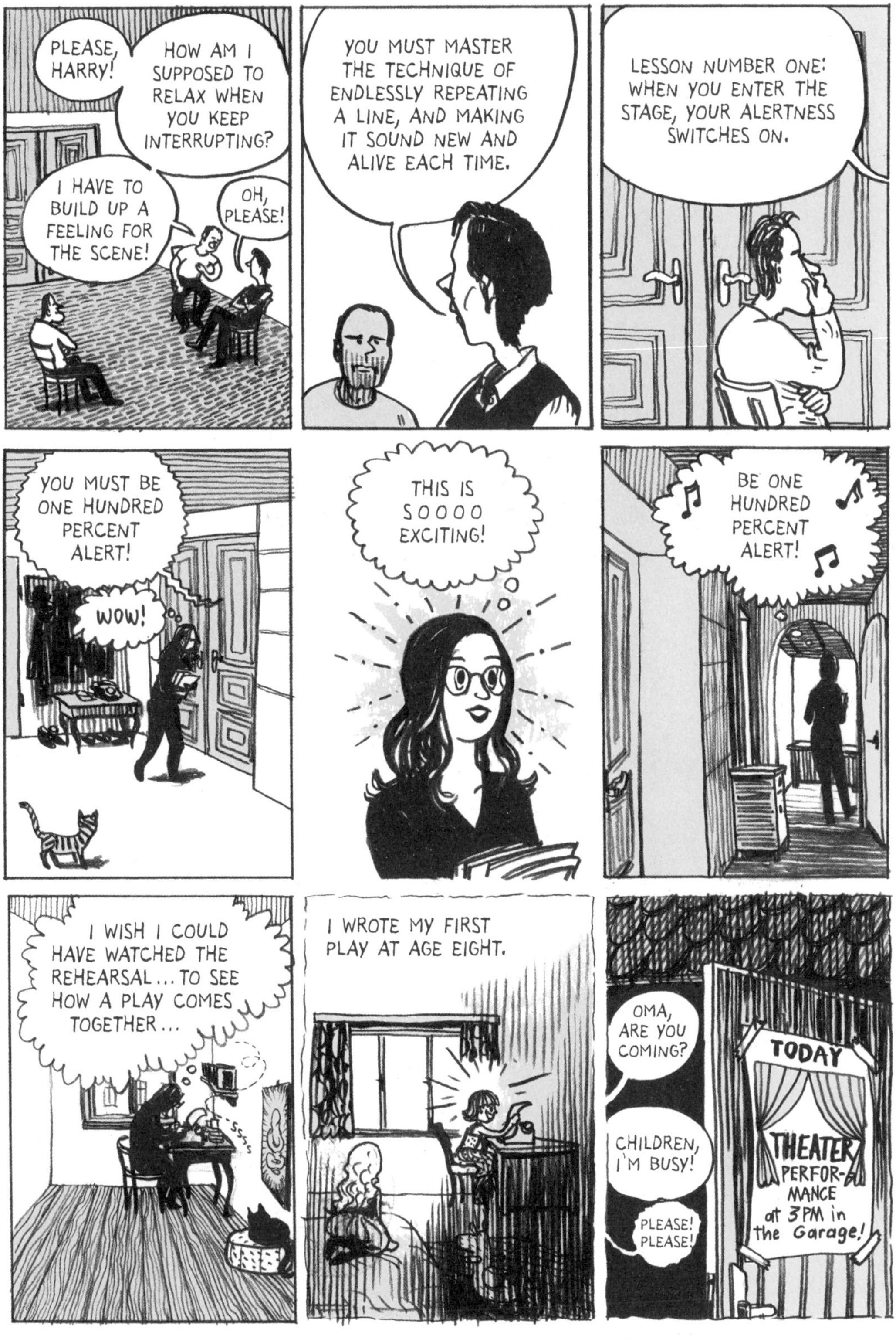
PLEASE, HARRY!
HOW AM I SUPPOSED TO RELAX WHEN YOU KEEP INTERRUPTING?
I HAVE TO BUILD UP A FEELING FOR THE SCENE!
OH, PLEASE!
YOU MUST MASTER THE TECHNIQUE OF ENDLESSLY REPEATING A LINE, AND MAKING IT SOUND NEW AND ALIVE EACH TIME.
LESSON NUMBER ONE: WHEN YOU ENTER THE STAGE, YOUR ALERTNESS SWITCHES ON.
YOU MUST BE ONE HUNDRED PERCENT ALERT!
WOW!
THIS IS SOOOO EXCITING!
BE ONE HUNDRED PERCENT ALERT!
I WISH I COULD HAVE WATCHED THE REHEARSAL... TO SEE HOW A PLAY COMES TOGETHER...
SSSS
I WROTE MY FIRST PLAY AT AGE EIGHT.
OMA, ARE YOU COMING?
CHILDREN, I'M BUSY!
PLEASE! PLEASE!
TODAY
THEATER PERFORMANCE at 3PM in the Garage!

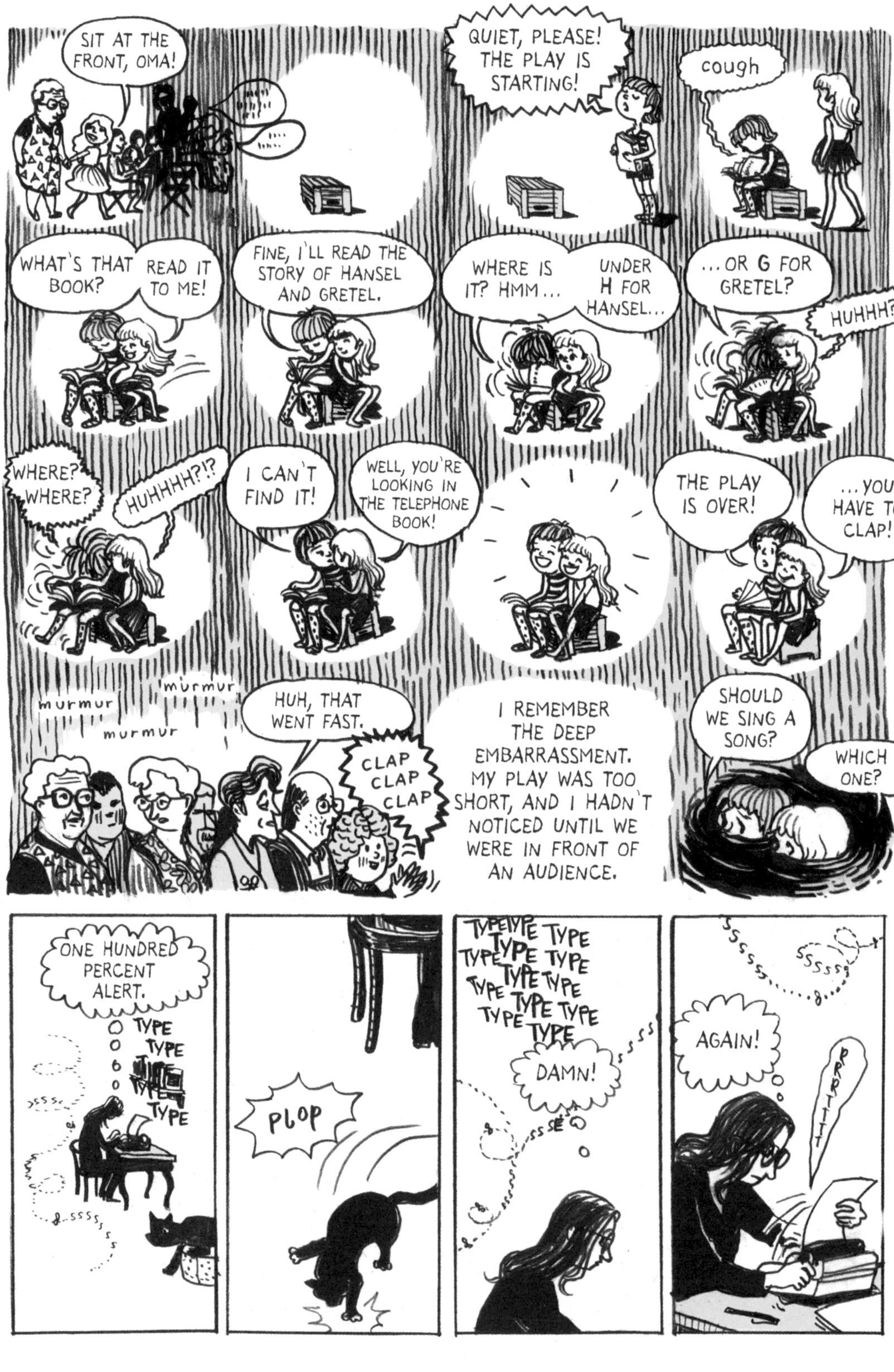
SIT AT THE FRONT, OMA!
QUIET, PLEASE! THE PLAY IS STARTING!
cough
WHAT'S THAT BOOK?
READ IT TO ME!
FINE, I'LL READ THE STORY OF HANSEL AND GRETEL.
WHERE IS IT? HMM...
UNDER H FOR HANSEL...
...OR G FOR GRETEL?
HUHHH??
WHERE? WHERE?
HUHHHH?!?
I CAN'T FIND IT!
WELL, YOU'RE LOOKING IN THE TELEPHONE BOOK!
THE PLAY IS OVER!
...YOU HAVE TO CLAP!
murmur
murmur
murmur
HUH, THAT WENT FAST.
CLAP CLAP CLAP
I REMEMBER THE DEEP EMBARRASSMENT. MY PLAY WAS TOO SHORT, AND I HADN'T NOTICED UNTIL WE WERE IN FRONT OF AN AUDIENCE.
SHOULD WE SING A SONG?
WHICH ONE?
ONE HUNDRED PERCENT ALERT.
TYPE TYPE TYPE
PLOP
TYPE TYPE TYPE TYPE TYPE TYPE TYPE TYPE TYPE TYPE TYPE TYPE
DAMN!
AGAIN!

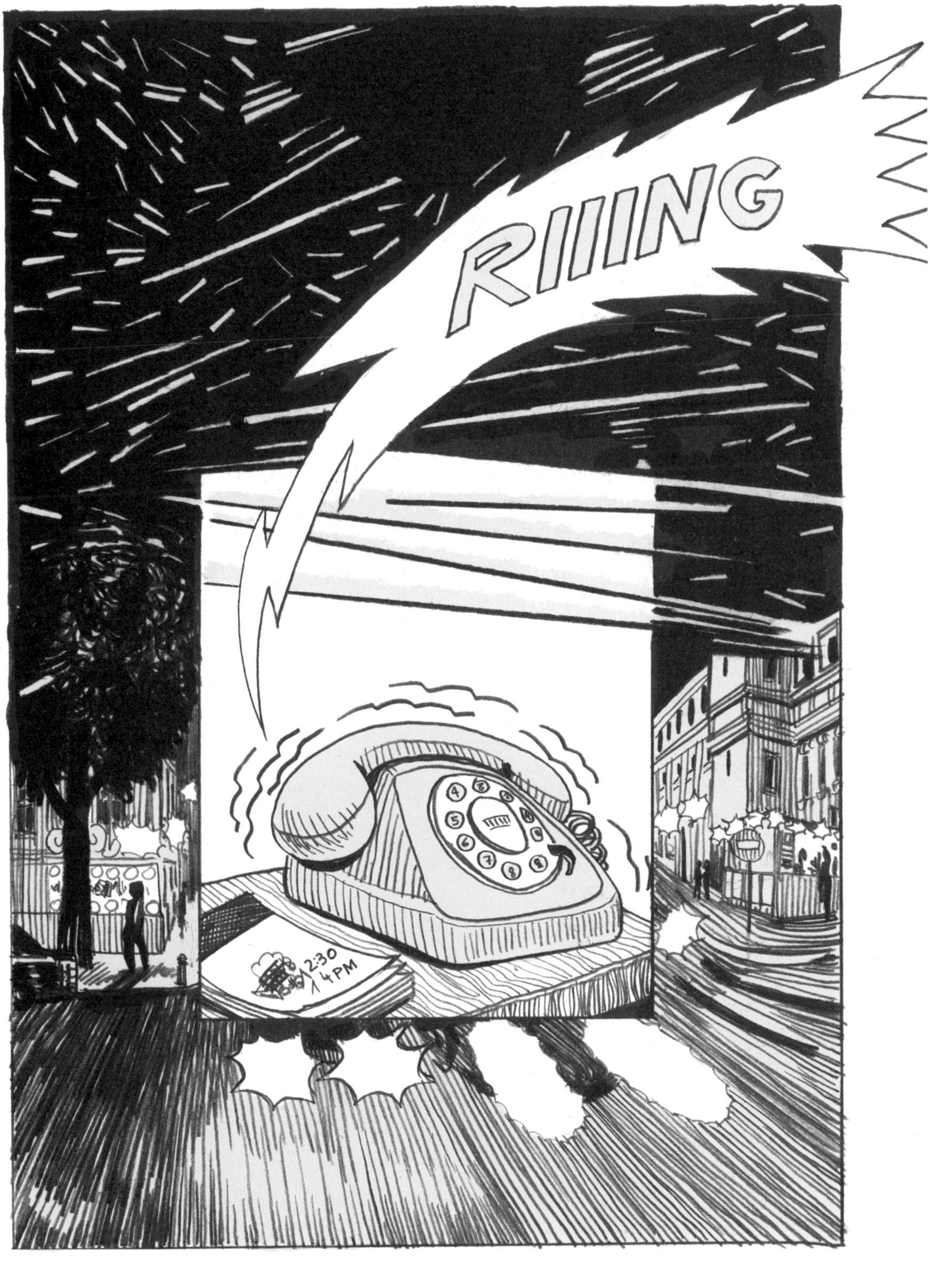
RIIING
2:30
4PM

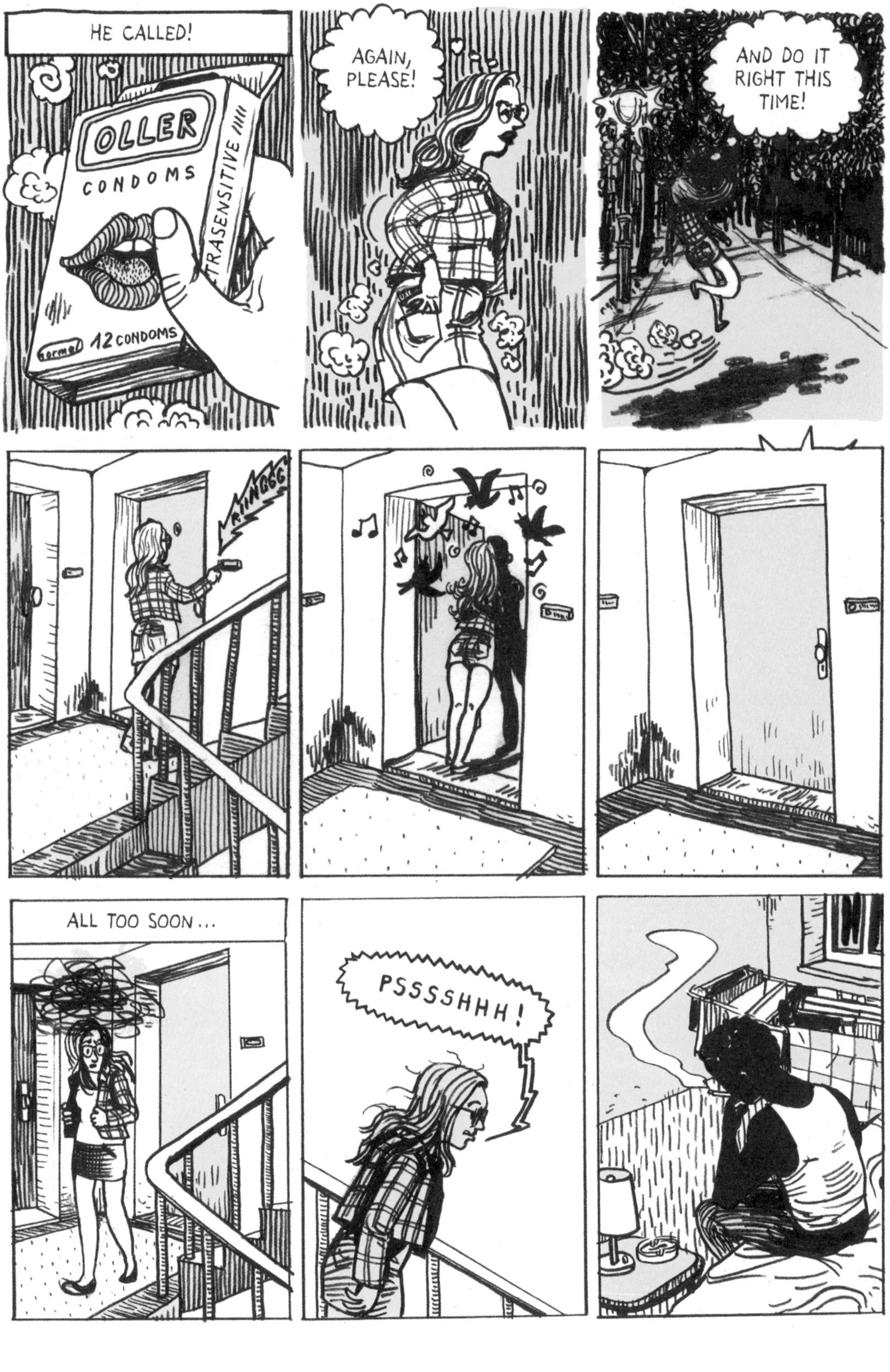
HE CALLED!
OLLER
CONDOMS
TRASENSITIVE
12 CONDOMS
AGAIN, PLEASE!
AND DO IT RIGHT THIS TIME!
ALL TOO SOON...
PSSSSHHH!

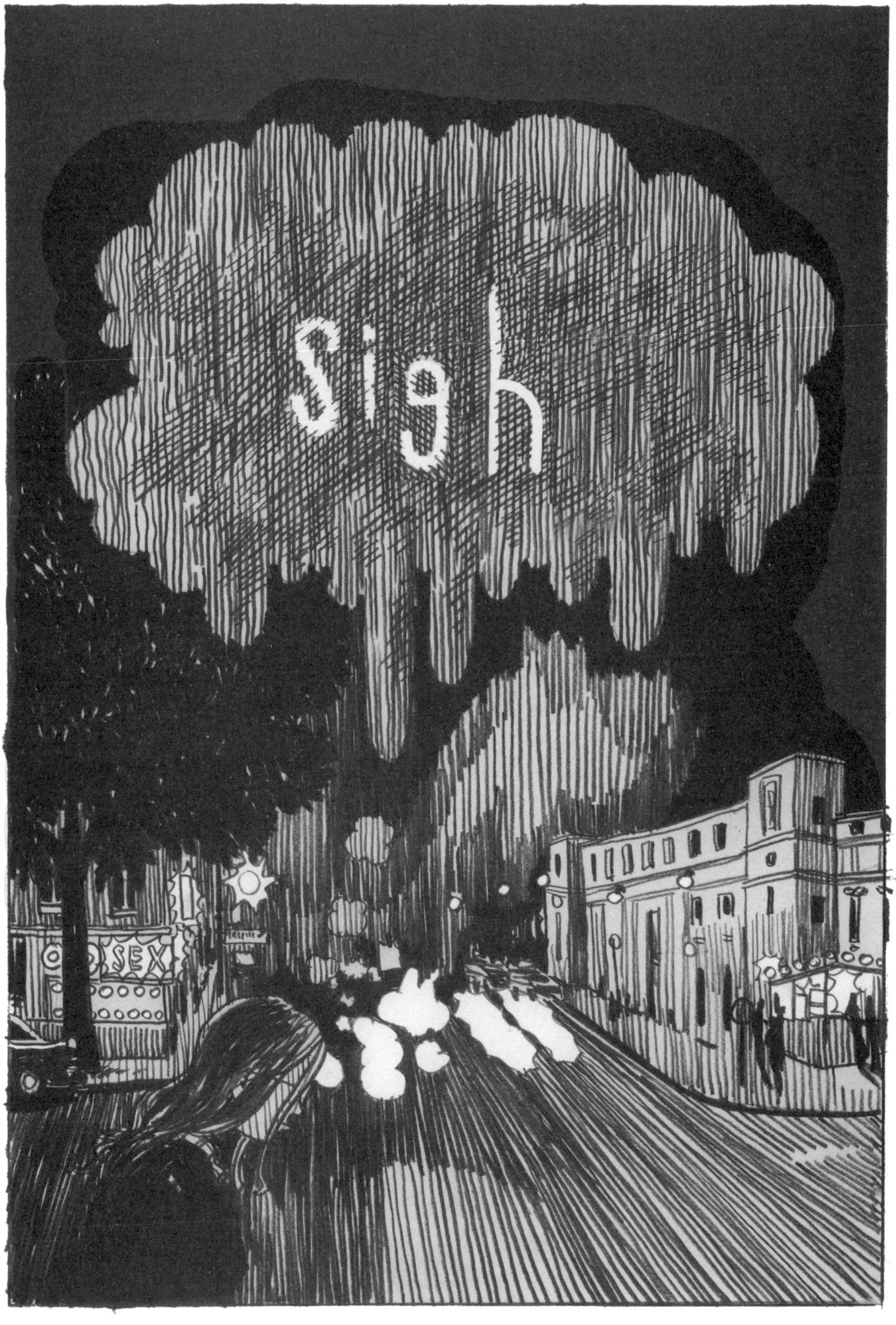
sigh
SEX

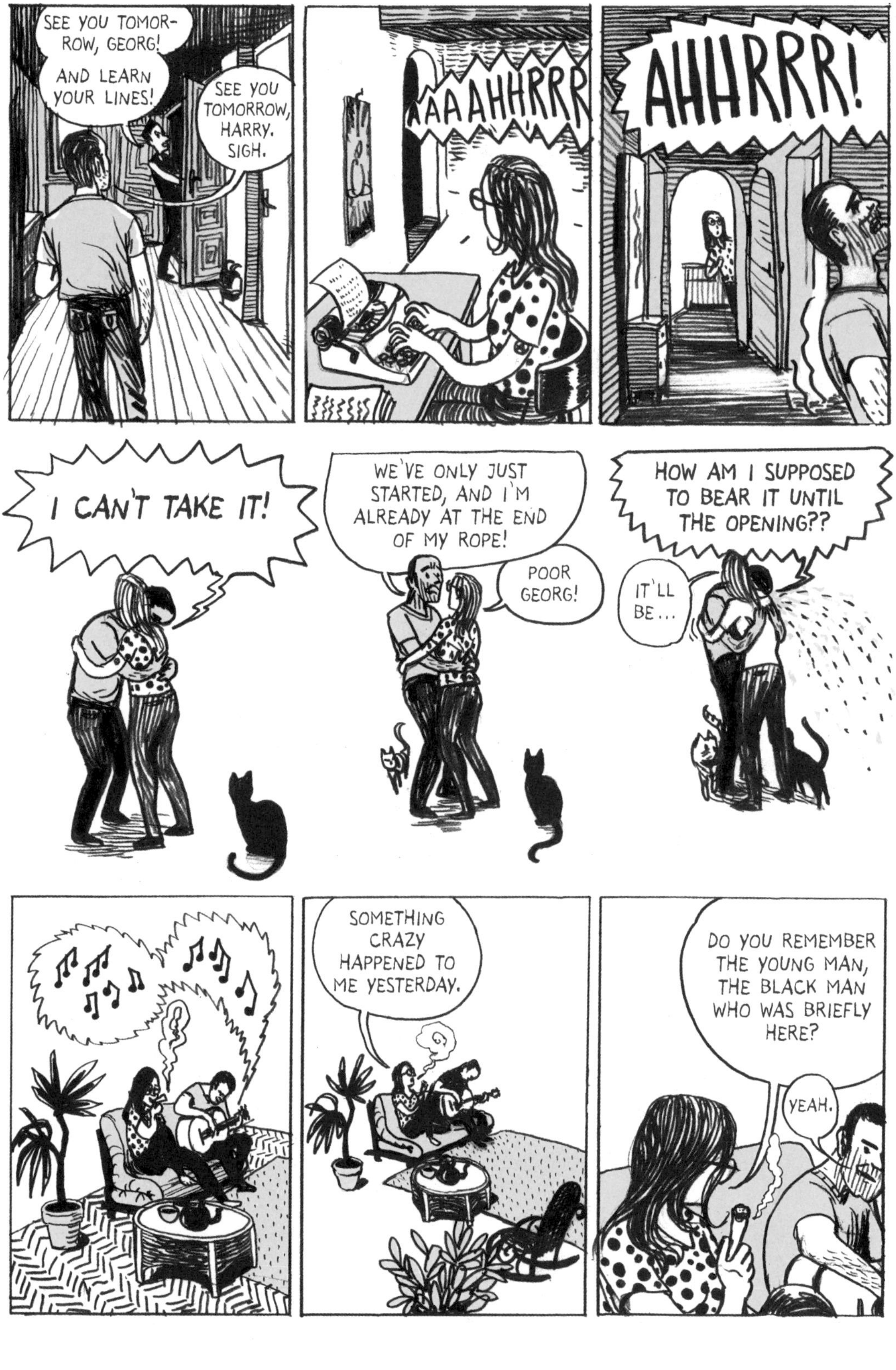
SEE YOU TOMOR-ROW, GEORG!
AND LEARN YOUR LINES!
SEE YOU TOMORROW, HARRY. SIGH.
AAAHHRRR
AHHRRR!
I CAN'T TAKE IT!
WE'VE ONLY JUST STARTED, AND I'M ALREADY AT THE END OF MY ROPE!
POOR GEORG!
HOW AM I SUPPOSED TO BEAR IT UNTIL THE OPENING??
IT'LL BE...
SOMETHING CRAZY HAPPENED TO ME YESTERDAY.
DO YOU REMEMBER THE YOUNG MAN, THE BLACK MAN WHO WAS BRIEFLY HERE?
YEAH.

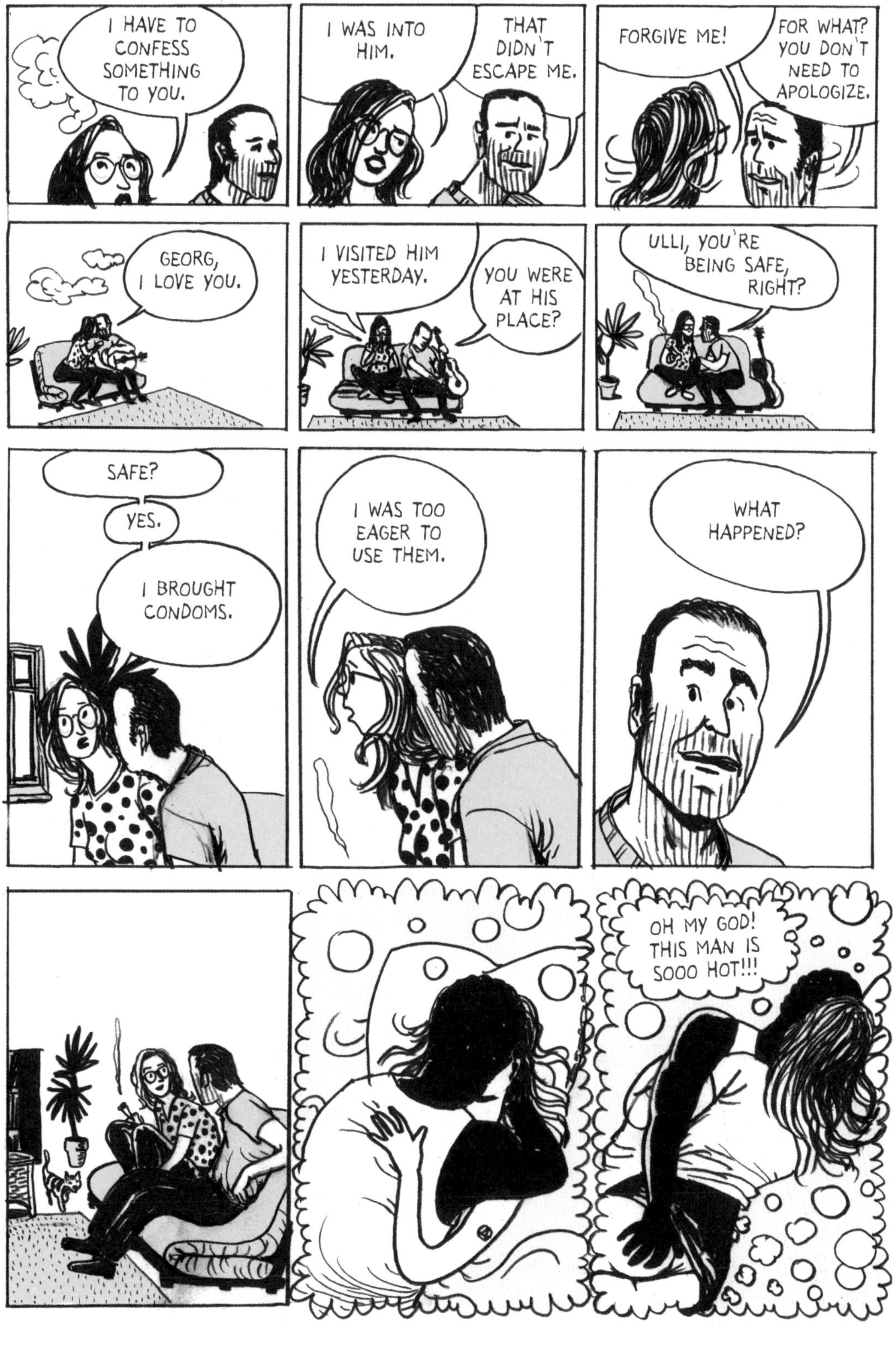
I HAVE TO CONFESS SOMETHING TO YOU.
I WAS INTO HIM.
THAT DIDN'T ESCAPE ME.
FORGIVE ME!
FOR WHAT? YOU DON'T NEED TO APOLOGIZE.
GEORG, I LOVE YOU.
I VISITED HIM YESTERDAY.
YOU WERE AT HIS PLACE?
ULLI, YOU'RE BEING SAFE, RIGHT?
SAFE?
YES.
I BROUGHT CONDOMS.
I WAS TOO EAGER TO USE THEM.
WHAT HAPPENED?
OH MY GOD! THIS MAN IS SOOO HOT!!!

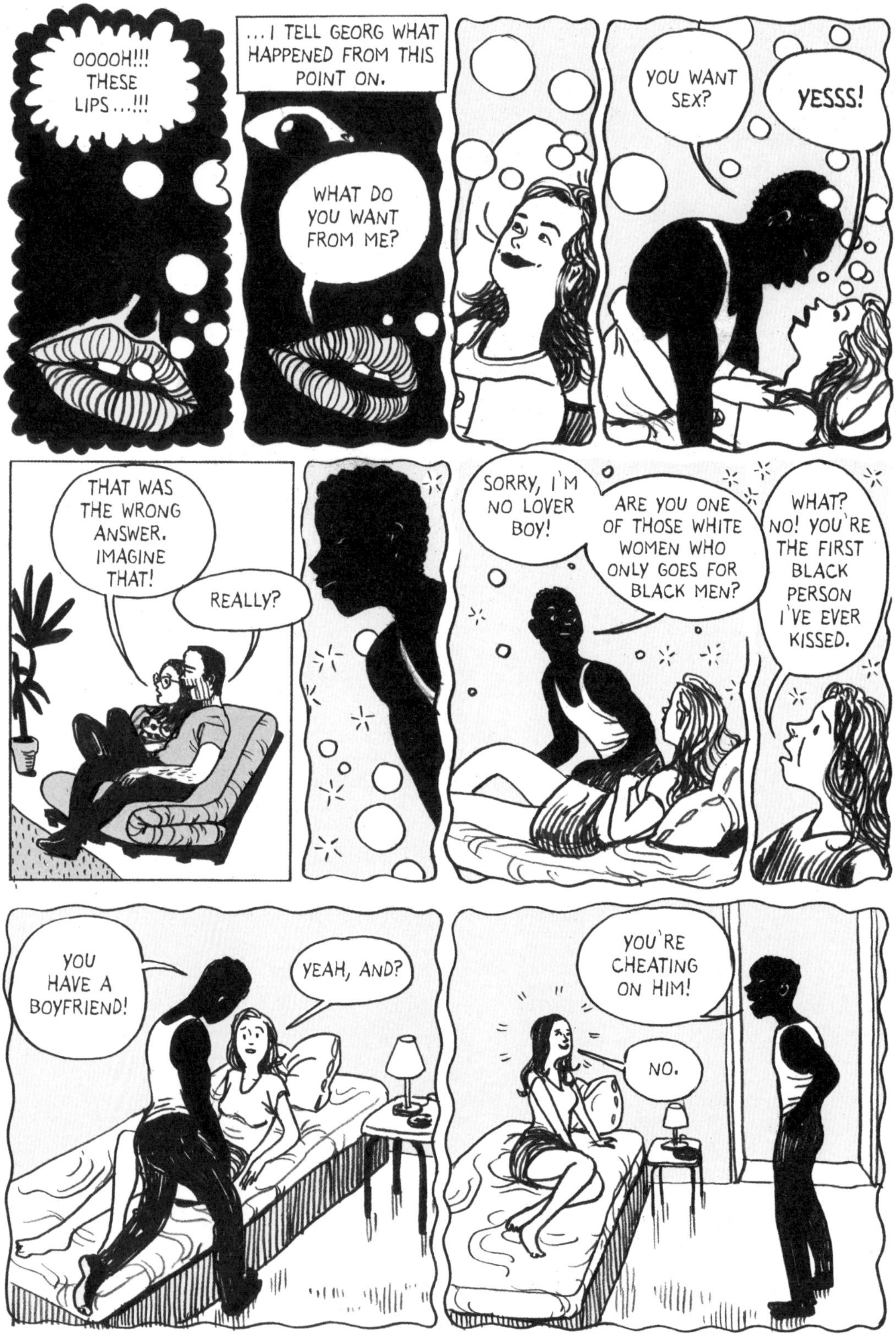
OOOOH!!! THESE LIPS...!!!
...I TELL GEORG WHAT HAPPENED FROM THIS POINT ON.
WHAT DO YOU WANT FROM ME?
YOU WANT SEX?
YESSS!
THAT WAS THE WRONG ANSWER. IMAGINE THAT!
REALLY?
SORRY, I'M NO LOVER BOY!
ARE YOU ONE OF THOSE WHITE WOMEN WHO ONLY GOES FOR BLACK MEN?
WHAT? NO! YOU'RE THE FIRST BLACK PERSON I'VE EVER KISSED.
YOU HAVE A BOYFRIEND!
YEAH, AND?
YOU'RE CHEATING ON HIM!
NO.

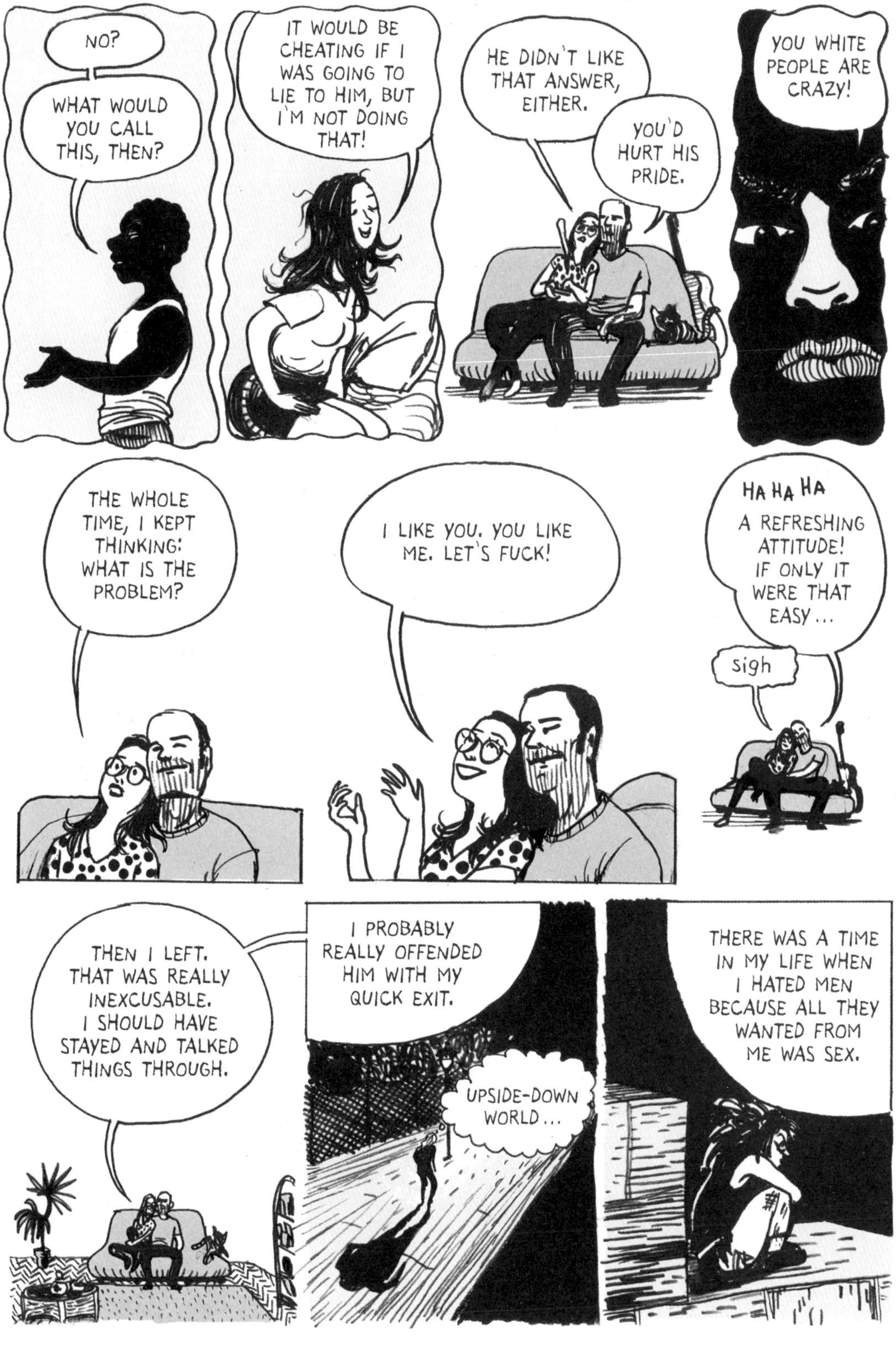
NO?
WHAT WOULD YOU CALL THIS, THEN?
IT WOULD BE CHEATING IF I WAS GOING TO LIE TO HIM, BUT I'M NOT DOING THAT!
HE DIDN'T LIKE THAT ANSWER, EITHER.
YOU'D HURT HIS PRIDE.
YOU WHITE PEOPLE ARE CRAZY!
THE WHOLE TIME, I KEPT THINKING: WHAT IS THE PROBLEM?
I LIKE YOU. YOU LIKE ME. LET'S FUCK!
HA HA HA
A REFRESHING ATTITUDE! IF ONLY IT WERE THAT EASY...
sigh
THEN I LEFT. THAT WAS REALLY INEXCUSABLE. I SHOULD HAVE STAYED AND TALKED THINGS THROUGH.
I PROBABLY REALLY OFFENDED HIM WITH MY QUICK EXIT.
UPSIDE-DOWN WORLD...
THERE WAS A TIME IN MY LIFE WHEN I HATED MEN BECAUSE ALL THEY WANTED FROM ME WAS SEX.

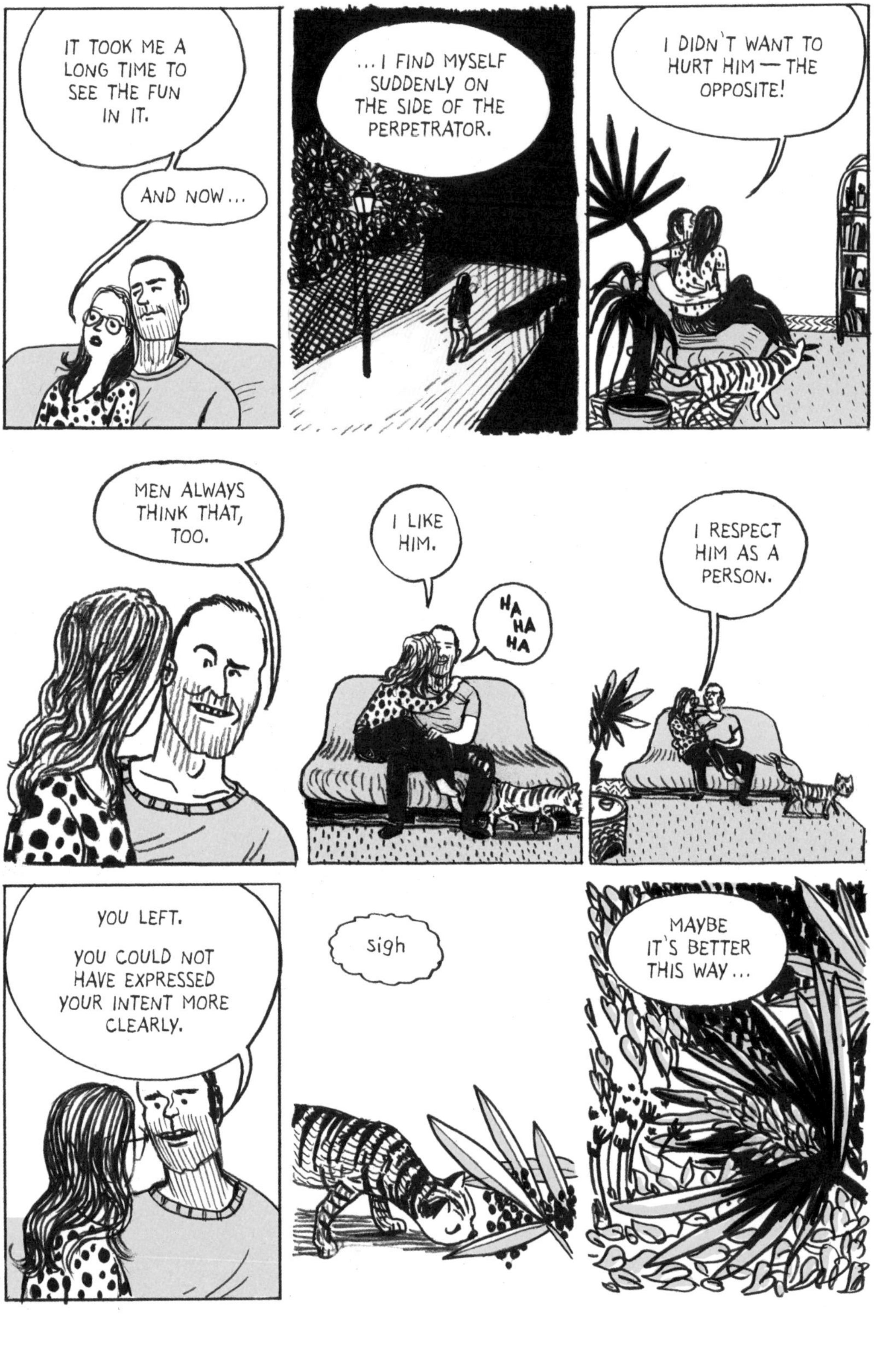
IT TOOK ME A LONG TIME TO SEE THE FUN IN IT.
AND NOW...
...I FIND MYSELF SUDDENLY ON THE SIDE OF THE PERPETRATOR.
I DIDN'T WANT TO HURT HIM — THE OPPOSITE!
MEN ALWAYS THINK THAT, TOO.
I LIKE HIM.
HA HA HA
I RESPECT HIM AS A PERSON.
YOU LEFT.
YOU COULD NOT HAVE EXPRESSED YOUR INTENT MORE CLEARLY.
sigh
MAYBE IT'S BETTER THIS WAY...

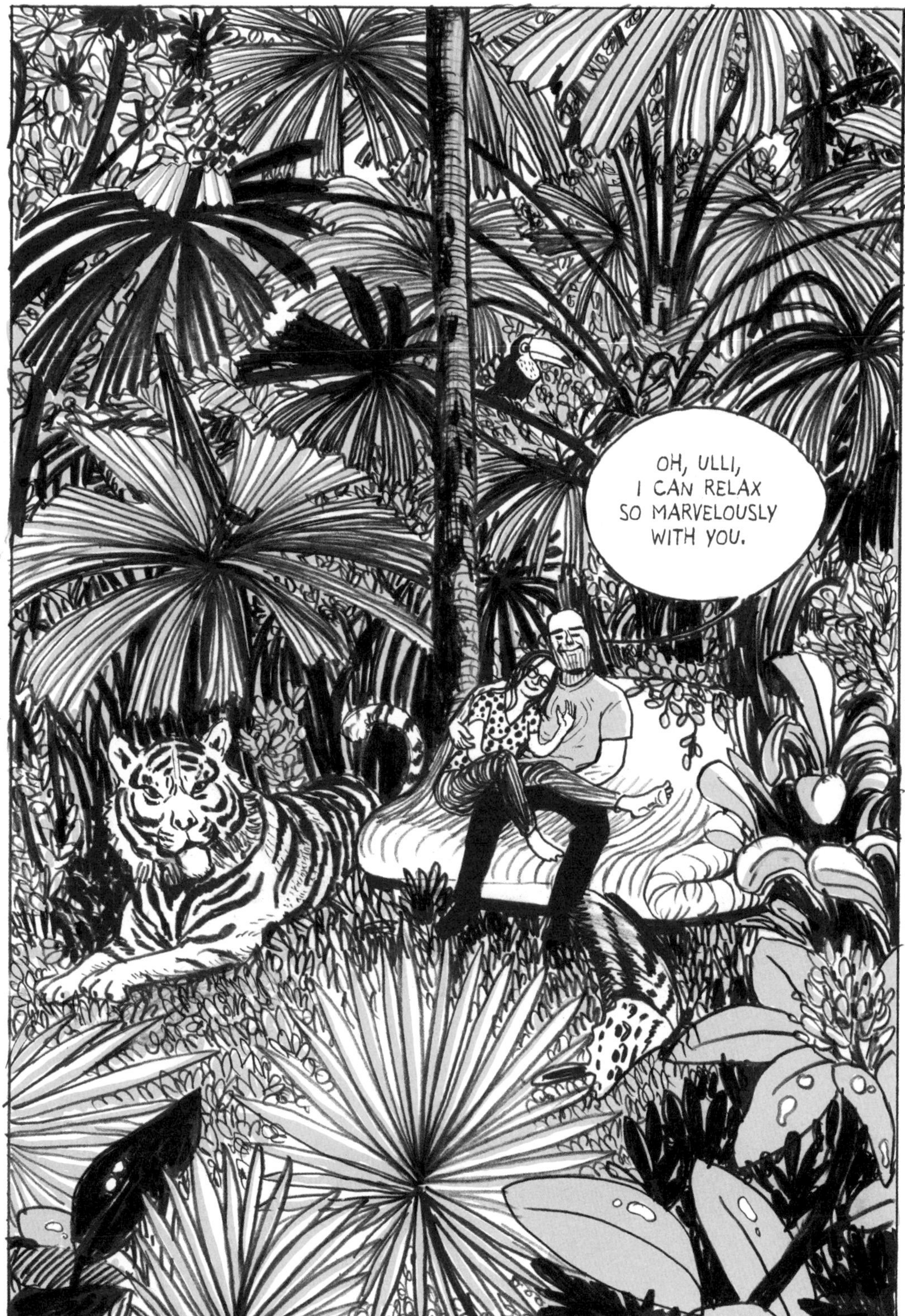
OH, ULLI, I CAN RELAX SO MARVELOUSLY WITH YOU.

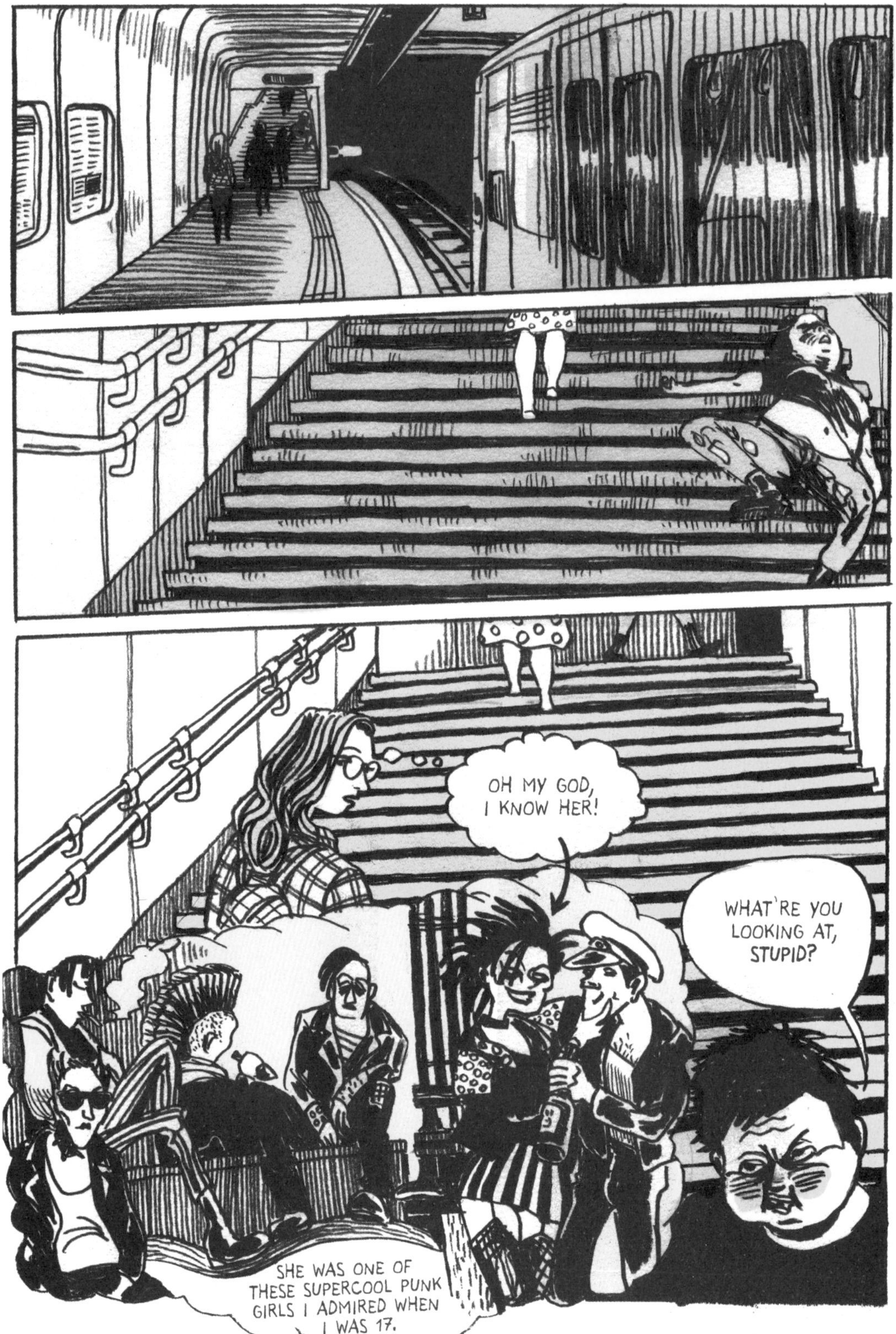
OH MY GOD, I KNOW HER!
WHAT'RE YOU LOOKING AT, STUPID?
SHE WAS ONE OF THESE SUPERCOOL PUNK GIRLS I ADMIRED WHEN I WAS 17.

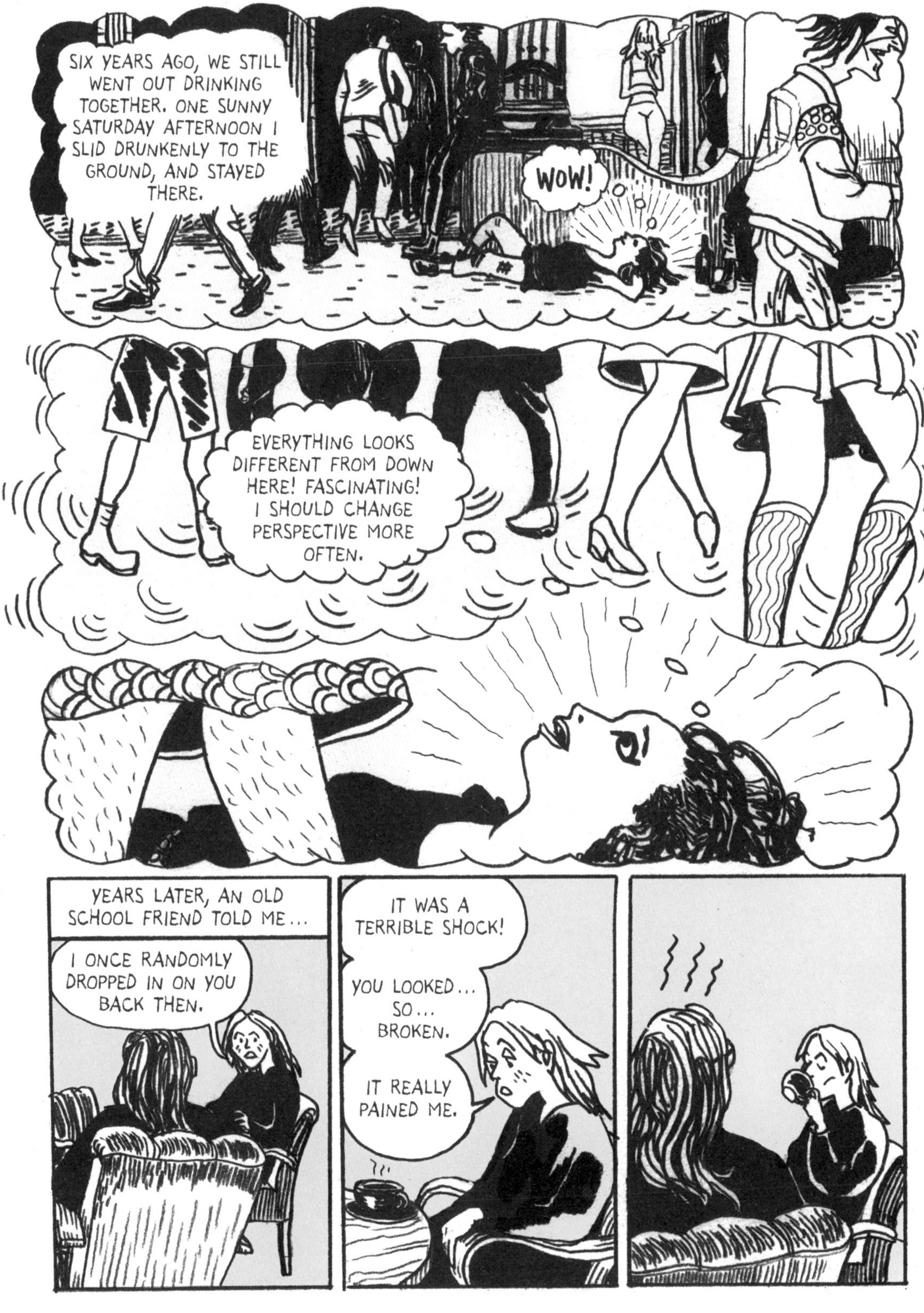
SIX YEARS AGO, WE STILL WENT OUT DRINKING TOGETHER. ONE SUNNY SATURDAY AFTERNOON I SLID DRUNKENLY TO THE GROUND, AND STAYED THERE.
WOW!
EVERYTHING LOOKS DIFFERENT FROM DOWN HERE! FASCINATING! I SHOULD CHANGE PERSPECTIVE MORE OFTEN.
YEARS LATER, AN OLD SCHOOL FRIEND TOLD ME...
I ONCE RANDOMLY DROPPED IN ON YOU BACK THEN.
IT WAS A TERRIBLE SHOCK!
YOU LOOKED... SO... BROKEN.
IT REALLY PAINED ME.

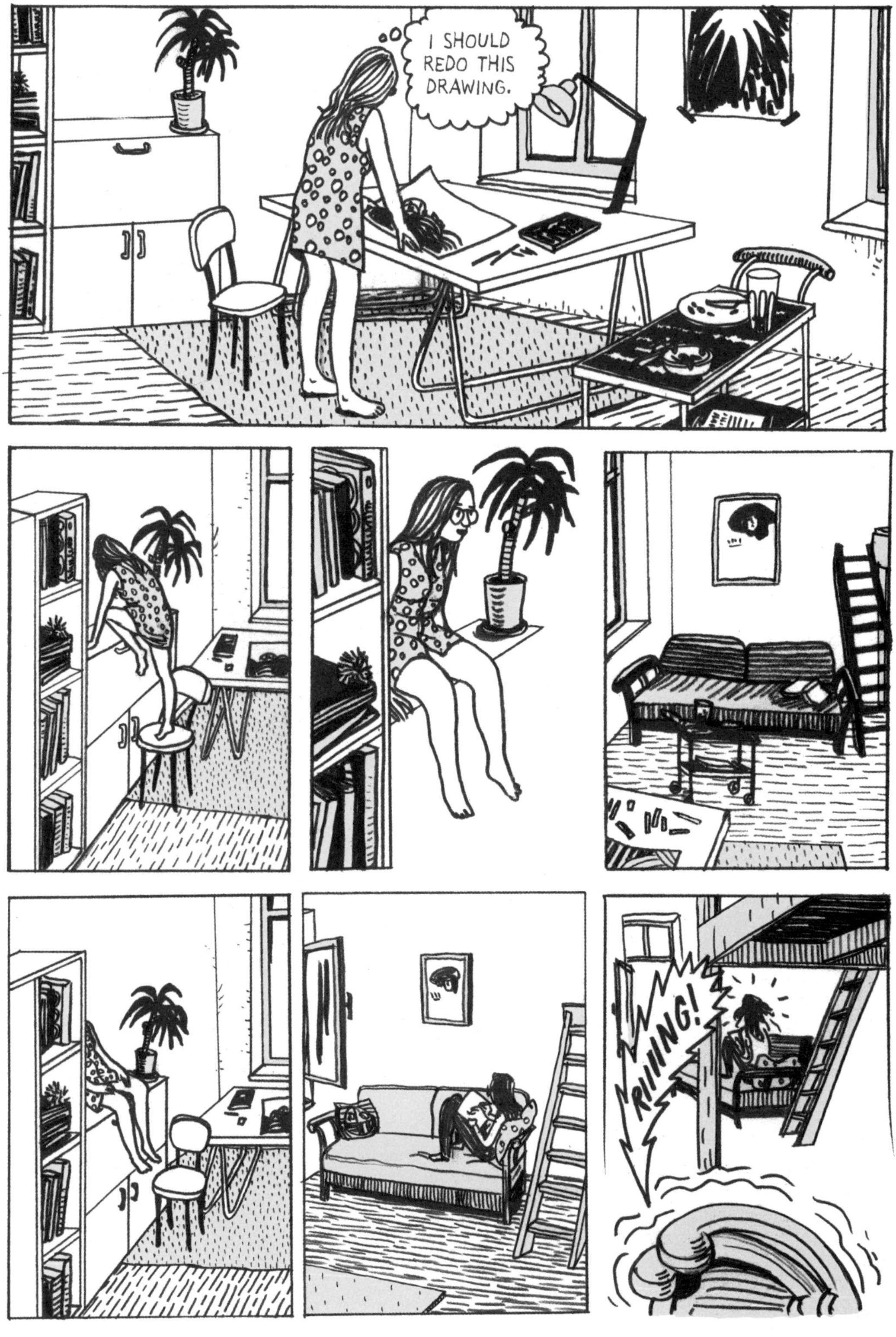
I SHOULD REDO THIS DRAWING.
RIIIING!

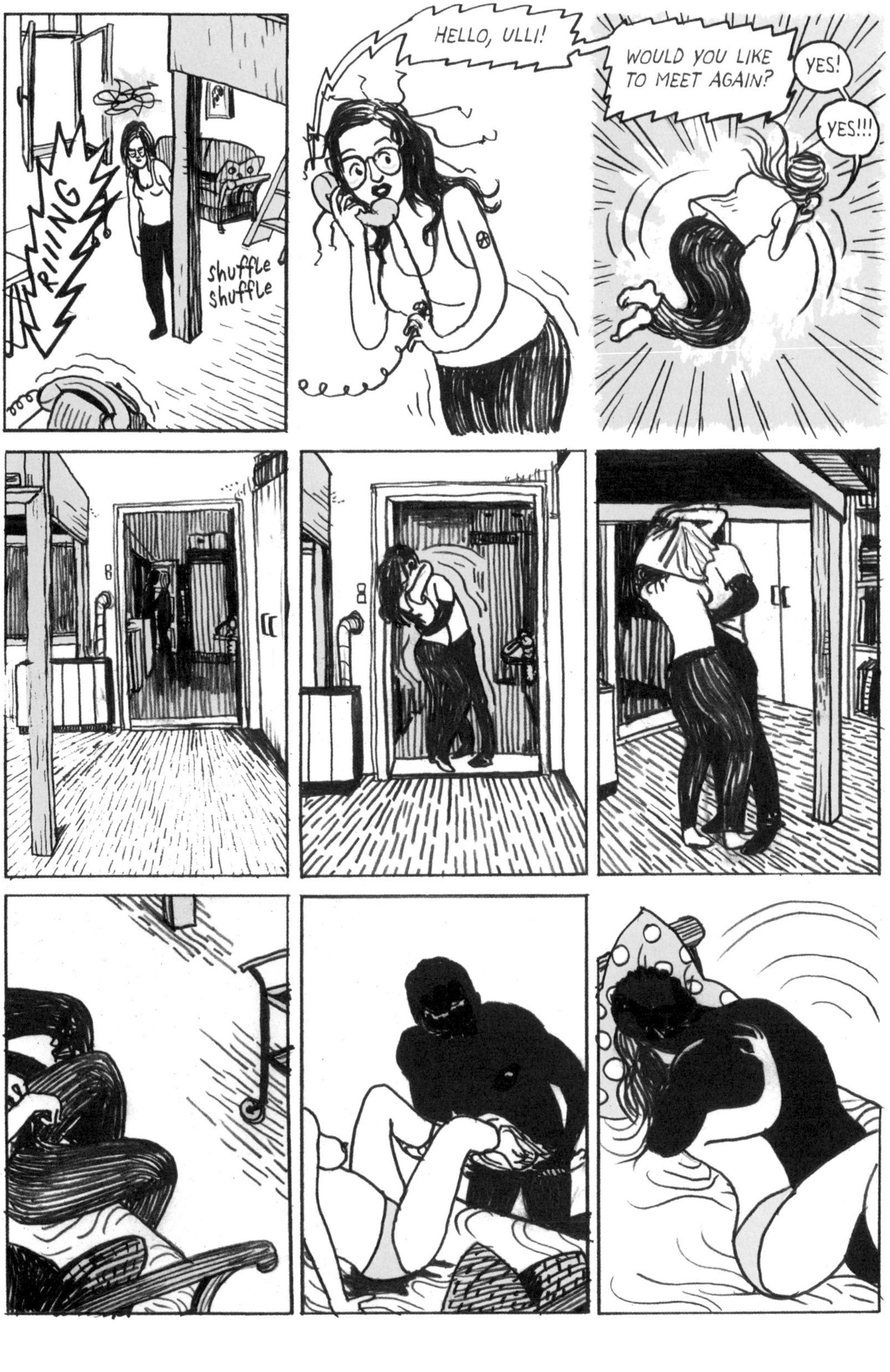
RIIIING
shuffle shuffle
HELLO, ULLI!
WOULD YOU LIKE TO MEET AGAIN?
YES!
YES!!!

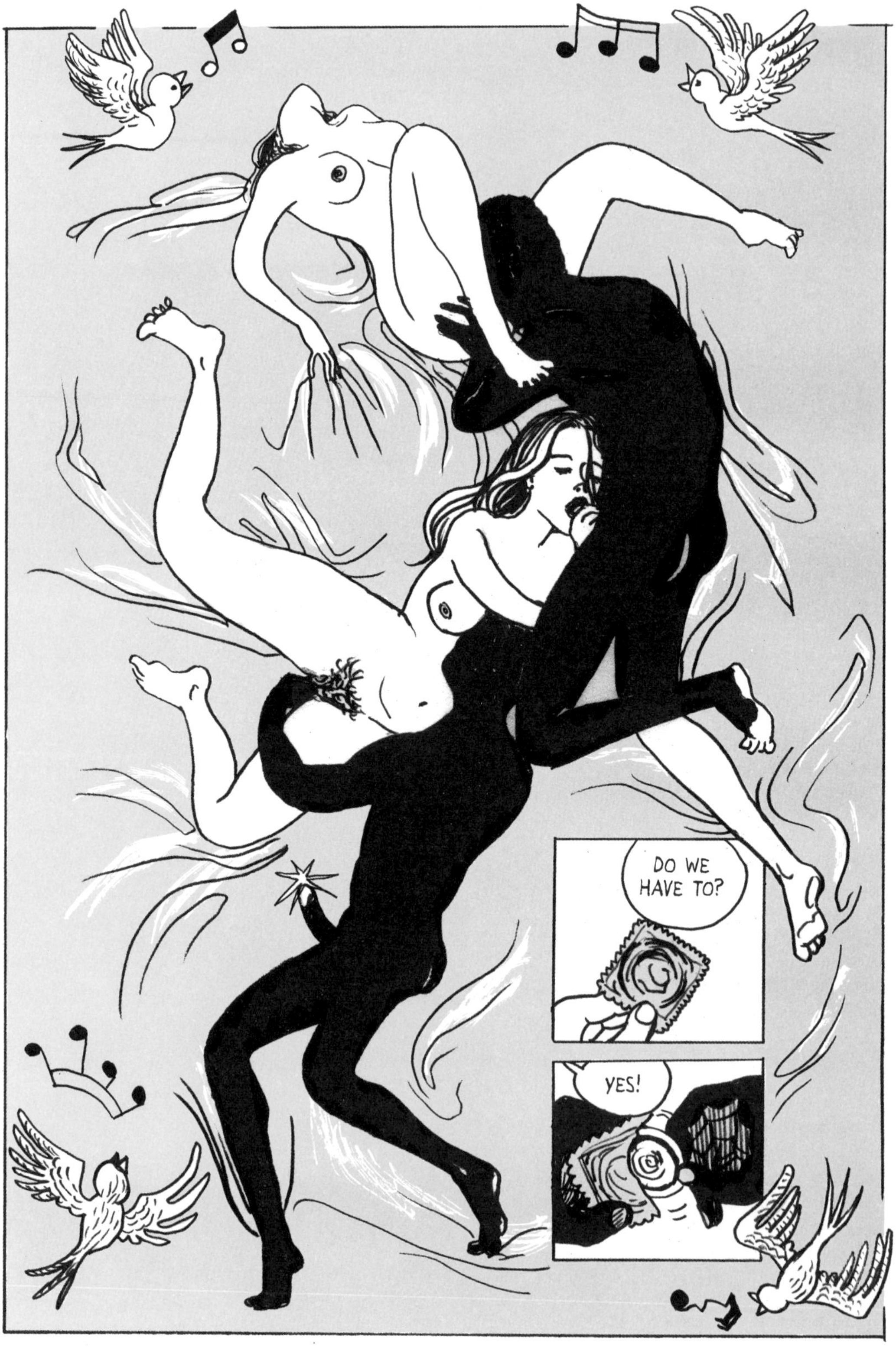
DO WE HAVE TO?
YES!

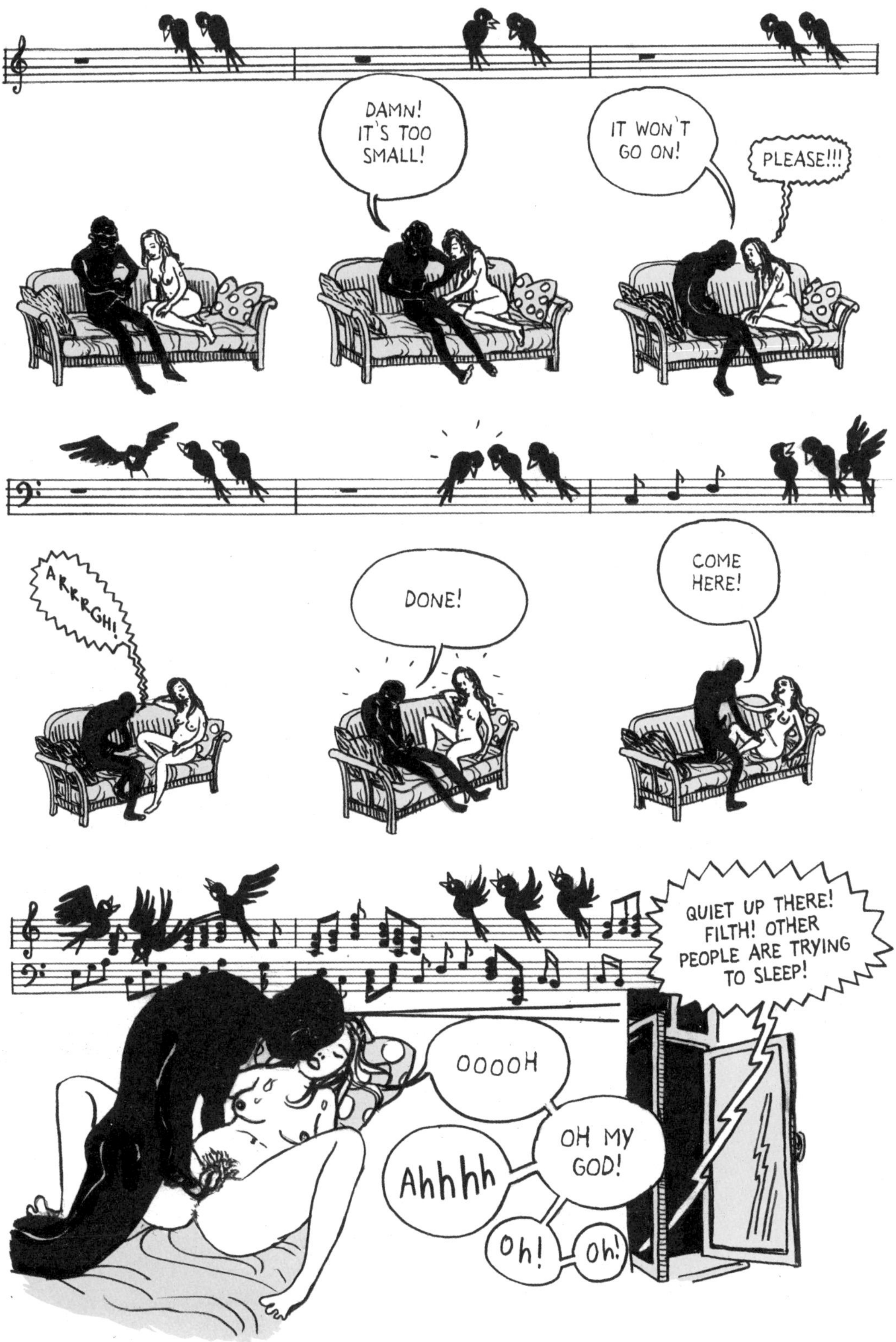
DAMN! IT'S TOO SMALL!
IT WON'T GO ON!
PLEASE!!!
ARRRGH!
DONE!
COME HERE!
QUIET UP THERE! FILTH! OTHER PEOPLE ARE TRYING TO SLEEP!
OOOOH
OH MY GOD!
Ahhhh
Oh!
Oh!

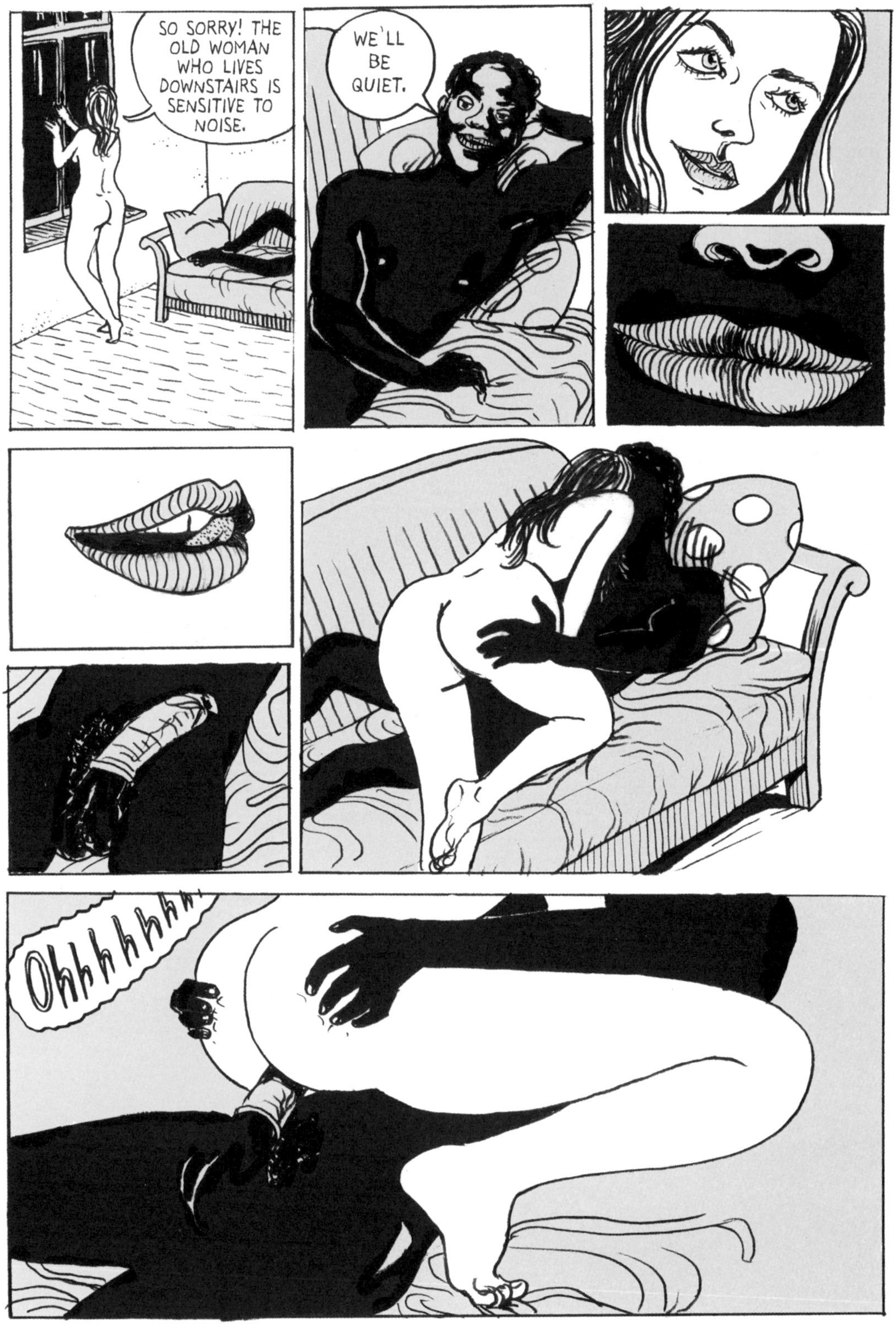
SO SORRY! THE OLD WOMAN WHO LIVES DOWNSTAIRS IS SENSITIVE TO NOISE.
WE'LL BE QUIET.
Ohhhhhh

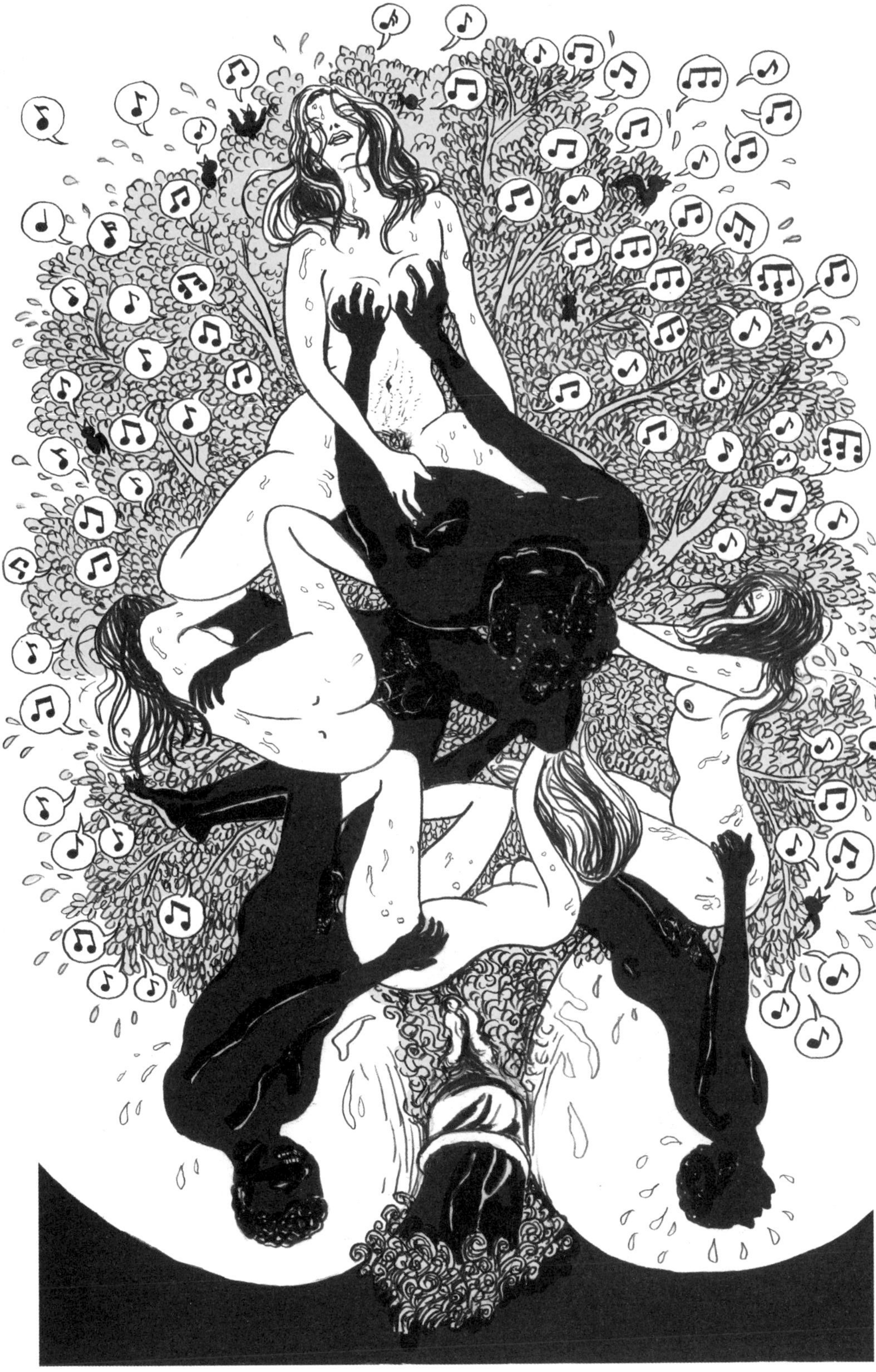

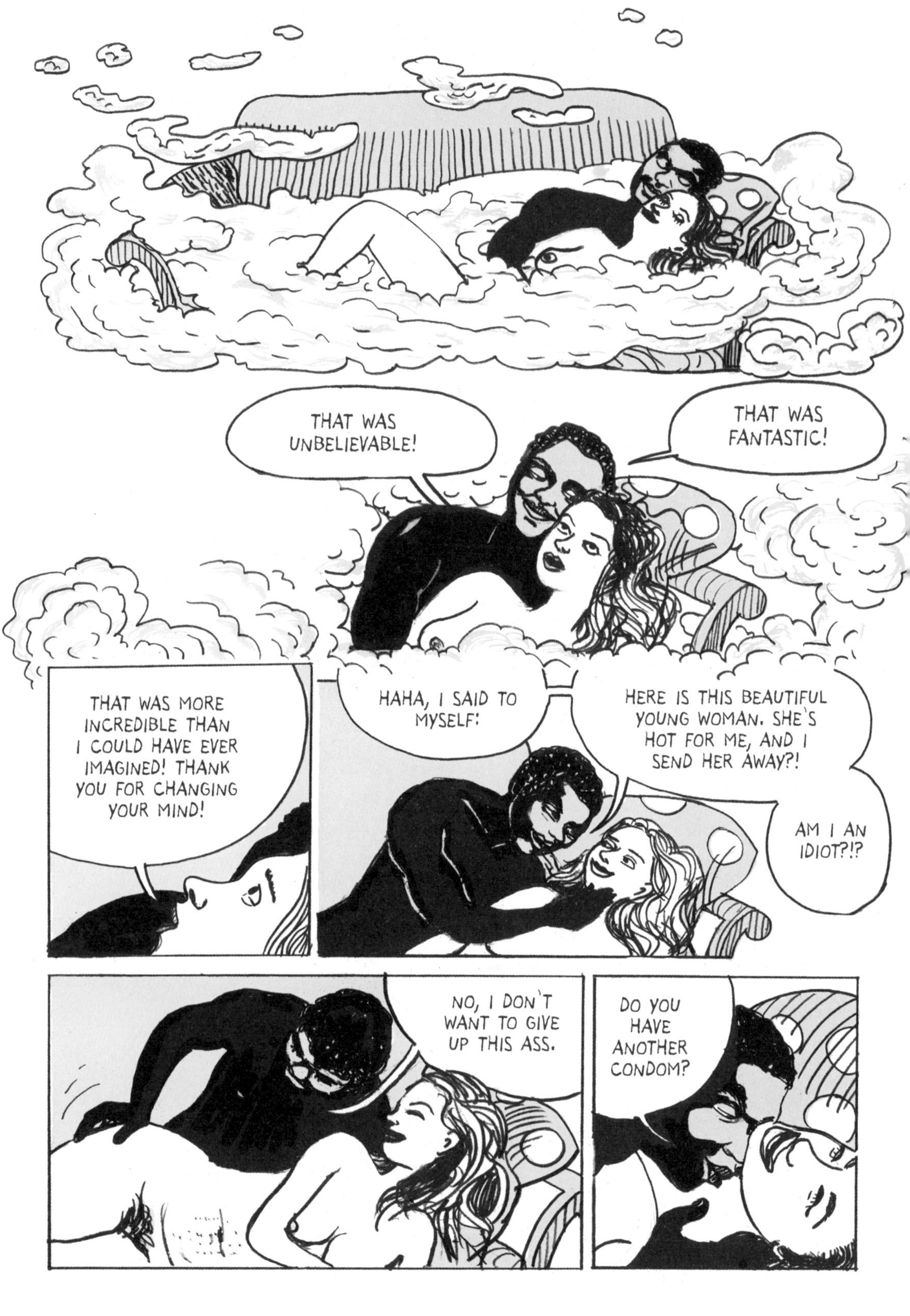

THAT WAS UNBELIEVABLE!
THAT WAS FANTASTIC!
THAT WAS MORE INCREDIBLE THAN I COULD HAVE EVER IMAGINED! THANK YOU FOR CHANGING YOUR MIND!
HAHA, I SAID TO MYSELF:
HERE IS THIS BEAUTIFUL YOUNG WOMAN. SHE'S HOT FOR ME, AND I SEND HER AWAY?!
AM I AN IDIOT?!?
NO, I DON'T WANT TO GIVE UP THIS ASS.
DO YOU HAVE ANOTHER CONDOM?

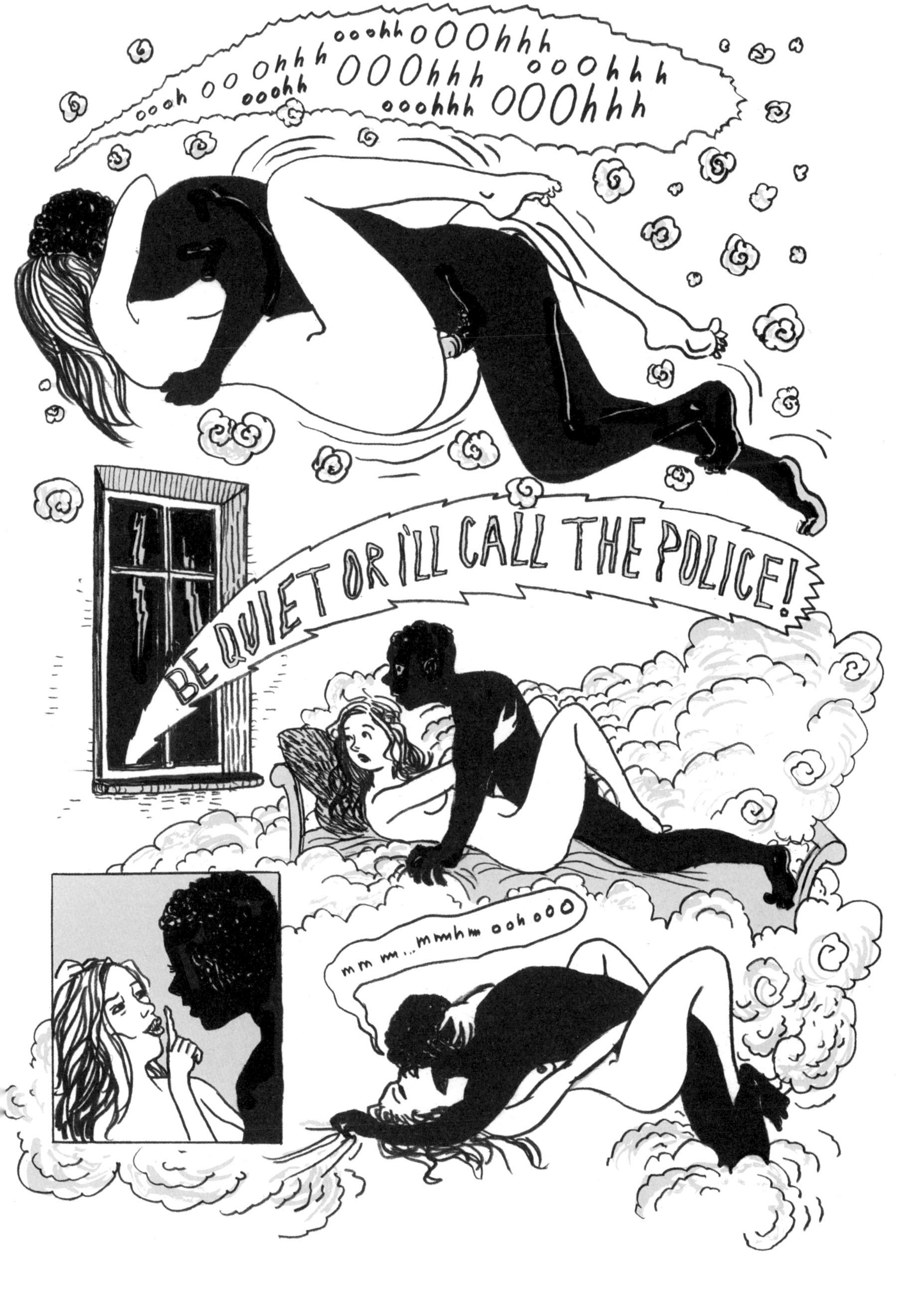
ooohh OOOhhh
oooh OO Ohhh OOOhhh oooOhhh
ooohh
ooohhh OOOhhh
BE QUIET OR I'LL CALL THE POLICE!
mm mm... mmhm oohooO

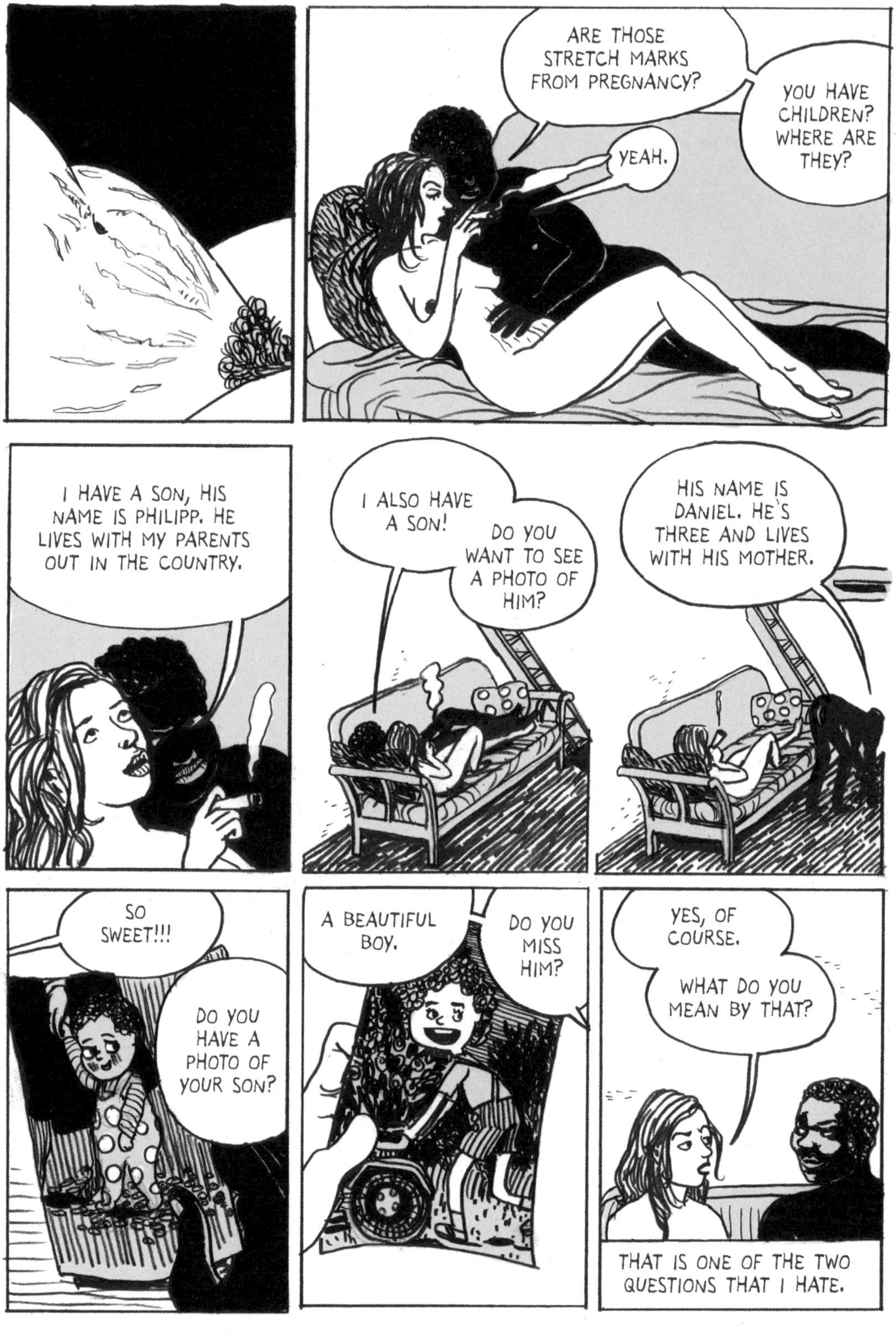
ARE THOSE STRETCH MARKS FROM PREGNANCY?
YEAH.
YOU HAVE CHILDREN? WHERE ARE THEY?
I HAVE A SON, HIS NAME IS PHILIPP. HE LIVES WITH MY PARENTS OUT IN THE COUNTRY.
I ALSO HAVE A SON!
DO YOU WANT TO SEE A PHOTO OF HIM?
HIS NAME IS DANIEL. HE'S THREE AND LIVES WITH HIS MOTHER.
SO SWEET!!!
DO YOU HAVE A PHOTO OF YOUR SON?
A BEAUTIFUL BOY.
DO YOU MISS HIM?
YES, OF COURSE.
WHAT DO YOU MEAN BY THAT?
THAT IS ONE OF THE TWO QUESTIONS THAT I HATE.

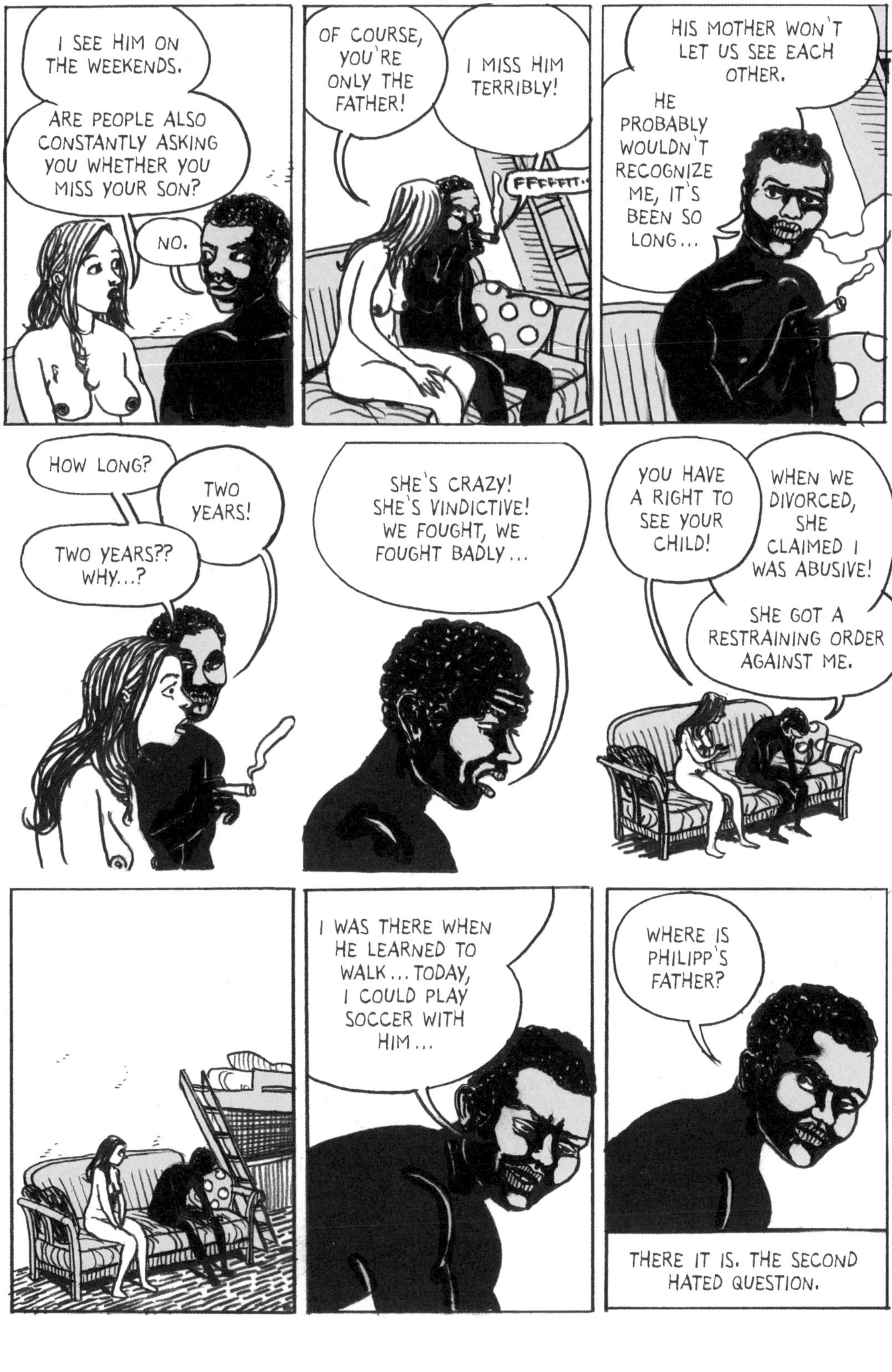
I SEE HIM ON THE WEEKENDS.
ARE PEOPLE ALSO CONSTANTLY ASKING YOU WHETHER YOU MISS YOUR SON?
NO.
OF COURSE, YOU'RE ONLY THE FATHER!
I MISS HIM TERRIBLY!
FFFFFTT
HIS MOTHER WON'T LET US SEE EACH OTHER.
HE PROBABLY WOULDN'T RECOGNIZE ME, IT'S BEEN SO LONG...
HOW LONG?
TWO YEARS!
TWO YEARS?? WHY...?
SHE'S CRAZY! SHE'S VINDICTIVE! WE FOUGHT, WE FOUGHT BADLY...
YOU HAVE A RIGHT TO SEE YOUR CHILD!
WHEN WE DIVORCED, SHE CLAIMED I WAS ABUSIVE!
SHE GOT A RESTRAINING ORDER AGAINST ME.
I WAS THERE WHEN HE LEARNED TO WALK... TODAY, I COULD PLAY SOCCER WITH HIM...
WHERE IS PHILIPP'S FATHER?
THERE IT IS. THE SECOND HATED QUESTION.

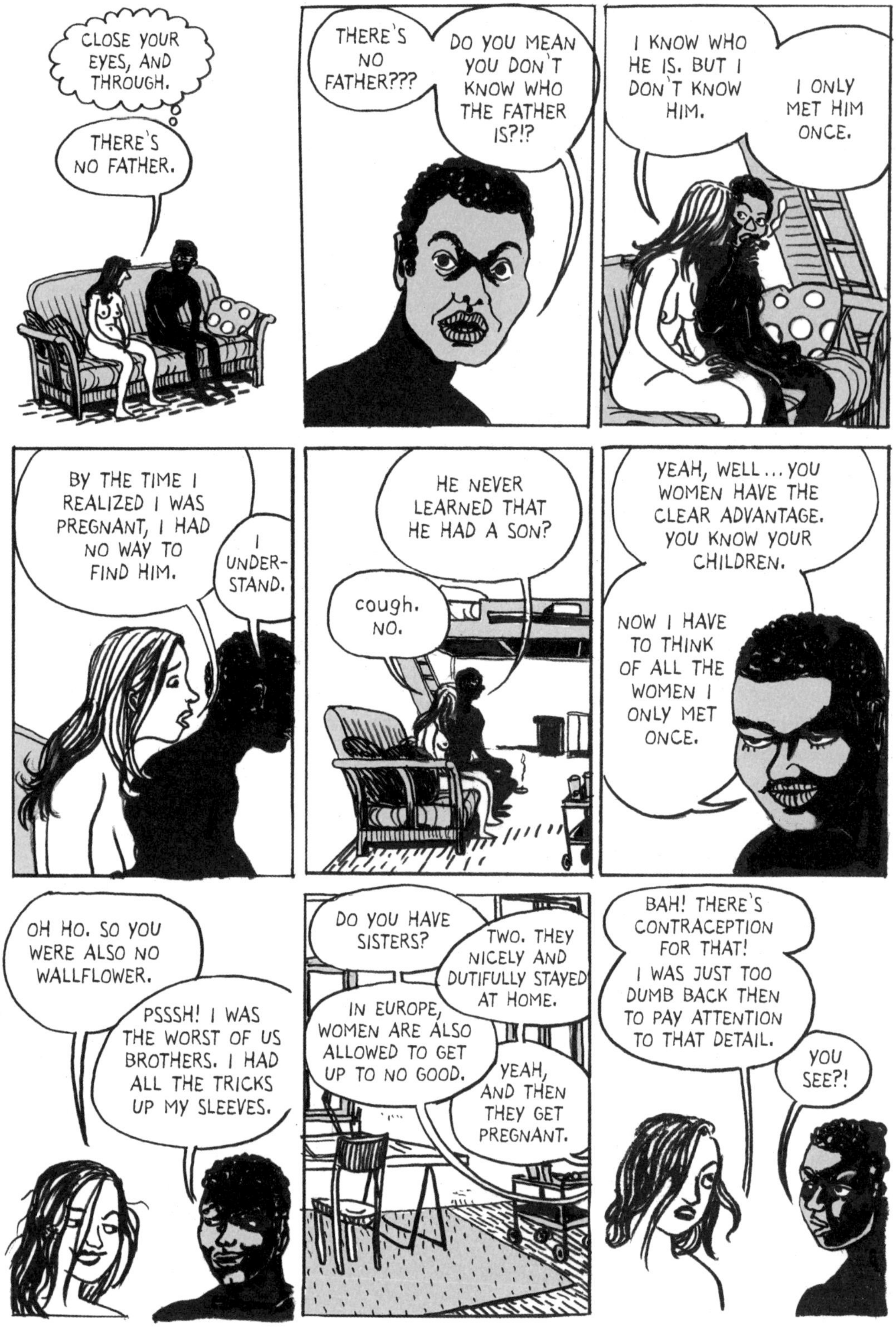
CLOSE YOUR EYES, AND THROUGH.
THERE'S NO FATHER.
THERE'S NO FATHER???
DO YOU MEAN YOU DON'T KNOW WHO THE FATHER IS?!?
I KNOW WHO HE IS. BUT I DON'T KNOW HIM.
I ONLY MET HIM ONCE.
BY THE TIME I REALIZED I WAS PREGNANT, I HAD NO WAY TO FIND HIM.
I UNDER-STAND.
HE NEVER LEARNED THAT HE HAD A SON?
cough. NO.
YEAH, WELL... YOU WOMEN HAVE THE CLEAR ADVANTAGE. YOU KNOW YOUR CHILDREN.
NOW I HAVE TO THINK OF ALL THE WOMEN I ONLY MET ONCE.
OH HO. SO YOU WERE ALSO NO WALLFLOWER.
PSSSH! I WAS THE WORST OF US BROTHERS. I HAD ALL THE TRICKS UP MY SLEEVES.
DO YOU HAVE SISTERS?
TWO. THEY NICELY AND DUTIFULLY STAYED AT HOME.
IN EUROPE, WOMEN ARE ALSO ALLOWED TO GET UP TO NO GOOD.
YEAH, AND THEN THEY GET PREGNANT.
BAH! THERE'S CONTRACEPTION FOR THAT! I WAS JUST TOO DUMB BACK THEN TO PAY ATTENTION TO THAT DETAIL.
YOU SEE?!

MY MOTHER NOTICED ME PUKING EVERY MORNING.
SHE KNEW TO READ THE SIGNS.

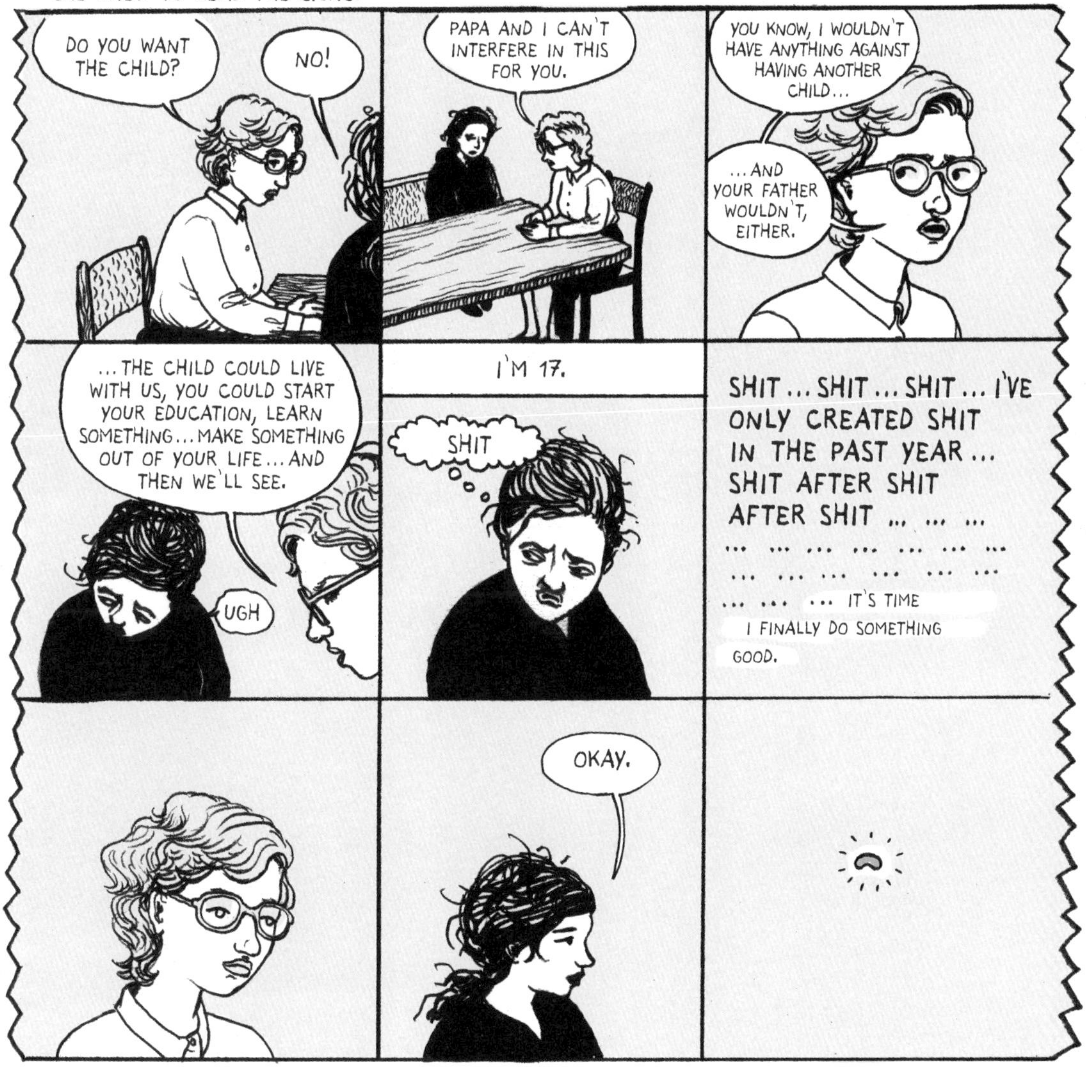
DO YOU WANT THE CHILD?
NO!
PAPA AND I CAN'T INTERFERE IN THIS FOR YOU.
YOU KNOW, I WOULDN'T HAVE ANYTHING AGAINST HAVING ANOTHER CHILD...
...AND YOUR FATHER WOULDN'T, EITHER.
...THE CHILD COULD LIVE WITH US, YOU COULD START YOUR EDUCATION, LEARN SOMETHING...MAKE SOMETHING OUT OF YOUR LIFE...AND THEN WE'LL SEE.
UGH
I'M 17.
SHIT
SHIT ... SHIT ... SHIT ... I'VE ONLY CREATED SHIT IN THE PAST YEAR ... SHIT AFTER SHIT AFTER SHIT ... ...
... IT'S TIME I FINALLY DO SOMETHING GOOD.
OKAY.

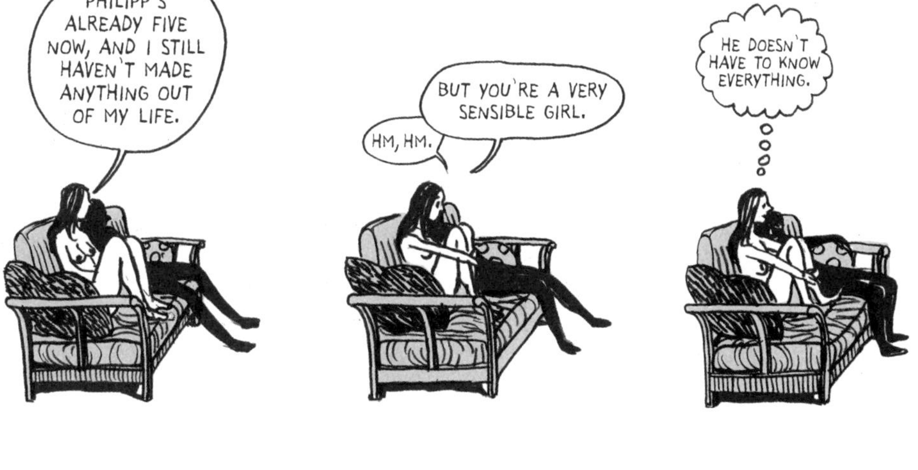
PHILIPP'S ALREADY FIVE NOW, AND I STILL HAVEN'T MADE ANYTHING OUT OF MY LIFE.
HM, HM.
BUT YOU'RE A VERY SENSIBLE GIRL.
HE DOESN'T HAVE TO KNOW EVERYTHING.

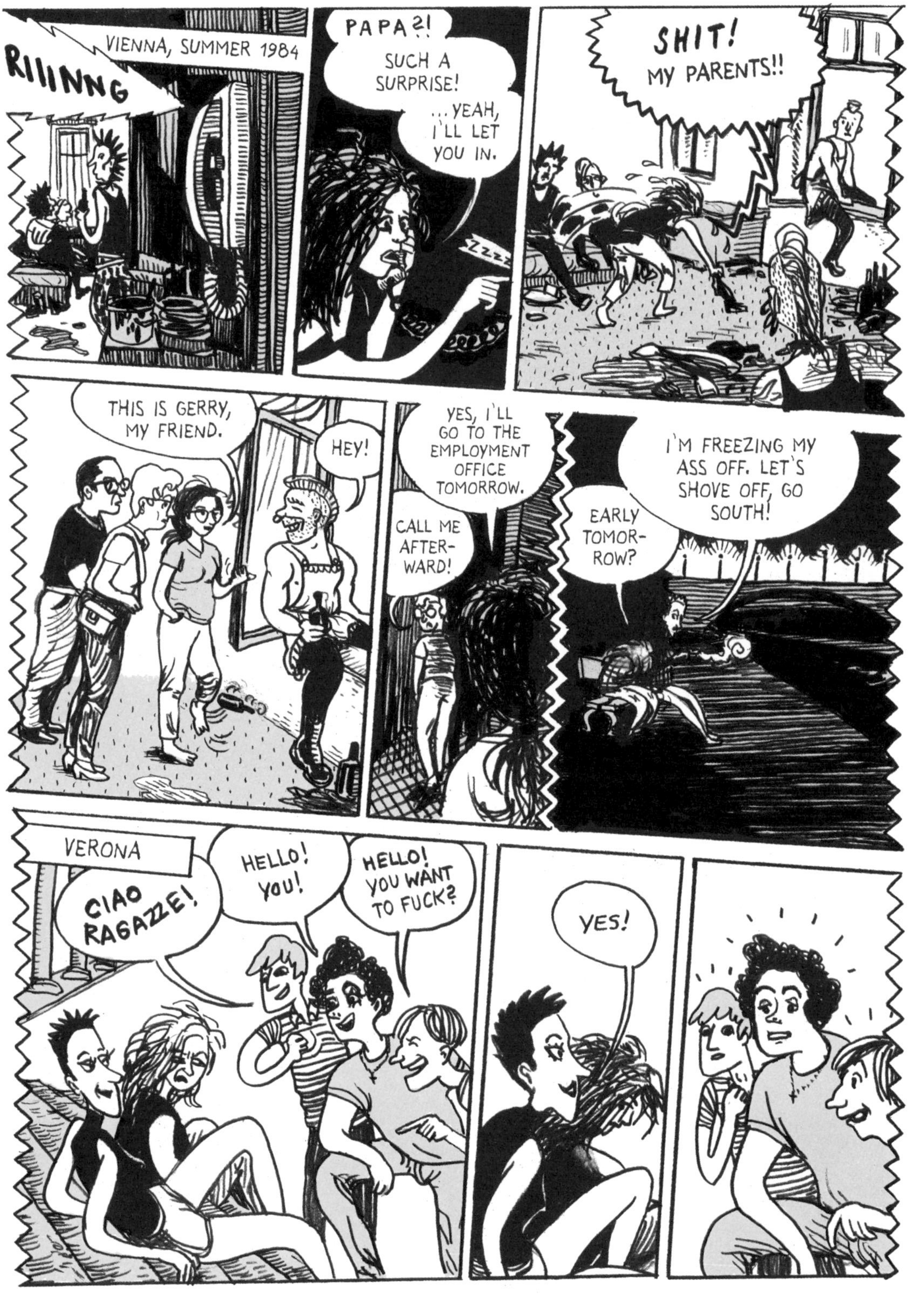
VIENNA, SUMMER 1984
RIIINNG
PAPA?!
SUCH A SURPRISE!
...YEAH, I'LL LET YOU IN.
ZZZZ
SHIT! MY PARENTS!!
THIS IS GERRY, MY FRIEND.
HEY!
YES, I'LL GO TO THE EMPLOYMENT OFFICE TOMORROW.
CALL ME AFTER-WARD!
I'M FREEZING MY ASS OFF. LET'S SHOVE OFF, GO SOUTH!
EARLY TOMOR-ROW?
VERONA
CIAO RAGAZZE!
HELLO! YOU!
HELLO! YOU WANT TO FUCK?
YES!

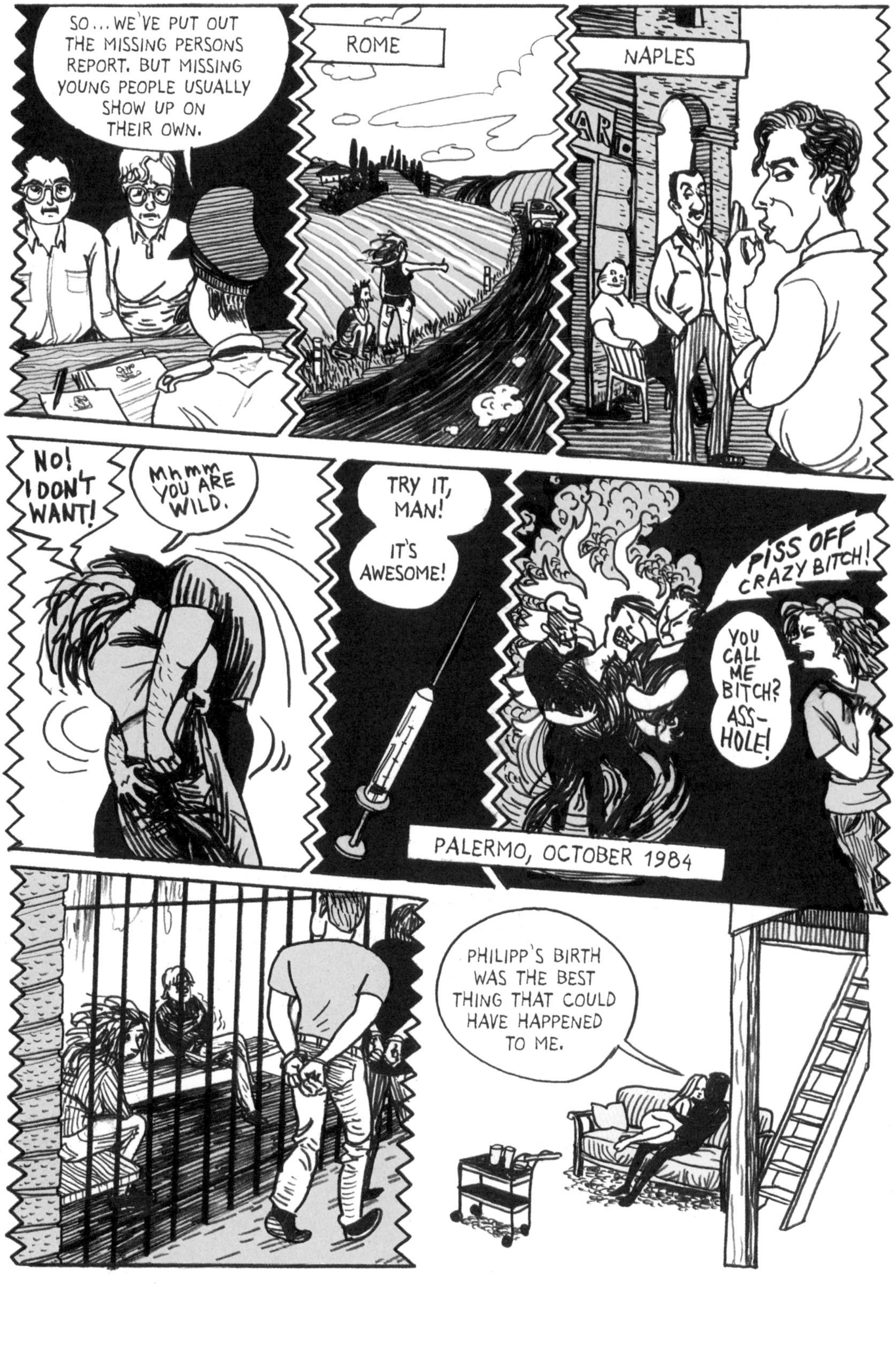
SO... WE'VE PUT OUT THE MISSING PERSONS REPORT. BUT MISSING YOUNG PEOPLE USUALLY SHOW UP ON THEIR OWN.
ROME
NAPLES
NO! I DON'T WANT!
Mhmm YOU ARE WILD.
TRY IT, MAN!
IT'S AWESOME!
PISS OFF CRAZY BITCH!
YOU CALL ME BITCH? ASS-HOLE!
PALERMO, OCTOBER 1984
PHILIPP'S BIRTH WAS THE BEST THING THAT COULD HAVE HAPPENED TO ME.

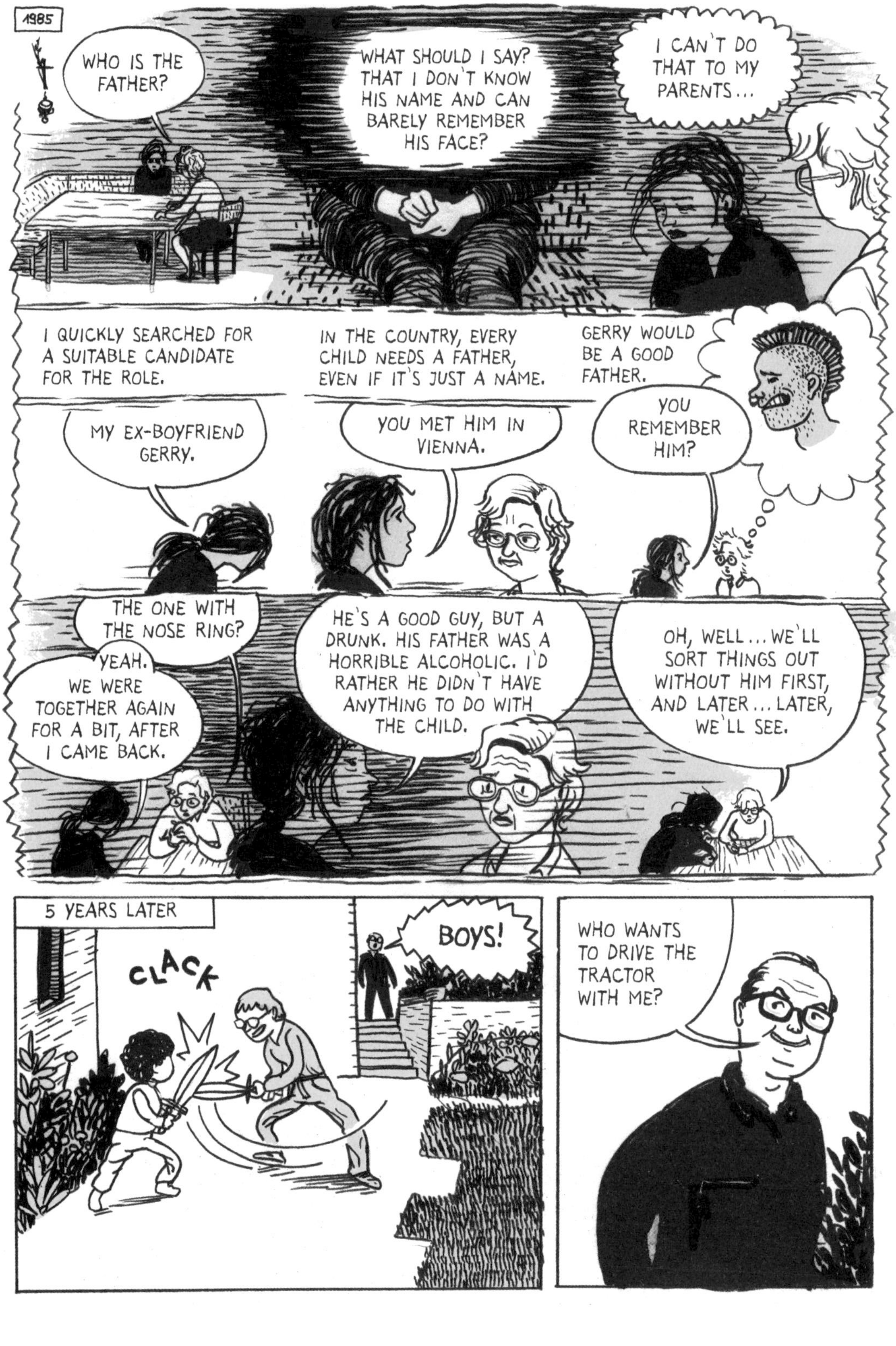
1985
WHO IS THE FATHER?
WHAT SHOULD I SAY? THAT I DON'T KNOW HIS NAME AND CAN BARELY REMEMBER HIS FACE?
I CAN'T DO THAT TO MY PARENTS...
I QUICKLY SEARCHED FOR A SUITABLE CANDIDATE FOR THE ROLE.
IN THE COUNTRY, EVERY CHILD NEEDS A FATHER, EVEN IF IT'S JUST A NAME.
GERRY WOULD BE A GOOD FATHER.
MY EX-BOYFRIEND GERRY.
YOU MET HIM IN VIENNA.
YOU REMEMBER HIM?
THE ONE WITH THE NOSE RING?
YEAH. WE WERE TOGETHER AGAIN FOR A BIT, AFTER I CAME BACK.
HE'S A GOOD GUY, BUT A DRUNK. HIS FATHER WAS A HORRIBLE ALCOHOLIC. I'D RATHER HE DIDN'T HAVE ANYTHING TO DO WITH THE CHILD.
OH, WELL... WE'LL SORT THINGS OUT WITHOUT HIM FIRST, AND LATER... LATER, WE'LL SEE.
5 YEARS LATER
CLACK
BOYS!
WHO WANTS TO DRIVE THE TRACTOR WITH ME?

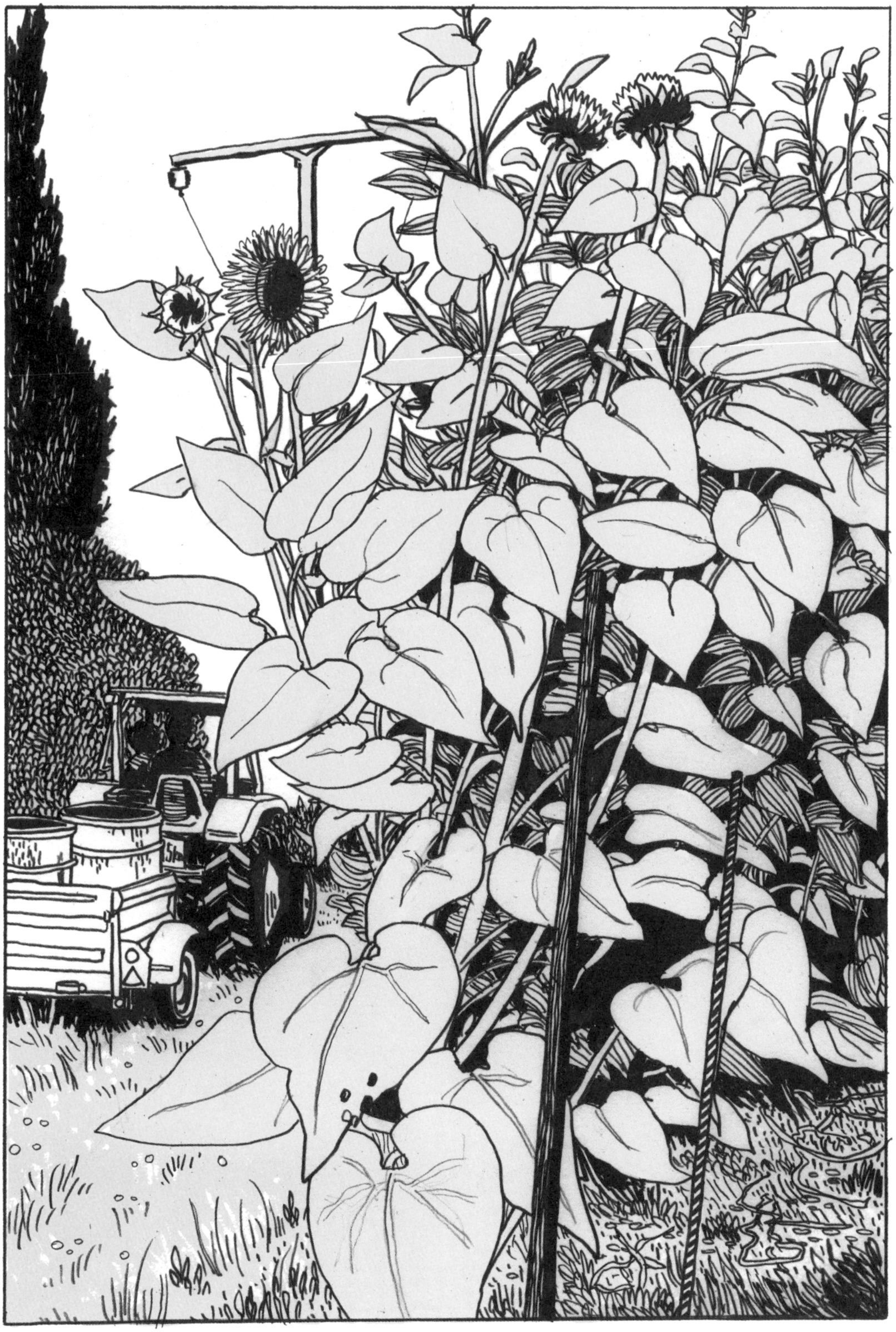

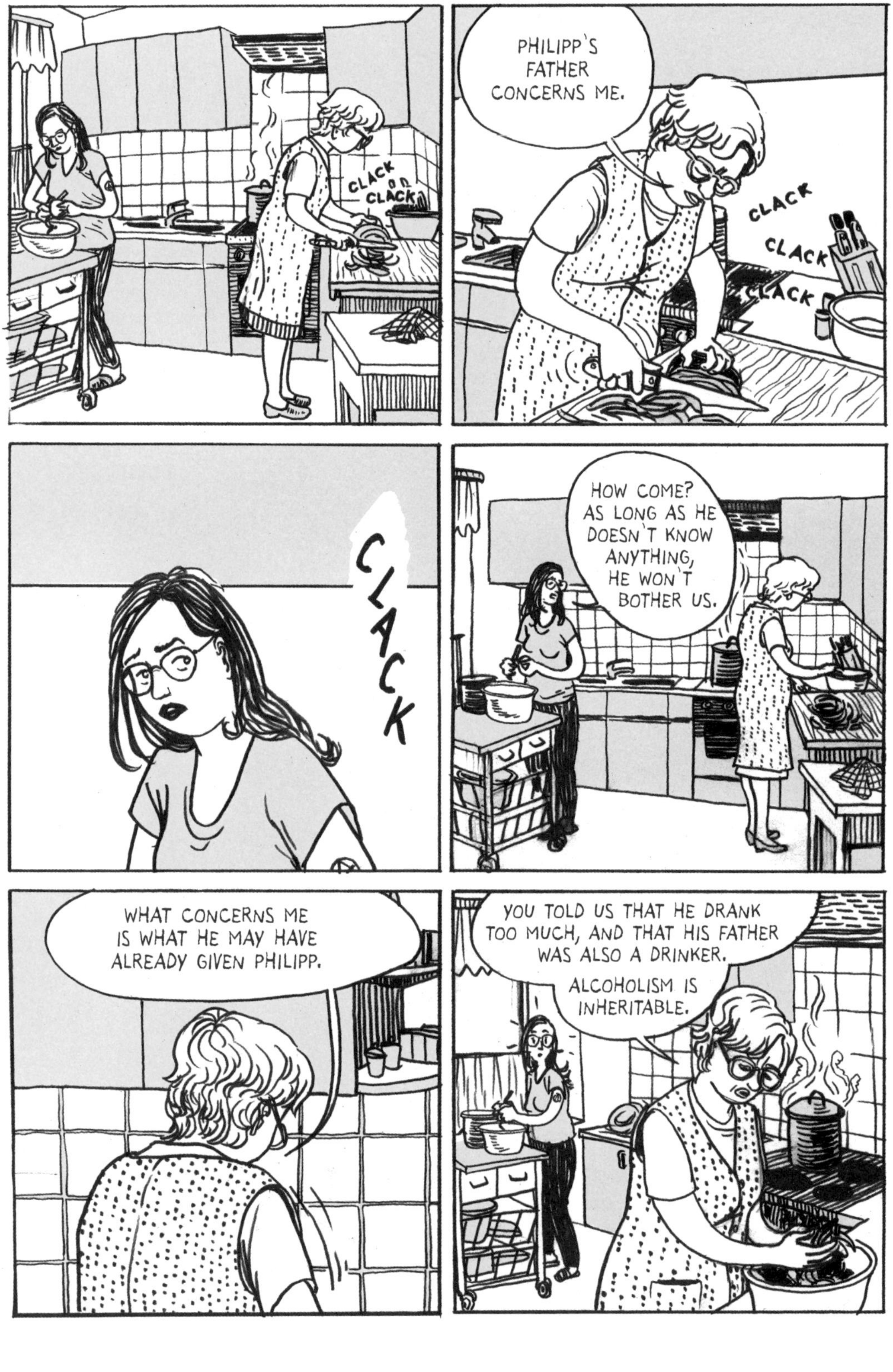
CLACK
CLACK
PHILIPP'S FATHER CONCERNS ME.
CLACK
CLACK
CLACK
CLACK
HOW COME? AS LONG AS HE DOESN'T KNOW ANYTHING, HE WON'T BOTHER US.
WHAT CONCERNS ME IS WHAT HE MAY HAVE ALREADY GIVEN PHILIPP.
YOU TOLD US THAT HE DRANK TOO MUCH, AND THAT HIS FATHER WAS ALSO A DRINKER.
ALCOHOLISM IS INHERITABLE.

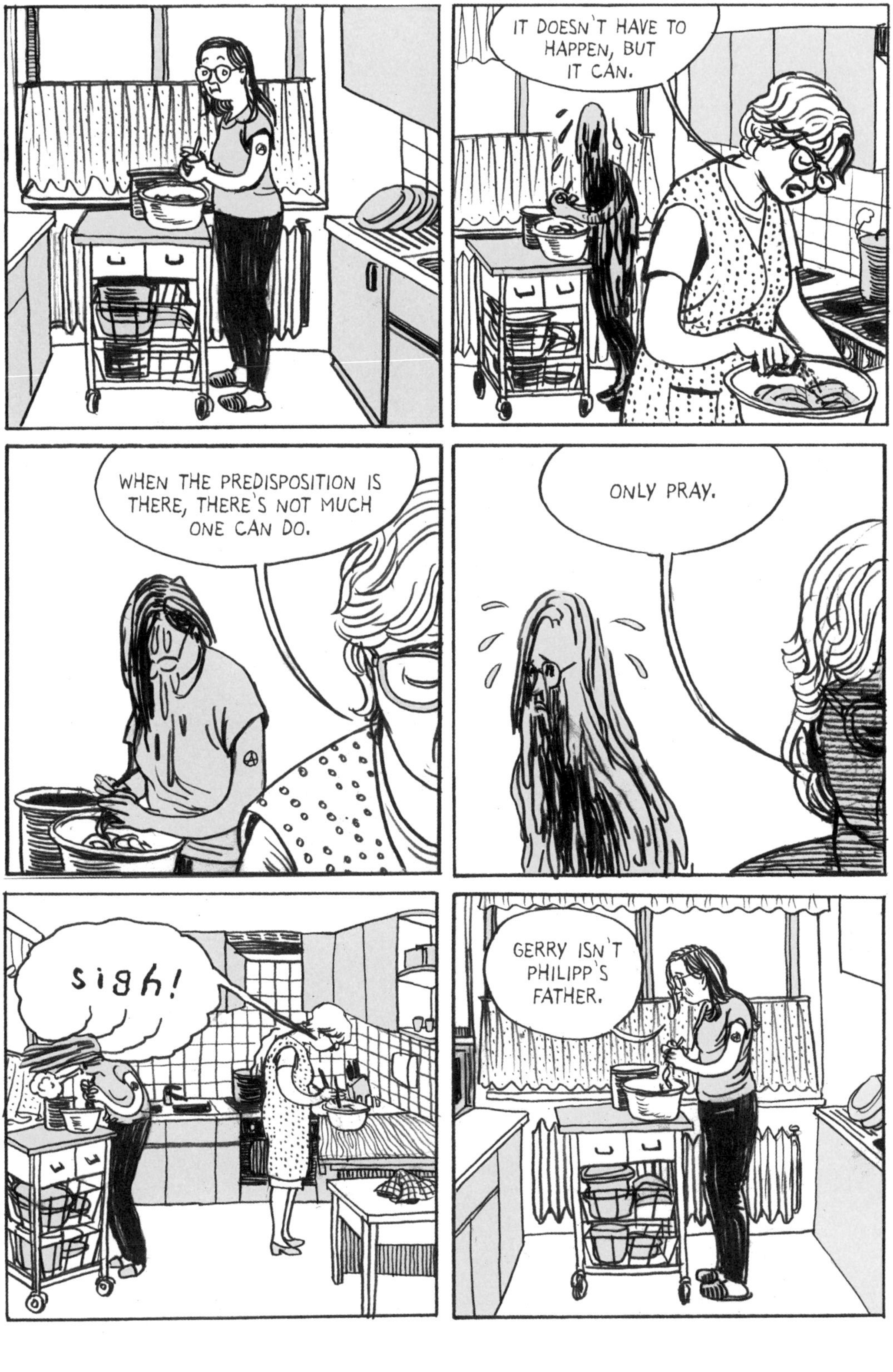
IT DOESN'T HAVE TO HAPPEN, BUT IT CAN.
WHEN THE PREDISPOSITION IS THERE, THERE'S NOT MUCH ONE CAN DO.
ONLY PRAY.
sigh!
GERRY ISN'T PHILIPP'S FATHER.

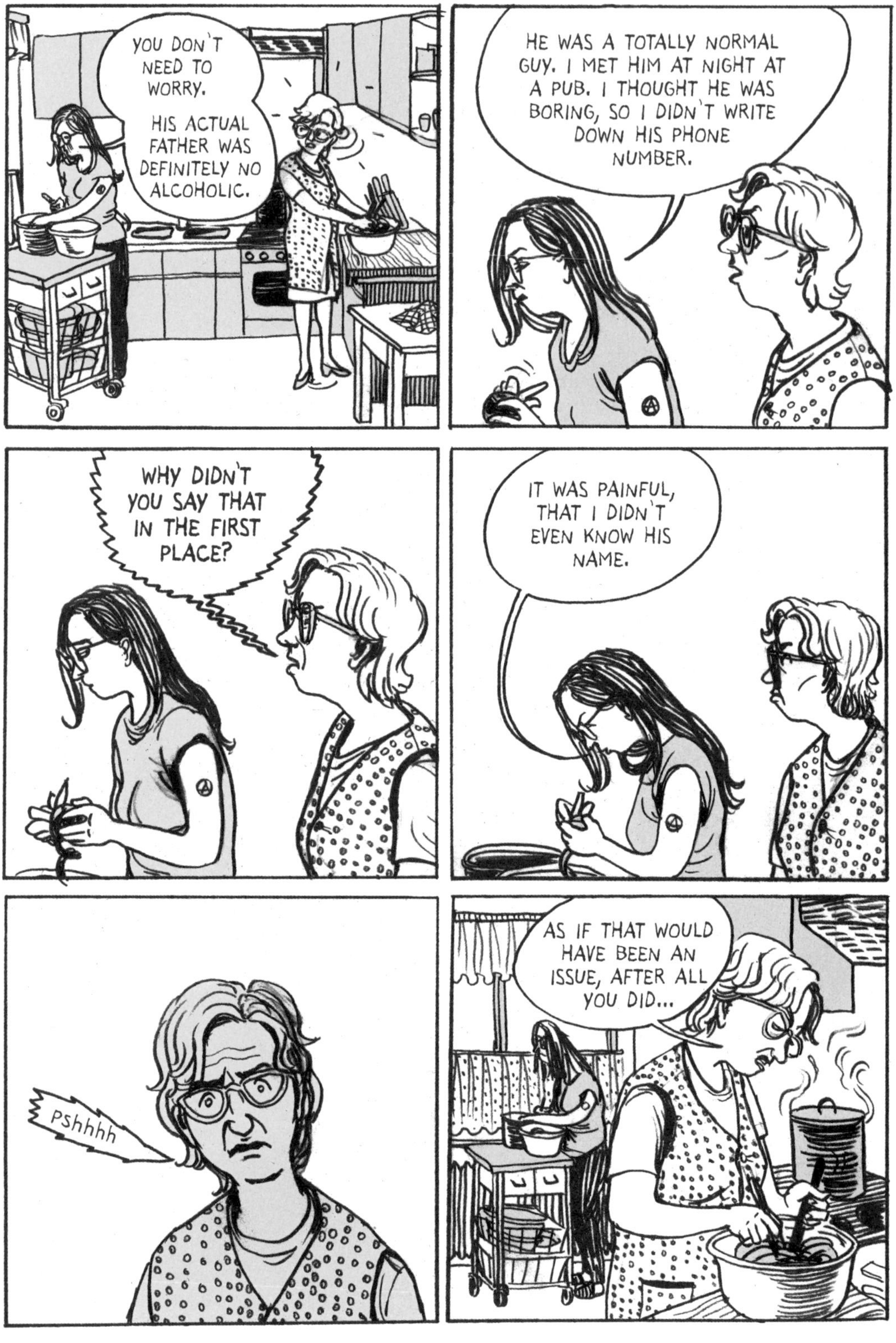
YOU DON'T NEED TO WORRY.
HIS ACTUAL FATHER WAS DEFINITELY NO ALCOHOLIC.
HE WAS A TOTALLY NORMAL GUY. I MET HIM AT NIGHT AT A PUB. I THOUGHT HE WAS BORING, SO I DIDN'T WRITE DOWN HIS PHONE NUMBER.
WHY DIDN'T YOU SAY THAT IN THE FIRST PLACE?
IT WAS PAINFUL, THAT I DIDN'T EVEN KNOW HIS NAME.
Pshhhh
AS IF THAT WOULD HAVE BEEN AN ISSUE, AFTER ALL YOU DID...

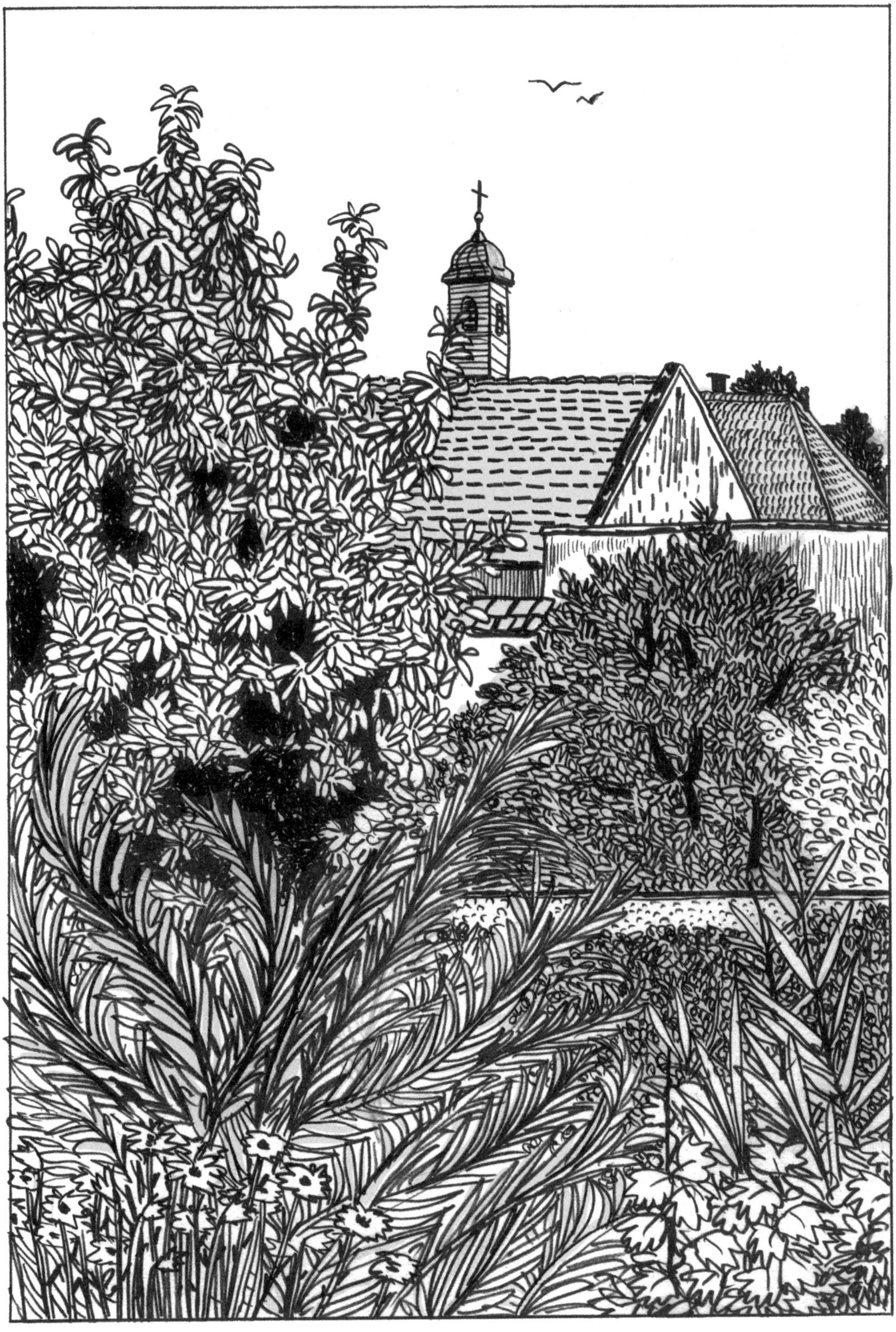

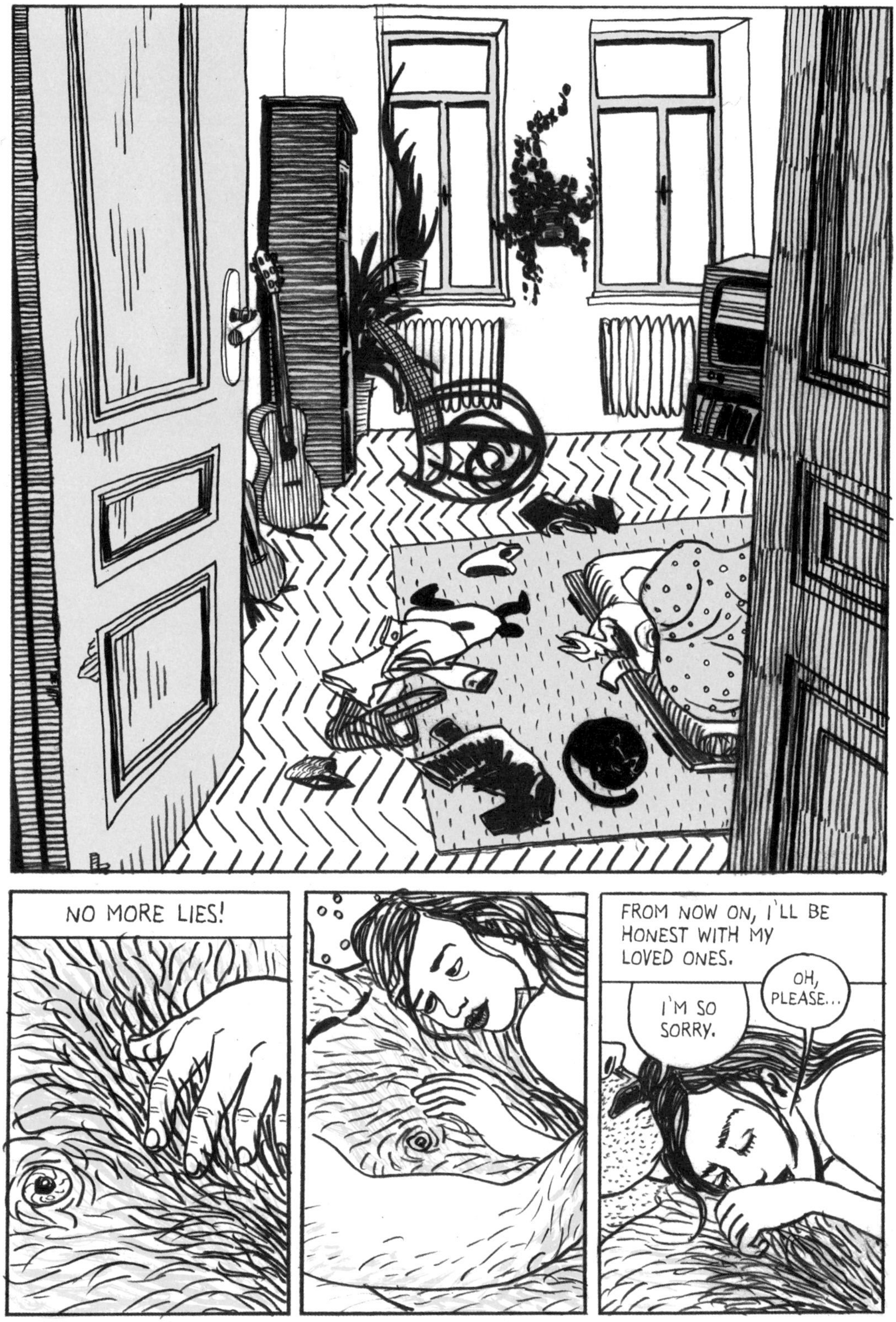
NO MORE LIES!
FROM NOW ON, I'LL BE HONEST WITH MY LOVED ONES.
I'M SO SORRY.
OH, PLEASE...

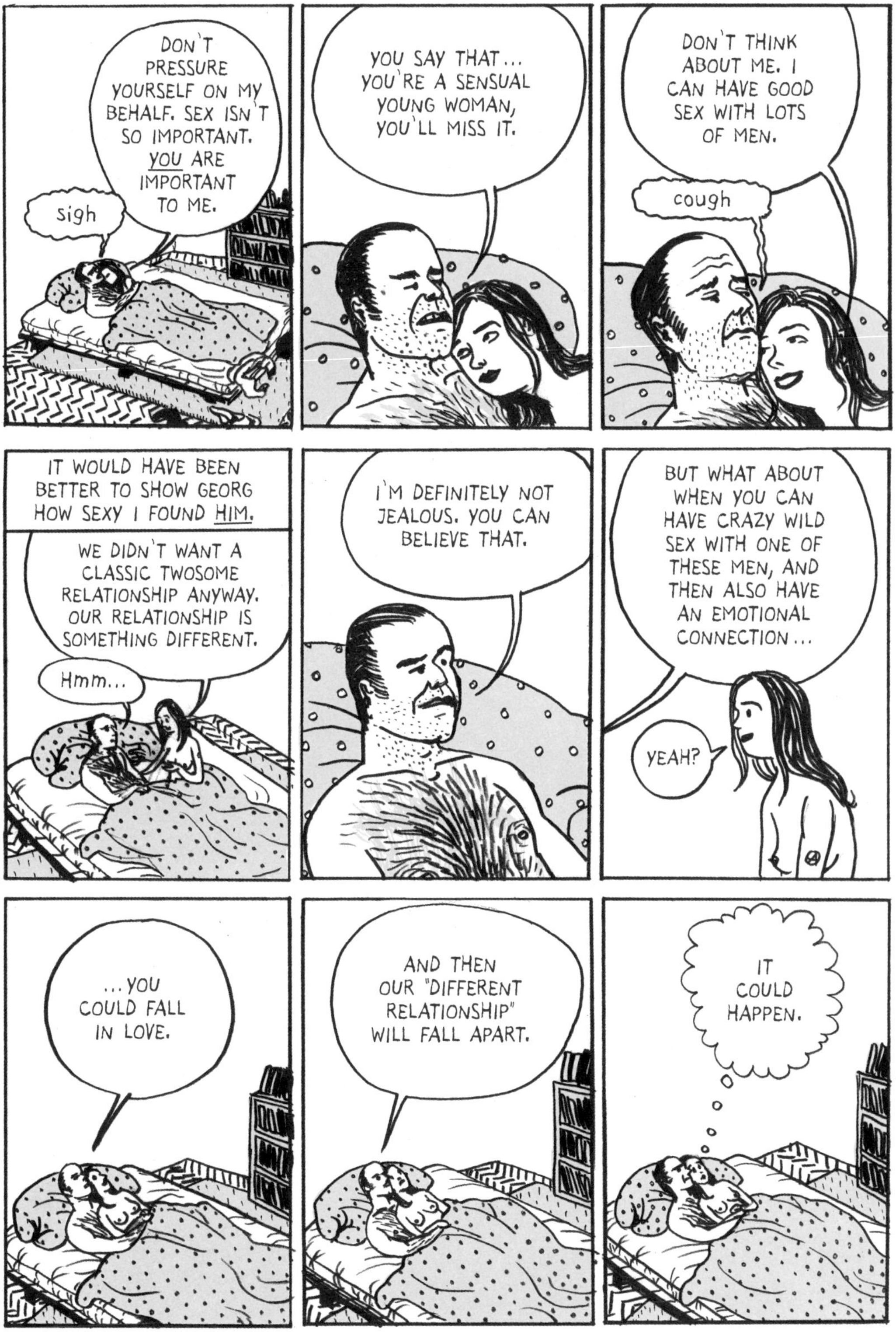
DON'T PRESSURE YOURSELF ON MY BEHALF. SEX ISN'T SO IMPORTANT. YOU ARE IMPORTANT TO ME.
sigh
YOU SAY THAT... YOU'RE A SENSUAL YOUNG WOMAN, YOU'LL MISS IT.
DON'T THINK ABOUT ME. I CAN HAVE GOOD SEX WITH LOTS OF MEN.
cough
IT WOULD HAVE BEEN BETTER TO SHOW GEORG HOW SEXY I FOUND HIM.
WE DIDN'T WANT A CLASSIC TWOSOME RELATIONSHIP ANYWAY. OUR RELATIONSHIP IS SOMETHING DIFFERENT.
Hmm...
I'M DEFINITELY NOT JEALOUS. YOU CAN BELIEVE THAT.
BUT WHAT ABOUT WHEN YOU CAN HAVE CRAZY WILD SEX WITH ONE OF THESE MEN, AND THEN ALSO HAVE AN EMOTIONAL CONNECTION...
YEAH?
...YOU COULD FALL IN LOVE.
AND THEN OUR "DIFFERENT RELATIONSHIP" WILL FALL APART.
IT COULD HAPPEN.

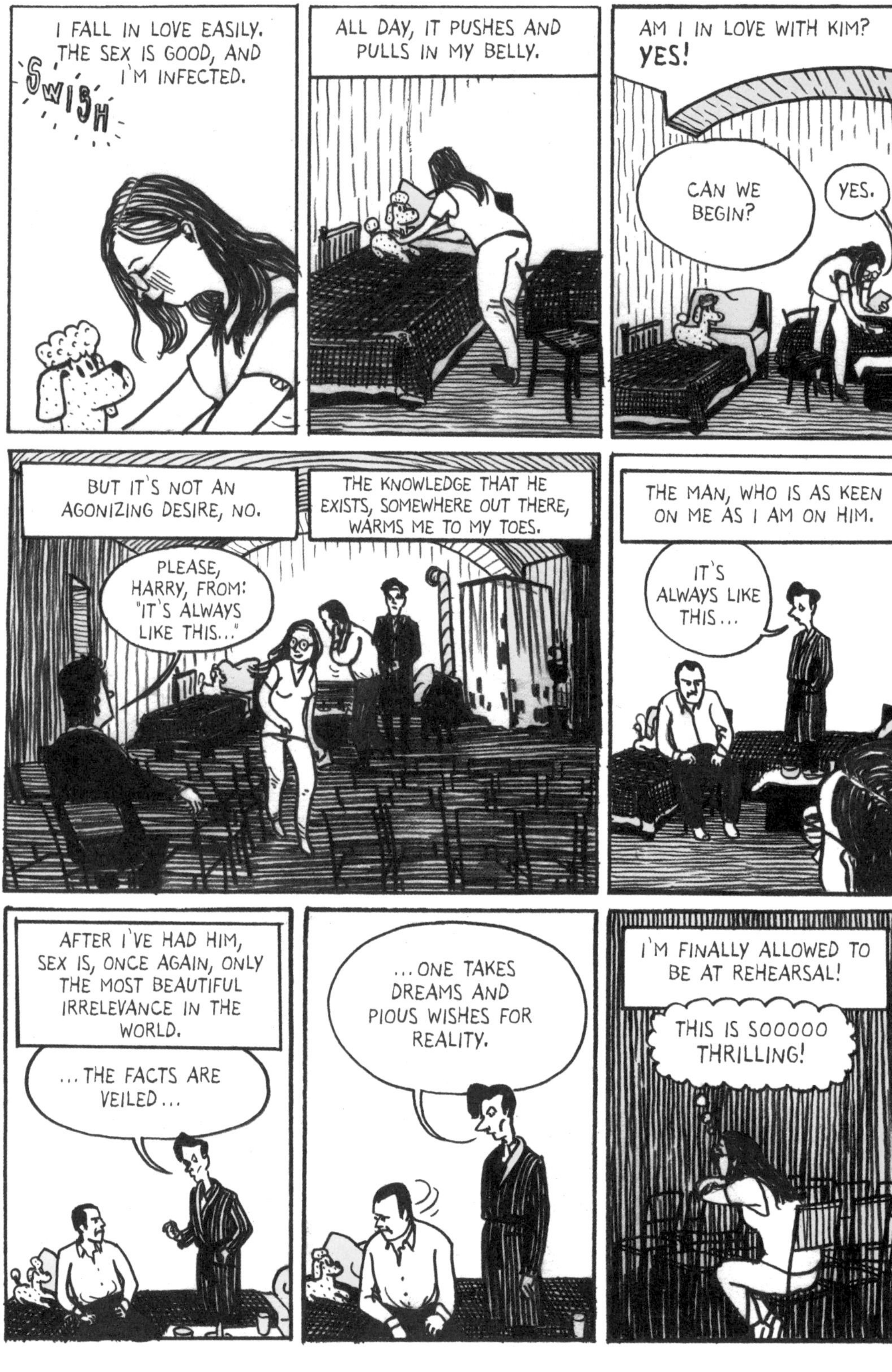
I FALL IN LOVE EASILY. THE SEX IS GOOD, AND I'M INFECTED.
SWISH
ALL DAY, IT PUSHES AND PULLS IN MY BELLY.
AM I IN LOVE WITH KIM? YES!
CAN WE BEGIN?
YES.
BUT IT'S NOT AN AGONIZING DESIRE, NO.
THE KNOWLEDGE THAT HE EXISTS, SOMEWHERE OUT THERE, WARMS ME TO MY TOES.
PLEASE, HARRY, FROM: "IT'S ALWAYS LIKE THIS..."
THE MAN, WHO IS AS KEEN ON ME AS I AM ON HIM.
IT'S ALWAYS LIKE THIS...
AFTER I'VE HAD HIM, SEX IS, ONCE AGAIN, ONLY THE MOST BEAUTIFUL IRRELEVANCE IN THE WORLD.
...THE FACTS ARE VEILED...
...ONE TAKES DREAMS AND PIOUS WISHES FOR REALITY.
I'M FINALLY ALLOWED TO BE AT REHEARSAL!
THIS IS SOOOOO THRILLING!

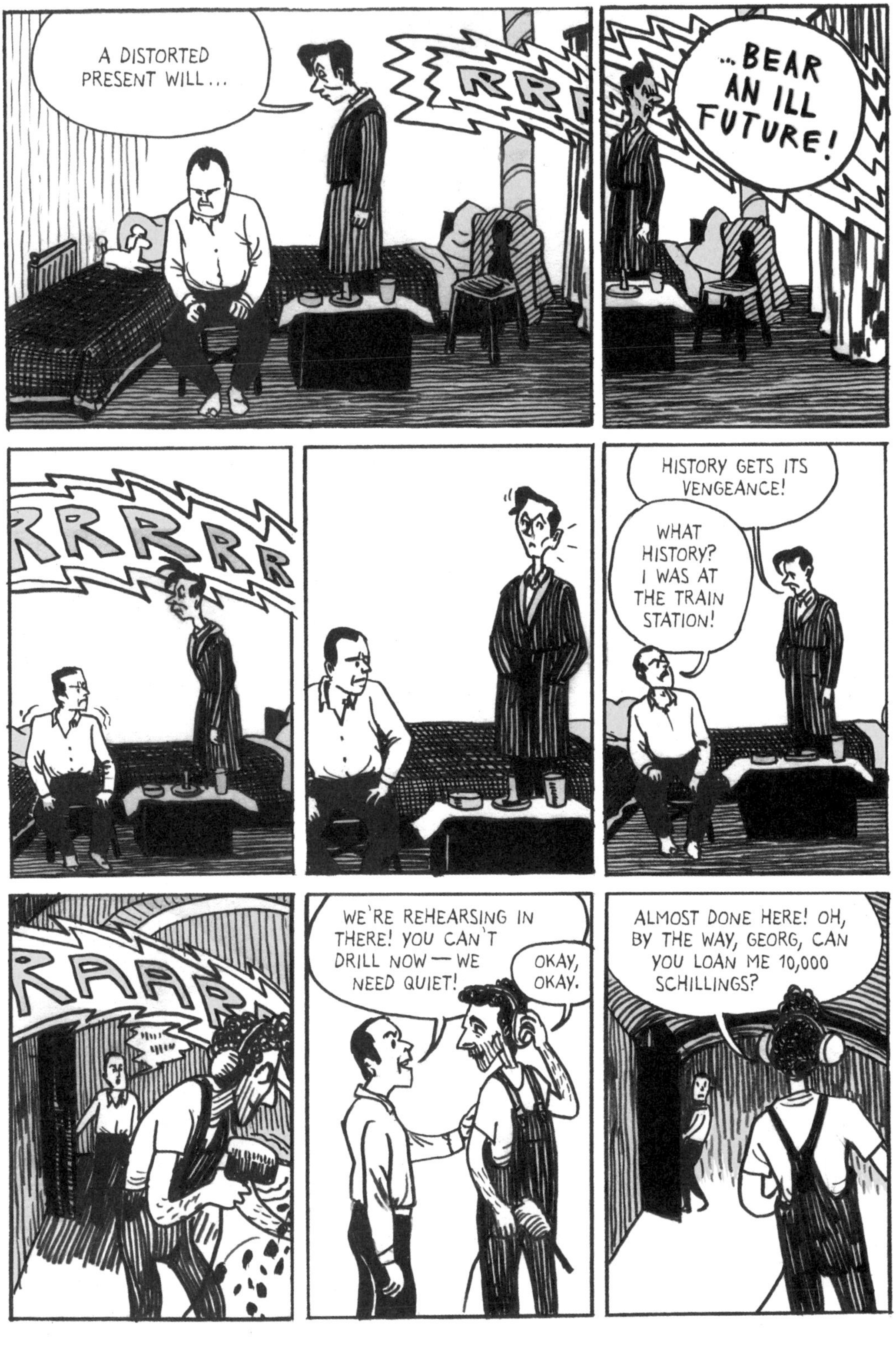
A DISTORTED PRESENT WILL...
RRR
...BEAR AN ILL FUTURE!
RRRRRR
HISTORY GETS ITS VENGEANCE!
WHAT HISTORY? I WAS AT THE TRAIN STATION!
RAAAR
WE'RE REHEARSING IN THERE! YOU CAN'T DRILL NOW — WE NEED QUIET!
OKAY, OKAY.
ALMOST DONE HERE! OH, BY THE WAY, GEORG, CAN YOU LOAN ME 10,000 SCHILLINGS?

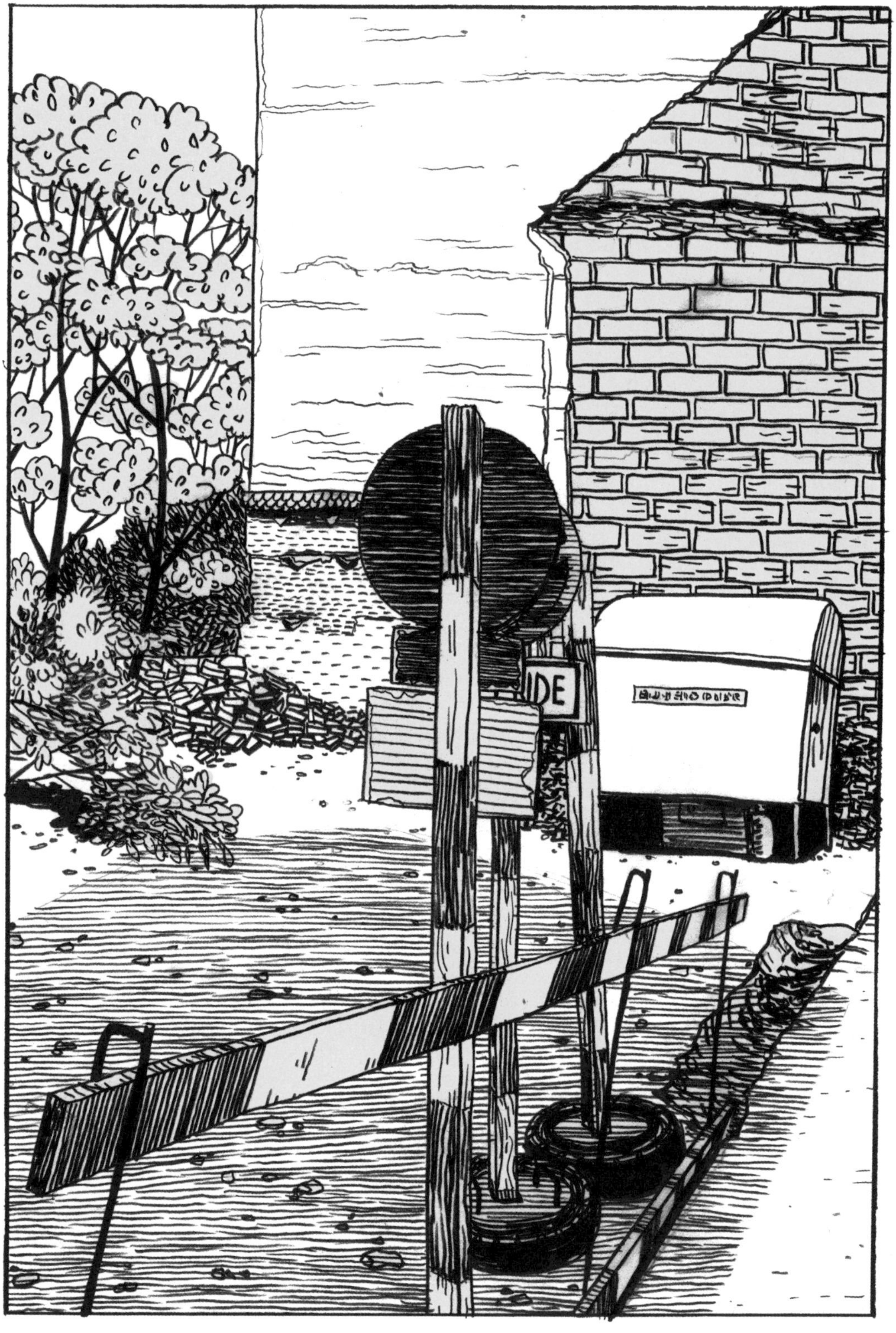
IDE

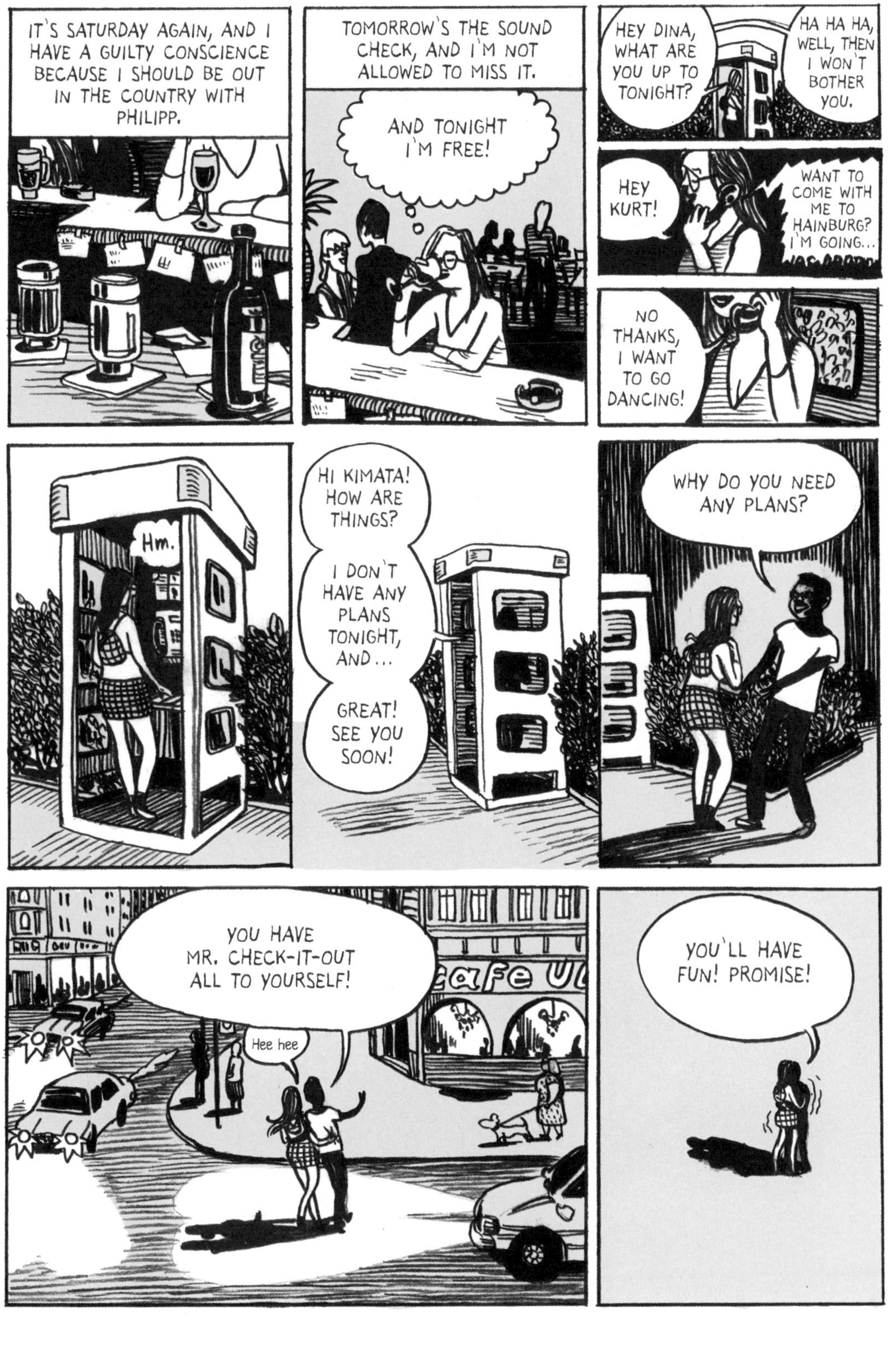
IT'S SATURDAY AGAIN, AND I HAVE A GUILTY CONSCIENCE BECAUSE I SHOULD BE OUT IN THE COUNTRY WITH PHILIPP.
TOMORROW'S THE SOUND CHECK, AND I'M NOT ALLOWED TO MISS IT.
AND TONIGHT I'M FREE!
HEY DINA, WHAT ARE YOU UP TO TONIGHT?
HA HA HA, WELL, THEN I WON'T BOTHER YOU.
HEY KURT!
WANT TO COME WITH ME TO HAINBURG? I'M GOING...
NO THANKS, I WANT TO GO DANCING!
Hm.
HI KIMATA! HOW ARE THINGS?
I DON'T HAVE ANY PLANS TONIGHT, AND...
GREAT! SEE YOU SOON!
WHY DO YOU NEED ANY PLANS?
YOU HAVE MR. CHECK-IT-OUT ALL TO YOURSELF!
Hee hee
YOU'LL HAVE FUN! PROMISE!

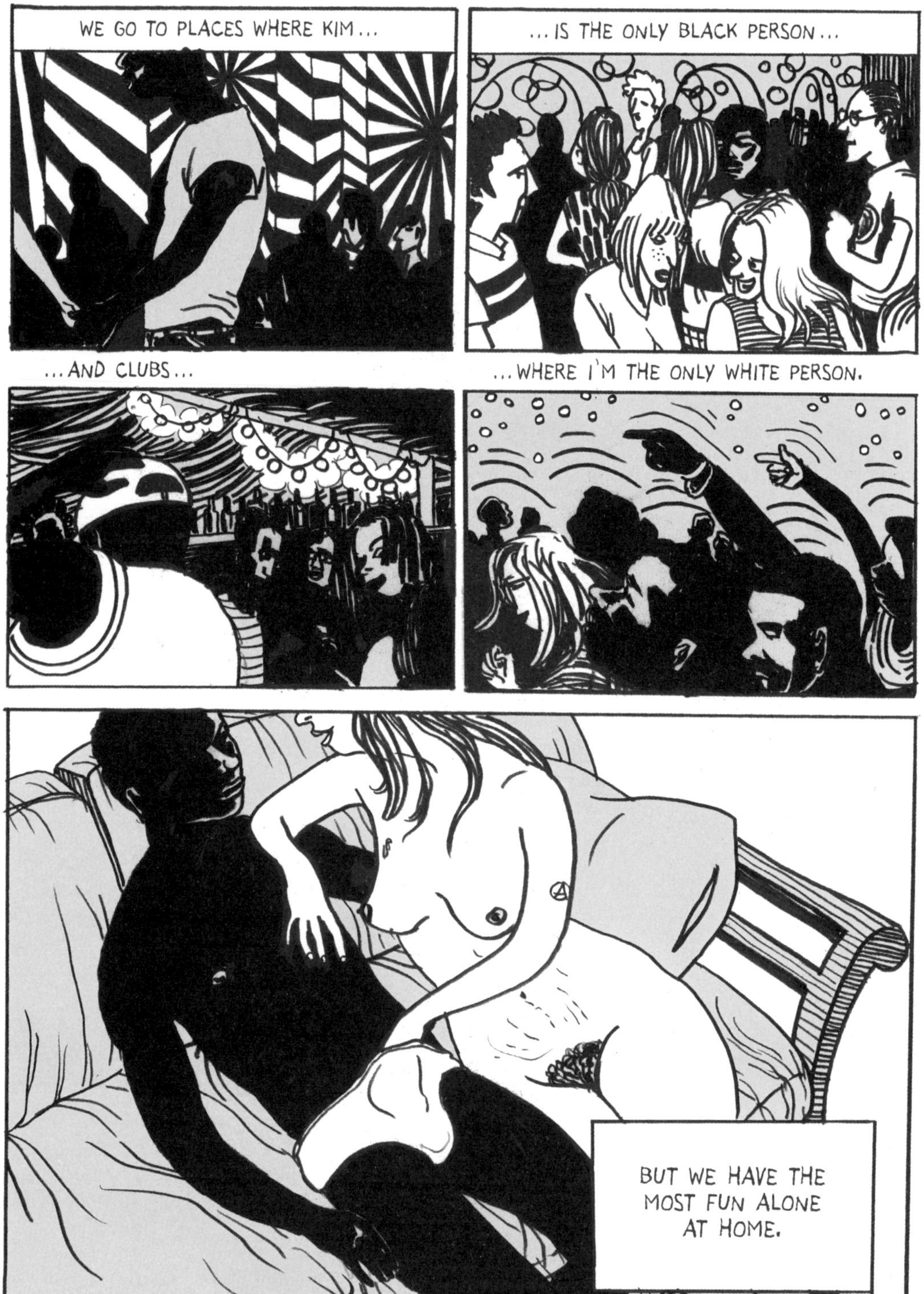
WE GO TO PLACES WHERE KIM...
...IS THE ONLY BLACK PERSON...
...AND CLUBS...
...WHERE I'M THE ONLY WHITE PERSON.
BUT WE HAVE THE MOST FUN ALONE AT HOME.

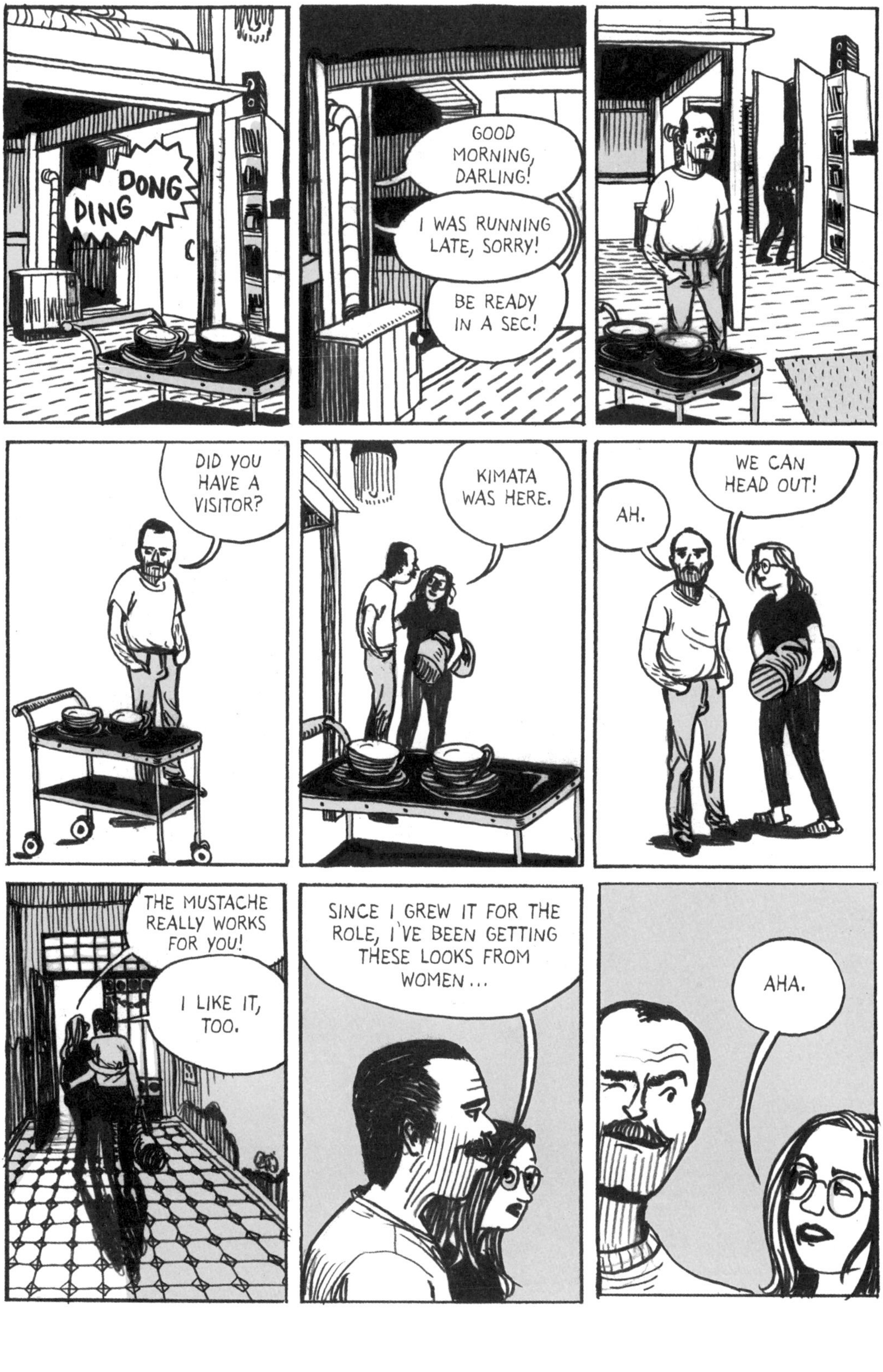
DING
DONG
GOOD MORNING, DARLING!
I WAS RUNNING LATE, SORRY!
BE READY IN A SEC!
DID YOU HAVE A VISITOR?
KIMATA WAS HERE.
AH.
WE CAN HEAD OUT!
THE MUSTACHE REALLY WORKS FOR YOU!
I LIKE IT, TOO.
SINCE I GREW IT FOR THE ROLE, I'VE BEEN GETTING THESE LOOKS FROM WOMEN...
AHA.

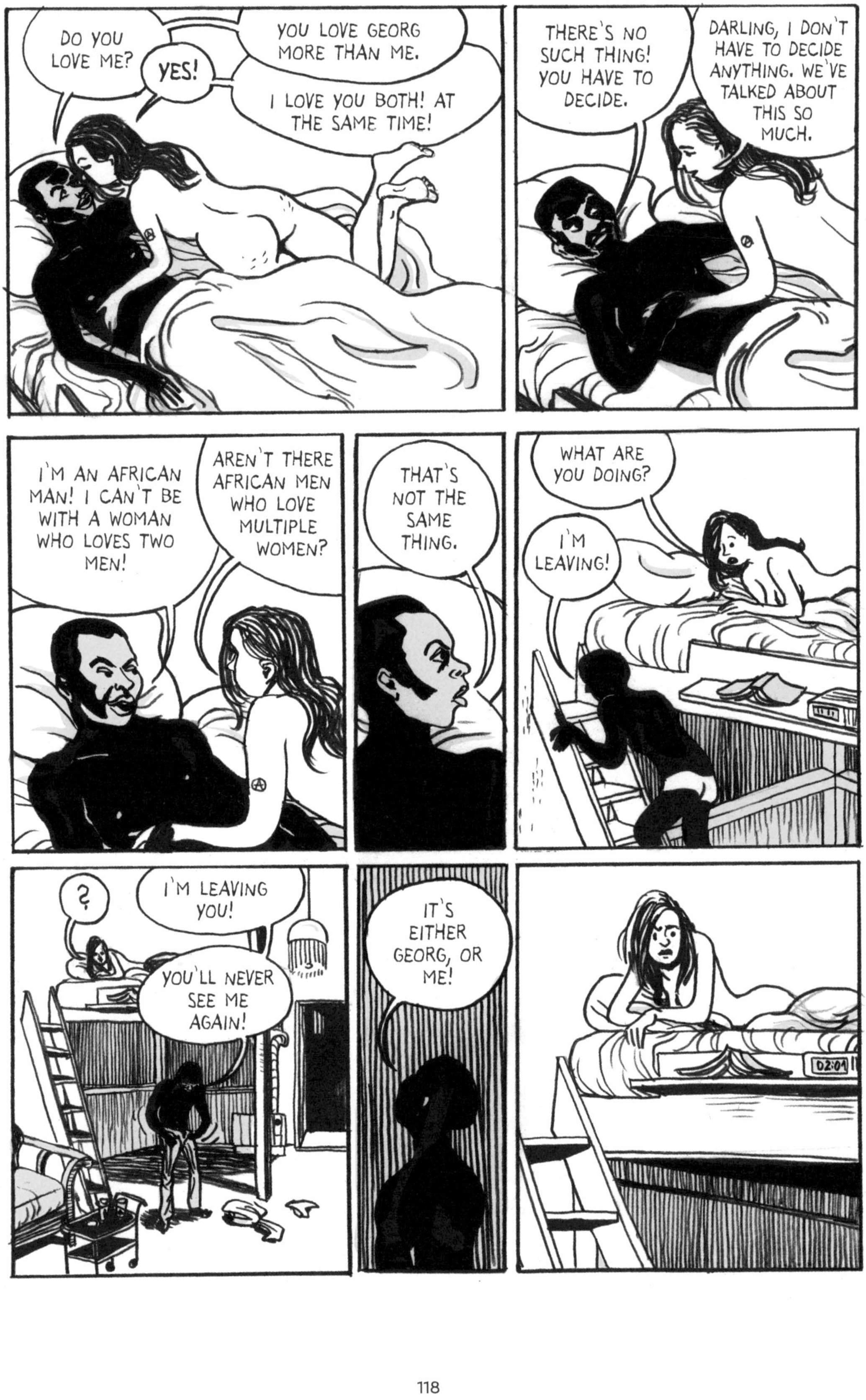
DO YOU LOVE ME?
YES!
YOU LOVE GEORG MORE THAN ME.
I LOVE YOU BOTH! AT THE SAME TIME!
THERE'S NO SUCH THING! YOU HAVE TO DECIDE.
DARLING, I DON'T HAVE TO DECIDE ANYTHING. WE'VE TALKED ABOUT THIS SO MUCH.
I'M AN AFRICAN MAN! I CAN'T BE WITH A WOMAN WHO LOVES TWO MEN!
AREN'T THERE AFRICAN MEN WHO LOVE MULTIPLE WOMEN?
THAT'S NOT THE SAME THING.
WHAT ARE YOU DOING?
I'M LEAVING!
?
I'M LEAVING YOU!
YOU'LL NEVER SEE ME AGAIN!
IT'S EITHER GEORG, OR ME!
02:01

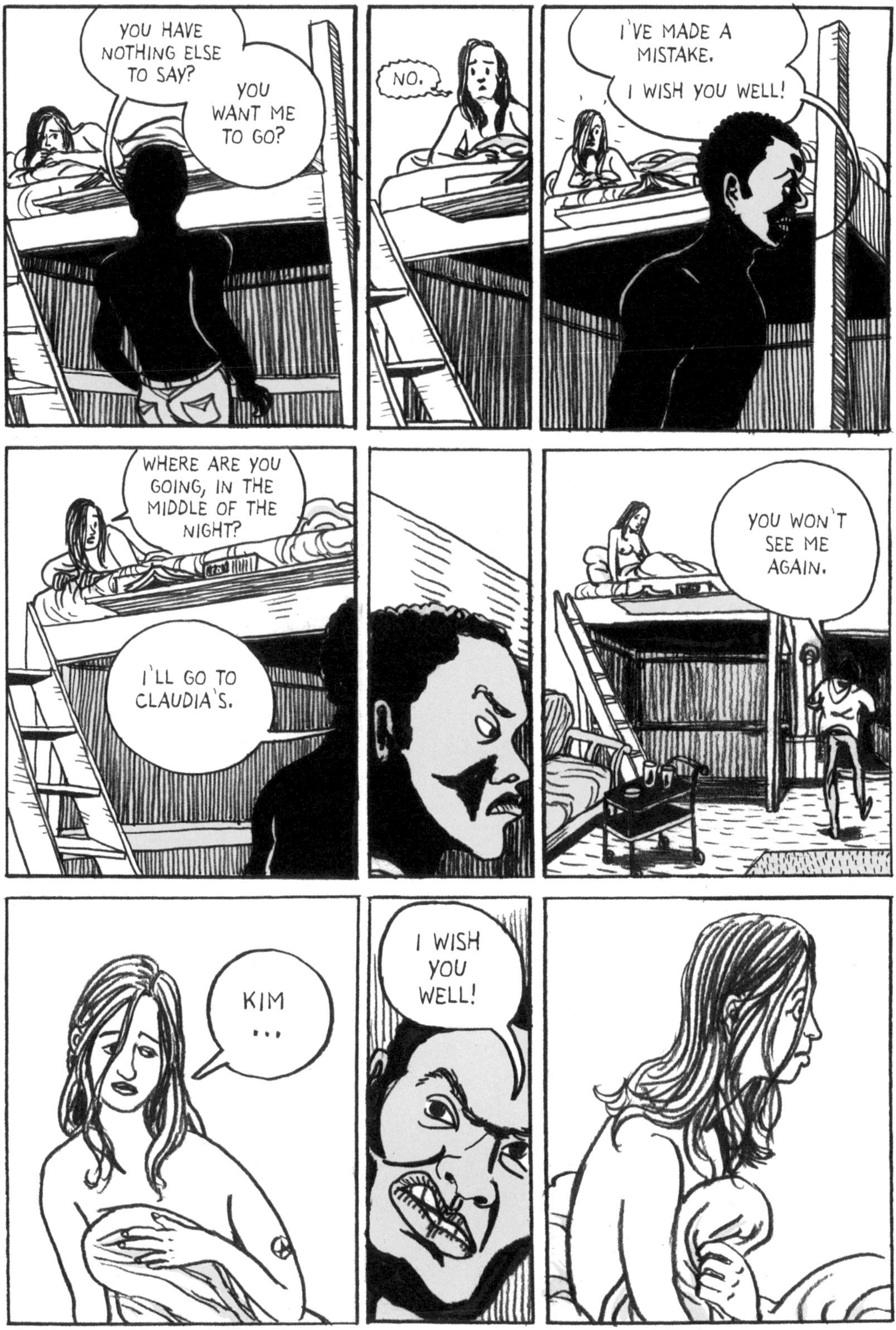
YOU HAVE NOTHING ELSE TO SAY?
YOU WANT ME TO GO?
NO.
I'VE MADE A MISTAKE.
I WISH YOU WELL!
WHERE ARE YOU GOING, IN THE MIDDLE OF THE NIGHT?
I'LL GO TO CLAUDIA'S.
YOU WON'T SEE ME AGAIN.
KIM ...
I WISH YOU WELL!

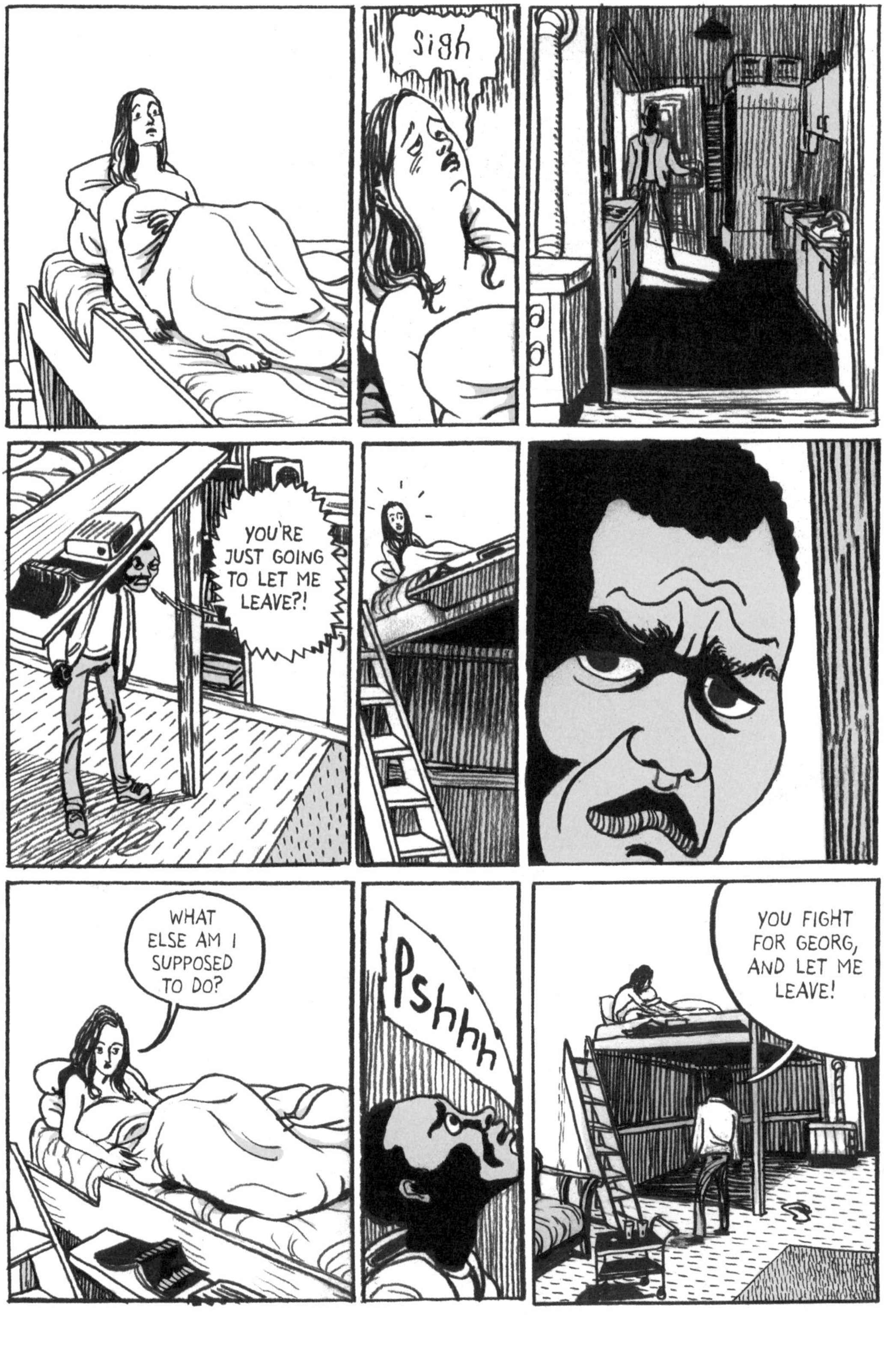
sigh
YOU'RE JUST GOING TO LET ME LEAVE?!
WHAT ELSE AM I SUPPOSED TO DO?
Pshhh
YOU FIGHT FOR GEORG, AND LET ME LEAVE!

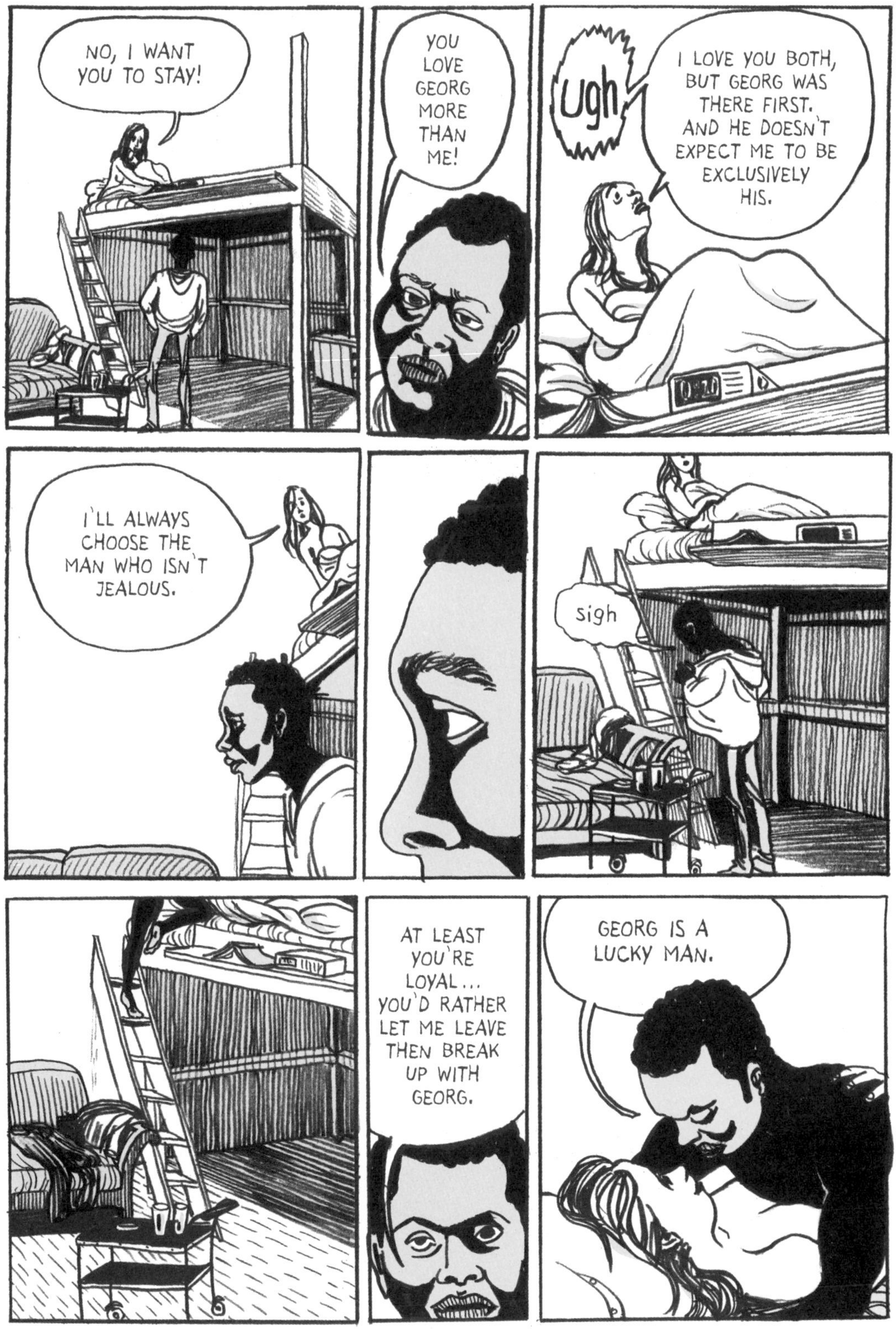
NO, I WANT YOU TO STAY!
YOU LOVE GEORG MORE THAN ME!
Ugh
I LOVE YOU BOTH, BUT GEORG WAS THERE FIRST. AND HE DOESN'T EXPECT ME TO BE EXCLUSIVELY HIS.
I'LL ALWAYS CHOOSE THE MAN WHO ISN'T JEALOUS.
sigh
AT LEAST YOU'RE LOYAL... YOU'D RATHER LET ME LEAVE THEN BREAK UP WITH GEORG.
GEORG IS A LUCKY MAN.

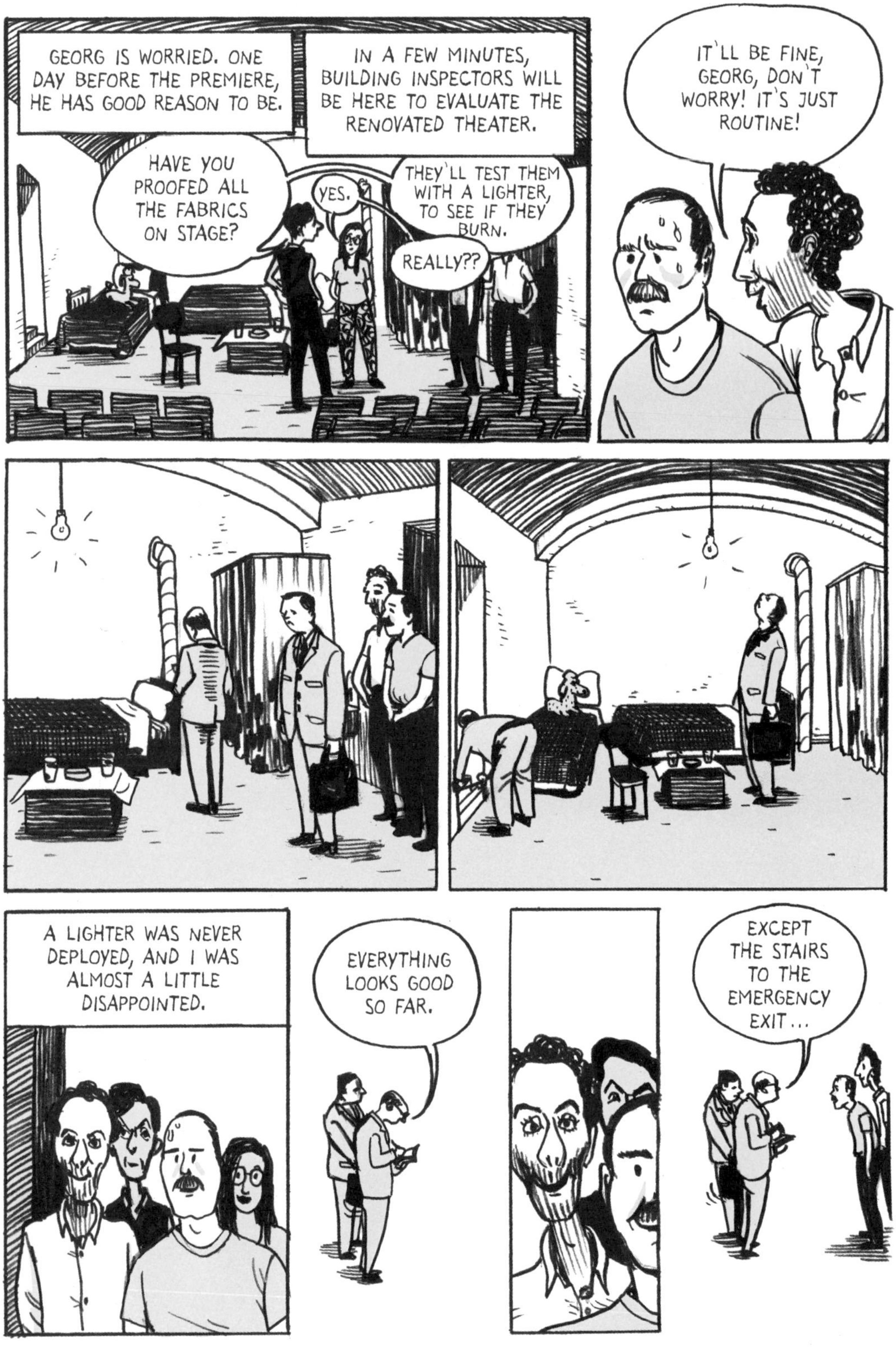
GEORG IS WORRIED. ONE DAY BEFORE THE PREMIERE, HE HAS GOOD REASON TO BE.
IN A FEW MINUTES, BUILDING INSPECTORS WILL BE HERE TO EVALUATE THE RENOVATED THEATER.
HAVE YOU PROOFED ALL THE FABRICS ON STAGE?
YES.
THEY'LL TEST THEM WITH A LIGHTER, TO SEE IF THEY BURN.
REALLY??
IT'LL BE FINE, GEORG, DON'T WORRY! IT'S JUST ROUTINE!
A LIGHTER WAS NEVER DEPLOYED, AND I WAS ALMOST A LITTLE DISAPPOINTED.
EVERYTHING LOOKS GOOD SO FAR.
EXCEPT THE STAIRS TO THE EMERGENCY EXIT...

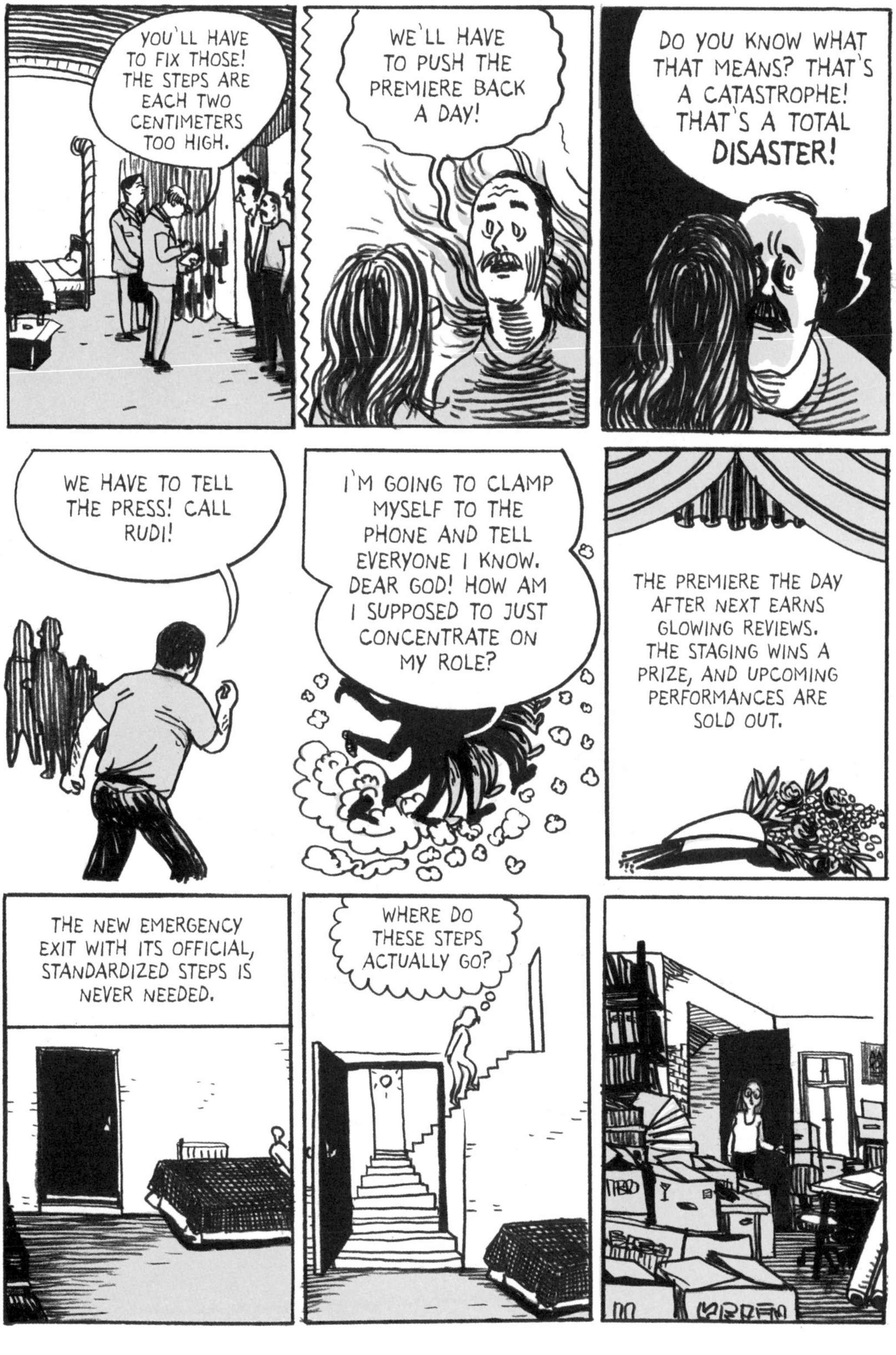
YOU'LL HAVE TO FIX THOSE! THE STEPS ARE EACH TWO CENTIMETERS TOO HIGH.
WE'LL HAVE TO PUSH THE PREMIERE BACK A DAY!
DO YOU KNOW WHAT THAT MEANS? THAT'S A CATASTROPHE! THAT'S A TOTAL DISASTER!
WE HAVE TO TELL THE PRESS! CALL RUDI!
I'M GOING TO CLAMP MYSELF TO THE PHONE AND TELL EVERYONE I KNOW. DEAR GOD! HOW AM I SUPPOSED TO JUST CONCENTRATE ON MY ROLE?
THE PREMIERE THE DAY AFTER NEXT EARNS GLOWING REVIEWS. THE STAGING WINS A PRIZE, AND UPCOMING PERFORMANCES ARE SOLD OUT.
THE NEW EMERGENCY EXIT WITH ITS OFFICIAL, STANDARDIZED STEPS IS NEVER NEEDED.
WHERE DO THESE STEPS ACTUALLY GO?

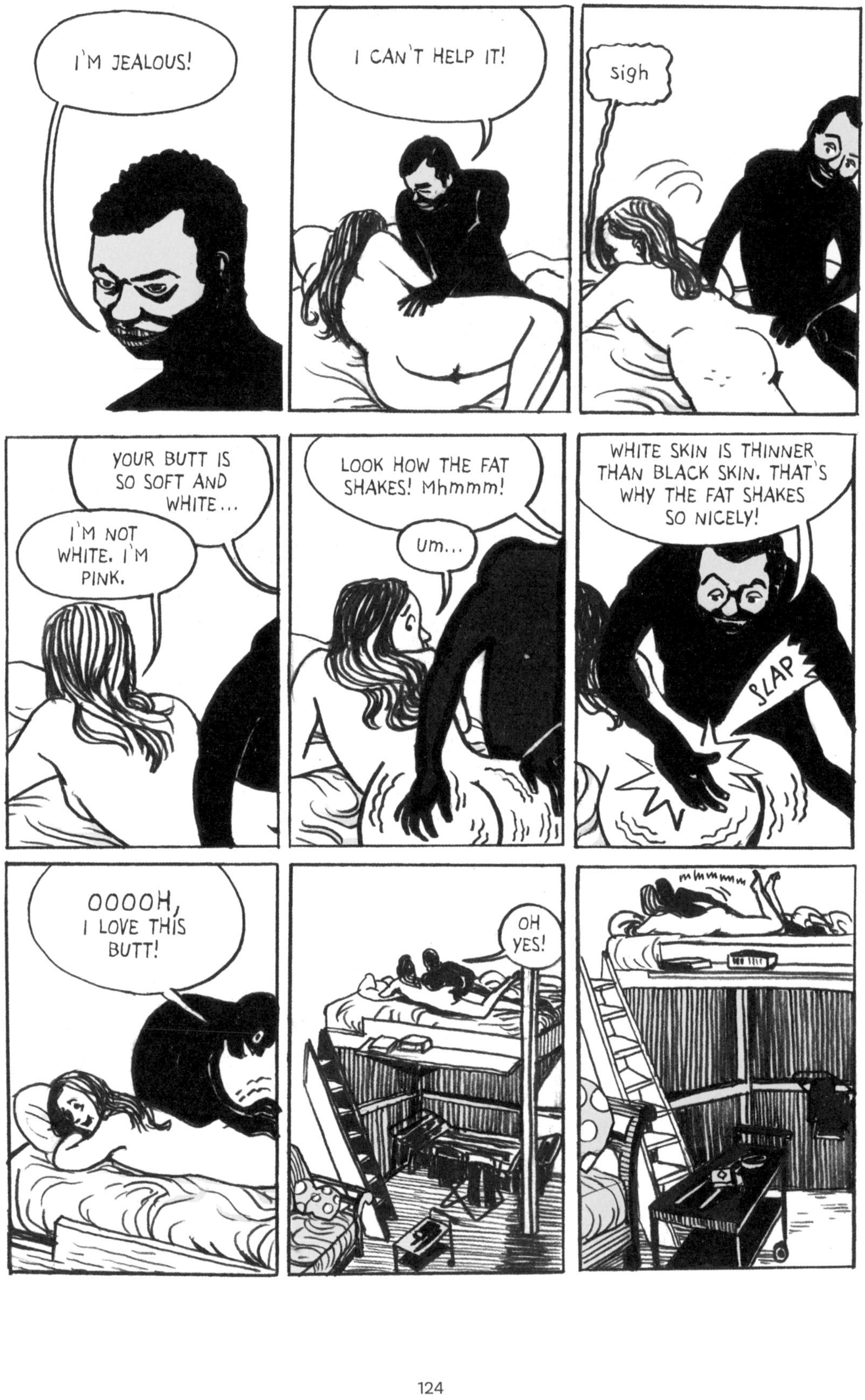
I'M JEALOUS!
I CAN'T HELP IT!
sigh
YOUR BUTT IS SO SOFT AND WHITE...
I'M NOT WHITE. I'M PINK.
LOOK HOW THE FAT SHAKES! Mhmmm!
um...
WHITE SKIN IS THINNER THAN BLACK SKIN. THAT'S WHY THE FAT SHAKES SO NICELY!
SLAP
OOOOH, I LOVE THIS BUTT!
OH YES!

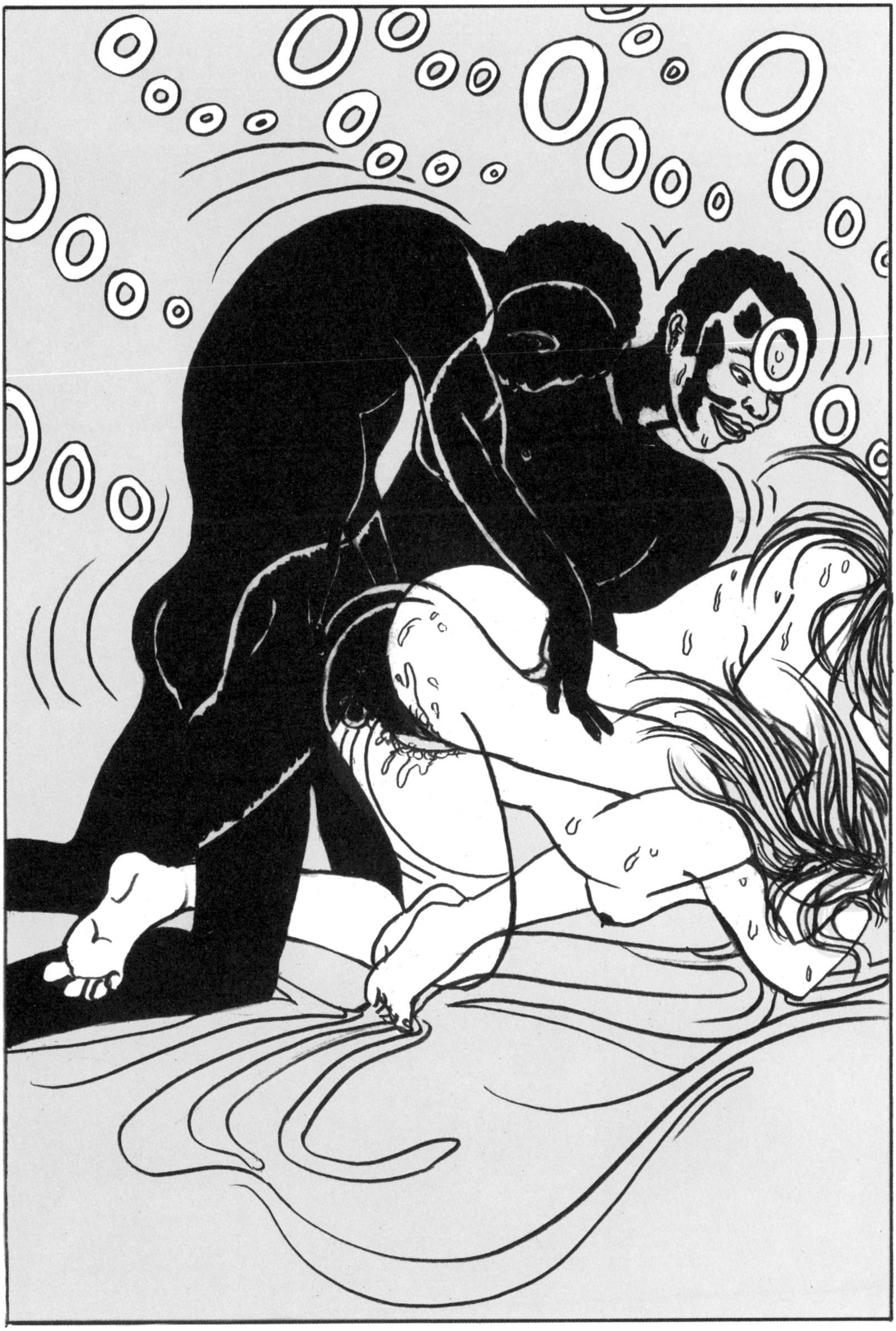

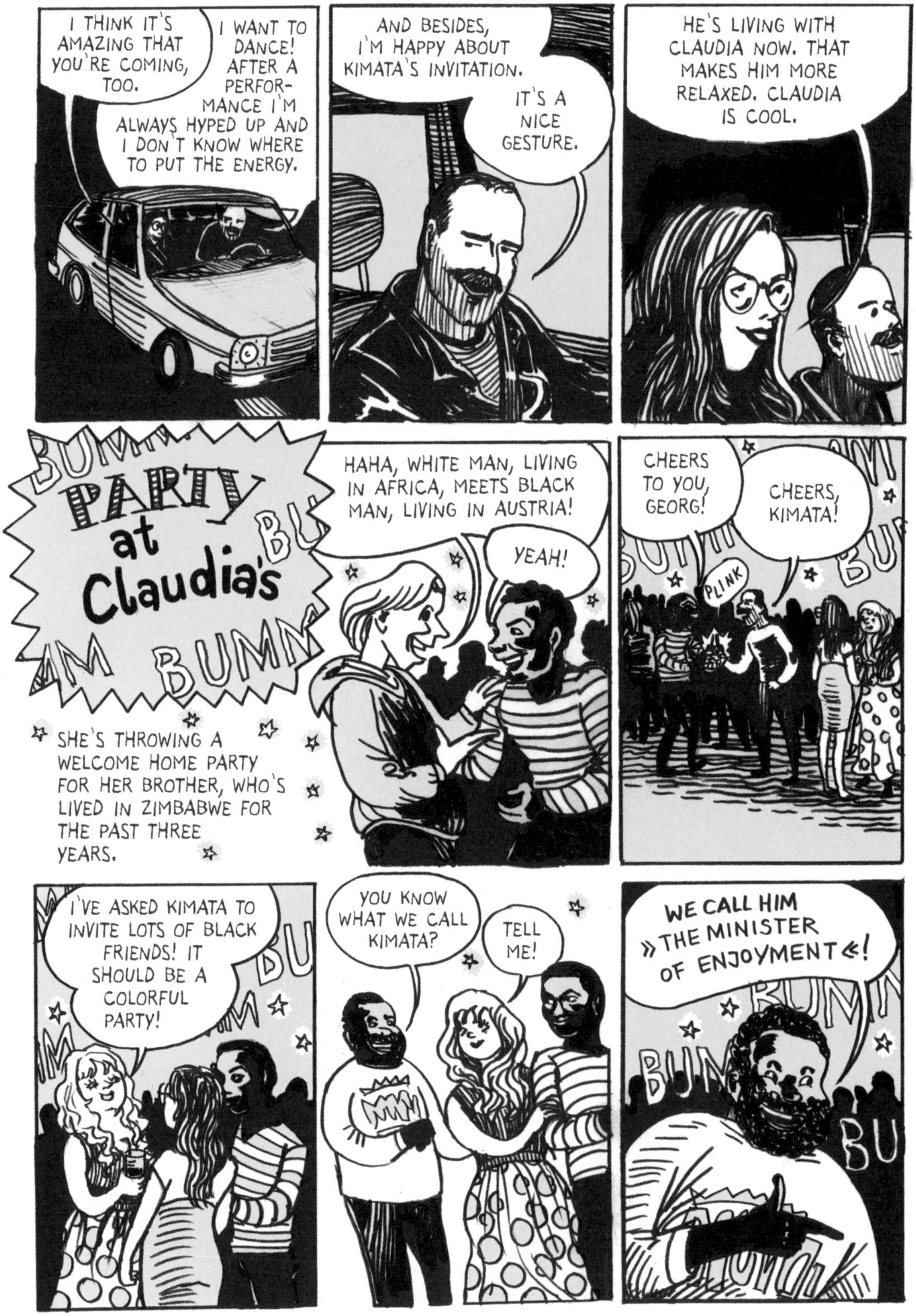

I THINK IT'S AMAZING THAT YOU'RE COMING, TOO.
I WANT TO DANCE! AFTER A PERFORMANCE I'M ALWAYS HYPED UP AND I DON'T KNOW WHERE TO PUT THE ENERGY.
AND BESIDES, I'M HAPPY ABOUT KIMATA'S INVITATION.
IT'S A NICE GESTURE.
HE'S LIVING WITH CLAUDIA NOW. THAT MAKES HIM MORE RELAXED. CLAUDIA IS COOL.
PARTY at Claudia's
BU
BUMM
SHE'S THROWING A WELCOME HOME PARTY FOR HER BROTHER, WHO'S LIVED IN ZIMBABWE FOR THE PAST THREE YEARS.
HAHA, WHITE MAN, LIVING IN AFRICA, MEETS BLACK MAN, LIVING IN AUSTRIA!
YEAH!
CHEERS TO YOU, GEORG!
CHEERS, KIMATA!
PLINK
I'VE ASKED KIMATA TO INVITE LOTS OF BLACK FRIENDS! IT SHOULD BE A COLORFUL PARTY!
YOU KNOW WHAT WE CALL KIMATA?
TELL ME!
WE CALL HIM »THE MINISTER OF ENJOYMENT«!
BU

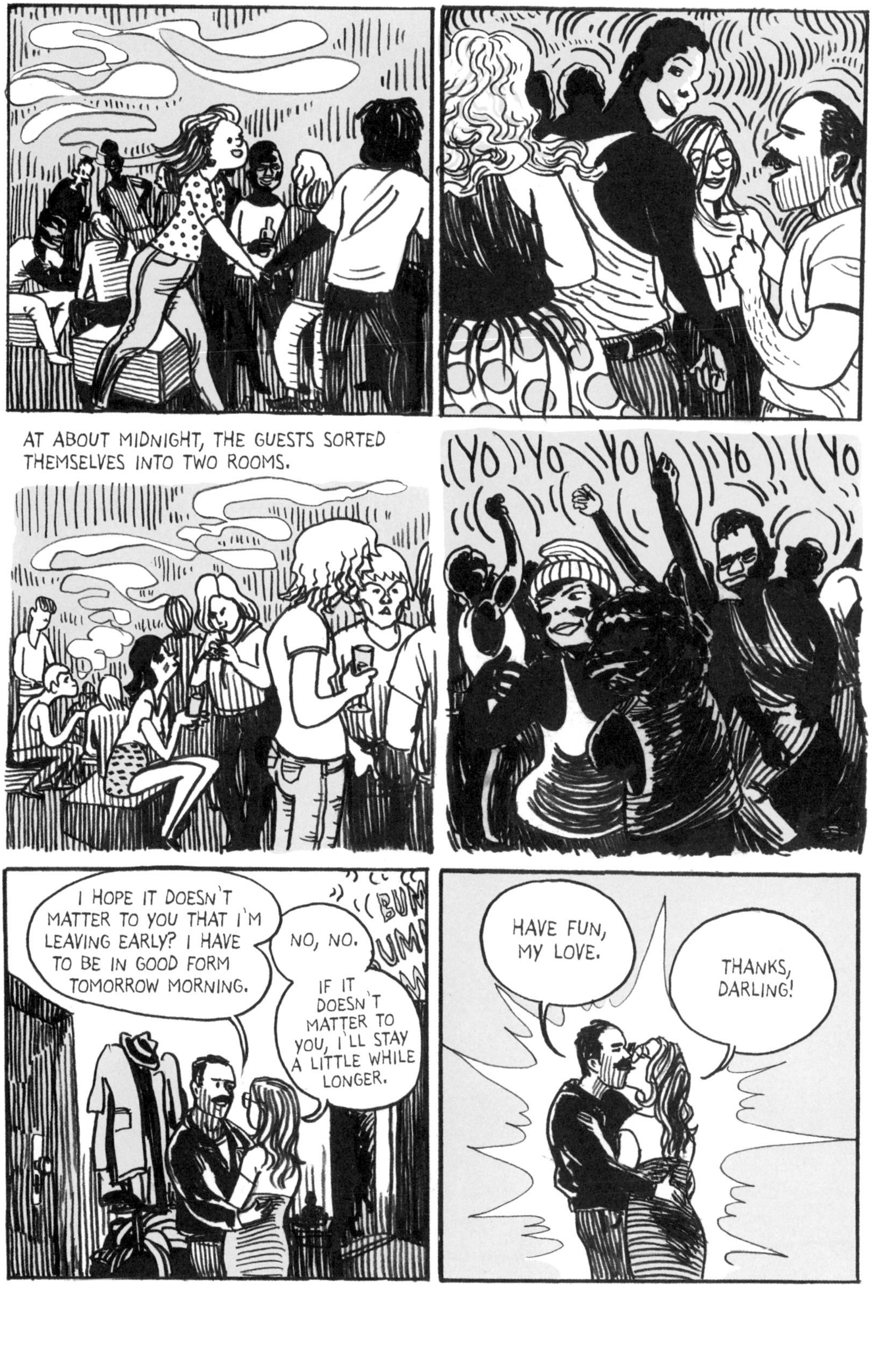
AT ABOUT MIDNIGHT, THE GUESTS SORTED THEMSELVES INTO TWO ROOMS.
YO YO YO YO YO
I HOPE IT DOESN'T MATTER TO YOU THAT I'M LEAVING EARLY? I HAVE TO BE IN GOOD FORM TOMORROW MORNING.
NO, NO.
IF IT DOESN'T MATTER TO YOU, I'LL STAY A LITTLE WHILE LONGER.
HAVE FUN, MY LOVE.
THANKS, DARLING!

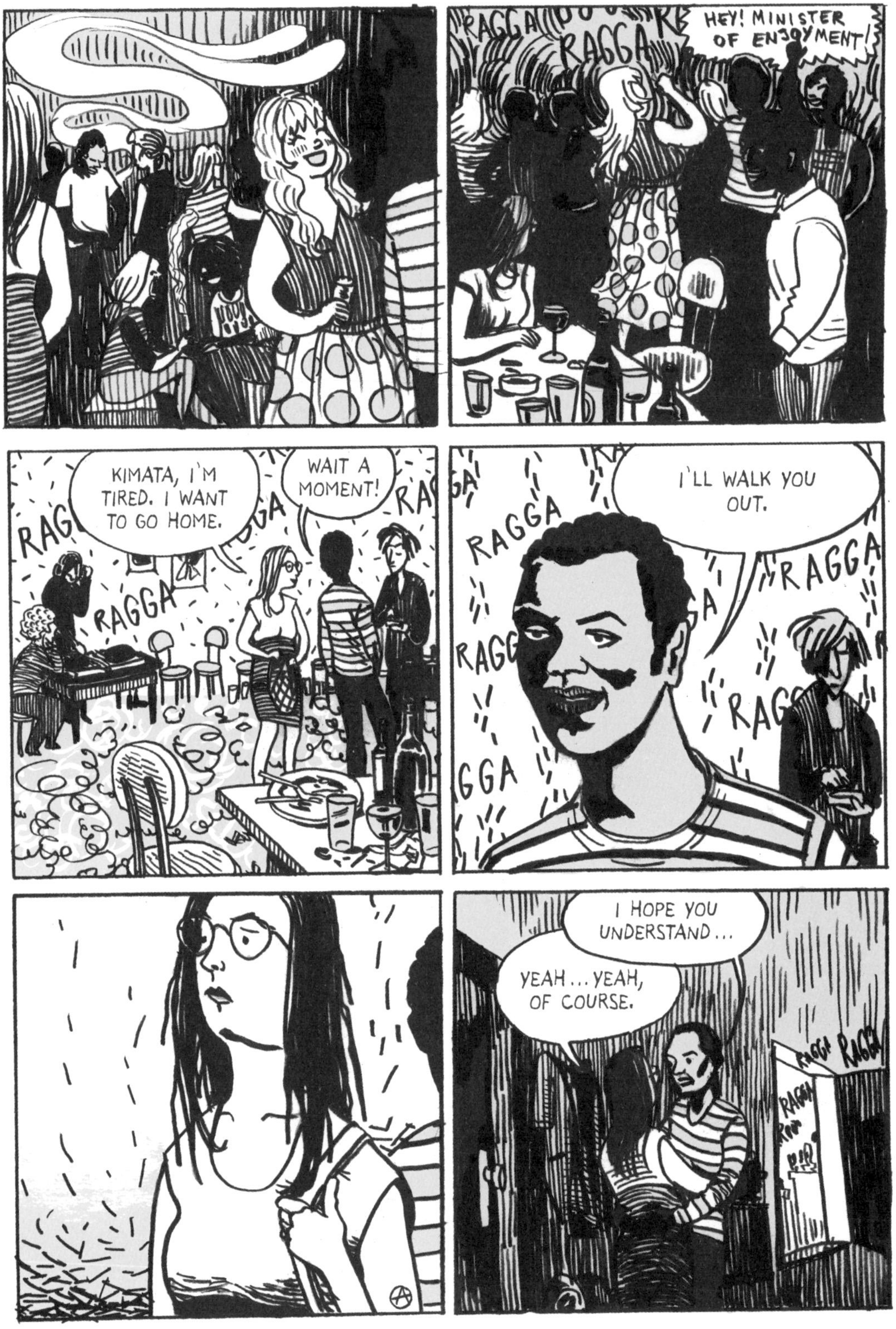
RAGGA
RAGGA
HEY! MINISTER OF ENJOYMENT!
RAGGA
KIMATA, I'M TIRED. I WANT TO GO HOME.
WAIT A MOMENT!
RAGGA
I'LL WALK YOU OUT.
RAGGA
RAGGA
I HOPE YOU UNDERSTAND...
YEAH... YEAH, OF COURSE.
RAGGA
RAGGA

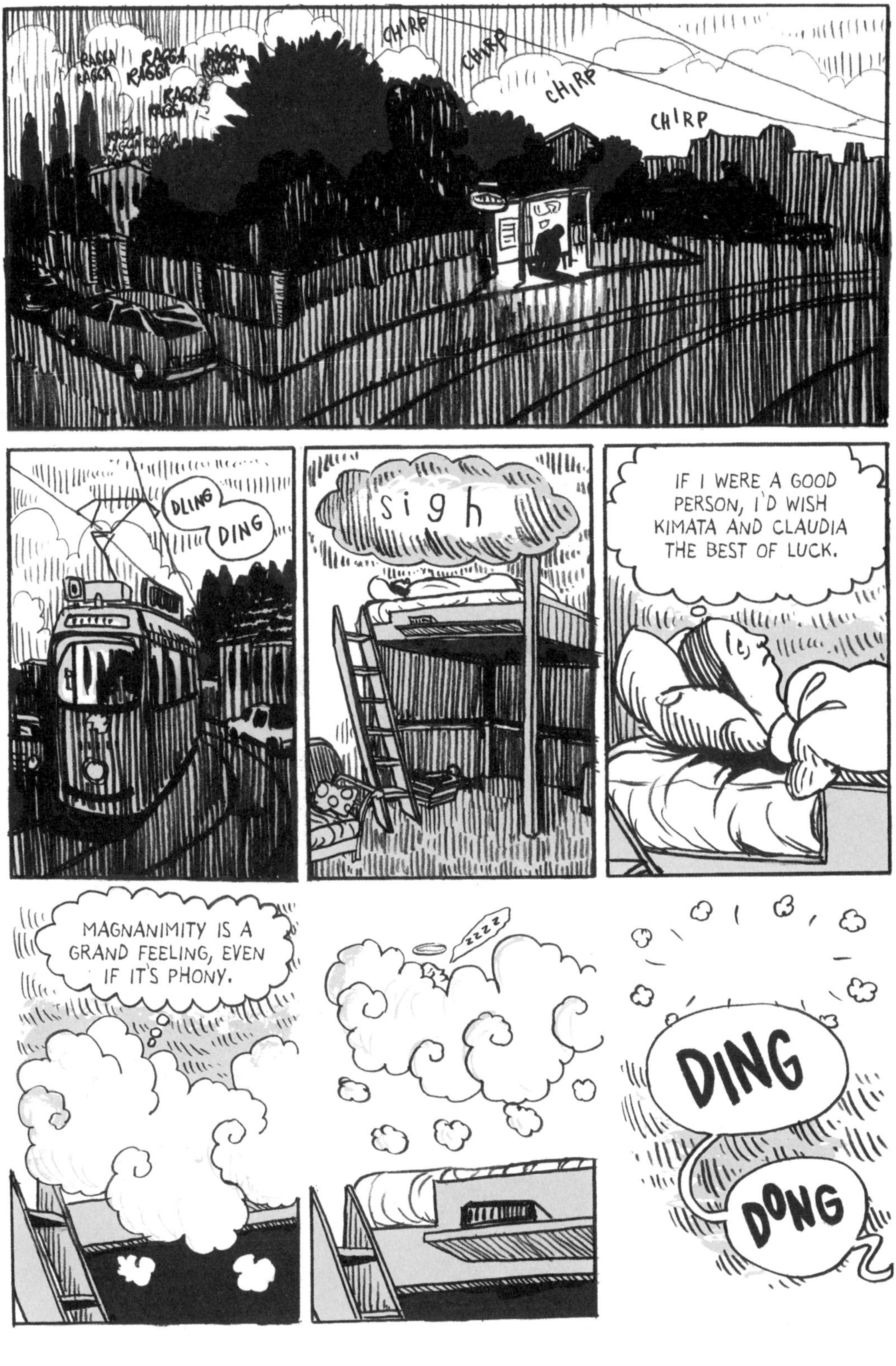
CHIRP
CHIRP
CHIRP
CHIRP
DLING
DING
sigh
IF I WERE A GOOD PERSON, I'D WISH KIMATA AND CLAUDIA THE BEST OF LUCK.
MAGNANIMITY IS A GRAND FEELING, EVEN IF IT'S PHONY.
DING
DONG

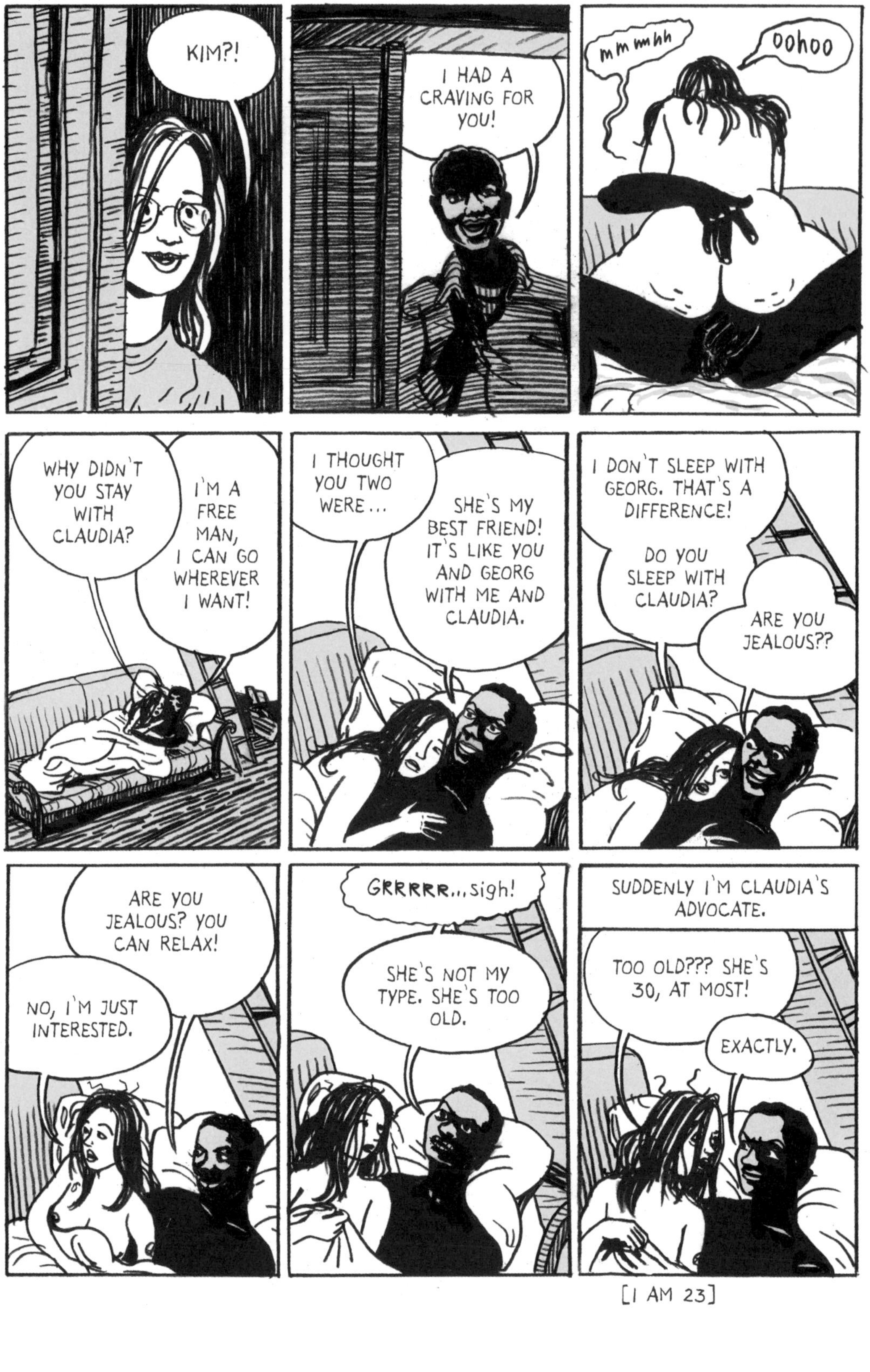
KIM?!
I HAD A CRAVING FOR YOU!
mmmhh
OOHOO
WHY DIDN'T YOU STAY WITH CLAUDIA?
I'M A FREE MAN, I CAN GO WHEREVER I WANT!
I THOUGHT YOU TWO WERE...
SHE'S MY BEST FRIEND! IT'S LIKE YOU AND GEORG WITH ME AND CLAUDIA.
I DON'T SLEEP WITH GEORG. THAT'S A DIFFERENCE!
DO YOU SLEEP WITH CLAUDIA?
ARE YOU JEALOUS??
ARE YOU JEALOUS? YOU CAN RELAX!
NO, I'M JUST INTERESTED.
GRRRRR... sigh!
SHE'S NOT MY TYPE. SHE'S TOO OLD.
SUDDENLY I'M CLAUDIA'S ADVOCATE.
TOO OLD??? SHE'S 30, AT MOST!
EXACTLY.
[I AM 23]

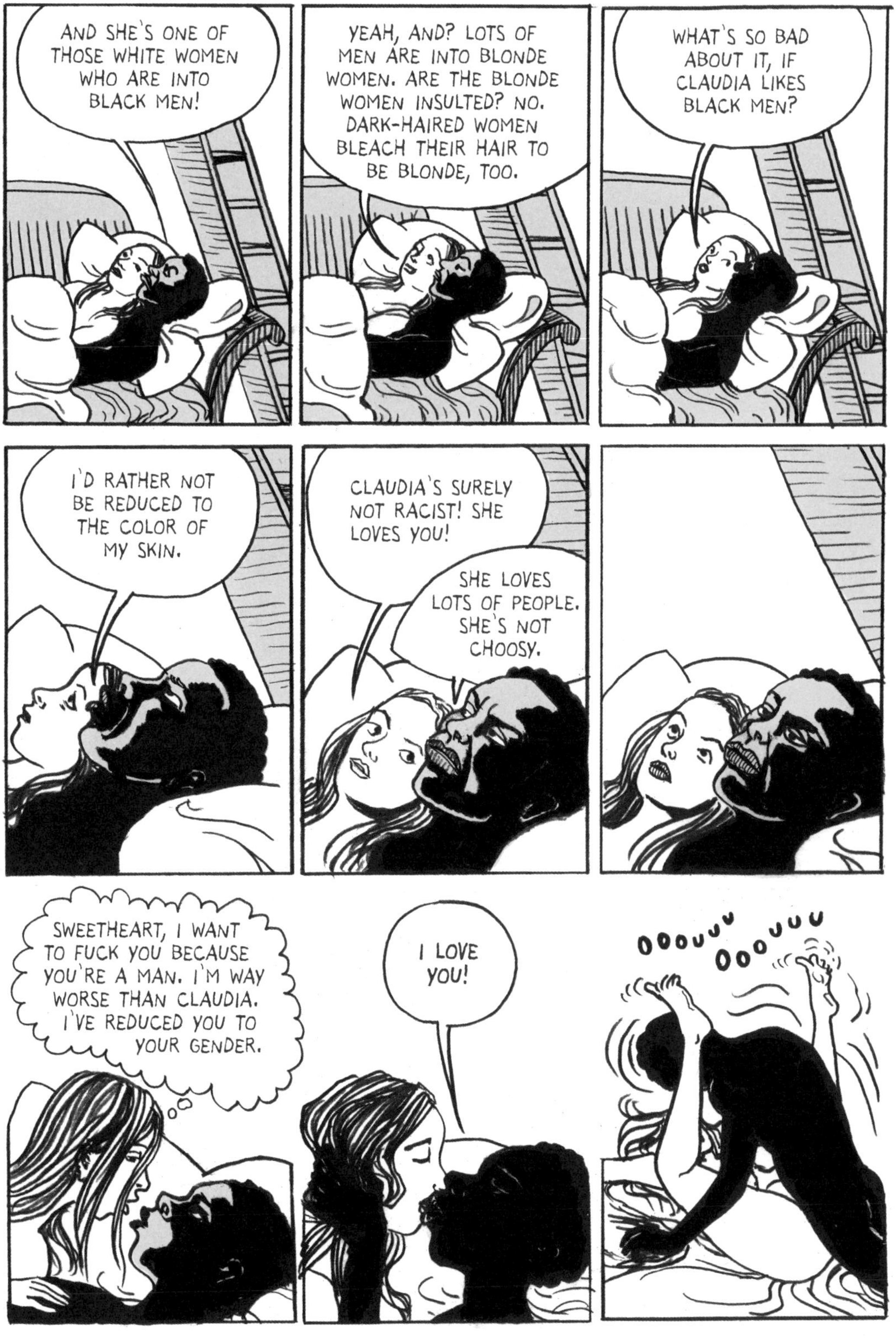
AND SHE'S ONE OF THOSE WHITE WOMEN WHO ARE INTO BLACK MEN!
YEAH, AND? LOTS OF MEN ARE INTO BLONDE WOMEN. ARE THE BLONDE WOMEN INSULTED? NO. DARK-HAIRED WOMEN BLEACH THEIR HAIR TO BE BLONDE, TOO.
WHAT'S SO BAD ABOUT IT, IF CLAUDIA LIKES BLACK MEN?
I'D RATHER NOT BE REDUCED TO THE COLOR OF MY SKIN.
CLAUDIA'S SURELY NOT RACIST! SHE LOVES YOU!
SHE LOVES LOTS OF PEOPLE. SHE'S NOT CHOOSY.
SWEETHEART, I WANT TO FUCK YOU BECAUSE YOU'RE A MAN. I'M WAY WORSE THAN CLAUDIA. I'VE REDUCED YOU TO YOUR GENDER.
I LOVE YOU!
OOOUUU OOOUUU

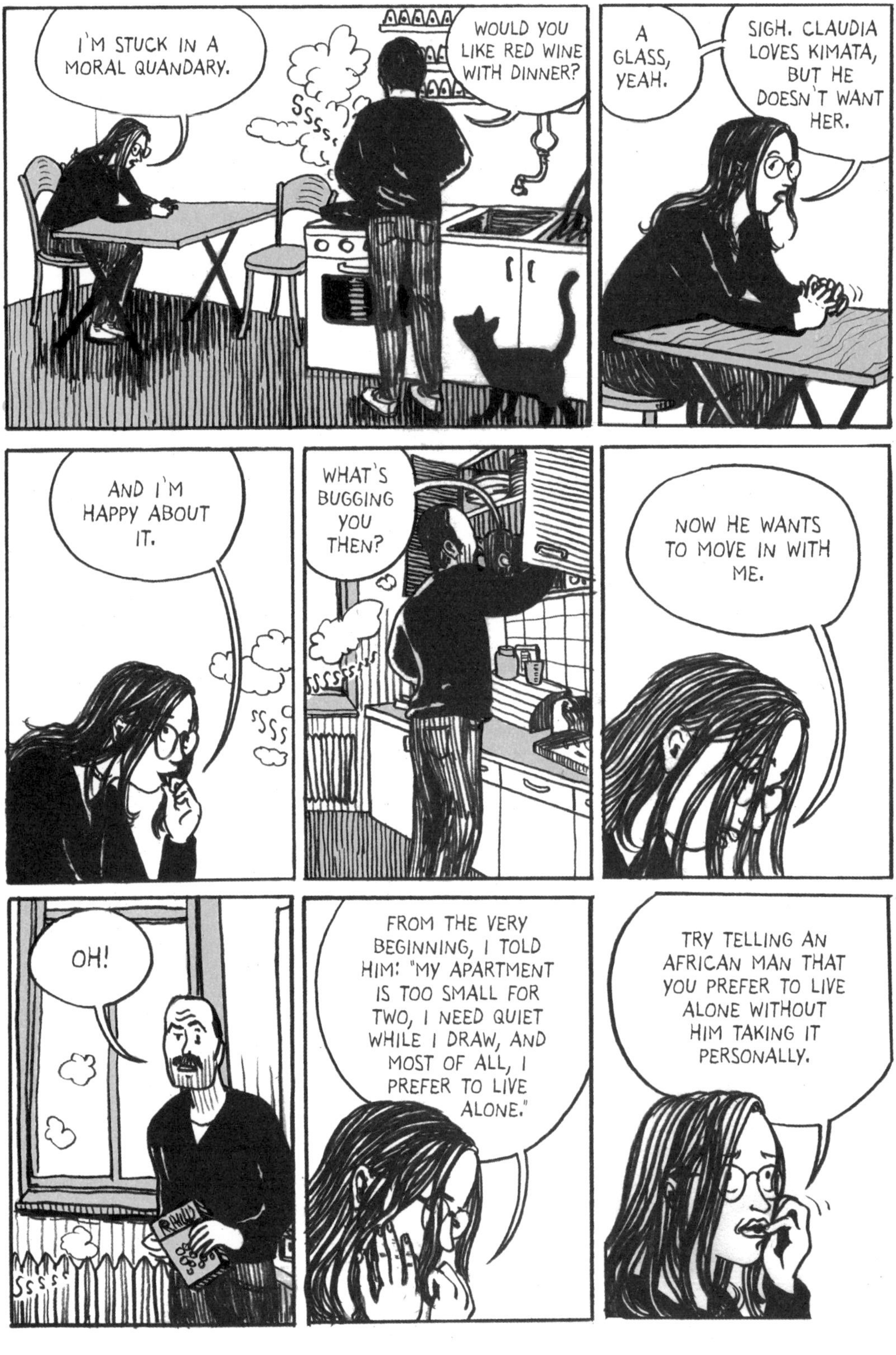
I'M STUCK IN A MORAL QUANDARY.
WOULD YOU LIKE RED WINE WITH DINNER?
SSSSS
A GLASS, YEAH.
SIGH. CLAUDIA LOVES KIMATA, BUT HE DOESN'T WANT HER.
AND I'M HAPPY ABOUT IT.
SSS
WHAT'S BUGGING YOU THEN?
SSSSSSSS
NOW HE WANTS TO MOVE IN WITH ME.
OH!
SSSS
FROM THE VERY BEGINNING, I TOLD HIM: "MY APARTMENT IS TOO SMALL FOR TWO, I NEED QUIET WHILE I DRAW, AND MOST OF ALL, I PREFER TO LIVE ALONE."
TRY TELLING AN AFRICAN MAN THAT YOU PREFER TO LIVE ALONE WITHOUT HIM TAKING IT PERSONALLY.

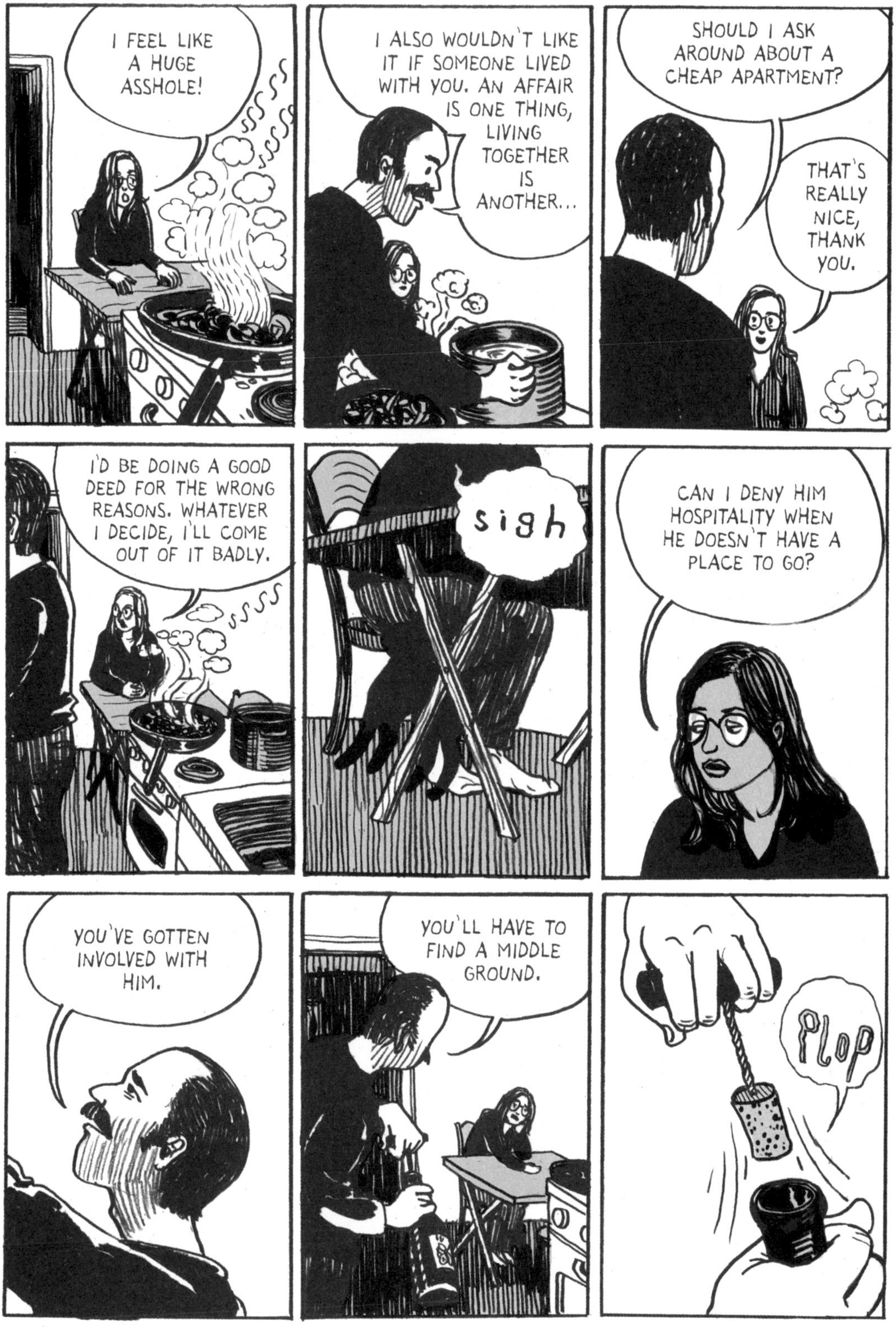

I FEEL LIKE A HUGE ASSHOLE!
SSSSSSSSS
I ALSO WOULDN'T LIKE IT IF SOMEONE LIVED WITH YOU. AN AFFAIR IS ONE THING, LIVING TOGETHER IS ANOTHER...
SHOULD I ASK AROUND ABOUT A CHEAP APARTMENT?
THAT'S REALLY NICE, THANK YOU.
I'D BE DOING A GOOD DEED FOR THE WRONG REASONS. WHATEVER I DECIDE, I'LL COME OUT OF IT BADLY.
SSSS
sigh
CAN I DENY HIM HOSPITALITY WHEN HE DOESN'T HAVE A PLACE TO GO?
YOU'VE GOTTEN INVOLVED WITH HIM.
YOU'LL HAVE TO FIND A MIDDLE GROUND.
PLOP

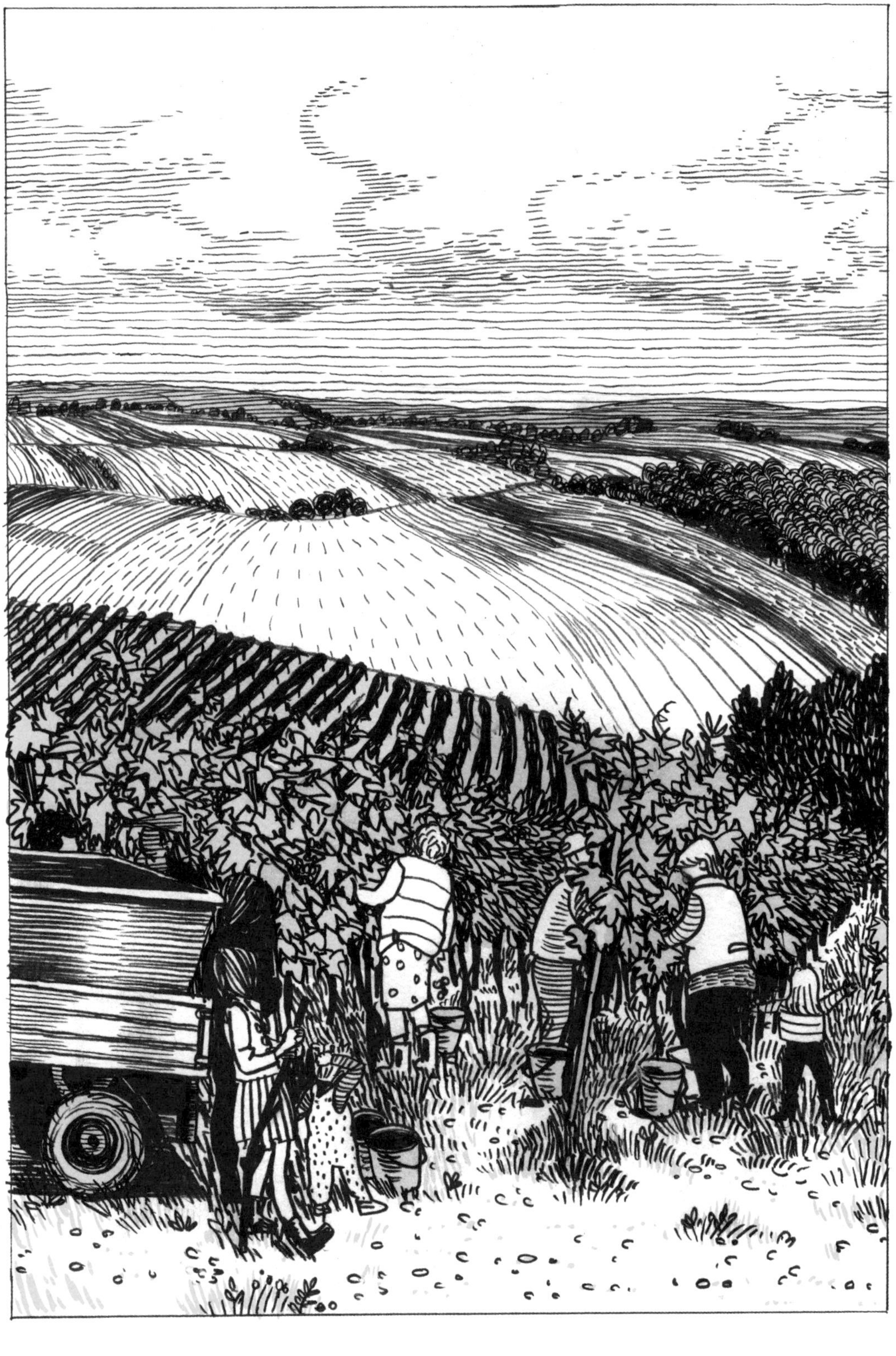

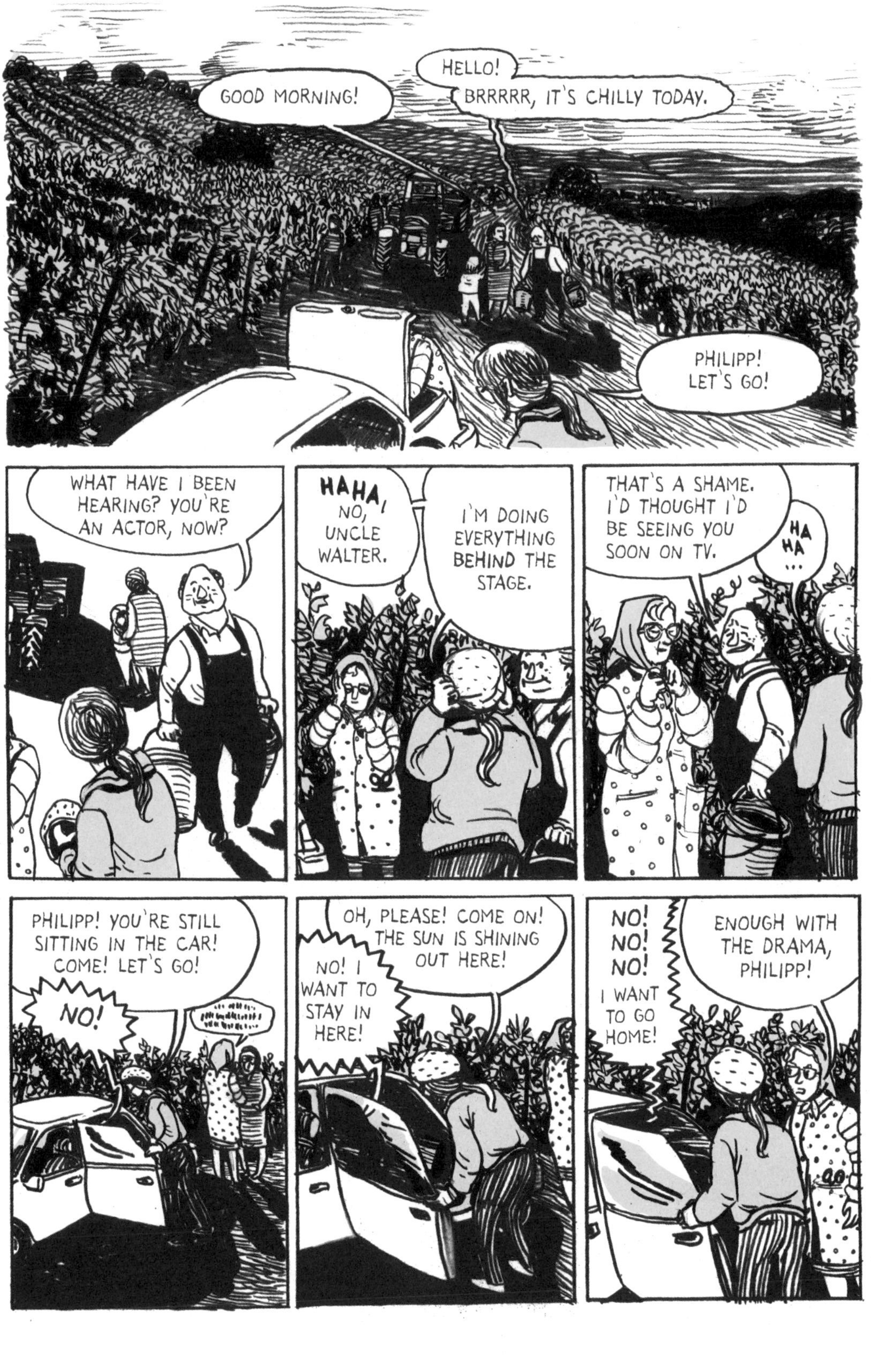
GOOD MORNING!
HELLO!
BRRRRR, IT'S CHILLY TODAY.
PHILIPP! LET'S GO!
WHAT HAVE I BEEN HEARING? YOU'RE AN ACTOR, NOW?
HAHA, NO, UNCLE WALTER.
I'M DOING EVERYTHING BEHIND THE STAGE.
THAT'S A SHAME. I'D THOUGHT I'D BE SEEING YOU SOON ON TV.
HA HA ...
PHILIPP! YOU'RE STILL SITTING IN THE CAR! COME! LET'S GO!
NO!
OH, PLEASE! COME ON! THE SUN IS SHINING OUT HERE!
NO! I WANT TO STAY IN HERE!
NO! NO! NO! I WANT TO GO HOME!
ENOUGH WITH THE DRAMA, PHILIPP!

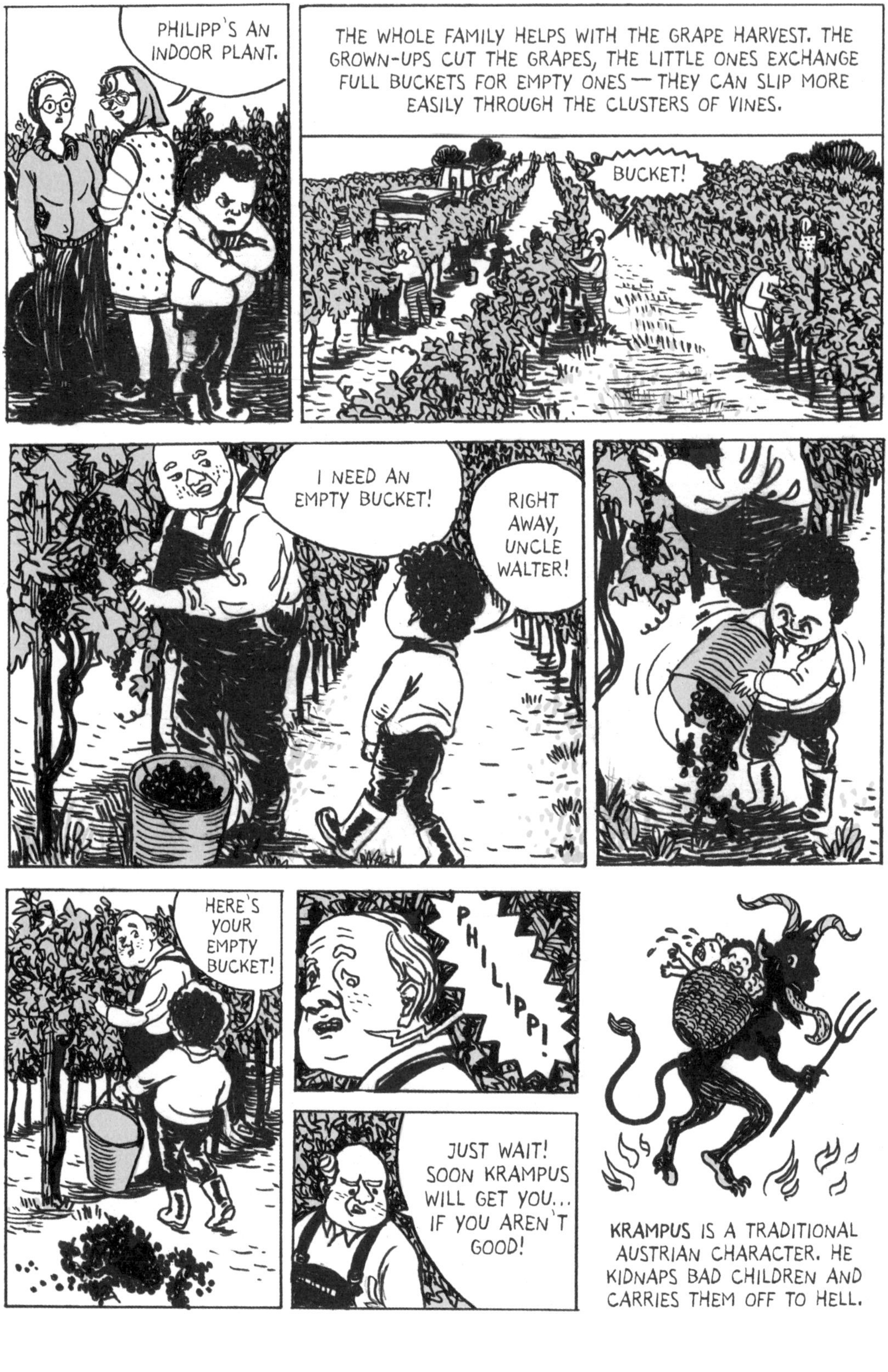
PHILIPP'S AN INDOOR PLANT.
THE WHOLE FAMILY HELPS WITH THE GRAPE HARVEST. THE GROWN-UPS CUT THE GRAPES, THE LITTLE ONES EXCHANGE FULL BUCKETS FOR EMPTY ONES — THEY CAN SLIP MORE EASILY THROUGH THE CLUSTERS OF VINES.
BUCKET!
I NEED AN EMPTY BUCKET!
RIGHT AWAY, UNCLE WALTER!
HERE'S YOUR EMPTY BUCKET!
PHILIPP!
JUST WAIT! SOON KRAMPUS WILL GET YOU... IF YOU AREN'T GOOD!
KRAMPUS IS A TRADITIONAL AUSTRIAN CHARACTER. HE KIDNAPS BAD CHILDREN AND CARRIES THEM OFF TO HELL.

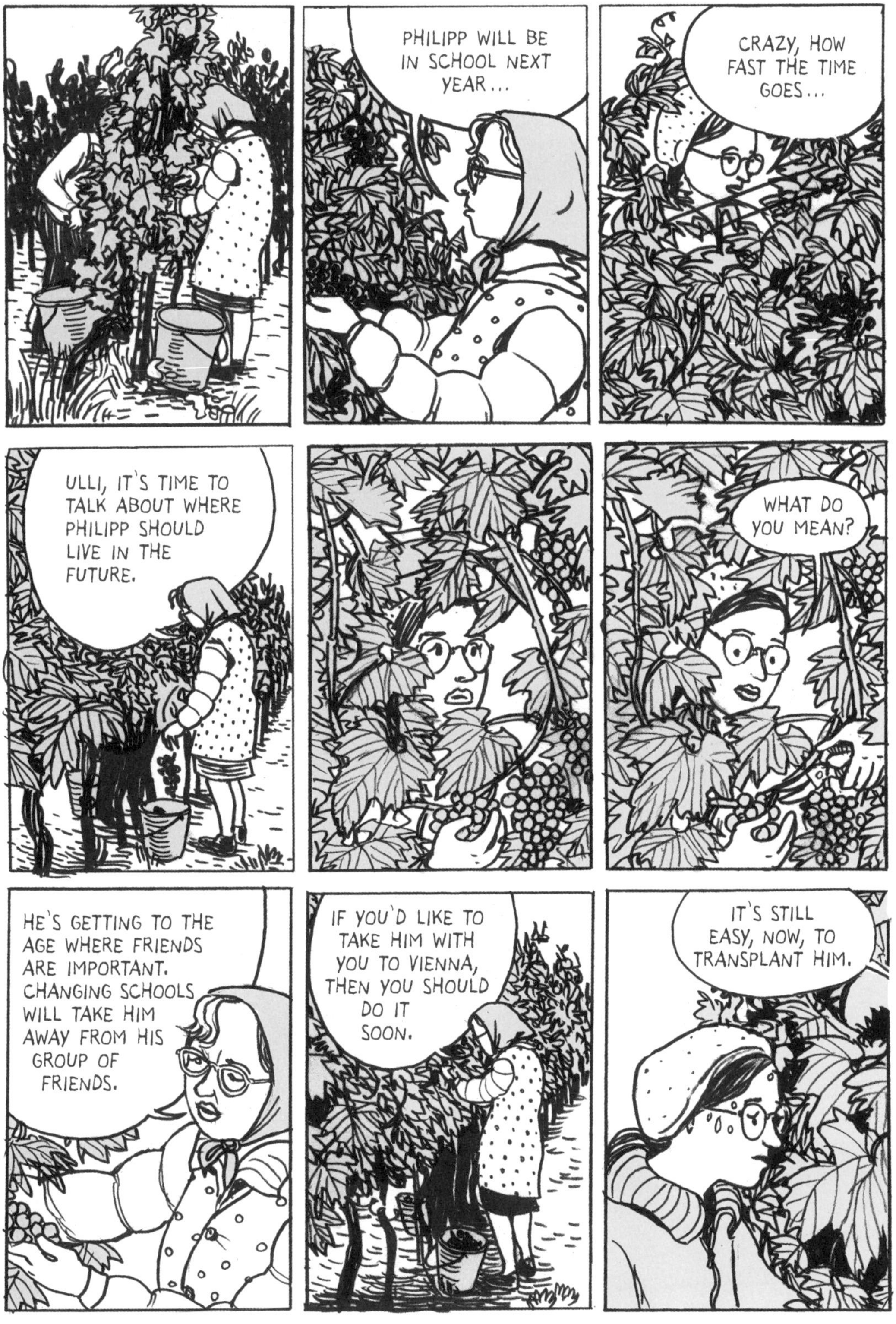
PHILIPP WILL BE IN SCHOOL NEXT YEAR...
CRAZY, HOW FAST THE TIME GOES...
ULLI, IT'S TIME TO TALK ABOUT WHERE PHILIPP SHOULD LIVE IN THE FUTURE.
WHAT DO YOU MEAN?
HE'S GETTING TO THE AGE WHERE FRIENDS ARE IMPORTANT. CHANGING SCHOOLS WILL TAKE HIM AWAY FROM HIS GROUP OF FRIENDS.
IF YOU'D LIKE TO TAKE HIM WITH YOU TO VIENNA, THEN YOU SHOULD DO IT SOON.
IT'S STILL EASY, NOW, TO TRANSPLANT HIM.

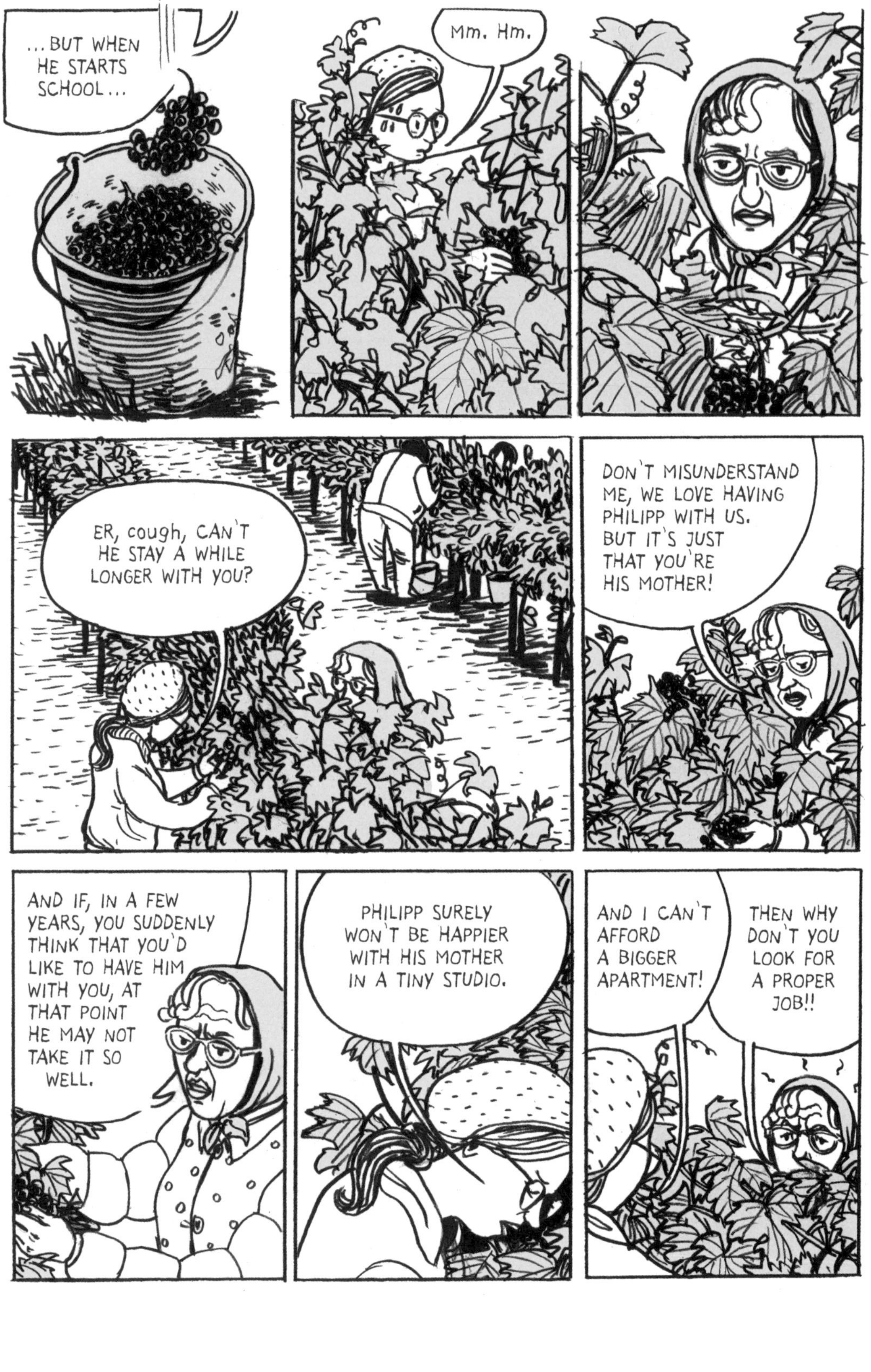
...BUT WHEN HE STARTS SCHOOL...
Mm. Hm.
ER, cough, CAN'T HE STAY A WHILE LONGER WITH YOU?
DON'T MISUNDERSTAND ME, WE LOVE HAVING PHILIPP WITH US. BUT IT'S JUST THAT YOU'RE HIS MOTHER!
AND IF, IN A FEW YEARS, YOU SUDDENLY THINK THAT YOU'D LIKE TO HAVE HIM WITH YOU, AT THAT POINT HE MAY NOT TAKE IT SO WELL.
PHILIPP SURELY WON'T BE HAPPIER WITH HIS MOTHER IN A TINY STUDIO.
AND I CAN'T AFFORD A BIGGER APARTMENT!
THEN WHY DON'T YOU LOOK FOR A PROPER JOB!!

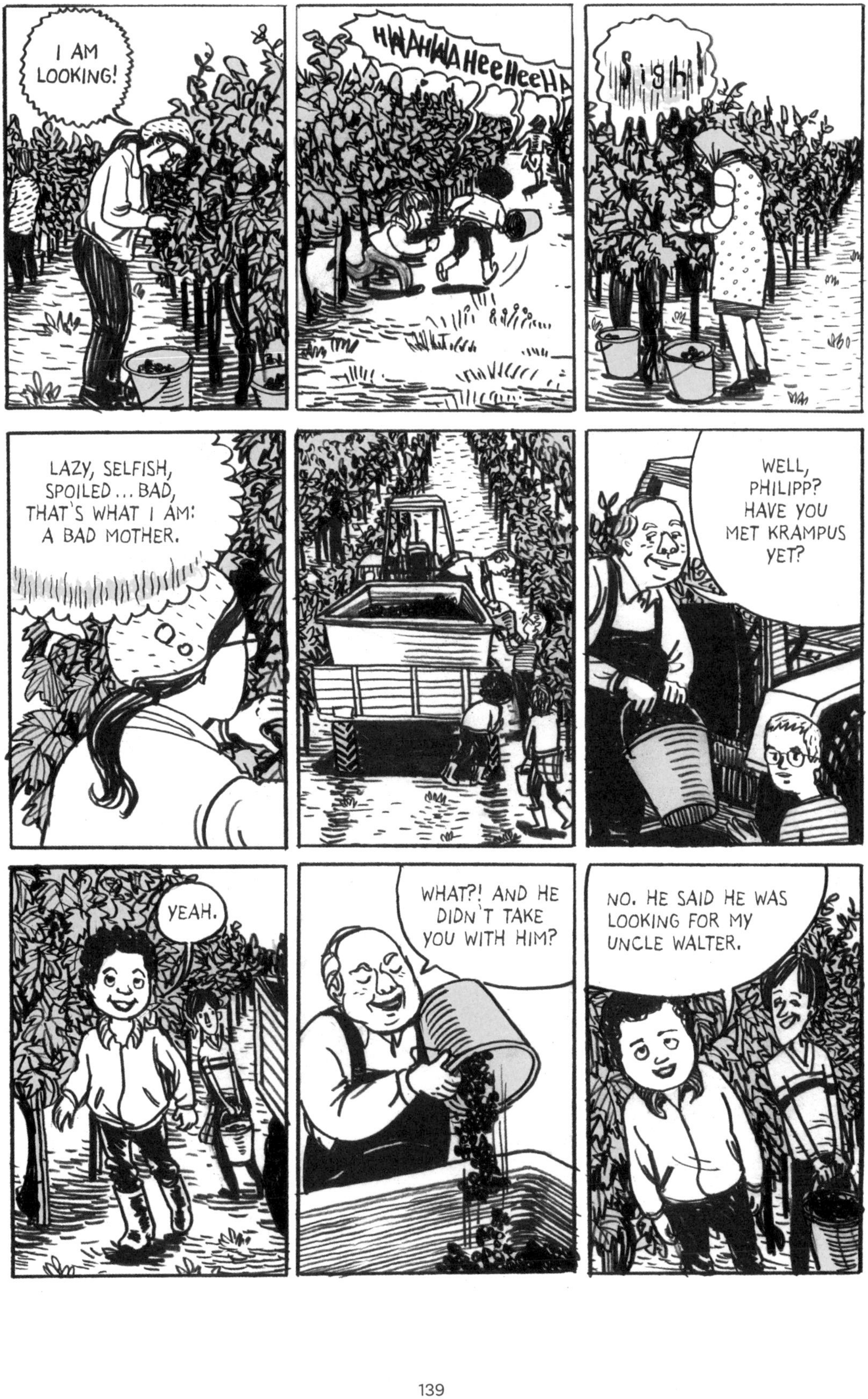
I AM LOOKING!
HAHAHAHAHeeHeeHA
Sigh!
LAZY, SELFISH, SPOILED... BAD, THAT'S WHAT I AM: A BAD MOTHER.
WELL, PHILIPP? HAVE YOU MET KRAMPUS YET?
YEAH.
WHAT?! AND HE DIDN'T TAKE YOU WITH HIM?
NO. HE SAID HE WAS LOOKING FOR MY UNCLE WALTER.

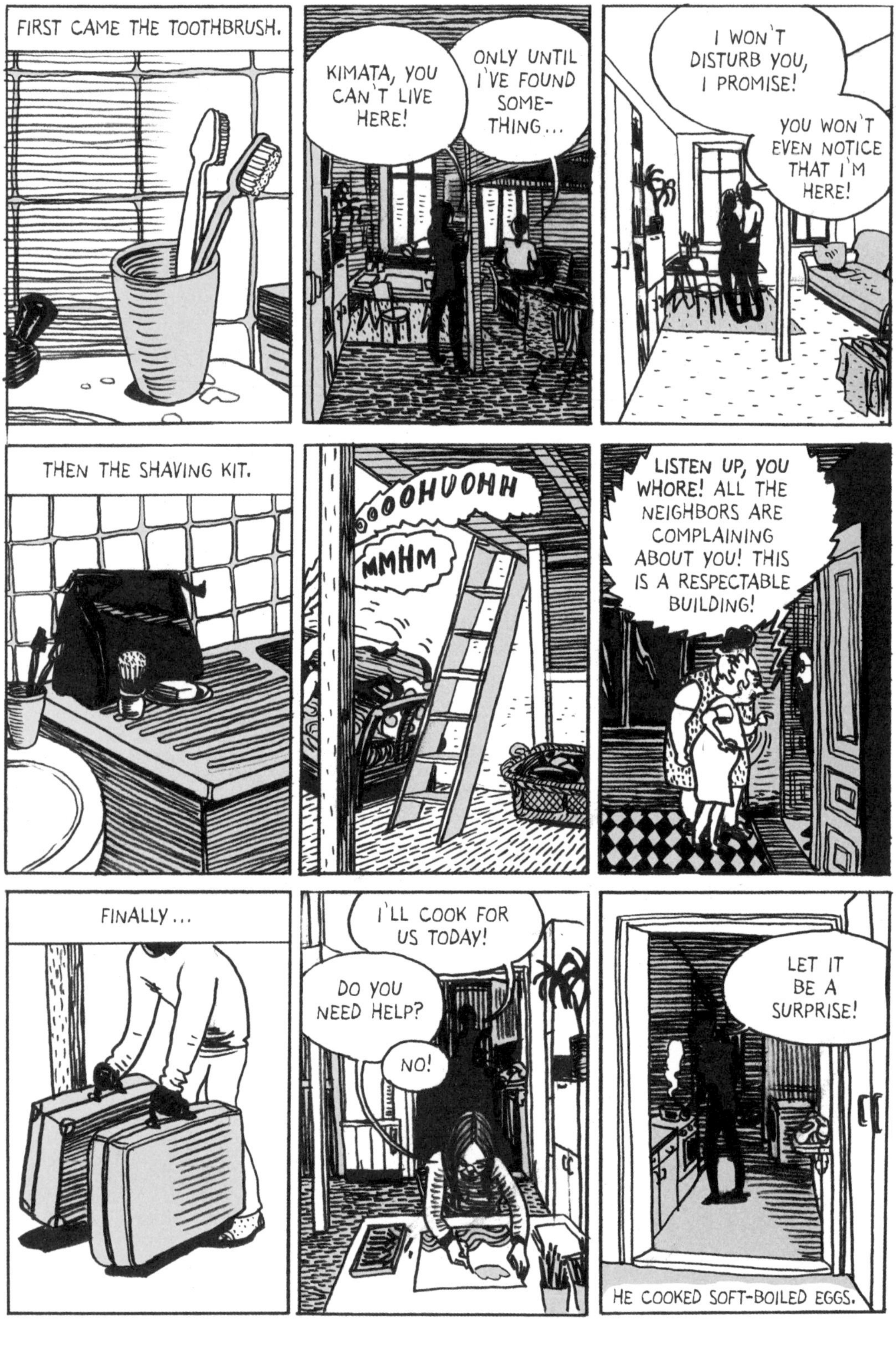
FIRST CAME THE TOOTHBRUSH.
KIMATA, YOU CAN'T LIVE HERE!
ONLY UNTIL I'VE FOUND SOME-THING...
I WON'T DISTURB YOU, I PROMISE!
YOU WON'T EVEN NOTICE THAT I'M HERE!
THEN THE SHAVING KIT.
OOOOHUOHH
MMHM
LISTEN UP, YOU WHORE! ALL THE NEIGHBORS ARE COMPLAINING ABOUT YOU! THIS IS A RESPECTABLE BUILDING!
FINALLY...
I'LL COOK FOR US TODAY!
DO YOU NEED HELP?
NO!
LET IT BE A SURPRISE!
HE COOKED SOFT-BOILED EGGS.

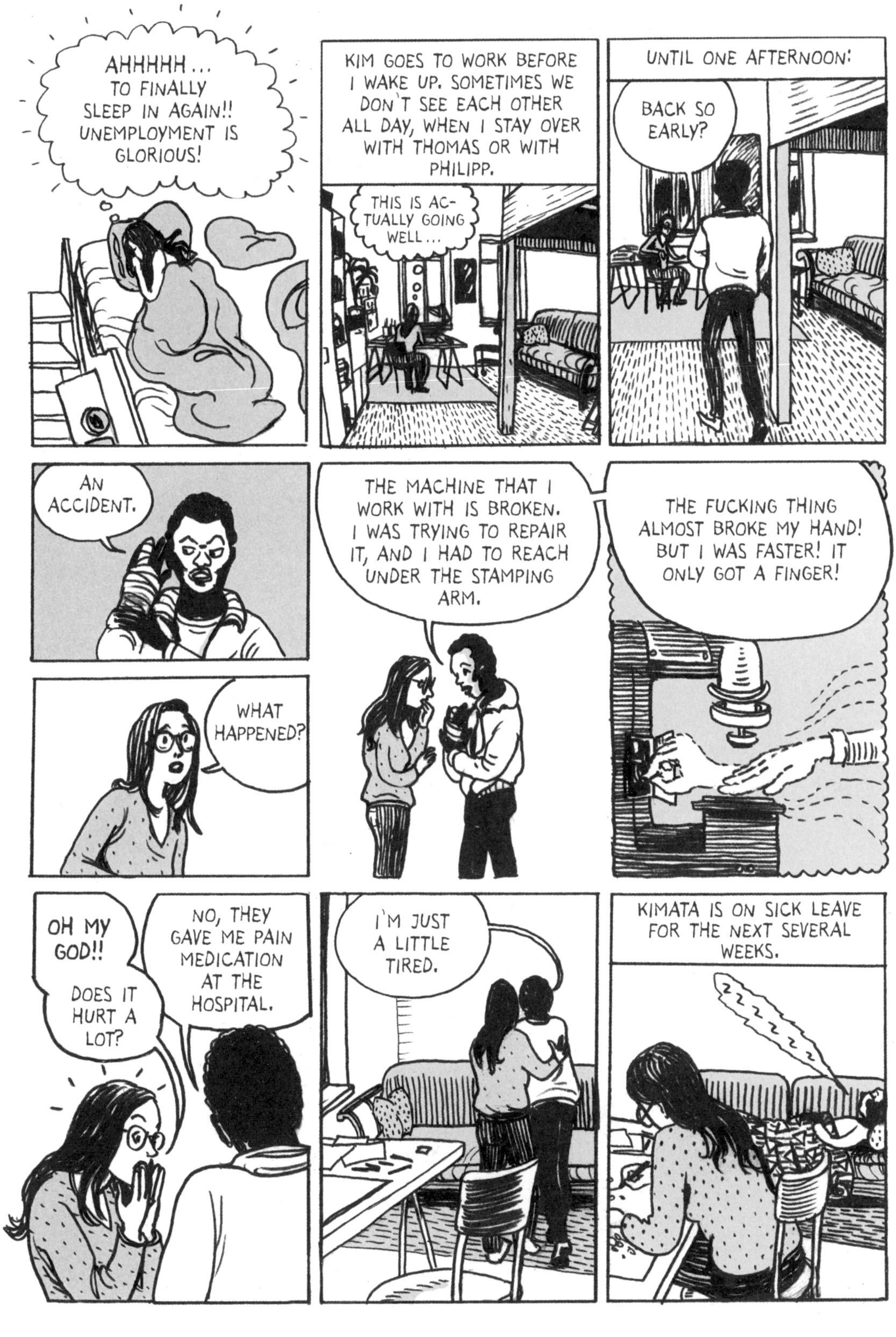

AHHHHH... TO FINALLY SLEEP IN AGAIN!! UNEMPLOYMENT IS GLORIOUS!
KIM GOES TO WORK BEFORE I WAKE UP. SOMETIMES WE DON'T SEE EACH OTHER ALL DAY, WHEN I STAY OVER WITH THOMAS OR WITH PHILIPP.
THIS IS ACTUALLY GOING WELL...
UNTIL ONE AFTERNOON:
BACK SO EARLY?
AN ACCIDENT.
THE MACHINE THAT I WORK WITH IS BROKEN. I WAS TRYING TO REPAIR IT, AND I HAD TO REACH UNDER THE STAMPING ARM.
THE FUCKING THING ALMOST BROKE MY HAND! BUT I WAS FASTER! IT ONLY GOT A FINGER!
WHAT HAPPENED?
OH MY GOD!!
DOES IT HURT A LOT?
NO, THEY GAVE ME PAIN MEDICATION AT THE HOSPITAL.
I'M JUST A LITTLE TIRED.
KIMATA IS ON SICK LEAVE FOR THE NEXT SEVERAL WEEKS.
ZZZZZZ

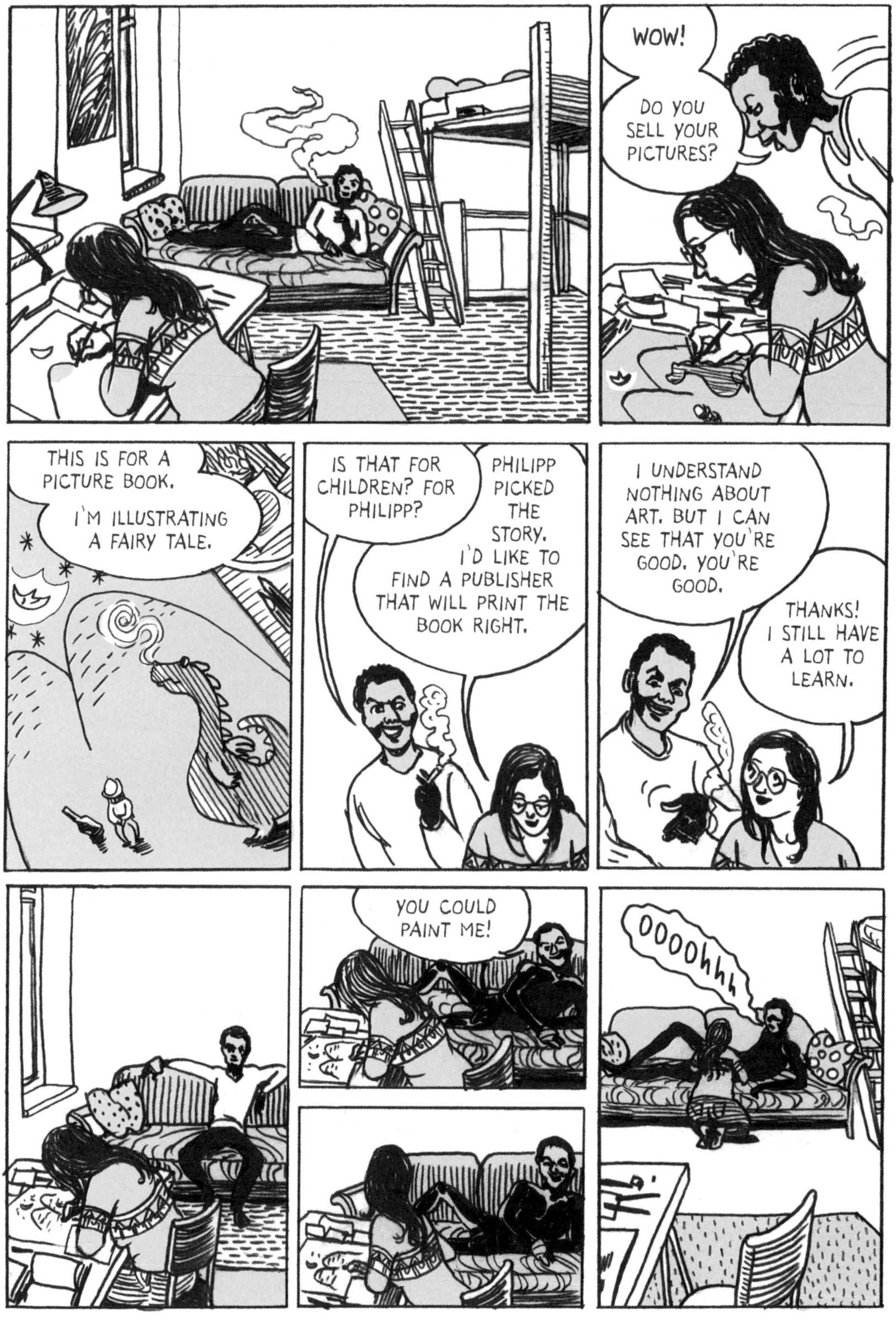
WOW!
DO YOU SELL YOUR PICTURES?
THIS IS FOR A PICTURE BOOK.
I'M ILLUSTRATING A FAIRY TALE.
IS THAT FOR CHILDREN? FOR PHILIPP?
PHILIPP PICKED THE STORY.
I'D LIKE TO FIND A PUBLISHER THAT WILL PRINT THE BOOK RIGHT.
I UNDERSTAND NOTHING ABOUT ART. BUT I CAN SEE THAT YOU'RE GOOD. YOU'RE GOOD.
THANKS! I STILL HAVE A LOT TO LEARN.
YOU COULD PAINT ME!
OOOOhhh

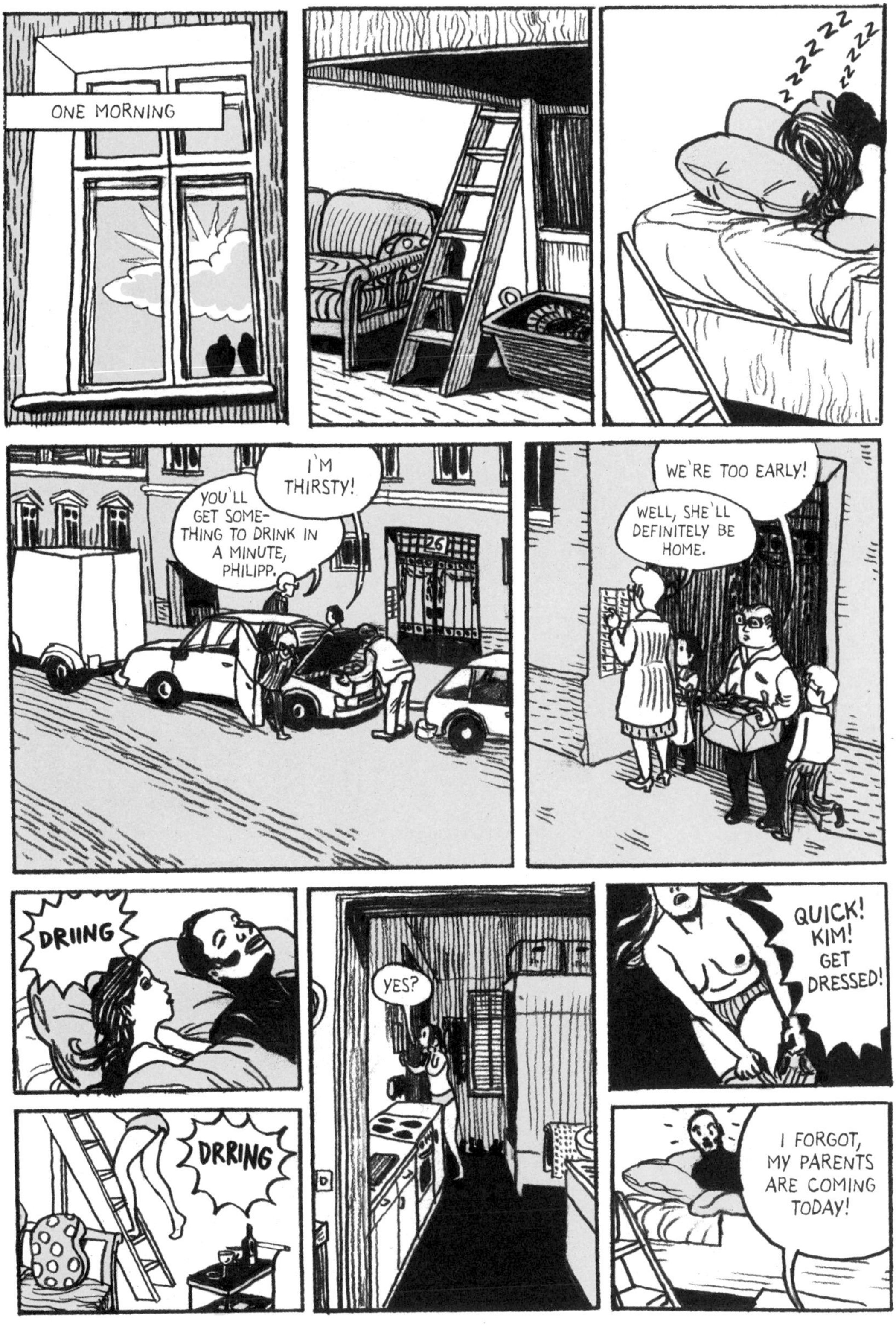
ONE MORNING
ZZZZZ
ZZZZZ
I'M THIRSTY!
YOU'LL GET SOME-THING TO DRINK IN A MINUTE, PHILIPP.
26
WE'RE TOO EARLY!
WELL, SHE'LL DEFINITELY BE HOME.
DRIING
DRRING
YES?
QUICK! KIM! GET DRESSED!
I FORGOT, MY PARENTS ARE COMING TODAY!

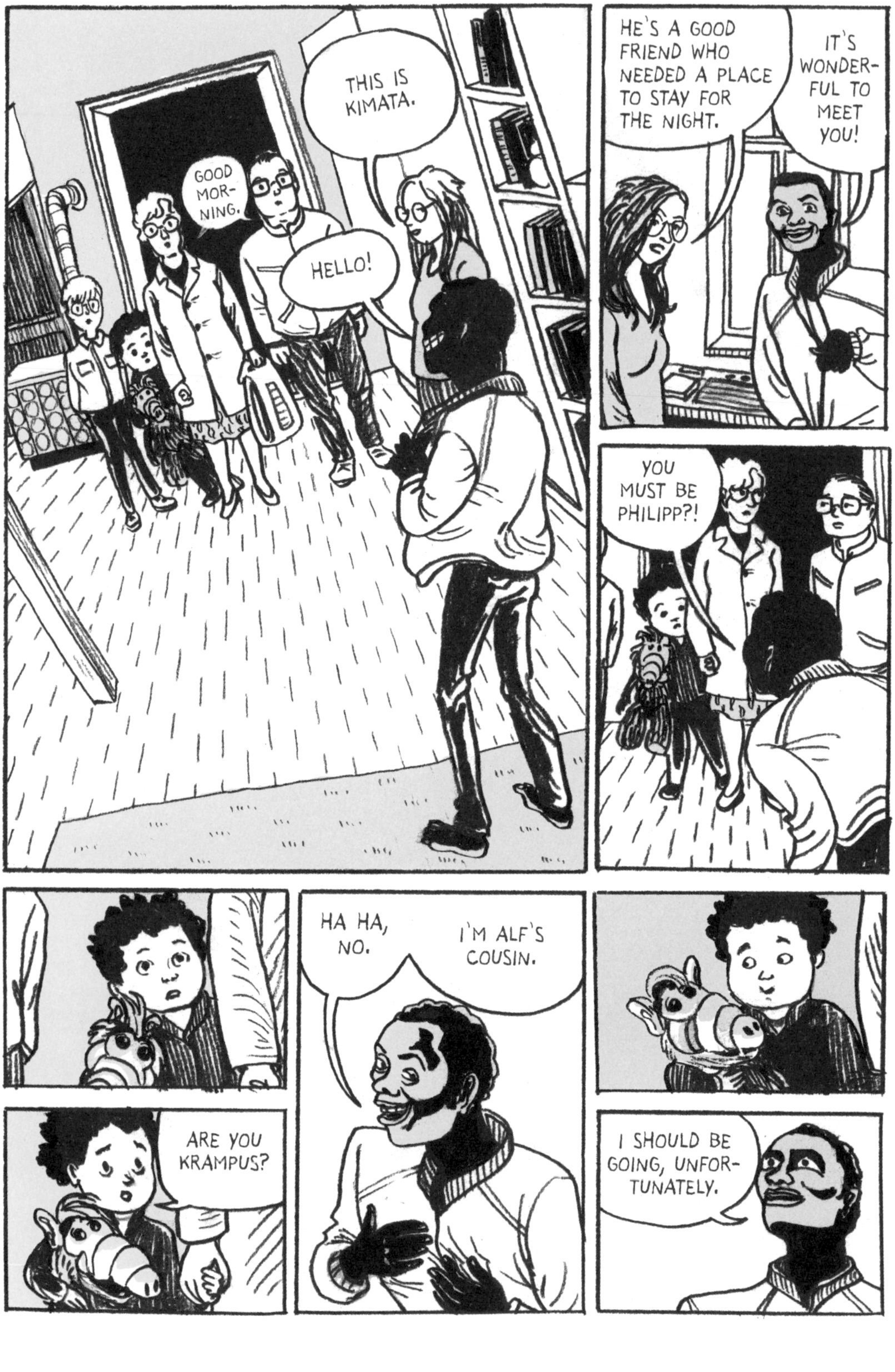
THIS IS KIMATA.
GOOD MOR-NING.
HELLO!
HE'S A GOOD FRIEND WHO NEEDED A PLACE TO STAY FOR THE NIGHT.
IT'S WONDER-FUL TO MEET YOU!
YOU MUST BE PHILIPP?!
ARE YOU KRAMPUS?
HA HA, NO.
I'M ALF'S COUSIN.
I SHOULD BE GOING, UNFOR-TUNATELY.

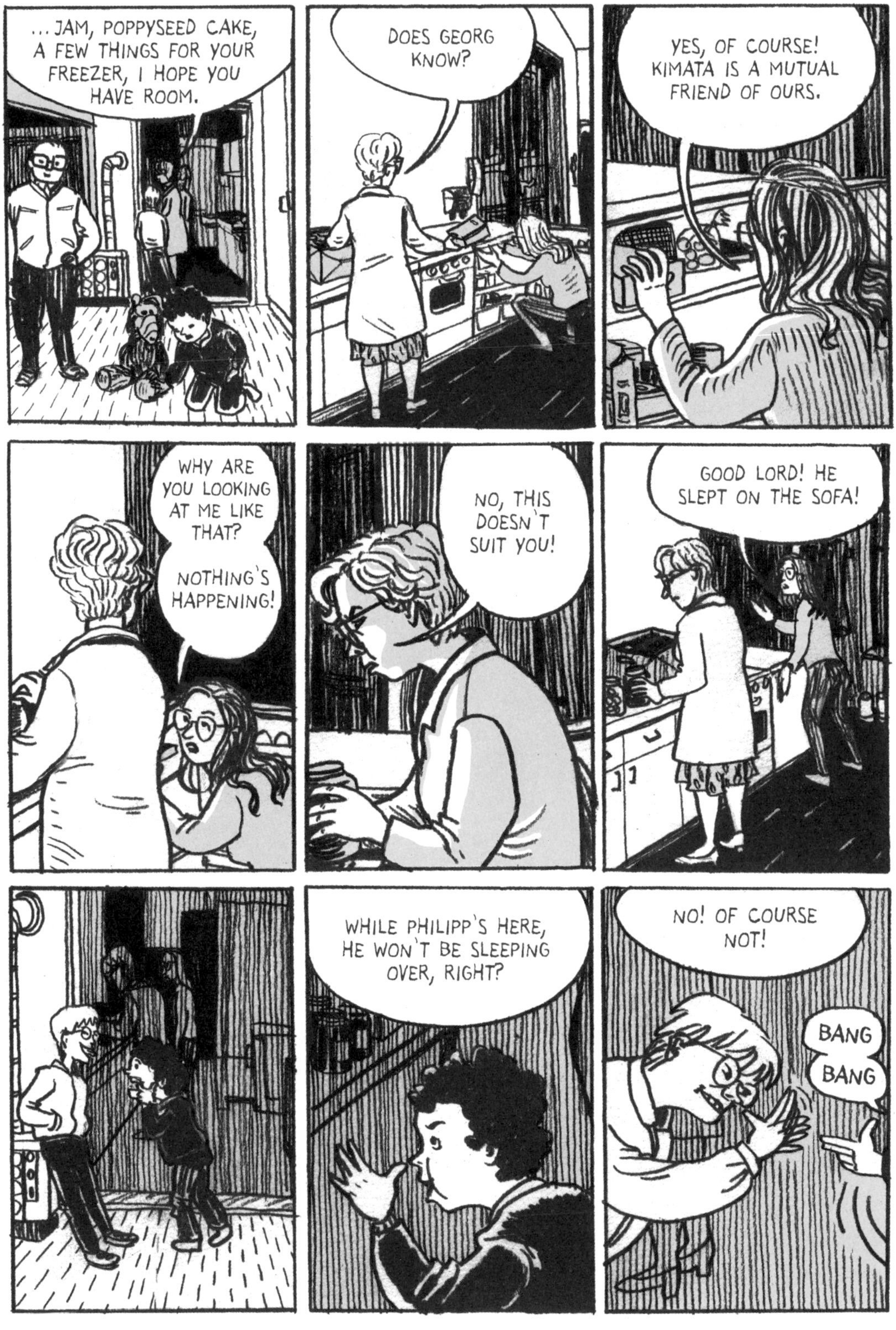
...JAM, POPPYSEED CAKE, A FEW THINGS FOR YOUR FREEZER, I HOPE YOU HAVE ROOM.
DOES GEORG KNOW?
YES, OF COURSE! KIMATA IS A MUTUAL FRIEND OF OURS.
WHY ARE YOU LOOKING AT ME LIKE THAT?
NOTHING'S HAPPENING!
NO, THIS DOESN'T SUIT YOU!
GOOD LORD! HE SLEPT ON THE SOFA!
WHILE PHILIPP'S HERE, HE WON'T BE SLEEPING OVER, RIGHT?
NO! OF COURSE NOT!
BANG
BANG

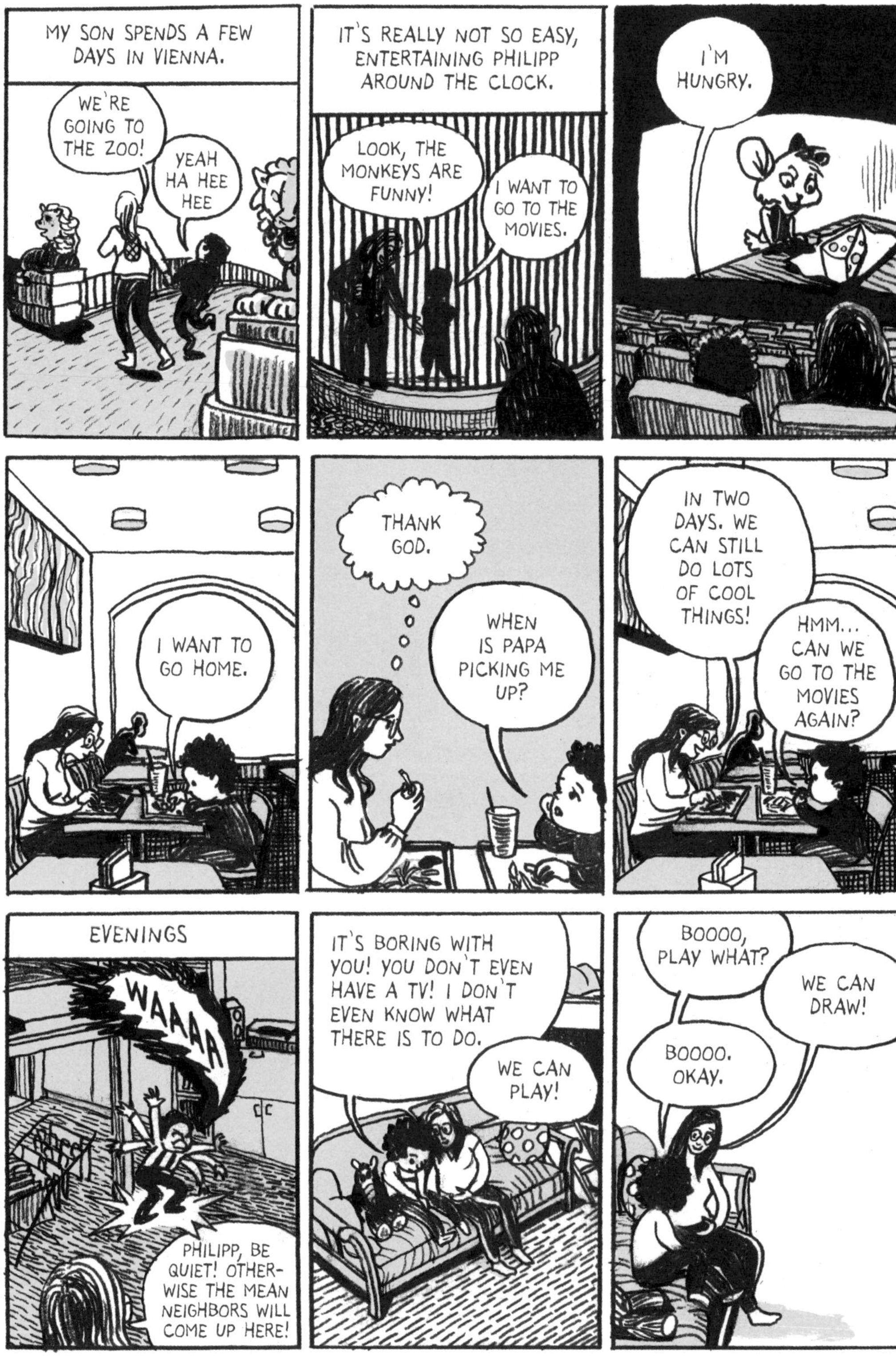
MY SON SPENDS A FEW DAYS IN VIENNA.
WE'RE GOING TO THE ZOO!
YEAH HA HEE HEE
IT'S REALLY NOT SO EASY, ENTERTAINING PHILIPP AROUND THE CLOCK.
LOOK, THE MONKEYS ARE FUNNY!
I WANT TO GO TO THE MOVIES.
I'M HUNGRY.
I WANT TO GO HOME.
THANK GOD.
WHEN IS PAPA PICKING ME UP?
IN TWO DAYS. WE CAN STILL DO LOTS OF COOL THINGS!
HMM... CAN WE GO TO THE MOVIES AGAIN?
EVENINGS
WAAAAA
PHILIPP, BE QUIET! OTHER-WISE THE MEAN NEIGHBORS WILL COME UP HERE!
IT'S BORING WITH YOU! YOU DON'T EVEN HAVE A TV! I DON'T EVEN KNOW WHAT THERE IS TO DO.
WE CAN PLAY!
BOOOO, PLAY WHAT?
WE CAN DRAW!
BOOOO. OKAY.

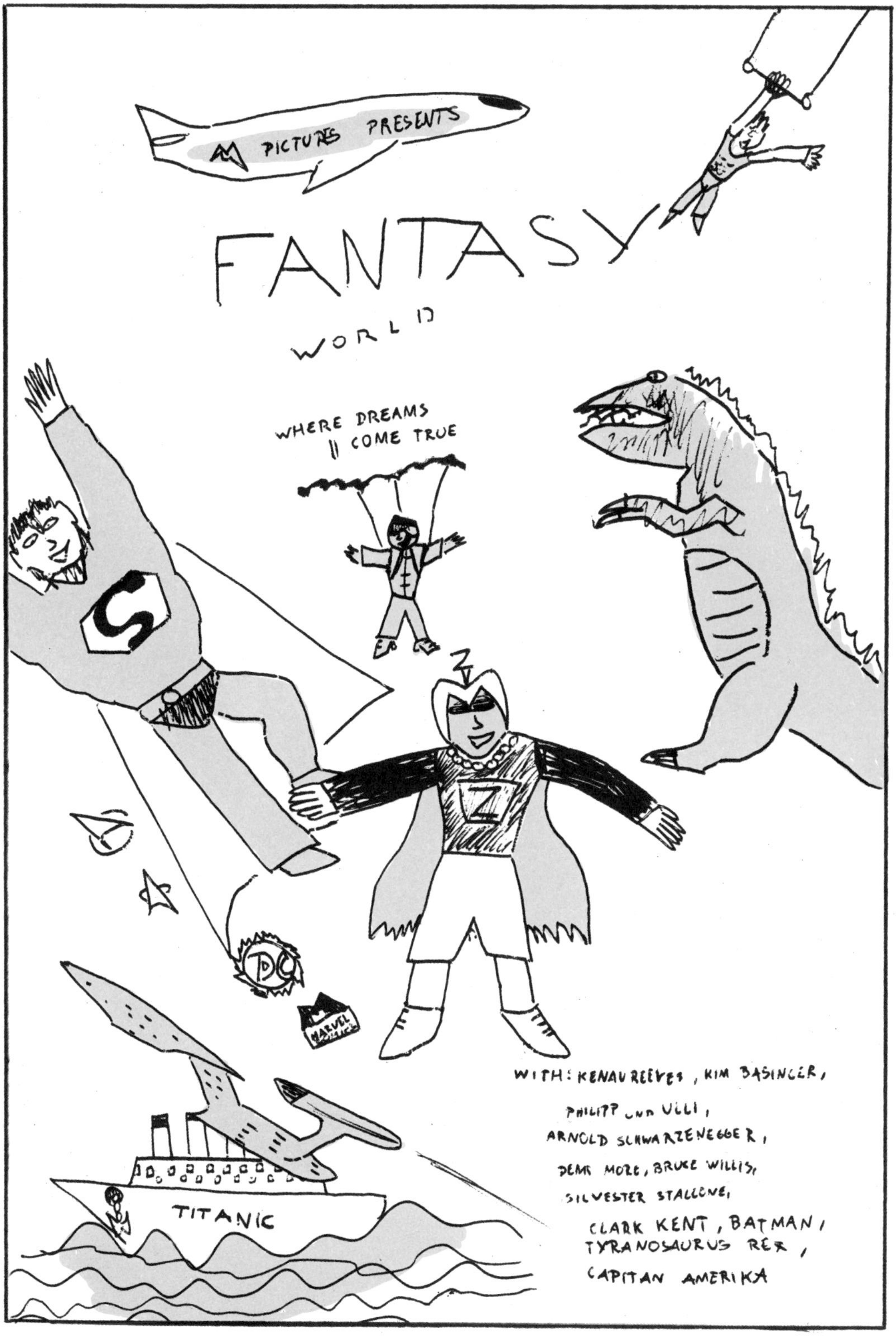
AM PICTURES PRESENTS
FANTASY
WORLD
WHERE DREAMS
COME TRUE
TITANIC
WITH: KENAU REEVES, KIM BASINGER,
PHILIPP UND ULLI,
ARNOLD SCHWARZENEGGER,
DEMI MORE, BRUKE WILLIS,
SILVESTER STALLONE,
CLARK KENT, BATMAN,
TYRANOSAURUS REX,
CAPITAN AMERIKA

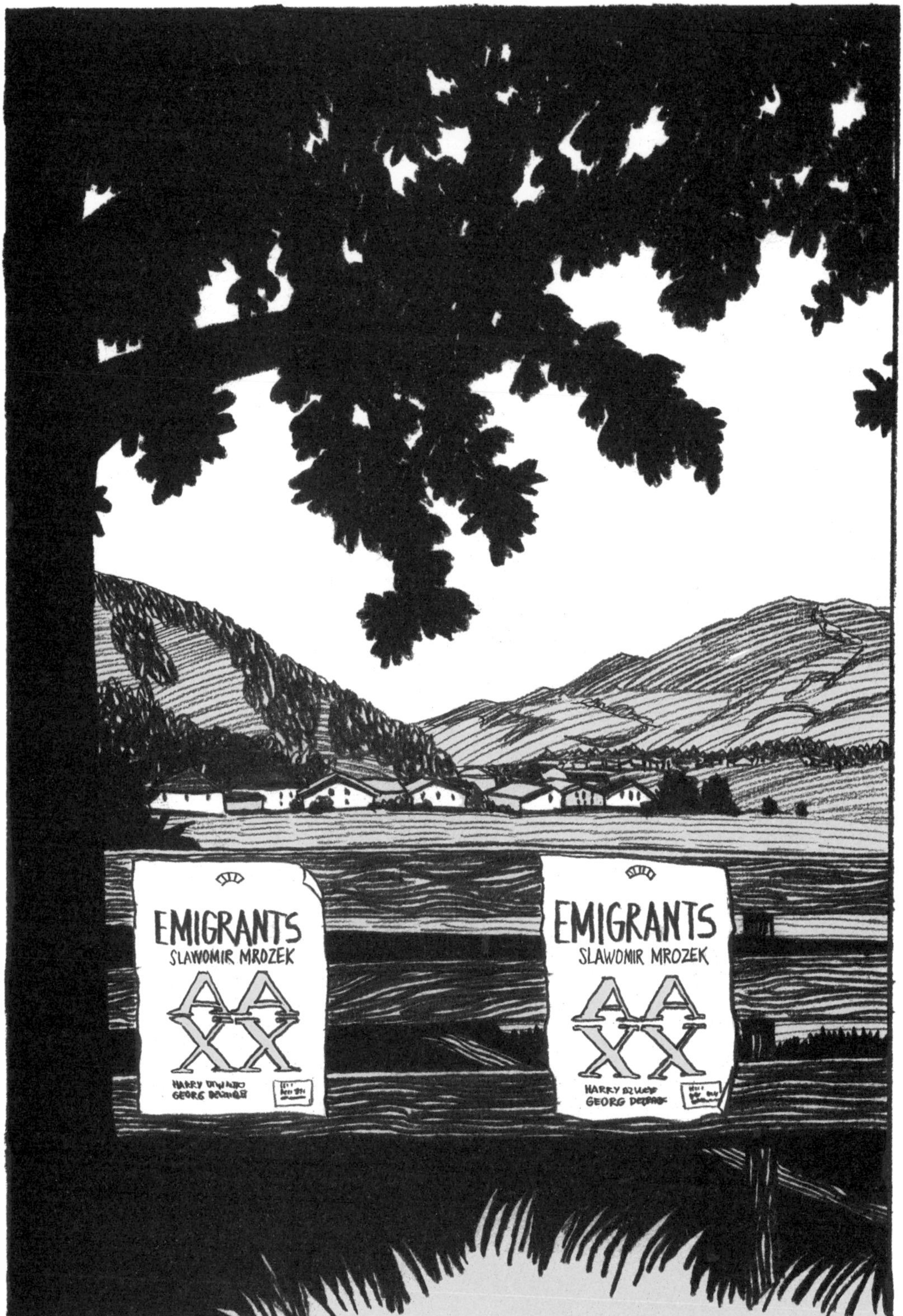
EMIGRANTS
SLAWOMIR MROZEK
EMIGRANTS
SLAWOMIR MROZEK

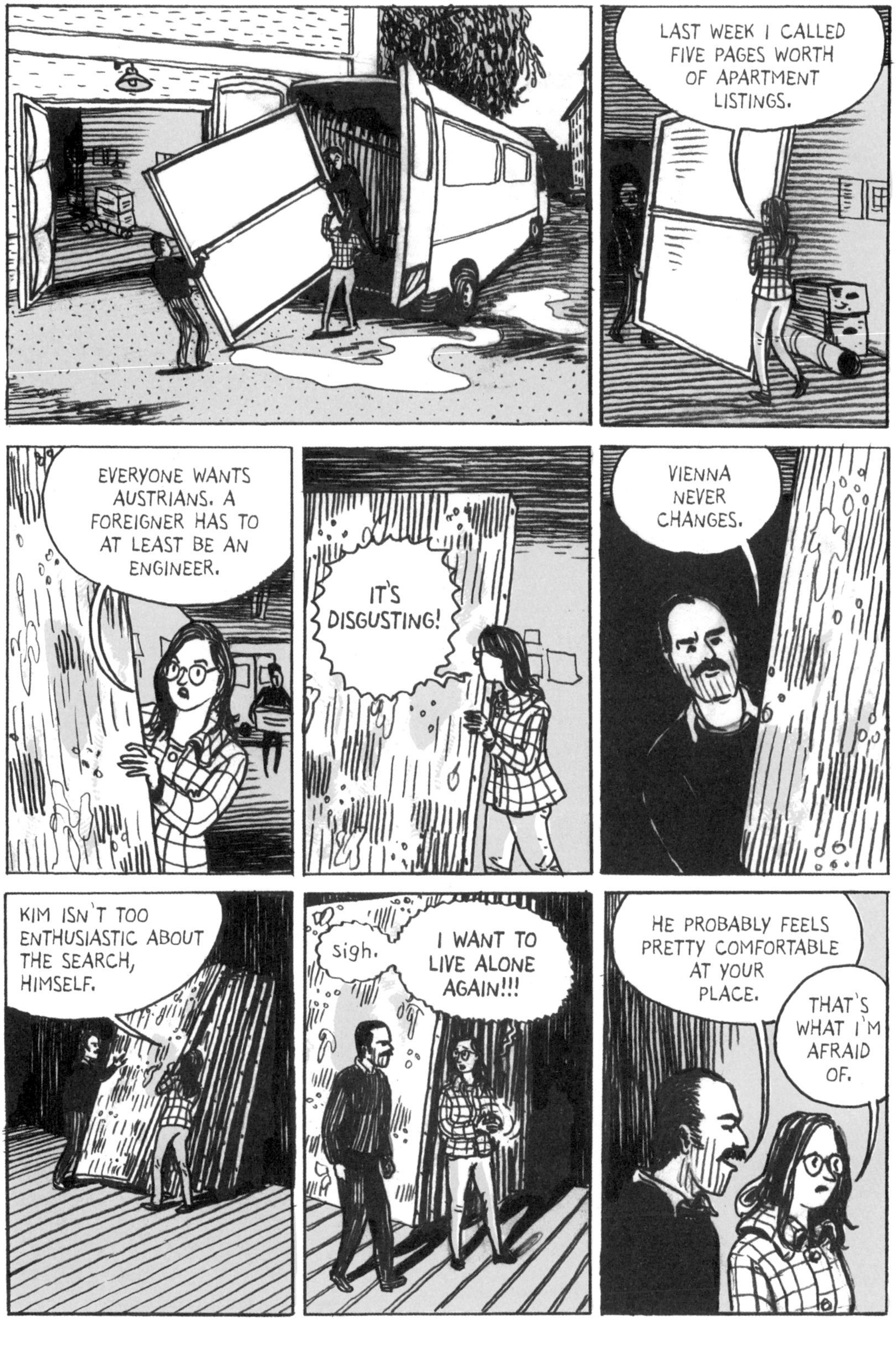
LAST WEEK I CALLED FIVE PAGES WORTH OF APARTMENT LISTINGS.
EVERYONE WANTS AUSTRIANS. A FOREIGNER HAS TO AT LEAST BE AN ENGINEER.
IT'S DISGUSTING!
VIENNA NEVER CHANGES.
KIM ISN'T TOO ENTHUSIASTIC ABOUT THE SEARCH, HIMSELF.
sigh.
I WANT TO LIVE ALONE AGAIN!!!
HE PROBABLY FEELS PRETTY COMFORTABLE AT YOUR PLACE.
THAT'S WHAT I'M AFRAID OF.

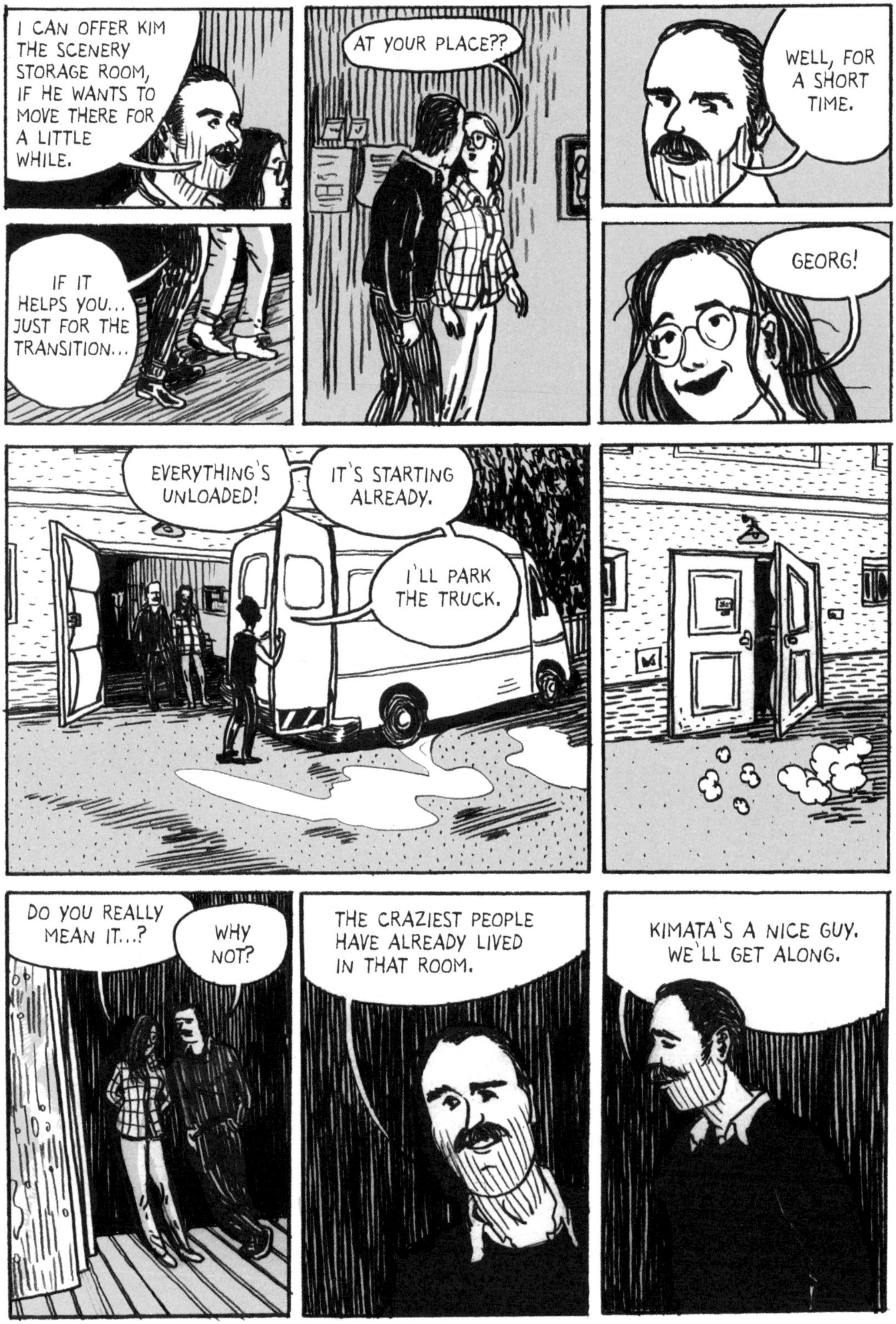
I CAN OFFER KIM THE SCENERY STORAGE ROOM, IF HE WANTS TO MOVE THERE FOR A LITTLE WHILE.
AT YOUR PLACE??
WELL, FOR A SHORT TIME.
IF IT HELPS YOU... JUST FOR THE TRANSITION...
GEORG!
EVERYTHING'S UNLOADED!
IT'S STARTING ALREADY.
I'LL PARK THE TRUCK.
DO YOU REALLY MEAN IT...?
WHY NOT?
THE CRAZIEST PEOPLE HAVE ALREADY LIVED IN THAT ROOM.
KIMATA'S A NICE GUY. WE'LL GET ALONG.

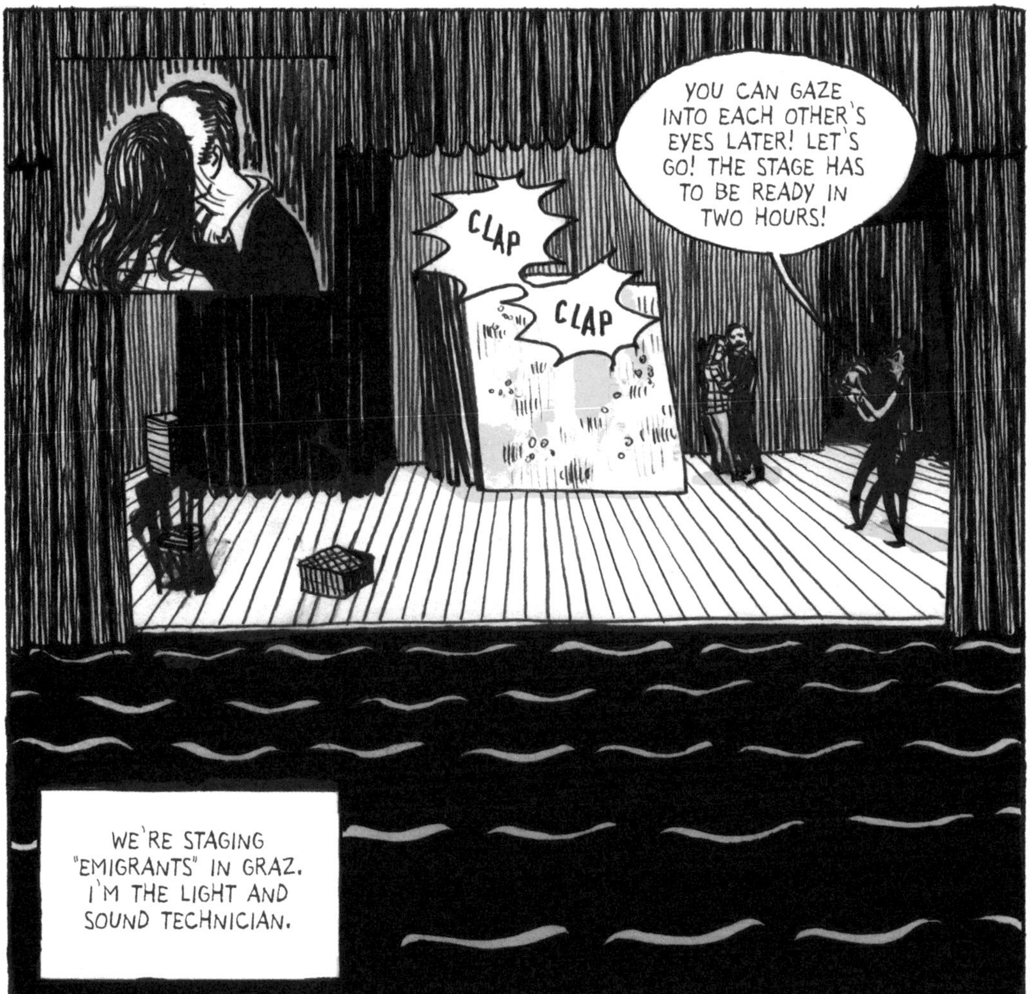
YOU CAN GAZE INTO EACH OTHER'S EYES LATER! LET'S GO! THE STAGE HAS TO BE READY IN TWO HOURS!
CLAP
CLAP
WE'RE STAGING "EMIGRANTS" IN GRAZ. I'M THE LIGHT AND SOUND TECHNICIAN.

GEORG IS A GENIUS AT ORGANIZING GUEST PERFORMANCES. LIKE A SMALL CIRCUS, WE PUT UP THE SET IN THE AFTERNOON, PERFORM IN THE EVENING, AND THEN STRIKE IT DOWN. IN BETWEEN, WE STORE THE SET PIECES IN GEORG'S APARTMENT. THE ROOM IS LARGE, LIGHT, AND HALF OF IT IS EMPTY.

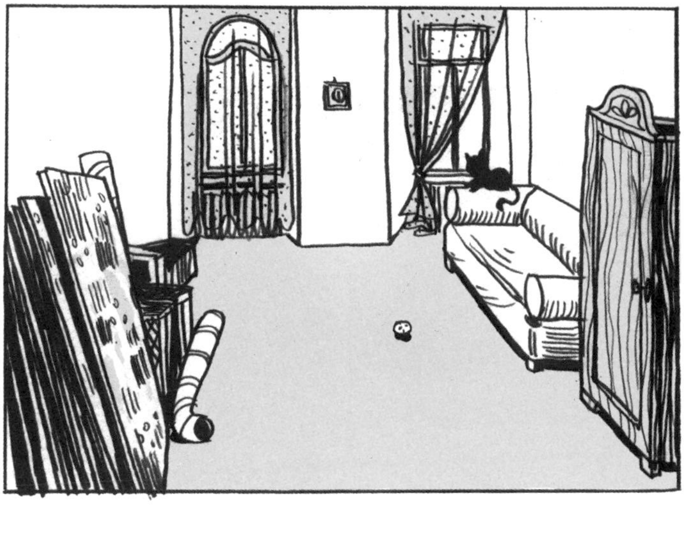

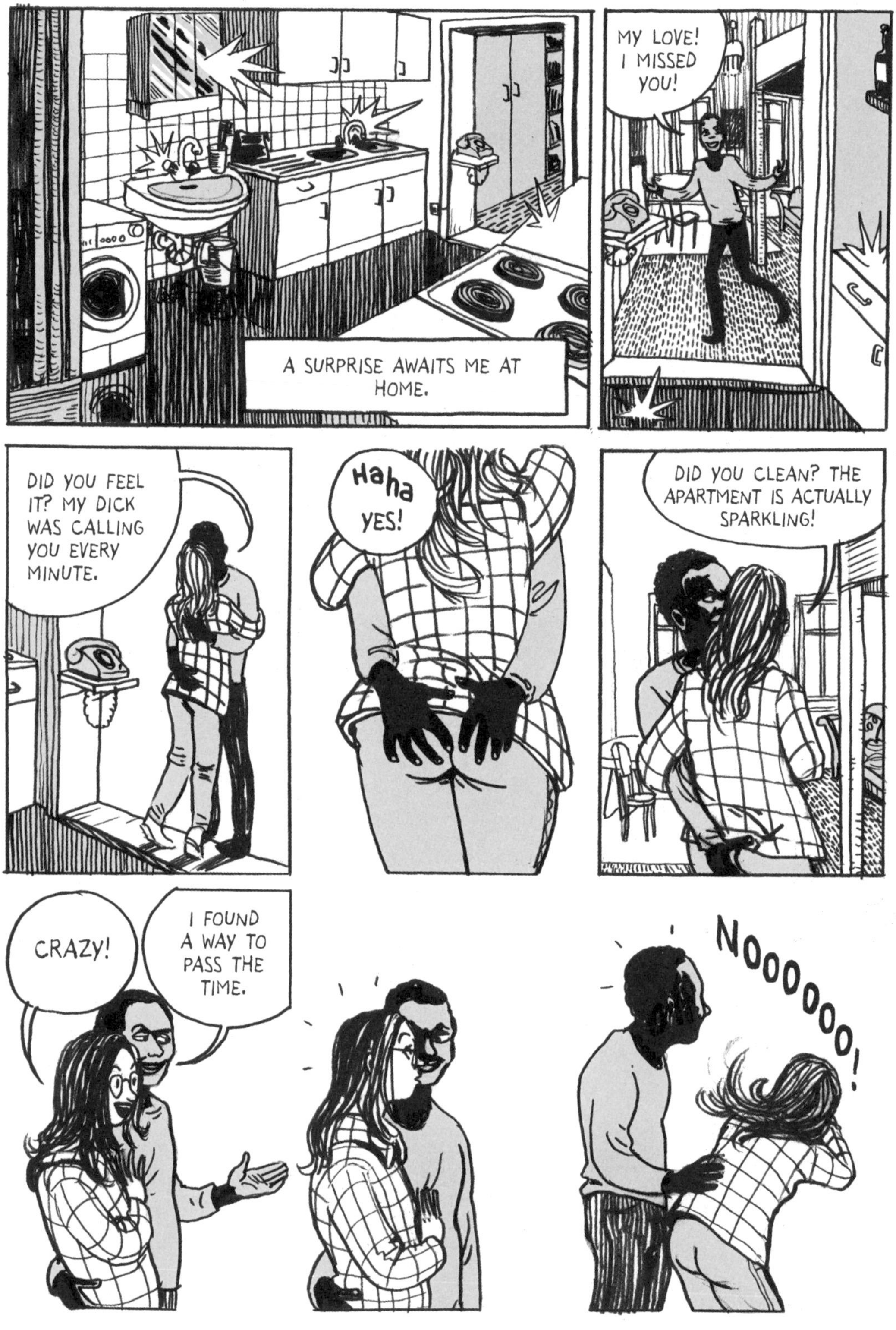
A SURPRISE AWAITS ME AT HOME.
MY LOVE! I MISSED YOU!
DID YOU FEEL IT? MY DICK WAS CALLING YOU EVERY MINUTE.
Haha YES!
DID YOU CLEAN? THE APARTMENT IS ACTUALLY SPARKLING!
CRAZY!
I FOUND A WAY TO PASS THE TIME.
NOOOOOO!

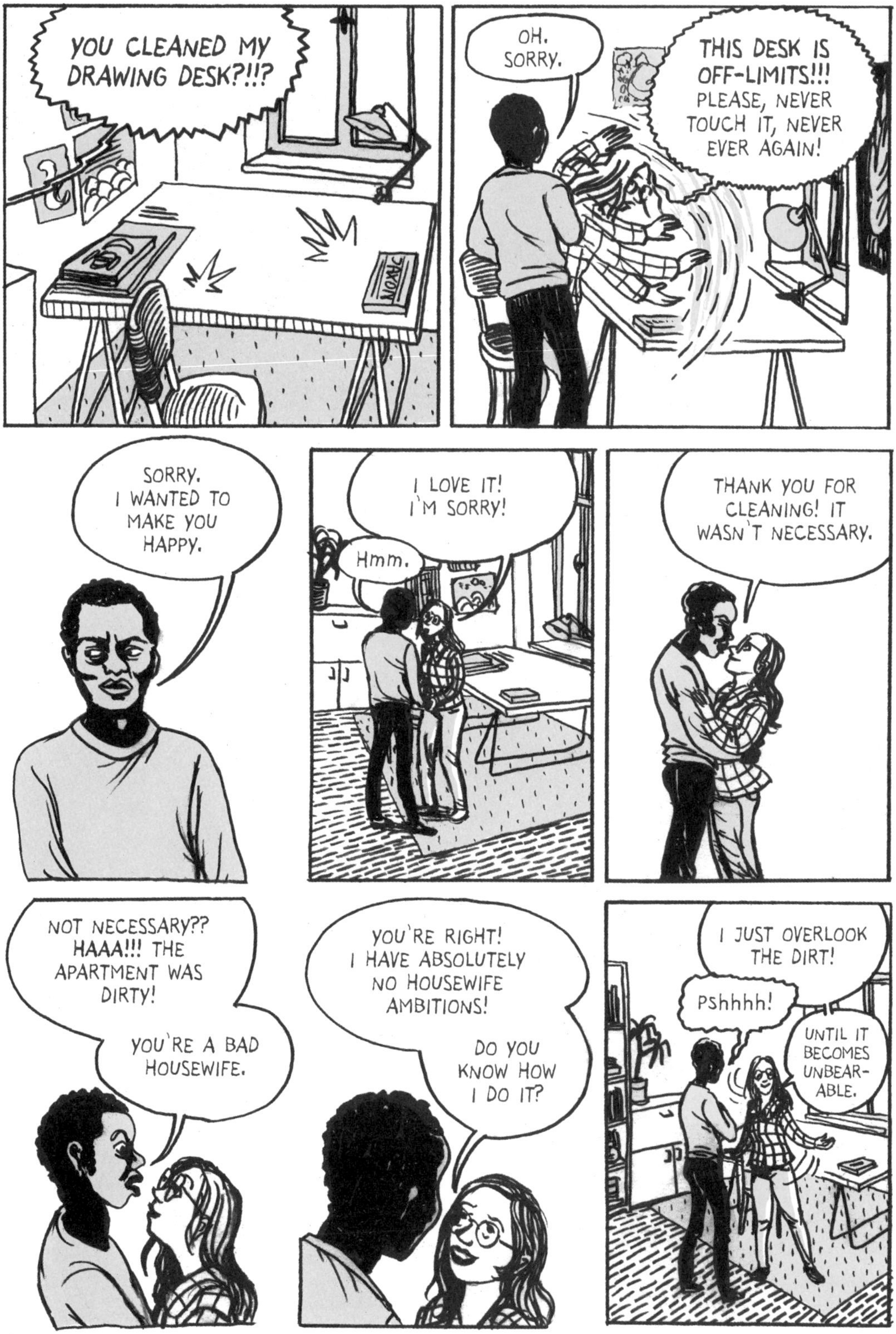
YOU CLEANED MY DRAWING DESK?!!?
OH. SORRY.
THIS DESK IS OFF-LIMITS!!! PLEASE, NEVER TOUCH IT, NEVER EVER AGAIN!
SORRY. I WANTED TO MAKE YOU HAPPY.
I LOVE IT! I'M SORRY!
Hmm.
THANK YOU FOR CLEANING! IT WASN'T NECESSARY.
NOT NECESSARY?? HAAA!!! THE APARTMENT WAS DIRTY!
YOU'RE A BAD HOUSEWIFE.
YOU'RE RIGHT! I HAVE ABSOLUTELY NO HOUSEWIFE AMBITIONS!
DO YOU KNOW HOW I DO IT?
I JUST OVERLOOK THE DIRT!
Pshhhh!
UNTIL IT BECOMES UNBEARABLE.

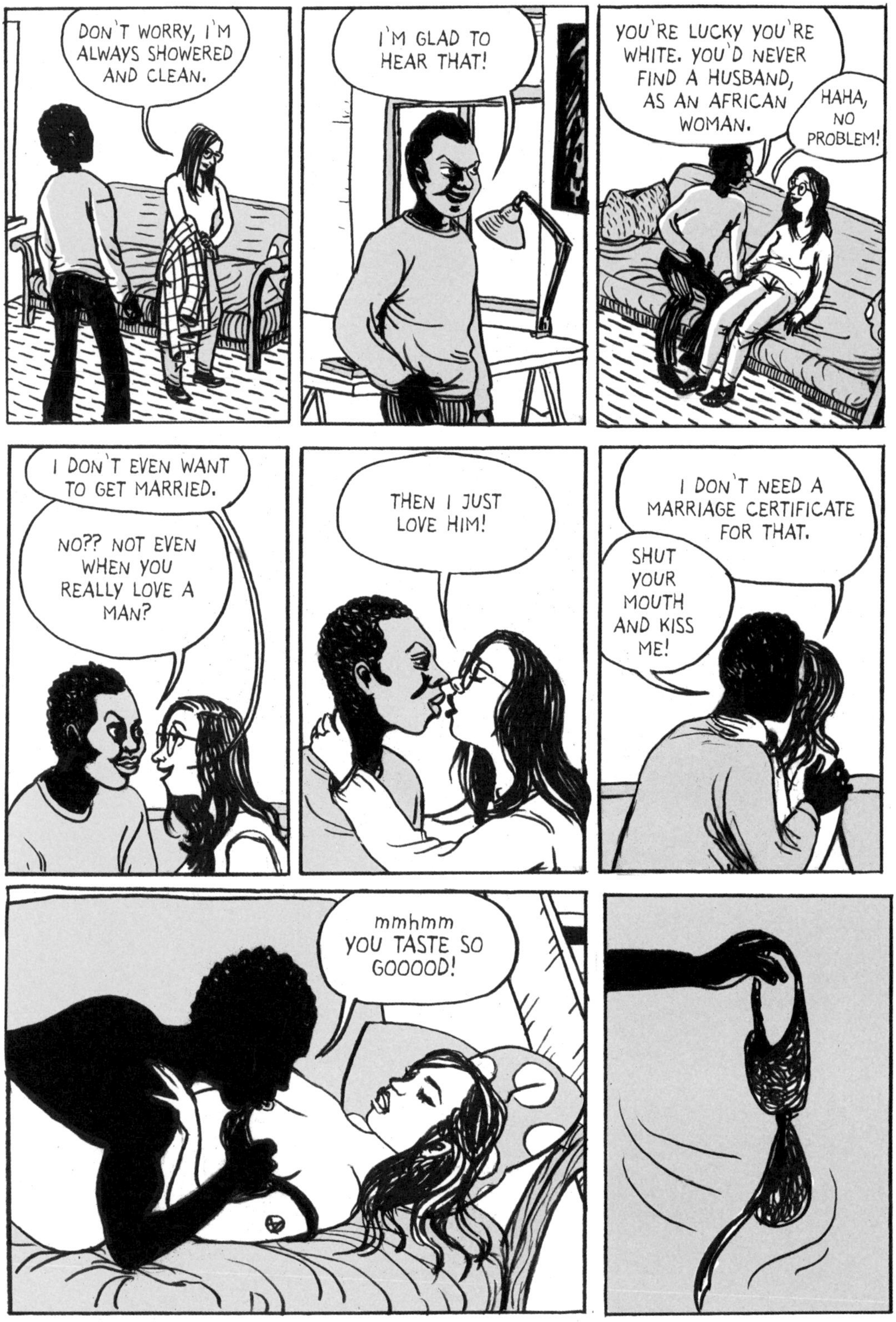
DON'T WORRY, I'M ALWAYS SHOWERED AND CLEAN.
I'M GLAD TO HEAR THAT!
YOU'RE LUCKY YOU'RE WHITE. YOU'D NEVER FIND A HUSBAND, AS AN AFRICAN WOMAN.
HAHA, NO PROBLEM!
I DON'T EVEN WANT TO GET MARRIED.
NO?? NOT EVEN WHEN YOU REALLY LOVE A MAN?
THEN I JUST LOVE HIM!
I DON'T NEED A MARRIAGE CERTIFICATE FOR THAT.
SHUT YOUR MOUTH AND KISS ME!
mmhmm YOU TASTE SO GOOOOD!

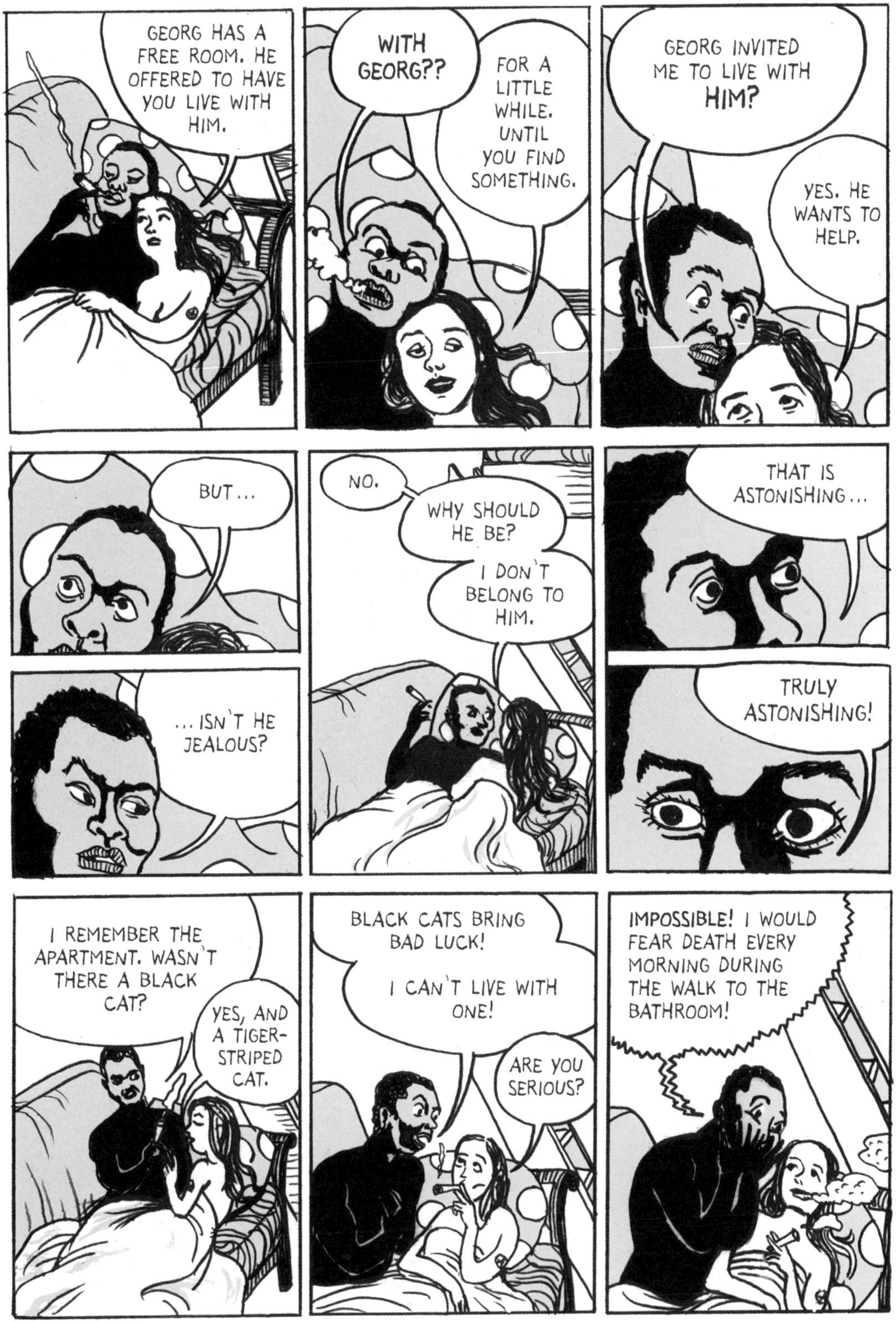
GEORG HAS A FREE ROOM. HE OFFERED TO HAVE YOU LIVE WITH HIM.
WITH GEORG??
FOR A LITTLE WHILE. UNTIL YOU FIND SOMETHING.
GEORG INVITED ME TO LIVE WITH HIM?
YES. HE WANTS TO HELP.
BUT...
...ISN'T HE JEALOUS?
NO.
WHY SHOULD HE BE?
I DON'T BELONG TO HIM.
THAT IS ASTONISHING...
TRULY ASTONISHING!
I REMEMBER THE APARTMENT. WASN'T THERE A BLACK CAT?
YES, AND A TIGER-STRIPED CAT.
BLACK CATS BRING BAD LUCK!
I CAN'T LIVE WITH ONE!
ARE YOU SERIOUS?
IMPOSSIBLE! I WOULD FEAR DEATH EVERY MORNING DURING THE WALK TO THE BATHROOM!

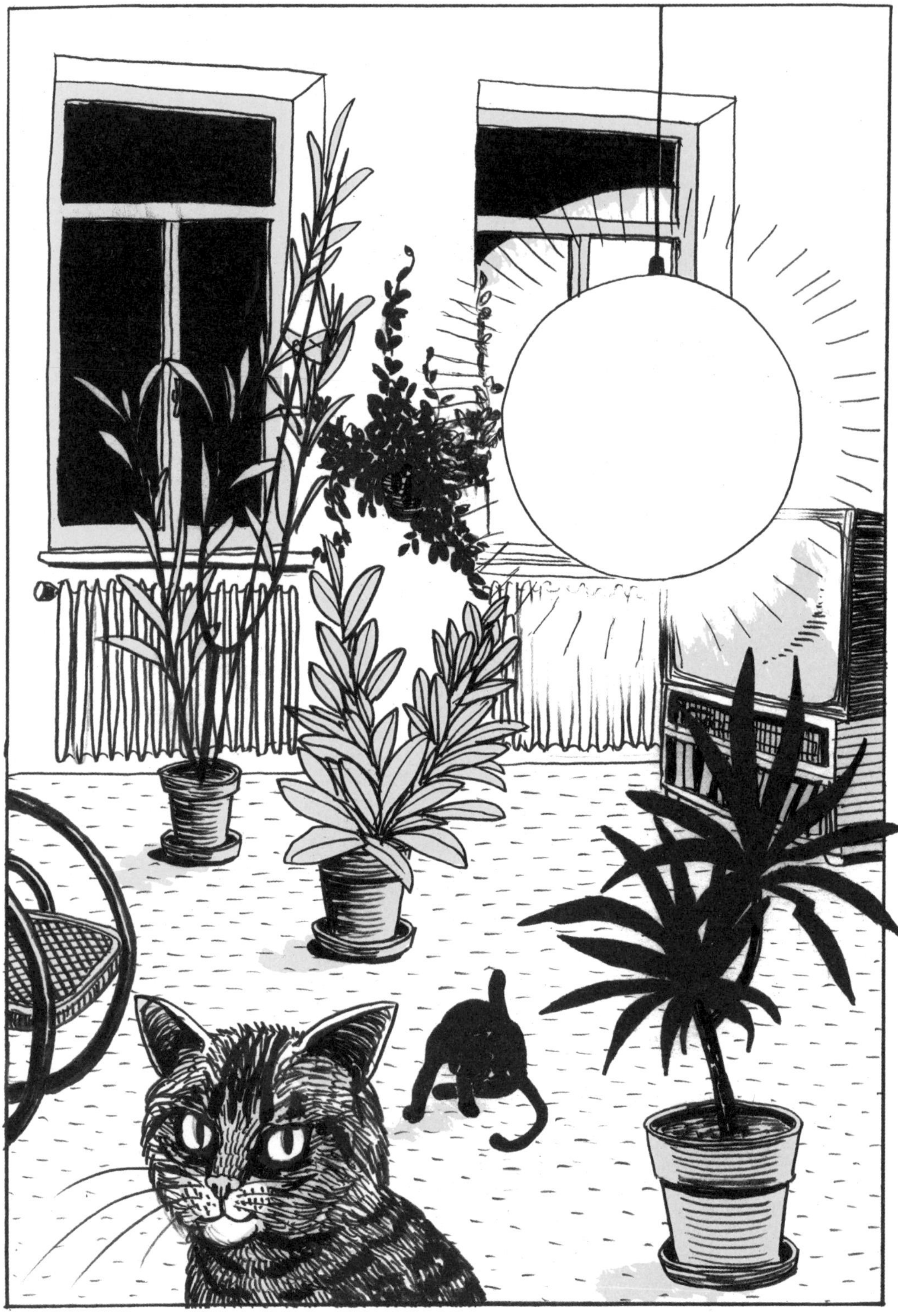

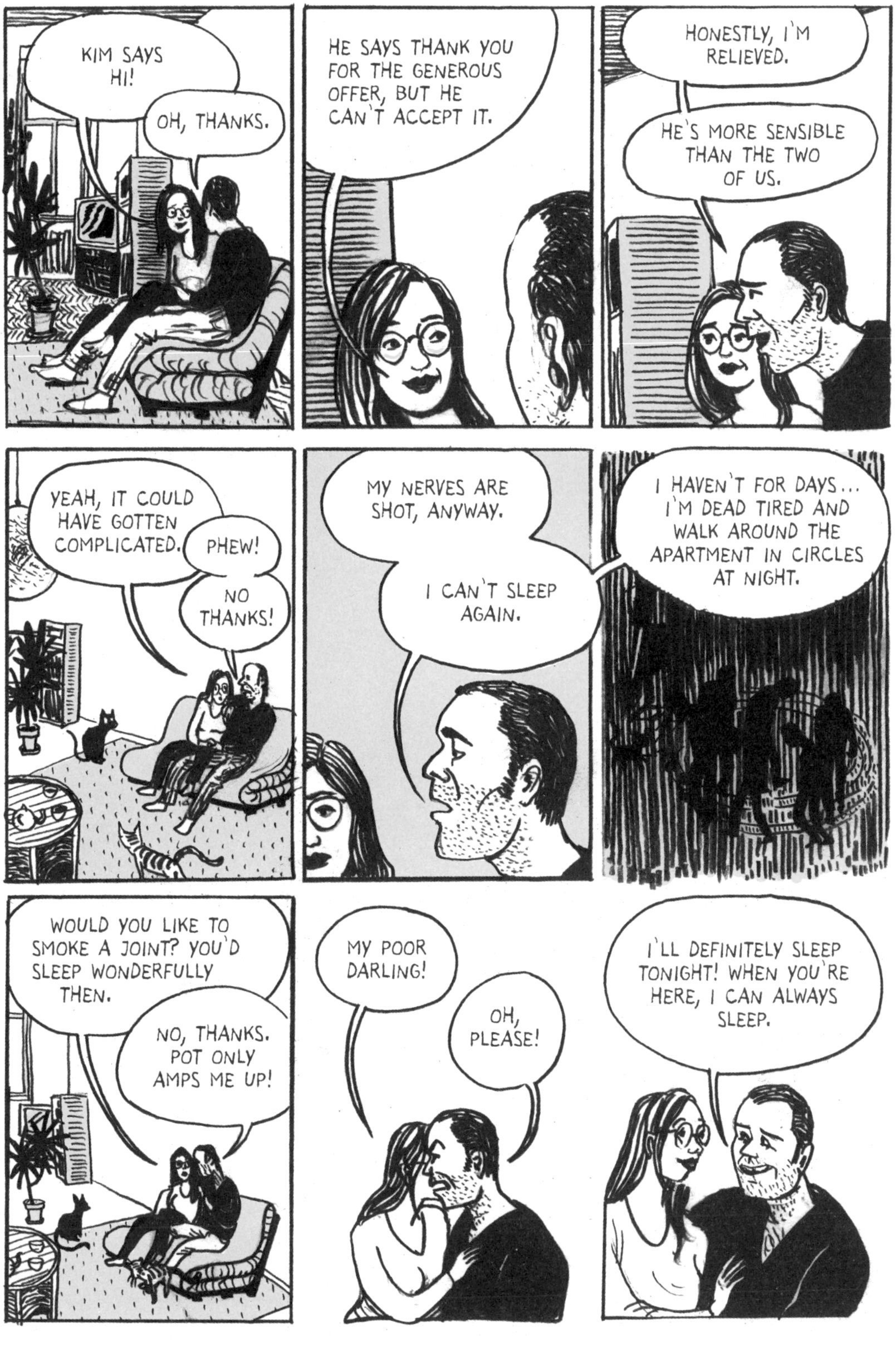
KIM SAYS HI!
OH, THANKS.
HE SAYS THANK YOU FOR THE GENEROUS OFFER, BUT HE CAN'T ACCEPT IT.
HONESTLY, I'M RELIEVED.
HE'S MORE SENSIBLE THAN THE TWO OF US.
YEAH, IT COULD HAVE GOTTEN COMPLICATED.
PHEW!
NO THANKS!
MY NERVES ARE SHOT, ANYWAY.
I CAN'T SLEEP AGAIN.
I HAVEN'T FOR DAYS... I'M DEAD TIRED AND WALK AROUND THE APARTMENT IN CIRCLES AT NIGHT.
WOULD YOU LIKE TO SMOKE A JOINT? YOU'D SLEEP WONDERFULLY THEN.
NO, THANKS. POT ONLY AMPS ME UP!
MY POOR DARLING!
OH, PLEASE!
I'LL DEFINITELY SLEEP TONIGHT! WHEN YOU'RE HERE, I CAN ALWAYS SLEEP.

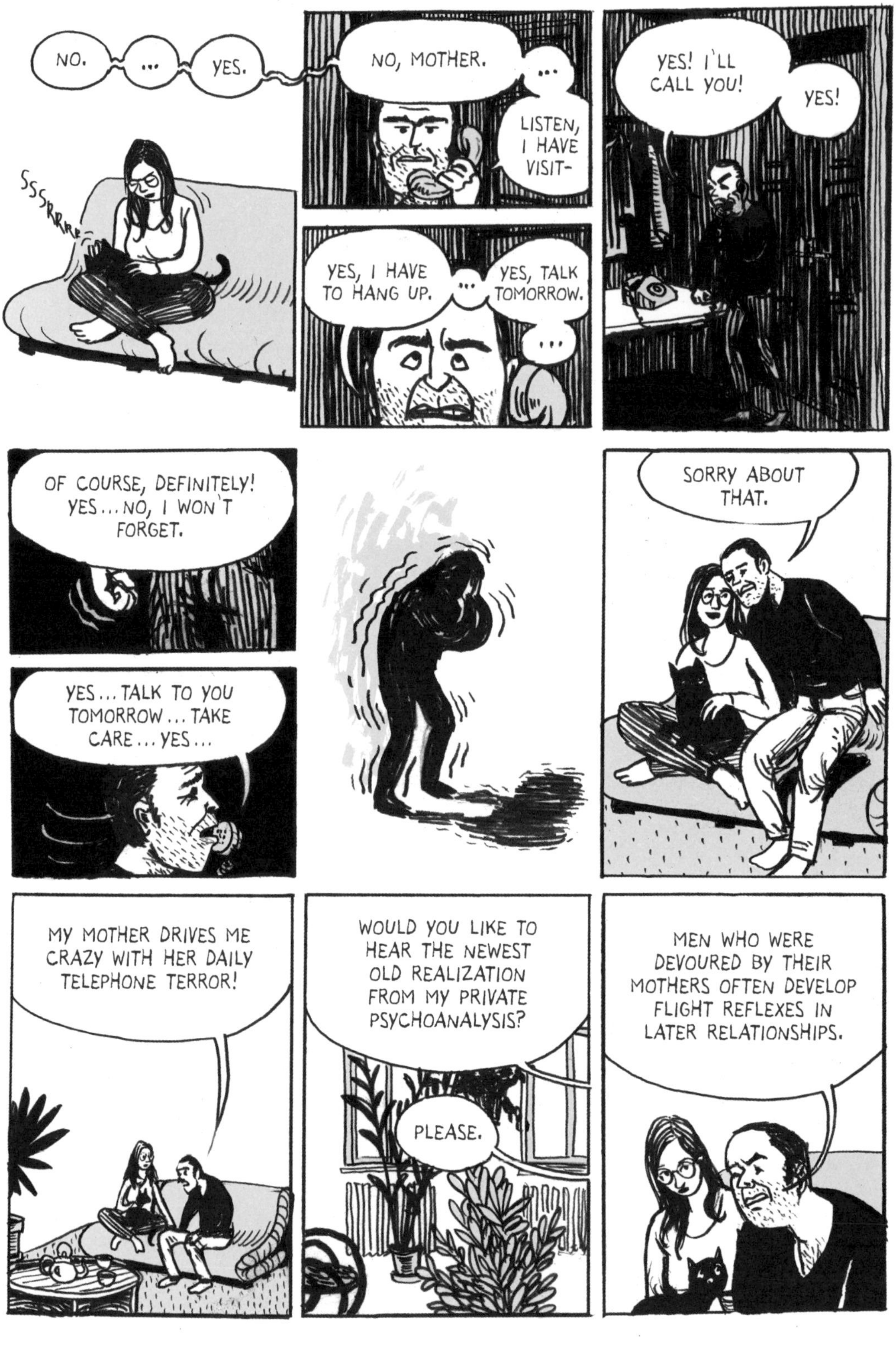
NO.
...
YES.
SSSRRRR
NO, MOTHER.
...
LISTEN, I HAVE VISIT-
YES, I HAVE TO HANG UP.
...
YES, TALK TOMORROW.
...
YES! I'LL CALL YOU!
YES!
OF COURSE, DEFINITELY! YES... NO, I WON'T FORGET.
YES... TALK TO YOU TOMORROW... TAKE CARE... YES...
SORRY ABOUT THAT.
MY MOTHER DRIVES ME CRAZY WITH HER DAILY TELEPHONE TERROR!
WOULD YOU LIKE TO HEAR THE NEWEST OLD REALIZATION FROM MY PRIVATE PSYCHOANALYSIS?
PLEASE.
MEN WHO WERE DEVOURED BY THEIR MOTHERS OFTEN DEVELOP FLIGHT REFLEXES IN LATER RELATIONSHIPS.

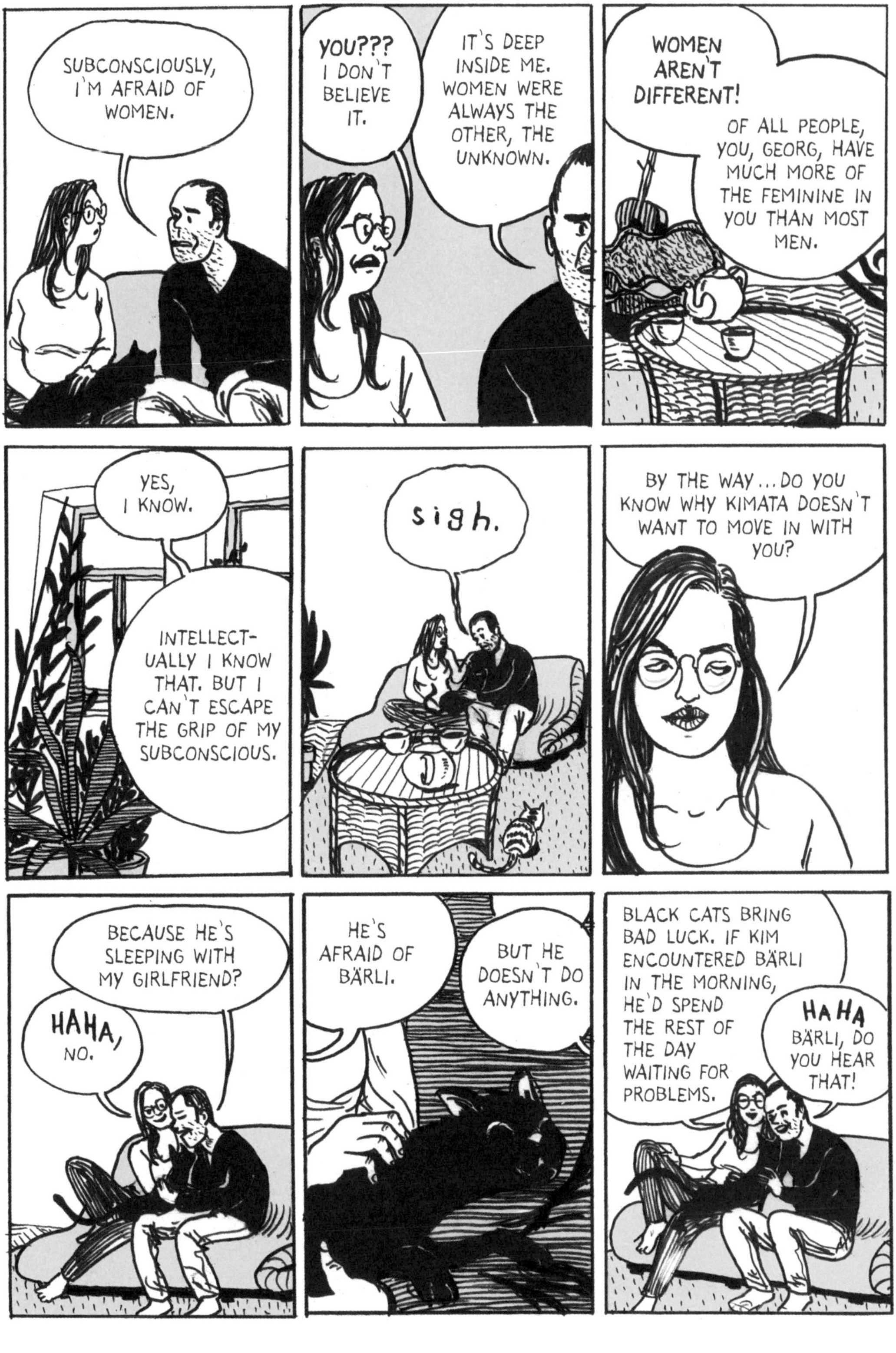
SUBCONSCIOUSLY, I'M AFRAID OF WOMEN.
YOU??? I DON'T BELIEVE IT.
IT'S DEEP INSIDE ME. WOMEN WERE ALWAYS THE OTHER, THE UNKNOWN.
WOMEN AREN'T DIFFERENT!
OF ALL PEOPLE, YOU, GEORG, HAVE MUCH MORE OF THE FEMININE IN YOU THAN MOST MEN.
YES, I KNOW.
INTELLECTUALLY I KNOW THAT. BUT I CAN'T ESCAPE THE GRIP OF MY SUBCONSCIOUS.
sigh.
BY THE WAY... DO YOU KNOW WHY KIMATA DOESN'T WANT TO MOVE IN WITH YOU?
BECAUSE HE'S SLEEPING WITH MY GIRLFRIEND?
HAHA, NO.
HE'S AFRAID OF BÄRLI.
BUT HE DOESN'T DO ANYTHING.
BLACK CATS BRING BAD LUCK. IF KIM ENCOUNTERED BÄRLI IN THE MORNING, HE'D SPEND THE REST OF THE DAY WAITING FOR PROBLEMS.
HAHA BÄRLI, DO YOU HEAR THAT!

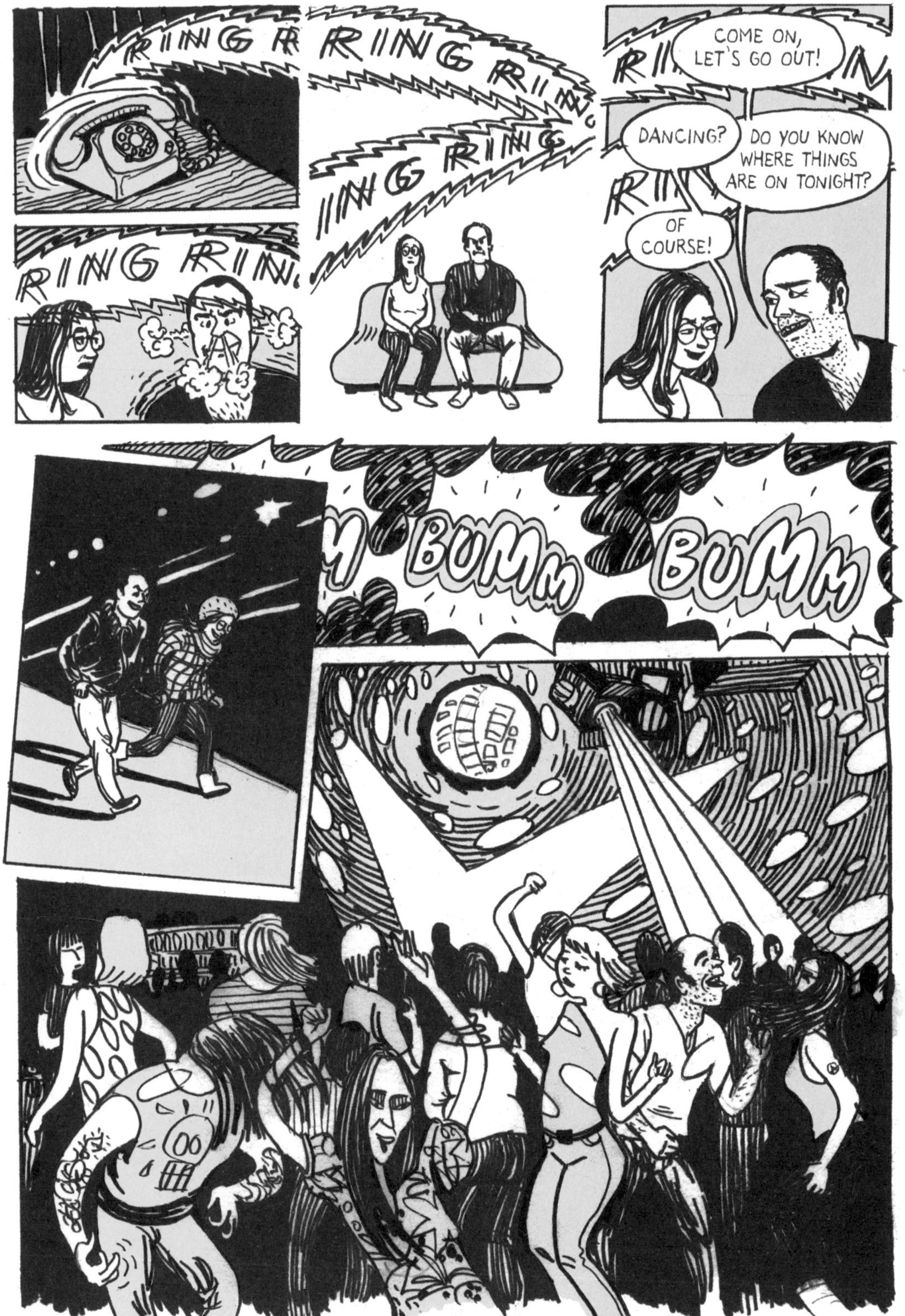
RING RING RING RIN
RING RIN
ING RING
RING RIN
COME ON, LET'S GO OUT!
DANCING?
DO YOU KNOW WHERE THINGS ARE ON TONIGHT?
OF COURSE!
BUMM BUMM

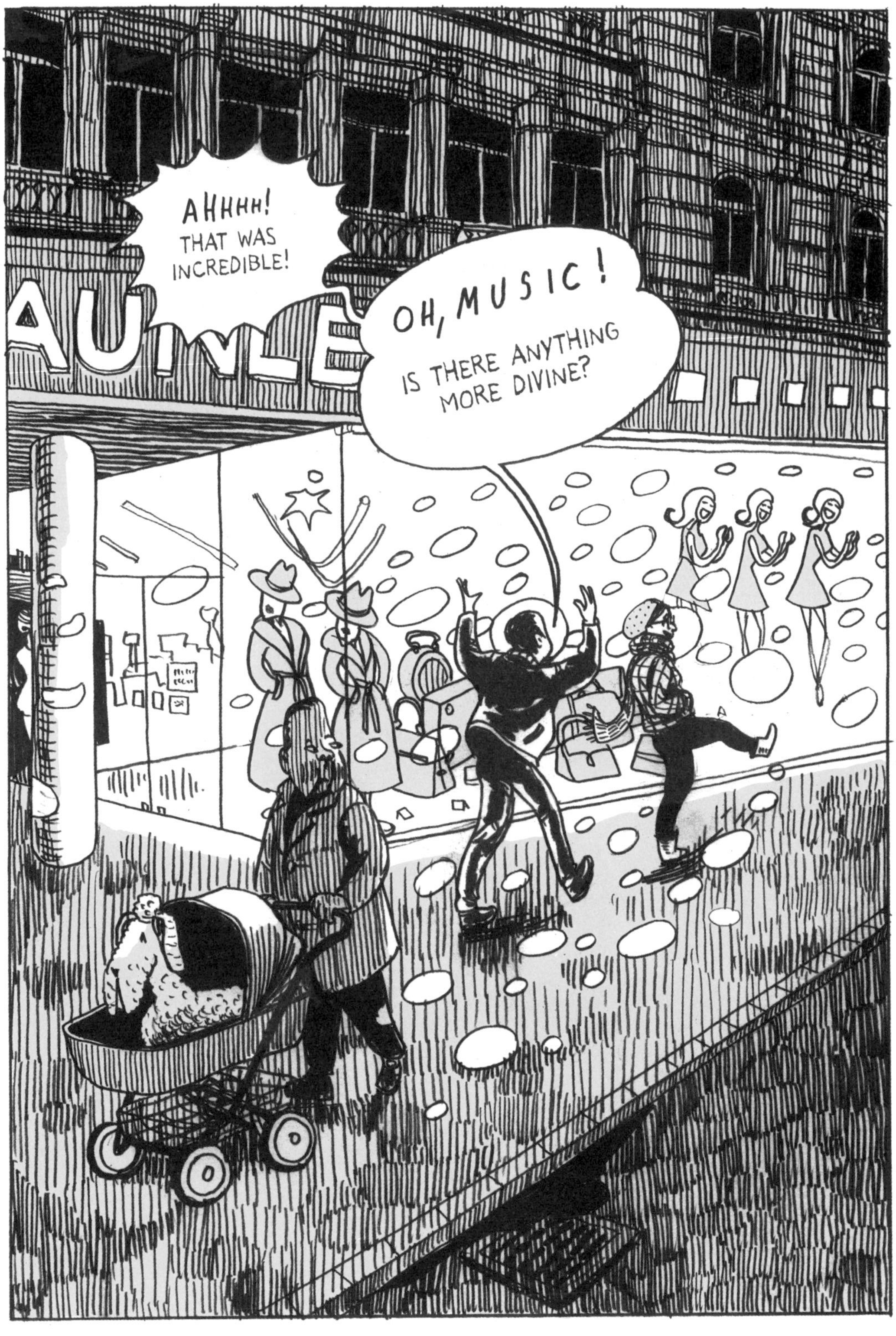
AHHHH! THAT WAS INCREDIBLE!
OH, MUSIC! IS THERE ANYTHING MORE DIVINE?

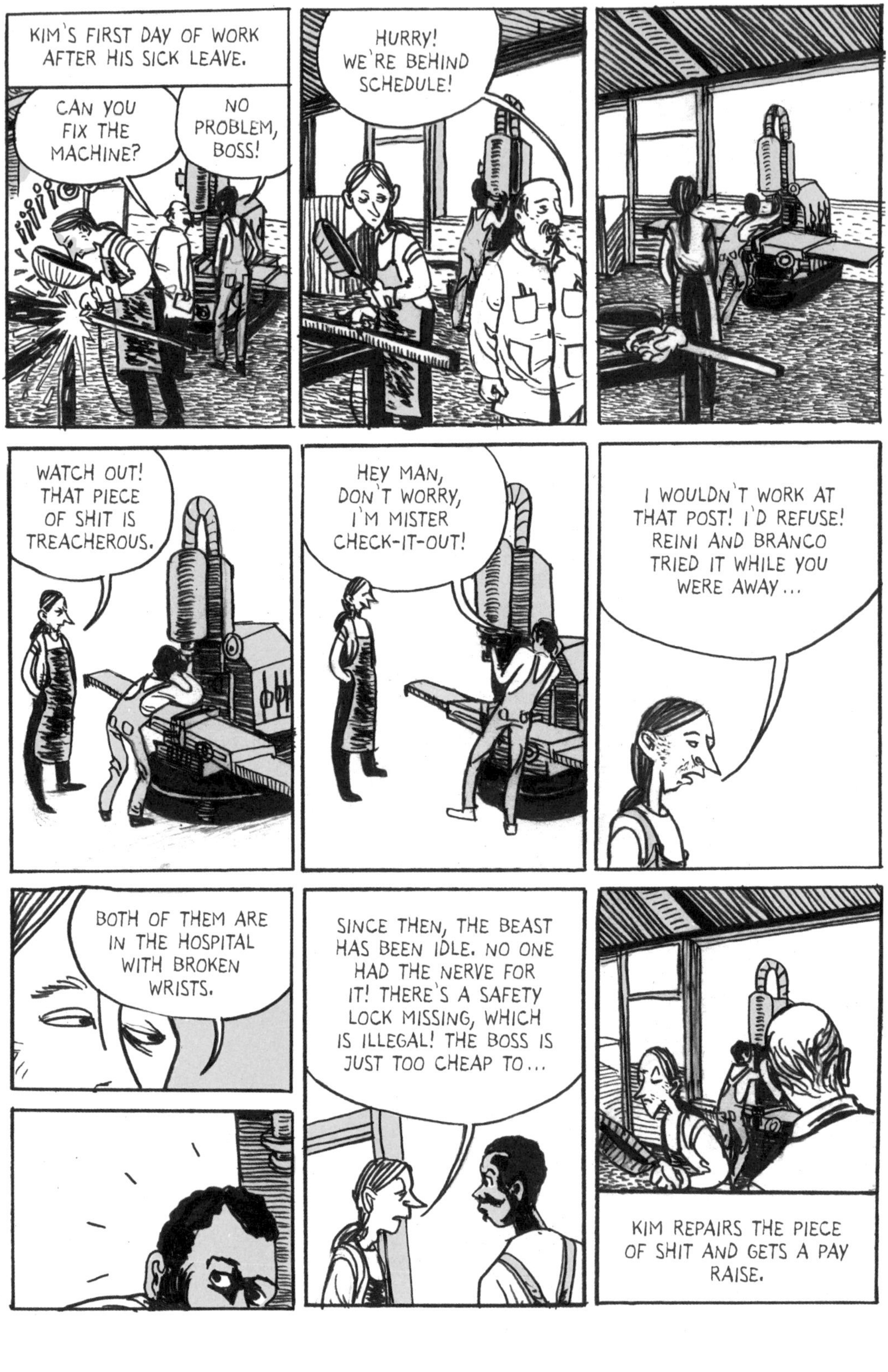

KIM'S FIRST DAY OF WORK AFTER HIS SICK LEAVE.
CAN YOU FIX THE MACHINE?
NO PROBLEM, BOSS!
HURRY! WE'RE BEHIND SCHEDULE!
WATCH OUT! THAT PIECE OF SHIT IS TREACHEROUS.
HEY MAN, DON'T WORRY, I'M MISTER CHECK-IT-OUT!
I WOULDN'T WORK AT THAT POST! I'D REFUSE! REINI AND BRANCO TRIED IT WHILE YOU WERE AWAY...
BOTH OF THEM ARE IN THE HOSPITAL WITH BROKEN WRISTS.
SINCE THEN, THE BEAST HAS BEEN IDLE. NO ONE HAD THE NERVE FOR IT! THERE'S A SAFETY LOCK MISSING, WHICH IS ILLEGAL! THE BOSS IS JUST TOO CHEAP TO...
KIM REPAIRS THE PIECE OF SHIT AND GETS A PAY RAISE.

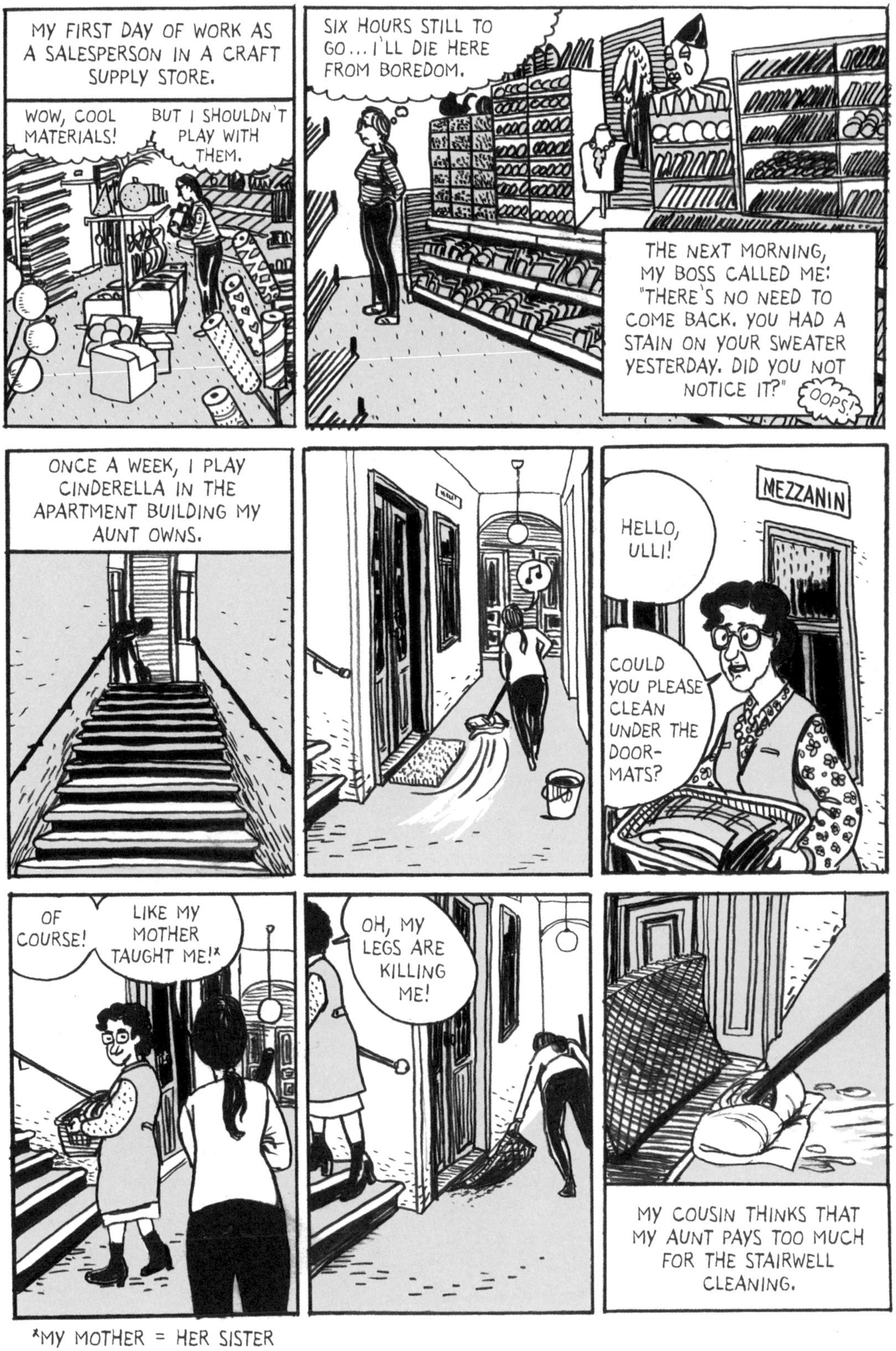
MY FIRST DAY OF WORK AS A SALESPERSON IN A CRAFT SUPPLY STORE.
WOW, COOL MATERIALS!
BUT I SHOULDN'T PLAY WITH THEM.
SIX HOURS STILL TO GO... I'LL DIE HERE FROM BOREDOM.
THE NEXT MORNING, MY BOSS CALLED ME: "THERE'S NO NEED TO COME BACK. YOU HAD A STAIN ON YOUR SWEATER YESTERDAY. DID YOU NOT NOTICE IT?"
OOPS!
ONCE A WEEK, I PLAY CINDERELLA IN THE APARTMENT BUILDING MY AUNT OWNS.
MEZZANIN
HELLO, ULLI!
COULD YOU PLEASE CLEAN UNDER THE DOOR-MATS?
OF COURSE!
LIKE MY MOTHER TAUGHT ME!*
OH, MY LEGS ARE KILLING ME!
MY COUSIN THINKS THAT MY AUNT PAYS TOO MUCH FOR THE STAIRWELL CLEANING.
*MY MOTHER = HER SISTER

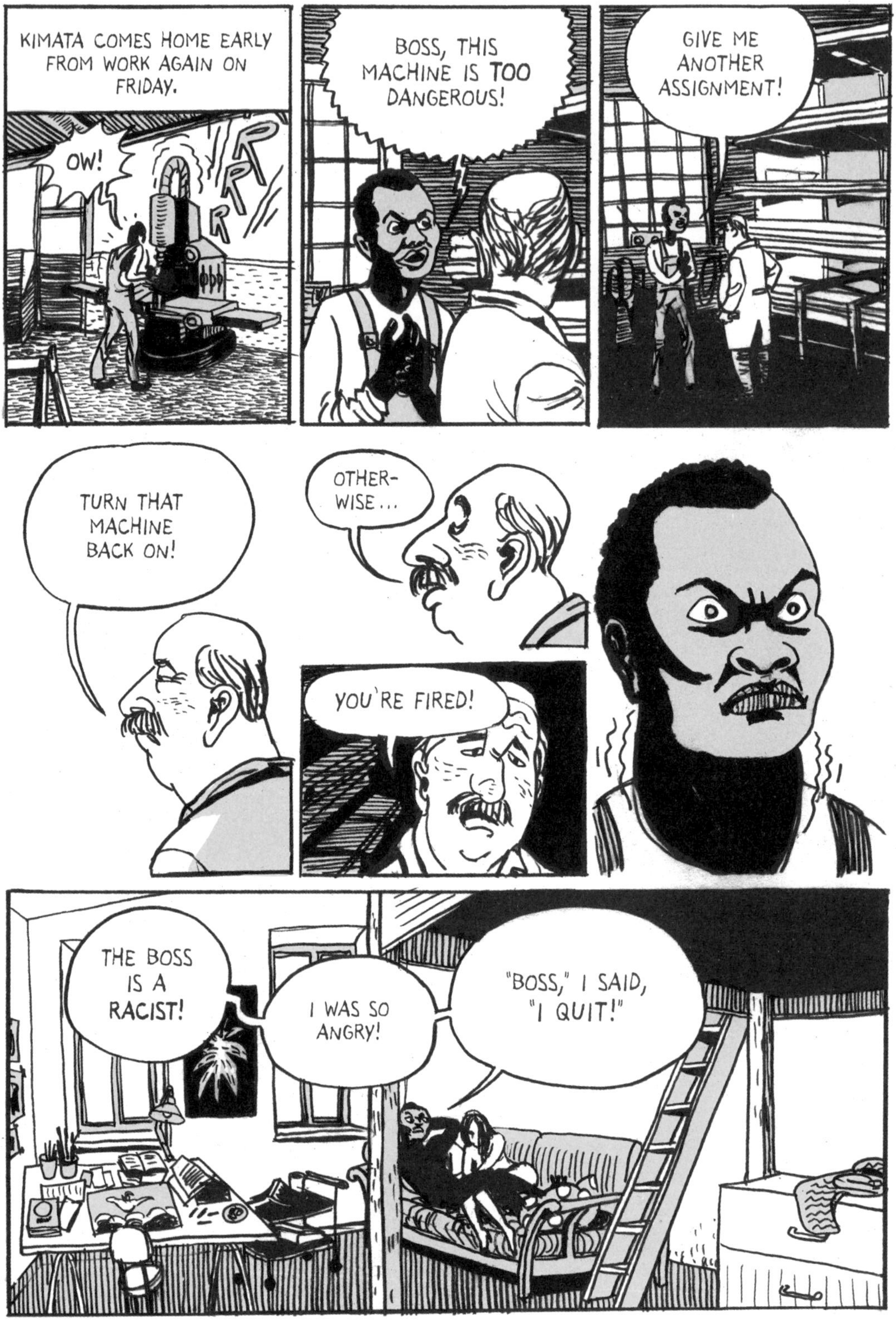
KIMATA COMES HOME EARLY FROM WORK AGAIN ON FRIDAY.
OW!
RRRR
BOSS, THIS MACHINE IS **TOO** DANGEROUS!
GIVE ME ANOTHER ASSIGNMENT!
TURN THAT MACHINE BACK ON!
OTHER-WISE...
YOU'RE FIRED!
THE BOSS IS A **RACIST**!
I WAS SO ANGRY!
"BOSS," I SAID, "I QUIT!"

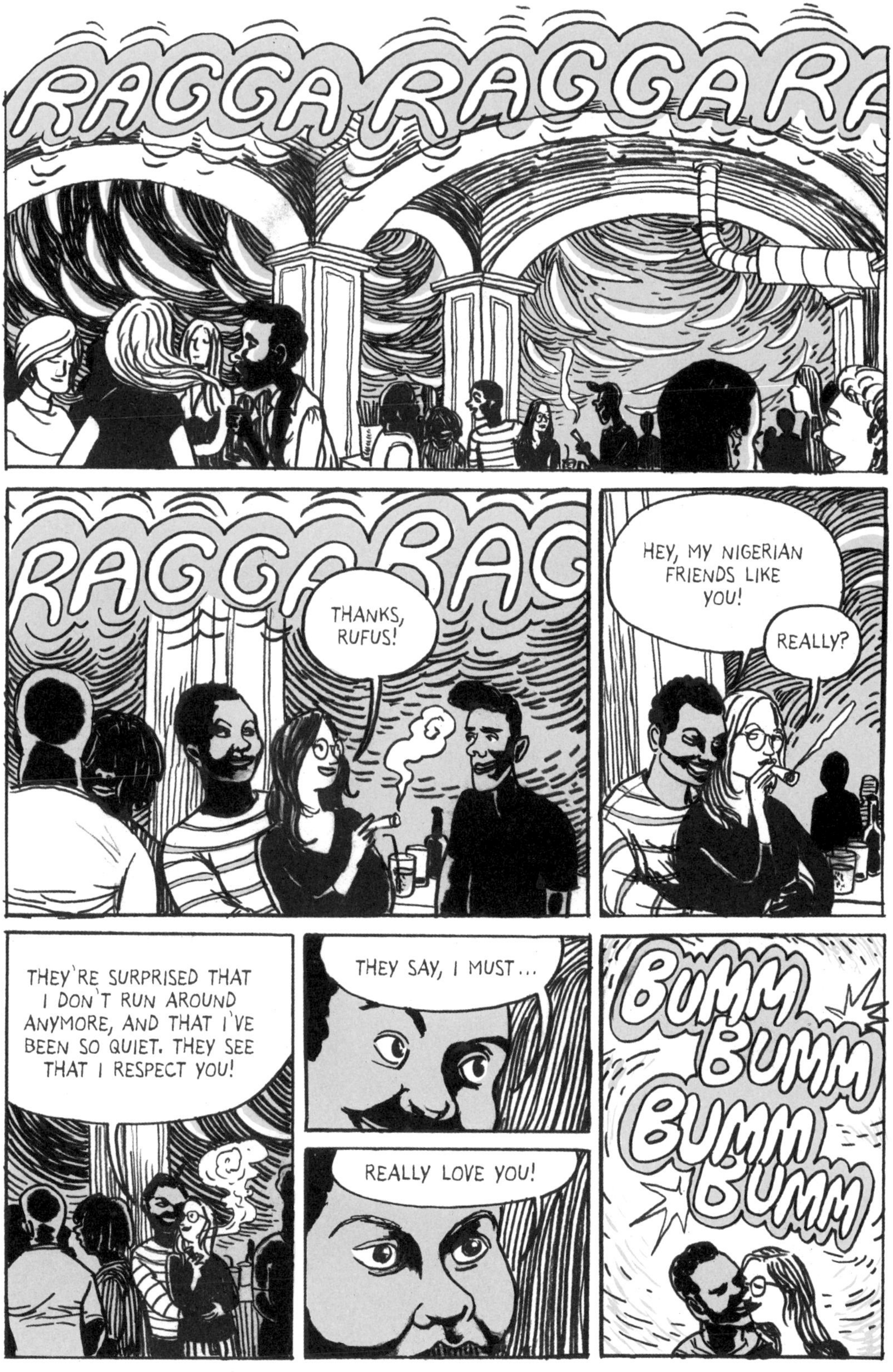
RAGGA RAGGA RA
RAGGA RAG
THANKS, RUFUS!
HEY, MY NIGERIAN FRIENDS LIKE YOU!
REALLY?
THEY'RE SURPRISED THAT I DON'T RUN AROUND ANYMORE, AND THAT I'VE BEEN SO QUIET. THEY SEE THAT I RESPECT YOU!
THEY SAY, I MUST...
REALLY LOVE YOU!
BUMM BUMM BUMM BUMM

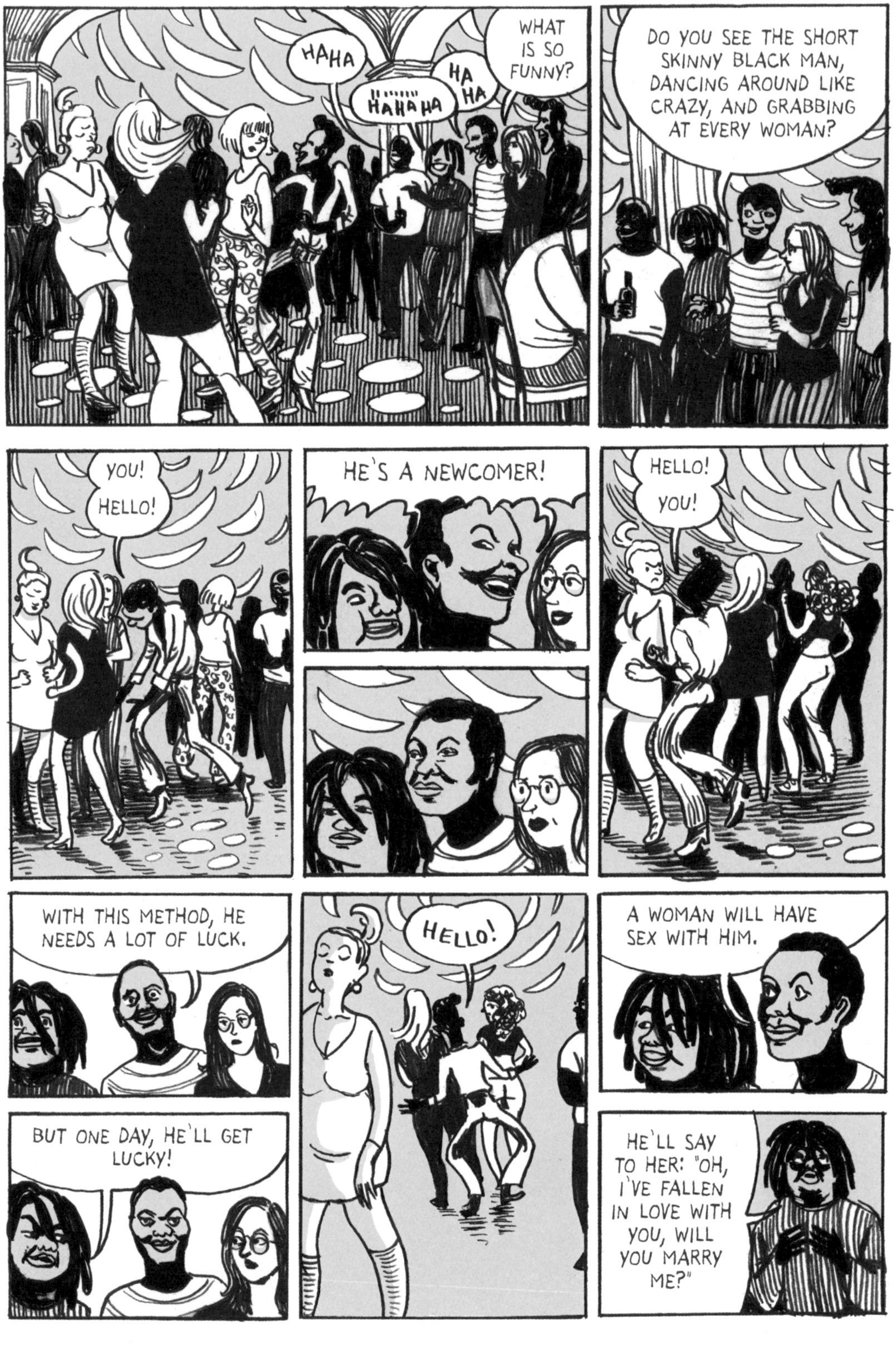
HAHA
HAHAHA
HA HA
WHAT IS SO FUNNY?
DO YOU SEE THE SHORT SKINNY BLACK MAN, DANCING AROUND LIKE CRAZY, AND GRABBING AT EVERY WOMAN?
YOU! HELLO!
HE'S A NEWCOMER!
HELLO! YOU!
WITH THIS METHOD, HE NEEDS A LOT OF LUCK.
BUT ONE DAY, HE'LL GET LUCKY!
HELLO!
A WOMAN WILL HAVE SEX WITH HIM.
HE'LL SAY TO HER: "OH, I'VE FALLEN IN LOVE WITH YOU, WILL YOU MARRY ME?"

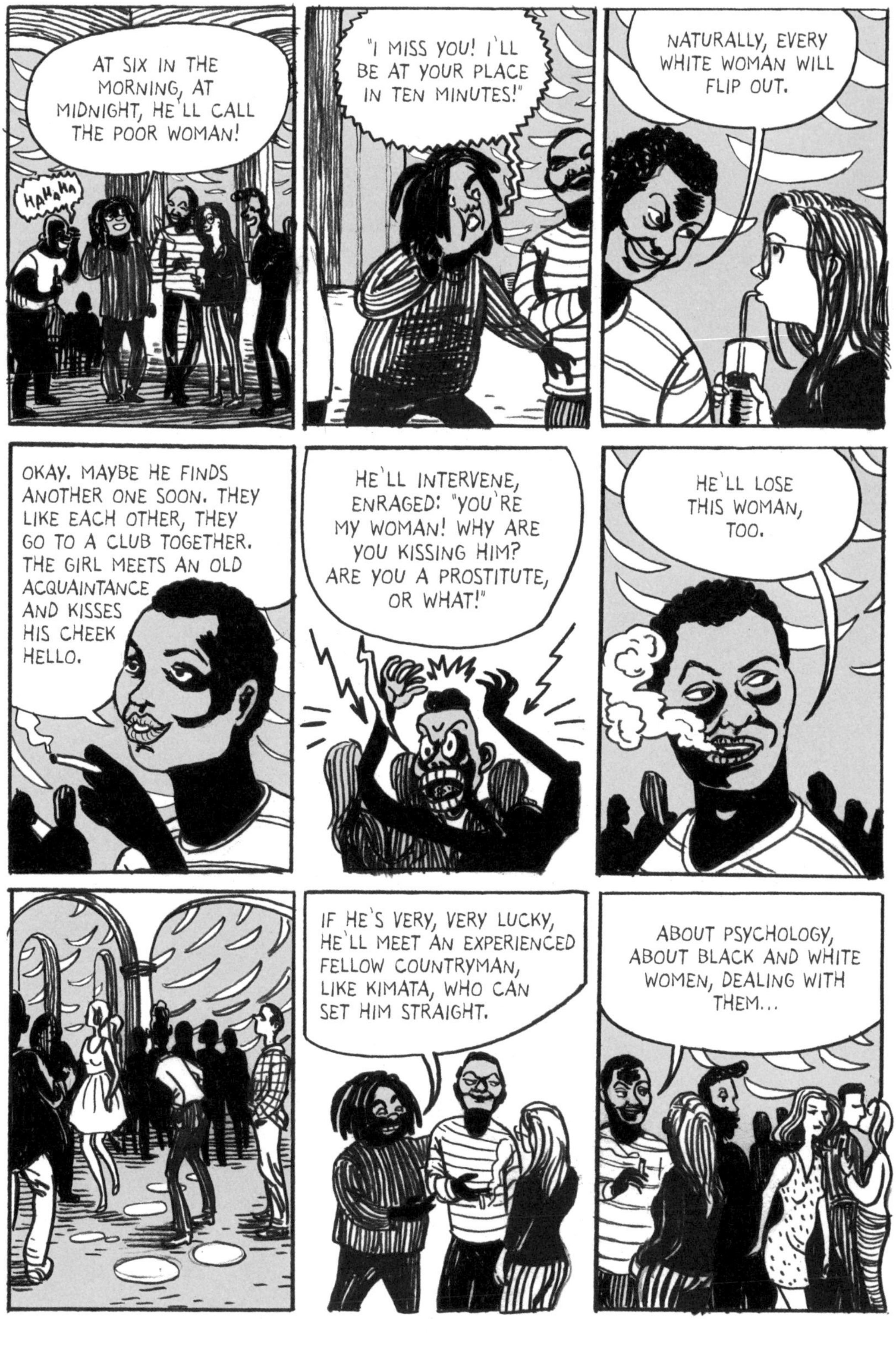
AT SIX IN THE MORNING, AT MIDNIGHT, HE'LL CALL THE POOR WOMAN!
HAHAHA
"I MISS YOU! I'LL BE AT YOUR PLACE IN TEN MINUTES!"
NATURALLY, EVERY WHITE WOMAN WILL FLIP OUT.
OKAY. MAYBE HE FINDS ANOTHER ONE SOON. THEY LIKE EACH OTHER, THEY GO TO A CLUB TOGETHER. THE GIRL MEETS AN OLD ACQUAINTANCE AND KISSES HIS CHEEK HELLO.
HE'LL INTERVENE, ENRAGED: "YOU'RE MY WOMAN! WHY ARE YOU KISSING HIM? ARE YOU A PROSTITUTE, OR WHAT!"
HE'LL LOSE THIS WOMAN, TOO.
IF HE'S VERY, VERY LUCKY, HE'LL MEET AN EXPERIENCED FELLOW COUNTRYMAN, LIKE KIMATA, WHO CAN SET HIM STRAIGHT.
ABOUT PSYCHOLOGY, ABOUT BLACK AND WHITE WOMEN, DEALING WITH THEM...

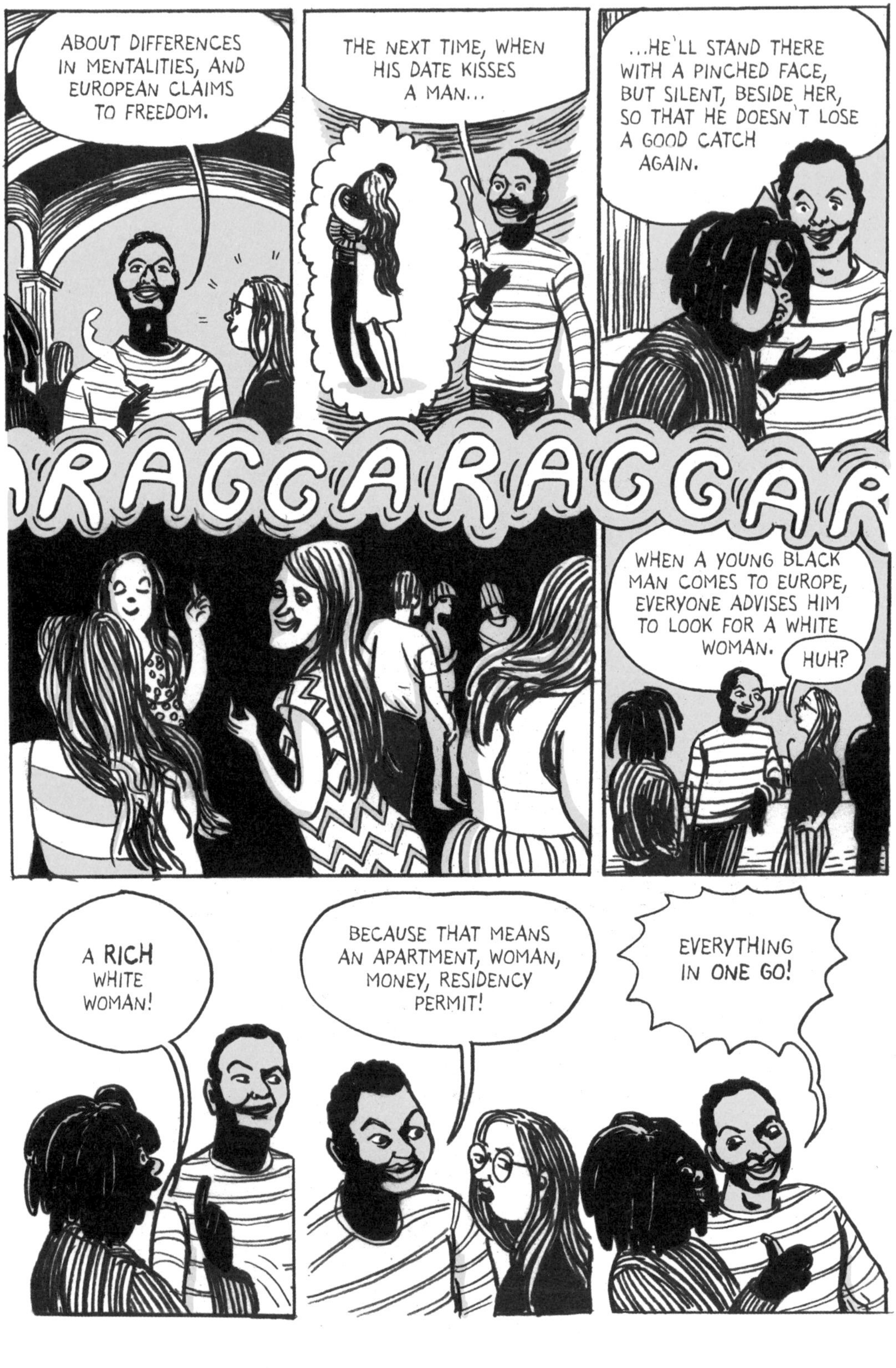
ABOUT DIFFERENCES IN MENTALITIES, AND EUROPEAN CLAIMS TO FREEDOM.
THE NEXT TIME, WHEN HIS DATE KISSES A MAN...
...HE'LL STAND THERE WITH A PINCHED FACE, BUT SILENT, BESIDE HER, SO THAT HE DOESN'T LOSE A GOOD CATCH AGAIN.
RAGGARAGGAR
WHEN A YOUNG BLACK MAN COMES TO EUROPE, EVERYONE ADVISES HIM TO LOOK FOR A WHITE WOMAN.
HUH?
A RICH WHITE WOMAN!
BECAUSE THAT MEANS AN APARTMENT, WOMAN, MONEY, RESIDENCY PERMIT!
EVERYTHING IN ONE GO!

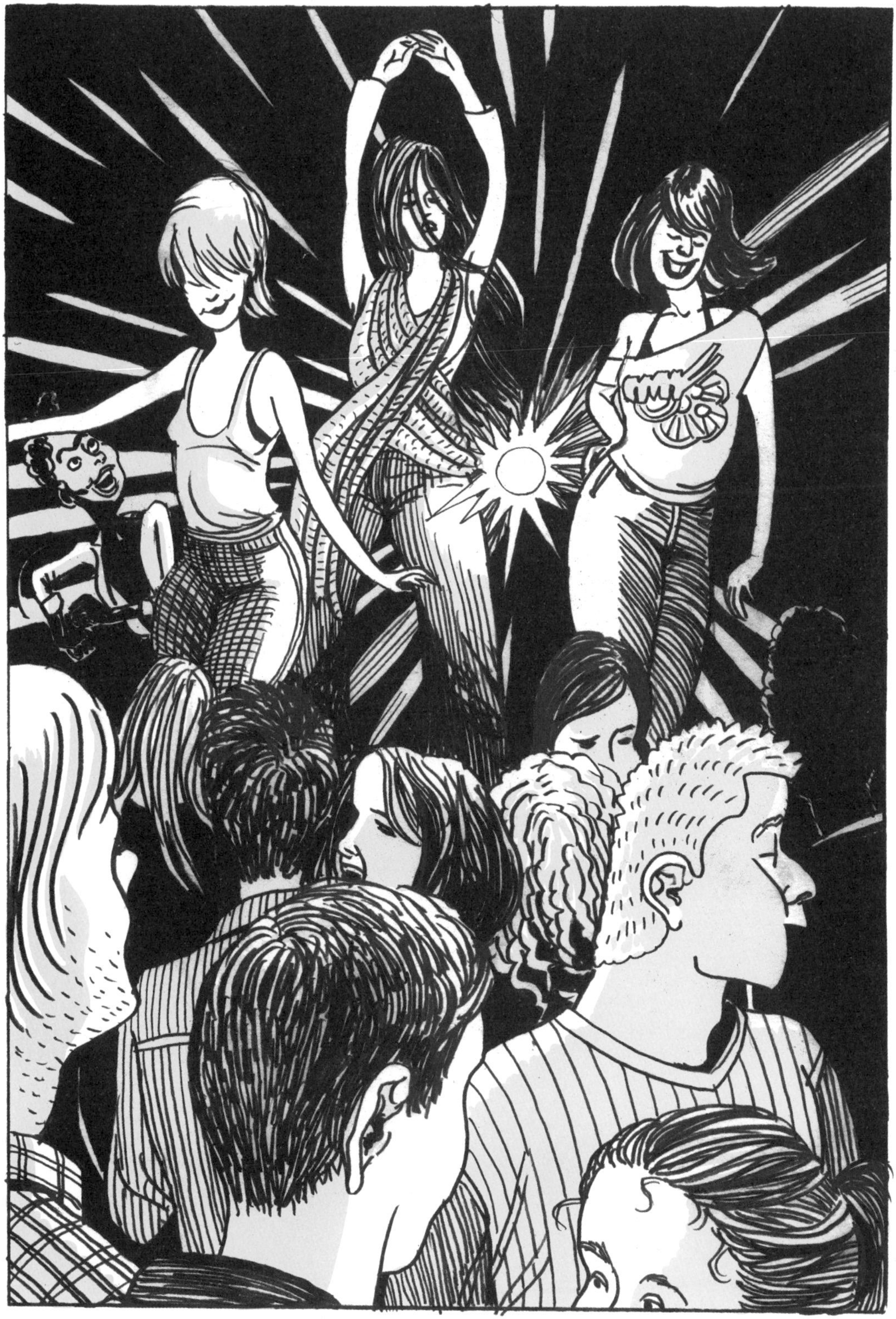

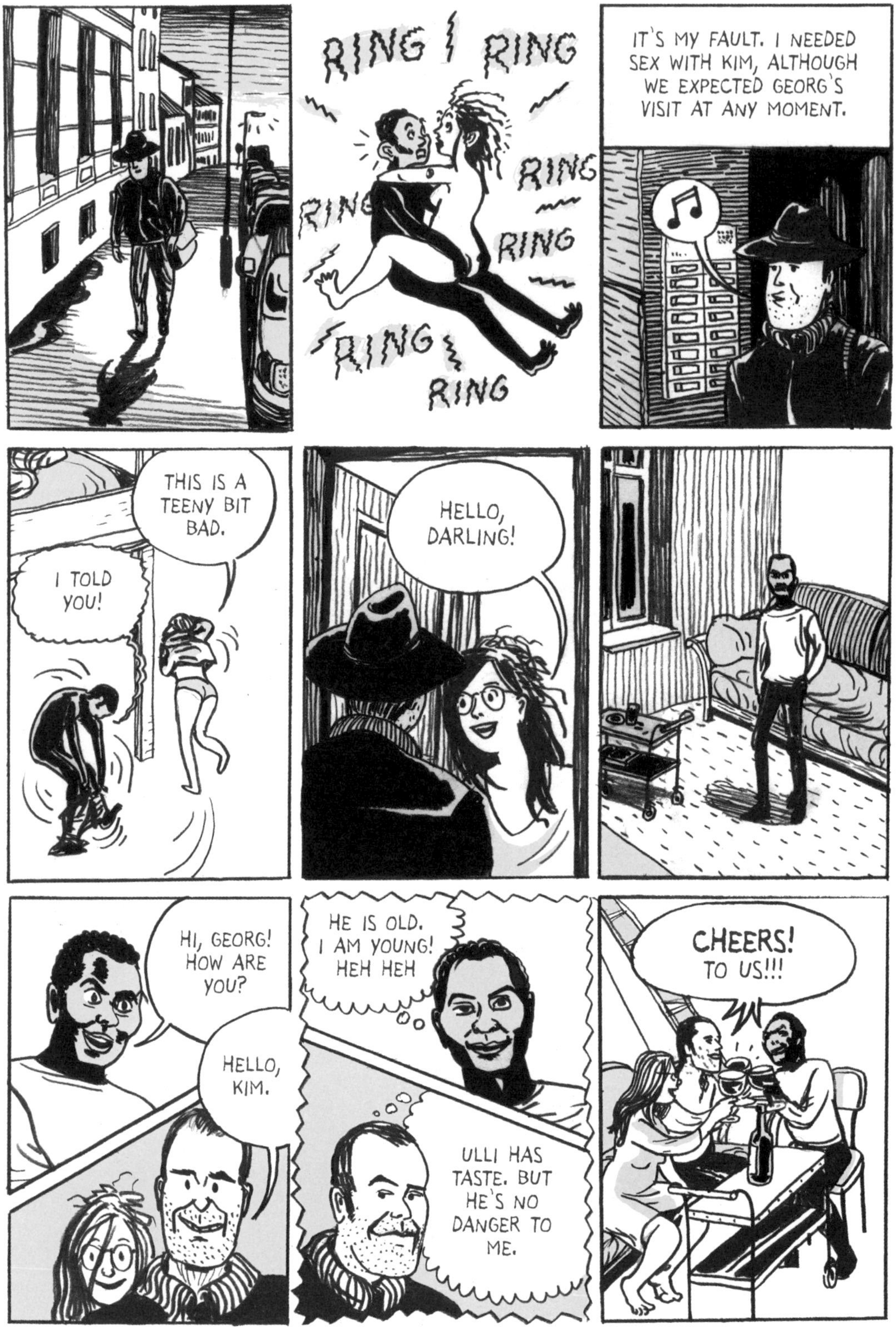
RING RING
RING
RING
RING
RING
RING
RING
IT'S MY FAULT. I NEEDED SEX WITH KIM, ALTHOUGH WE EXPECTED GEORG'S VISIT AT ANY MOMENT.
THIS IS A TEENY BIT BAD.
I TOLD YOU!
HELLO, DARLING!
HI, GEORG! HOW ARE YOU?
HELLO, KIM.
HE IS OLD. I AM YOUNG! HEH HEH
ULLI HAS TASTE. BUT HE'S NO DANGER TO ME.
CHEERS! TO US!!!

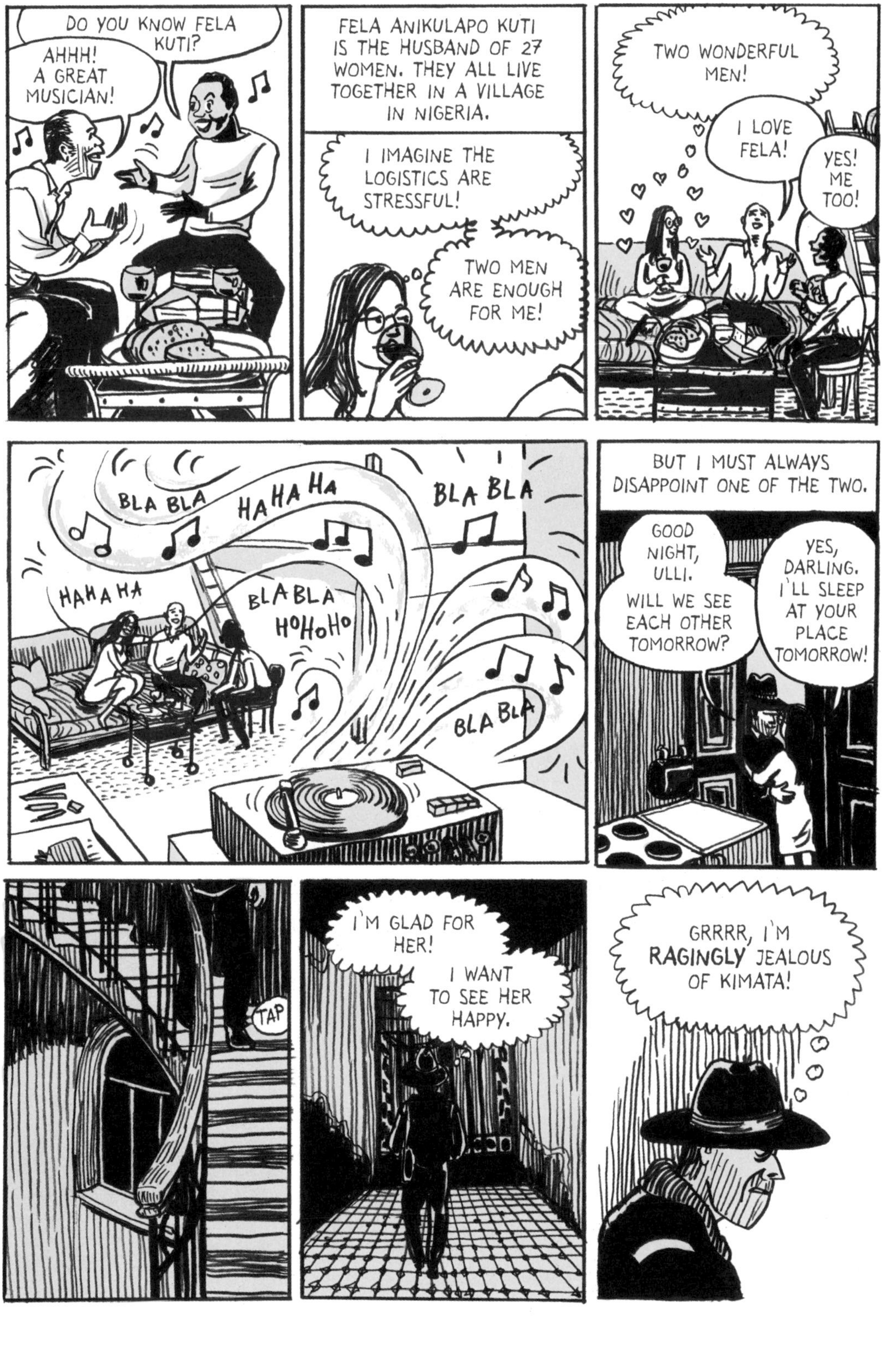
DO YOU KNOW FELA KUTI?
AHHH! A GREAT MUSICIAN!
FELA ANIKULAPO KUTI IS THE HUSBAND OF 27 WOMEN. THEY ALL LIVE TOGETHER IN A VILLAGE IN NIGERIA.
I IMAGINE THE LOGISTICS ARE STRESSFUL!
TWO MEN ARE ENOUGH FOR ME!
TWO WONDERFUL MEN!
I LOVE FELA!
YES! ME TOO!
BLA BLA
HAHAHA
BLA BLA
HAHAHA
BLABLA
HOHOHO
BLA BLA
BUT I MUST ALWAYS DISAPPOINT ONE OF THE TWO.
GOOD NIGHT, ULLI. WILL WE SEE EACH OTHER TOMORROW?
YES, DARLING. I'LL SLEEP AT YOUR PLACE TOMORROW!
TAP
I'M GLAD FOR HER!
I WANT TO SEE HER HAPPY.
GRRRR, I'M RAGINGLY JEALOUS OF KIMATA!

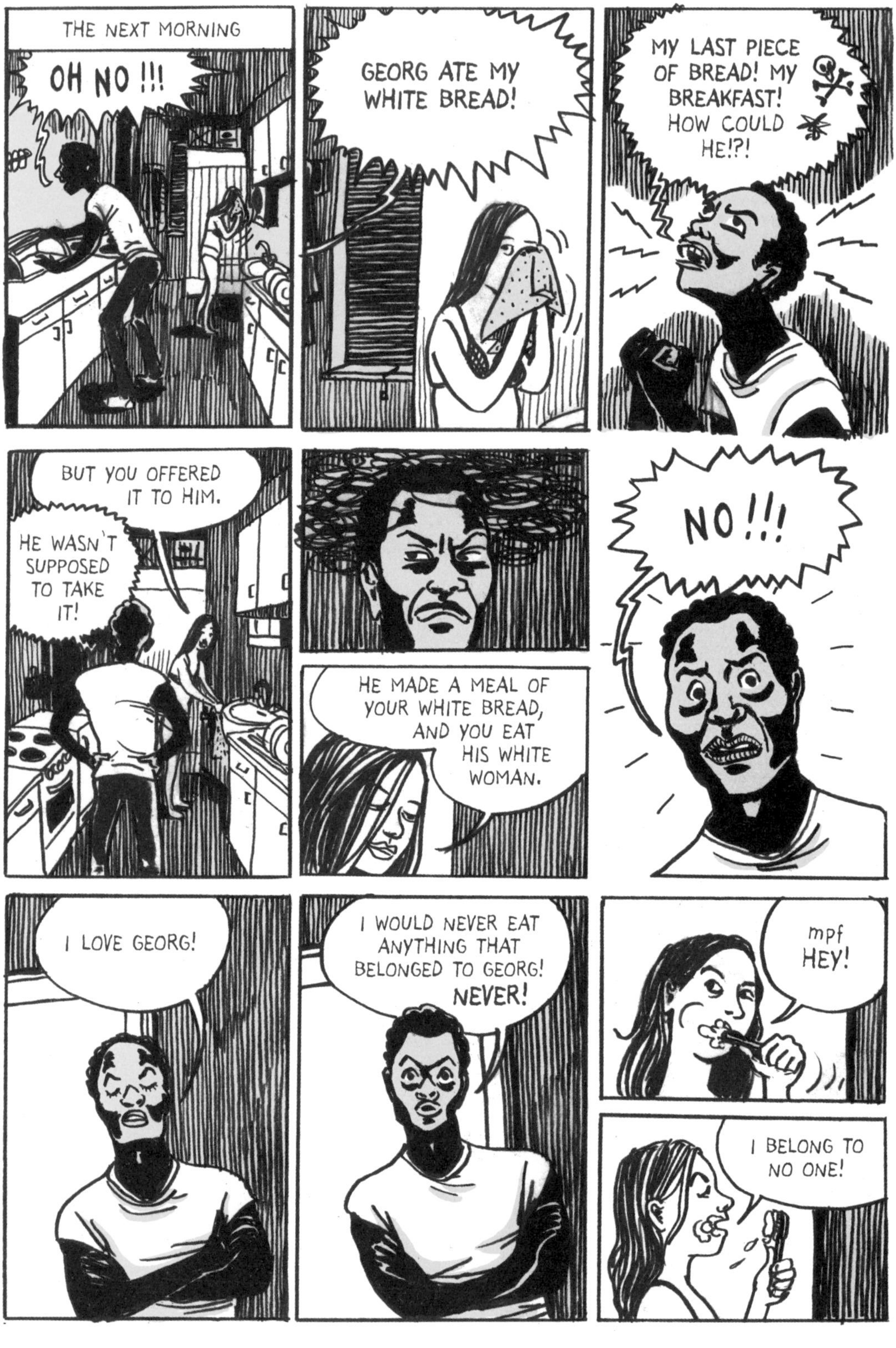
THE NEXT MORNING
OH NO !!!
GEORG ATE MY WHITE BREAD!
MY LAST PIECE OF BREAD! MY BREAKFAST! HOW COULD HE!?!
BUT YOU OFFERED IT TO HIM.
HE WASN'T SUPPOSED TO TAKE IT!
HE MADE A MEAL OF YOUR WHITE BREAD, AND YOU EAT HIS WHITE WOMAN.
NO !!!
I LOVE GEORG!
I WOULD NEVER EAT ANYTHING THAT BELONGED TO GEORG! NEVER!
mpf HEY!
I BELONG TO NO ONE!

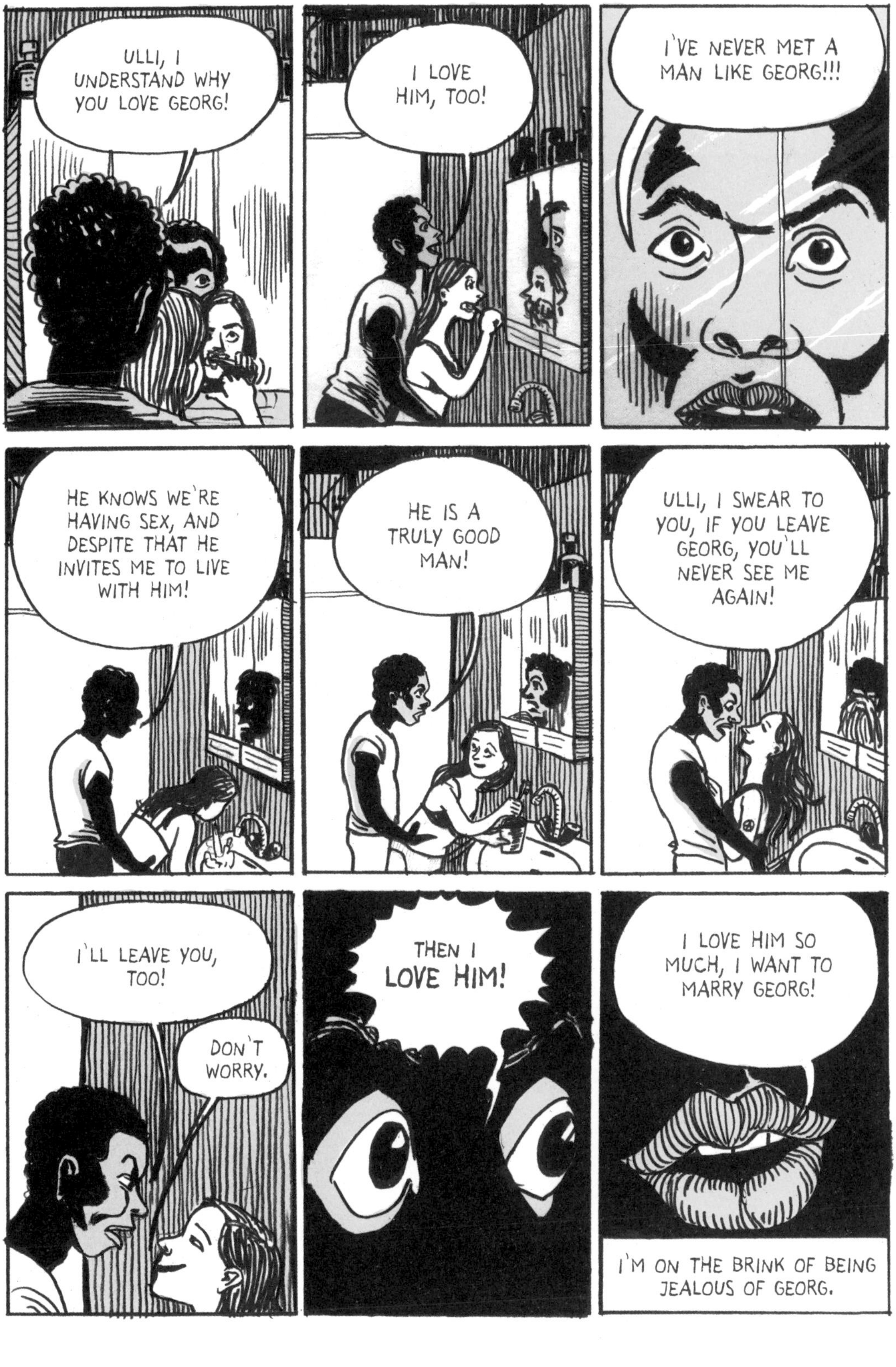
ULLI, I UNDERSTAND WHY YOU LOVE GEORG!
I LOVE HIM, TOO!
I'VE NEVER MET A MAN LIKE GEORG!!!
HE KNOWS WE'RE HAVING SEX, AND DESPITE THAT HE INVITES ME TO LIVE WITH HIM!
HE IS A TRULY GOOD MAN!
ULLI, I SWEAR TO YOU, IF YOU LEAVE GEORG, YOU'LL NEVER SEE ME AGAIN!
I'LL LEAVE YOU, TOO!
DON'T WORRY.
THEN I LOVE HIM!
I LOVE HIM SO MUCH, I WANT TO MARRY GEORG!
I'M ON THE BRINK OF BEING JEALOUS OF GEORG.

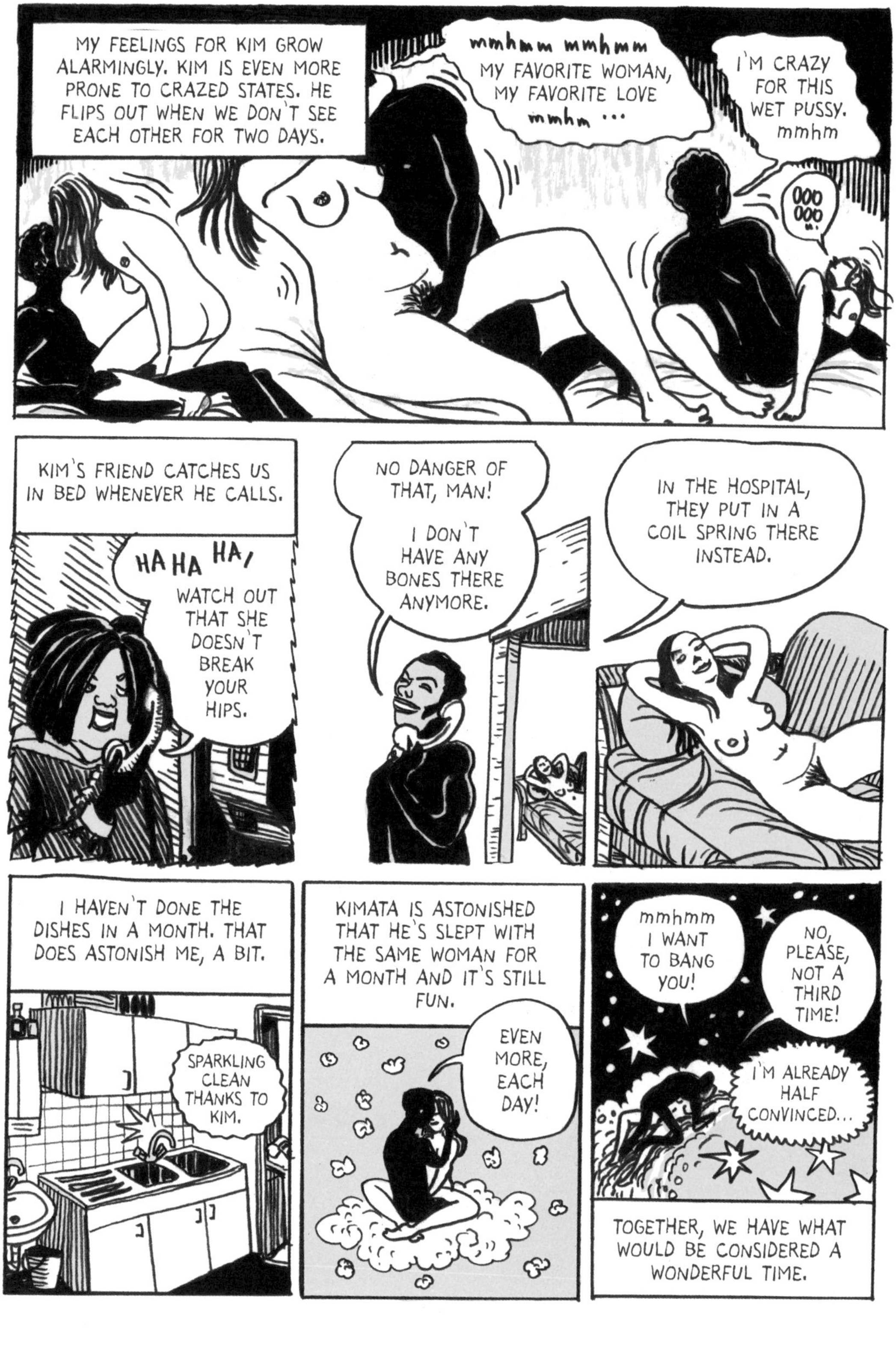
MY FEELINGS FOR KIM GROW ALARMINGLY. KIM IS EVEN MORE PRONE TO CRAZED STATES. HE FLIPS OUT WHEN WE DON'T SEE EACH OTHER FOR TWO DAYS.
mmhmm mmhmm MY FAVORITE WOMAN, MY FAVORITE LOVE mmhm ...
I'M CRAZY FOR THIS WET PUSSY. mmhm
KIM'S FRIEND CATCHES US IN BED WHENEVER HE CALLS.
HA HA HA!
WATCH OUT THAT SHE DOESN'T BREAK YOUR HIPS.
NO DANGER OF THAT, MAN!
I DON'T HAVE ANY BONES THERE ANYMORE.
IN THE HOSPITAL, THEY PUT IN A COIL SPRING THERE INSTEAD.
I HAVEN'T DONE THE DISHES IN A MONTH. THAT DOES ASTONISH ME, A BIT.
SPARKLING CLEAN THANKS TO KIM.
KIMATA IS ASTONISHED THAT HE'S SLEPT WITH THE SAME WOMAN FOR A MONTH AND IT'S STILL FUN.
EVEN MORE, EACH DAY!
mmhmm I WANT TO BANG YOU!
NO, PLEASE, NOT A THIRD TIME!
I'M ALREADY HALF CONVINCED...
TOGETHER, WE HAVE WHAT WOULD BE CONSIDERED A WONDERFUL TIME.

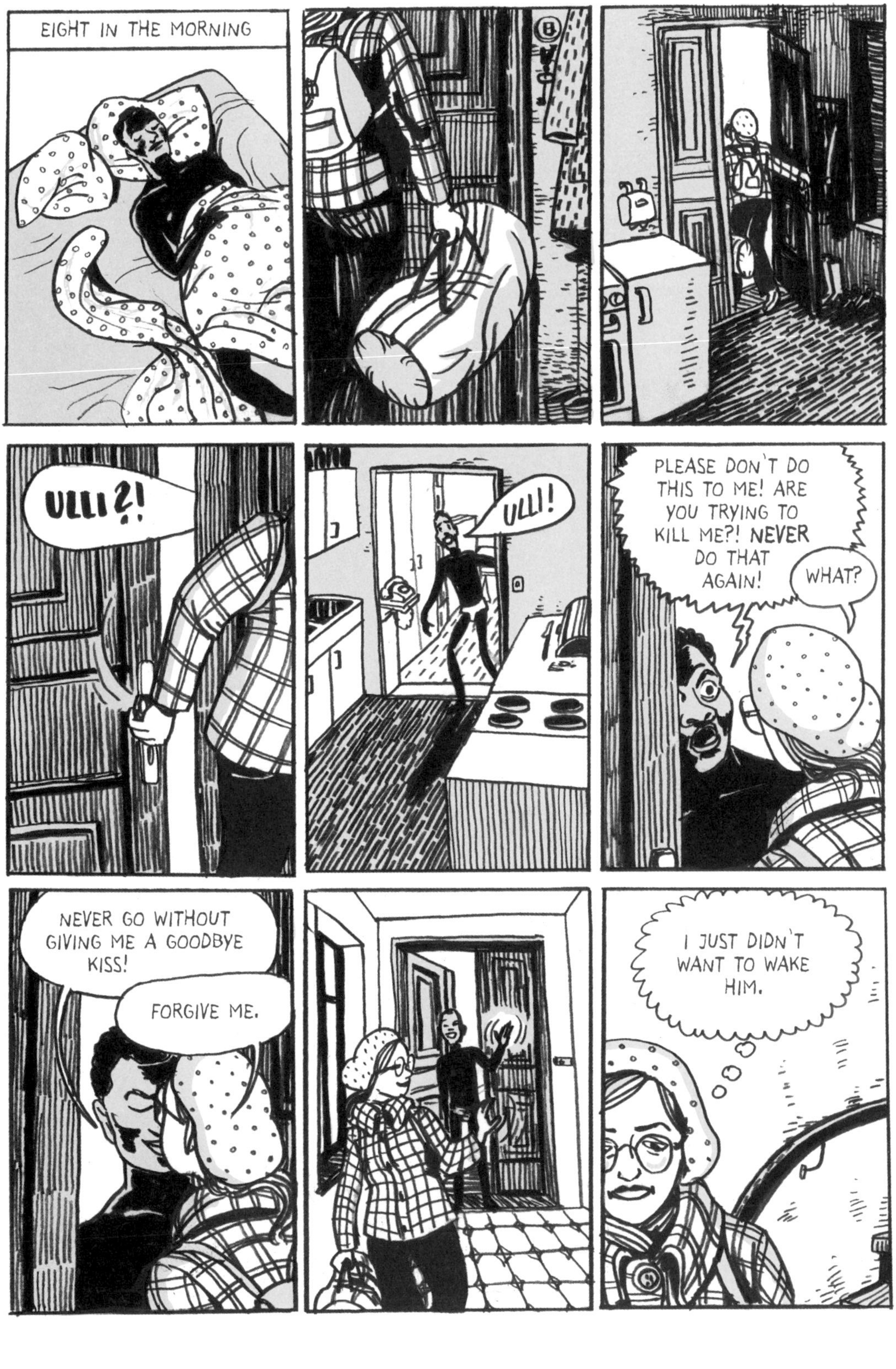
EIGHT IN THE MORNING
ULLI?!
ULLI!
PLEASE DON'T DO THIS TO ME! ARE YOU TRYING TO KILL ME?! NEVER DO THAT AGAIN!
WHAT?
NEVER GO WITHOUT GIVING ME A GOODBYE KISS!
FORGIVE ME.
I JUST DIDN'T WANT TO WAKE HIM.

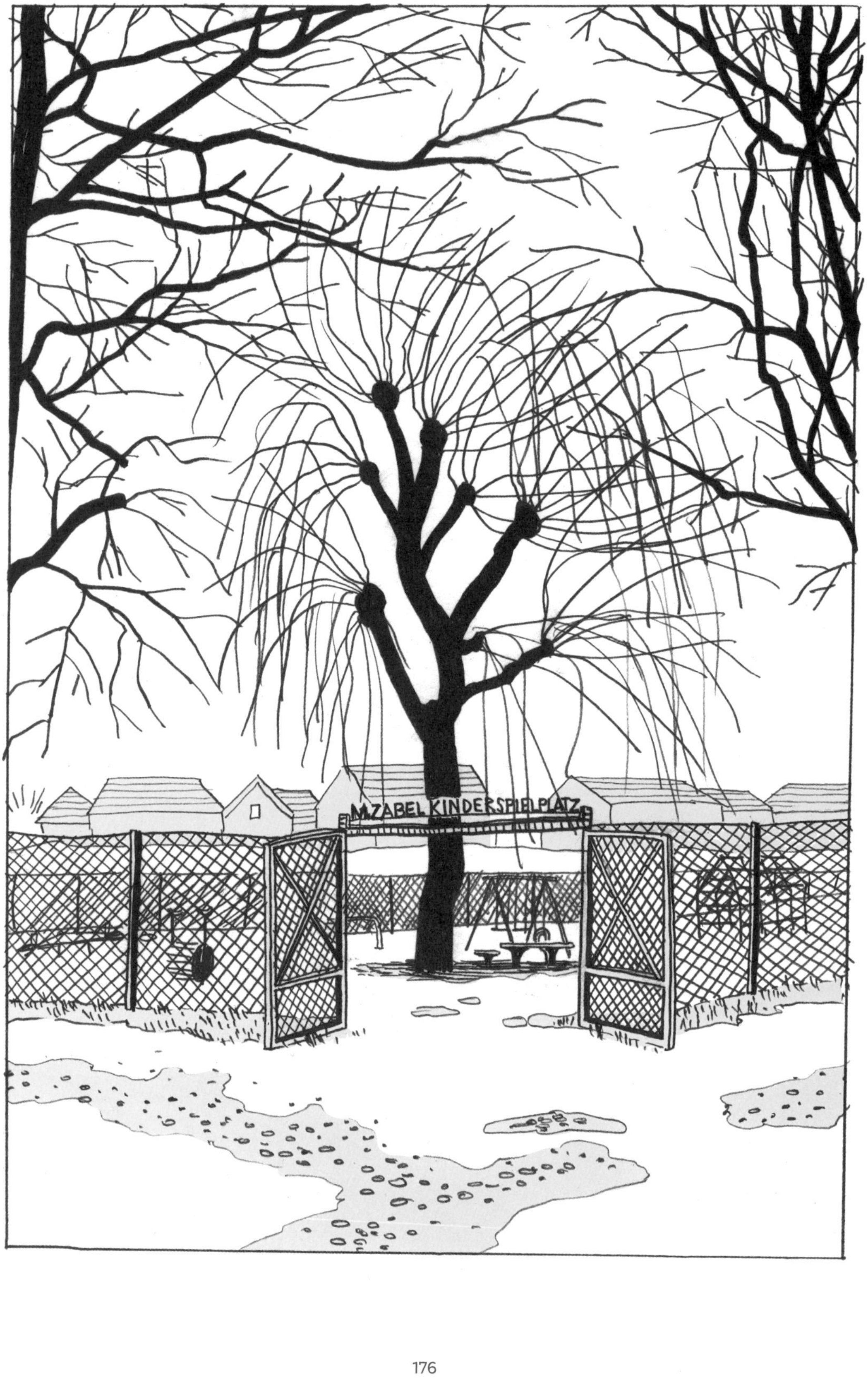
M.ZABEL KINDERSPIELPLATZ

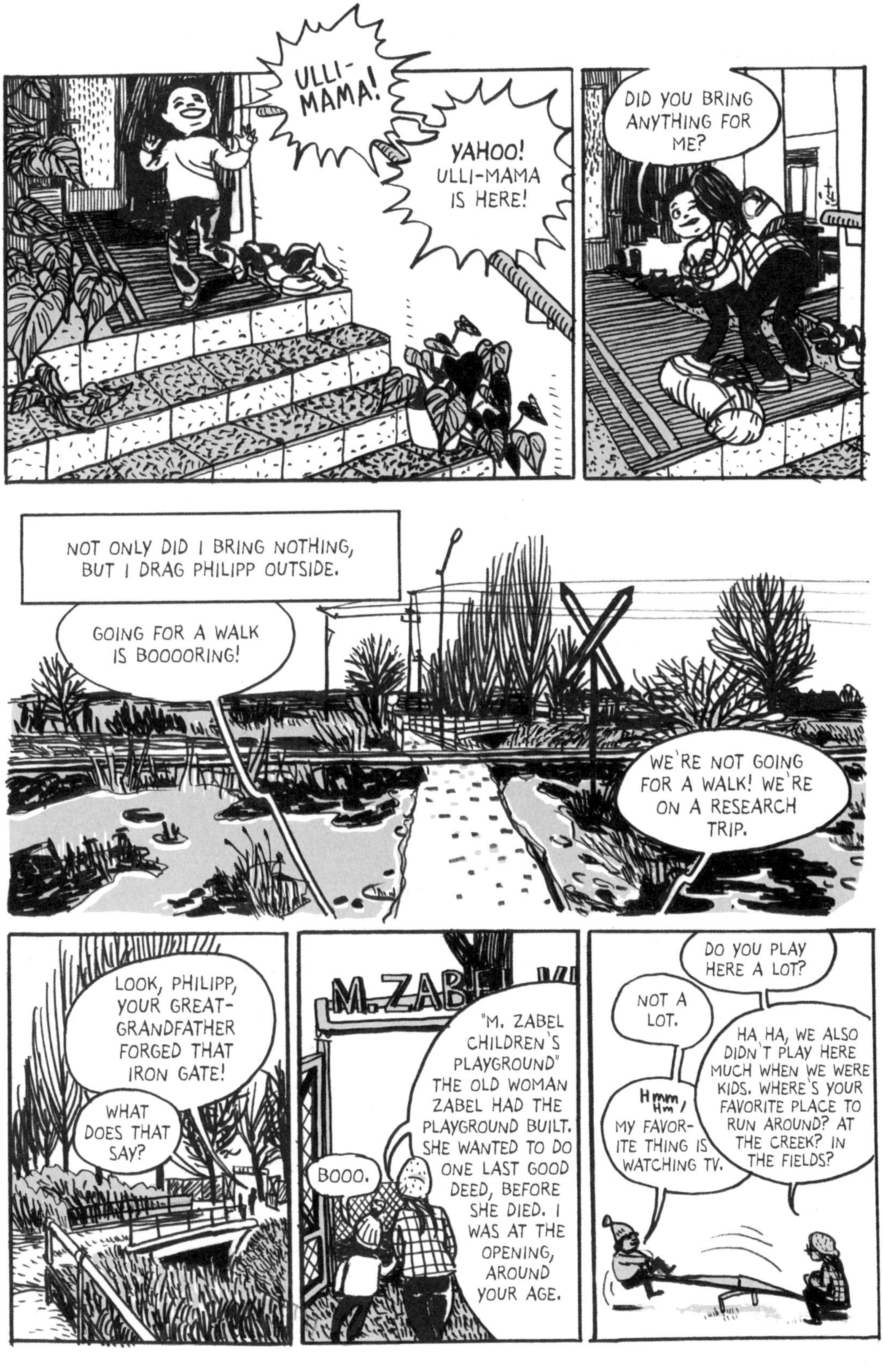

ULLI-MAMA!
YAHOO! ULLI-MAMA IS HERE!
DID YOU BRING ANYTHING FOR ME?
NOT ONLY DID I BRING NOTHING, BUT I DRAG PHILIPP OUTSIDE.
GOING FOR A WALK IS BOOOORING!
WE'RE NOT GOING FOR A WALK! WE'RE ON A RESEARCH TRIP.
LOOK, PHILIPP, YOUR GREAT-GRANDFATHER FORGED THAT IRON GATE!
WHAT DOES THAT SAY?
M. ZAB
"M. ZABEL CHILDREN'S PLAYGROUND" THE OLD WOMAN ZABEL HAD THE PLAYGROUND BUILT. SHE WANTED TO DO ONE LAST GOOD DEED, BEFORE SHE DIED. I WAS AT THE OPENING, AROUND YOUR AGE.
BOOO.
DO YOU PLAY HERE A LOT?
NOT A LOT.
HA HA, WE ALSO DIDN'T PLAY HERE MUCH WHEN WE WERE KIDS. WHERE'S YOUR FAVORITE PLACE TO RUN AROUND? AT THE CREEK? IN THE FIELDS?
Hmm, Hm, MY FAVORITE THING IS WATCHING TV.

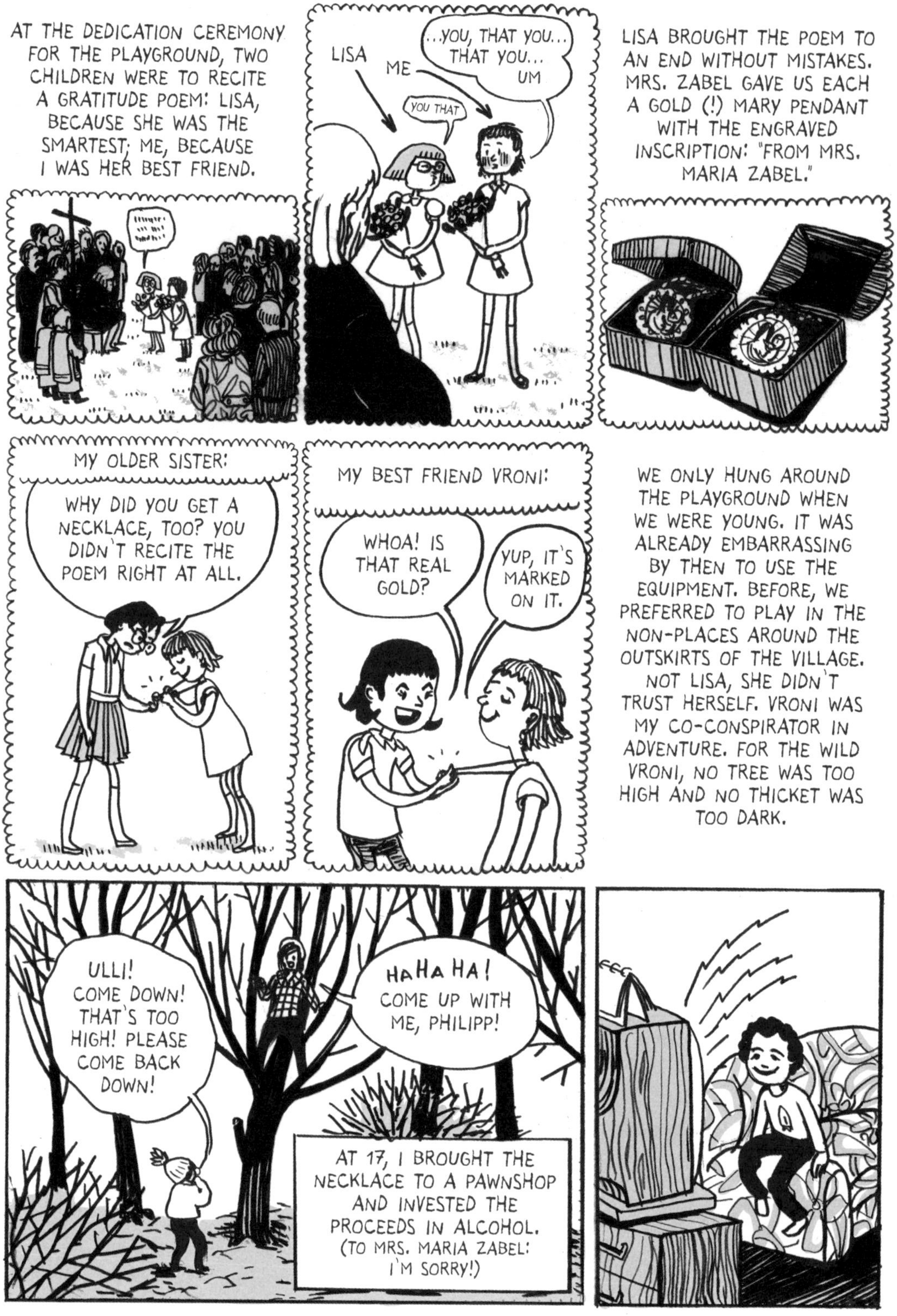
AT THE DEDICATION CEREMONY FOR THE PLAYGROUND, TWO CHILDREN WERE TO RECITE A GRATITUDE POEM: LISA, BECAUSE SHE WAS THE SMARTEST; ME, BECAUSE I WAS HER BEST FRIEND.
LISA
ME
...YOU, THAT YOU... THAT YOU... UM
YOU THAT
LISA BROUGHT THE POEM TO AN END WITHOUT MISTAKES. MRS. ZABEL GAVE US EACH A GOLD (!) MARY PENDANT WITH THE ENGRAVED INSCRIPTION: "FROM MRS. MARIA ZABEL."
MY OLDER SISTER:
WHY DID YOU GET A NECKLACE, TOO? YOU DIDN'T RECITE THE POEM RIGHT AT ALL.
MY BEST FRIEND VRONI:
WHOA! IS THAT REAL GOLD?
YUP, IT'S MARKED ON IT.
WE ONLY HUNG AROUND THE PLAYGROUND WHEN WE WERE YOUNG. IT WAS ALREADY EMBARRASSING BY THEN TO USE THE EQUIPMENT. BEFORE, WE PREFERRED TO PLAY IN THE NON-PLACES AROUND THE OUTSKIRTS OF THE VILLAGE. NOT LISA, SHE DIDN'T TRUST HERSELF. VRONI WAS MY CO-CONSPIRATOR IN ADVENTURE. FOR THE WILD VRONI, NO TREE WAS TOO HIGH AND NO THICKET WAS TOO DARK.
ULLI! COME DOWN! THAT'S TOO HIGH! PLEASE COME BACK DOWN!
HAHAHA! COME UP WITH ME, PHILIPP!
AT 17, I BROUGHT THE NECKLACE TO A PAWNSHOP AND INVESTED THE PROCEEDS IN ALCOHOL. (TO MRS. MARIA ZABEL: I'M SORRY!)

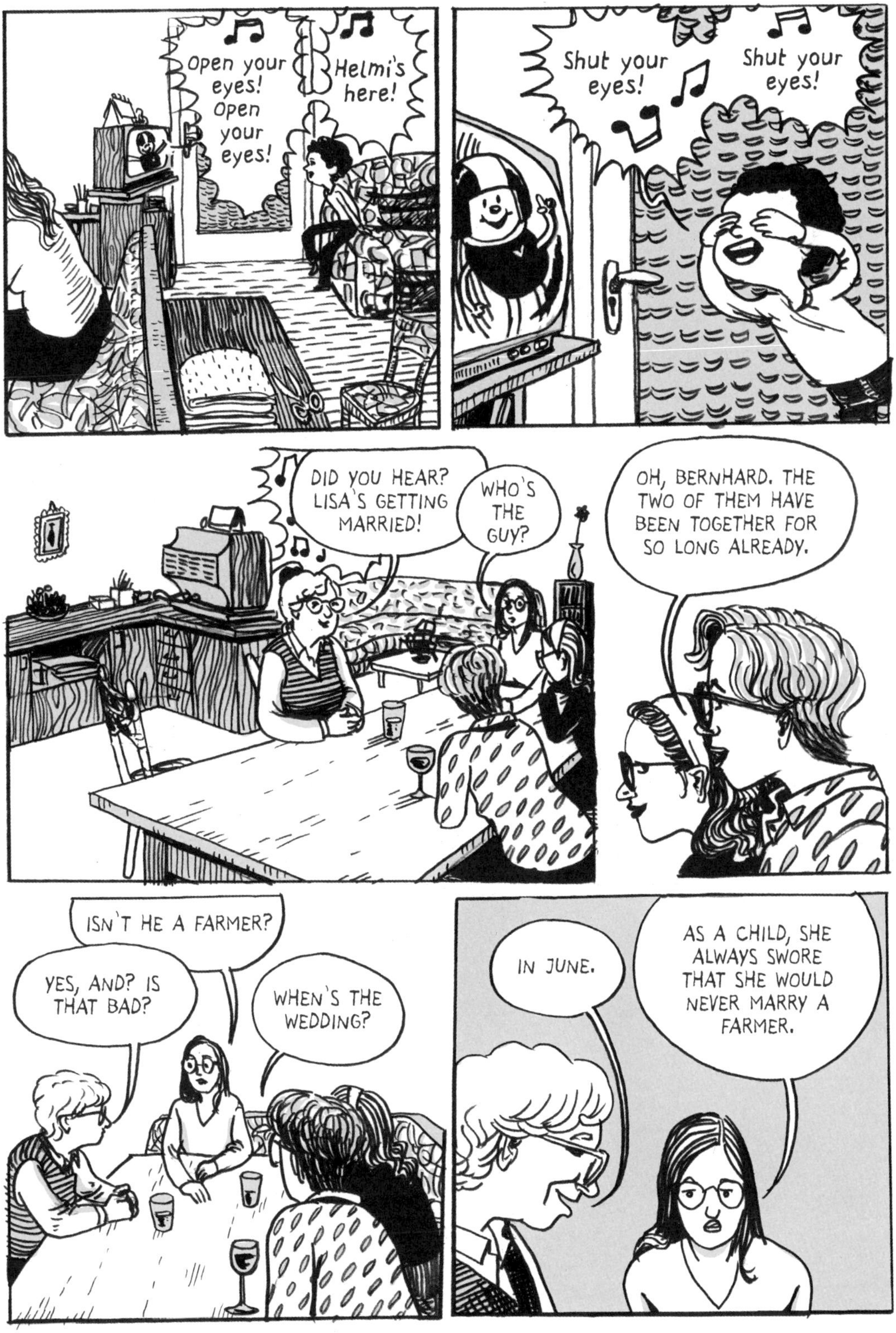
Open your eyes! Open your eyes!
Helmi's here!
Shut your eyes!
Shut your eyes!
DID YOU HEAR? LISA'S GETTING MARRIED!
WHO'S THE GUY?
OH, BERNHARD. THE TWO OF THEM HAVE BEEN TOGETHER FOR SO LONG ALREADY.
ISN'T HE A FARMER?
YES, AND? IS THAT BAD?
WHEN'S THE WEDDING?
IN JUNE.
AS A CHILD, SHE ALWAYS SWORE THAT SHE WOULD NEVER MARRY A FARMER.

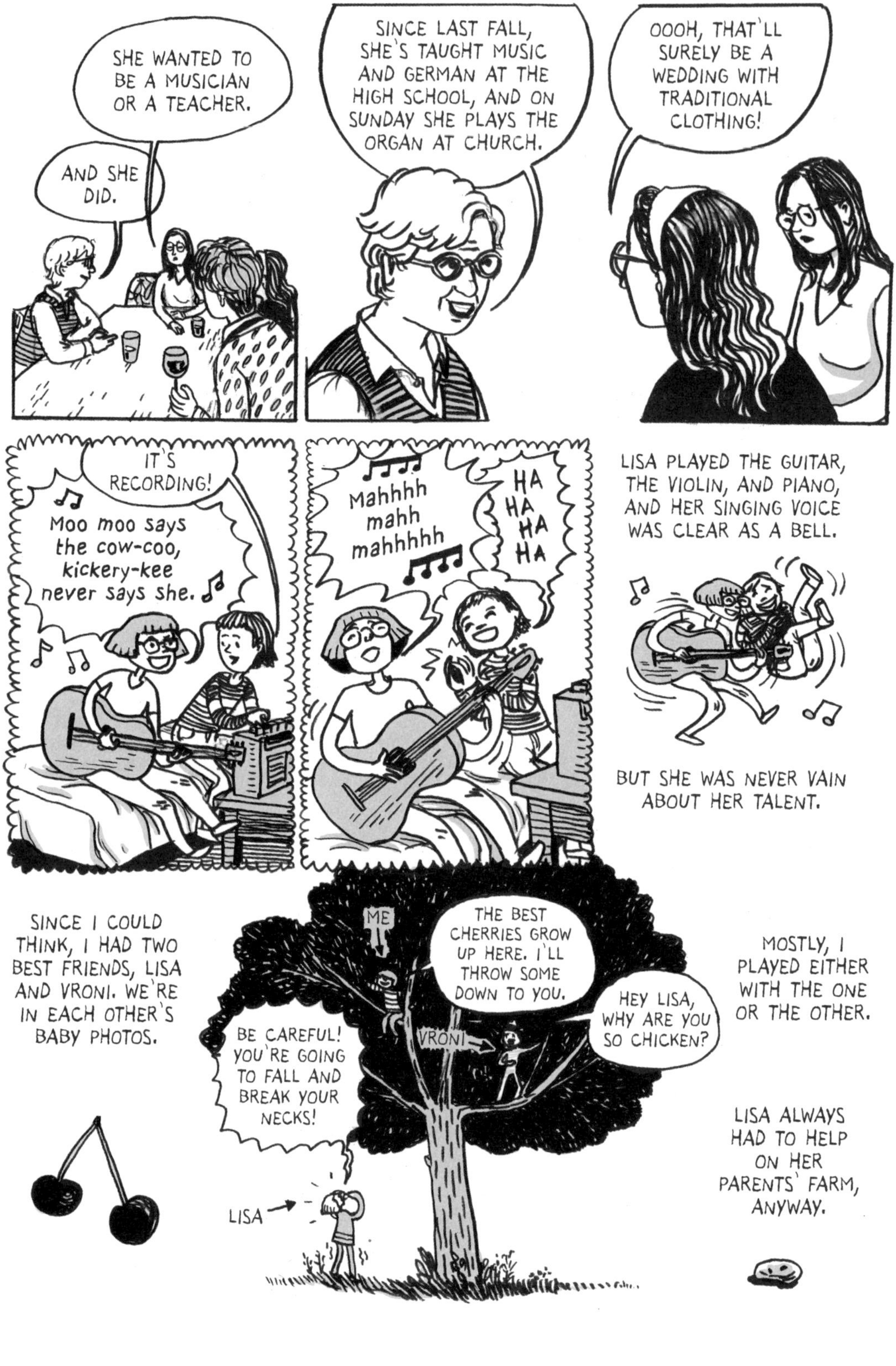
SHE WANTED TO BE A MUSICIAN OR A TEACHER.
AND SHE DID.
SINCE LAST FALL, SHE'S TAUGHT MUSIC AND GERMAN AT THE HIGH SCHOOL, AND ON SUNDAY SHE PLAYS THE ORGAN AT CHURCH.
OOOH, THAT'LL SURELY BE A WEDDING WITH TRADITIONAL CLOTHING!
IT'S RECORDING!
Moo moo says the cow-coo, kickery-kee never says she.
Mahhhh mahh mahhhhh
HA HA HA HA
LISA PLAYED THE GUITAR, THE VIOLIN, AND PIANO, AND HER SINGING VOICE WAS CLEAR AS A BELL.
BUT SHE WAS NEVER VAIN ABOUT HER TALENT.
SINCE I COULD THINK, I HAD TWO BEST FRIENDS, LISA AND VRONI. WE'RE IN EACH OTHER'S BABY PHOTOS.
ME
THE BEST CHERRIES GROW UP HERE. I'LL THROW SOME DOWN TO YOU.
HEY LISA, WHY ARE YOU SO CHICKEN?
VRONI
BE CAREFUL! YOU'RE GOING TO FALL AND BREAK YOUR NECKS!
LISA
MOSTLY, I PLAYED EITHER WITH THE ONE OR THE OTHER.
LISA ALWAYS HAD TO HELP ON HER PARENTS' FARM, ANYWAY.

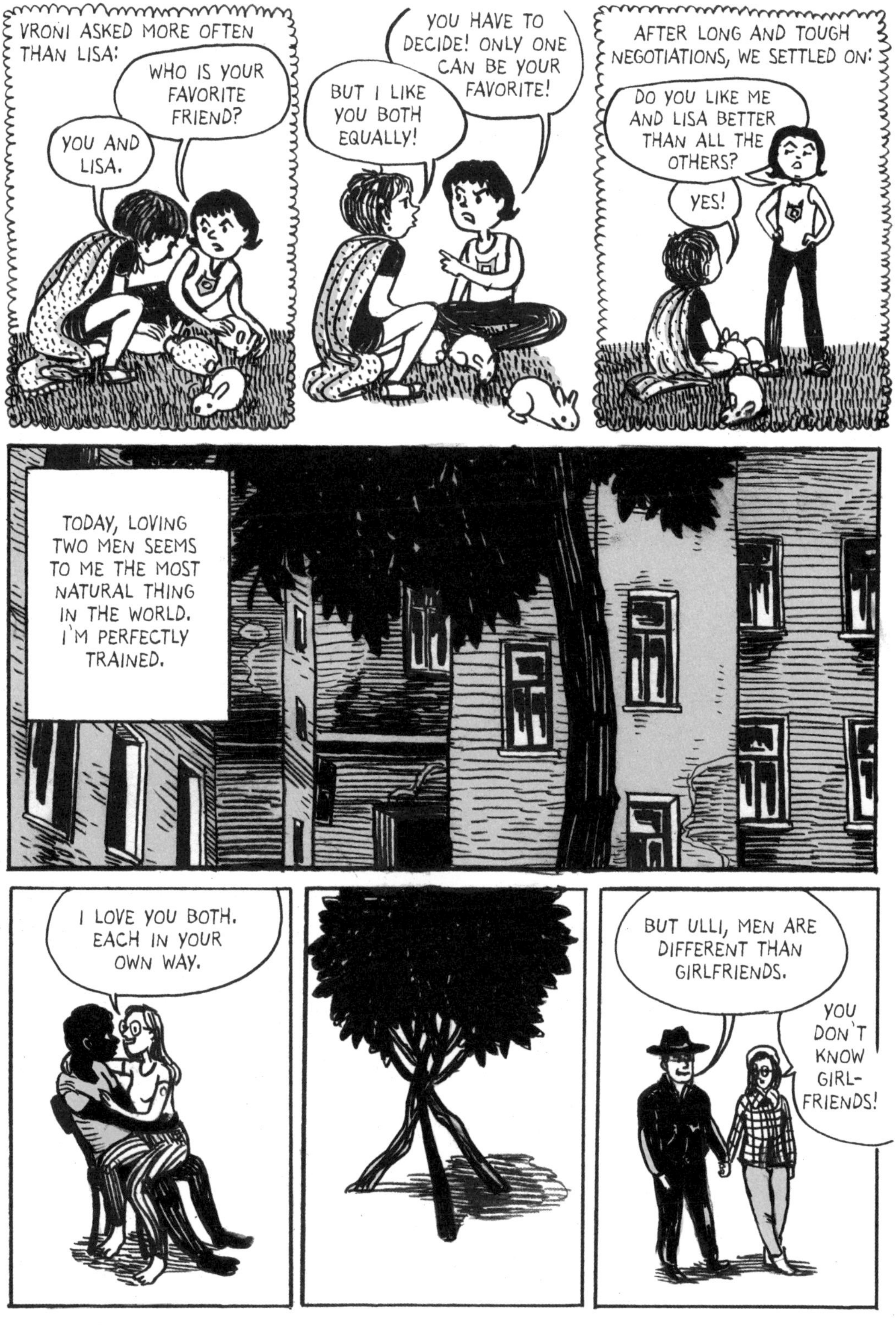
VRONI ASKED MORE OFTEN THAN LISA:
WHO IS YOUR FAVORITE FRIEND?
YOU AND LISA.
YOU HAVE TO DECIDE! ONLY ONE CAN BE YOUR FAVORITE!
BUT I LIKE YOU BOTH EQUALLY!
AFTER LONG AND TOUGH NEGOTIATIONS, WE SETTLED ON:
DO YOU LIKE ME AND LISA BETTER THAN ALL THE OTHERS?
YES!
TODAY, LOVING TWO MEN SEEMS TO ME THE MOST NATURAL THING IN THE WORLD. I'M PERFECTLY TRAINED.
I LOVE YOU BOTH. EACH IN YOUR OWN WAY.
BUT ULLI, MEN ARE DIFFERENT THAN GIRLFRIENDS.
YOU DON'T KNOW GIRL-FRIENDS!

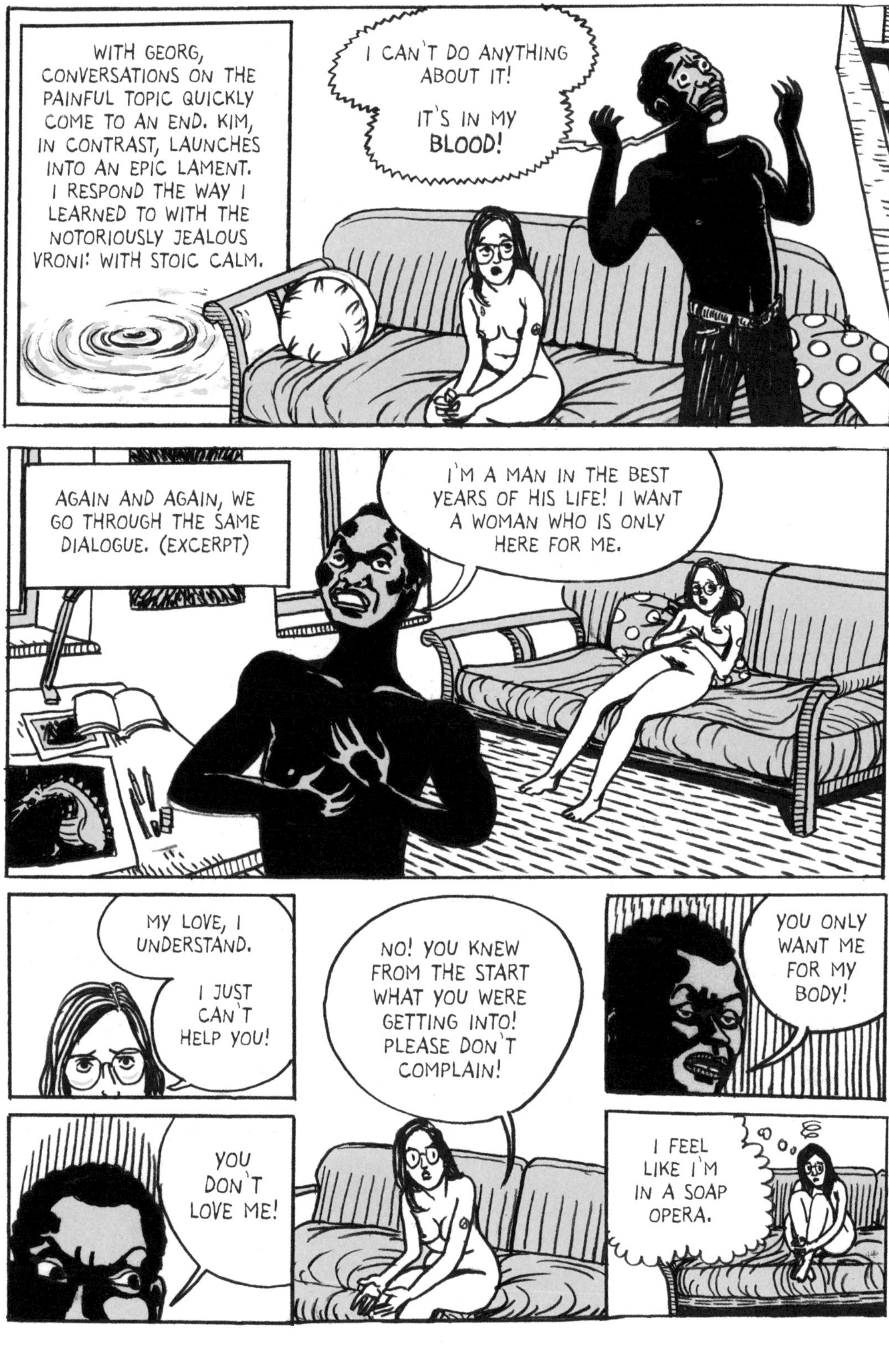
WITH GEORG, CONVERSATIONS ON THE PAINFUL TOPIC QUICKLY COME TO AN END. KIM, IN CONTRAST, LAUNCHES INTO AN EPIC LAMENT. I RESPOND THE WAY I LEARNED TO WITH THE NOTORIOUSLY JEALOUS VRONI: WITH STOIC CALM.
I CAN'T DO ANYTHING ABOUT IT! IT'S IN MY BLOOD!
AGAIN AND AGAIN, WE GO THROUGH THE SAME DIALOGUE. (EXCERPT)
I'M A MAN IN THE BEST YEARS OF HIS LIFE! I WANT A WOMAN WHO IS ONLY HERE FOR ME.
MY LOVE, I UNDERSTAND. I JUST CAN'T HELP YOU!
NO! YOU KNEW FROM THE START WHAT YOU WERE GETTING INTO! PLEASE DON'T COMPLAIN!
YOU ONLY WANT ME FOR MY BODY!
YOU DON'T LOVE ME!
I FEEL LIKE I'M IN A SOAP OPERA.

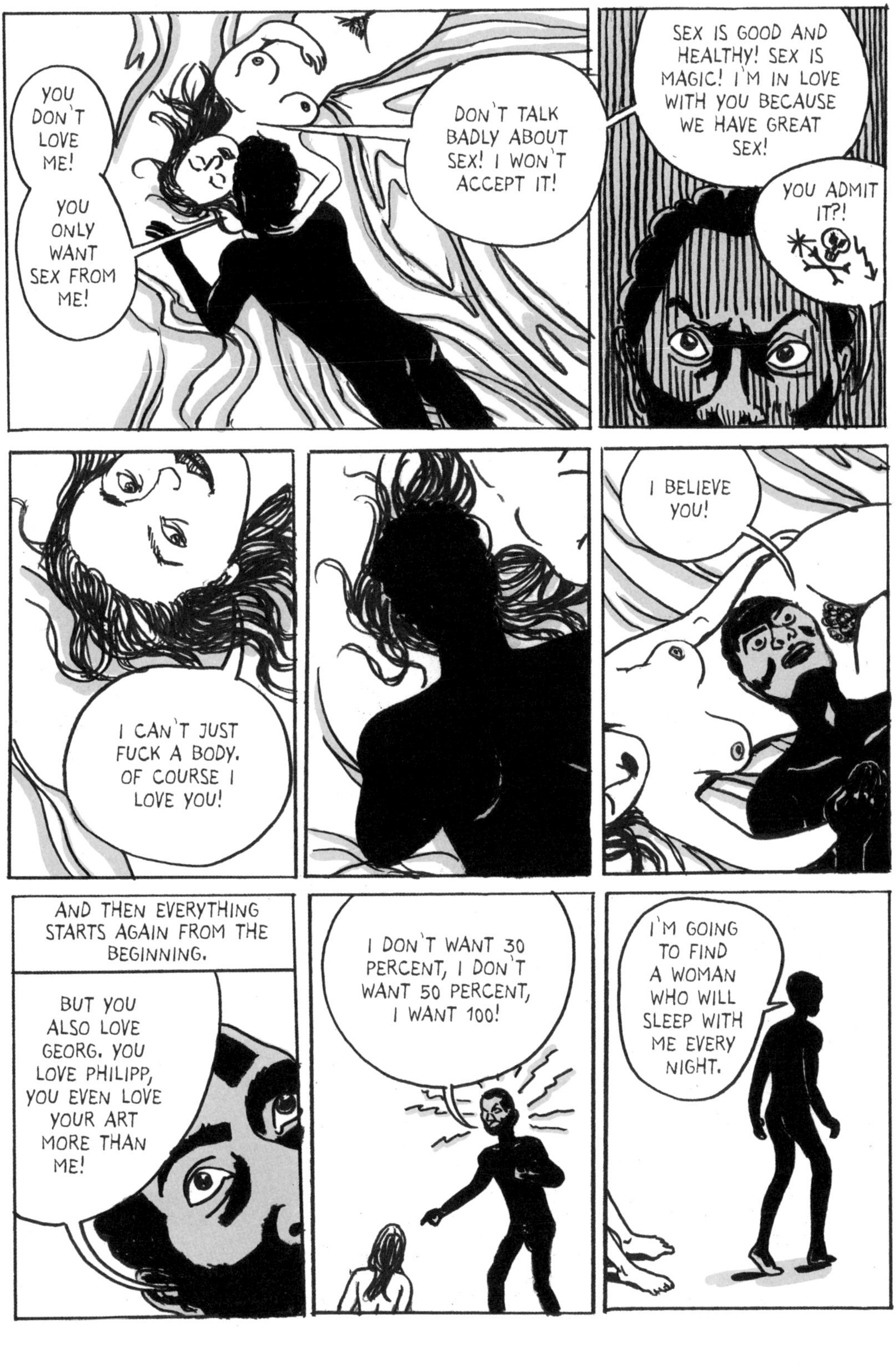

YOU DON'T LOVE ME!
YOU ONLY WANT SEX FROM ME!
DON'T TALK BADLY ABOUT SEX! I WON'T ACCEPT IT!
SEX IS GOOD AND HEALTHY! SEX IS MAGIC! I'M IN LOVE WITH YOU BECAUSE WE HAVE GREAT SEX!
YOU ADMIT IT?!
I CAN'T JUST FUCK A BODY. OF COURSE I LOVE YOU!
I BELIEVE YOU!
AND THEN EVERYTHING STARTS AGAIN FROM THE BEGINNING.
BUT YOU ALSO LOVE GEORG. YOU LOVE PHILIPP, YOU EVEN LOVE YOUR ART MORE THAN ME!
I DON'T WANT 30 PERCENT, I DON'T WANT 50 PERCENT, I WANT 100!
I'M GOING TO FIND A WOMAN WHO WILL SLEEP WITH ME EVERY NIGHT.

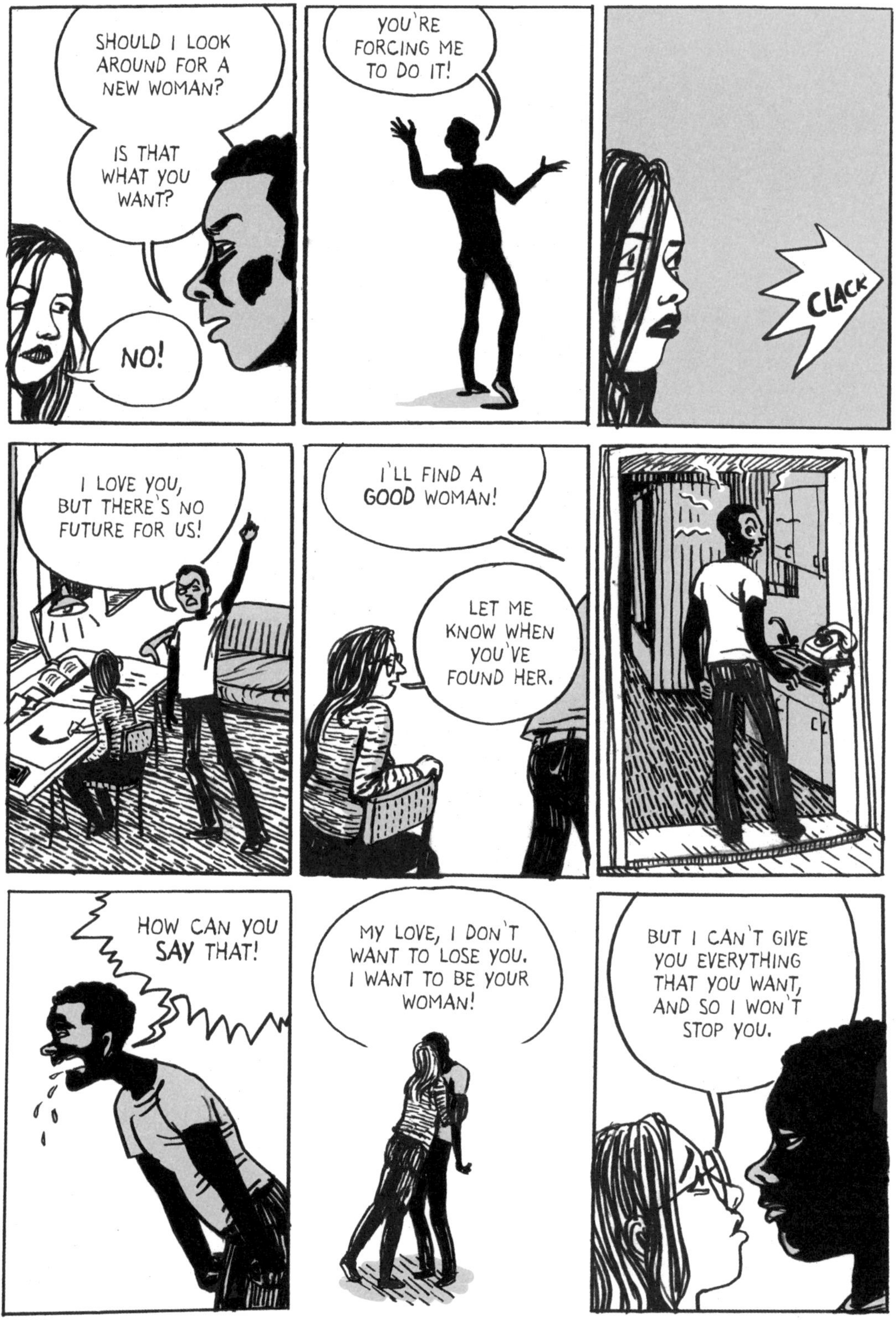
SHOULD I LOOK AROUND FOR A NEW WOMAN?
IS THAT WHAT YOU WANT?
NO!
YOU'RE FORCING ME TO DO IT!
CLACK
I LOVE YOU, BUT THERE'S NO FUTURE FOR US!
I'LL FIND A GOOD WOMAN!
LET ME KNOW WHEN YOU'VE FOUND HER.
HOW CAN YOU SAY THAT!
MY LOVE, I DON'T WANT TO LOSE YOU. I WANT TO BE YOUR WOMAN!
BUT I CAN'T GIVE YOU EVERYTHING THAT YOU WANT, AND SO I WON'T STOP YOU.

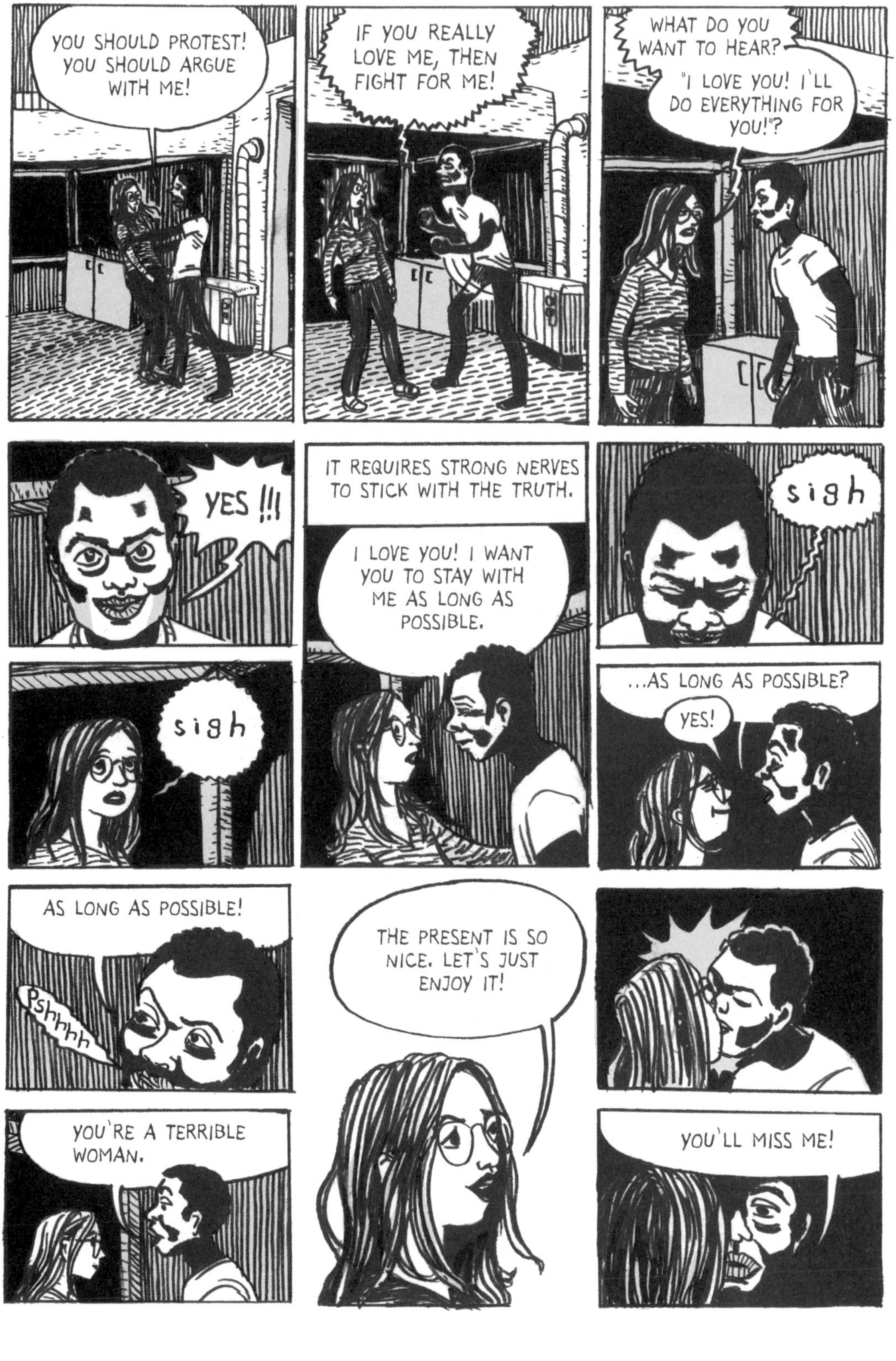
YOU SHOULD PROTEST! YOU SHOULD ARGUE WITH ME!
IF YOU REALLY LOVE ME, THEN FIGHT FOR ME!
WHAT DO YOU WANT TO HEAR?
"I LOVE YOU! I'LL DO EVERYTHING FOR YOU!"?
YES !!!
IT REQUIRES STRONG NERVES TO STICK WITH THE TRUTH.
I LOVE YOU! I WANT YOU TO STAY WITH ME AS LONG AS POSSIBLE.
sigh
sigh
...AS LONG AS POSSIBLE?
YES!
AS LONG AS POSSIBLE!
Pshhhh
THE PRESENT IS SO NICE. LET'S JUST ENJOY IT!
YOU'RE A TERRIBLE WOMAN.
YOU'LL MISS ME!

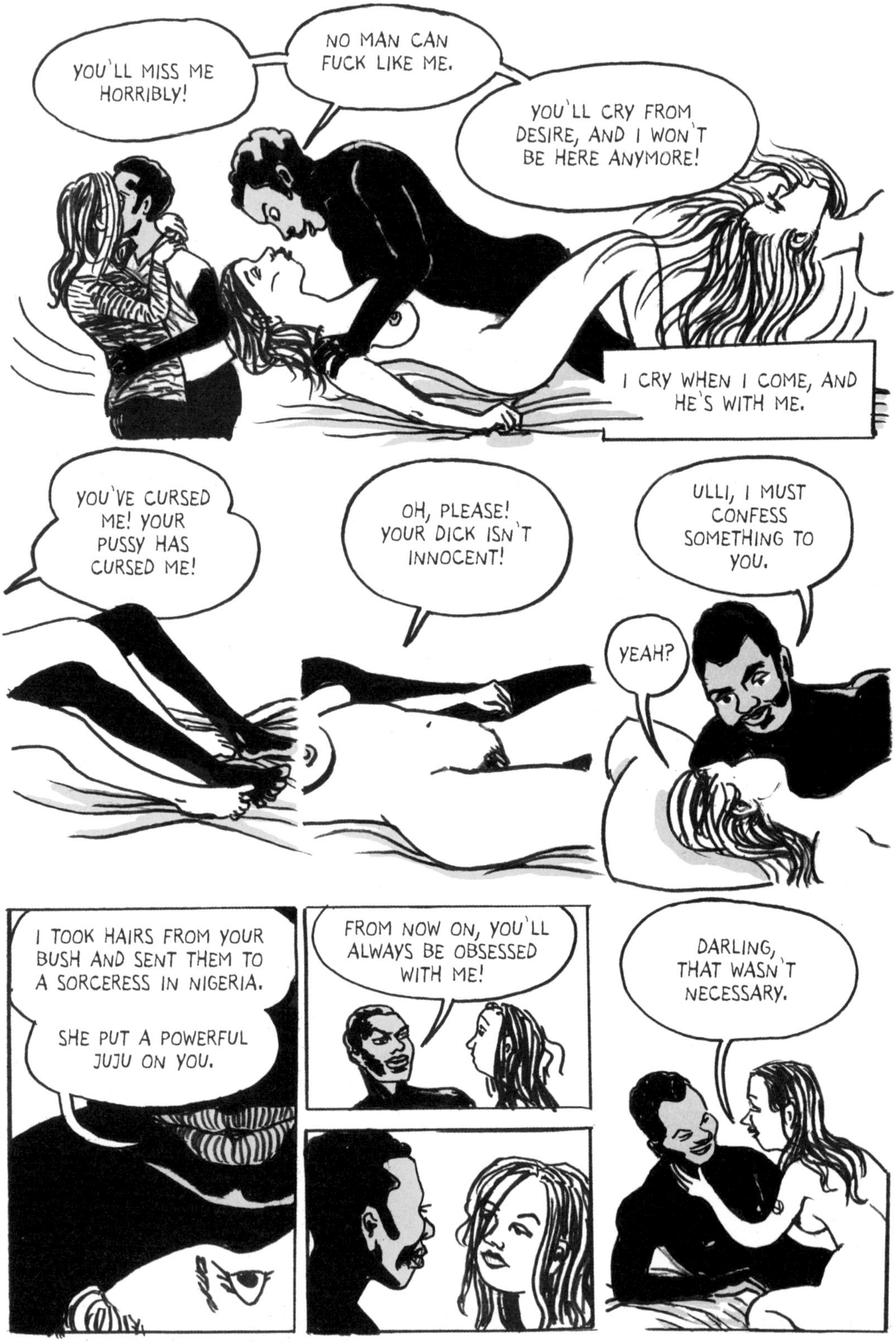
YOU'LL MISS ME HORRIBLY!
NO MAN CAN FUCK LIKE ME.
YOU'LL CRY FROM DESIRE, AND I WON'T BE HERE ANYMORE!
I CRY WHEN I COME, AND HE'S WITH ME.
YOU'VE CURSED ME! YOUR PUSSY HAS CURSED ME!
OH, PLEASE! YOUR DICK ISN'T INNOCENT!
ULLI, I MUST CONFESS SOMETHING TO YOU.
YEAH?
I TOOK HAIRS FROM YOUR BUSH AND SENT THEM TO A SORCERESS IN NIGERIA.
SHE PUT A POWERFUL JUJU ON YOU.
FROM NOW ON, YOU'LL ALWAYS BE OBSESSED WITH ME!
DARLING, THAT WASN'T NECESSARY.

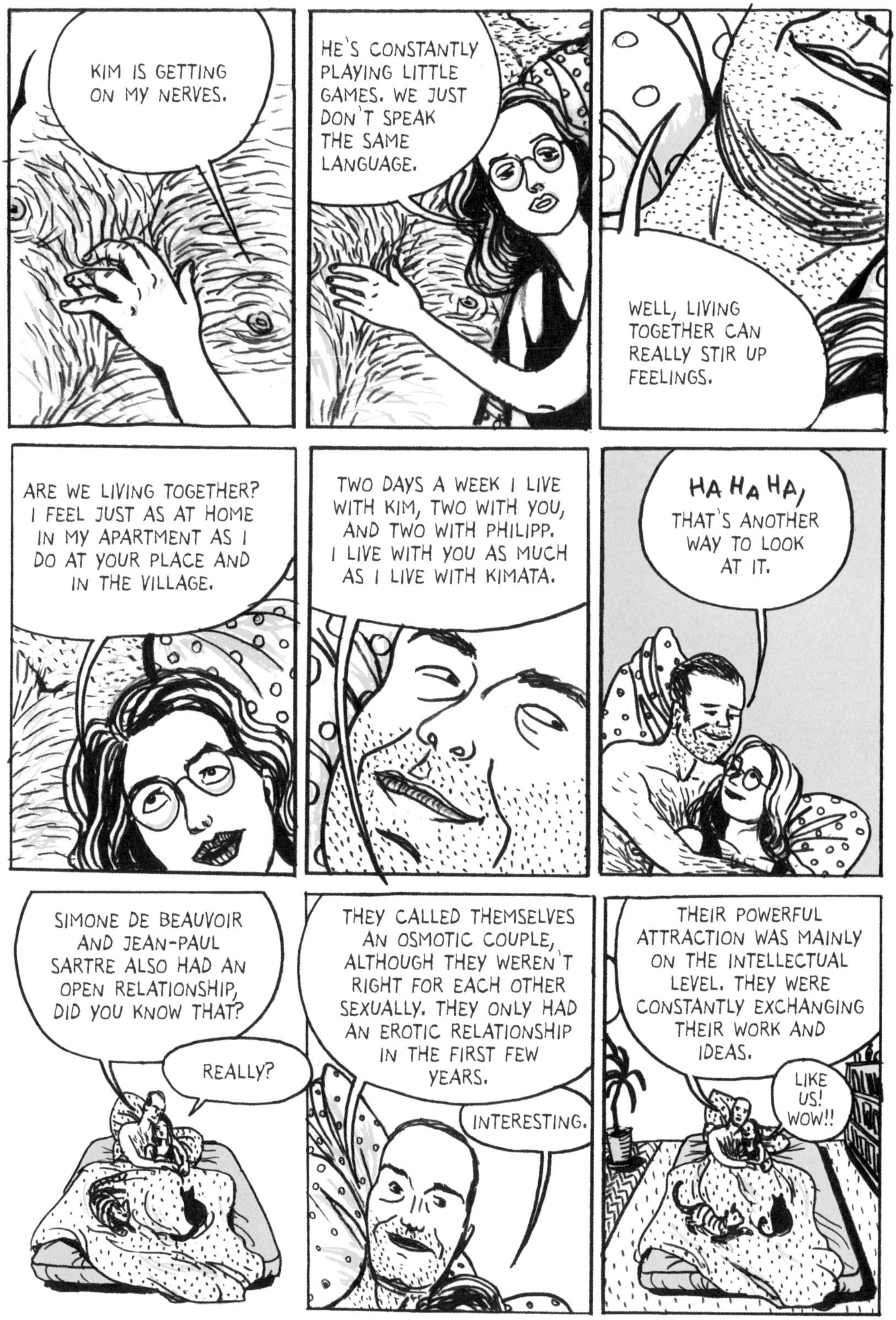
KIM IS GETTING ON MY NERVES.
HE'S CONSTANTLY PLAYING LITTLE GAMES. WE JUST DON'T SPEAK THE SAME LANGUAGE.
WELL, LIVING TOGETHER CAN REALLY STIR UP FEELINGS.
ARE WE LIVING TOGETHER? I FEEL JUST AS AT HOME IN MY APARTMENT AS I DO AT YOUR PLACE AND IN THE VILLAGE.
TWO DAYS A WEEK I LIVE WITH KIM, TWO WITH YOU, AND TWO WITH PHILIPP. I LIVE WITH YOU AS MUCH AS I LIVE WITH KIMATA.
HA HA HA, THAT'S ANOTHER WAY TO LOOK AT IT.
SIMONE DE BEAUVOIR AND JEAN-PAUL SARTRE ALSO HAD AN OPEN RELATIONSHIP, DID YOU KNOW THAT?
REALLY?
THEY CALLED THEMSELVES AN OSMOTIC COUPLE, ALTHOUGH THEY WEREN'T RIGHT FOR EACH OTHER SEXUALLY. THEY ONLY HAD AN EROTIC RELATIONSHIP IN THE FIRST FEW YEARS.
INTERESTING.
THEIR POWERFUL ATTRACTION WAS MAINLY ON THE INTELLECTUAL LEVEL. THEY WERE CONSTANTLY EXCHANGING THEIR WORK AND IDEAS.
LIKE US! WOW!!

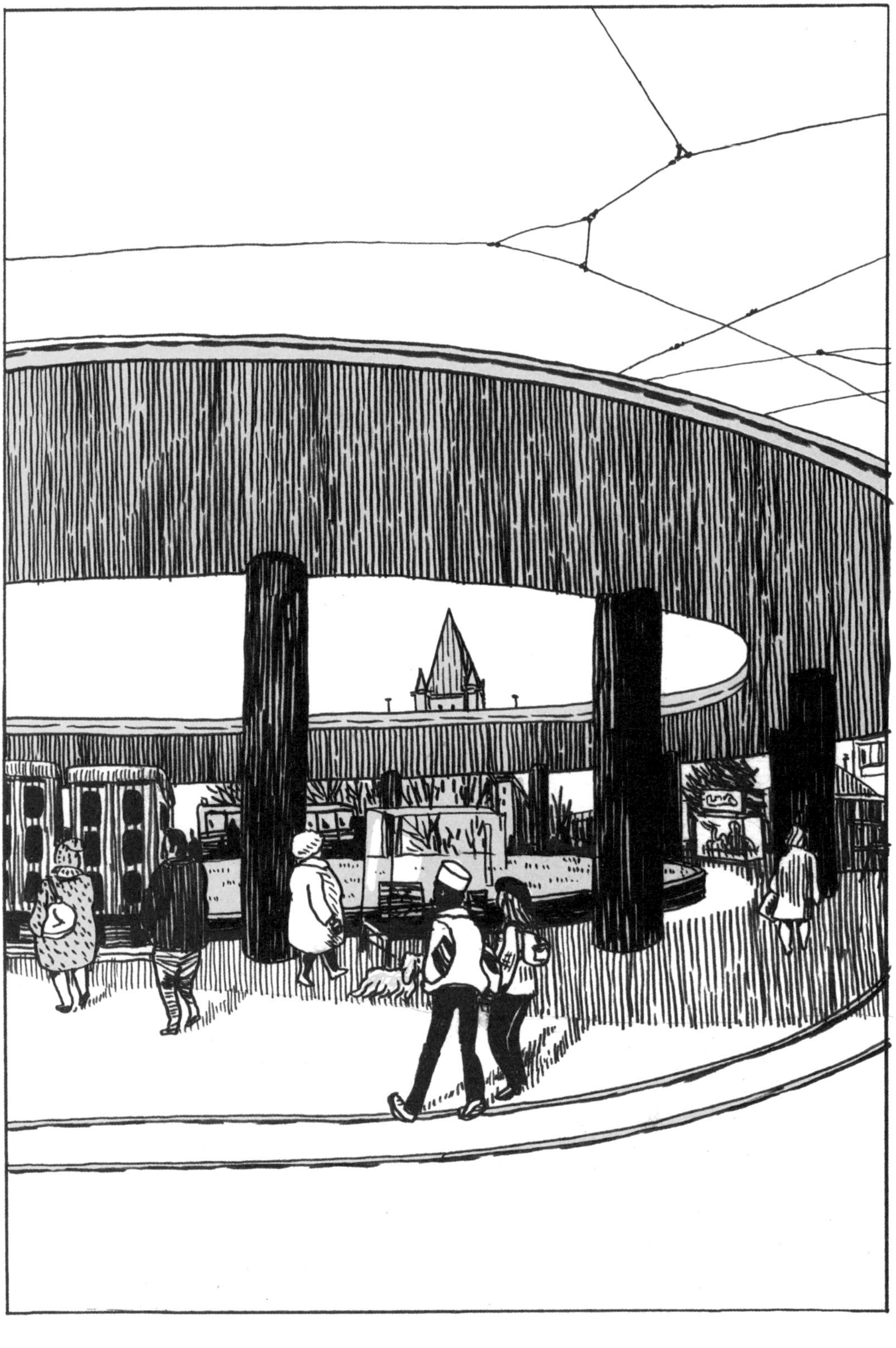

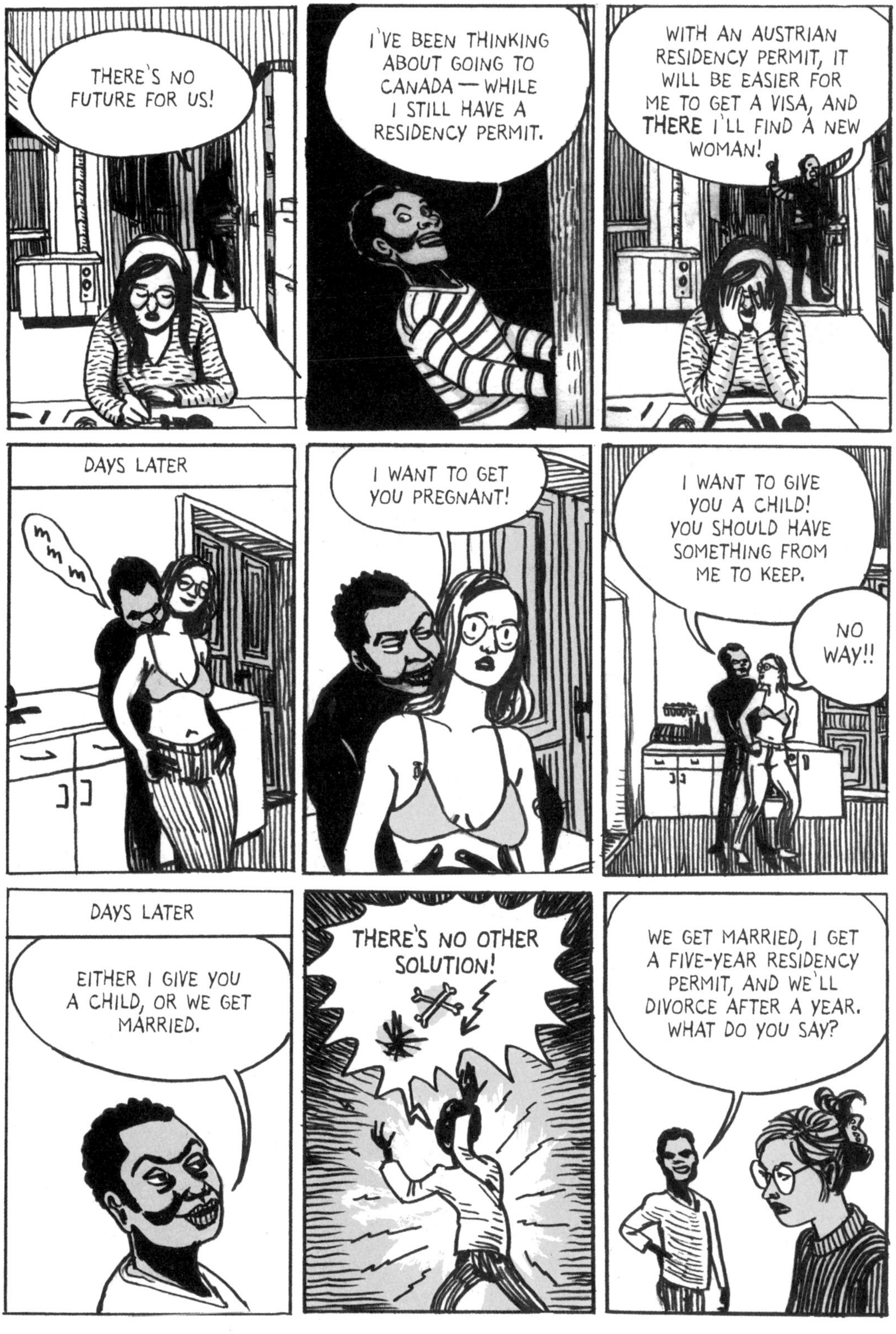
THERE'S NO FUTURE FOR US!
I'VE BEEN THINKING ABOUT GOING TO CANADA — WHILE I STILL HAVE A RESIDENCY PERMIT.
WITH AN AUSTRIAN RESIDENCY PERMIT, IT WILL BE EASIER FOR ME TO GET A VISA, AND THERE I'LL FIND A NEW WOMAN!
DAYS LATER
mmm
I WANT TO GET YOU PREGNANT!
I WANT TO GIVE YOU A CHILD! YOU SHOULD HAVE SOMETHING FROM ME TO KEEP.
NO WAY!!
DAYS LATER
EITHER I GIVE YOU A CHILD, OR WE GET MARRIED.
THERE'S NO OTHER SOLUTION!
WE GET MARRIED, I GET A FIVE-YEAR RESIDENCY PERMIT, AND WE'LL DIVORCE AFTER A YEAR. WHAT DO YOU SAY?

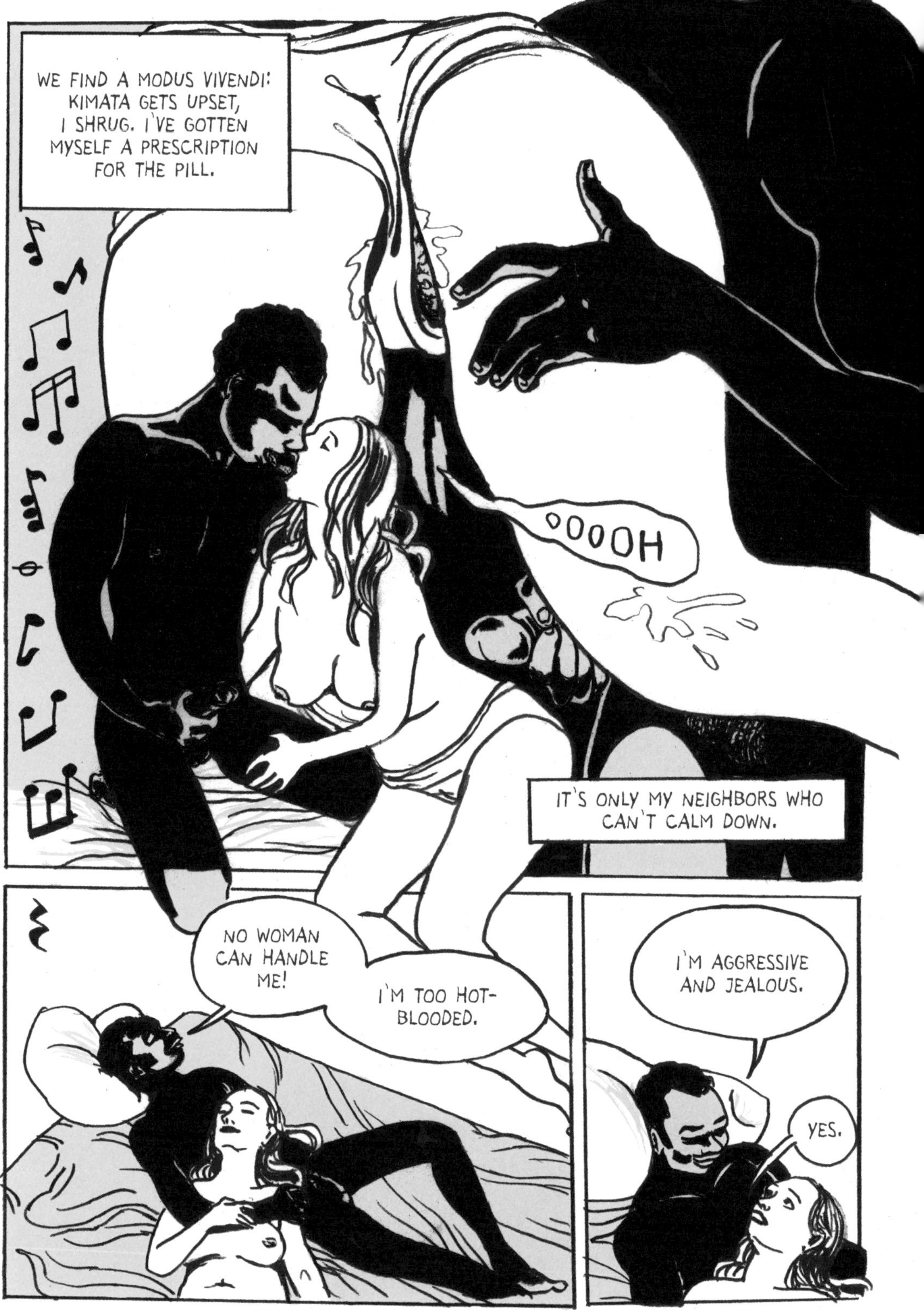
WE FIND A MODUS VIVENDI: KIMATA GETS UPSET, I SHRUG. I'VE GOTTEN MYSELF A PRESCRIPTION FOR THE PILL.
OOOOH
IT'S ONLY MY NEIGHBORS WHO CAN'T CALM DOWN.
NO WOMAN CAN HANDLE ME!
I'M TOO HOT-BLOODED.
I'M AGGRESSIVE AND JEALOUS.
YES.

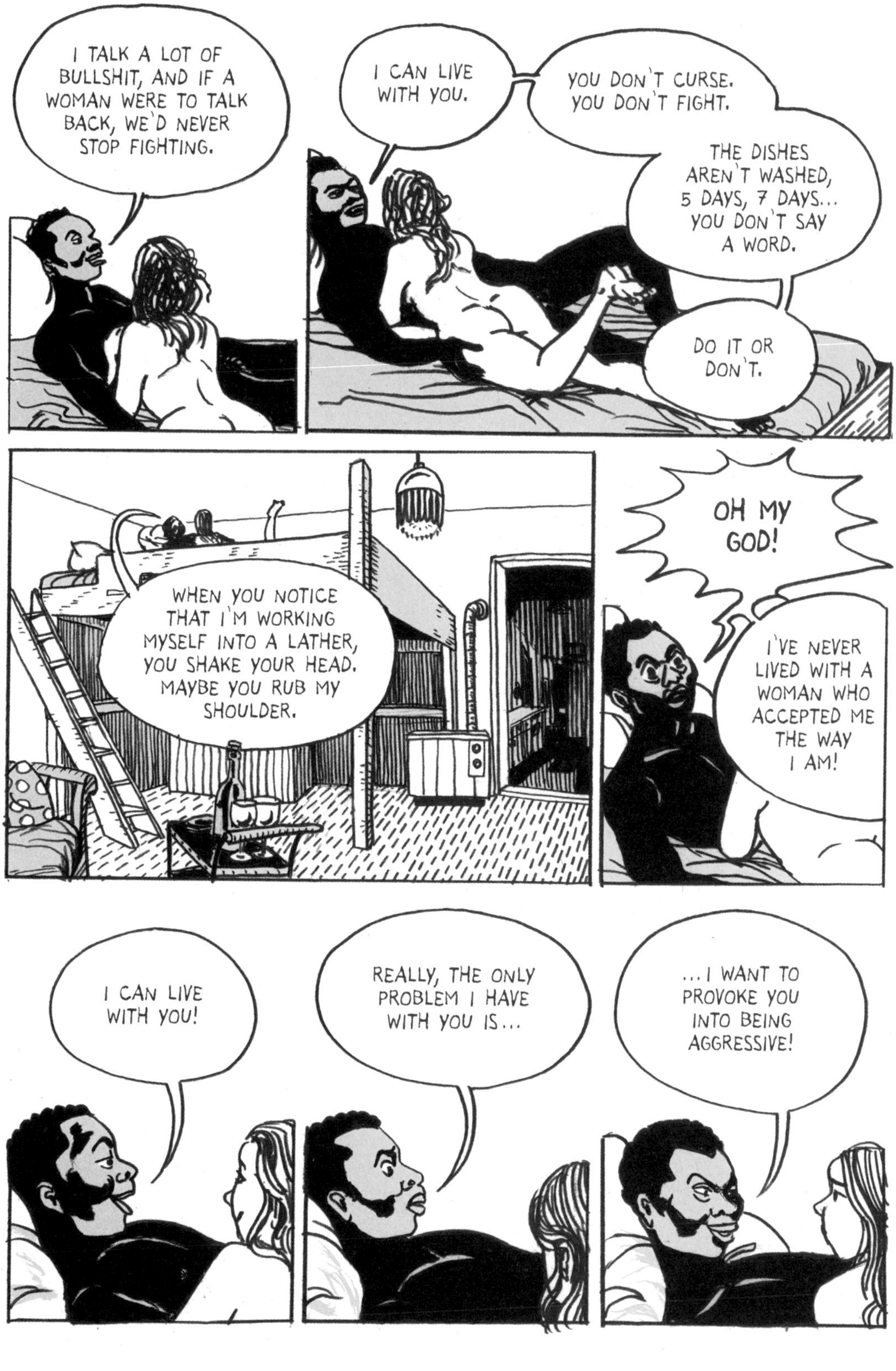
I TALK A LOT OF BULLSHIT, AND IF A WOMAN WERE TO TALK BACK, WE'D NEVER STOP FIGHTING.
I CAN LIVE WITH YOU.
YOU DON'T CURSE. YOU DON'T FIGHT.
THE DISHES AREN'T WASHED, 5 DAYS, 7 DAYS... YOU DON'T SAY A WORD.
DO IT OR DON'T.
WHEN YOU NOTICE THAT I'M WORKING MYSELF INTO A LATHER, YOU SHAKE YOUR HEAD. MAYBE YOU RUB MY SHOULDER.
OH MY GOD!
I'VE NEVER LIVED WITH A WOMAN WHO ACCEPTED ME THE WAY I AM!
I CAN LIVE WITH YOU!
REALLY, THE ONLY PROBLEM I HAVE WITH YOU IS...
...I WANT TO PROVOKE YOU INTO BEING AGGRESSIVE!

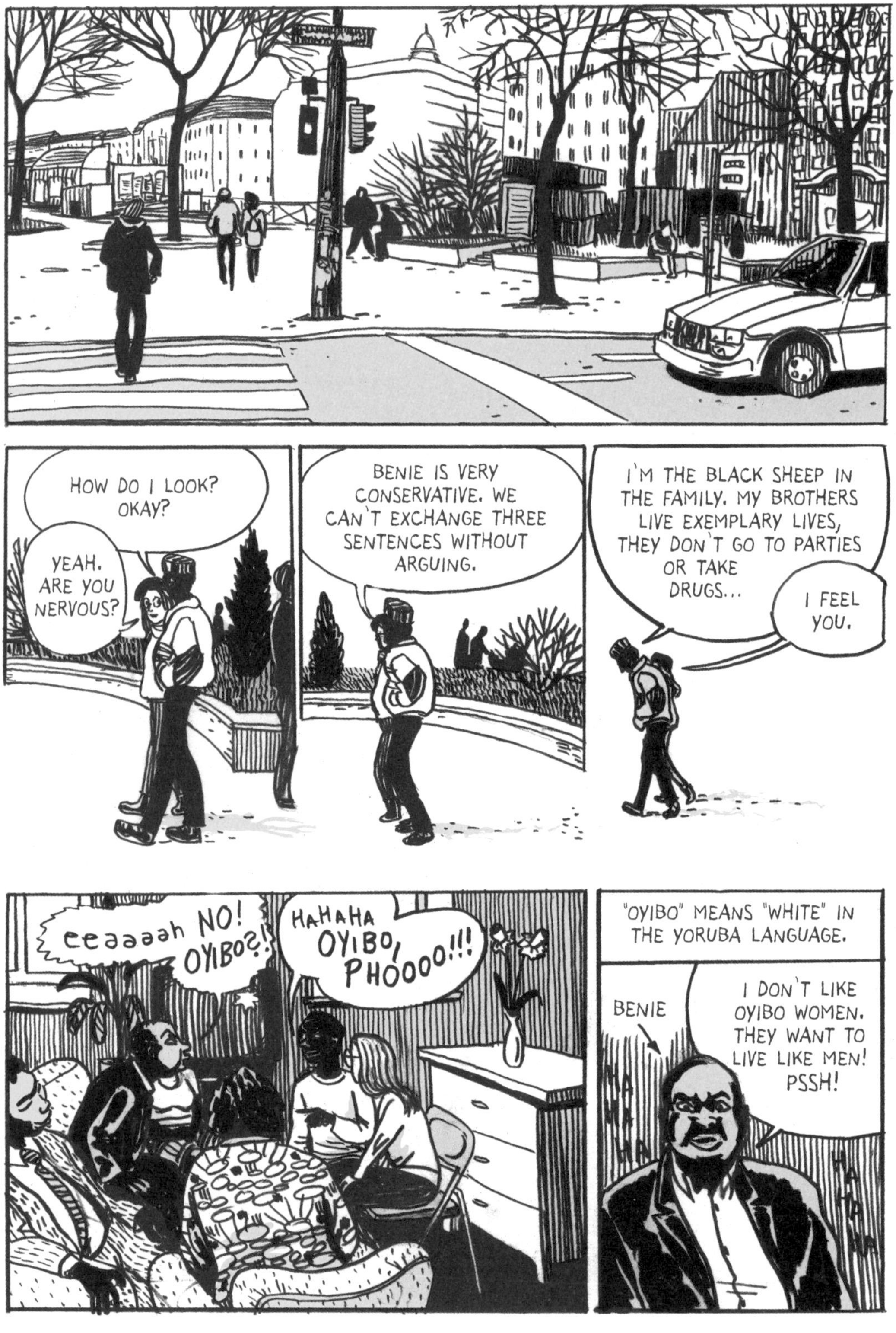
HOW DO I LOOK? OKAY?
YEAH. ARE YOU NERVOUS?
BENIE IS VERY CONSERVATIVE. WE CAN'T EXCHANGE THREE SENTENCES WITHOUT ARGUING.
I'M THE BLACK SHEEP IN THE FAMILY. MY BROTHERS LIVE EXEMPLARY LIVES, THEY DON'T GO TO PARTIES OR TAKE DRUGS...
I FEEL YOU.
eeaaaah NO! OYIBO?!
HAHAHA OYIBO, PHOOOO!!!
"OYIBO" MEANS "WHITE" IN THE YORUBA LANGUAGE.
BENIE
I DON'T LIKE OYIBO WOMEN. THEY WANT TO LIVE LIKE MEN! PSSH!
HA HA HA
HA HA HA HA

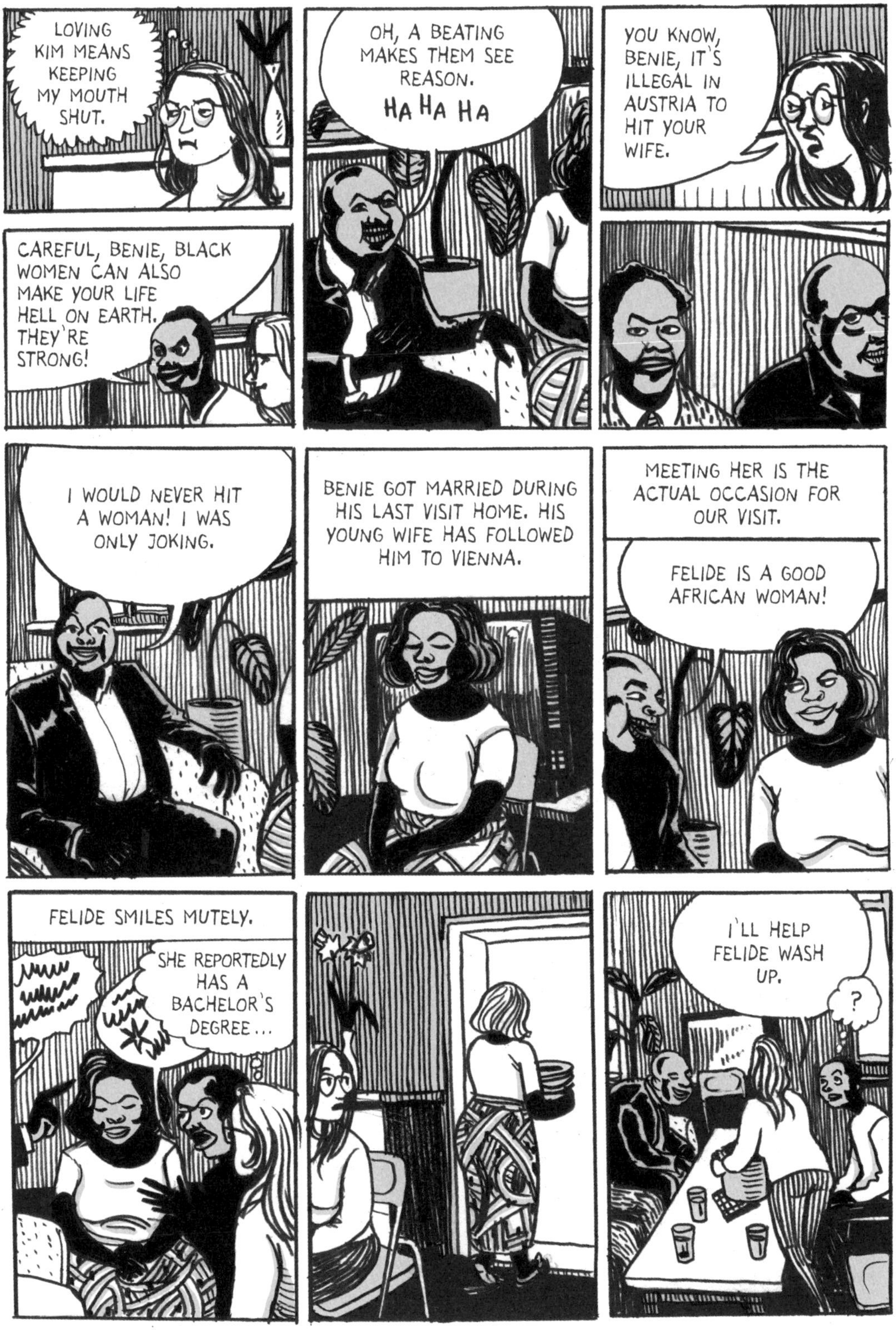
LOVING KIM MEANS KEEPING MY MOUTH SHUT.
OH, A BEATING MAKES THEM SEE REASON.
HA HA HA
YOU KNOW, BENIE, IT'S ILLEGAL IN AUSTRIA TO HIT YOUR WIFE.
CAREFUL, BENIE, BLACK WOMEN CAN ALSO MAKE YOUR LIFE HELL ON EARTH. THEY'RE STRONG!
I WOULD NEVER HIT A WOMAN! I WAS ONLY JOKING.
BENIE GOT MARRIED DURING HIS LAST VISIT HOME. HIS YOUNG WIFE HAS FOLLOWED HIM TO VIENNA.
MEETING HER IS THE ACTUAL OCCASION FOR OUR VISIT.
FELIDE IS A GOOD AFRICAN WOMAN!
FELIDE SMILES MUTELY.
SHE REPORTEDLY HAS A BACHELOR'S DEGREE...
I'LL HELP FELIDE WASH UP.
?

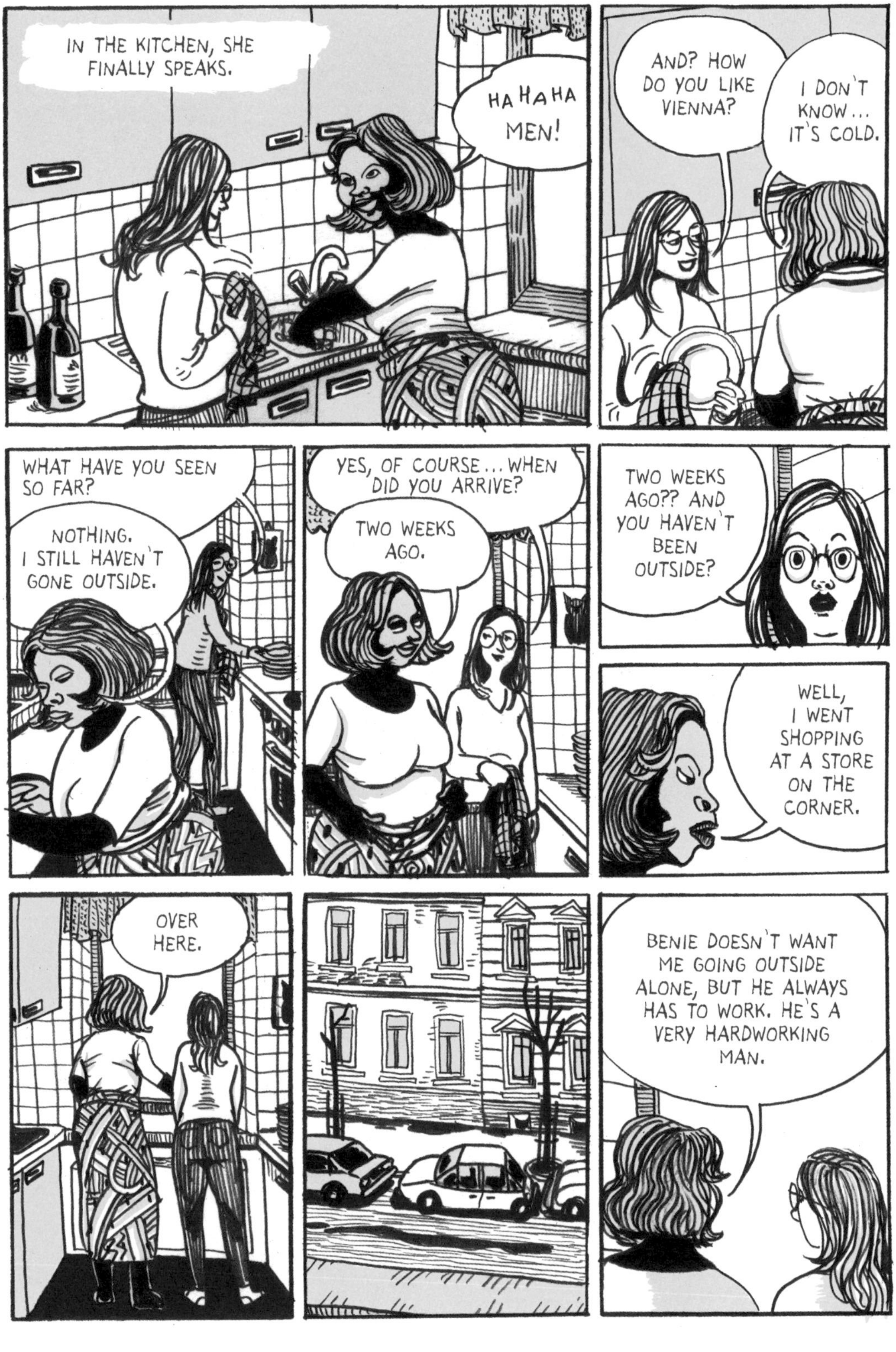
IN THE KITCHEN, SHE FINALLY SPEAKS.
HA HA HA MEN!
AND? HOW DO YOU LIKE VIENNA?
I DON'T KNOW... IT'S COLD.
WHAT HAVE YOU SEEN SO FAR?
NOTHING. I STILL HAVEN'T GONE OUTSIDE.
YES, OF COURSE... WHEN DID YOU ARRIVE?
TWO WEEKS AGO.
TWO WEEKS AGO?? AND YOU HAVEN'T BEEN OUTSIDE?
WELL, I WENT SHOPPING AT A STORE ON THE CORNER.
OVER HERE.
BENIE DOESN'T WANT ME GOING OUTSIDE ALONE, BUT HE ALWAYS HAS TO WORK. HE'S A VERY HARDWORKING MAN.

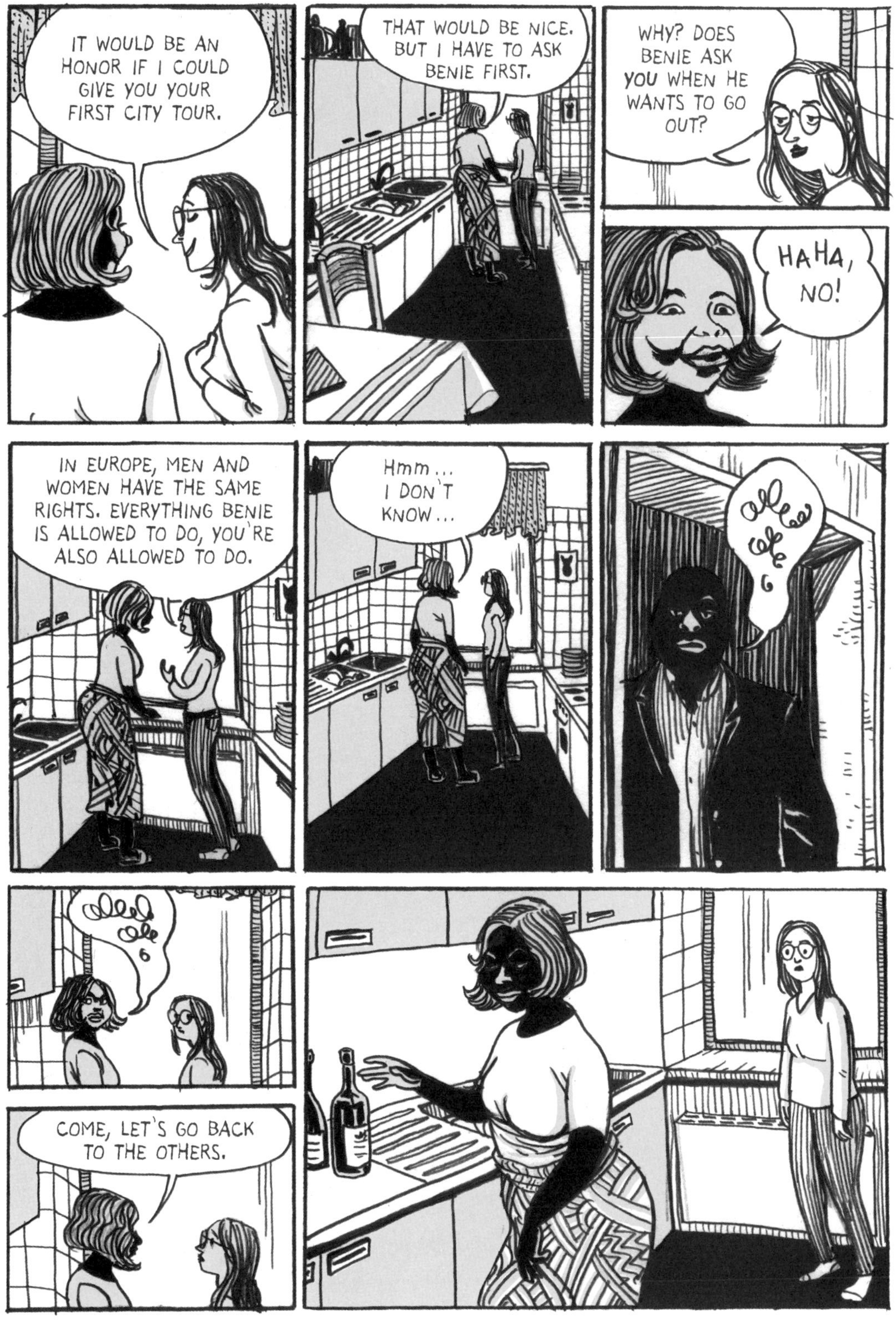
IT WOULD BE AN HONOR IF I COULD GIVE YOU YOUR FIRST CITY TOUR.
THAT WOULD BE NICE. BUT I HAVE TO ASK BENIE FIRST.
WHY? DOES BENIE ASK YOU WHEN HE WANTS TO GO OUT?
HAHA, NO!
IN EUROPE, MEN AND WOMEN HAVE THE SAME RIGHTS. EVERYTHING BENIE IS ALLOWED TO DO, YOU'RE ALSO ALLOWED TO DO.
Hmm... I DON'T KNOW...
COME, LET'S GO BACK TO THE OTHERS.

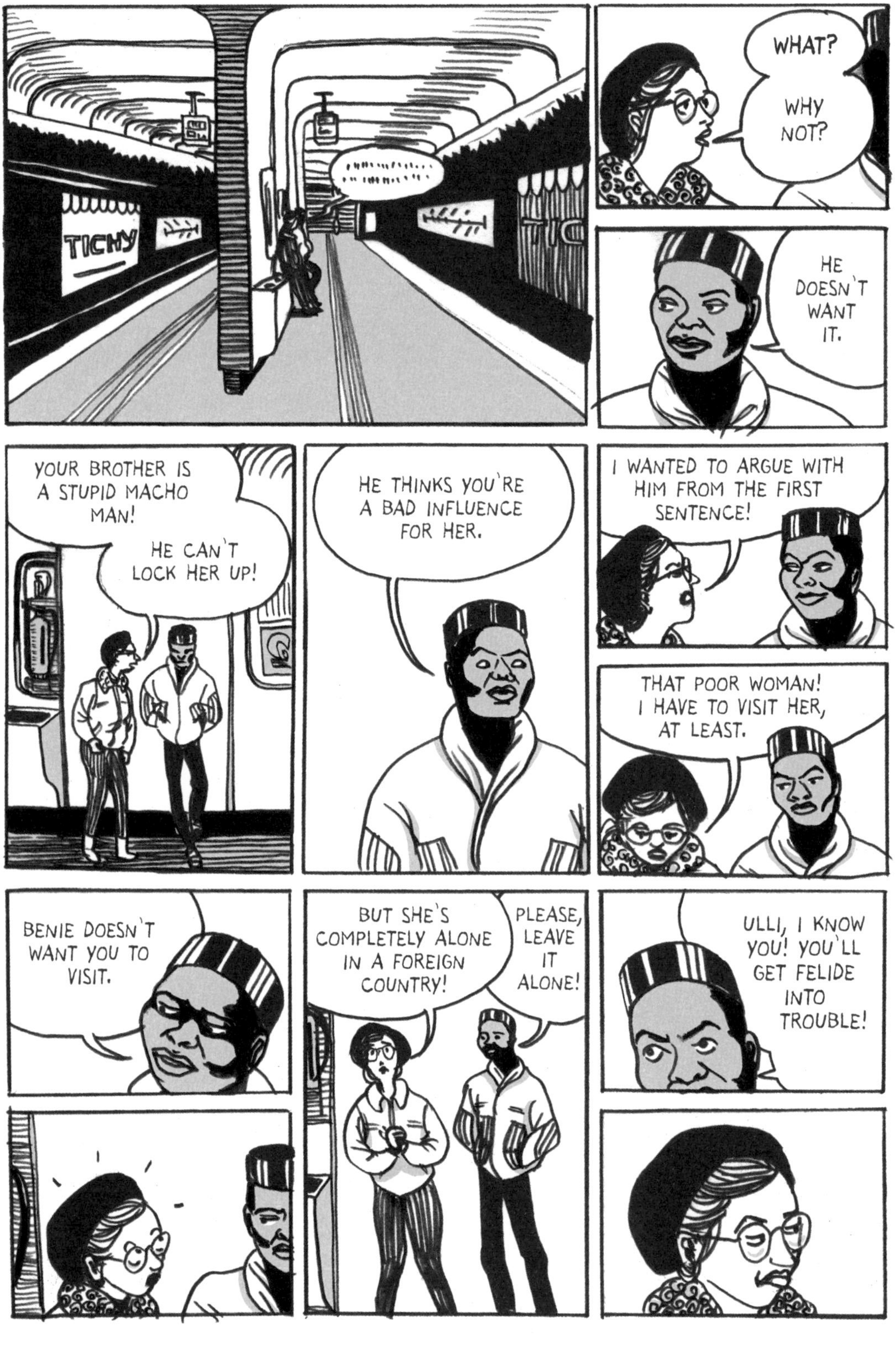
TICHY
WHAT?
WHY NOT?
HE DOESN'T WANT IT.
YOUR BROTHER IS A STUPID MACHO MAN!
HE CAN'T LOCK HER UP!
HE THINKS YOU'RE A BAD INFLUENCE FOR HER.
I WANTED TO ARGUE WITH HIM FROM THE FIRST SENTENCE!
THAT POOR WOMAN! I HAVE TO VISIT HER, AT LEAST.
BENIE DOESN'T WANT YOU TO VISIT.
BUT SHE'S COMPLETELY ALONE IN A FOREIGN COUNTRY!
PLEASE, LEAVE IT ALONE!
ULLI, I KNOW YOU! YOU'LL GET FELIDE INTO TROUBLE!

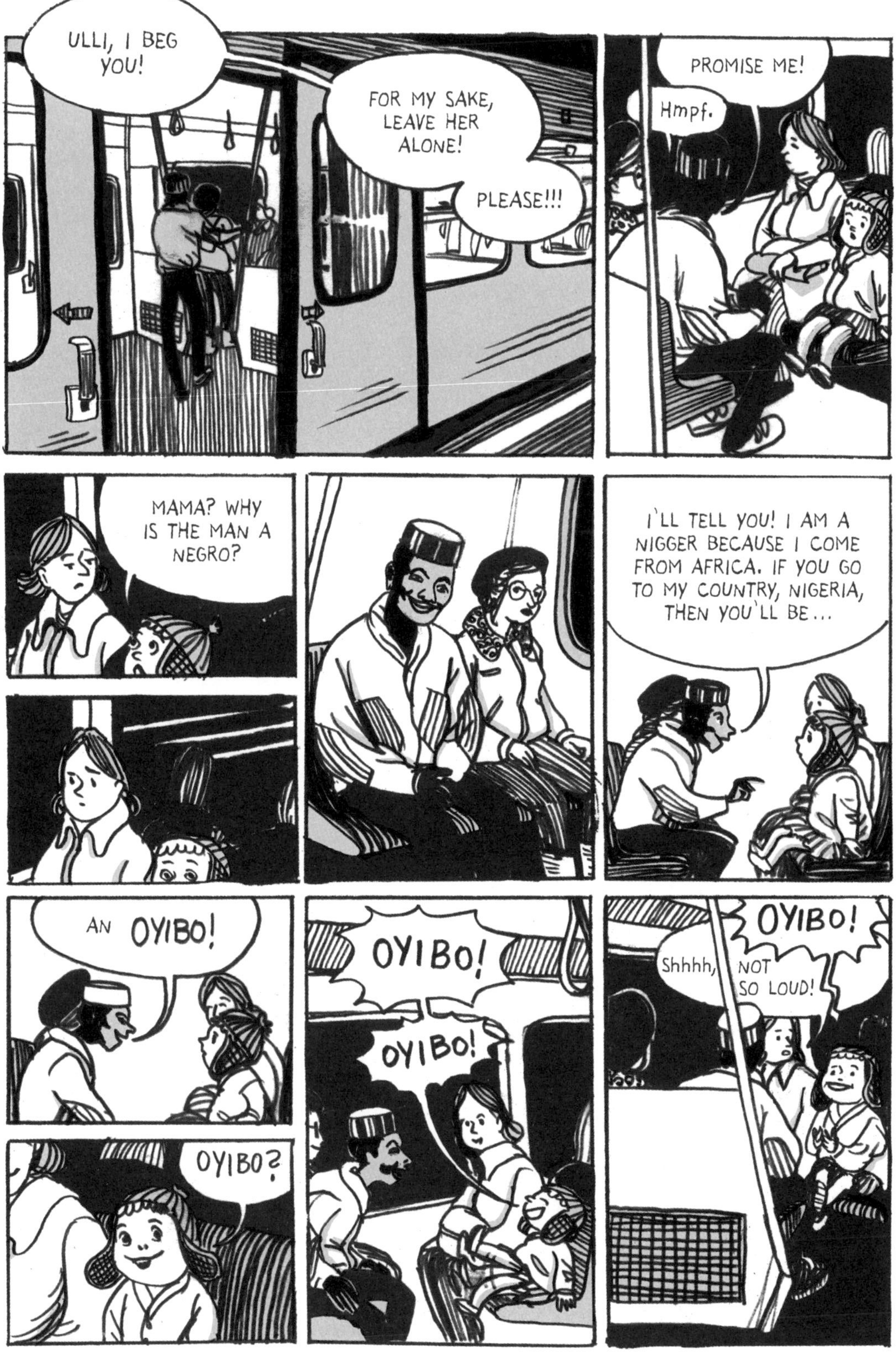
ULLI, I BEG YOU!
FOR MY SAKE, LEAVE HER ALONE!
PLEASE!!!
PROMISE ME!
Hmpf.
MAMA? WHY IS THE MAN A NEGRO?
I'LL TELL YOU! I AM A NIGGER BECAUSE I COME FROM AFRICA. IF YOU GO TO MY COUNTRY, NIGERIA, THEN YOU'LL BE...
AN OYIBO!
OYIBO?
OYIBO!
OYIBO!
OYIBO!
Shhhh, NOT SO LOUD!

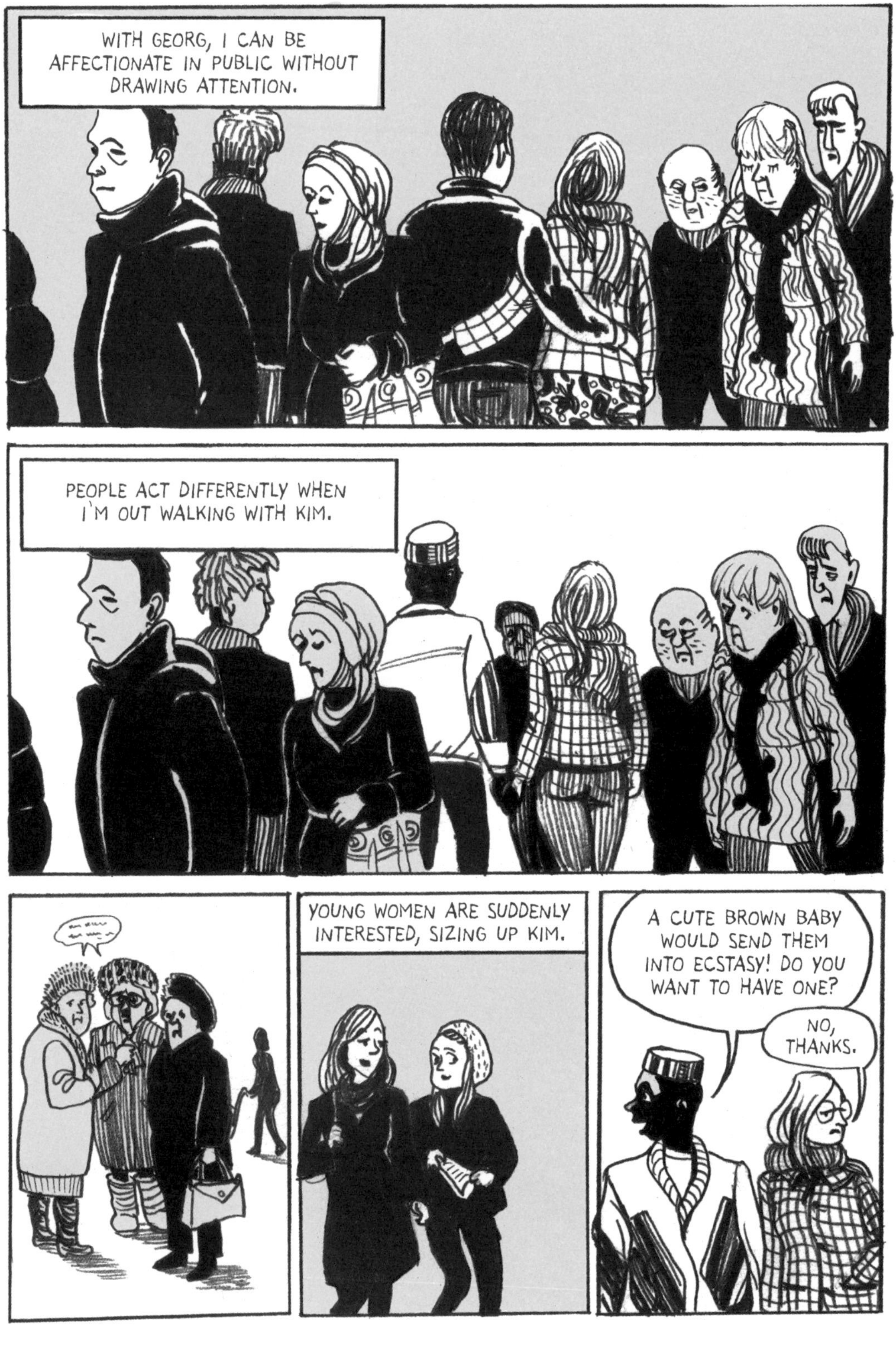
WITH GEORG, I CAN BE AFFECTIONATE IN PUBLIC WITHOUT DRAWING ATTENTION.
PEOPLE ACT DIFFERENTLY WHEN I'M OUT WALKING WITH KIM.
YOUNG WOMEN ARE SUDDENLY INTERESTED, SIZING UP KIM.
A CUTE BROWN BABY WOULD SEND THEM INTO ECSTASY! DO YOU WANT TO HAVE ONE?
NO, THANKS.

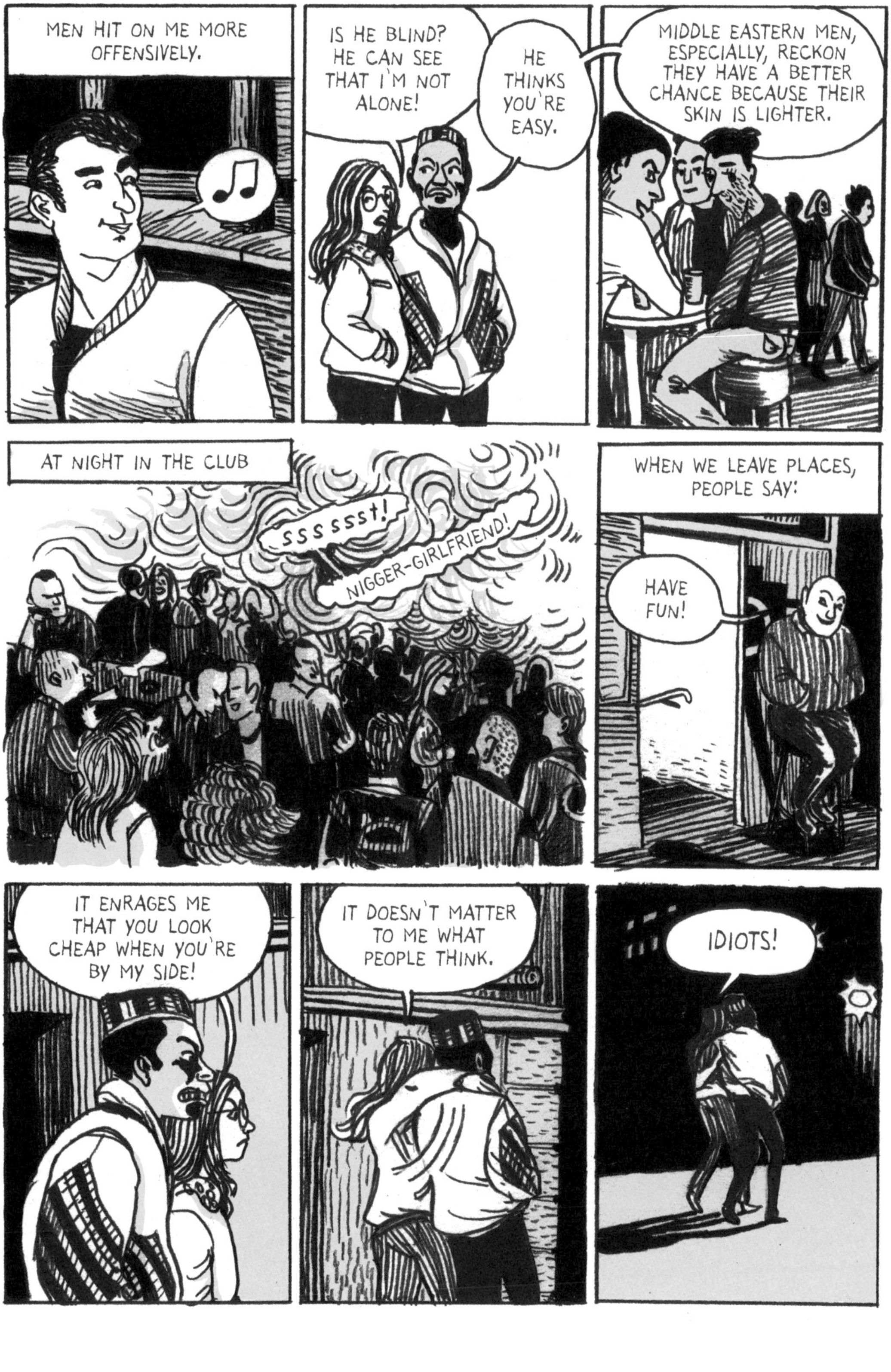
MEN HIT ON ME MORE OFFENSIVELY.
IS HE BLIND? HE CAN SEE THAT I'M NOT ALONE!
HE THINKS YOU'RE EASY.
MIDDLE EASTERN MEN, ESPECIALLY, RECKON THEY HAVE A BETTER CHANCE BECAUSE THEIR SKIN IS LIGHTER.
AT NIGHT IN THE CLUB
SSSSSST!
NIGGER-GIRLFRIEND!
WHEN WE LEAVE PLACES, PEOPLE SAY:
HAVE FUN!
IT ENRAGES ME THAT YOU LOOK CHEAP WHEN YOU'RE BY MY SIDE!
IT DOESN'T MATTER TO ME WHAT PEOPLE THINK.
IDIOTS!

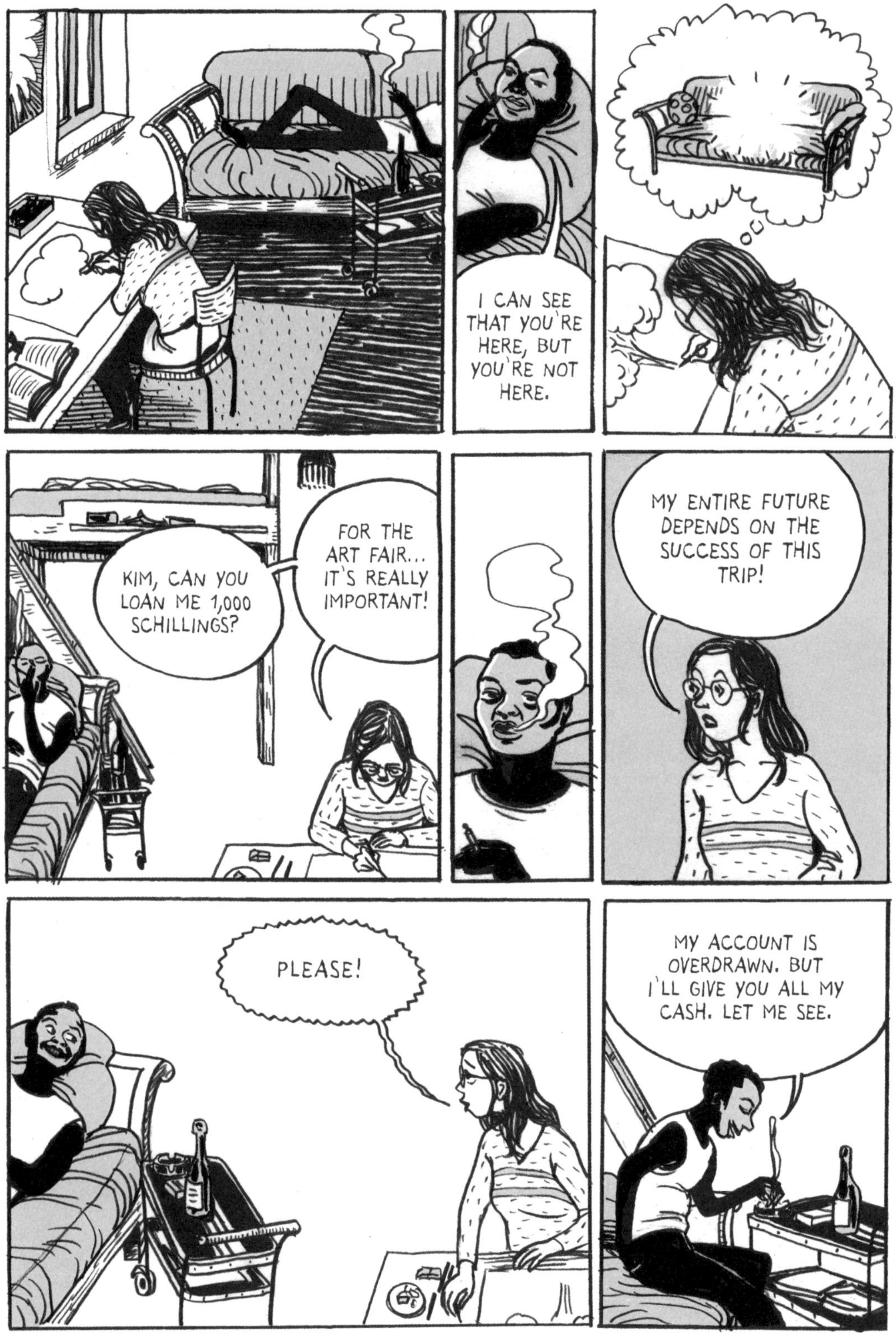
I CAN SEE THAT YOU'RE HERE, BUT YOU'RE NOT HERE.
KIM, CAN YOU LOAN ME 1,000 SCHILLINGS?
FOR THE ART FAIR... IT'S REALLY IMPORTANT!
MY ENTIRE FUTURE DEPENDS ON THE SUCCESS OF THIS TRIP!
PLEASE!
MY ACCOUNT IS OVERDRAWN. BUT I'LL GIVE YOU ALL MY CASH. LET ME SEE.

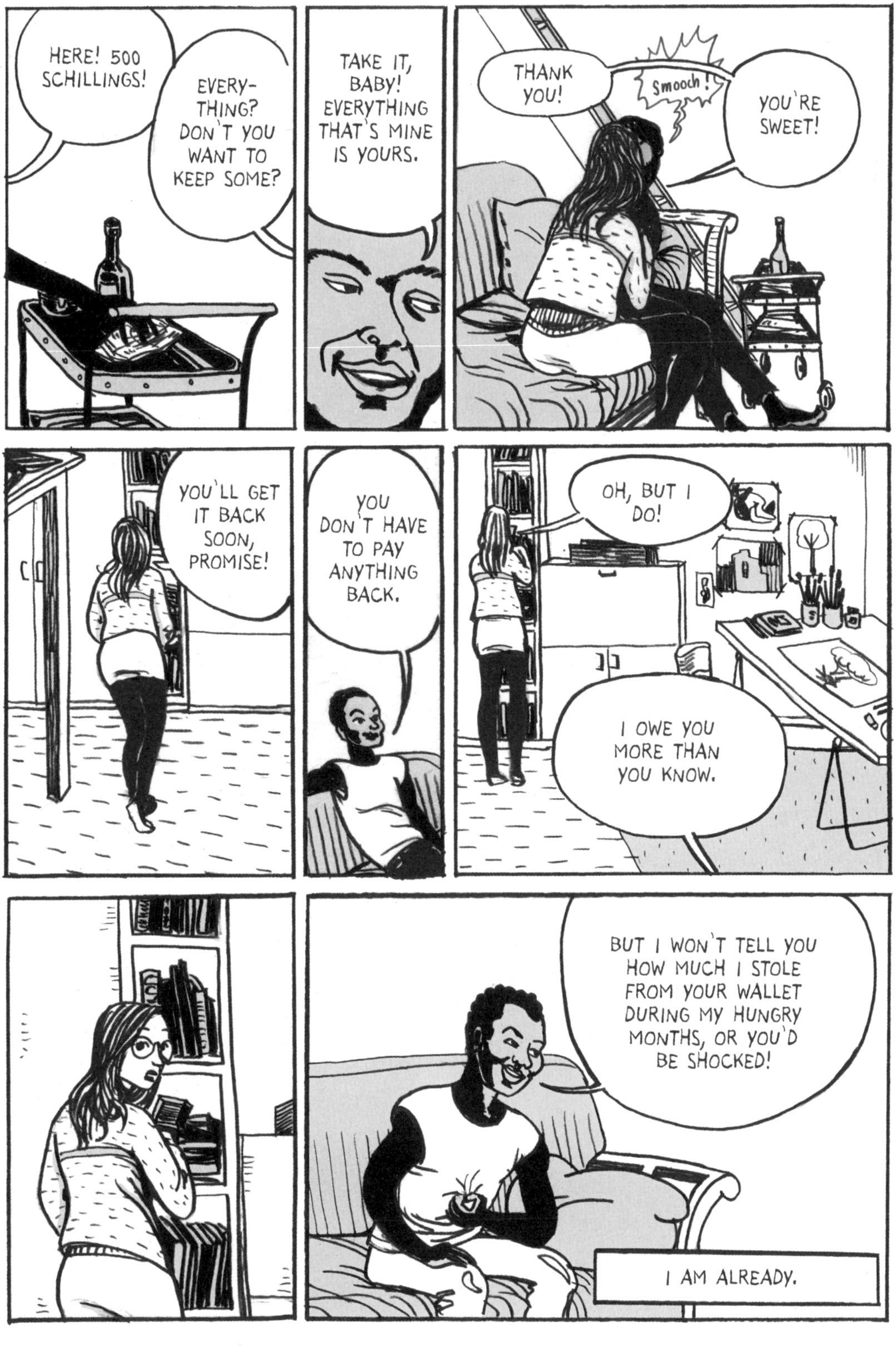
HERE! 500 SCHILLINGS!
EVERY-THING? DON'T YOU WANT TO KEEP SOME?
TAKE IT, BABY! EVERYTHING THAT'S MINE IS YOURS.
THANK YOU!
Smooch!
YOU'RE SWEET!
YOU'LL GET IT BACK SOON, PROMISE!
YOU DON'T HAVE TO PAY ANYTHING BACK.
OH, BUT I DO!
I OWE YOU MORE THAN YOU KNOW.
BUT I WON'T TELL YOU HOW MUCH I STOLE FROM YOUR WALLET DURING MY HUNGRY MONTHS, OR YOU'D BE SHOCKED!
I AM ALREADY.

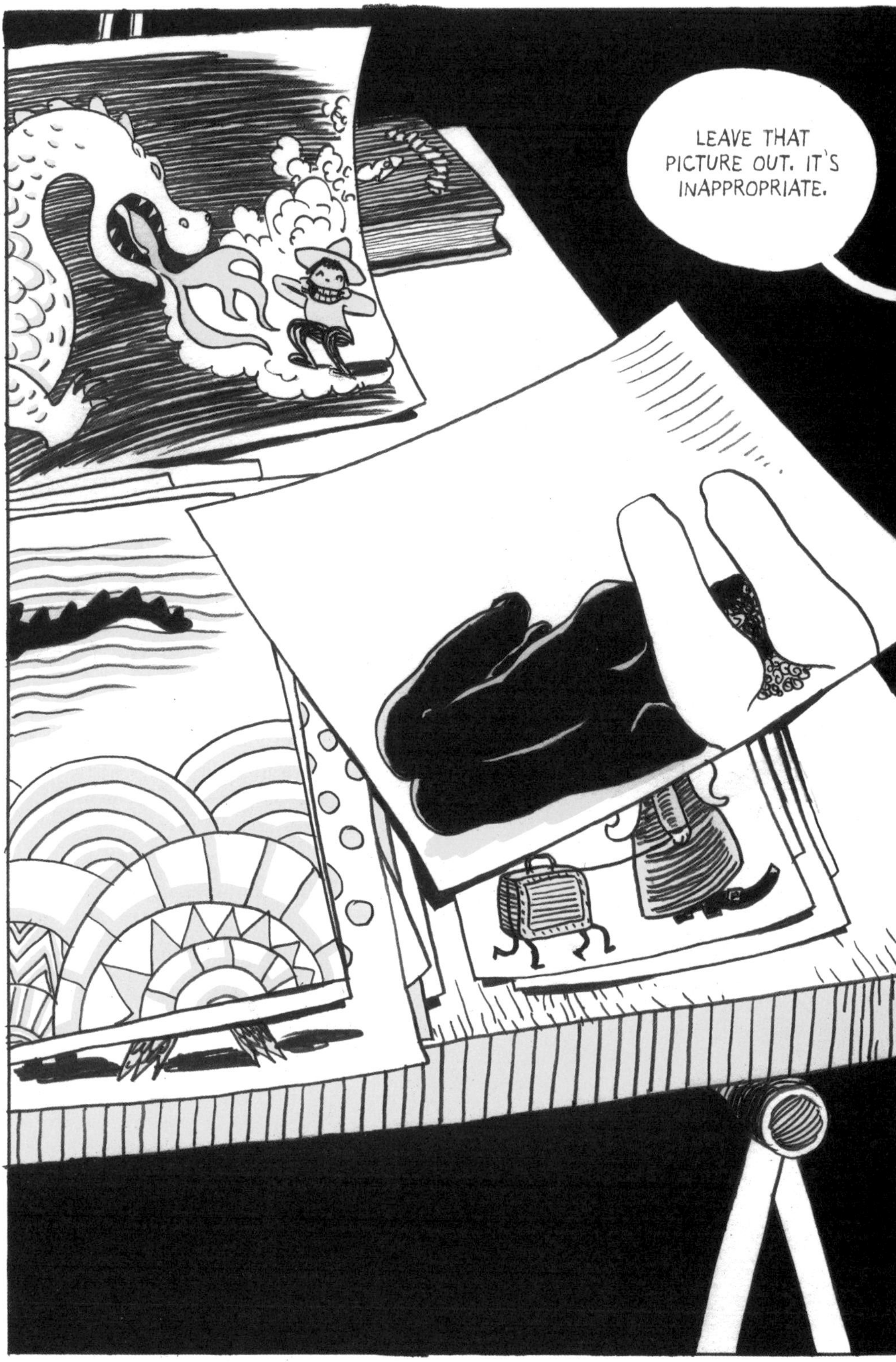
LEAVE THAT PICTURE OUT. IT'S INAPPROPRIATE.

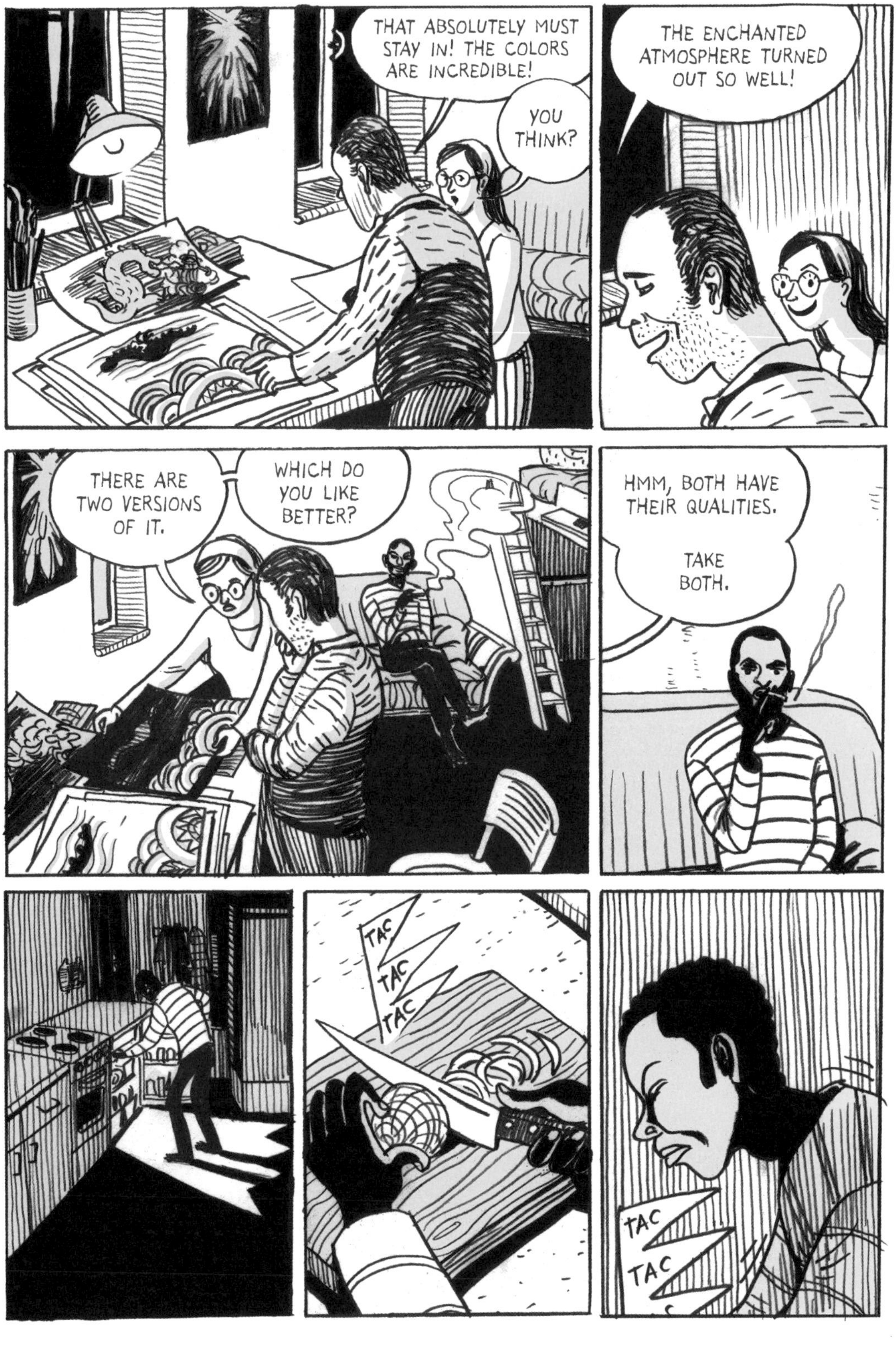
THAT ABSOLUTELY MUST STAY IN! THE COLORS ARE INCREDIBLE!
YOU THINK?
THE ENCHANTED ATMOSPHERE TURNED OUT SO WELL!
THERE ARE TWO VERSIONS OF IT.
WHICH DO YOU LIKE BETTER?
HMM, BOTH HAVE THEIR QUALITIES.
TAKE BOTH.
TAC
TAC
TAC
TAC
TAC

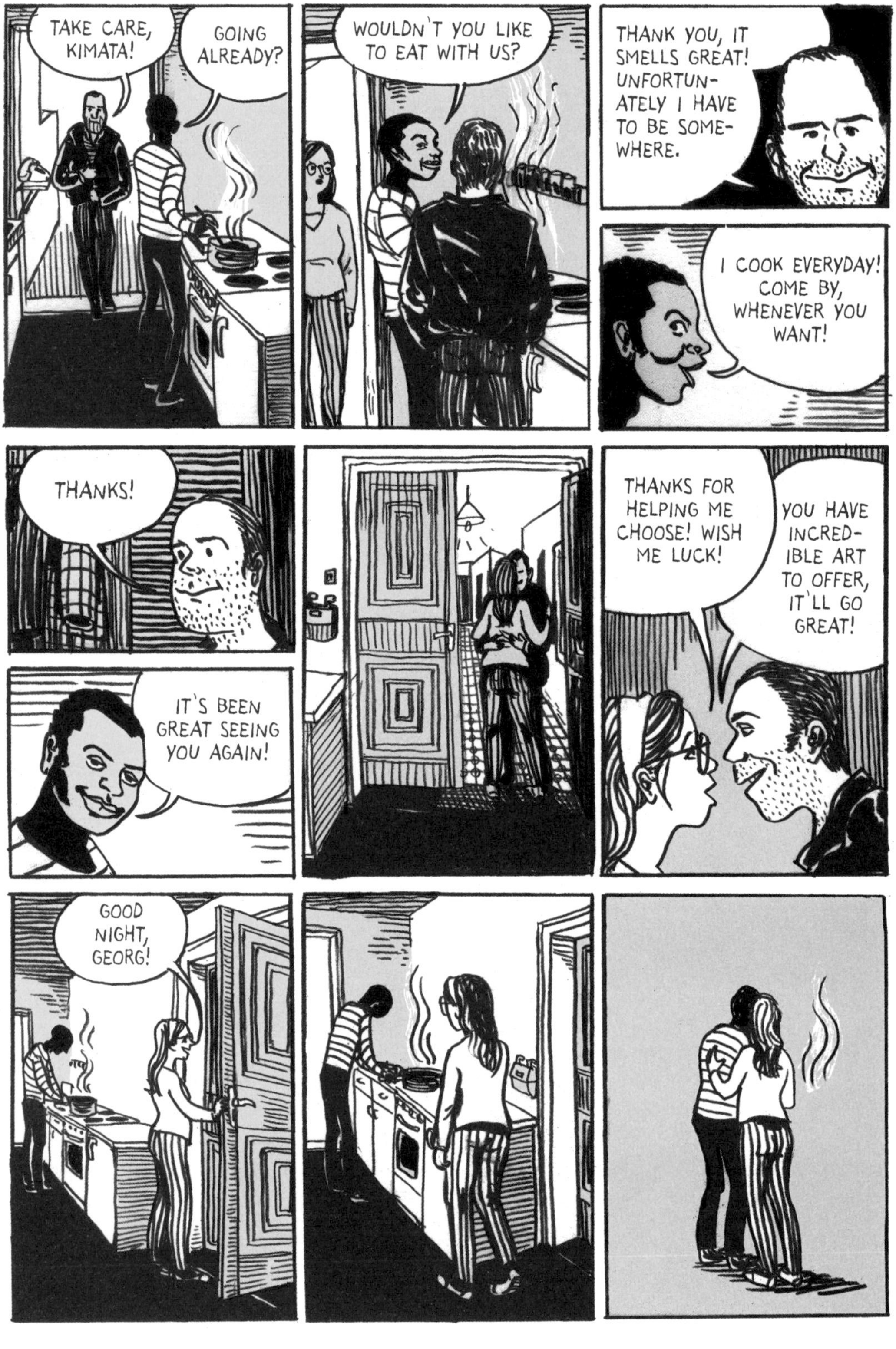
TAKE CARE, KIMATA!
GOING ALREADY?
WOULDN'T YOU LIKE TO EAT WITH US?
THANK YOU, IT SMELLS GREAT! UNFORTUNATELY I HAVE TO BE SOMEWHERE.
I COOK EVERYDAY! COME BY, WHENEVER YOU WANT!
THANKS!
IT'S BEEN GREAT SEEING YOU AGAIN!
THANKS FOR HELPING ME CHOOSE! WISH ME LUCK!
YOU HAVE INCREDIBLE ART TO OFFER, IT'LL GO GREAT!
GOOD NIGHT, GEORG!

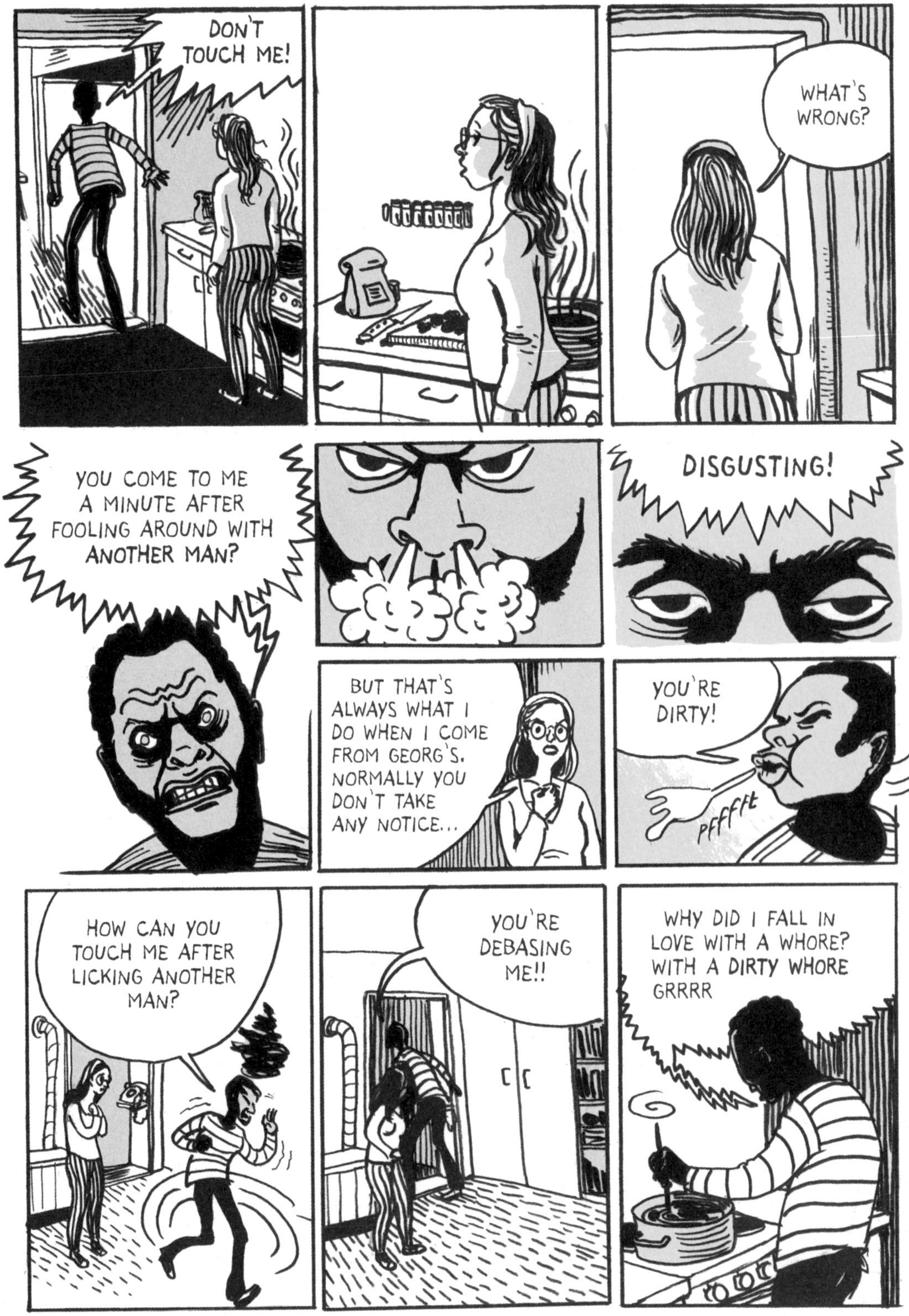
DON'T TOUCH ME!
WHAT'S WRONG?
YOU COME TO ME A MINUTE AFTER FOOLING AROUND WITH ANOTHER MAN?
DISGUSTING!
BUT THAT'S ALWAYS WHAT I DO WHEN I COME FROM GEORG'S. NORMALLY YOU DON'T TAKE ANY NOTICE...
YOU'RE DIRTY!
pffffft
HOW CAN YOU TOUCH ME AFTER LICKING ANOTHER MAN?
YOU'RE DEBASING ME!!
WHY DID I FALL IN LOVE WITH A WHORE? WITH A DIRTY WHORE GRRRR

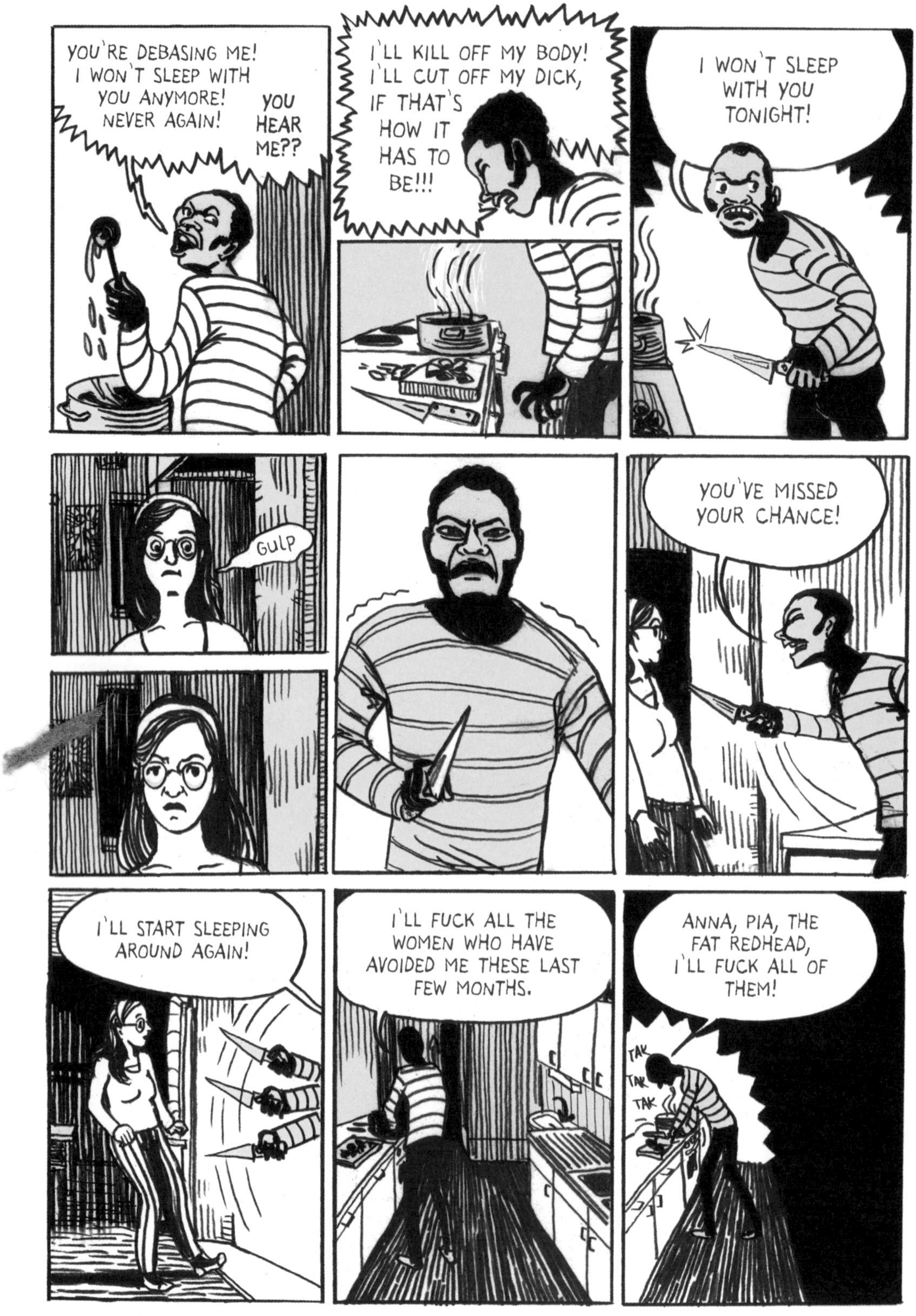
YOU'RE DEBASING ME! I WON'T SLEEP WITH YOU ANYMORE! NEVER AGAIN!
YOU HEAR ME??
I'LL KILL OFF MY BODY! I'LL CUT OFF MY DICK, IF THAT'S HOW IT HAS TO BE!!!
I WON'T SLEEP WITH YOU TONIGHT!
GULP
YOU'VE MISSED YOUR CHANCE!
I'LL START SLEEPING AROUND AGAIN!
I'LL FUCK ALL THE WOMEN WHO HAVE AVOIDED ME THESE LAST FEW MONTHS.
ANNA, PIA, THE FAT REDHEAD, I'LL FUCK ALL OF THEM!
TAK
TAK
TAK

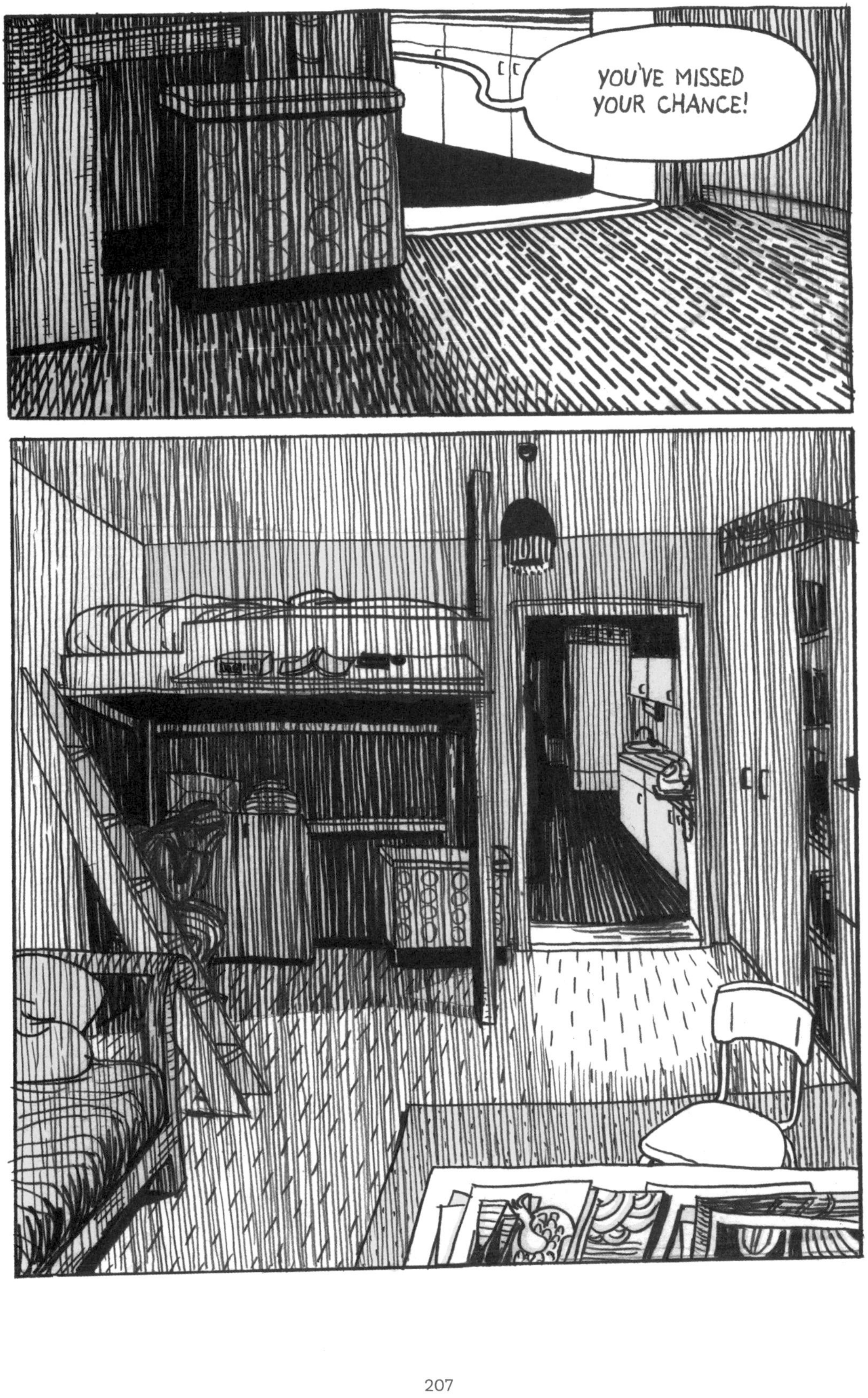
YOU'VE MISSED YOUR CHANCE!

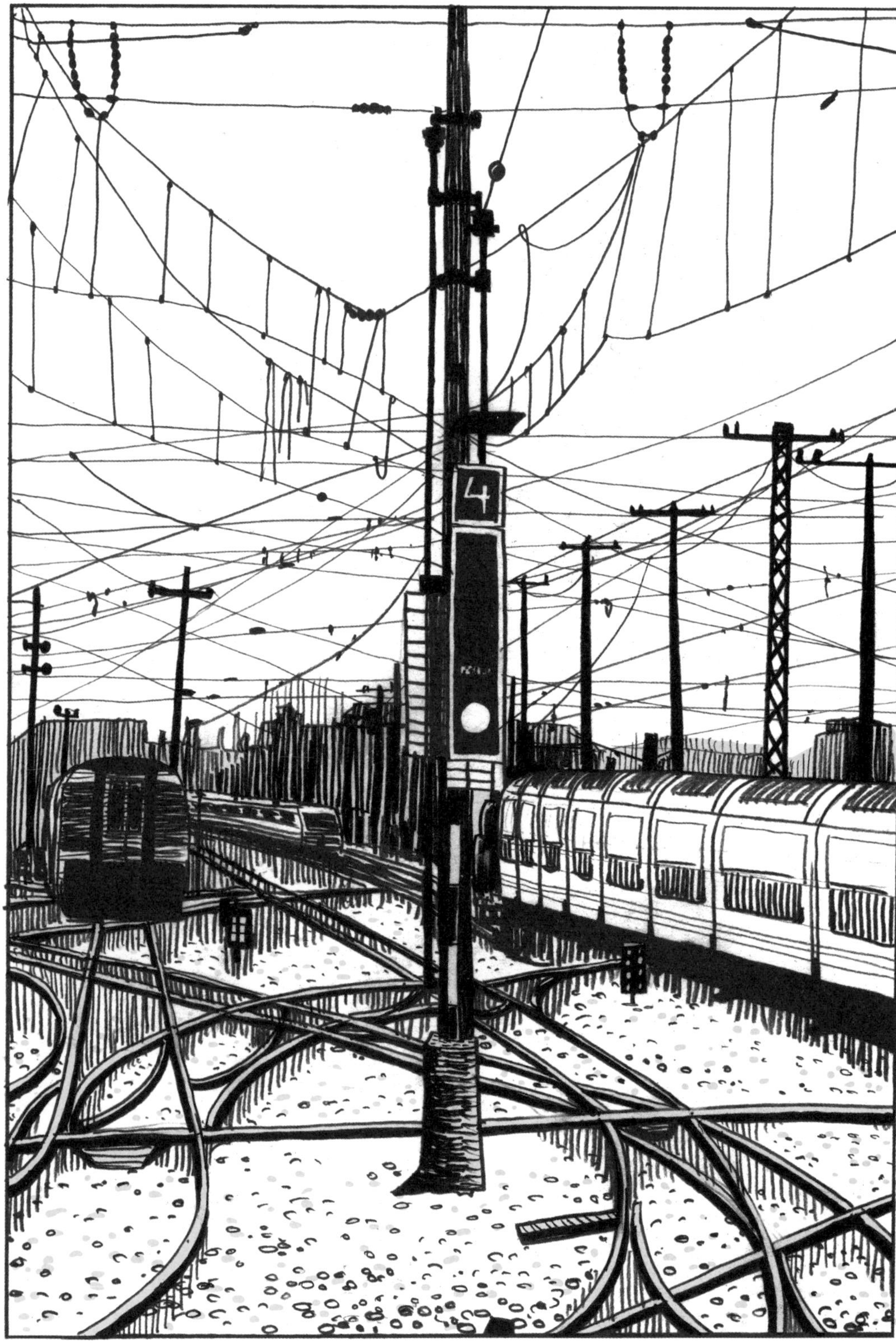
4

THE DINING CAR ON THE OVERNIGHT TRAIN.

WOULD YOU LIKE ANYTHING ELSE?

NO, THANK YOU!

THIS IS MY PORTFOLIO FOLDER, A REAL, PROFESSIONAL PRESENTATION FOLDER, BLACK LEATHER.

IT WAS EXPENSIVE. I FELT IMPORTANT JUST BUYING IT. OF COURSE I TOOK IT WITH ME IN THE DINING CAR.

IN IT, THERE WAS A PRINT-READY PICTURE BOOK — A YEAR'S WORK.

WOOOOOEEE

WOOOOOOOEEEEEEE

ON THE WAY INTO THE STATION I STARTED FEELING SICK. MY STOMACH TURNED INSIDE OUT, AN INNOCENT-LOOKING VEGETABLE DISH ENDED UP IN A STORM DRAIN. EITHER I'M PREGNANT, OR IT'S THE ANXIETY.

KIM HAD CALMED DOWN AGAIN. I'D BEEN CAUTIOUS AND KEPT FROM HIM THAT I HAD NO IDEA WHERE I'D STAY IN BOLOGNA. MY BUDGET ONLY COVERED PROVISIONS.

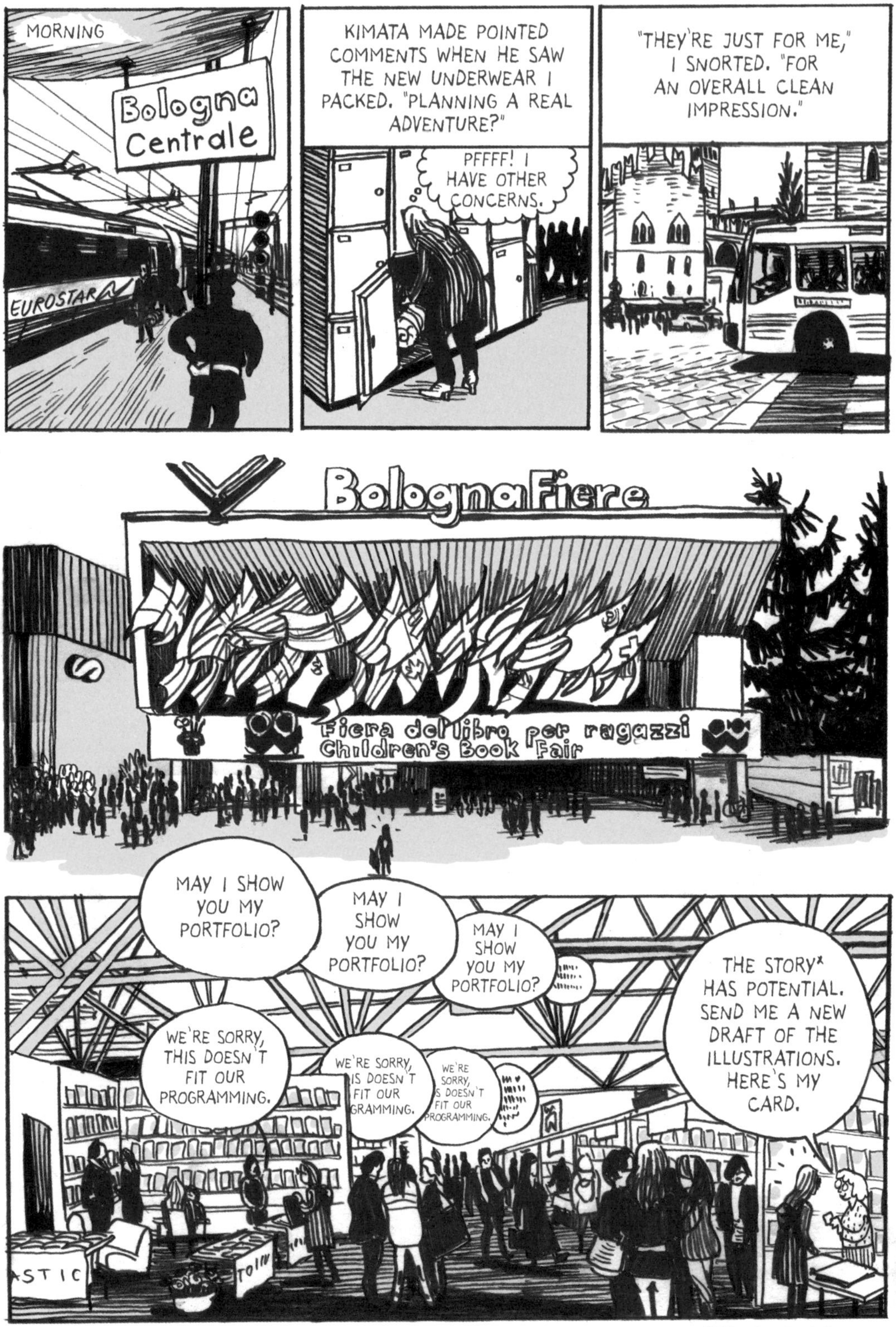
MORNING
Bologna Centrale
EUROSTAR
KIMATA MADE POINTED COMMENTS WHEN HE SAW THE NEW UNDERWEAR I PACKED. "PLANNING A REAL ADVENTURE?"
PFFFF! I HAVE OTHER CONCERNS.
"THEY'RE JUST FOR ME," I SNORTED. "FOR AN OVERALL CLEAN IMPRESSION."
BolognaFiere
Fiera del libro per ragazzi
Children's Book Fair
MAY I SHOW YOU MY PORTFOLIO?
MAY I SHOW YOU MY PORTFOLIO?
MAY I SHOW YOU MY PORTFOLIO?
WE'RE SORRY, THIS DOESN'T FIT OUR PROGRAMMING.
WE'RE SORRY, IS DOESN'T FIT OUR GRAMMING.
WE'RE SORRY, S DOESN'T FIT OUR PROGRAMMING.
THE STORY* HAS POTENTIAL. SEND ME A NEW DRAFT OF THE ILLUSTRATIONS. HERE'S MY CARD.
STIC

*THE TEXT IS BY KÄTHE RECHEIS AND FRIEDL HOFBAUER.

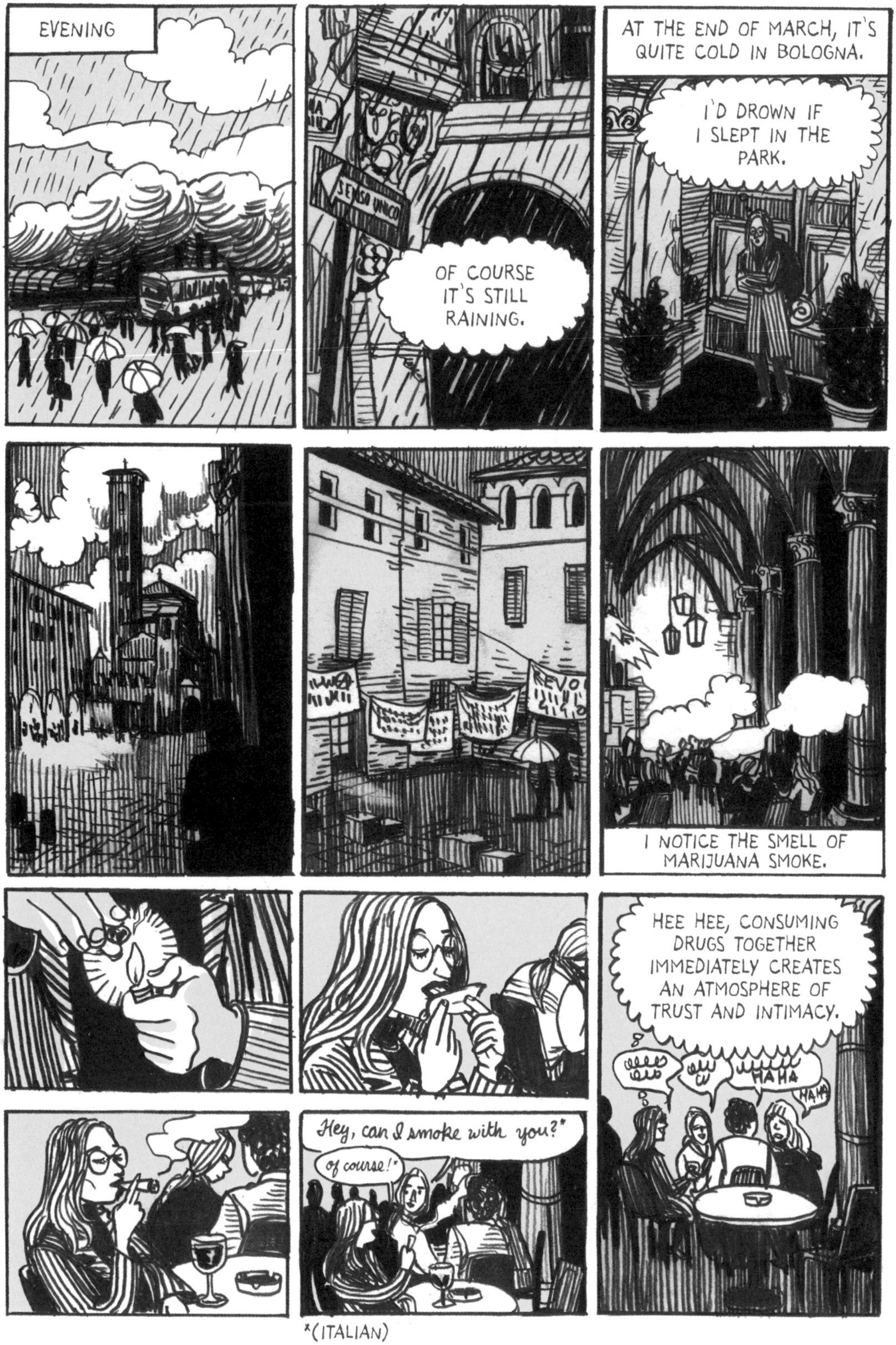
EVENING
OF COURSE IT'S STILL RAINING.
AT THE END OF MARCH, IT'S QUITE COLD IN BOLOGNA.
I'D DROWN IF I SLEPT IN THE PARK.
REVO
I NOTICE THE SMELL OF MARIJUANA SMOKE.
HEE HEE, CONSUMING DRUGS TOGETHER IMMEDIATELY CREATES AN ATMOSPHERE OF TRUST AND INTIMACY.
HA HA
HA HA
Hey, can I smoke with you?*
of course!*

*(ITALIAN)

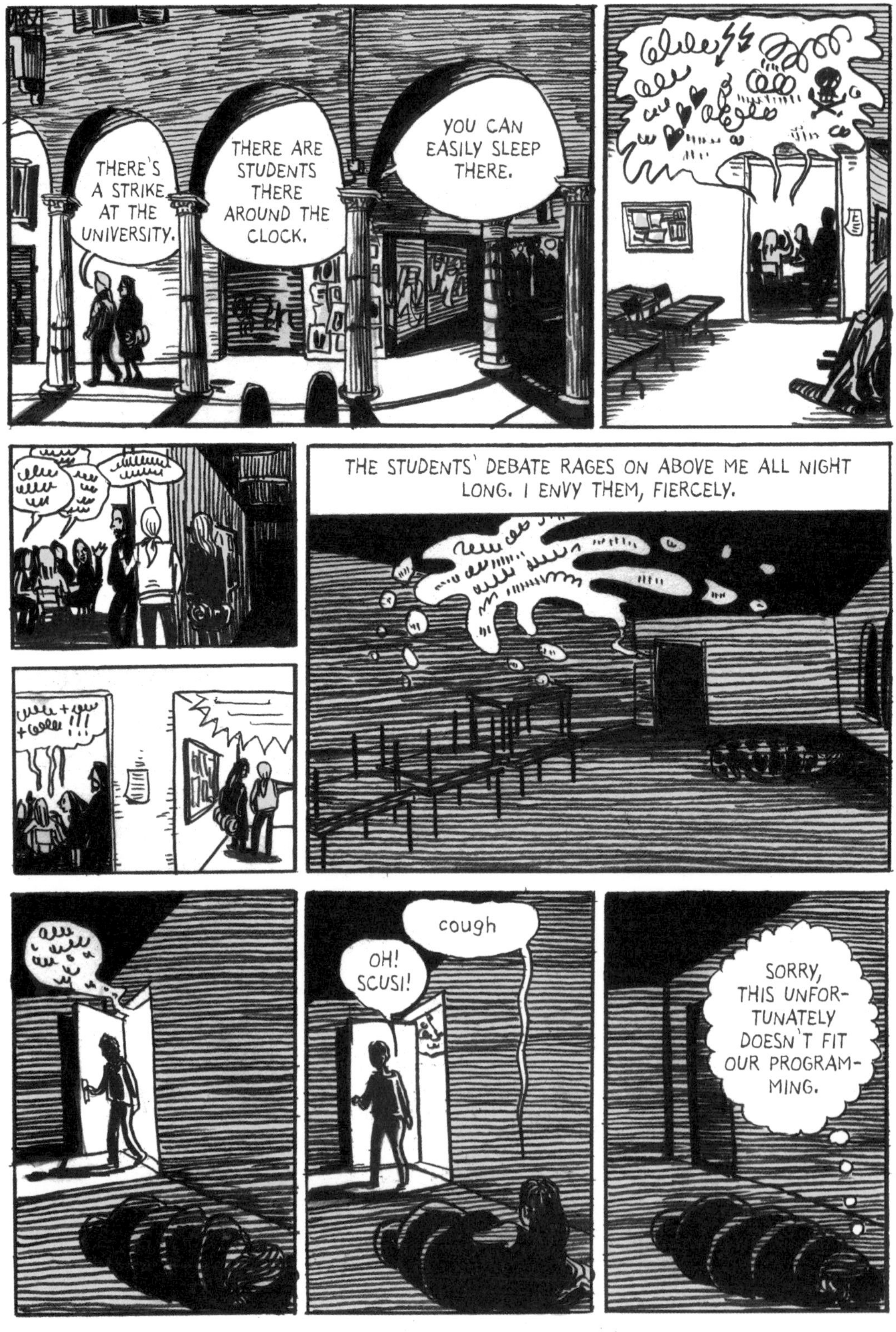
THERE'S A STRIKE AT THE UNIVERSITY.
THERE ARE STUDENTS THERE AROUND THE CLOCK.
YOU CAN EASILY SLEEP THERE.
THE STUDENTS' DEBATE RAGES ON ABOVE ME ALL NIGHT LONG. I ENVY THEM, FIERCELY.
cough
OH! SCUSI!
SORRY, THIS UNFORTUNATELY DOESN'T FIT OUR PROGRAMMING.

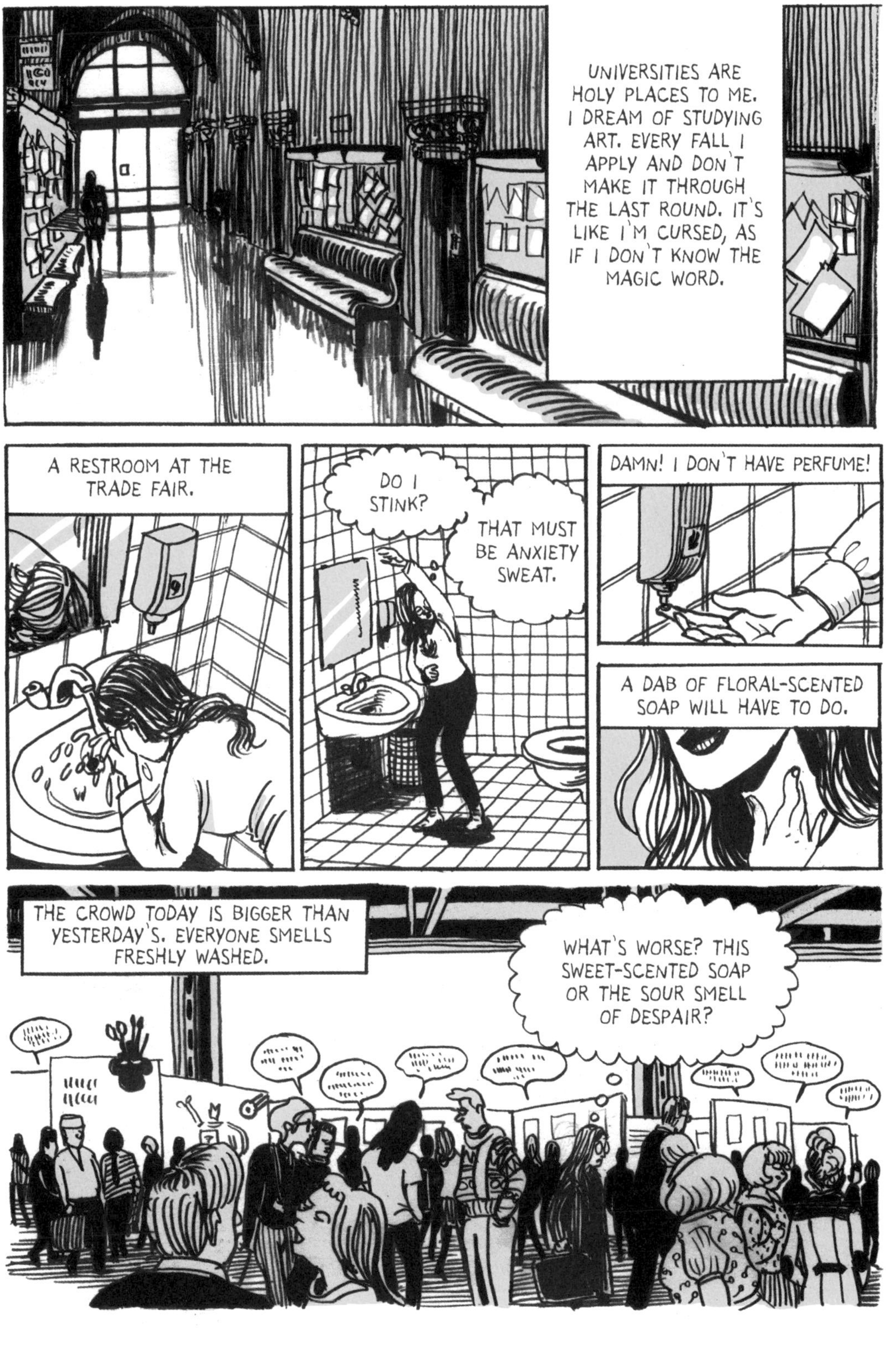
UNIVERSITIES ARE HOLY PLACES TO ME. I DREAM OF STUDYING ART. EVERY FALL I APPLY AND DON'T MAKE IT THROUGH THE LAST ROUND. IT'S LIKE I'M CURSED, AS IF I DON'T KNOW THE MAGIC WORD.
A RESTROOM AT THE TRADE FAIR.
DO I STINK?
THAT MUST BE ANXIETY SWEAT.
DAMN! I DON'T HAVE PERFUME!
A DAB OF FLORAL-SCENTED SOAP WILL HAVE TO DO.
THE CROWD TODAY IS BIGGER THAN YESTERDAY'S. EVERYONE SMELLS FRESHLY WASHED.
WHAT'S WORSE? THIS SWEET-SCENTED SOAP OR THE SOUR SMELL OF DESPAIR?

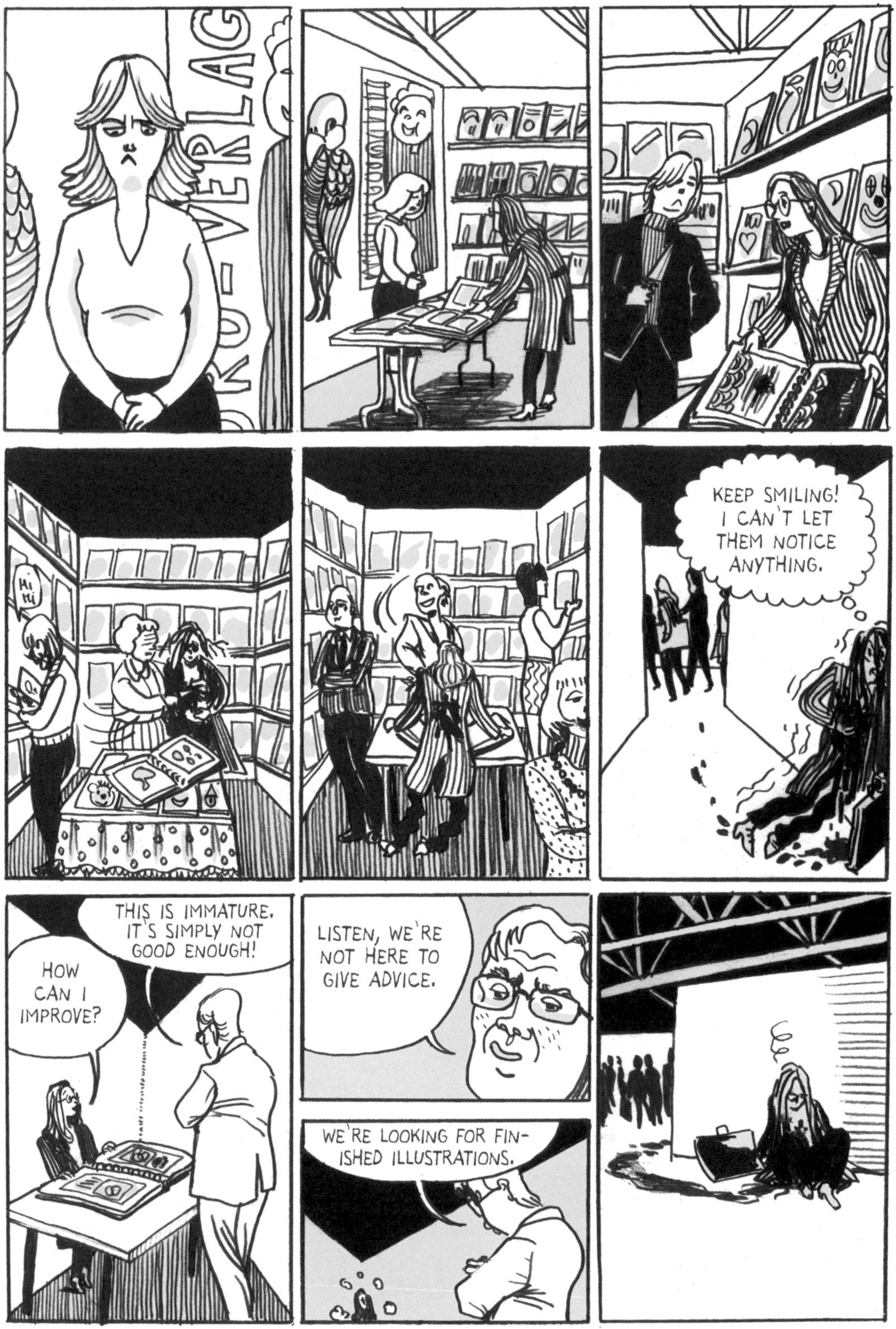

RO-VERLAG
HI HI
KEEP SMILING! I CAN'T LET THEM NOTICE ANYTHING.
HOW CAN I IMPROVE?
THIS IS IMMATURE. IT'S SIMPLY NOT GOOD ENOUGH!
LISTEN, WE'RE NOT HERE TO GIVE ADVICE.
WE'RE LOOKING FOR FIN-ISHED ILLUSTRATIONS.

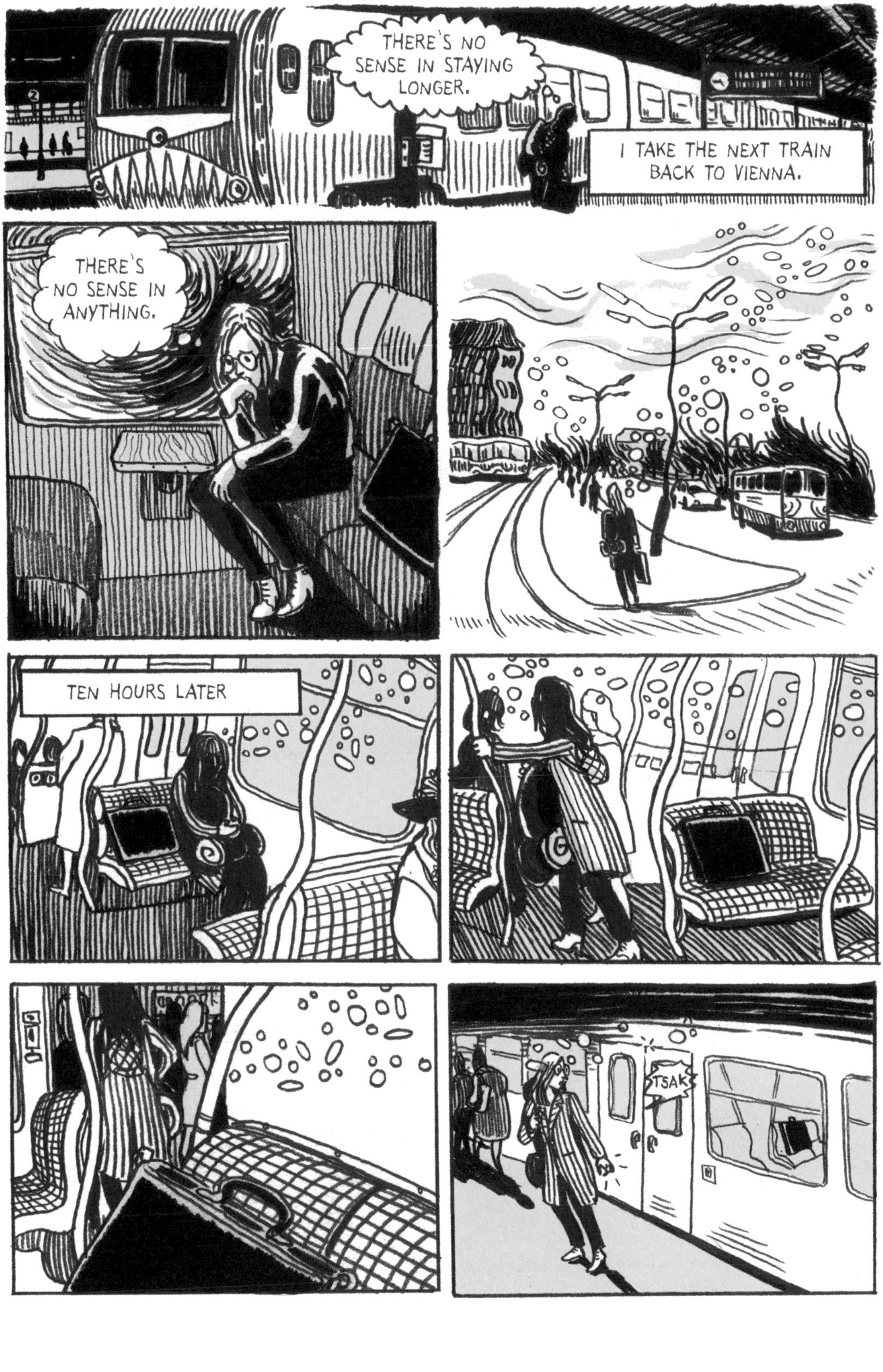
THERE'S NO SENSE IN STAYING LONGER.
I TAKE THE NEXT TRAIN BACK TO VIENNA.
THERE'S NO SENSE IN ANYTHING.
TEN HOURS LATER
TSAK

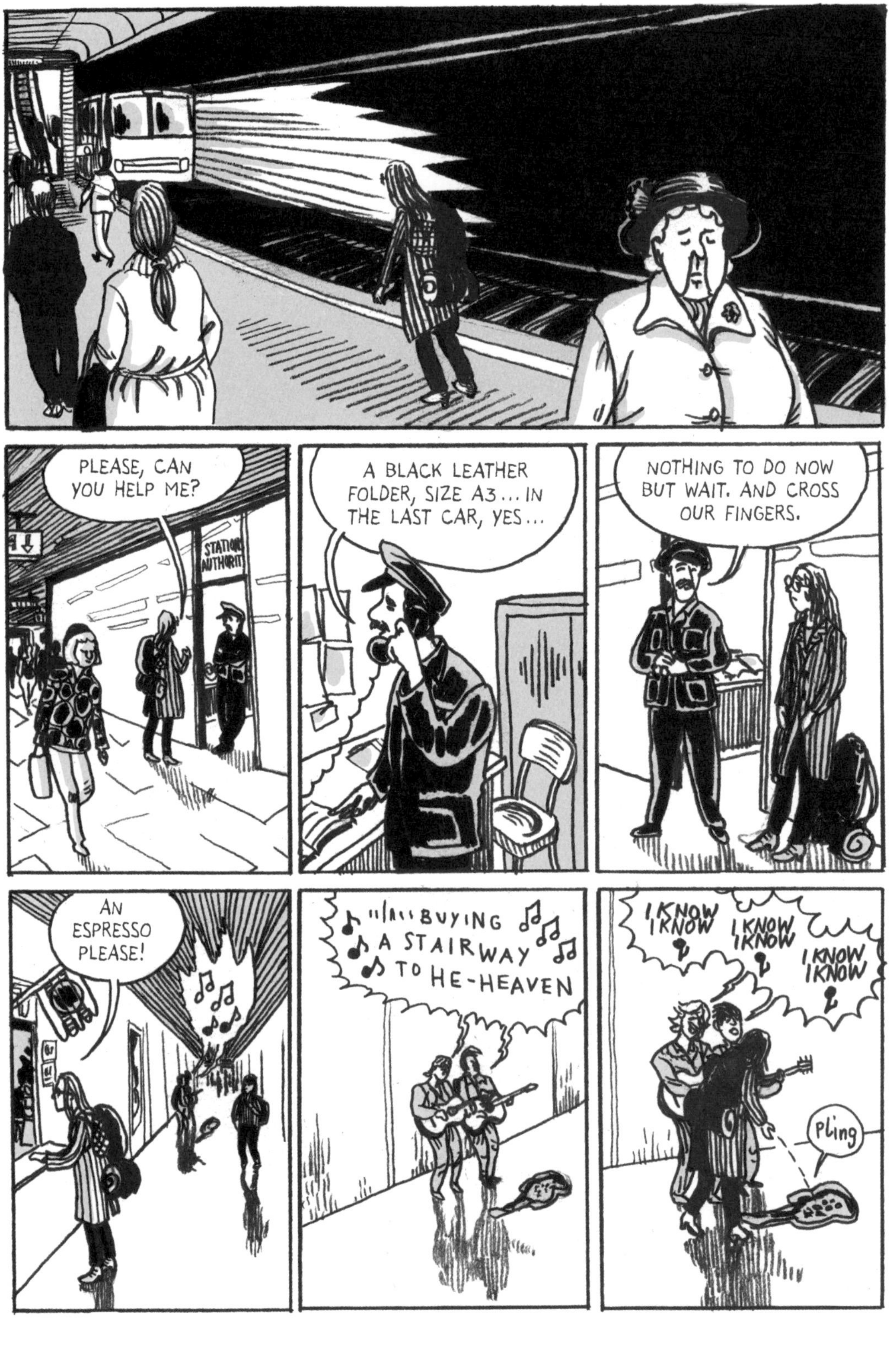
PLEASE, CAN YOU HELP ME?
A BLACK LEATHER FOLDER, SIZE A3... IN THE LAST CAR, YES...
NOTHING TO DO NOW BUT WAIT. AND CROSS OUR FINGERS.
AN ESPRESSO PLEASE!
BUYING A STAIRWAY TO HE-HEAVEN
I KNOW I KNOW
I KNOW I KNOW
I KNOW I KNOW
Pling

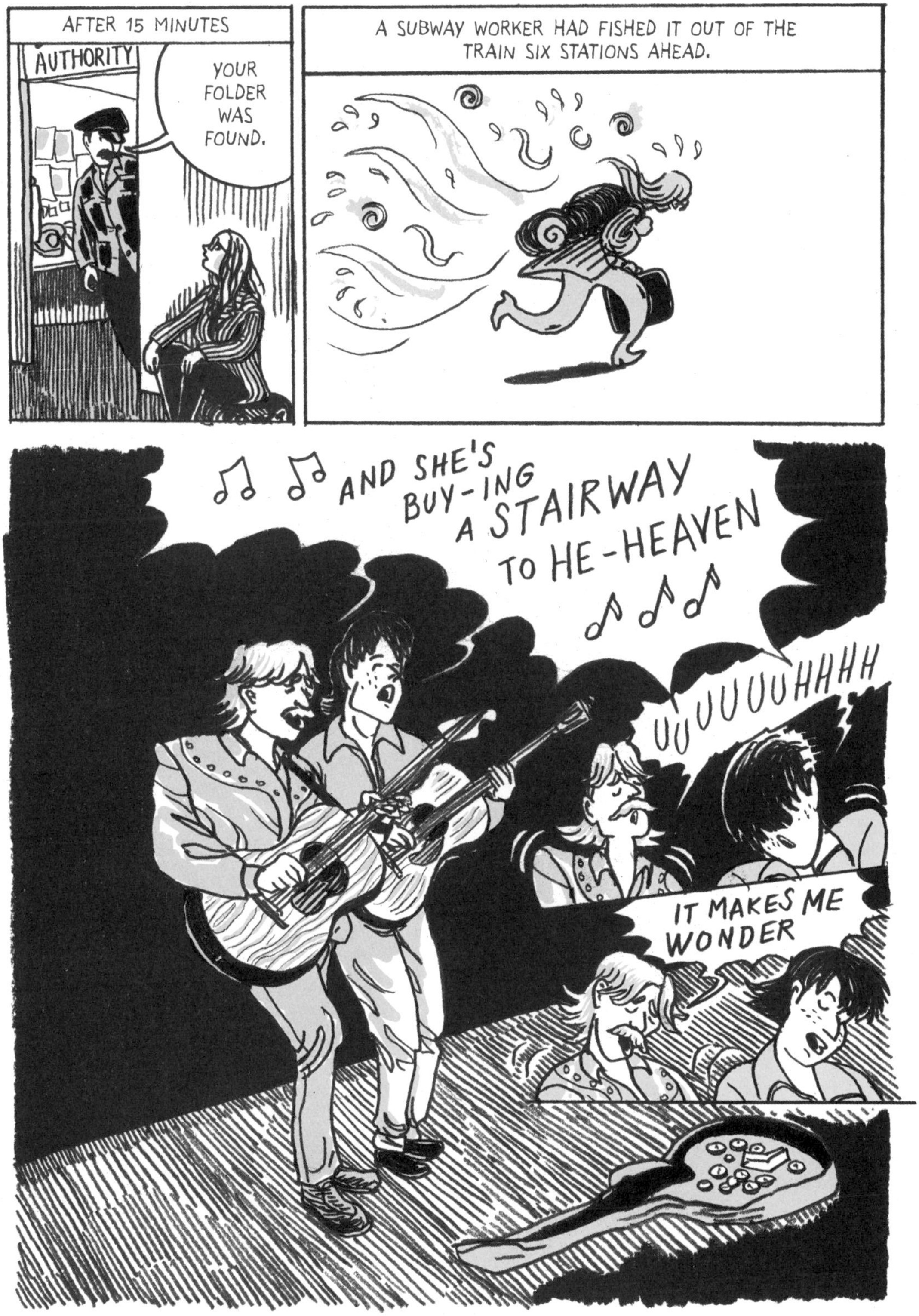
AFTER 15 MINUTES
AUTHORITY
YOUR FOLDER WAS FOUND.
A SUBWAY WORKER HAD FISHED IT OUT OF THE TRAIN SIX STATIONS AHEAD.
AND SHE'S BUY-ING A STAIRWAY TO HE-HEAVEN
UUUUUUHHHH
IT MAKES ME WONDER

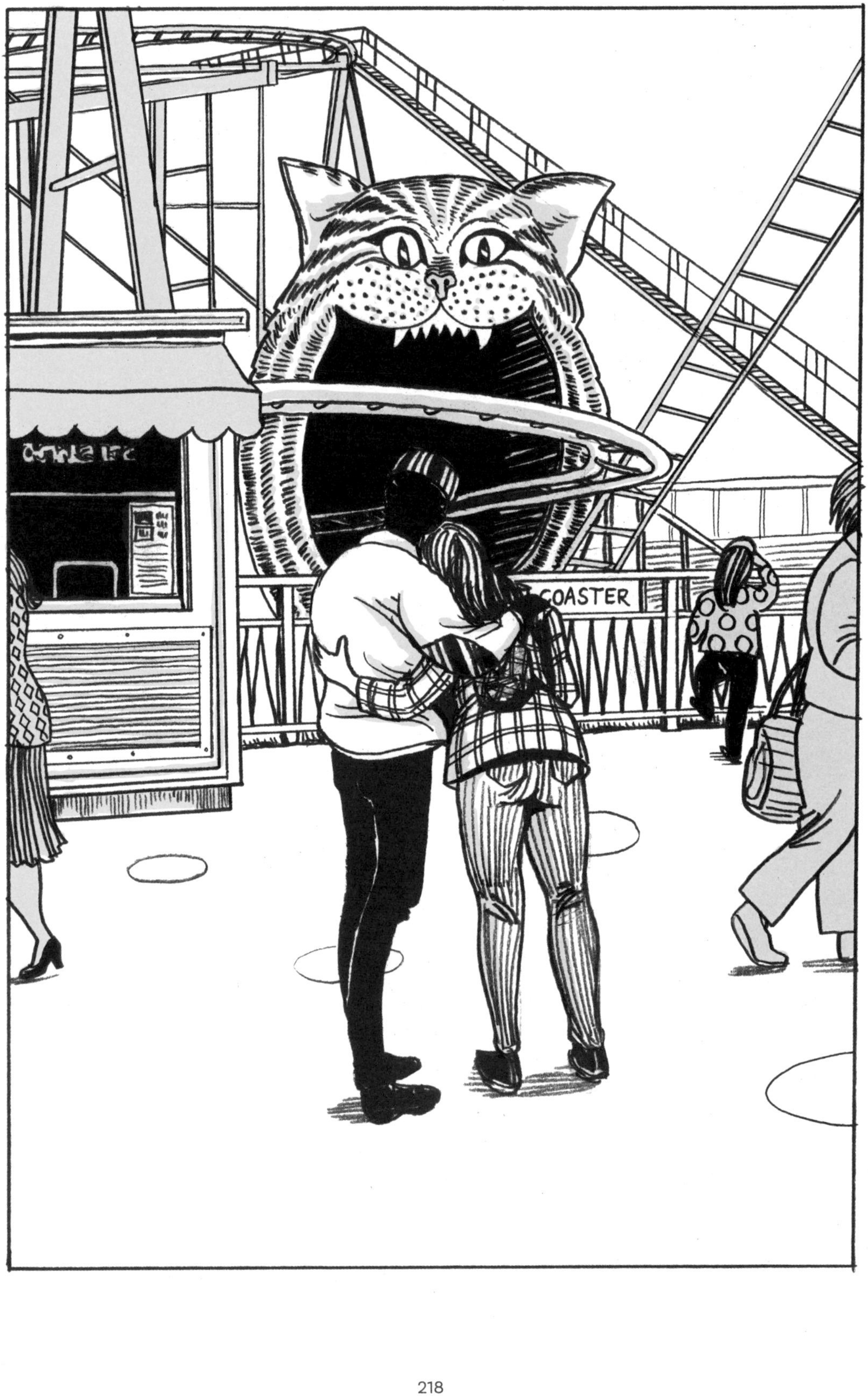
COASTER

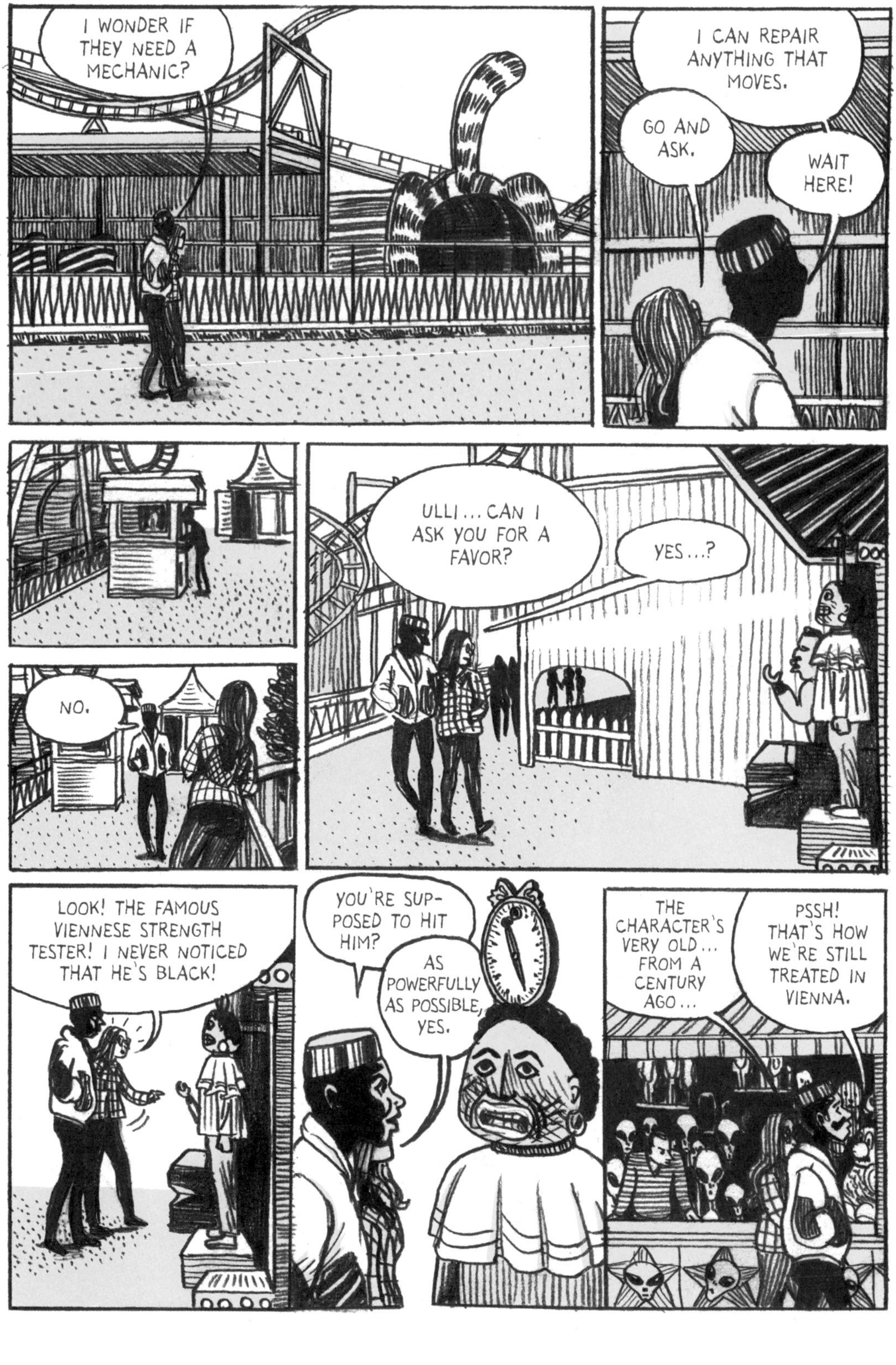
I WONDER IF THEY NEED A MECHANIC?
I CAN REPAIR ANYTHING THAT MOVES.
GO AND ASK.
WAIT HERE!
ULLI... CAN I ASK YOU FOR A FAVOR?
YES...?
NO.
LOOK! THE FAMOUS VIENNESE STRENGTH TESTER! I NEVER NOTICED THAT HE'S BLACK!
YOU'RE SUP-POSED TO HIT HIM?
AS POWERFULLY AS POSSIBLE, YES.
THE CHARACTER'S VERY OLD... FROM A CENTURY AGO...
PSSH! THAT'S HOW WE'RE STILL TREATED IN VIENNA.

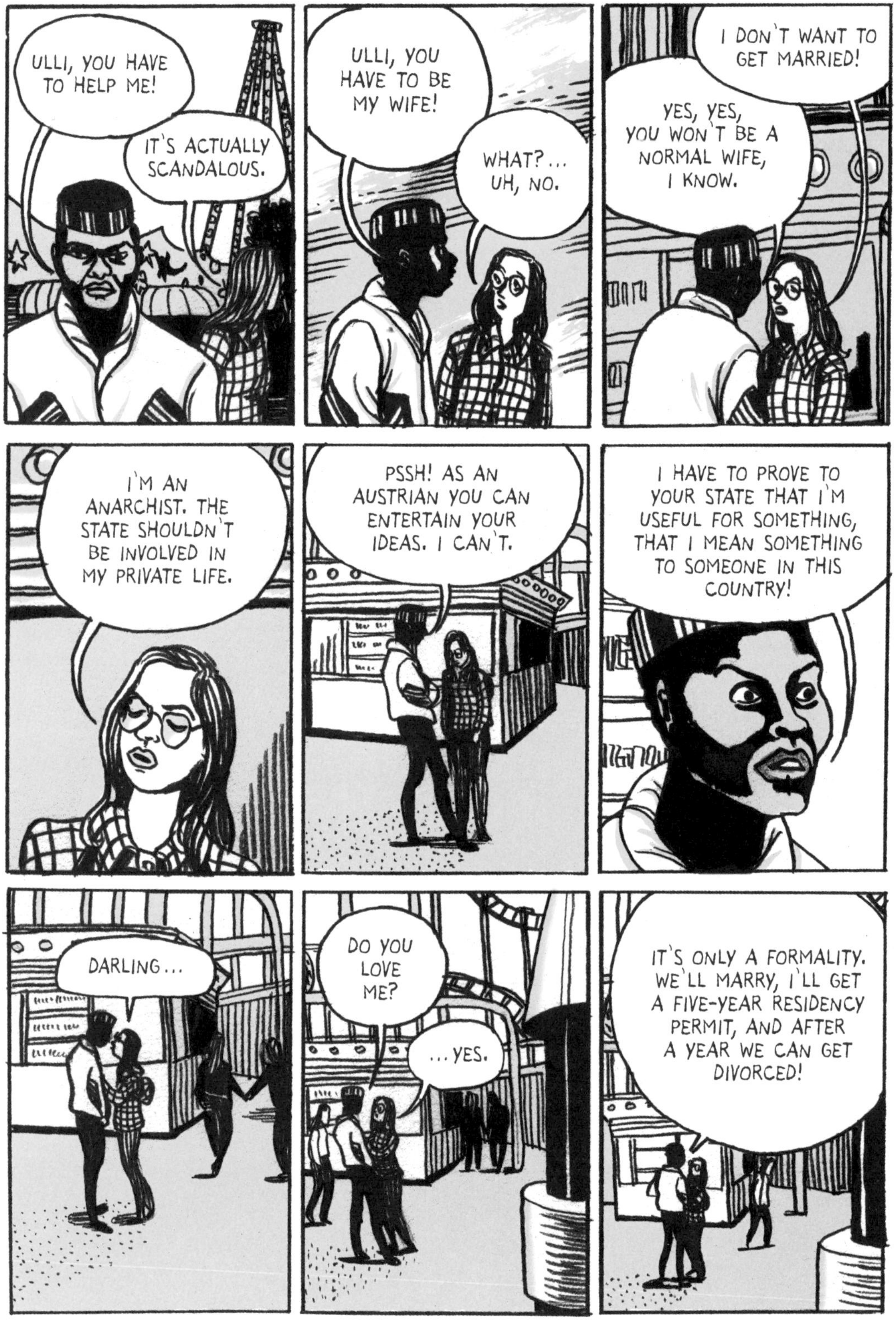
ULLI, YOU HAVE TO HELP ME!
IT'S ACTUALLY SCANDALOUS.
ULLI, YOU HAVE TO BE MY WIFE!
WHAT?... UH, NO.
I DON'T WANT TO GET MARRIED!
YES, YES, YOU WON'T BE A NORMAL WIFE, I KNOW.
I'M AN ANARCHIST. THE STATE SHOULDN'T BE INVOLVED IN MY PRIVATE LIFE.
PSSH! AS AN AUSTRIAN YOU CAN ENTERTAIN YOUR IDEAS. I CAN'T.
I HAVE TO PROVE TO YOUR STATE THAT I'M USEFUL FOR SOMETHING, THAT I MEAN SOMETHING TO SOMEONE IN THIS COUNTRY!
DARLING...
DO YOU LOVE ME?
...YES.
IT'S ONLY A FORMALITY. WE'LL MARRY, I'LL GET A FIVE-YEAR RESIDENCY PERMIT, AND AFTER A YEAR WE CAN GET DIVORCED!

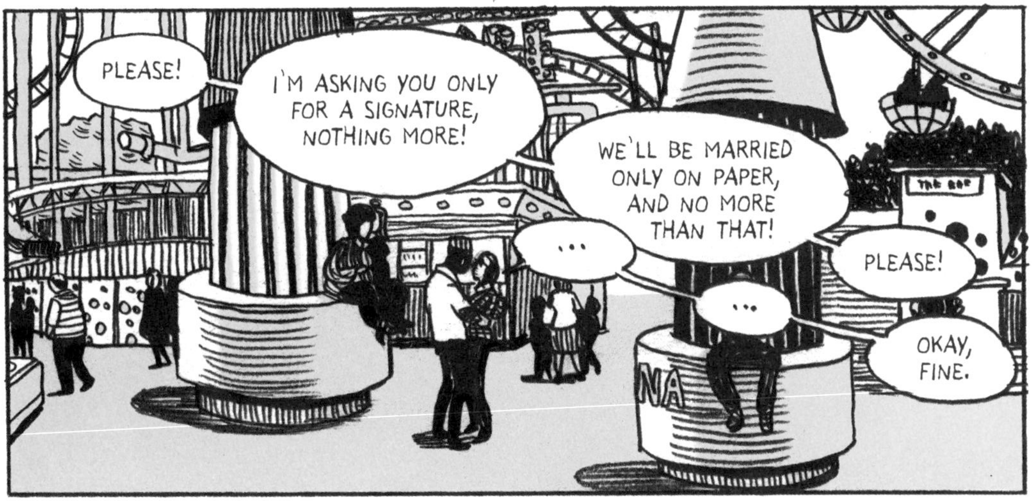
PLEASE!
I'M ASKING YOU ONLY FOR A SIGNATURE, NOTHING MORE!
WE'LL BE MARRIED ONLY ON PAPER, AND NO MORE THAN THAT!
...
PLEASE!
...
OKAY, FINE.
NA

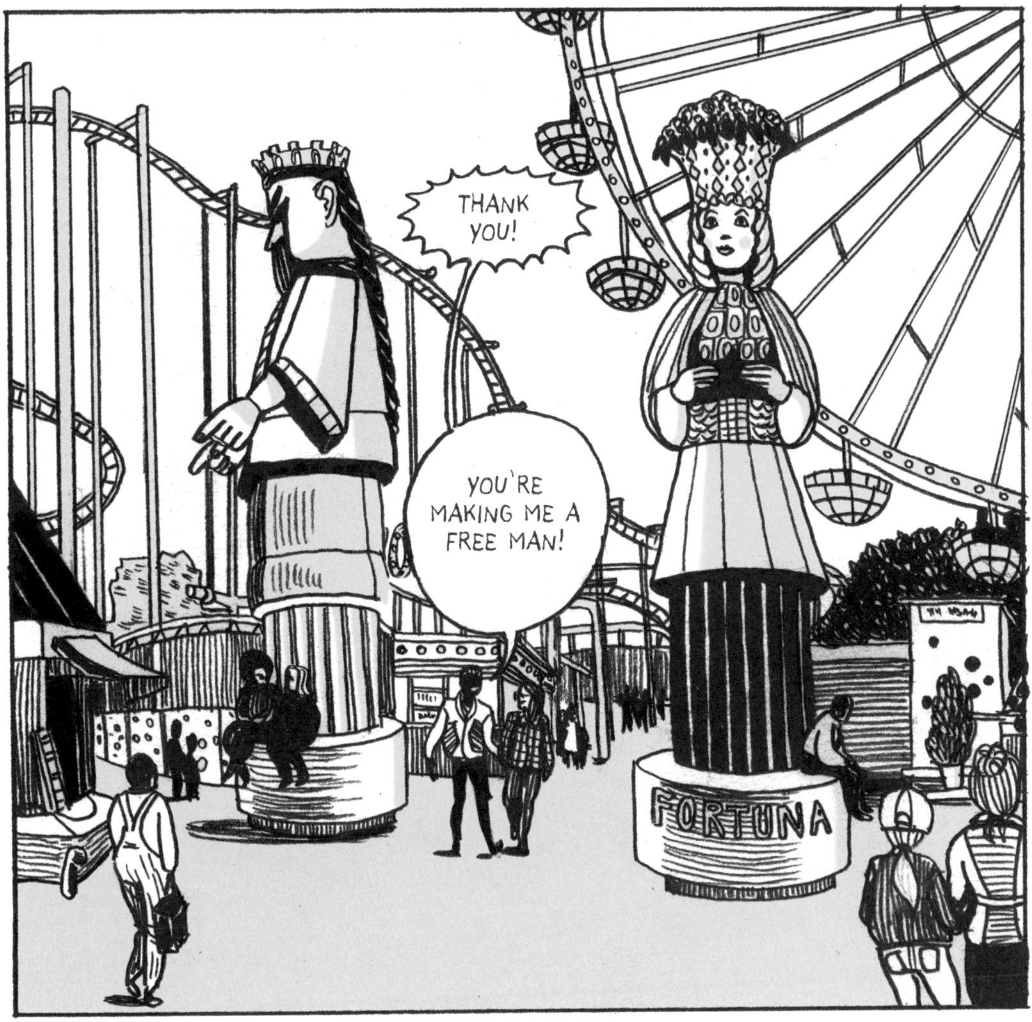
THANK YOU!
YOU'RE MAKING ME A FREE MAN!
FORTUNA

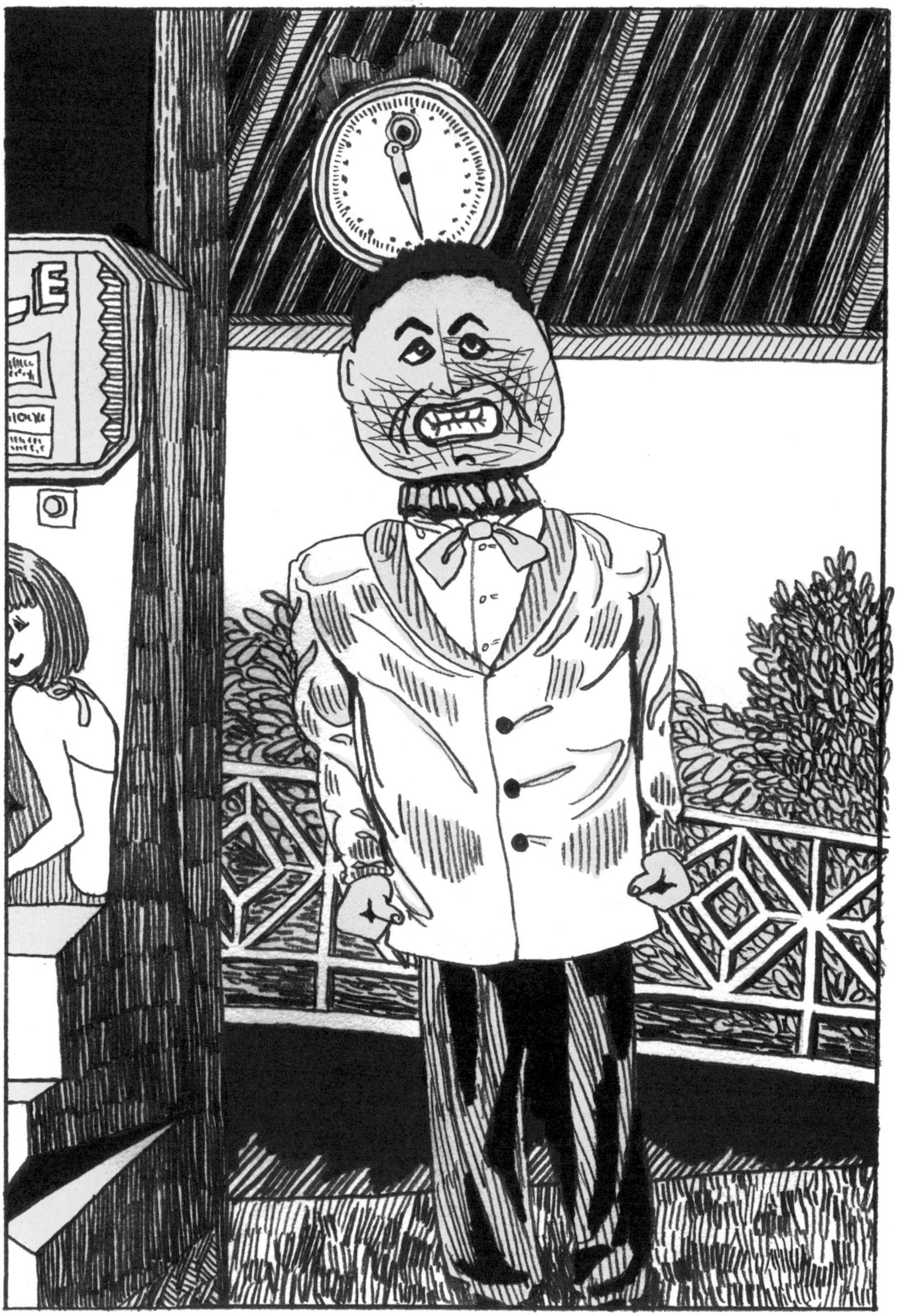

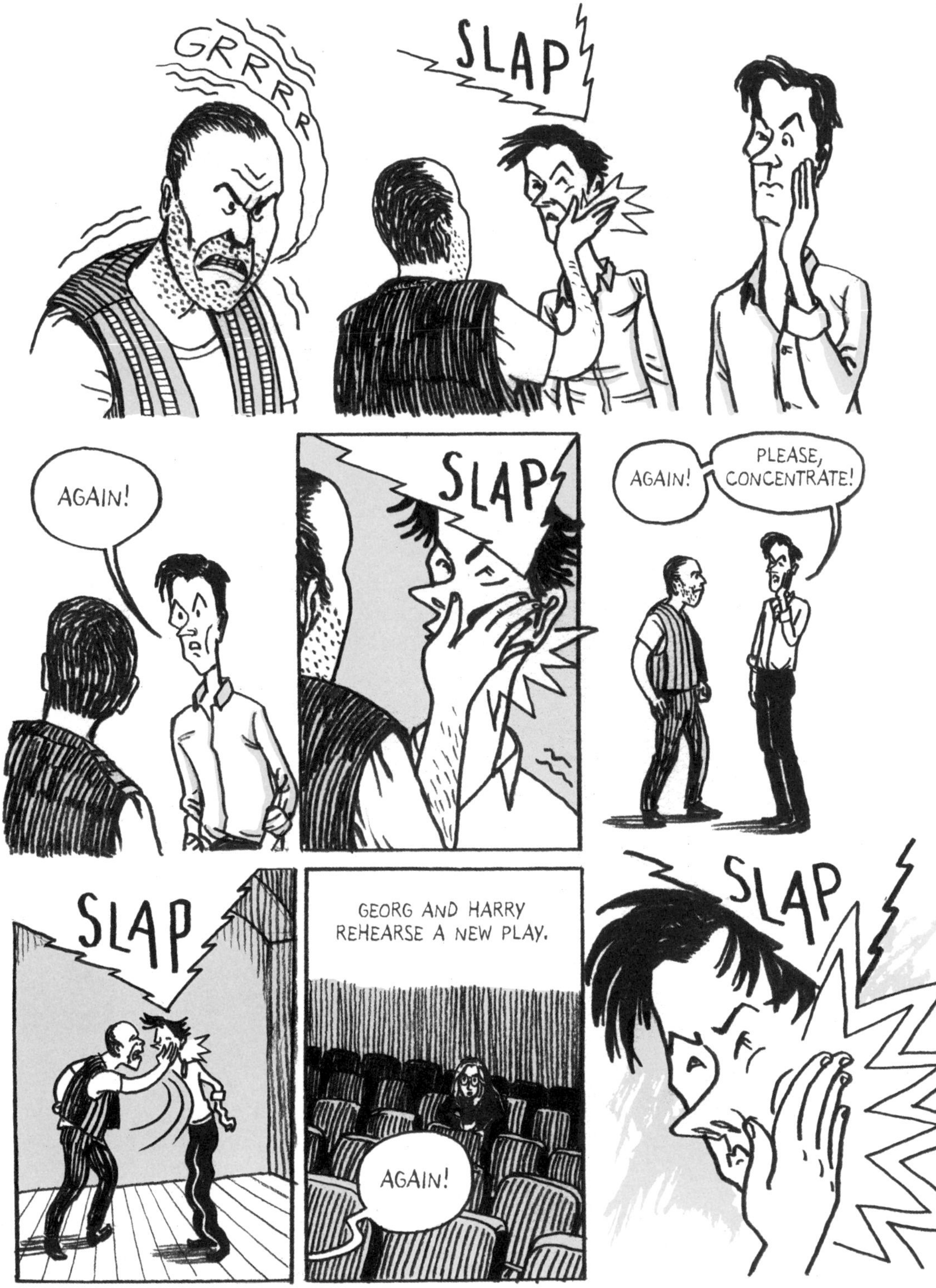
GRRRRR
SLAP
AGAIN!
SLAP
AGAIN!
PLEASE, CONCENTRATE!
SLAP
GEORG AND HARRY REHEARSE A NEW PLAY.
AGAIN!
SLAP

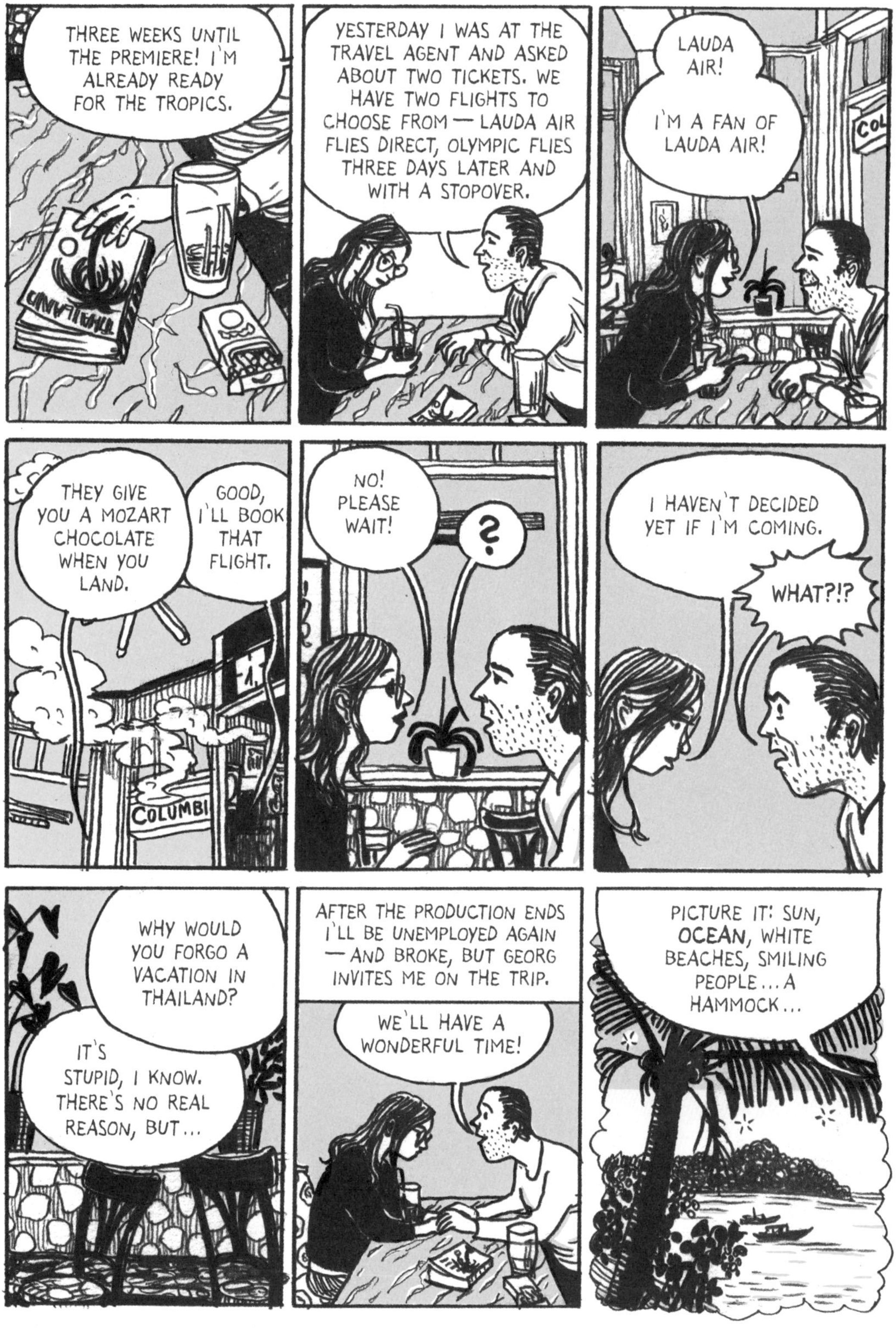
THREE WEEKS UNTIL THE PREMIERE! I'M ALREADY READY FOR THE TROPICS.
THAILAND
YESTERDAY I WAS AT THE TRAVEL AGENT AND ASKED ABOUT TWO TICKETS. WE HAVE TWO FLIGHTS TO CHOOSE FROM — LAUDA AIR FLIES DIRECT, OLYMPIC FLIES THREE DAYS LATER AND WITH A STOPOVER.
LAUDA AIR!
I'M A FAN OF LAUDA AIR!
THEY GIVE YOU A MOZART CHOCOLATE WHEN YOU LAND.
GOOD, I'LL BOOK THAT FLIGHT.
COLUMBI
NO! PLEASE WAIT!
?
I HAVEN'T DECIDED YET IF I'M COMING.
WHAT?!?
WHY WOULD YOU FORGO A VACATION IN THAILAND?
IT'S STUPID, I KNOW. THERE'S NO REAL REASON, BUT...
AFTER THE PRODUCTION ENDS I'LL BE UNEMPLOYED AGAIN — AND BROKE, BUT GEORG INVITES ME ON THE TRIP.
WE'LL HAVE A WONDERFUL TIME!
PICTURE IT: SUN, OCEAN, WHITE BEACHES, SMILING PEOPLE... A HAMMOCK...

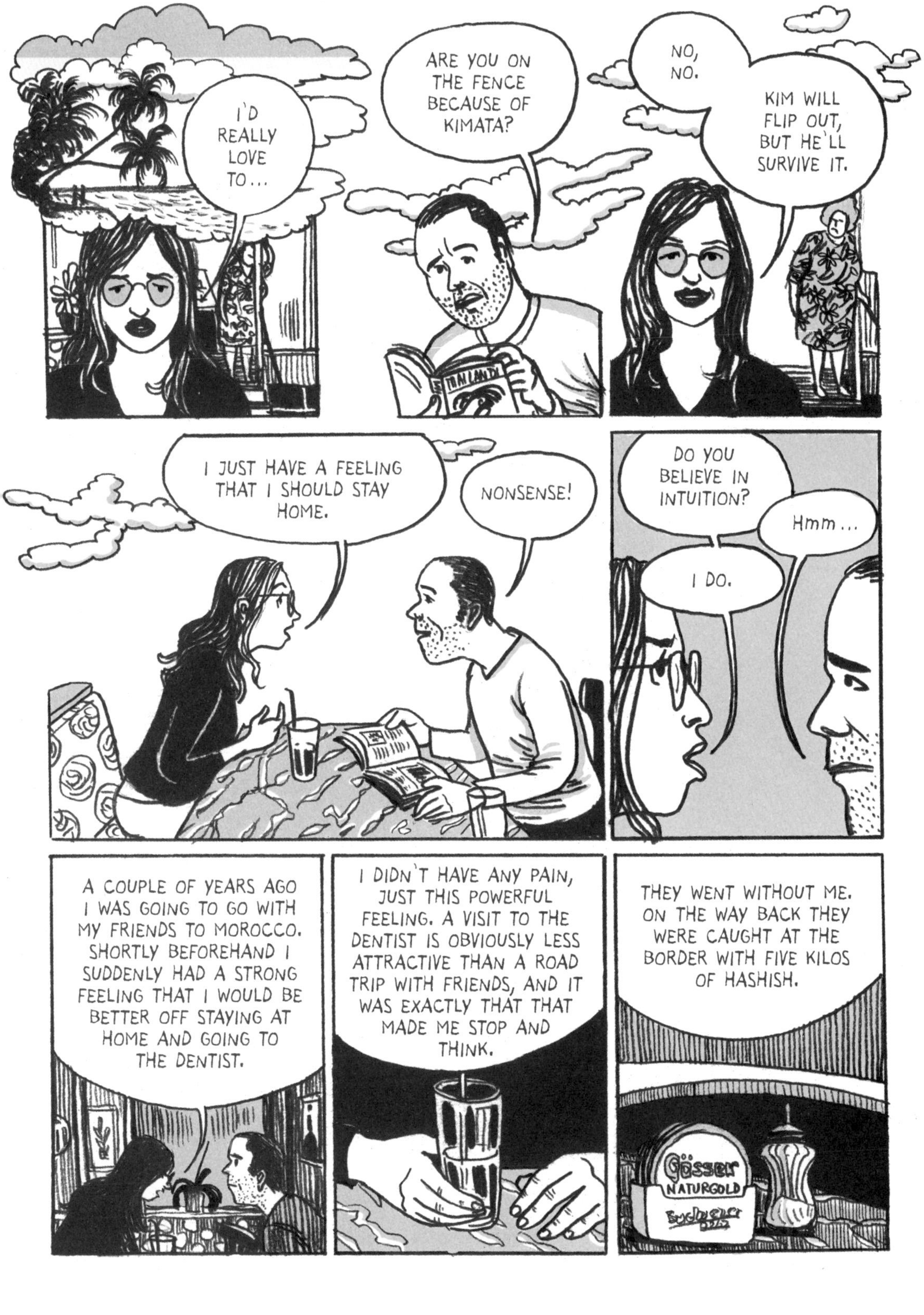
I'D REALLY LOVE TO...
ARE YOU ON THE FENCE BECAUSE OF KIMATA?
NO, NO.
KIM WILL FLIP OUT, BUT HE'LL SURVIVE IT.
I JUST HAVE A FEELING THAT I SHOULD STAY HOME.
NONSENSE!
DO YOU BELIEVE IN INTUITION?
Hmm...
I DO.
A COUPLE OF YEARS AGO I WAS GOING TO GO WITH MY FRIENDS TO MOROCCO. SHORTLY BEFOREHAND I SUDDENLY HAD A STRONG FEELING THAT I WOULD BE BETTER OFF STAYING AT HOME AND GOING TO THE DENTIST.
I DIDN'T HAVE ANY PAIN, JUST THIS POWERFUL FEELING. A VISIT TO THE DENTIST IS OBVIOUSLY LESS ATTRACTIVE THAN A ROAD TRIP WITH FRIENDS, AND IT WAS EXACTLY THAT THAT MADE ME STOP AND THINK.
THEY WENT WITHOUT ME. ON THE WAY BACK THEY WERE CAUGHT AT THE BORDER WITH FIVE KILOS OF HASHISH.
Gösser
NATURGOLD

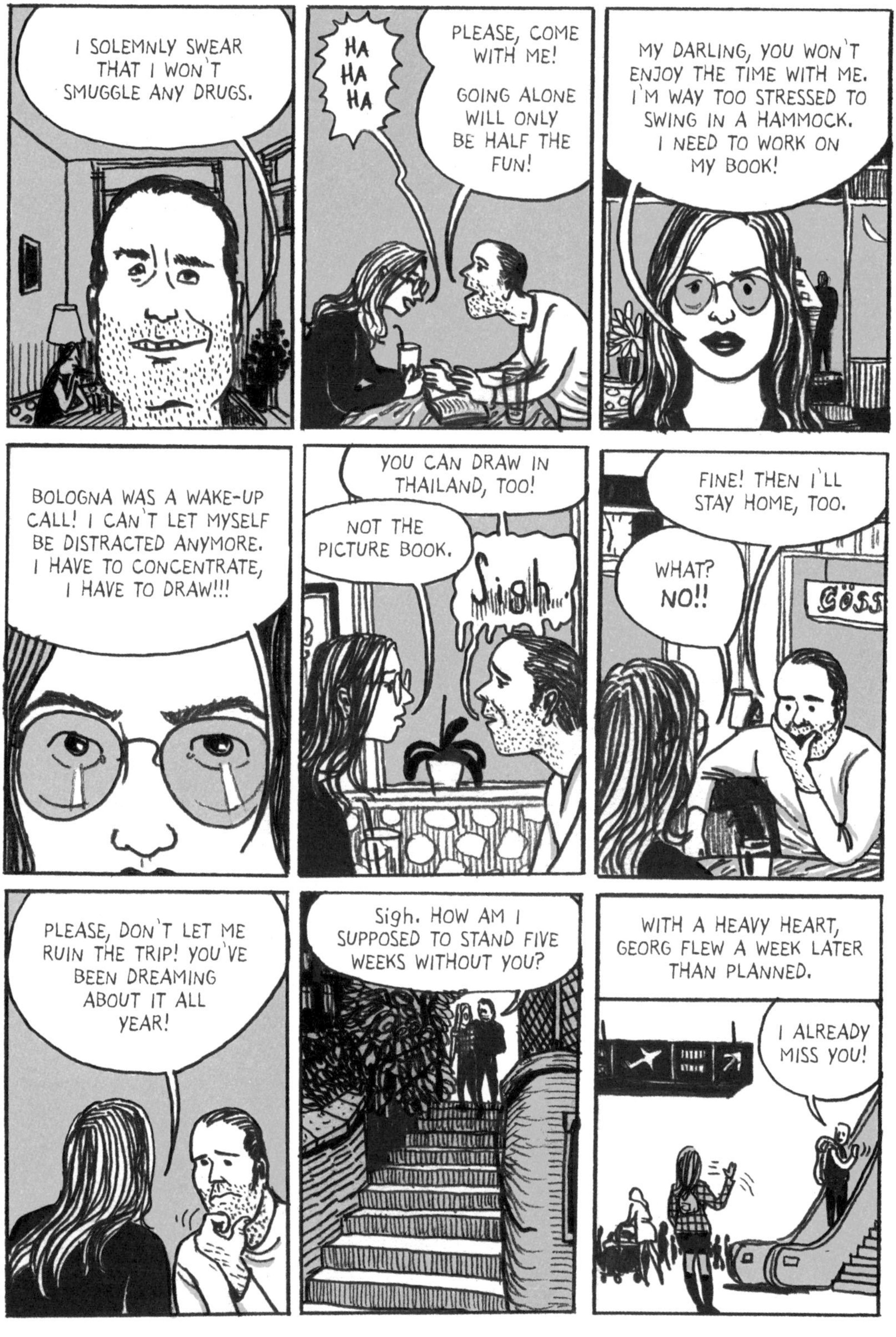
I SOLEMNLY SWEAR THAT I WON'T SMUGGLE ANY DRUGS.
HA HA HA
PLEASE, COME WITH ME!
GOING ALONE WILL ONLY BE HALF THE FUN!
MY DARLING, YOU WON'T ENJOY THE TIME WITH ME. I'M WAY TOO STRESSED TO SWING IN A HAMMOCK. I NEED TO WORK ON MY BOOK!
BOLOGNA WAS A WAKE-UP CALL! I CAN'T LET MYSELF BE DISTRACTED ANYMORE. I HAVE TO CONCENTRATE, I HAVE TO DRAW!!!
YOU CAN DRAW IN THAILAND, TOO!
NOT THE PICTURE BOOK.
Sigh...
FINE! THEN I'LL STAY HOME, TOO.
WHAT? NO!!
GÖSS
PLEASE, DON'T LET ME RUIN THE TRIP! YOU'VE BEEN DREAMING ABOUT IT ALL YEAR!
Sigh. HOW AM I SUPPOSED TO STAND FIVE WEEKS WITHOUT YOU?
WITH A HEAVY HEART, GEORG FLEW A WEEK LATER THAN PLANNED.
I ALREADY MISS YOU!

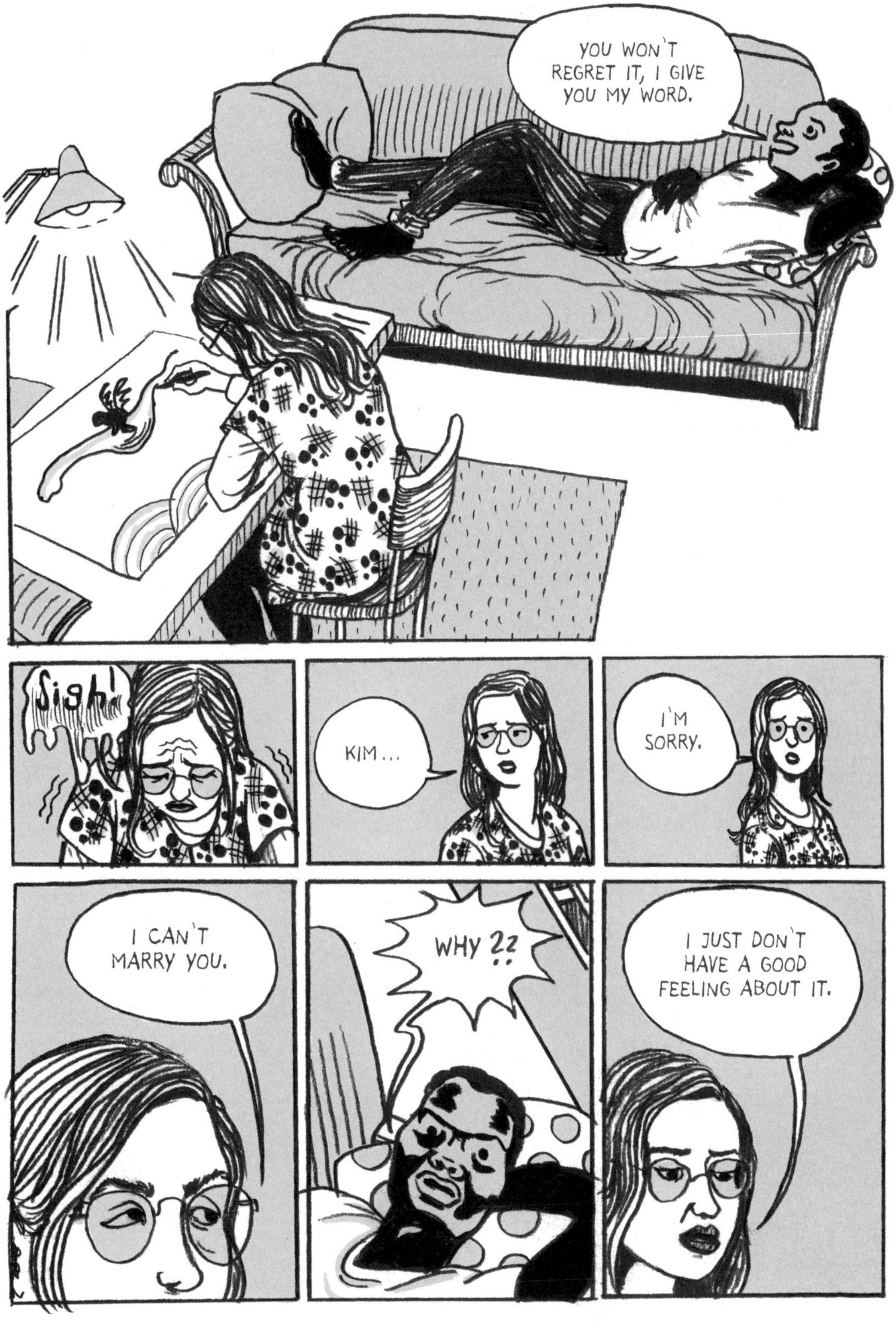
YOU WON'T REGRET IT, I GIVE YOU MY WORD.
SIGH!
KIM...
I'M SORRY.
I CAN'T MARRY YOU.
WHY ??
I JUST DON'T HAVE A GOOD FEELING ABOUT IT.

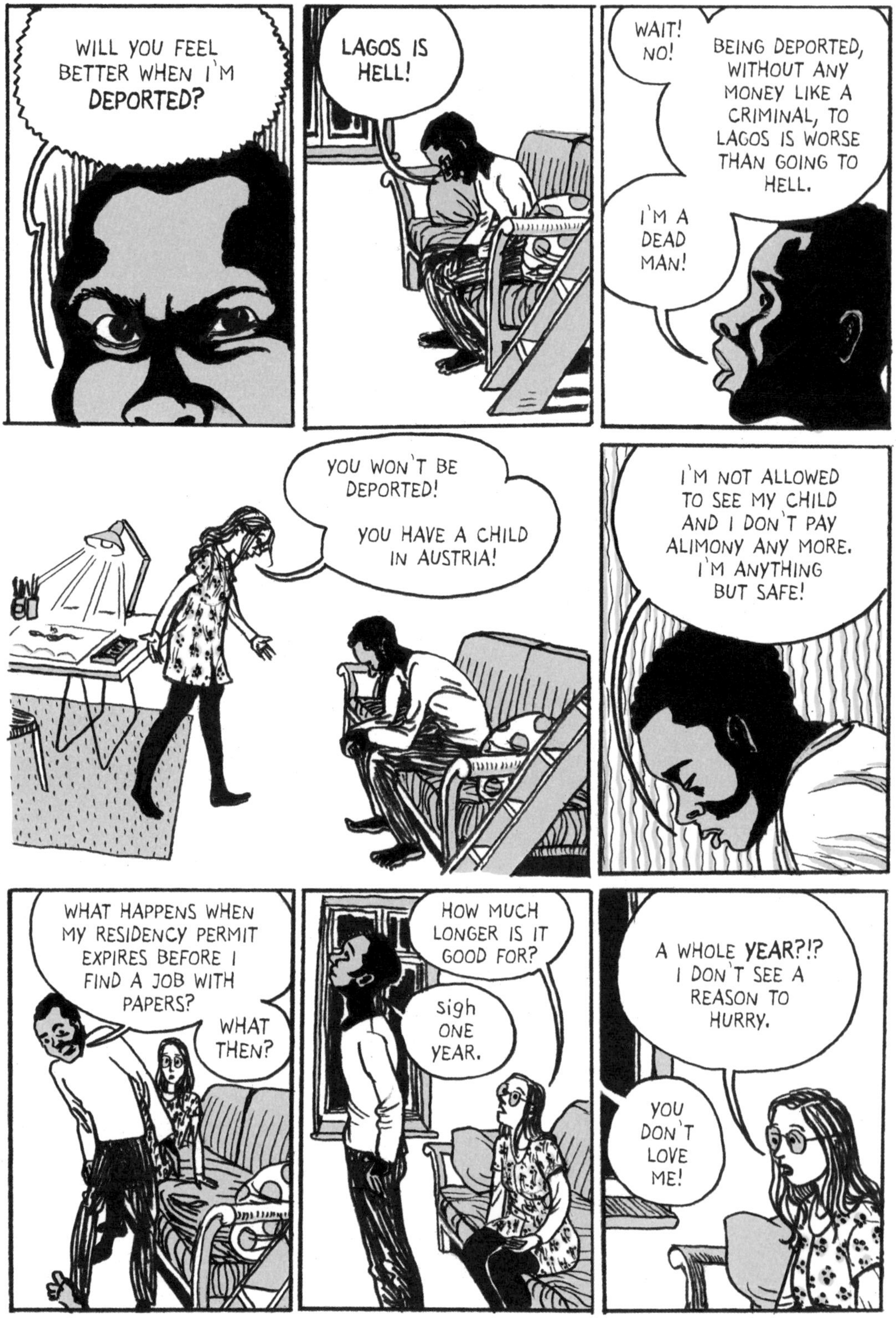
WILL YOU FEEL BETTER WHEN I'M DEPORTED?
LAGOS IS HELL!
WAIT! NO!
BEING DEPORTED, WITHOUT ANY MONEY LIKE A CRIMINAL, TO LAGOS IS WORSE THAN GOING TO HELL.
I'M A DEAD MAN!
YOU WON'T BE DEPORTED!
YOU HAVE A CHILD IN AUSTRIA!
I'M NOT ALLOWED TO SEE MY CHILD AND I DON'T PAY ALIMONY ANY MORE. I'M ANYTHING BUT SAFE!
WHAT HAPPENS WHEN MY RESIDENCY PERMIT EXPIRES BEFORE I FIND A JOB WITH PAPERS?
WHAT THEN?
HOW MUCH LONGER IS IT GOOD FOR?
sigh ONE YEAR.
A WHOLE YEAR?!? I DON'T SEE A REASON TO HURRY.
YOU DON'T LOVE ME!

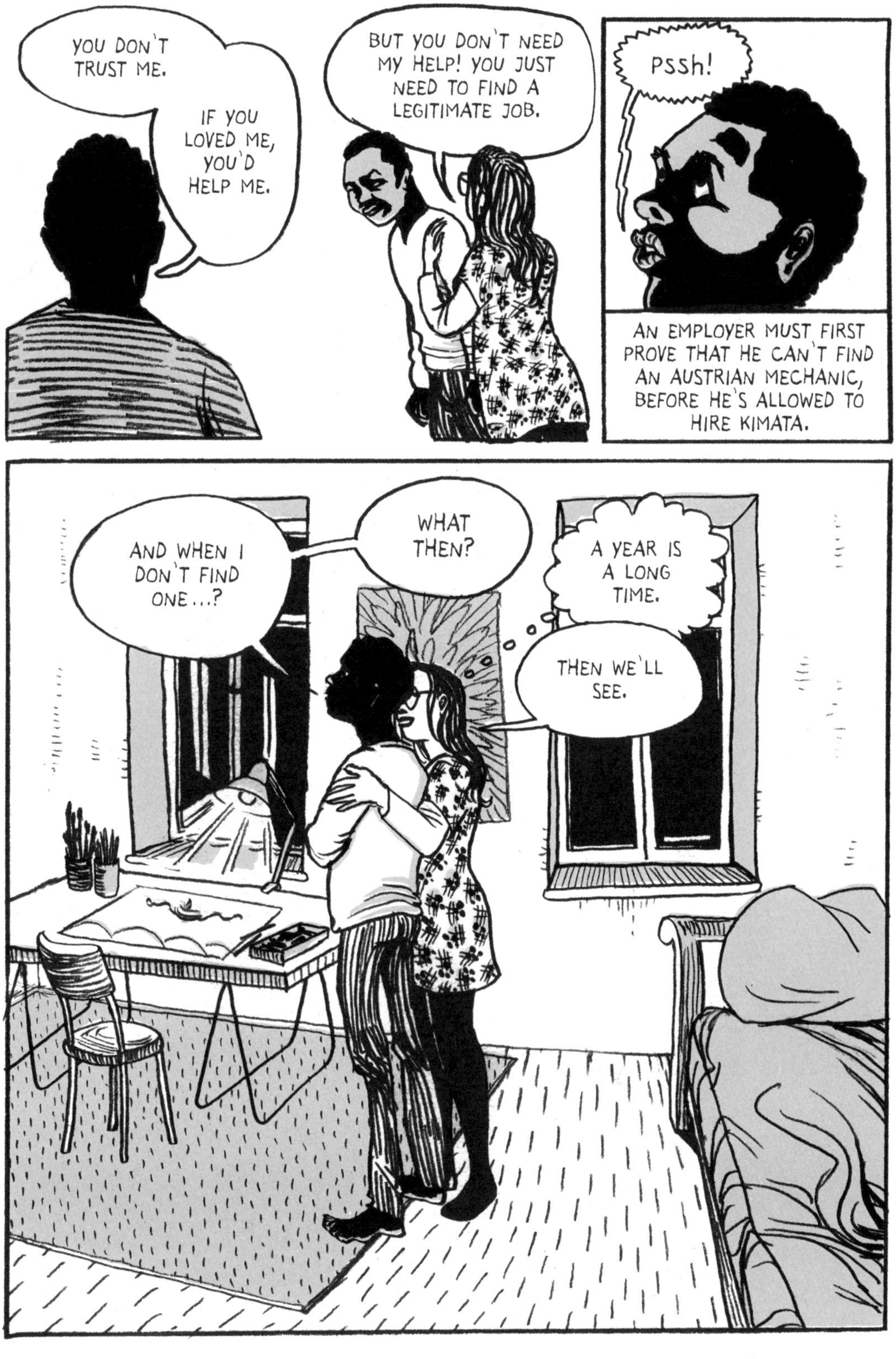
YOU DON'T TRUST ME.
IF YOU LOVED ME, YOU'D HELP ME.
BUT YOU DON'T NEED MY HELP! YOU JUST NEED TO FIND A LEGITIMATE JOB.
PSSH!
AN EMPLOYER MUST FIRST PROVE THAT HE CAN'T FIND AN AUSTRIAN MECHANIC, BEFORE HE'S ALLOWED TO HIRE KIMATA.
AND WHEN I DON'T FIND ONE...?
WHAT THEN?
A YEAR IS A LONG TIME.
THEN WE'LL SEE.

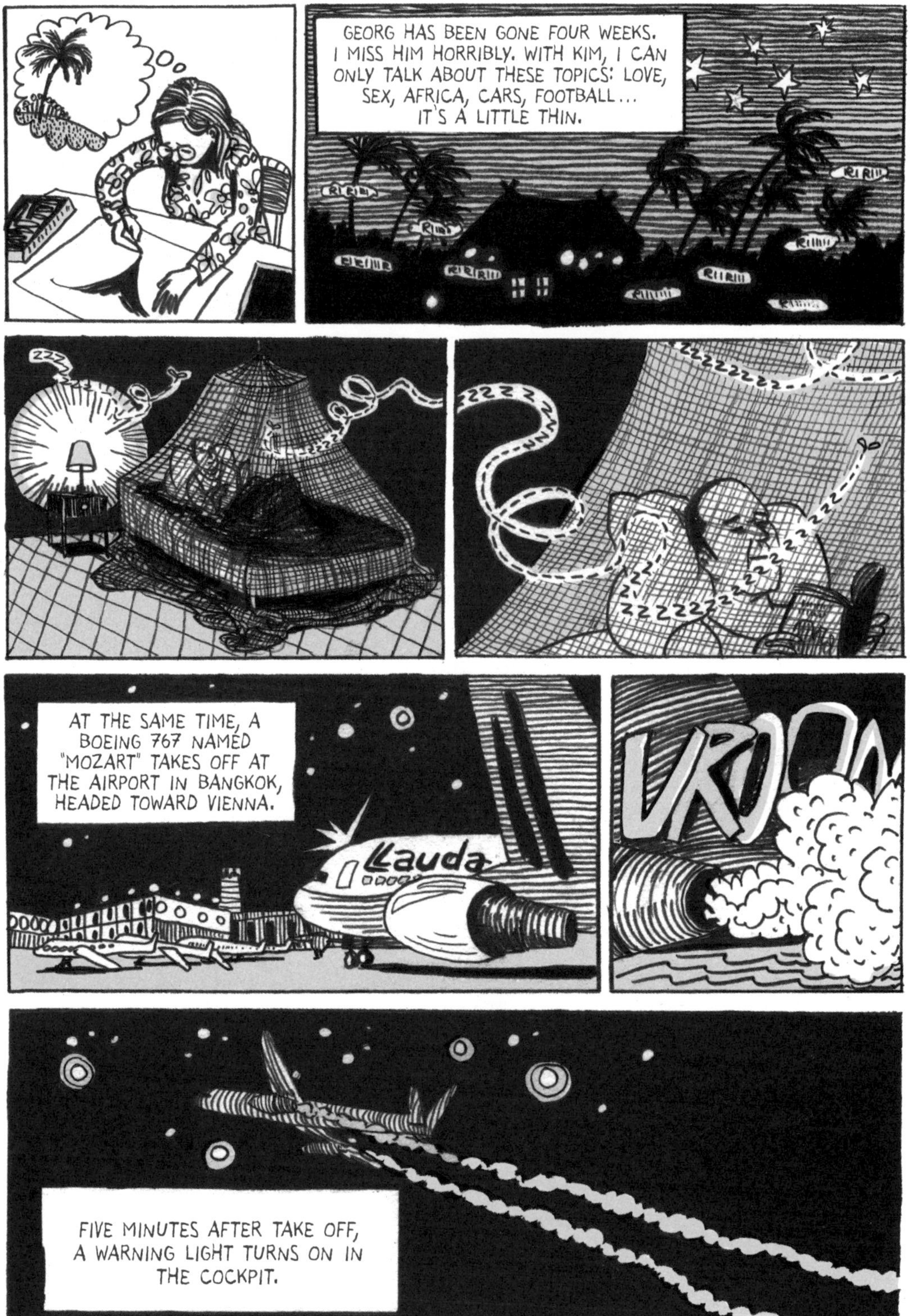
GEORG HAS BEEN GONE FOUR WEEKS. I MISS HIM HORRIBLY. WITH KIM, I CAN ONLY TALK ABOUT THESE TOPICS: LOVE, SEX, AFRICA, CARS, FOOTBALL... IT'S A LITTLE THIN.
AT THE SAME TIME, A BOEING 767 NAMED "MOZART" TAKES OFF AT THE AIRPORT IN BANGKOK, HEADED TOWARD VIENNA.
Lauda
VROO
FIVE MINUTES AFTER TAKE OFF, A WARNING LIGHT TURNS ON IN THE COCKPIT.

THE BLACK BOX RECORDING:

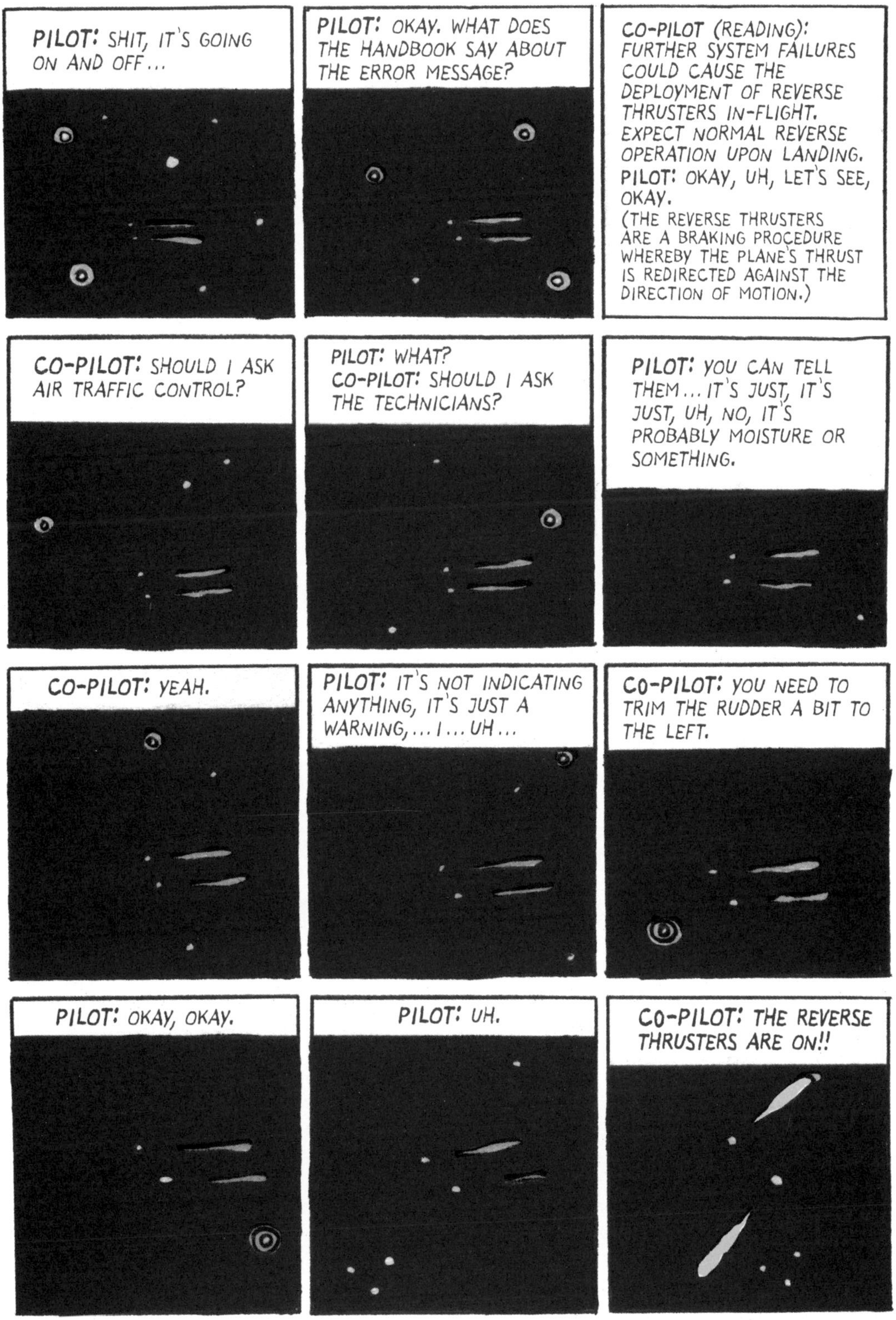
PILOT: SHIT, IT'S GOING ON AND OFF...
PILOT: OKAY. WHAT DOES THE HANDBOOK SAY ABOUT THE ERROR MESSAGE?
CO-PILOT (READING): FURTHER SYSTEM FAILURES COULD CAUSE THE DEPLOYMENT OF REVERSE THRUSTERS IN-FLIGHT. EXPECT NORMAL REVERSE OPERATION UPON LANDING.
PILOT: OKAY, UH, LET'S SEE, OKAY.
(THE REVERSE THRUSTERS ARE A BRAKING PROCEDURE WHEREBY THE PLANE'S THRUST IS REDIRECTED AGAINST THE DIRECTION OF MOTION.)
CO-PILOT: SHOULD I ASK AIR TRAFFIC CONTROL?
PILOT: WHAT?
CO-PILOT: SHOULD I ASK THE TECHNICIANS?
PILOT: YOU CAN TELL THEM... IT'S JUST, IT'S JUST, UH, NO, IT'S PROBABLY MOISTURE OR SOMETHING.
CO-PILOT: YEAH.
PILOT: IT'S NOT INDICATING ANYTHING, IT'S JUST A WARNING,... I... UH...
CO-PILOT: YOU NEED TO TRIM THE RUDDER A BIT TO THE LEFT.
PILOT: OKAY, OKAY.
PILOT: UH.
CO-PILOT: THE REVERSE THRUSTERS ARE ON!!

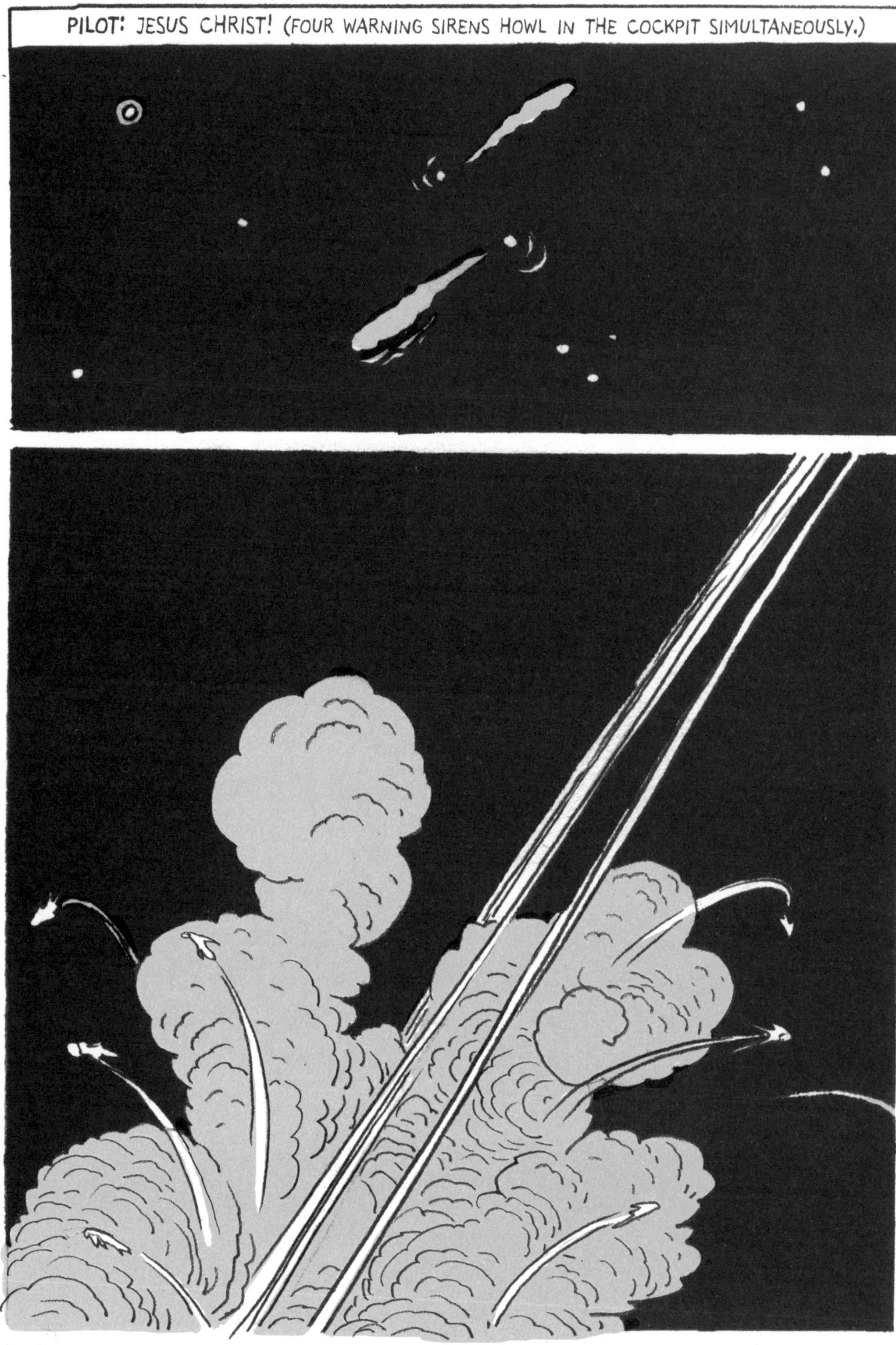
PILOT: JESUS CHRIST! (FOUR WARNING SIRENS HOWL IN THE COCKPIT SIMULTANEOUSLY.)

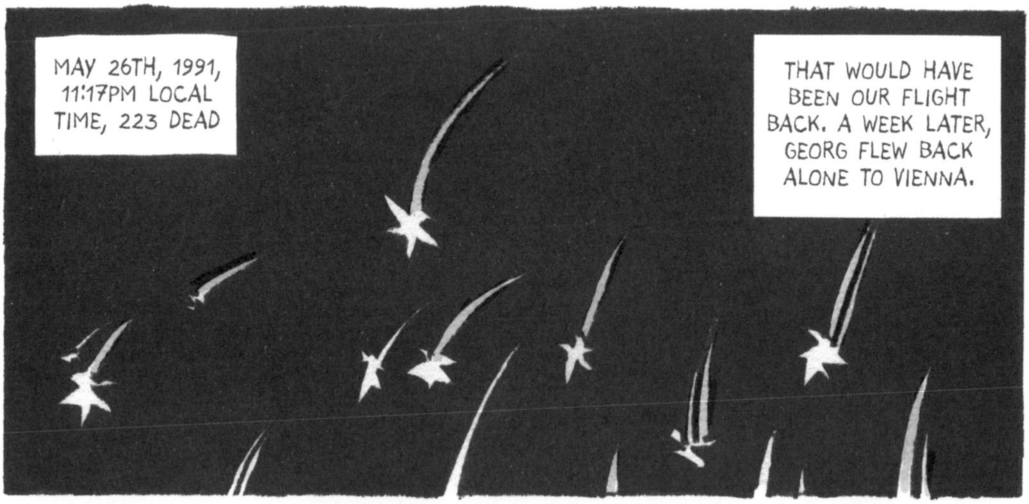
MAY 26TH, 1991, 11:17PM LOCAL TIME, 223 DEAD
THAT WOULD HAVE BEEN OUR FLIGHT BACK. A WEEK LATER, GEORG FLEW BACK ALONE TO VIENNA.

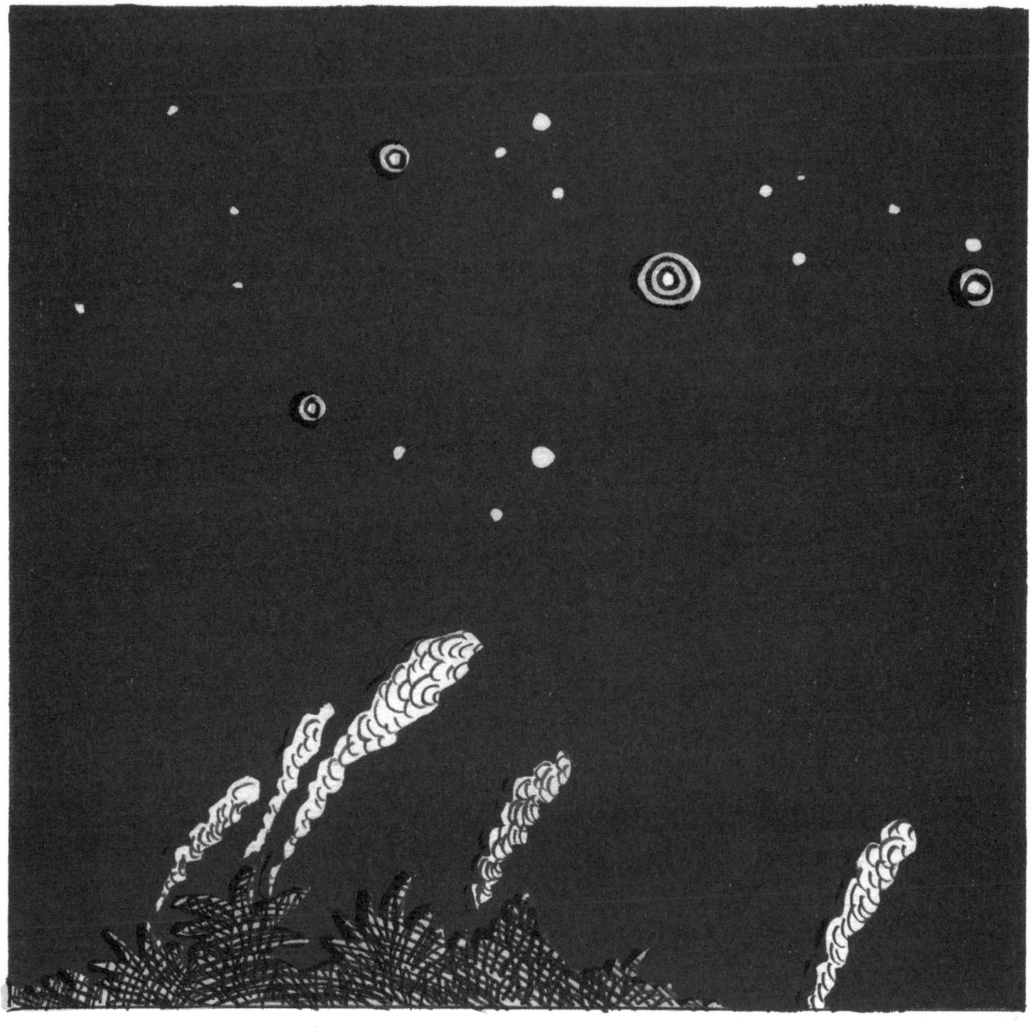

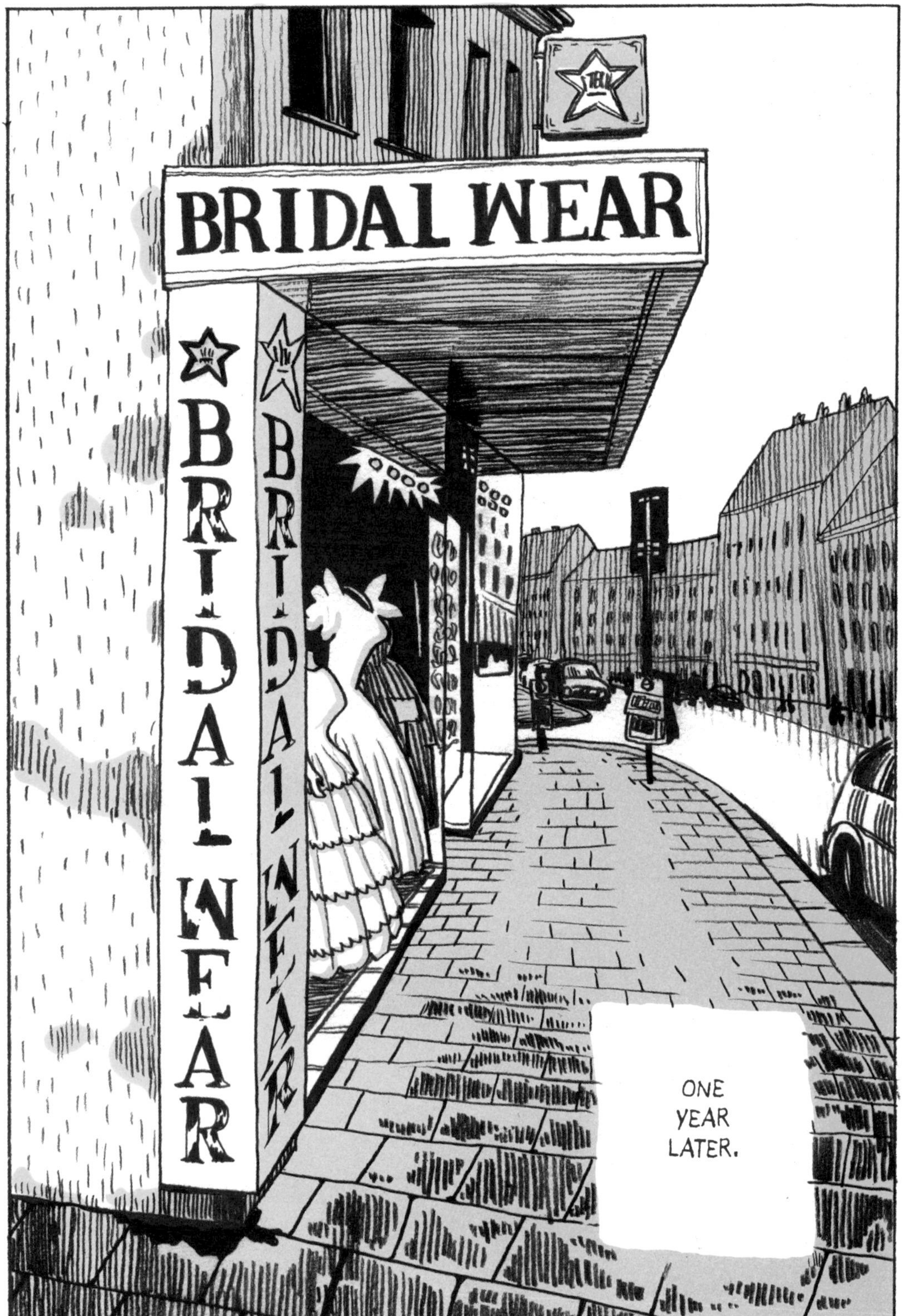
BRIDAL WEAR
BRIDAL WEAR
BRIDAL WEAR
ONE YEAR LATER.

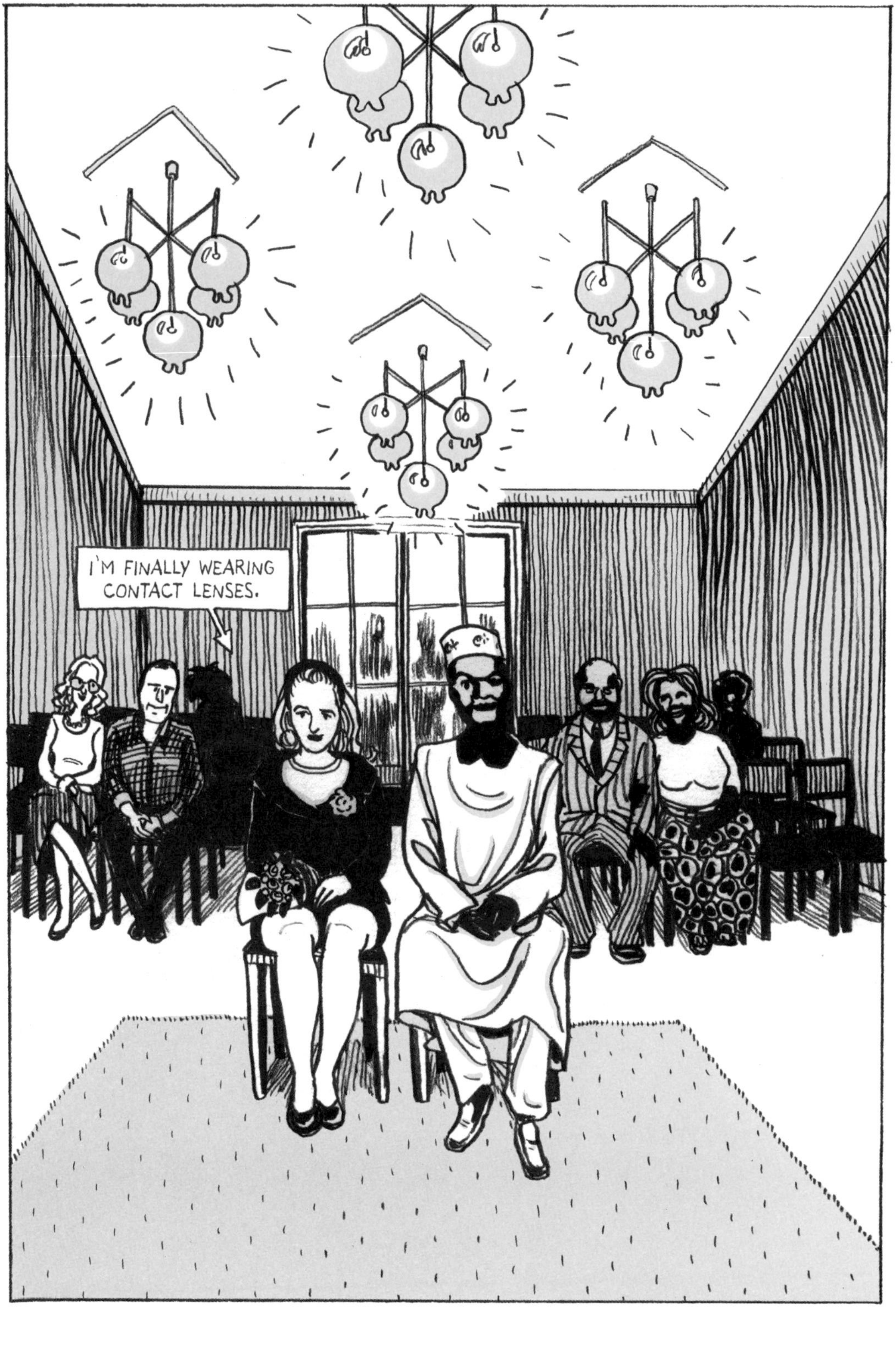
I'M FINALLY WEARING CONTACT LENSES.

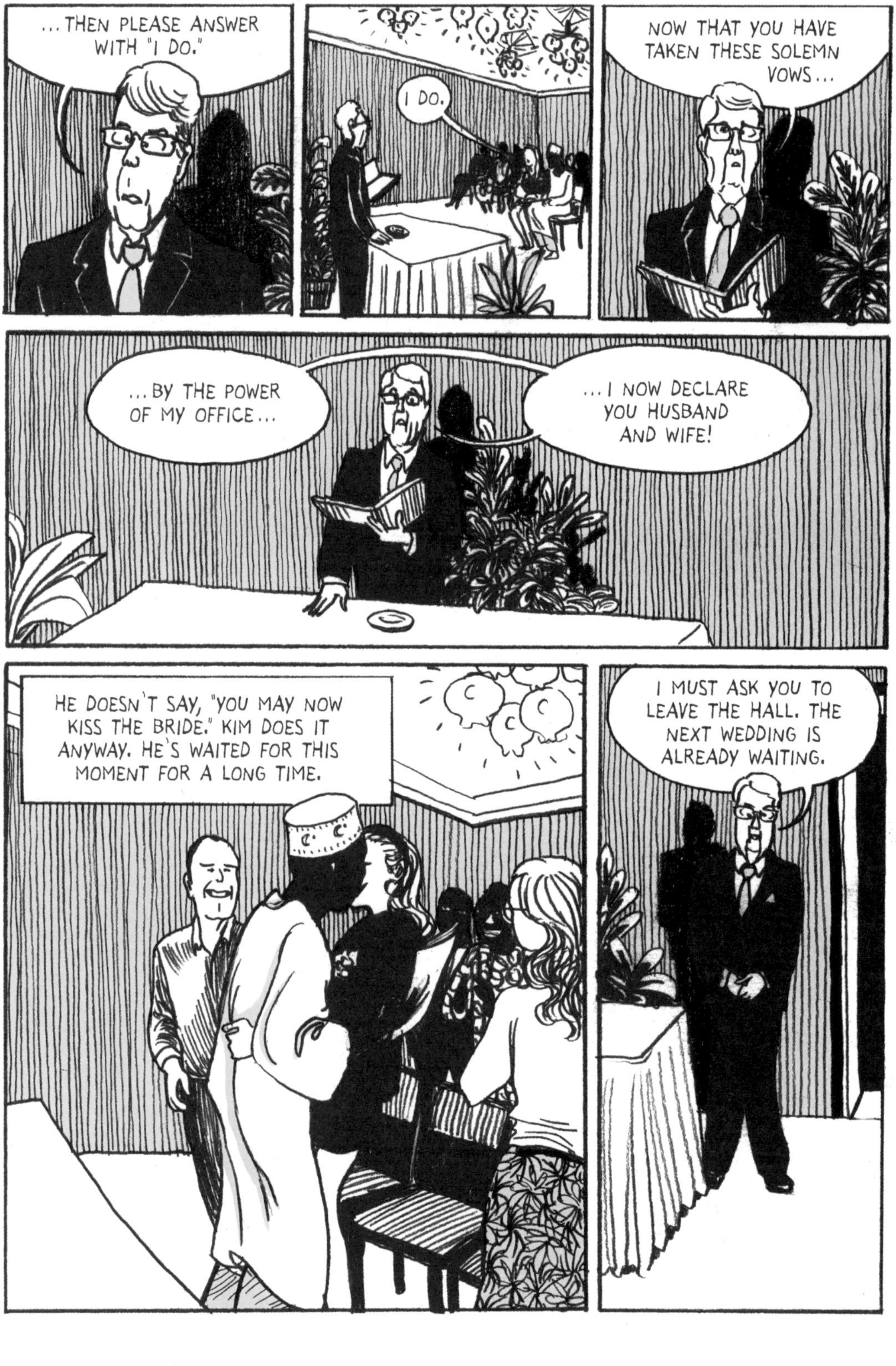
...THEN PLEASE ANSWER WITH "I DO."
I DO.
NOW THAT YOU HAVE TAKEN THESE SOLEMN VOWS...
...BY THE POWER OF MY OFFICE...
...I NOW DECLARE YOU HUSBAND AND WIFE!
HE DOESN'T SAY, "YOU MAY NOW KISS THE BRIDE." KIM DOES IT ANYWAY. HE'S WAITED FOR THIS MOMENT FOR A LONG TIME.
I MUST ASK YOU TO LEAVE THE HALL. THE NEXT WEDDING IS ALREADY WAITING.

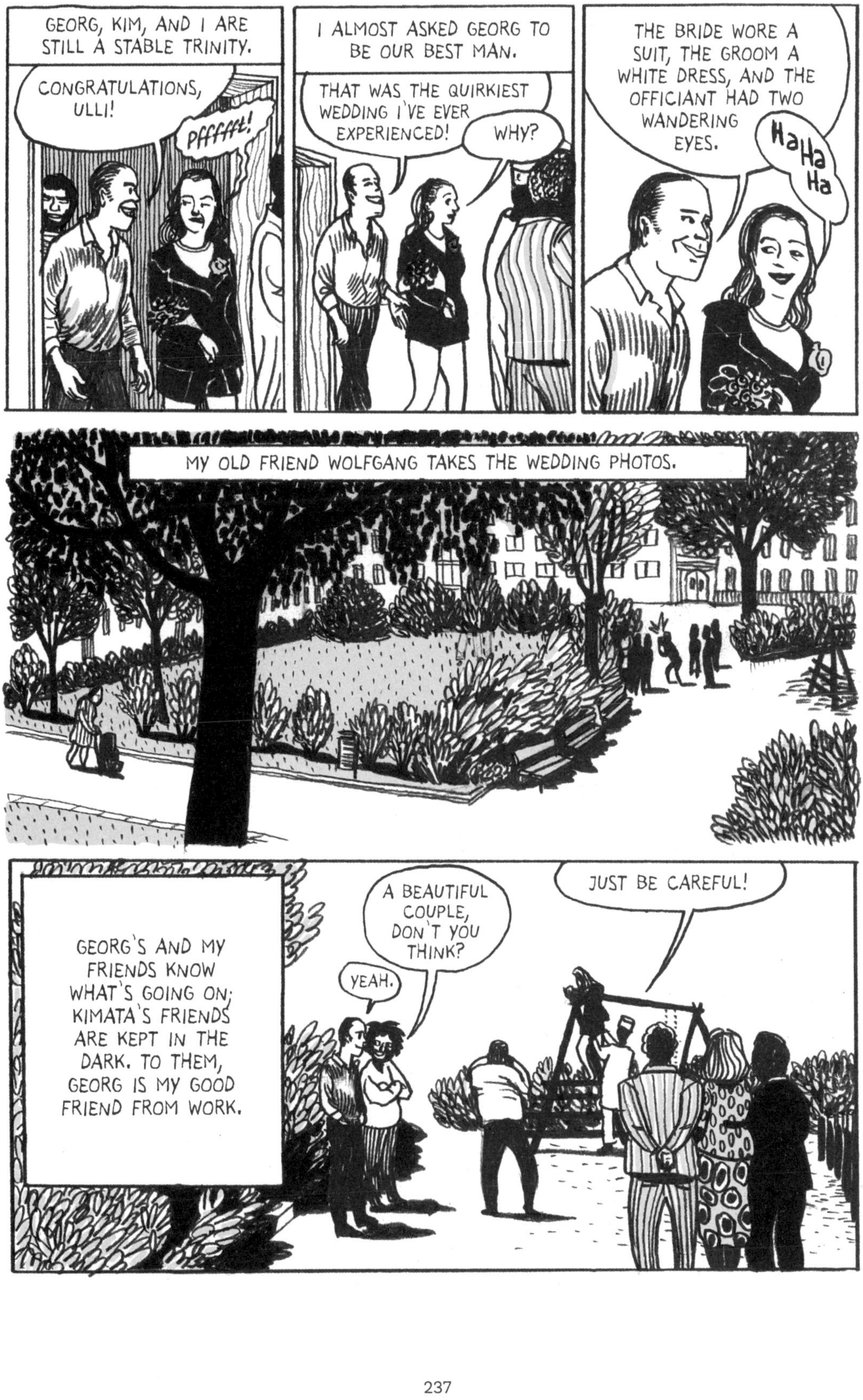
GEORG, KIM, AND I ARE STILL A STABLE TRINITY.
CONGRATULATIONS, ULLI!
PFFFFFT!
I ALMOST ASKED GEORG TO BE OUR BEST MAN.
THAT WAS THE QUIRKIEST WEDDING I'VE EVER EXPERIENCED!
WHY?
THE BRIDE WORE A SUIT, THE GROOM A WHITE DRESS, AND THE OFFICIANT HAD TWO WANDERING EYES.
HA HA HA
MY OLD FRIEND WOLFGANG TAKES THE WEDDING PHOTOS.
GEORG'S AND MY FRIENDS KNOW WHAT'S GOING ON; KIMATA'S FRIENDS ARE KEPT IN THE DARK. TO THEM, GEORG IS MY GOOD FRIEND FROM WORK.
A BEAUTIFUL COUPLE, DON'T YOU THINK?
YEAH.
JUST BE CAREFUL!

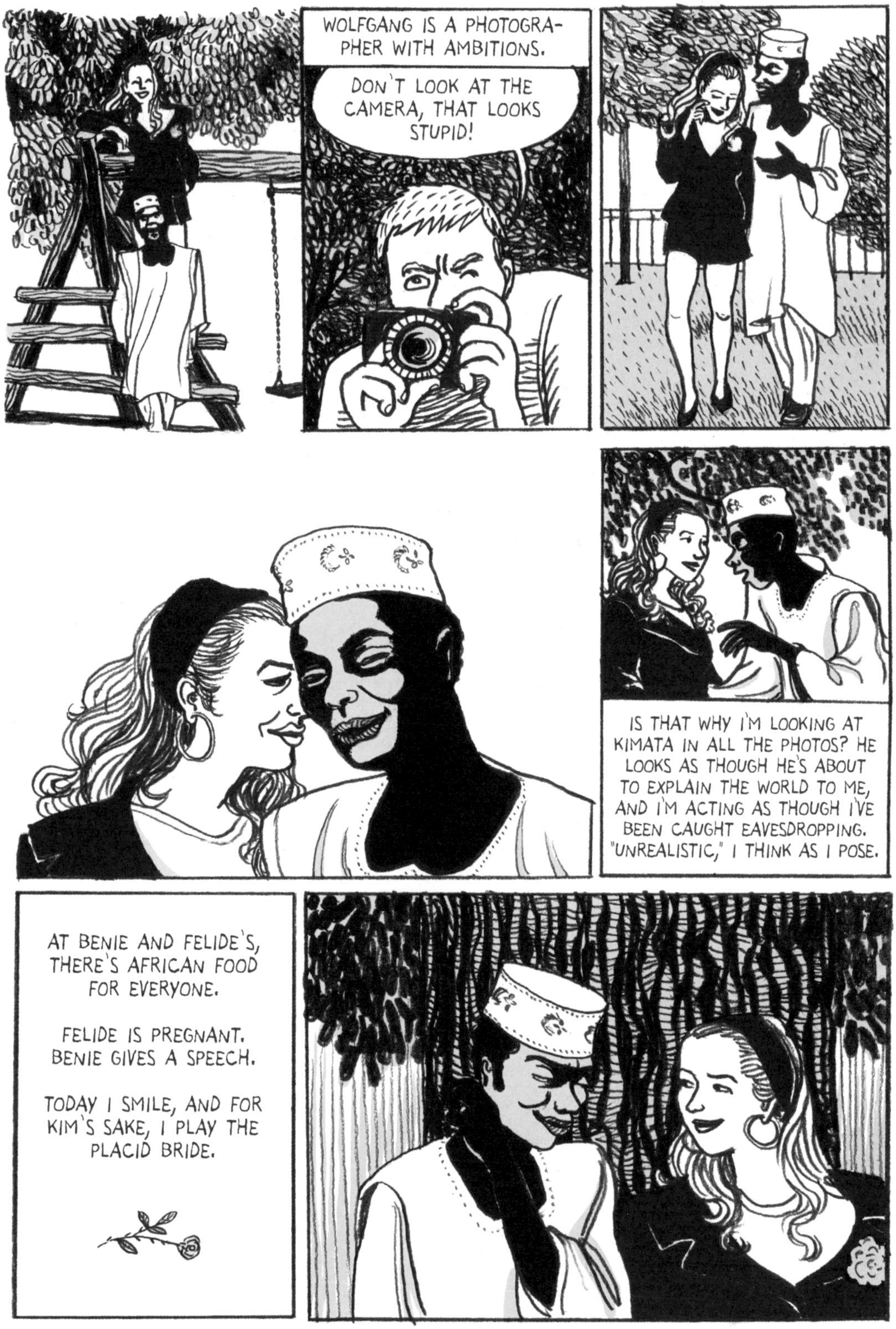
WOLFGANG IS A PHOTOGRAPHER WITH AMBITIONS.
DON'T LOOK AT THE CAMERA, THAT LOOKS STUPID!
IS THAT WHY I'M LOOKING AT KIMATA IN ALL THE PHOTOS? HE LOOKS AS THOUGH HE'S ABOUT TO EXPLAIN THE WORLD TO ME, AND I'M ACTING AS THOUGH I'VE BEEN CAUGHT EAVESDROPPING. "UNREALISTIC," I THINK AS I POSE.
AT BENIE AND FELIDE'S, THERE'S AFRICAN FOOD FOR EVERYONE.
FELIDE IS PREGNANT. BENIE GIVES A SPEECH.
TODAY I SMILE, AND FOR KIM'S SAKE, I PLAY THE PLACID BRIDE.

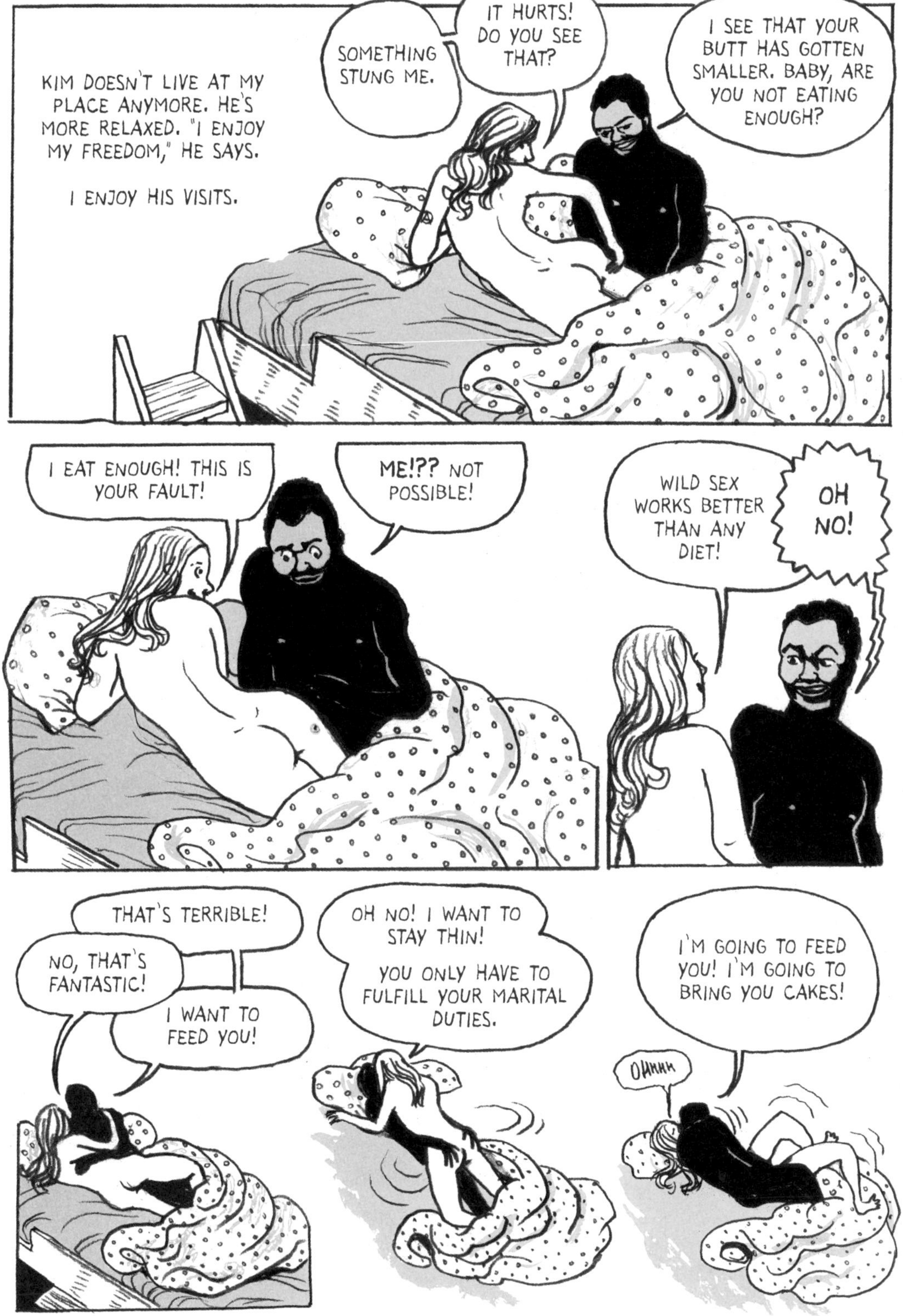
KIM DOESN'T LIVE AT MY PLACE ANYMORE. HE'S MORE RELAXED. "I ENJOY MY FREEDOM," HE SAYS.
I ENJOY HIS VISITS.
SOMETHING STUNG ME.
IT HURTS! DO YOU SEE THAT?
I SEE THAT YOUR BUTT HAS GOTTEN SMALLER. BABY, ARE YOU NOT EATING ENOUGH?
I EAT ENOUGH! THIS IS YOUR FAULT!
ME!?? NOT POSSIBLE!
WILD SEX WORKS BETTER THAN ANY DIET!
OH NO!
THAT'S TERRIBLE!
NO, THAT'S FANTASTIC!
I WANT TO FEED YOU!
OH NO! I WANT TO STAY THIN!
YOU ONLY HAVE TO FULFILL YOUR MARITAL DUTIES.
OHHHH
I'M GOING TO FEED YOU! I'M GOING TO BRING YOU CAKES!

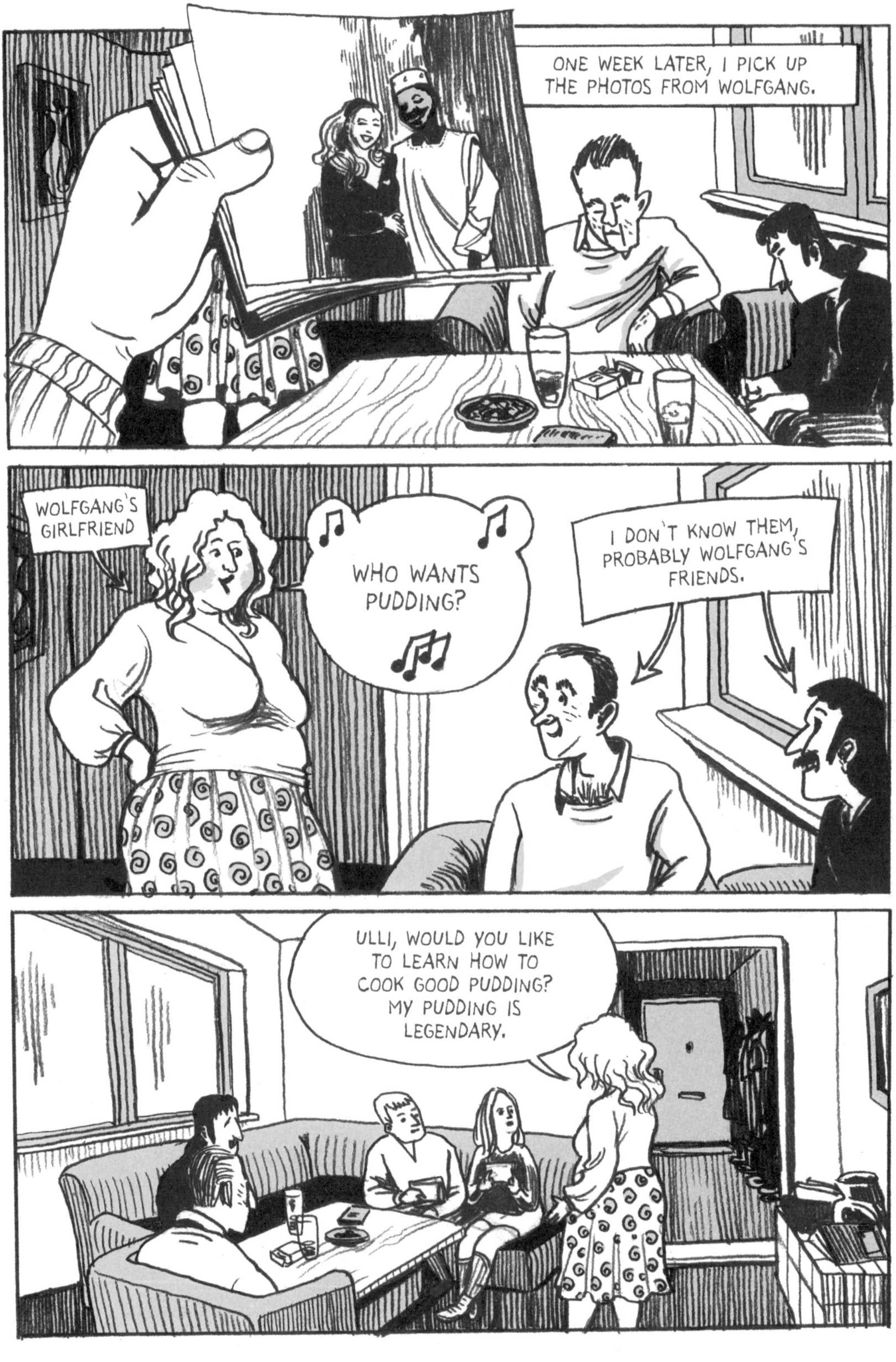

ONE WEEK LATER, I PICK UP THE PHOTOS FROM WOLFGANG.
WOLFGANG'S GIRLFRIEND
WHO WANTS PUDDING?
I DON'T KNOW THEM, PROBABLY WOLFGANG'S FRIENDS.
ULLI, WOULD YOU LIKE TO LEARN HOW TO COOK GOOD PUDDING? MY PUDDING IS LEGENDARY.

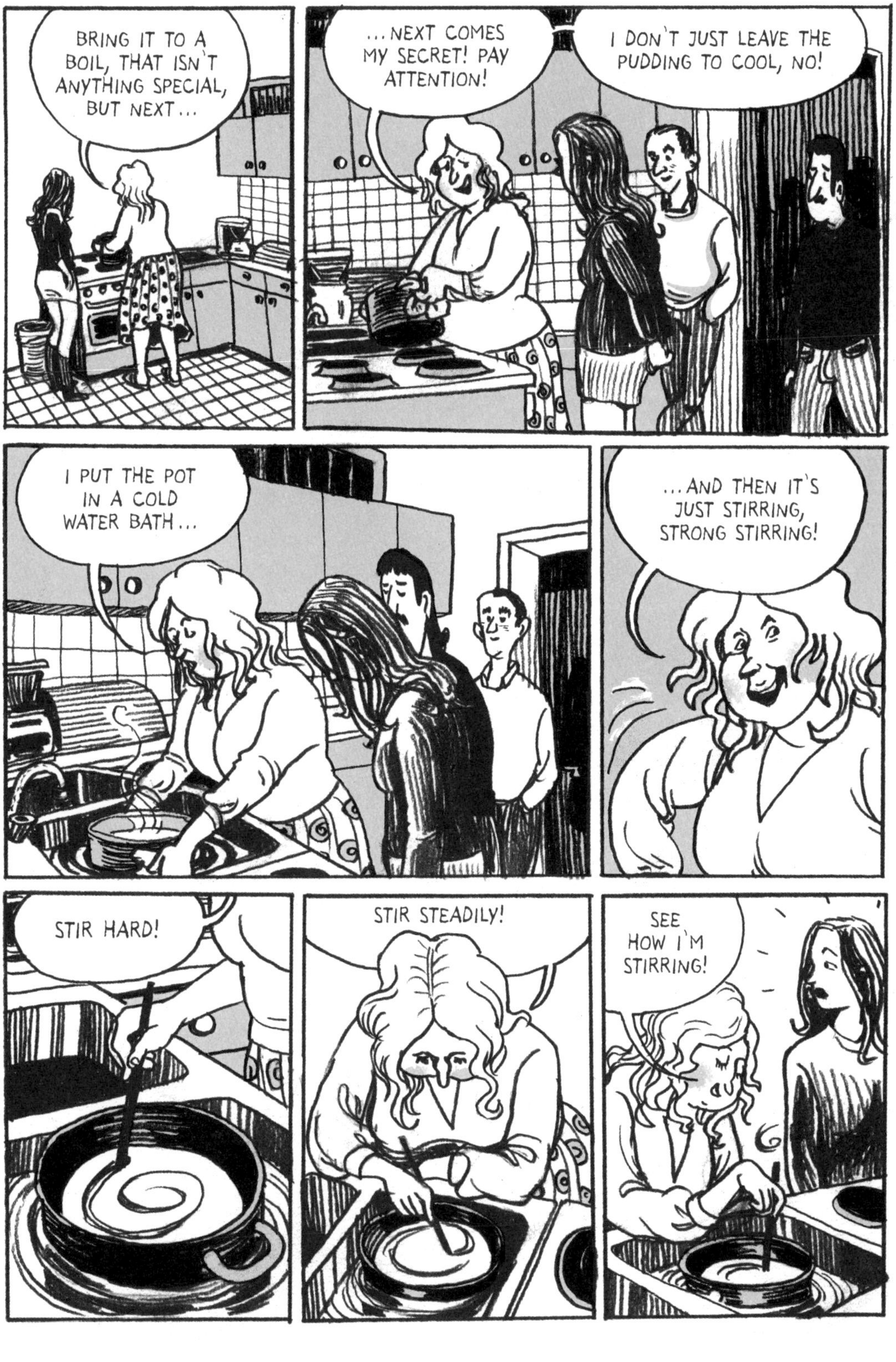

BRING IT TO A BOIL, THAT ISN'T ANYTHING SPECIAL, BUT NEXT...
...NEXT COMES MY SECRET! PAY ATTENTION!
I DON'T JUST LEAVE THE PUDDING TO COOL, NO!
I PUT THE POT IN A COLD WATER BATH...
...AND THEN IT'S JUST STIRRING, STRONG STIRRING!
STIR HARD!
STIR STEADILY!
SEE HOW I'M STIRRING!

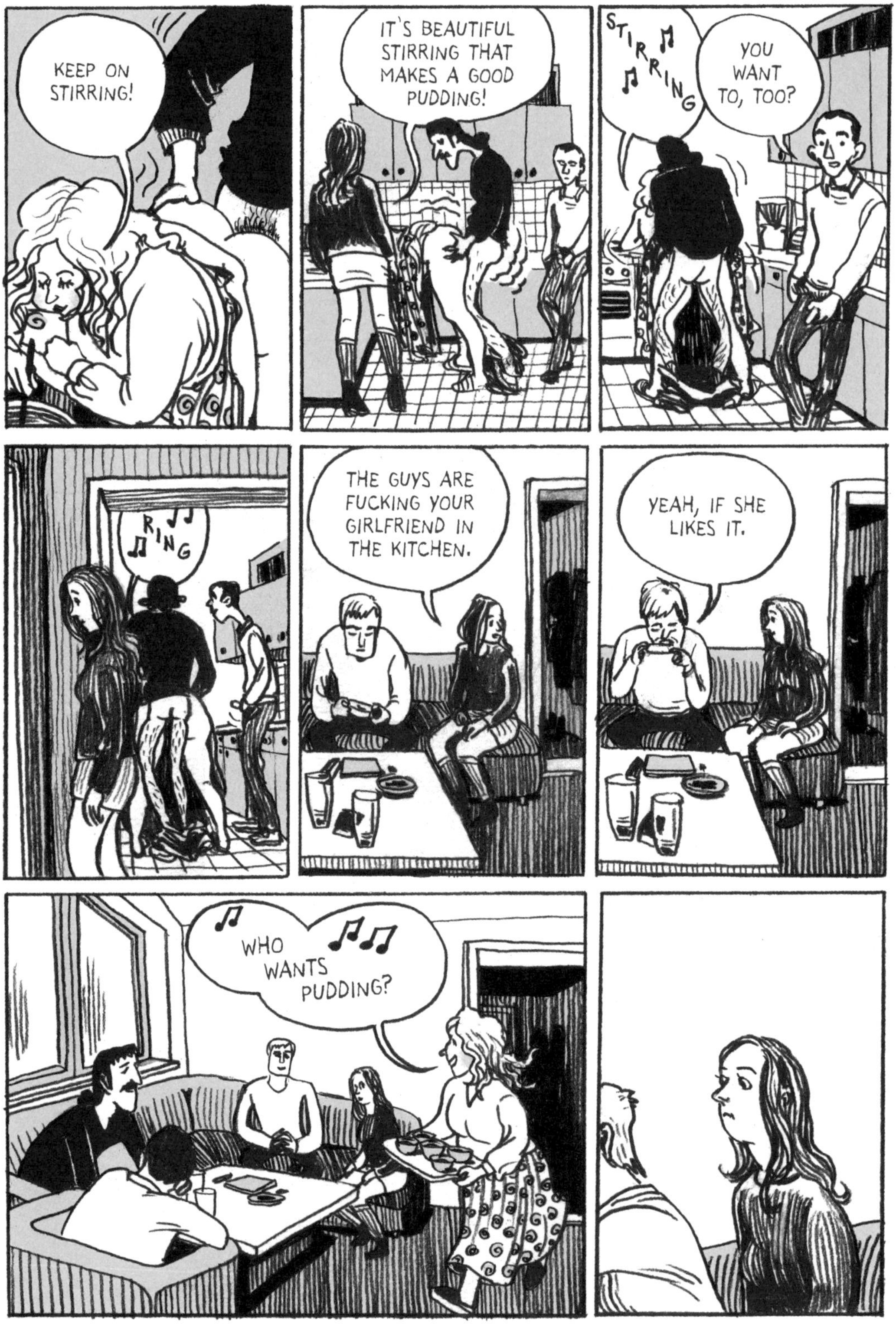
KEEP ON STIRRING!
IT'S BEAUTIFUL STIRRING THAT MAKES A GOOD PUDDING!
STIRRING
YOU WANT TO, TOO?
RING
THE GUYS ARE FUCKING YOUR GIRLFRIEND IN THE KITCHEN.
YEAH, IF SHE LIKES IT.
WHO WANTS PUDDING?

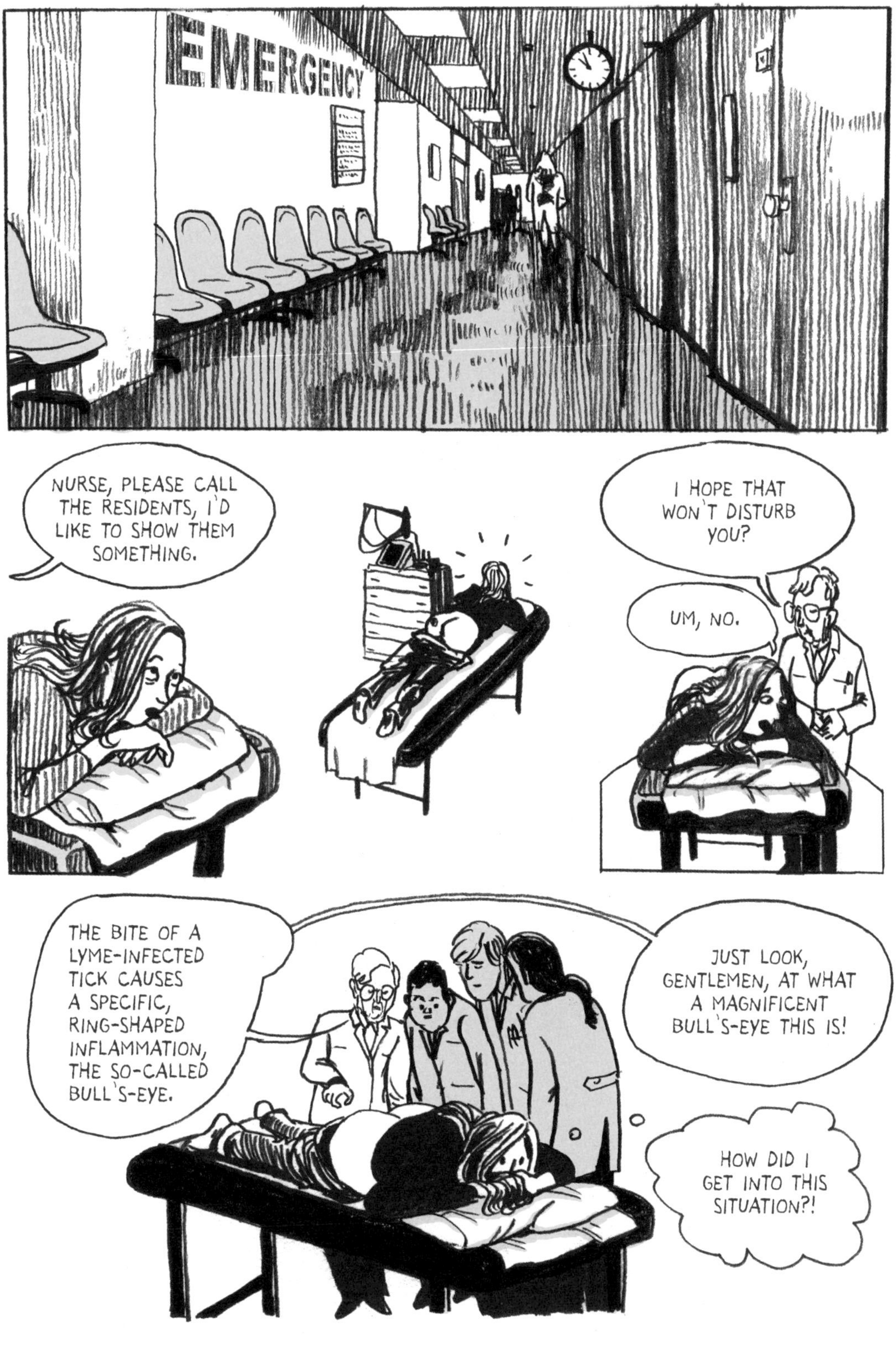
EMERGENCY
NURSE, PLEASE CALL THE RESIDENTS, I'D LIKE TO SHOW THEM SOMETHING.
I HOPE THAT WON'T DISTURB YOU?
UM, NO.
THE BITE OF A LYME-INFECTED TICK CAUSES A SPECIFIC, RING-SHAPED INFLAMMATION, THE SO-CALLED BULL'S-EYE.
JUST LOOK, GENTLEMEN, AT WHAT A MAGNIFICENT BULL'S-EYE THIS IS!
HOW DID I GET INTO THIS SITUATION?!

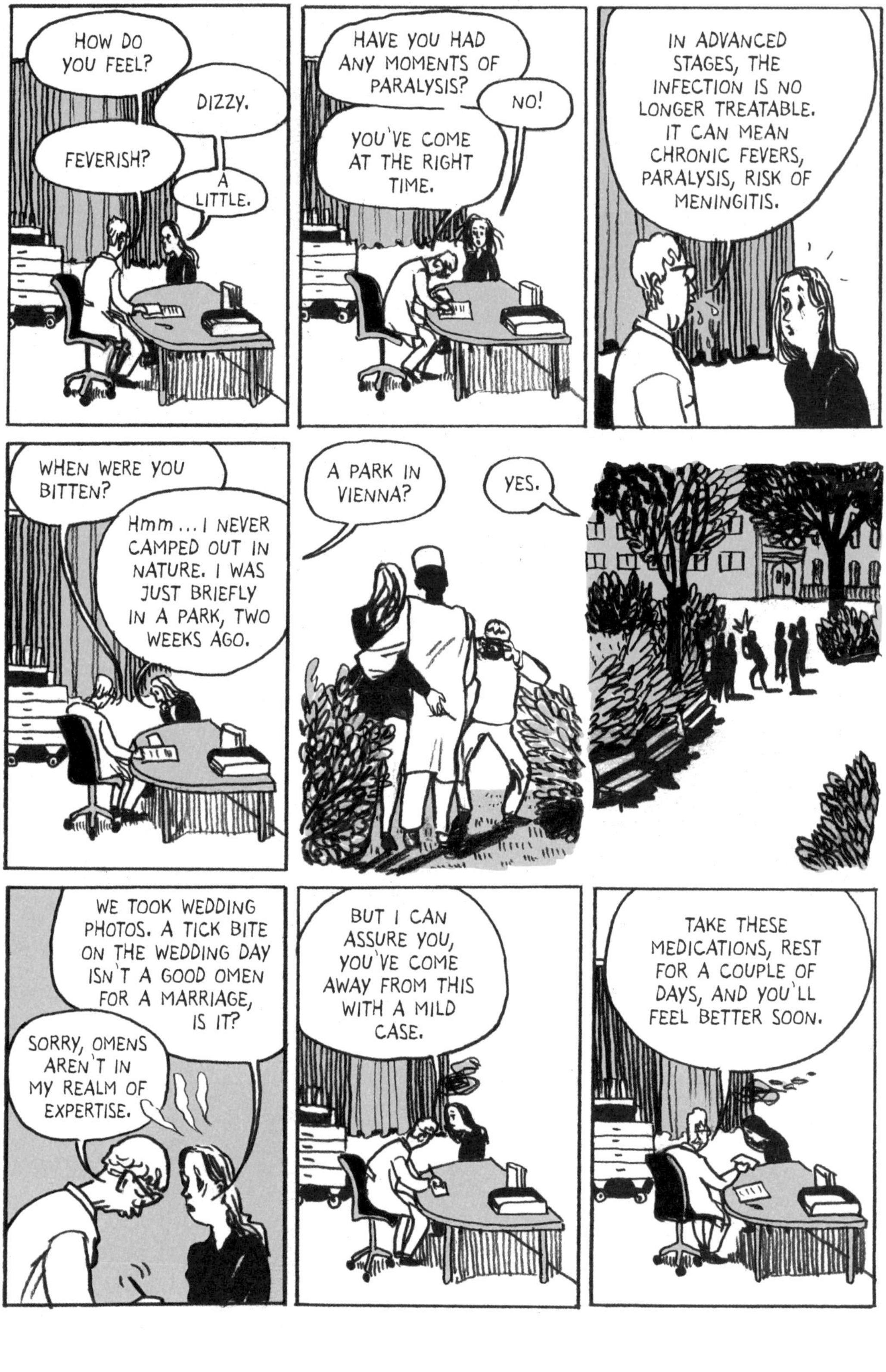
HOW DO YOU FEEL?
DIZZY.
FEVERISH?
A LITTLE.
HAVE YOU HAD ANY MOMENTS OF PARALYSIS?
NO!
YOU'VE COME AT THE RIGHT TIME.
IN ADVANCED STAGES, THE INFECTION IS NO LONGER TREATABLE. IT CAN MEAN CHRONIC FEVERS, PARALYSIS, RISK OF MENINGITIS.
WHEN WERE YOU BITTEN?
Hmm... I NEVER CAMPED OUT IN NATURE. I WAS JUST BRIEFLY IN A PARK, TWO WEEKS AGO.
A PARK IN VIENNA?
YES.
WE TOOK WEDDING PHOTOS. A TICK BITE ON THE WEDDING DAY ISN'T A GOOD OMEN FOR A MARRIAGE, IS IT?
SORRY, OMENS AREN'T IN MY REALM OF EXPERTISE.
BUT I CAN ASSURE YOU, YOU'VE COME AWAY FROM THIS WITH A MILD CASE.
TAKE THESE MEDICATIONS, REST FOR A COUPLE OF DAYS, AND YOU'LL FEEL BETTER SOON.

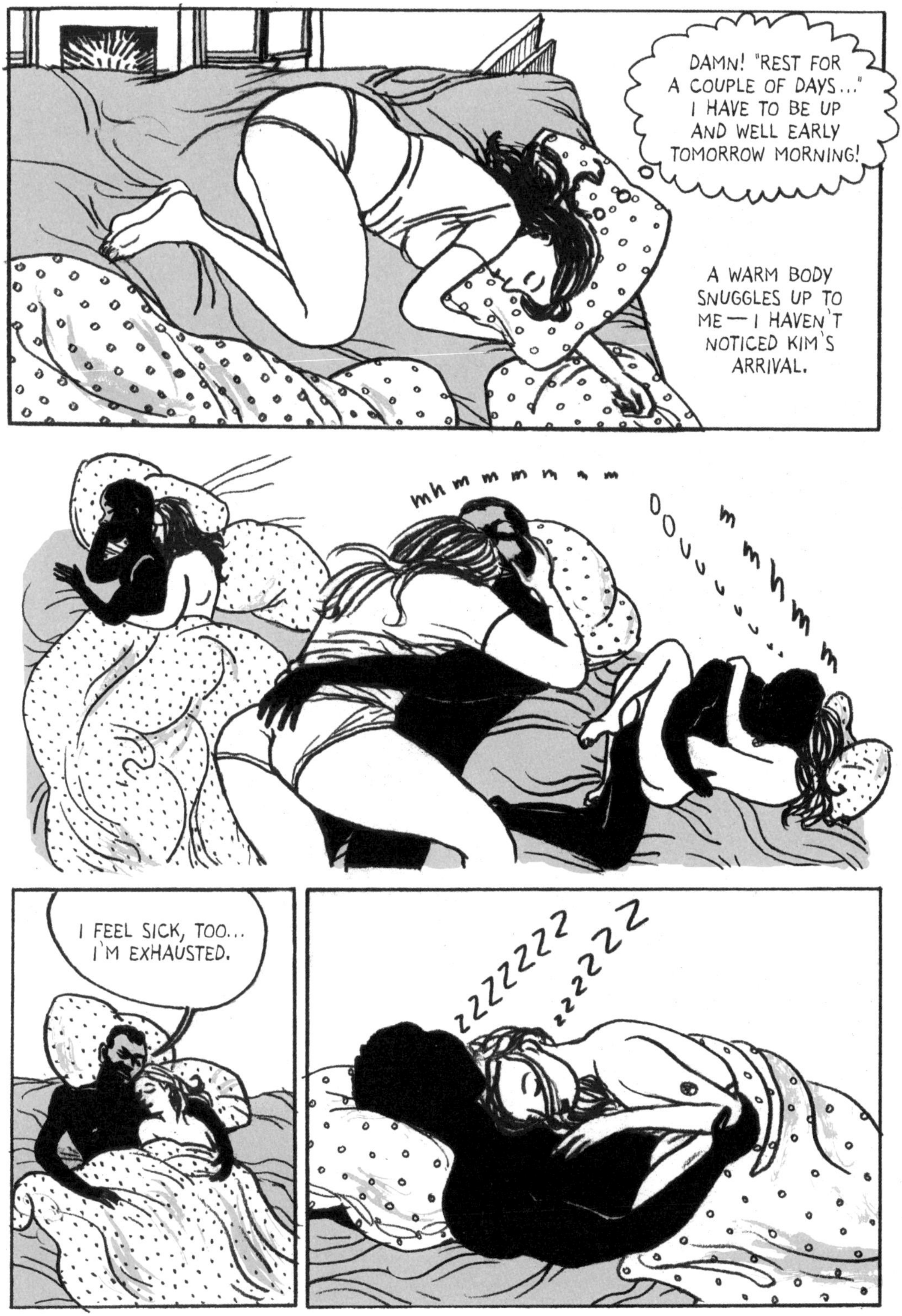
DAMN! "REST FOR A COUPLE OF DAYS..." I HAVE TO BE UP AND WELL EARLY TOMORROW MORNING!
A WARM BODY SNUGGLES UP TO ME — I HAVEN'T NOTICED KIM'S ARRIVAL.
I FEEL SICK, TOO... I'M EXHAUSTED.

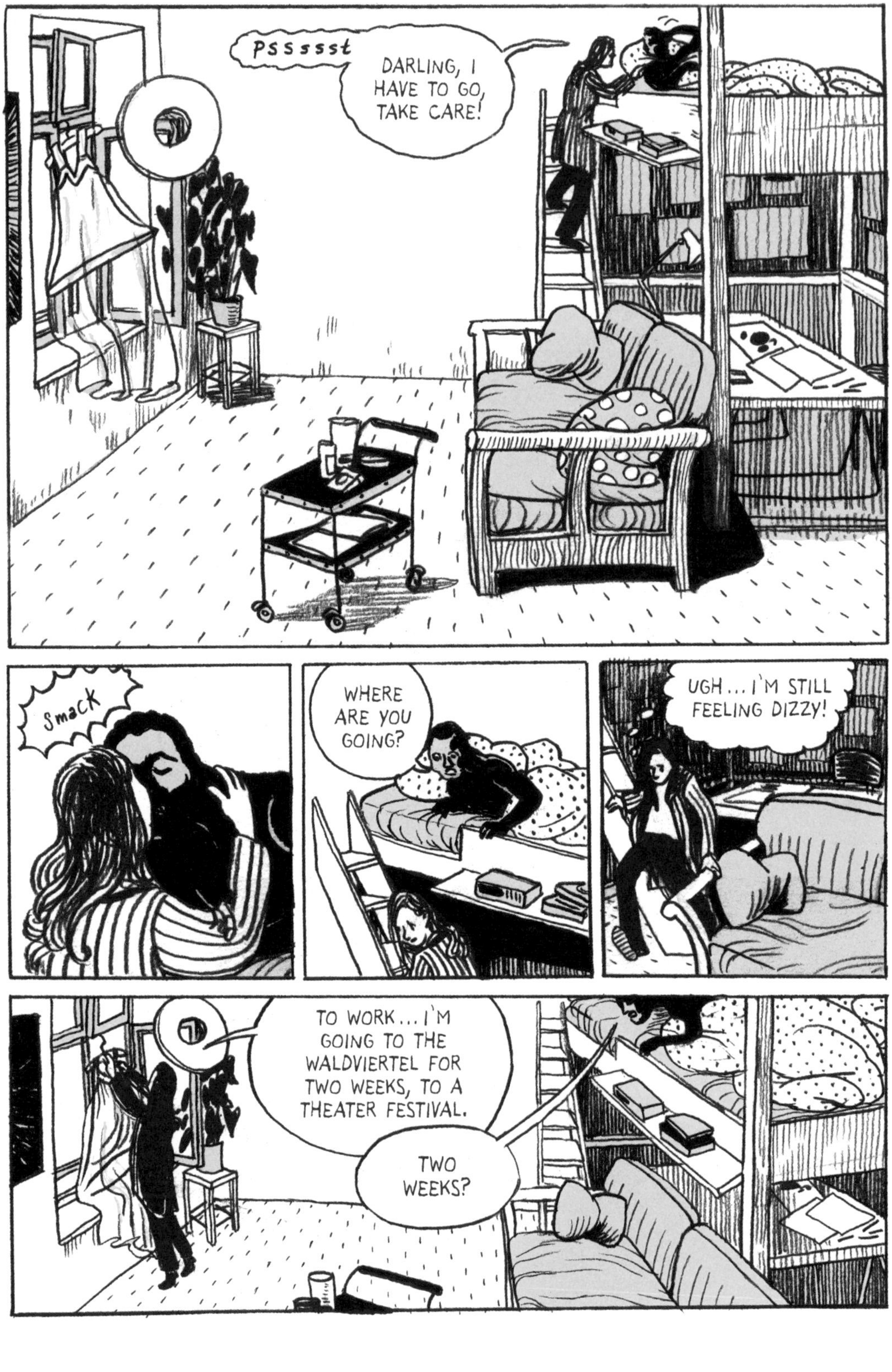
PSSSSST
DARLING, I HAVE TO GO, TAKE CARE!
SMACK
WHERE ARE YOU GOING?
UGH... I'M STILL FEELING DIZZY!
TO WORK... I'M GOING TO THE WALDVIERTEL FOR TWO WEEKS, TO A THEATER FESTIVAL.
TWO WEEKS?

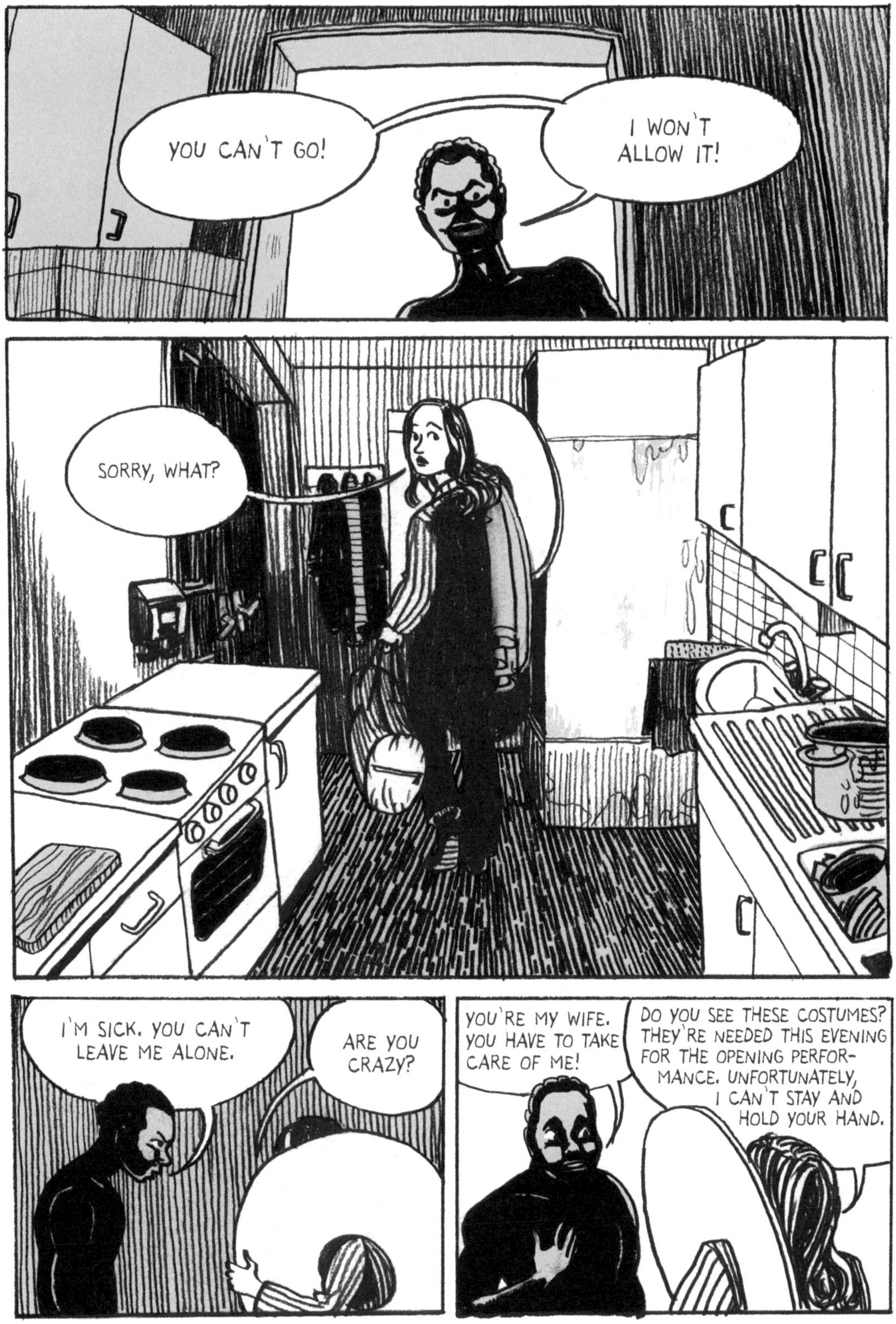
YOU CAN'T GO!
I WON'T ALLOW IT!
SORRY, WHAT?
I'M SICK. YOU CAN'T LEAVE ME ALONE.
ARE YOU CRAZY?
YOU'RE MY WIFE. YOU HAVE TO TAKE CARE OF ME!
DO YOU SEE THESE COSTUMES? THEY'RE NEEDED THIS EVENING FOR THE OPENING PERFORMANCE. UNFORTUNATELY, I CAN'T STAY AND HOLD YOUR HAND.

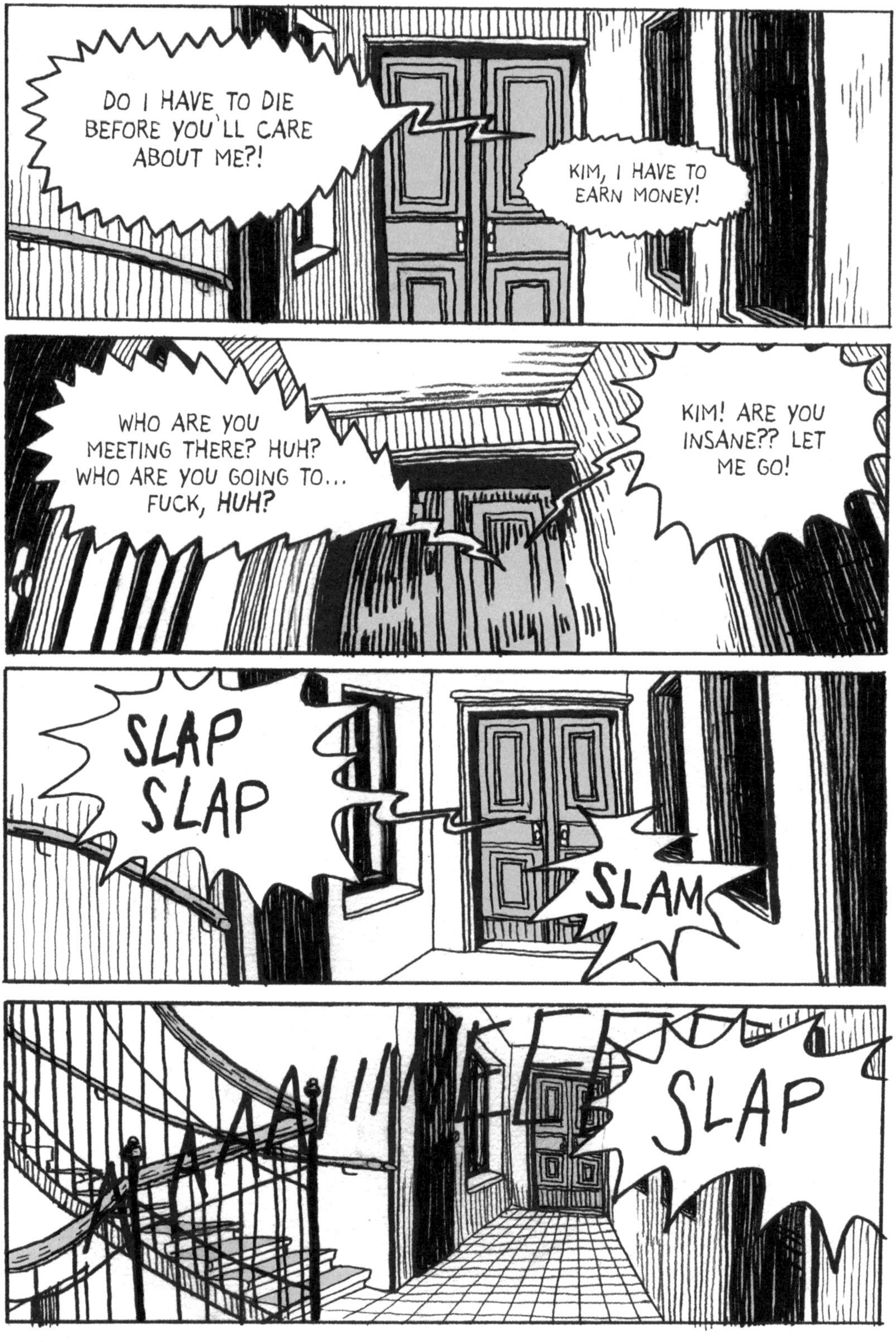
DO I HAVE TO DIE BEFORE YOU'LL CARE ABOUT ME?!
KIM, I HAVE TO EARN MONEY!
WHO ARE YOU MEETING THERE? HUH? WHO ARE YOU GOING TO... FUCK, HUH?
KIM! ARE YOU INSANE?? LET ME GO!
SLAP SLAP
SLAM
AAAAIIIIIEEE
SLAP

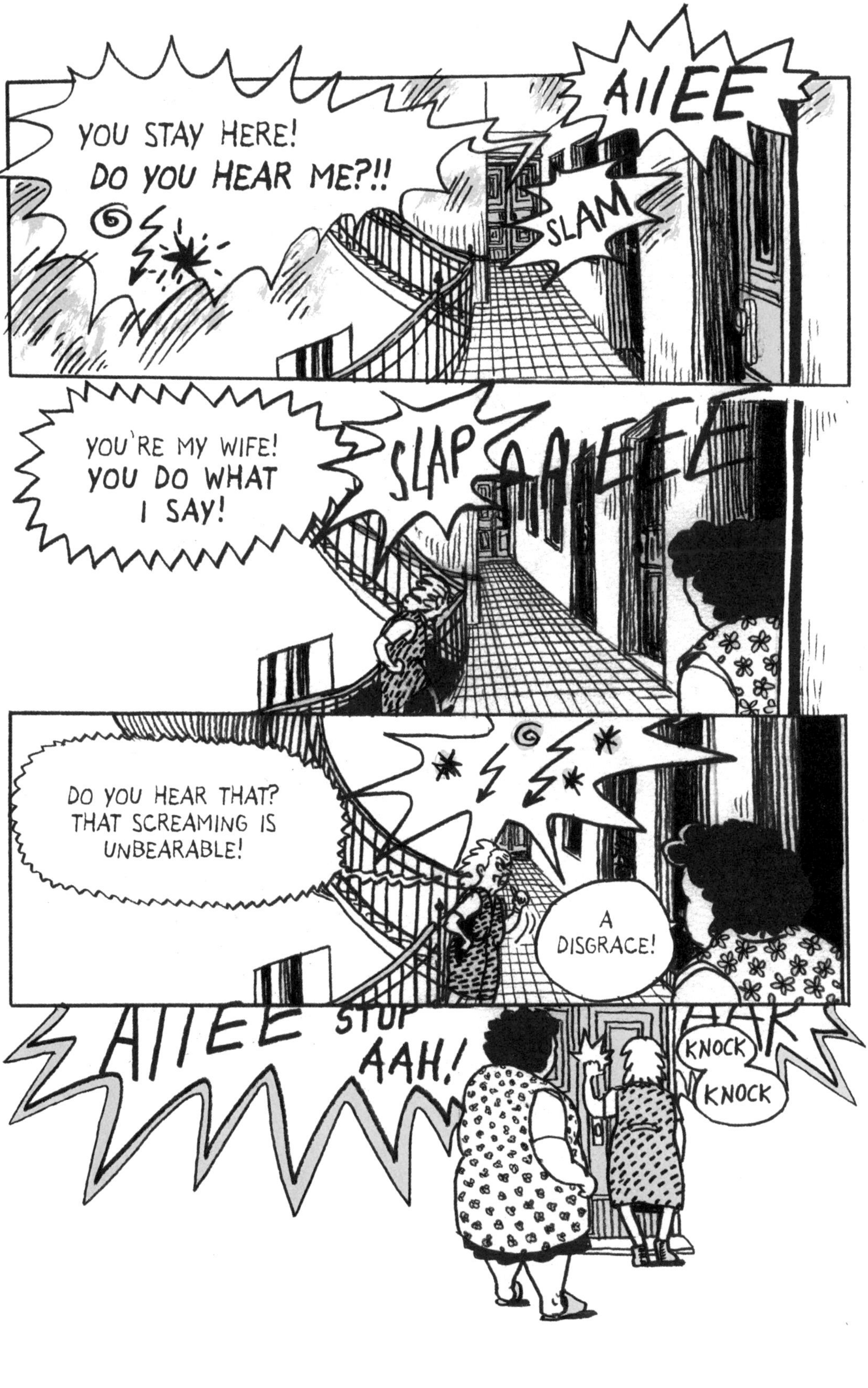
YOU STAY HERE!
DO YOU HEAR ME?!!
AIIEE
SLAM
YOU'RE MY WIFE! YOU DO WHAT I SAY!
SLAP
DO YOU HEAR THAT? THAT SCREAMING IS UNBEARABLE!
A DISGRACE!
AIIEE
AAH!
KNOCK
KNOCK

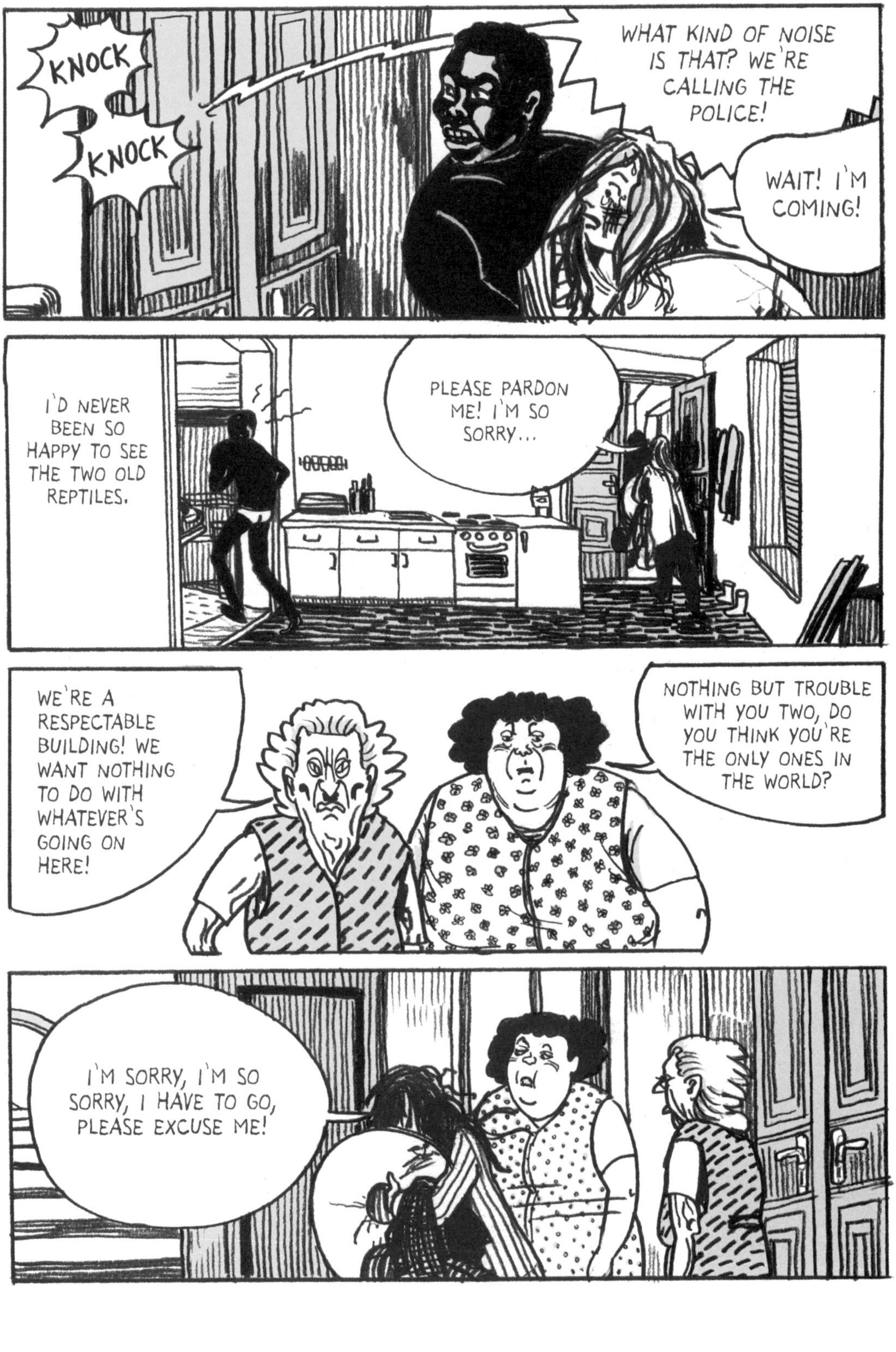
KNOCK
KNOCK
WHAT KIND OF NOISE IS THAT? WE'RE CALLING THE POLICE!
WAIT! I'M COMING!
I'D NEVER BEEN SO HAPPY TO SEE THE TWO OLD REPTILES.
PLEASE PARDON ME! I'M SO SORRY...
WE'RE A RESPECTABLE BUILDING! WE WANT NOTHING TO DO WITH WHATEVER'S GOING ON HERE!
NOTHING BUT TROUBLE WITH YOU TWO, DO YOU THINK YOU'RE THE ONLY ONES IN THE WORLD?
I'M SORRY, I'M SO SORRY, I HAVE TO GO, PLEASE EXCUSE ME!

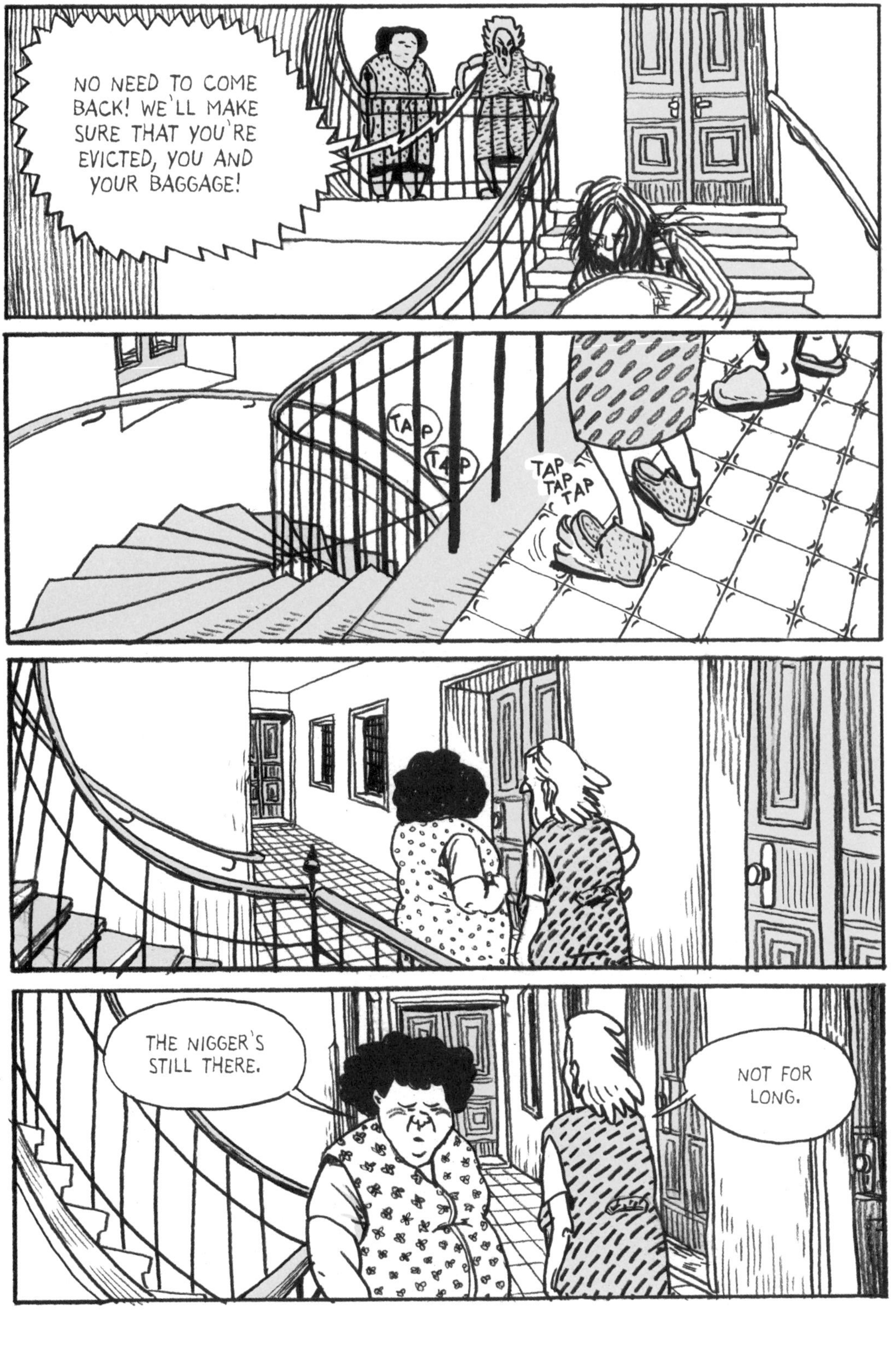
NO NEED TO COME BACK! WE'LL MAKE SURE THAT YOU'RE EVICTED, YOU AND YOUR BAGGAGE!
TAP
TAP
TAP TAP TAP
THE NIGGER'S STILL THERE.
NOT FOR LONG.

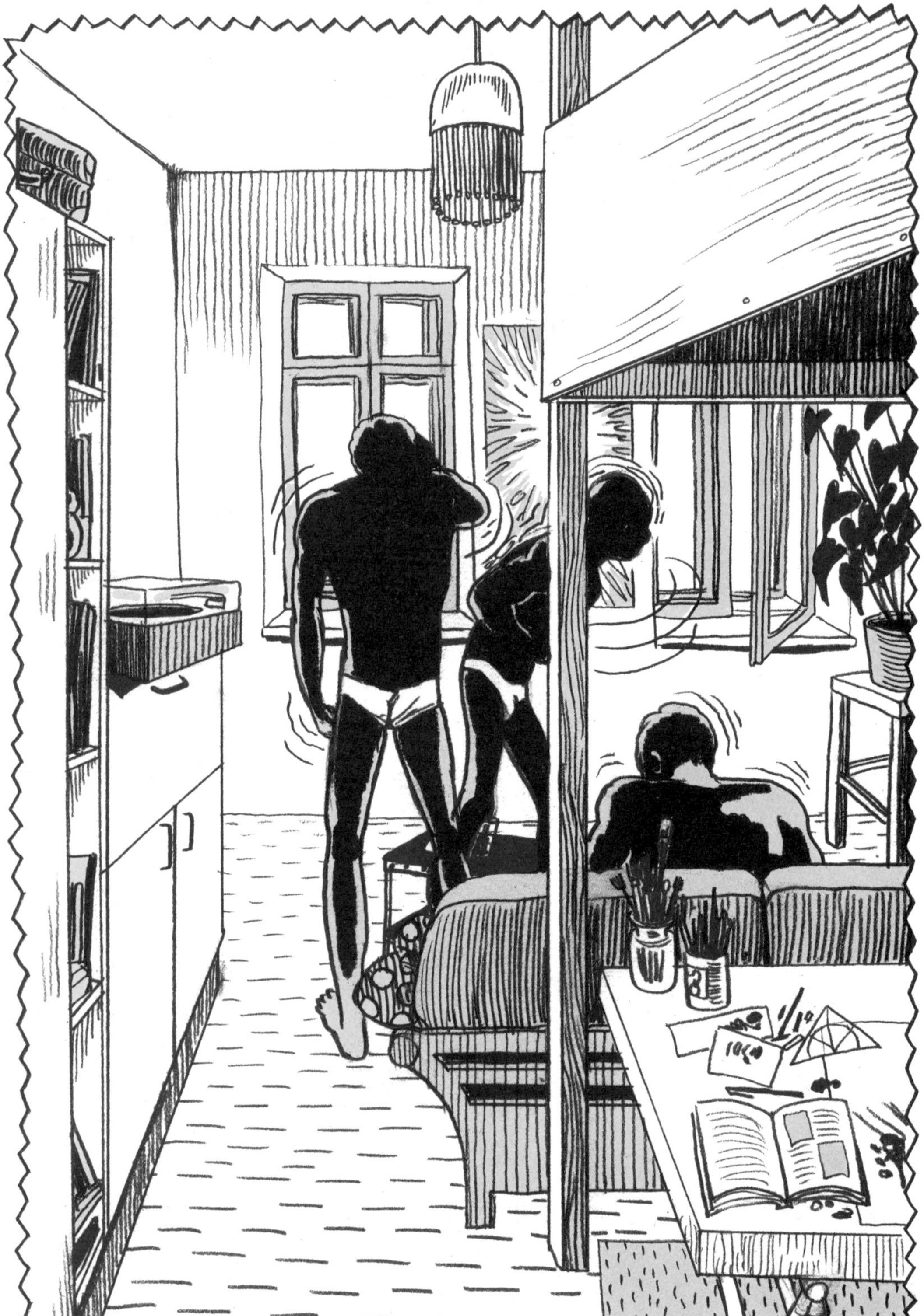

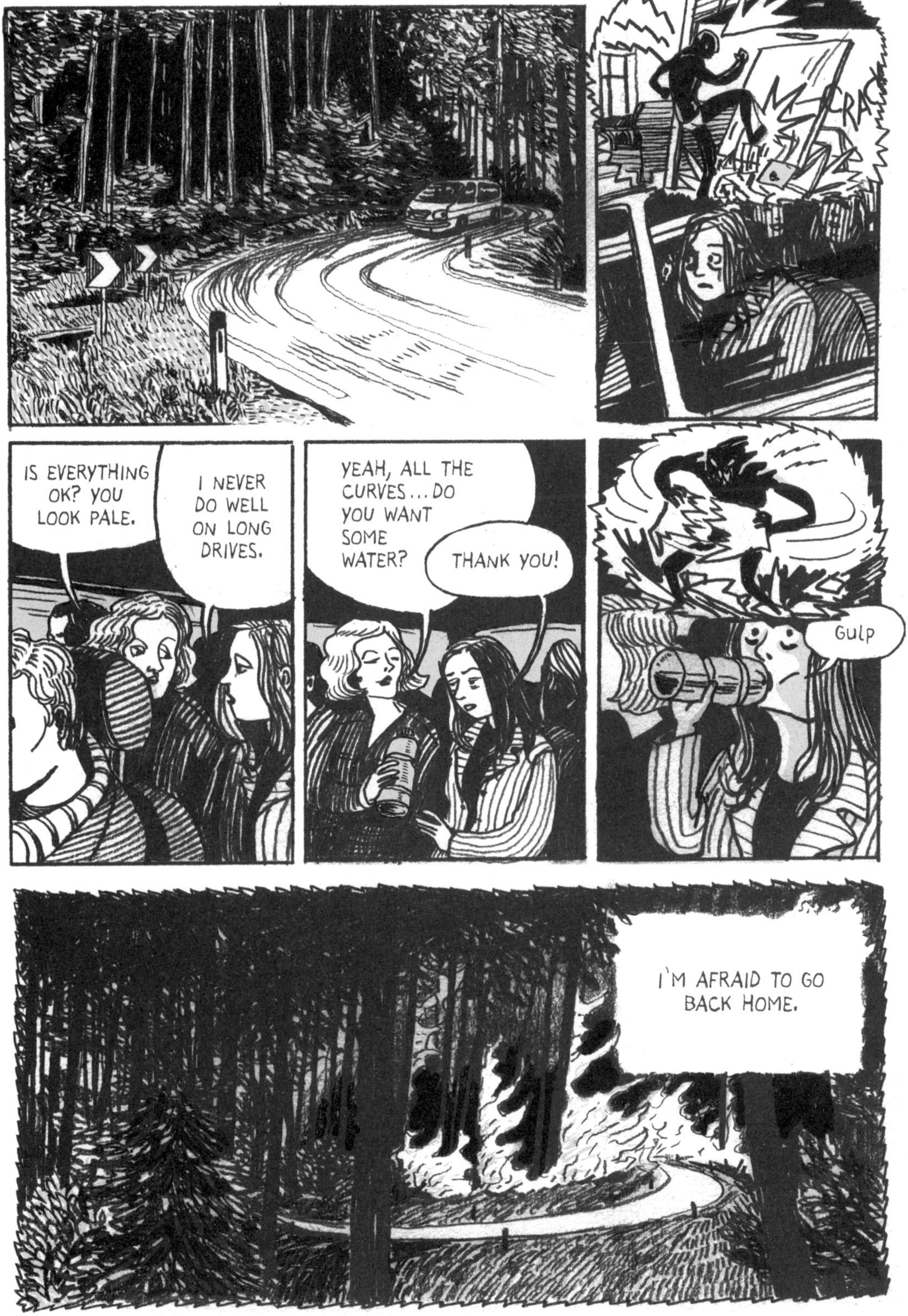
IS EVERYTHING OK? YOU LOOK PALE.
I NEVER DO WELL ON LONG DRIVES.
YEAH, ALL THE CURVES... DO YOU WANT SOME WATER?
THANK YOU!
Gulp
I'M AFRAID TO GO BACK HOME.

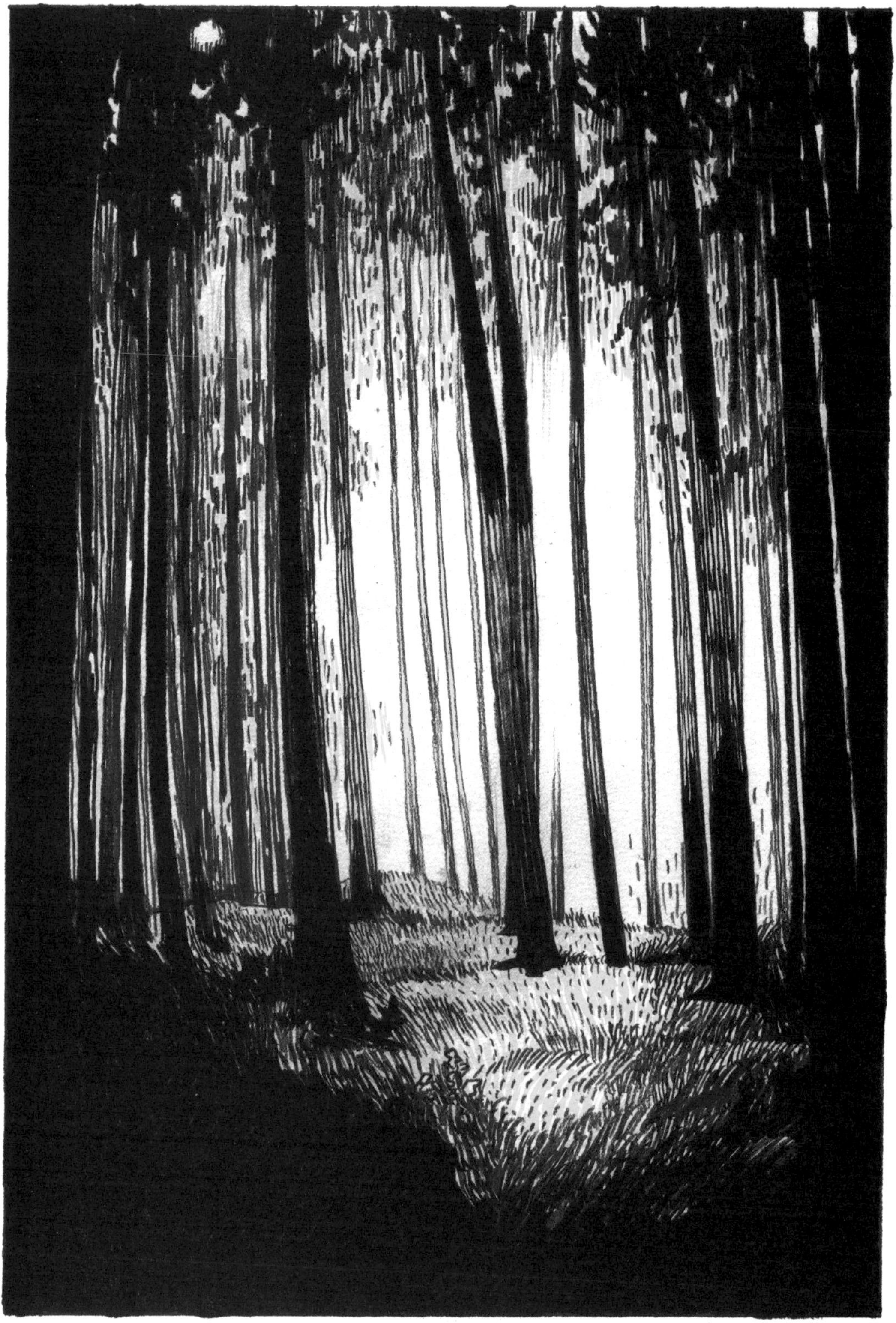

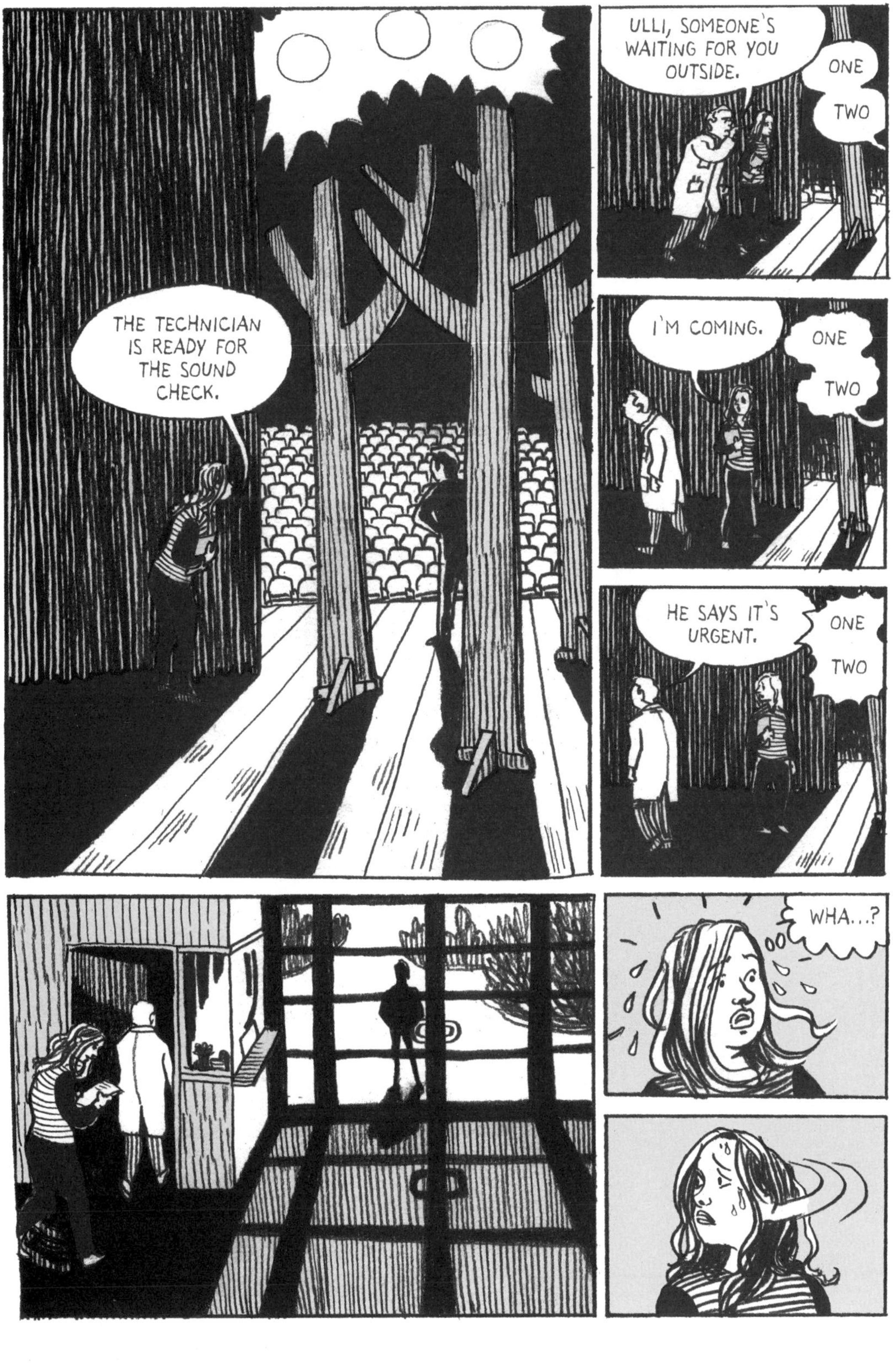
THE TECHNICIAN IS READY FOR THE SOUND CHECK.
ULLI, SOMEONE'S WAITING FOR YOU OUTSIDE.
ONE
TWO
I'M COMING.
ONE
TWO
HE SAYS IT'S URGENT.
ONE
TWO
WHA...?

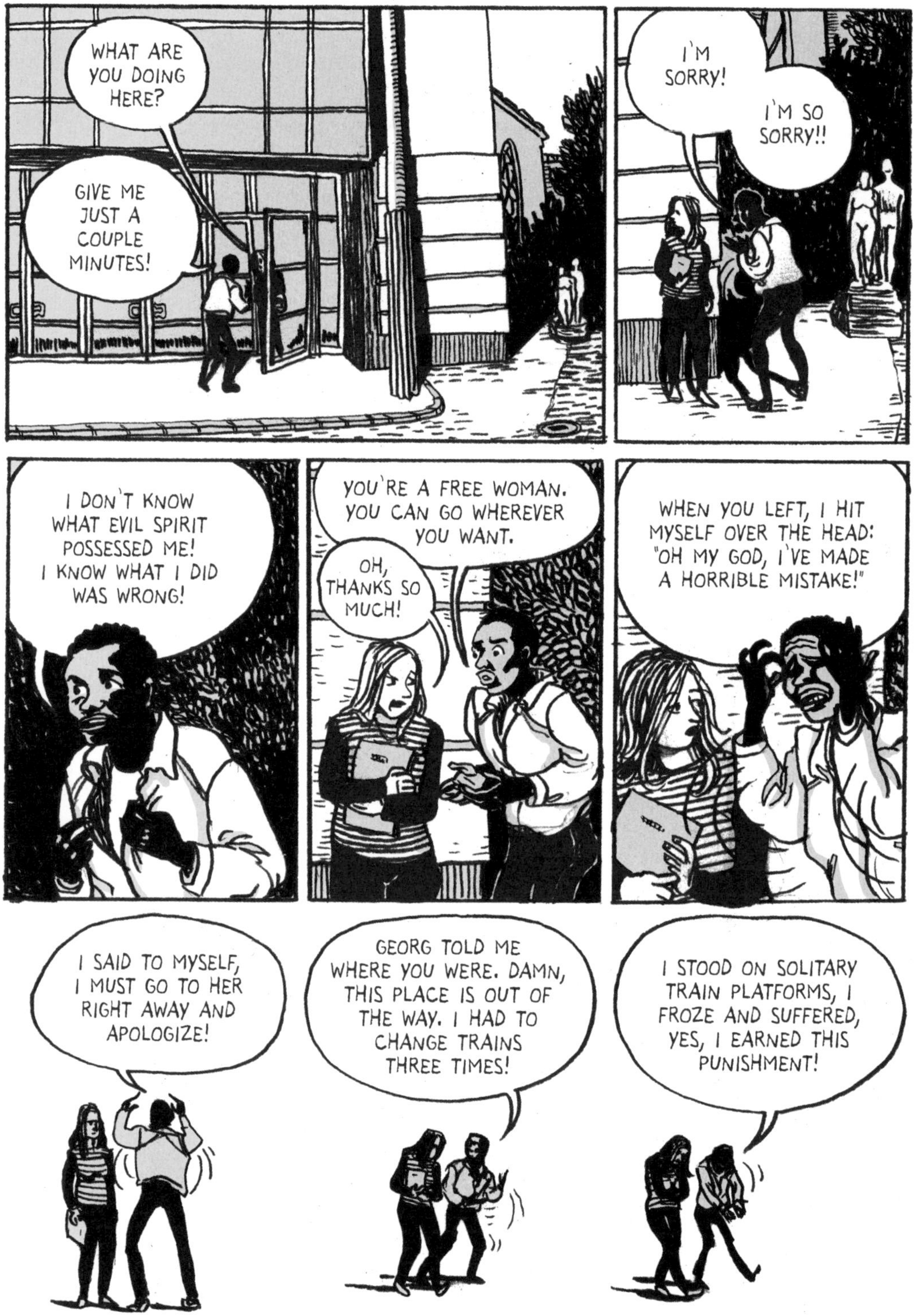
WHAT ARE YOU DOING HERE?
GIVE ME JUST A COUPLE MINUTES!
I'M SORRY!
I'M SO SORRY!!
I DON'T KNOW WHAT EVIL SPIRIT POSSESSED ME! I KNOW WHAT I DID WAS WRONG!
YOU'RE A FREE WOMAN. YOU CAN GO WHEREVER YOU WANT.
OH, THANKS SO MUCH!
WHEN YOU LEFT, I HIT MYSELF OVER THE HEAD: "OH MY GOD, I'VE MADE A HORRIBLE MISTAKE!"
I SAID TO MYSELF, I MUST GO TO HER RIGHT AWAY AND APOLOGIZE!
GEORG TOLD ME WHERE YOU WERE. DAMN, THIS PLACE IS OUT OF THE WAY. I HAD TO CHANGE TRAINS THREE TIMES!
I STOOD ON SOLITARY TRAIN PLATFORMS, I FROZE AND SUFFERED, YES, I EARNED THIS PUNISHMENT!

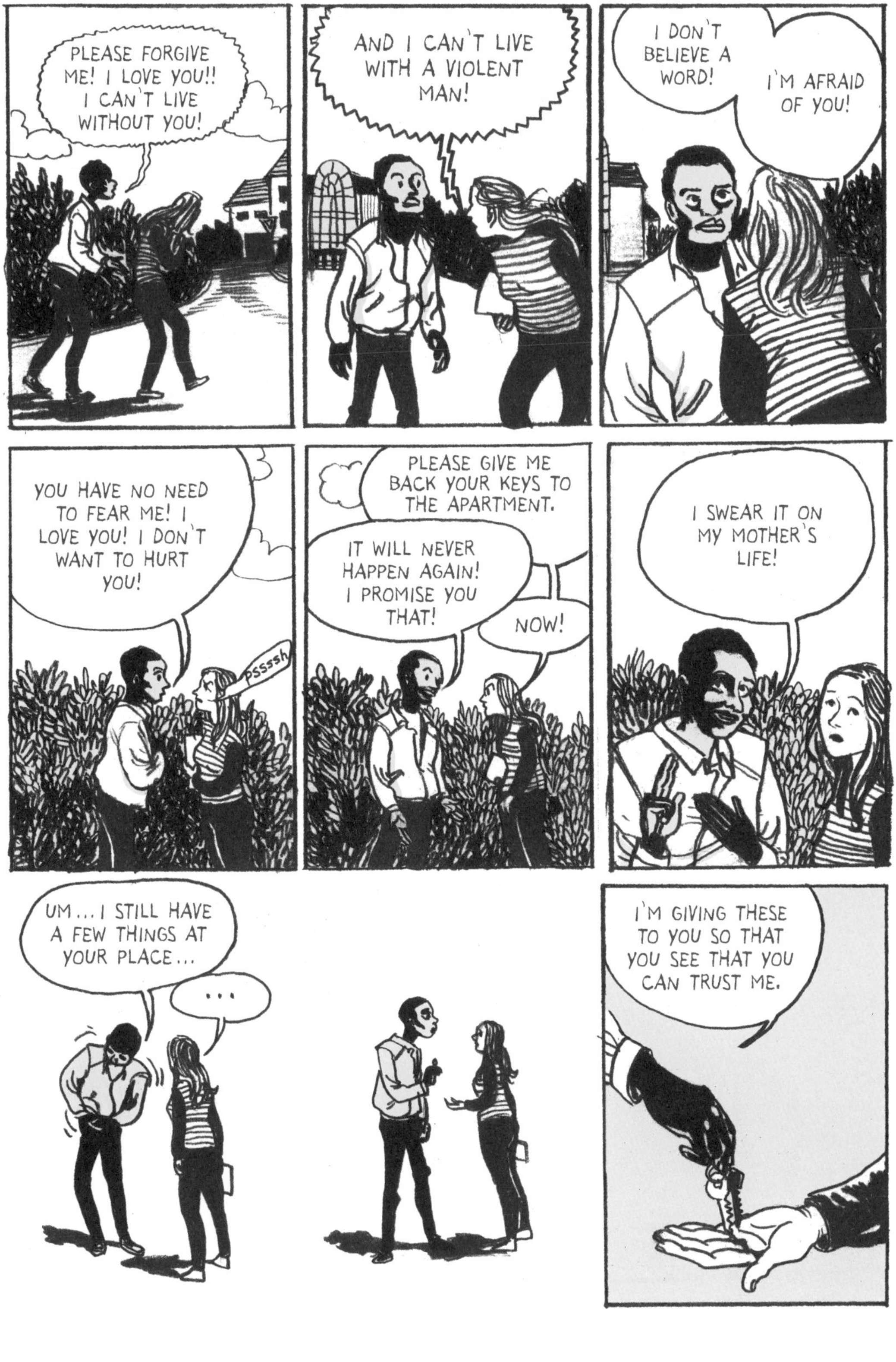
PLEASE FORGIVE ME! I LOVE YOU!! I CAN'T LIVE WITHOUT YOU!
AND I CAN'T LIVE WITH A VIOLENT MAN!
I DON'T BELIEVE A WORD!
I'M AFRAID OF YOU!
YOU HAVE NO NEED TO FEAR ME! I LOVE YOU! I DON'T WANT TO HURT YOU!
PSSSSH
PLEASE GIVE ME BACK YOUR KEYS TO THE APARTMENT.
IT WILL NEVER HAPPEN AGAIN! I PROMISE YOU THAT!
NOW!
I SWEAR IT ON MY MOTHER'S LIFE!
UM... I STILL HAVE A FEW THINGS AT YOUR PLACE...
...
I'M GIVING THESE TO YOU SO THAT YOU SEE THAT YOU CAN TRUST ME.

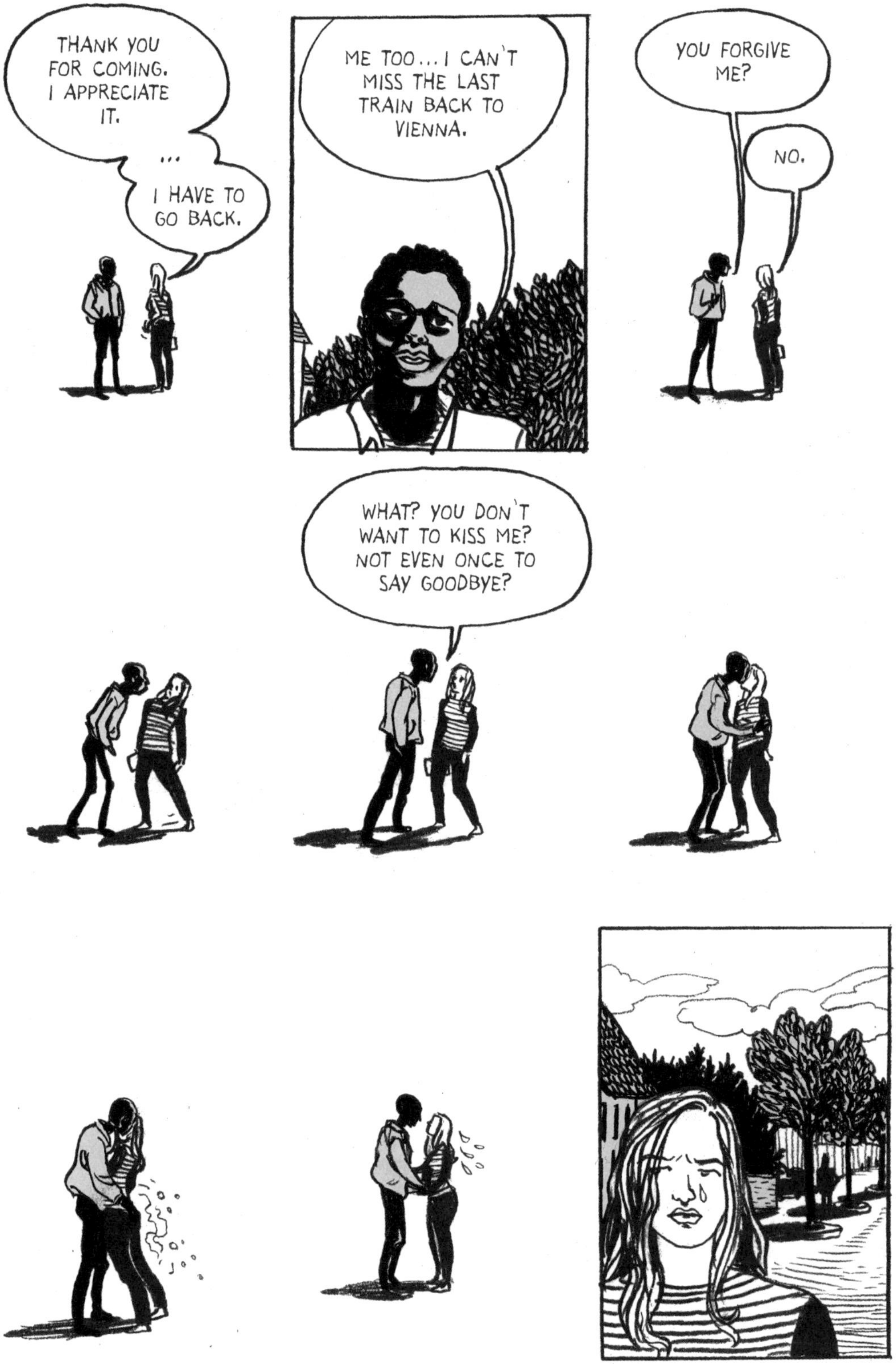
THANK YOU FOR COMING. I APPRECIATE IT.
...
I HAVE TO GO BACK.
ME TOO... I CAN'T MISS THE LAST TRAIN BACK TO VIENNA.
YOU FORGIVE ME?
NO.
WHAT? YOU DON'T WANT TO KISS ME? NOT EVEN ONCE TO SAY GOODBYE?

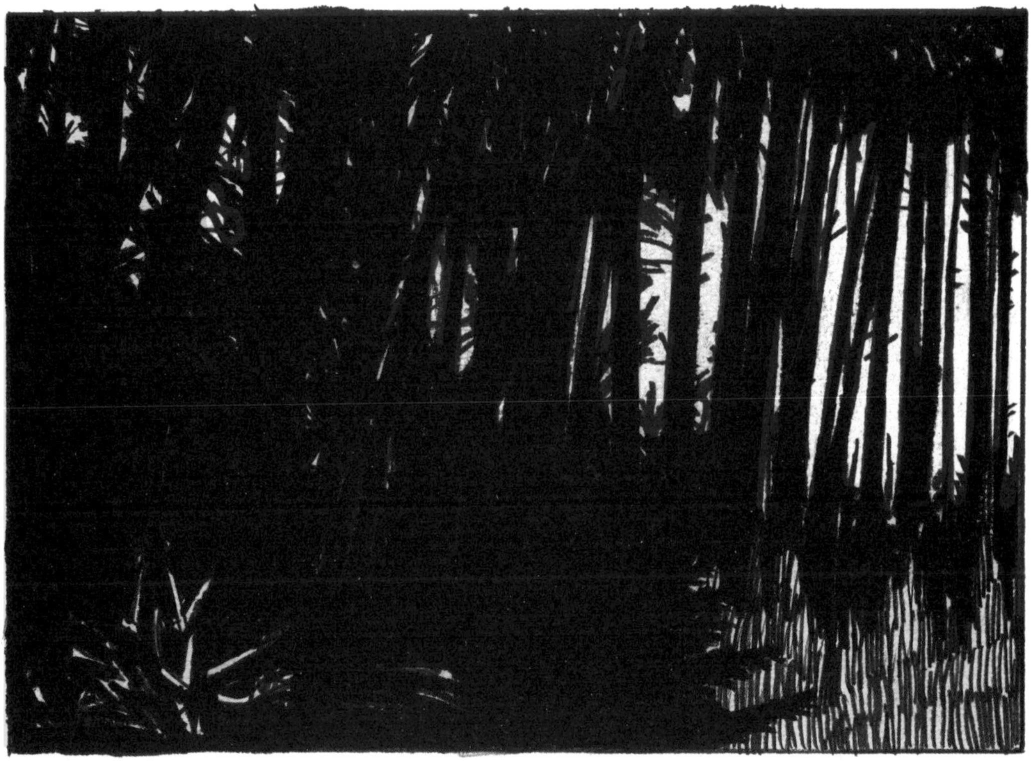

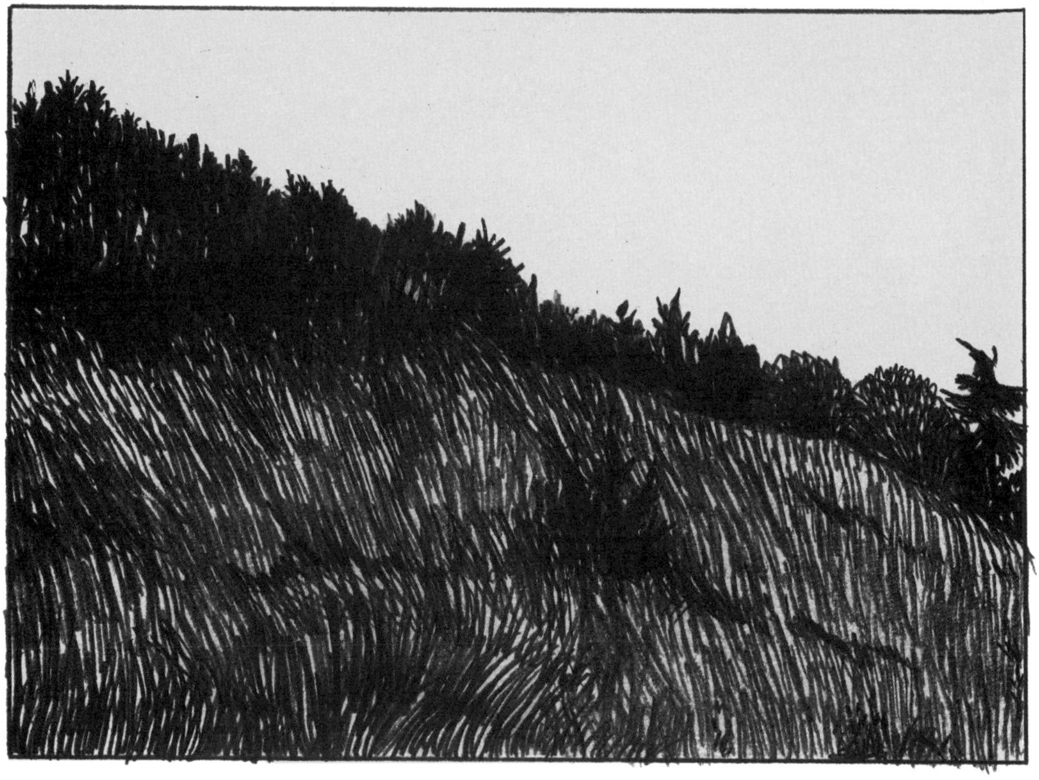

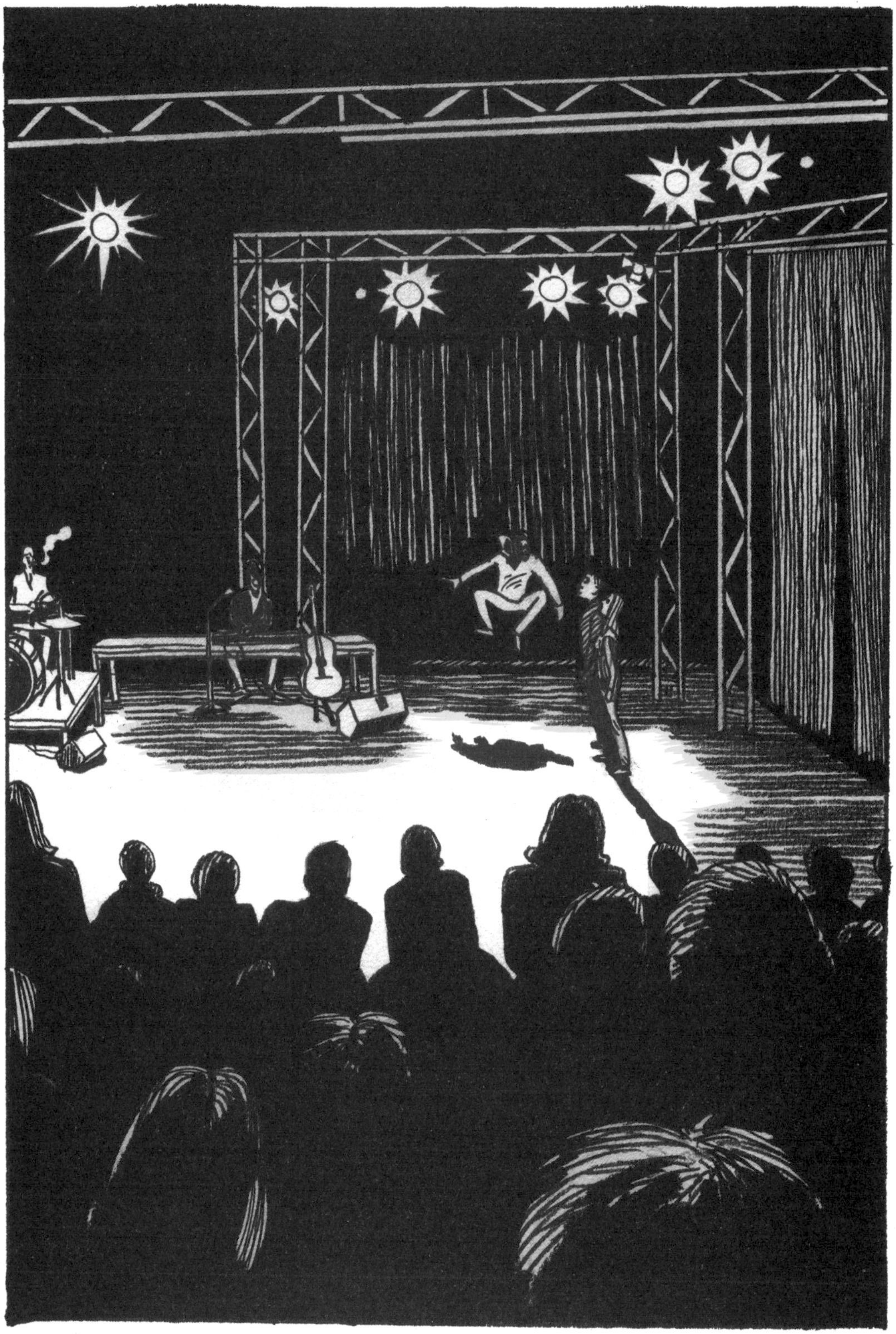

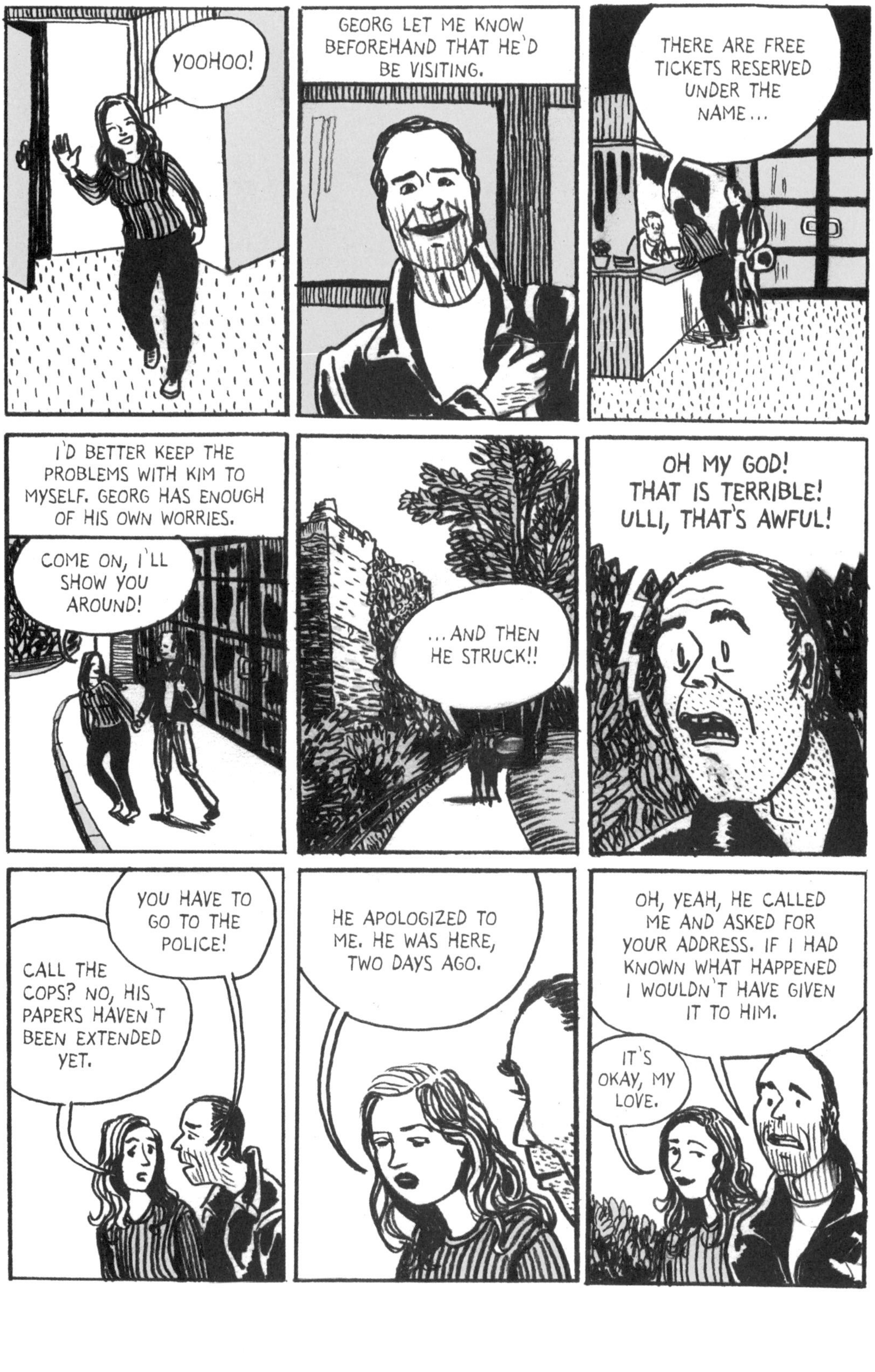
YOOHOO!
GEORG LET ME KNOW BEFOREHAND THAT HE'D BE VISITING.
THERE ARE FREE TICKETS RESERVED UNDER THE NAME...
I'D BETTER KEEP THE PROBLEMS WITH KIM TO MYSELF. GEORG HAS ENOUGH OF HIS OWN WORRIES.
COME ON, I'LL SHOW YOU AROUND!
...AND THEN HE STRUCK!!
OH MY GOD! THAT IS TERRIBLE! ULLI, THAT'S AWFUL!
YOU HAVE TO GO TO THE POLICE!
CALL THE COPS? NO, HIS PAPERS HAVEN'T BEEN EXTENDED YET.
HE APOLOGIZED TO ME. HE WAS HERE, TWO DAYS AGO.
OH, YEAH, HE CALLED ME AND ASKED FOR YOUR ADDRESS. IF I HAD KNOWN WHAT HAPPENED I WOULDN'T HAVE GIVEN IT TO HIM.
IT'S OKAY, MY LOVE.

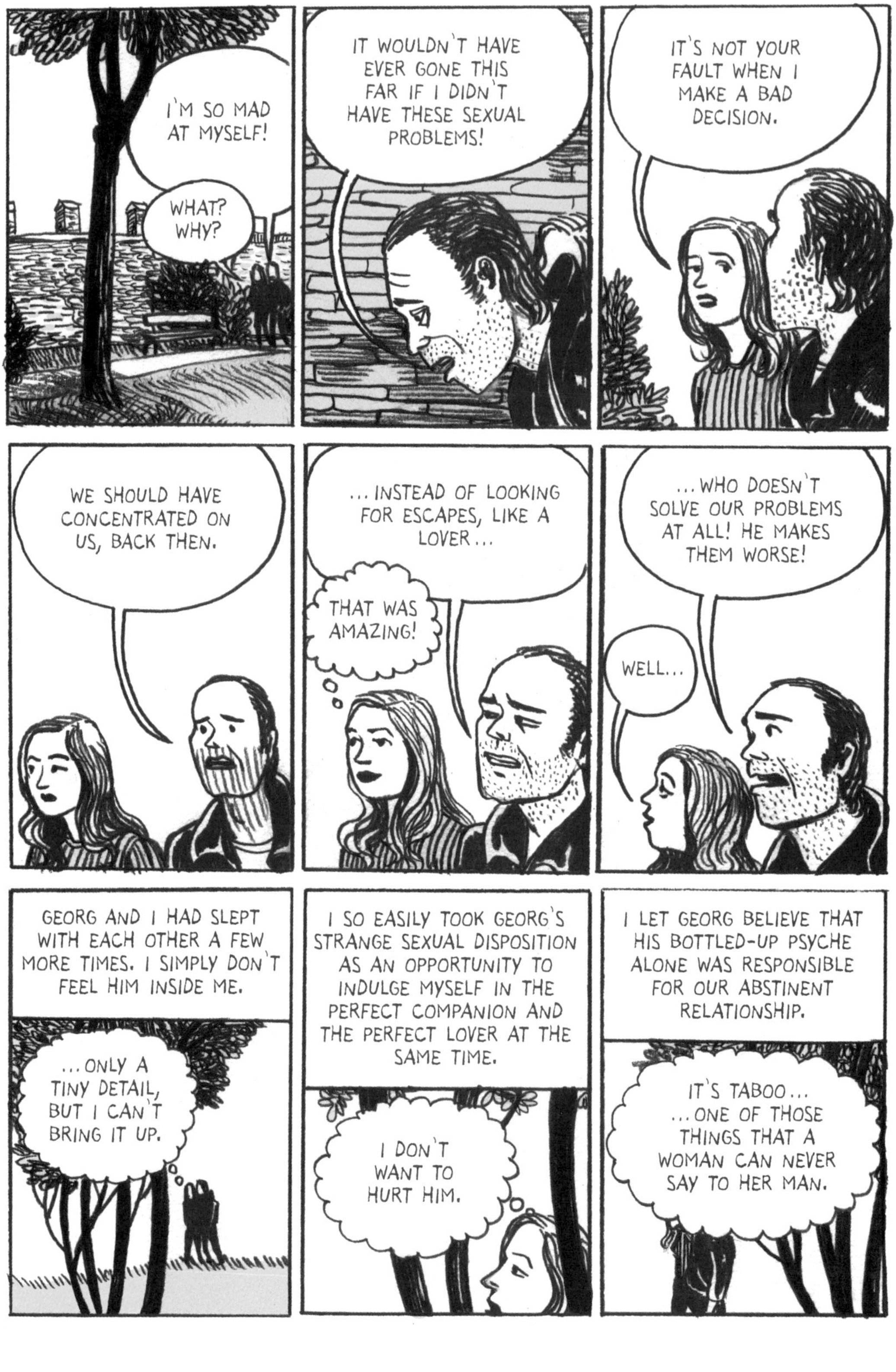
I'M SO MAD AT MYSELF!
WHAT? WHY?
IT WOULDN'T HAVE EVER GONE THIS FAR IF I DIDN'T HAVE THESE SEXUAL PROBLEMS!
IT'S NOT YOUR FAULT WHEN I MAKE A BAD DECISION.
WE SHOULD HAVE CONCENTRATED ON US, BACK THEN.
...INSTEAD OF LOOKING FOR ESCAPES, LIKE A LOVER...
THAT WAS AMAZING!
...WHO DOESN'T SOLVE OUR PROBLEMS AT ALL! HE MAKES THEM WORSE!
WELL...
GEORG AND I HAD SLEPT WITH EACH OTHER A FEW MORE TIMES. I SIMPLY DON'T FEEL HIM INSIDE ME.
...ONLY A TINY DETAIL, BUT I CAN'T BRING IT UP.
I SO EASILY TOOK GEORG'S STRANGE SEXUAL DISPOSITION AS AN OPPORTUNITY TO INDULGE MYSELF IN THE PERFECT COMPANION AND THE PERFECT LOVER AT THE SAME TIME.
I DON'T WANT TO HURT HIM.
I LET GEORG BELIEVE THAT HIS BOTTLED-UP PSYCHE ALONE WAS RESPONSIBLE FOR OUR ABSTINENT RELATIONSHIP.
IT'S TABOO... ...ONE OF THOSE THINGS THAT A WOMAN CAN NEVER SAY TO HER MAN.

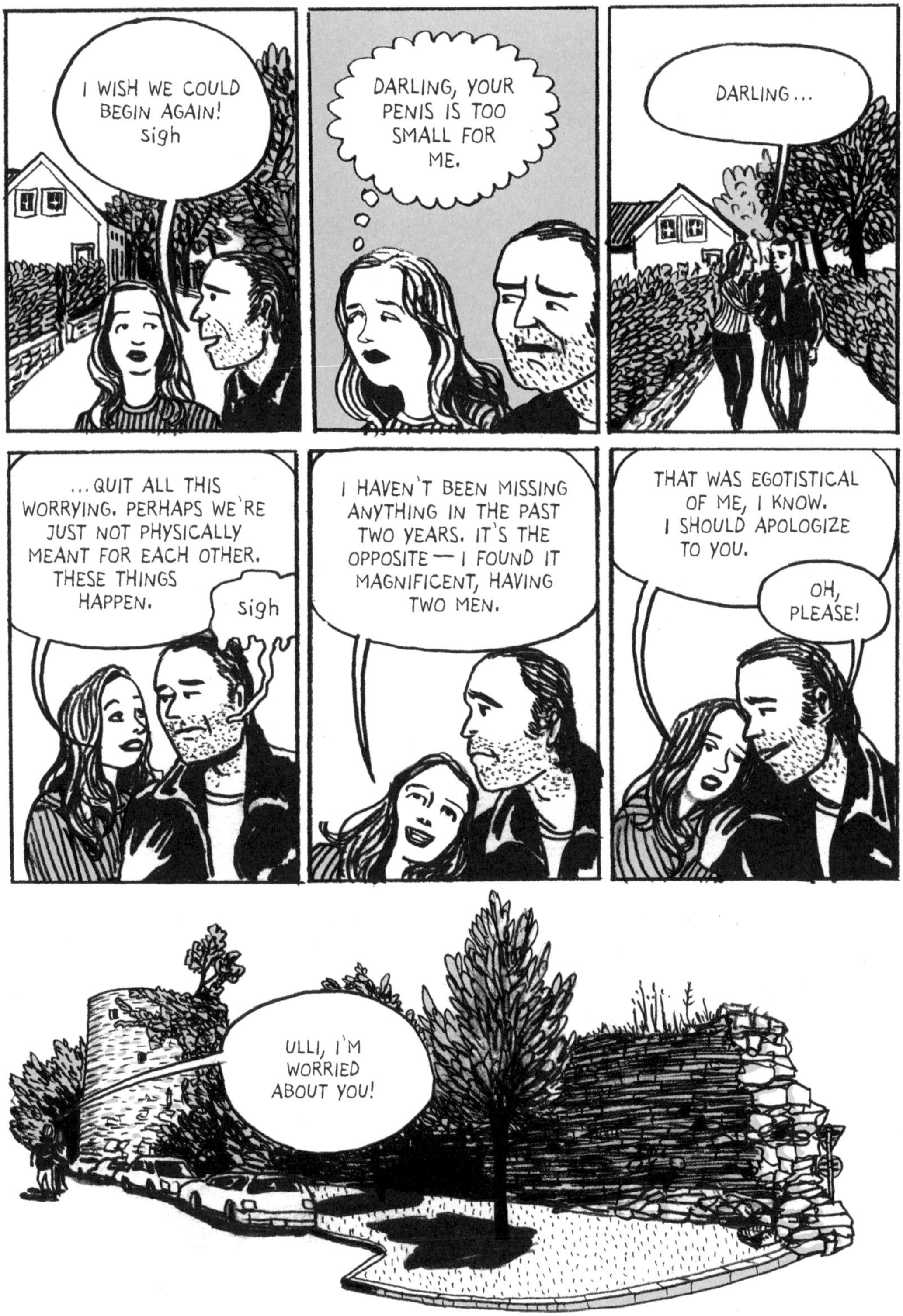
I WISH WE COULD BEGIN AGAIN! sigh
DARLING, YOUR PENIS IS TOO SMALL FOR ME.
DARLING...
...QUIT ALL THIS WORRYING. PERHAPS WE'RE JUST NOT PHYSICALLY MEANT FOR EACH OTHER. THESE THINGS HAPPEN.
sigh
I HAVEN'T BEEN MISSING ANYTHING IN THE PAST TWO YEARS. IT'S THE OPPOSITE — I FOUND IT MAGNIFICENT, HAVING TWO MEN.
THAT WAS EGOTISTICAL OF ME, I KNOW. I SHOULD APOLOGIZE TO YOU.
OH, PLEASE!
ULLI, I'M WORRIED ABOUT YOU!

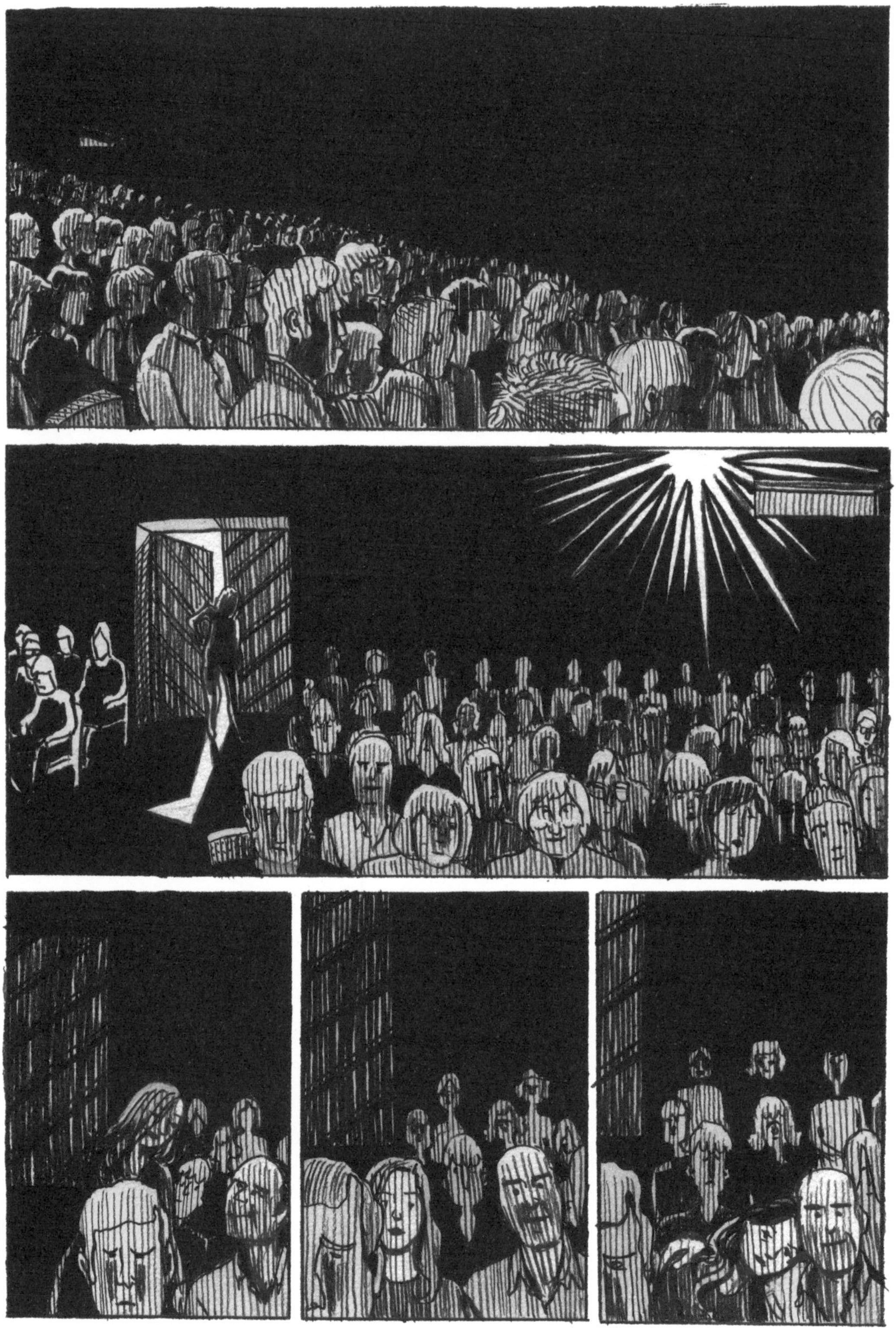

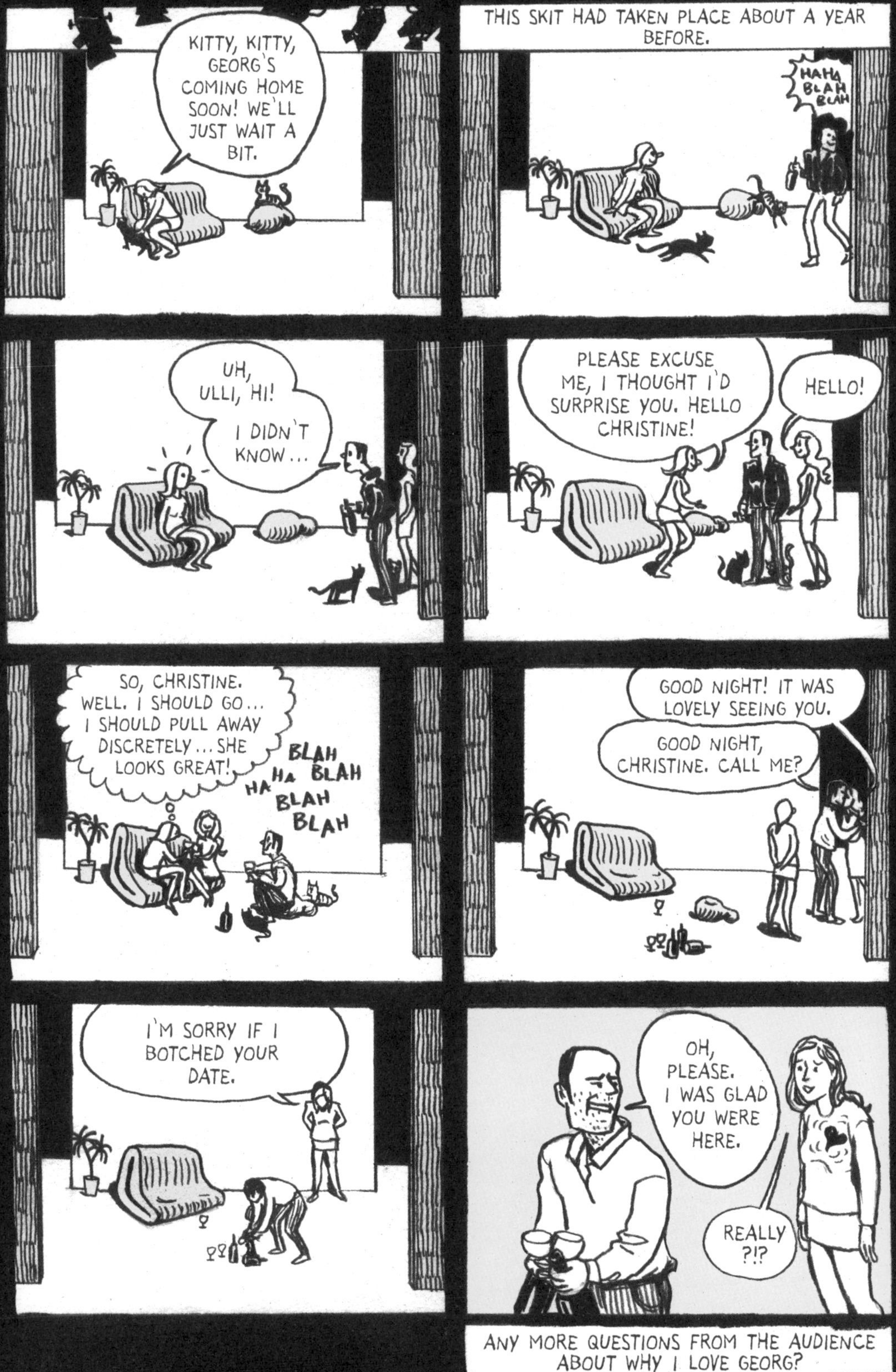
KITTY, KITTY, GEORG'S COMING HOME SOON! WE'LL JUST WAIT A BIT.
THIS SKIT HAD TAKEN PLACE ABOUT A YEAR BEFORE.
HAHA BLAH BLAH
UH, ULLI, HI!
I DIDN'T KNOW...
PLEASE EXCUSE ME, I THOUGHT I'D SURPRISE YOU. HELLO CHRISTINE!
HELLO!
SO, CHRISTINE. WELL. I SHOULD GO... I SHOULD PULL AWAY DISCRETELY... SHE LOOKS GREAT!
BLAH HA HA BLAH BLAH BLAH
GOOD NIGHT! IT WAS LOVELY SEEING YOU.
GOOD NIGHT, CHRISTINE. CALL ME?
I'M SORRY IF I BOTCHED YOUR DATE.
OH, PLEASE. I WAS GLAD YOU WERE HERE.
REALLY ?!?
ANY MORE QUESTIONS FROM THE AUDIENCE ABOUT WHY I LOVE GEORG?

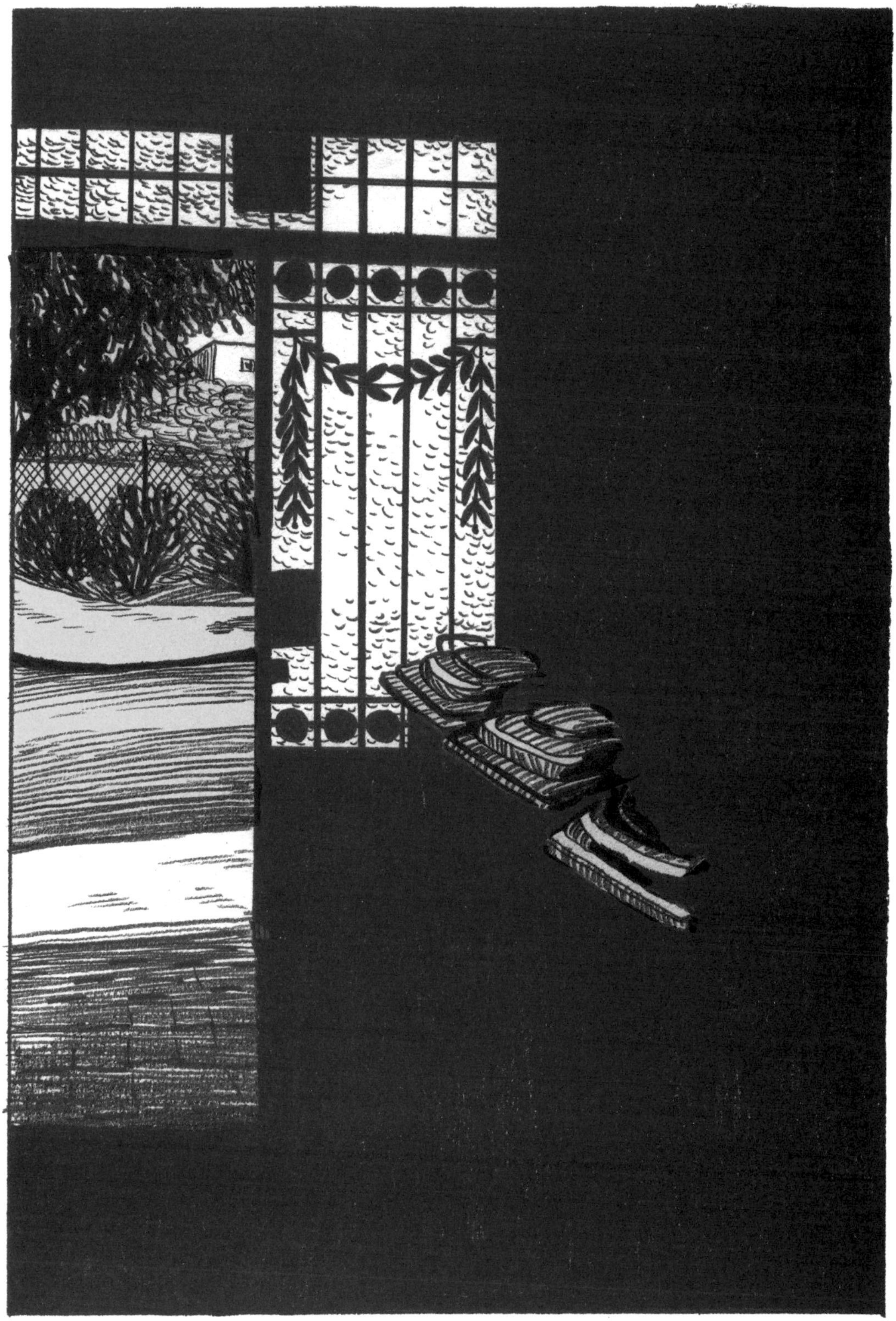

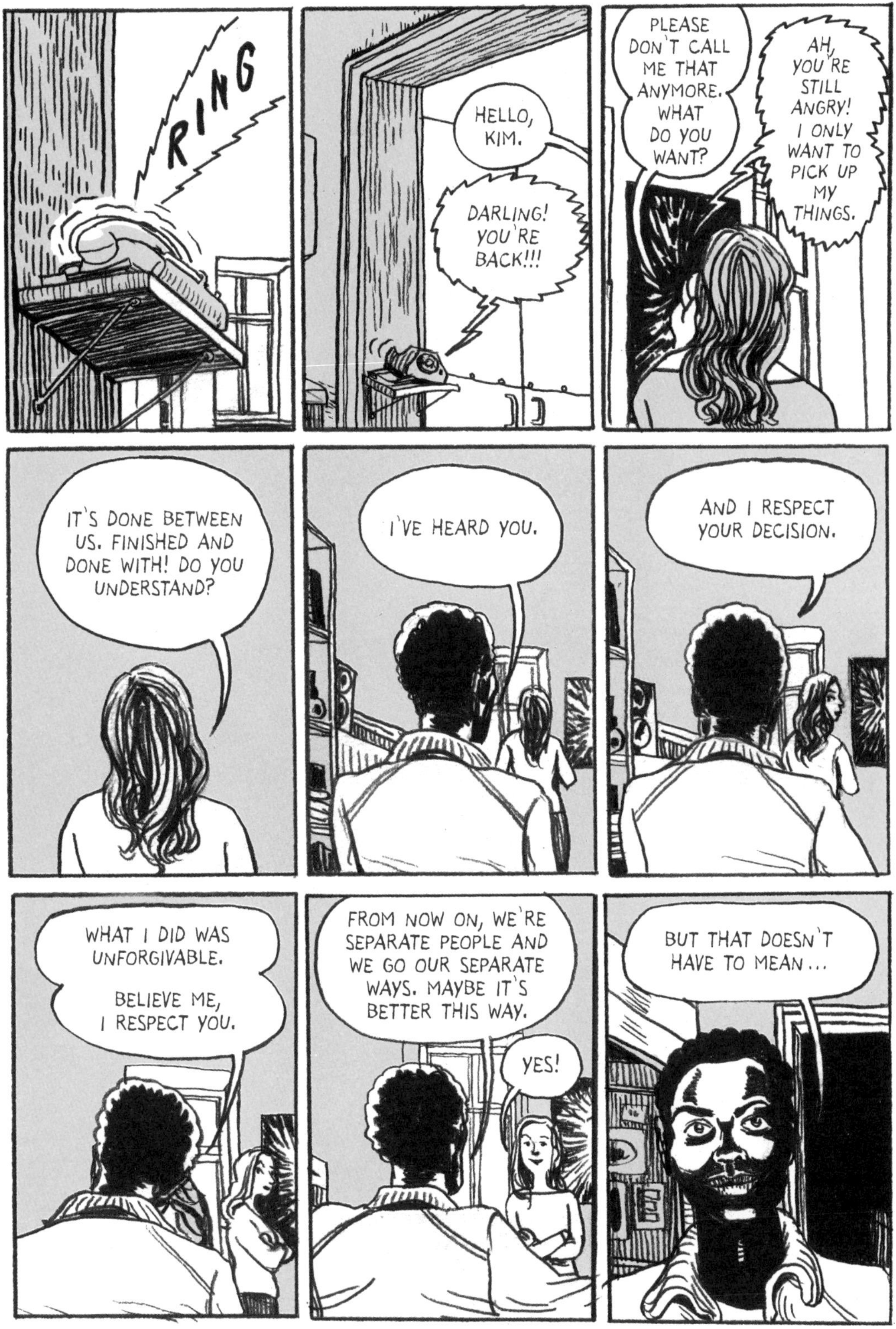
RING
HELLO, KIM.
DARLING! YOU'RE BACK!!!
PLEASE DON'T CALL ME THAT ANYMORE. WHAT DO YOU WANT?
AH, YOU'RE STILL ANGRY! I ONLY WANT TO PICK UP MY THINGS.
IT'S DONE BETWEEN US. FINISHED AND DONE WITH! DO YOU UNDERSTAND?
I'VE HEARD YOU.
AND I RESPECT YOUR DECISION.
WHAT I DID WAS UNFORGIVABLE.
BELIEVE ME, I RESPECT YOU.
FROM NOW ON, WE'RE SEPARATE PEOPLE AND WE GO OUR SEPARATE WAYS. MAYBE IT'S BETTER THIS WAY.
YES!
BUT THAT DOESN'T HAVE TO MEAN...

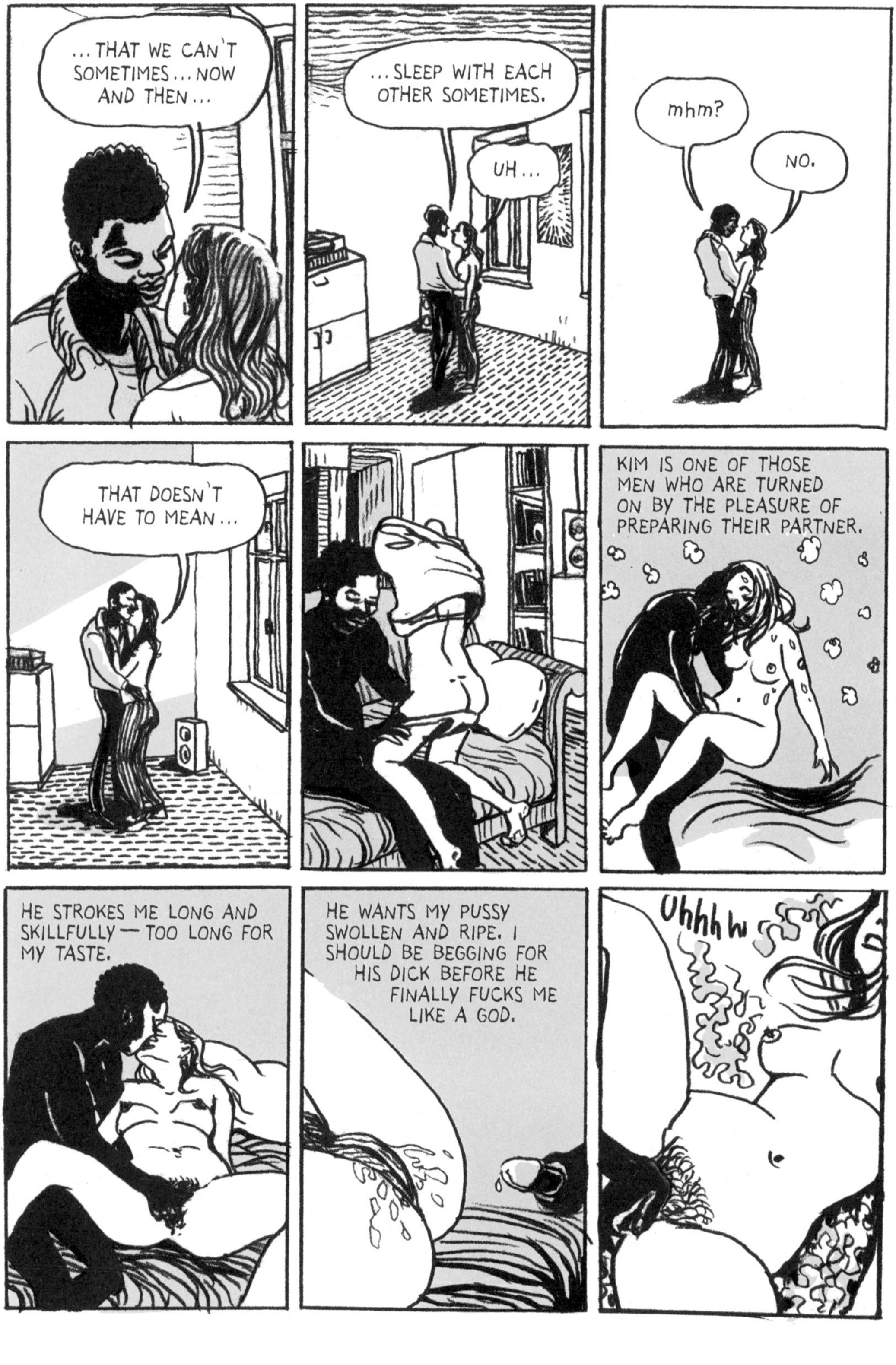

...THAT WE CAN'T SOMETIMES...NOW AND THEN...
...SLEEP WITH EACH OTHER SOMETIMES.
UH...
mhm?
NO.
THAT DOESN'T HAVE TO MEAN...
KIM IS ONE OF THOSE MEN WHO ARE TURNED ON BY THE PLEASURE OF PREPARING THEIR PARTNER.
HE STROKES ME LONG AND SKILLFULLY—TOO LONG FOR MY TASTE.
HE WANTS MY PUSSY SWOLLEN AND RIPE. I SHOULD BE BEGGING FOR HIS DICK BEFORE HE FINALLY FUCKS ME LIKE A GOD.
Uhhhw

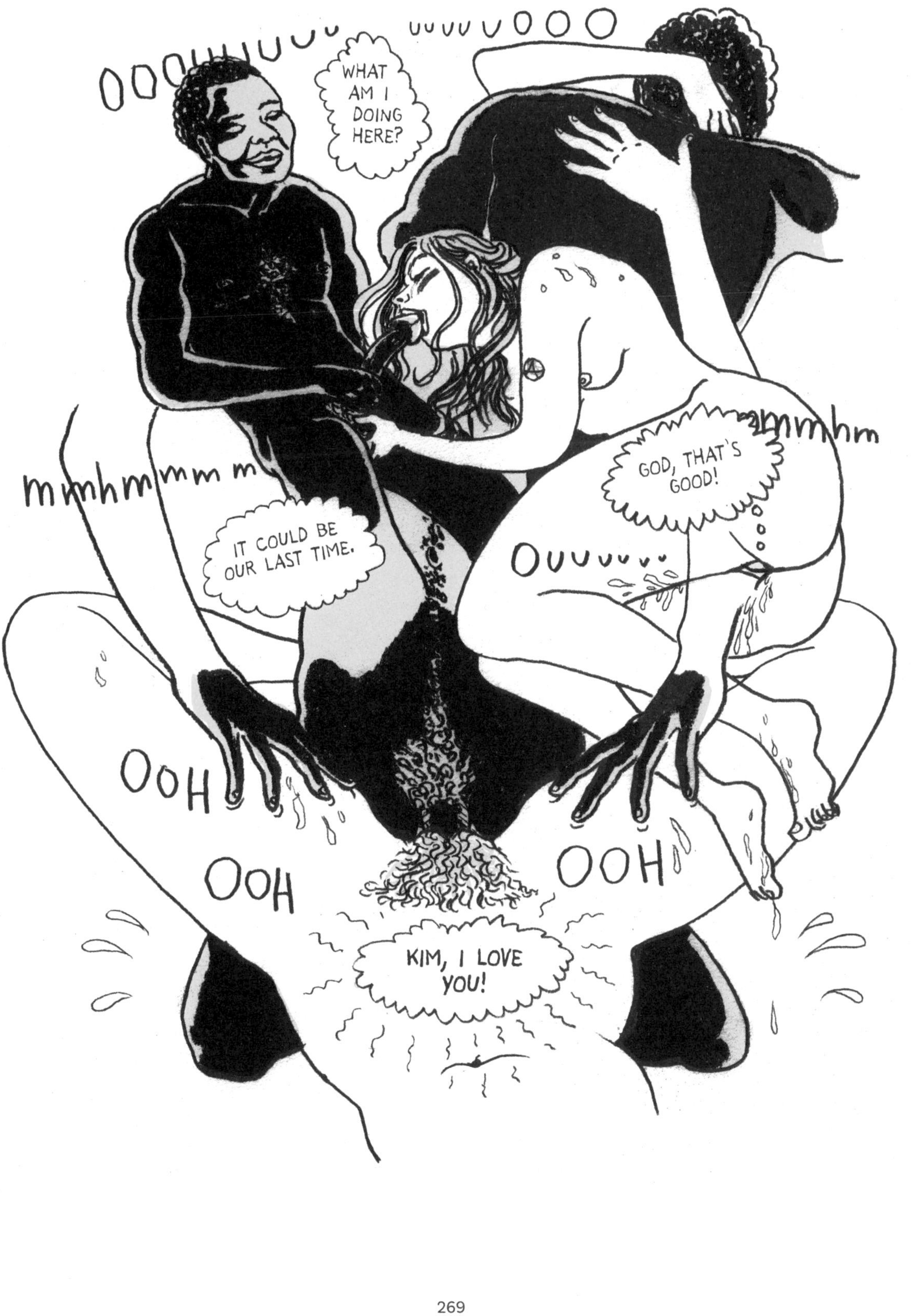
WHAT AM I DOING HERE?
GOD, THAT'S GOOD!
IT COULD BE OUR LAST TIME.
OOH
OOH
OOH
KIM, I LOVE YOU!

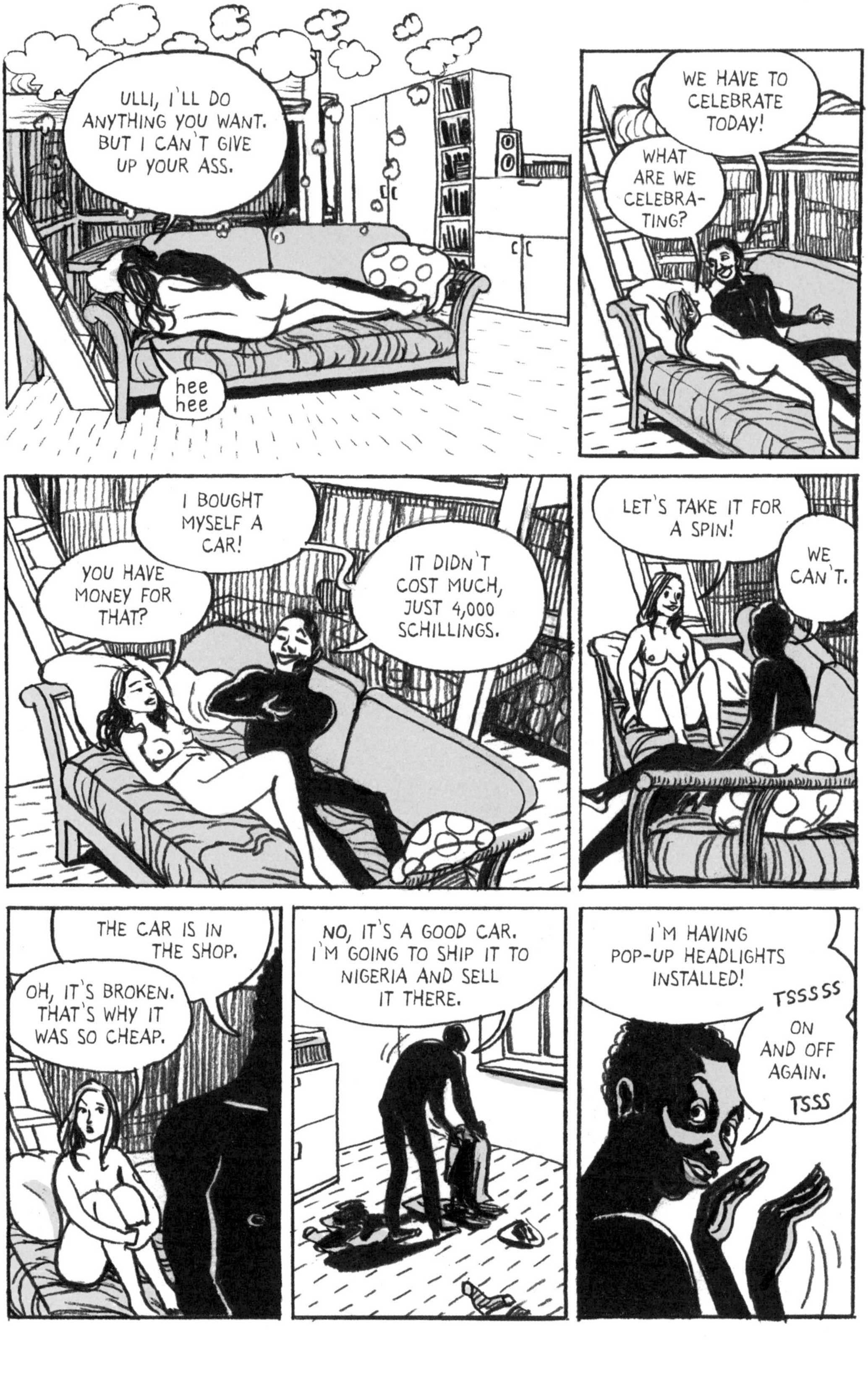
ULLI, I'LL DO ANYTHING YOU WANT. BUT I CAN'T GIVE UP YOUR ASS.
hee hee
WE HAVE TO CELEBRATE TODAY!
WHAT ARE WE CELEBRA-TING?
I BOUGHT MYSELF A CAR!
YOU HAVE MONEY FOR THAT?
IT DIDN'T COST MUCH, JUST 4,000 SCHILLINGS.
LET'S TAKE IT FOR A SPIN!
WE CAN'T.
THE CAR IS IN THE SHOP.
OH, IT'S BROKEN. THAT'S WHY IT WAS SO CHEAP.
NO, IT'S A GOOD CAR. I'M GOING TO SHIP IT TO NIGERIA AND SELL IT THERE.
I'M HAVING POP-UP HEADLIGHTS INSTALLED!
TSSSSS
ON AND OFF AGAIN.
TSSS

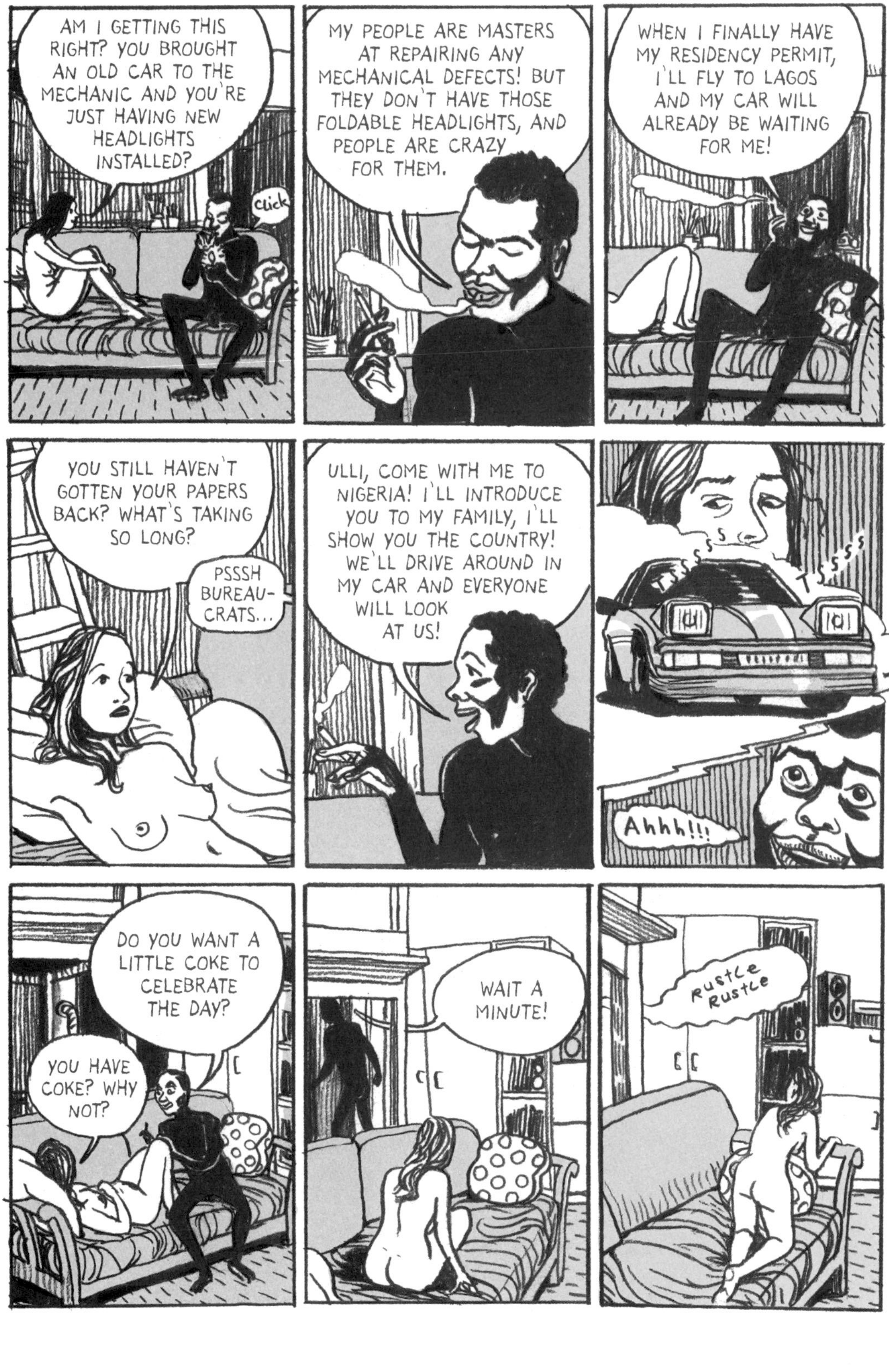
AM I GETTING THIS RIGHT? YOU BROUGHT AN OLD CAR TO THE MECHANIC AND YOU'RE JUST HAVING NEW HEADLIGHTS INSTALLED?
Click
MY PEOPLE ARE MASTERS AT REPAIRING ANY MECHANICAL DEFECTS! BUT THEY DON'T HAVE THOSE FOLDABLE HEADLIGHTS, AND PEOPLE ARE CRAZY FOR THEM.
WHEN I FINALLY HAVE MY RESIDENCY PERMIT, I'LL FLY TO LAGOS AND MY CAR WILL ALREADY BE WAITING FOR ME!
YOU STILL HAVEN'T GOTTEN YOUR PAPERS BACK? WHAT'S TAKING SO LONG?
PSSSH BUREAU-CRATS...
ULLI, COME WITH ME TO NIGERIA! I'LL INTRODUCE YOU TO MY FAMILY, I'LL SHOW YOU THE COUNTRY! WE'LL DRIVE AROUND IN MY CAR AND EVERYONE WILL LOOK AT US!
TSSSS
TSSSS
Ahhh!!!
DO YOU WANT A LITTLE COKE TO CELEBRATE THE DAY?
YOU HAVE COKE? WHY NOT?
WAIT A MINUTE!
Rustle Rustle

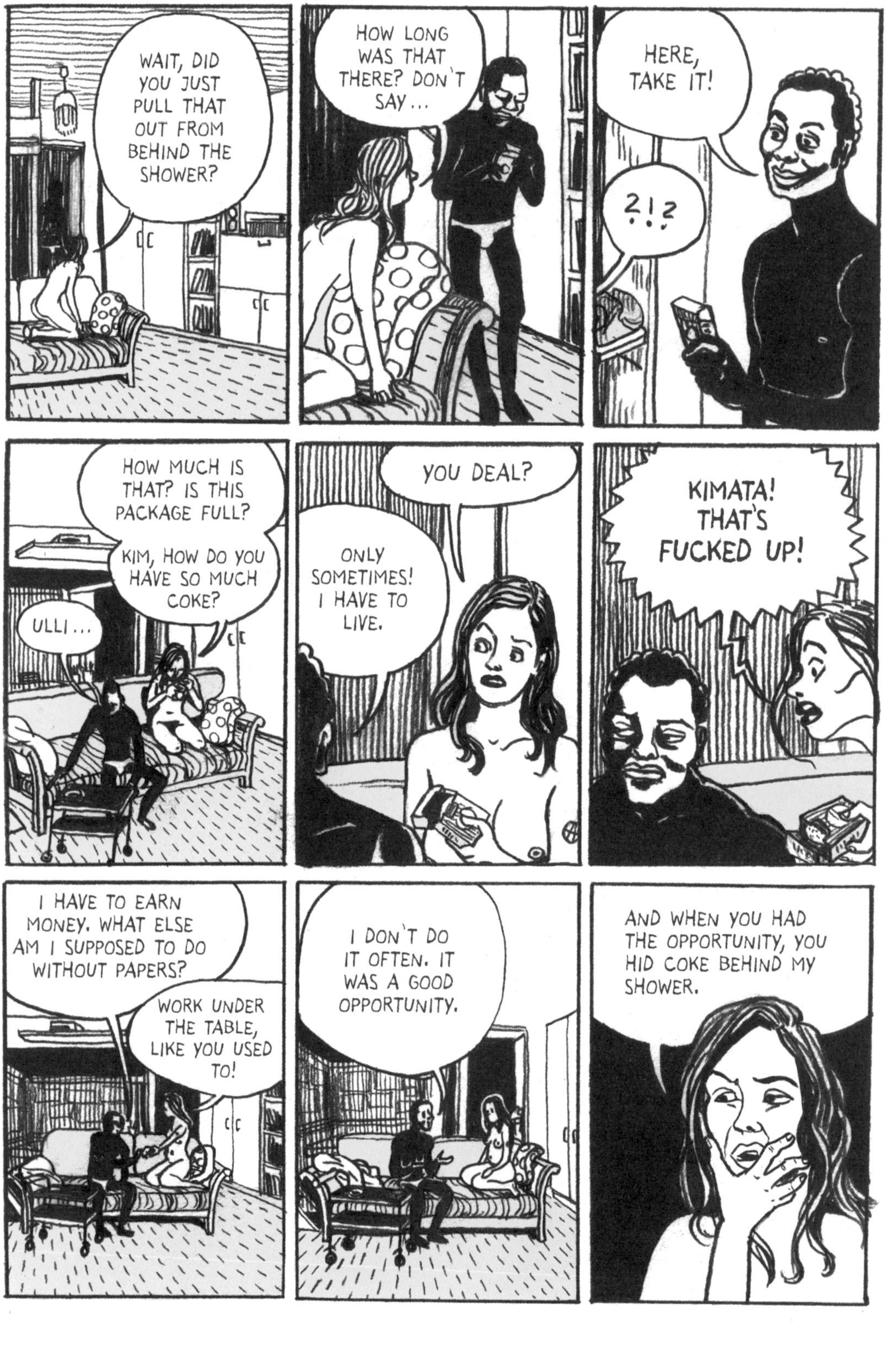
WAIT, DID YOU JUST PULL THAT OUT FROM BEHIND THE SHOWER?
HOW LONG WAS THAT THERE? DON'T SAY...
HERE, TAKE IT!
?!?
HOW MUCH IS THAT? IS THIS PACKAGE FULL?
KIM, HOW DO YOU HAVE SO MUCH COKE?
ULLI...
YOU DEAL?
ONLY SOMETIMES! I HAVE TO LIVE.
KIMATA! THAT'S FUCKED UP!
I HAVE TO EARN MONEY. WHAT ELSE AM I SUPPOSED TO DO WITHOUT PAPERS?
WORK UNDER THE TABLE, LIKE YOU USED TO!
I DON'T DO IT OFTEN. IT WAS A GOOD OPPORTUNITY.
AND WHEN YOU HAD THE OPPORTUNITY, YOU HID COKE BEHIND MY SHOWER.

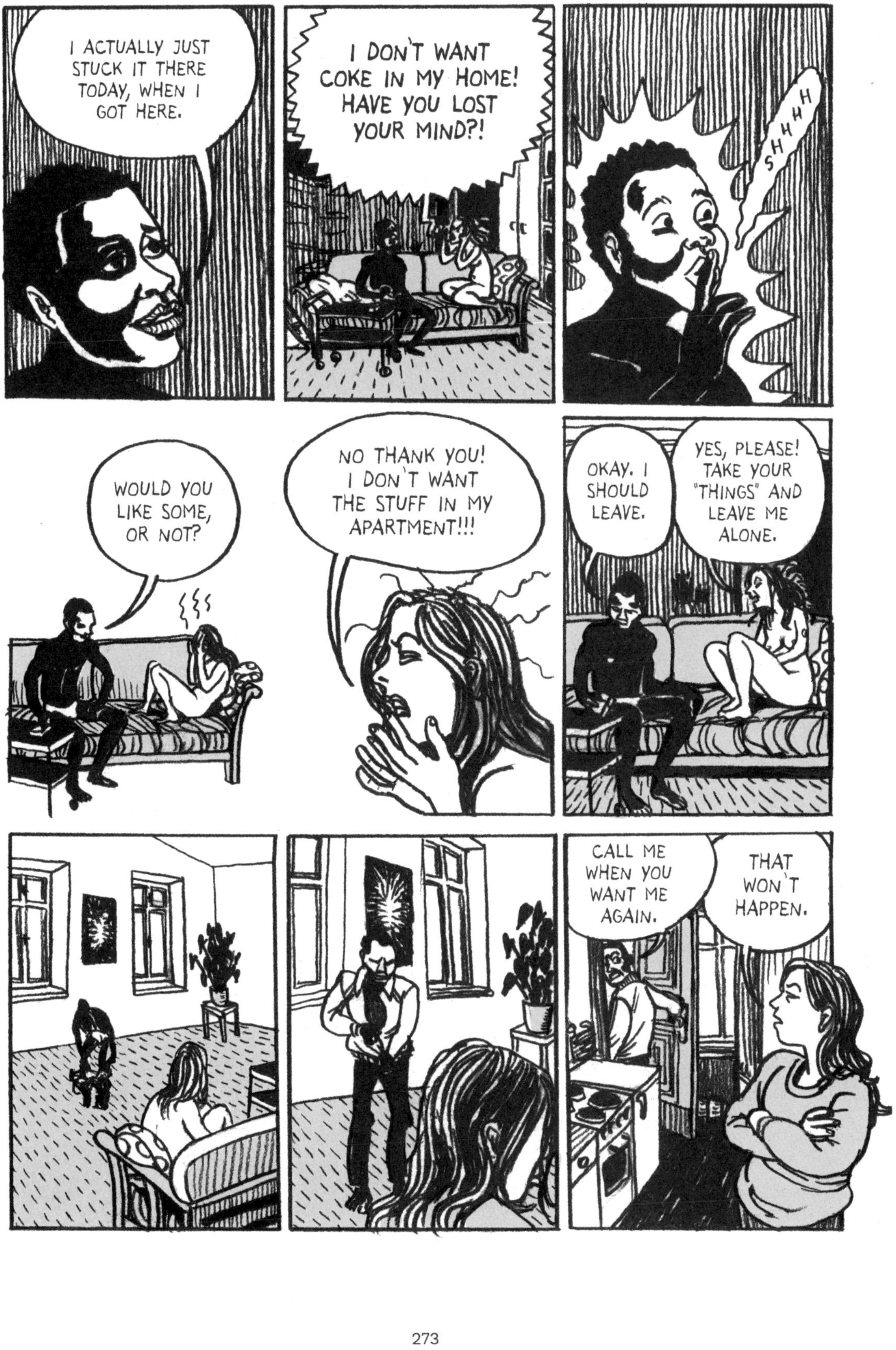
I ACTUALLY JUST STUCK IT THERE TODAY, WHEN I GOT HERE.
I DON'T WANT COKE IN MY HOME! HAVE YOU LOST YOUR MIND?!
SHHHH
WOULD YOU LIKE SOME, OR NOT?
NO THANK YOU! I DON'T WANT THE STUFF IN MY APARTMENT!!!
OKAY. I SHOULD LEAVE.
YES, PLEASE! TAKE YOUR "THINGS" AND LEAVE ME ALONE.
CALL ME WHEN YOU WANT ME AGAIN.
THAT WON'T HAPPEN.

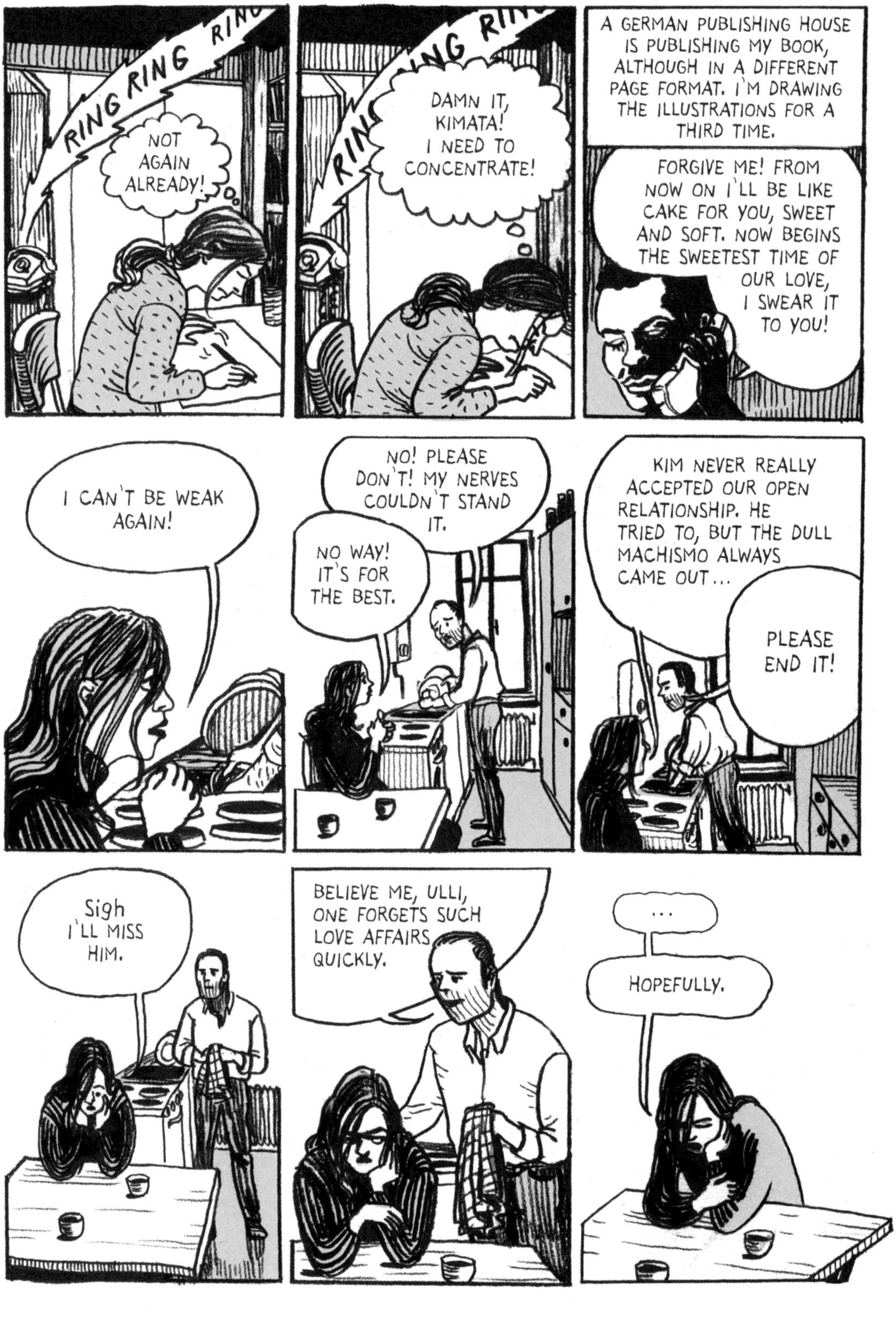
RING RING RING
NOT AGAIN ALREADY!
RING RING RING
DAMN IT, KIMATA! I NEED TO CONCENTRATE!
A GERMAN PUBLISHING HOUSE IS PUBLISHING MY BOOK, ALTHOUGH IN A DIFFERENT PAGE FORMAT. I'M DRAWING THE ILLUSTRATIONS FOR A THIRD TIME.
FORGIVE ME! FROM NOW ON I'LL BE LIKE CAKE FOR YOU, SWEET AND SOFT. NOW BEGINS THE SWEETEST TIME OF OUR LOVE, I SWEAR IT TO YOU!
I CAN'T BE WEAK AGAIN!
NO! PLEASE DON'T! MY NERVES COULDN'T STAND IT.
NO WAY! IT'S FOR THE BEST.
KIM NEVER REALLY ACCEPTED OUR OPEN RELATIONSHIP. HE TRIED TO, BUT THE DULL MACHISMO ALWAYS CAME OUT...
PLEASE END IT!
Sigh I'LL MISS HIM.
BELIEVE ME, ULLI, ONE FORGETS SUCH LOVE AFFAIRS QUICKLY.
...
HOPEFULLY.

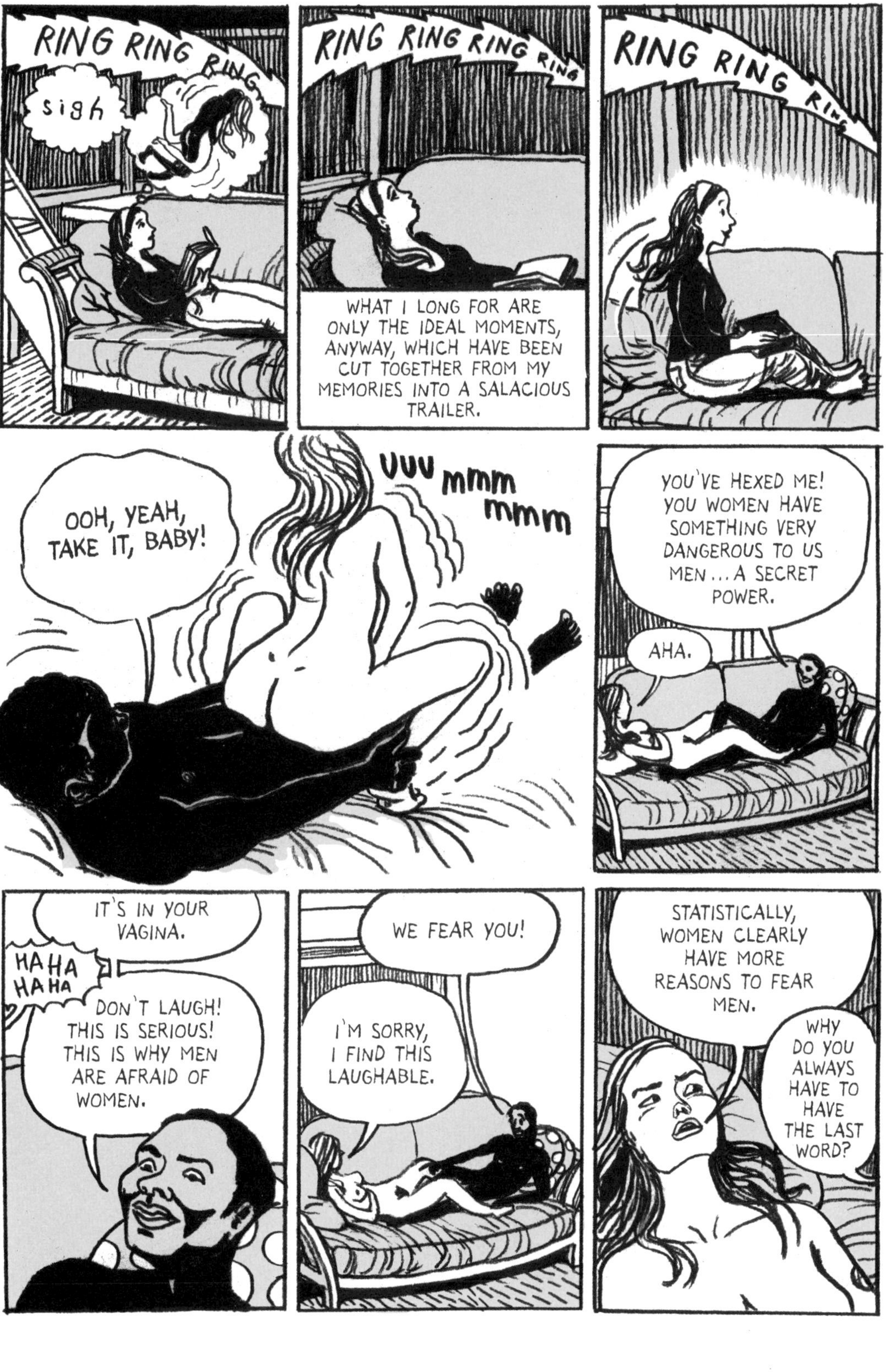
RING RING RING
sigh
RING RING RING RING
WHAT I LONG FOR ARE ONLY THE IDEAL MOMENTS, ANYWAY, WHICH HAVE BEEN CUT TOGETHER FROM MY MEMORIES INTO A SALACIOUS TRAILER.
RING RING RING
OOH, YEAH, TAKE IT, BABY!
UUU mmm mmm
YOU'VE HEXED ME! YOU WOMEN HAVE SOMETHING VERY DANGEROUS TO US MEN... A SECRET POWER.
AHA.
IT'S IN YOUR VAGINA.
HA HA HA HA
DON'T LAUGH! THIS IS SERIOUS! THIS IS WHY MEN ARE AFRAID OF WOMEN.
WE FEAR YOU!
I'M SORRY, I FIND THIS LAUGHABLE.
STATISTICALLY, WOMEN CLEARLY HAVE MORE REASONS TO FEAR MEN.
WHY DO YOU ALWAYS HAVE TO HAVE THE LAST WORD?

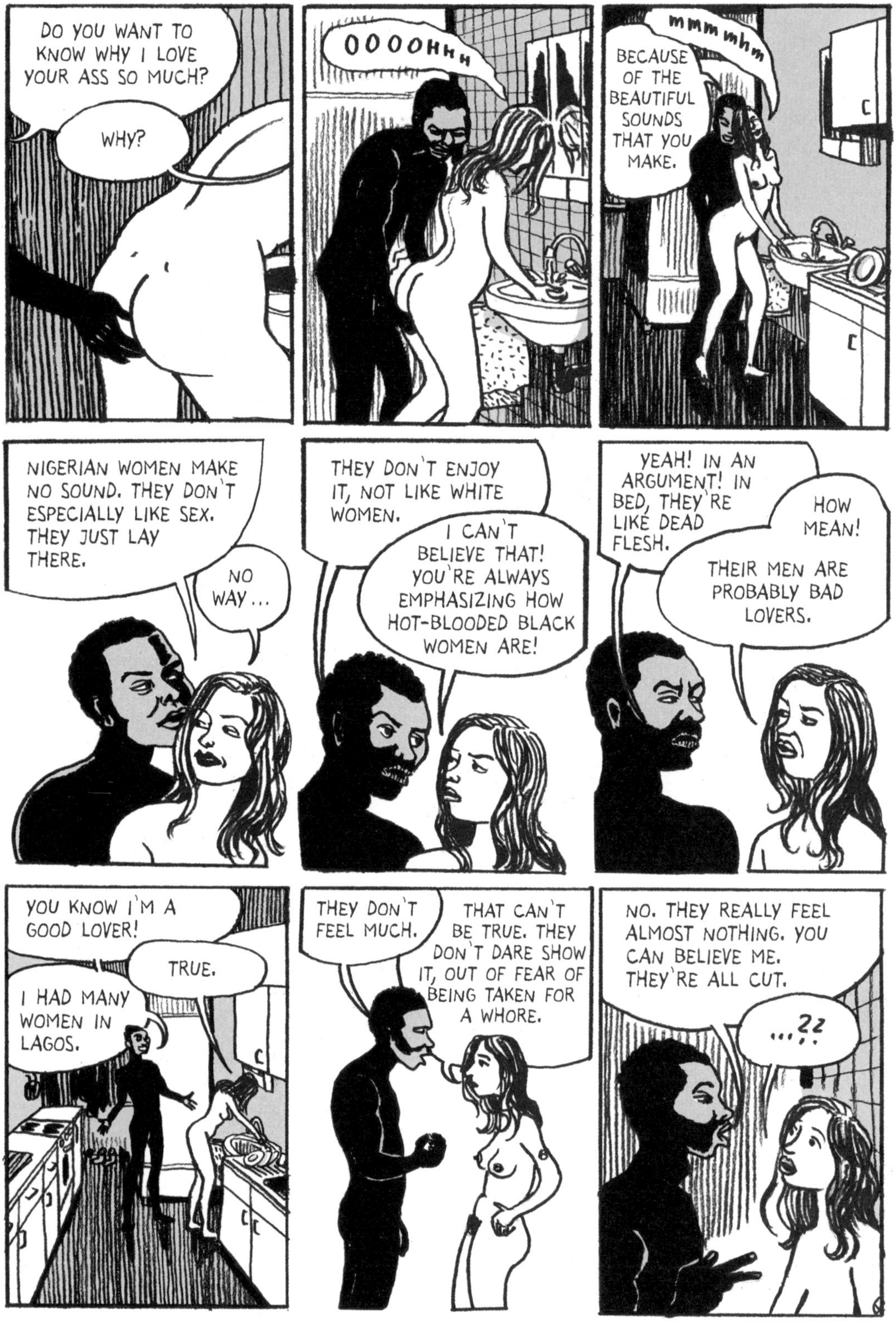
DO YOU WANT TO KNOW WHY I LOVE YOUR ASS SO MUCH?
WHY?
OOOOHHH
mmmmhm
BECAUSE OF THE BEAUTIFUL SOUNDS THAT YOU MAKE.
NIGERIAN WOMEN MAKE NO SOUND. THEY DON'T ESPECIALLY LIKE SEX. THEY JUST LAY THERE.
NO WAY...
THEY DON'T ENJOY IT, NOT LIKE WHITE WOMEN.
I CAN'T BELIEVE THAT! YOU'RE ALWAYS EMPHASIZING HOW HOT-BLOODED BLACK WOMEN ARE!
YEAH! IN AN ARGUMENT! IN BED, THEY'RE LIKE DEAD FLESH.
HOW MEAN!
THEIR MEN ARE PROBABLY BAD LOVERS.
YOU KNOW I'M A GOOD LOVER!
TRUE.
I HAD MANY WOMEN IN LAGOS.
THEY DON'T FEEL MUCH.
THAT CAN'T BE TRUE. THEY DON'T DARE SHOW IT, OUT OF FEAR OF BEING TAKEN FOR A WHORE.
NO. THEY REALLY FEEL ALMOST NOTHING. YOU CAN BELIEVE ME. THEY'RE ALL CUT.
...??

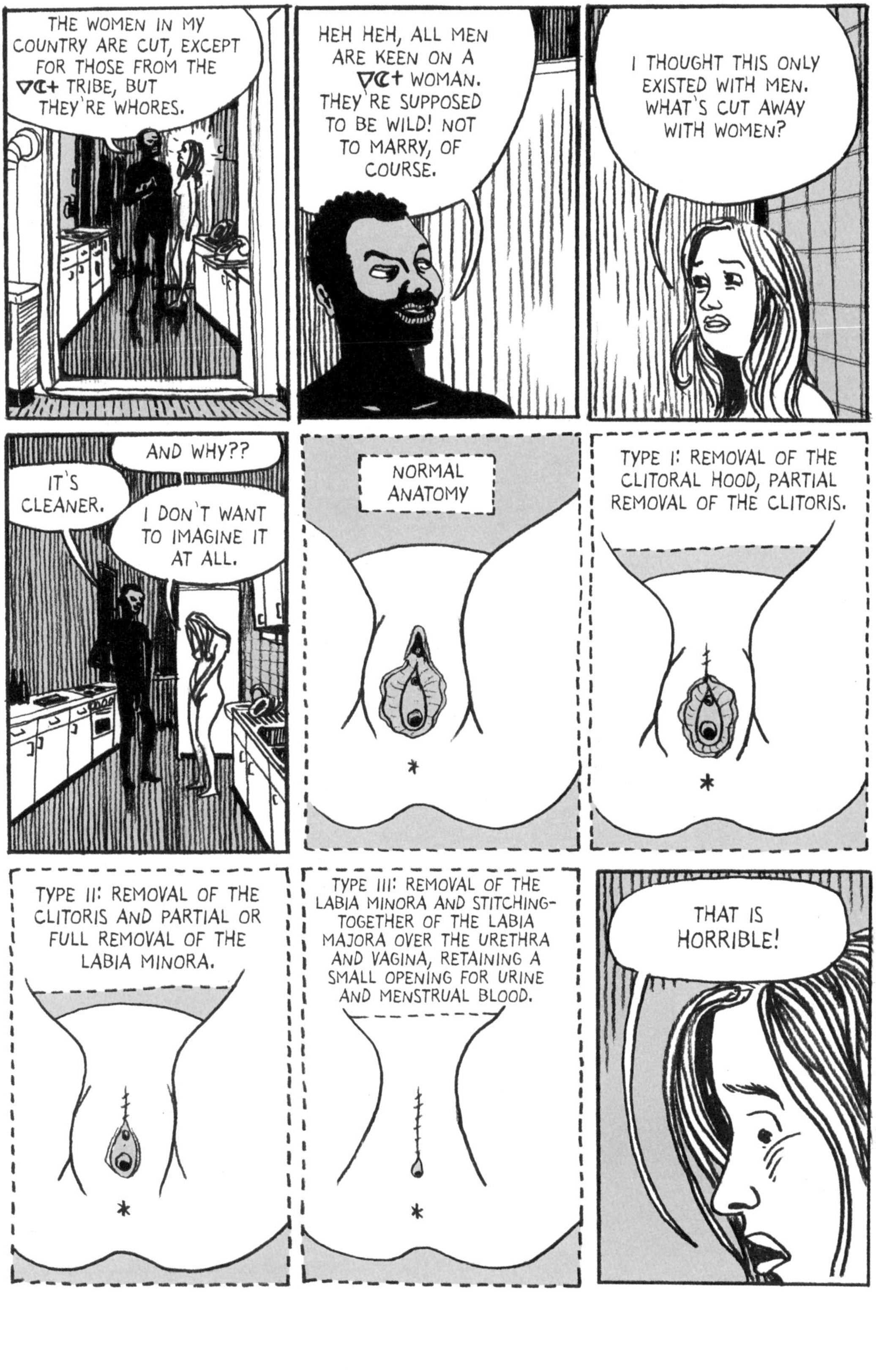
THE WOMEN IN MY COUNTRY ARE CUT, EXCEPT FOR THOSE FROM THE ▽☾+ TRIBE, BUT THEY'RE WHORES.
HEH HEH, ALL MEN ARE KEEN ON A ▽☾+ WOMAN. THEY'RE SUPPOSED TO BE WILD! NOT TO MARRY, OF COURSE.
I THOUGHT THIS ONLY EXISTED WITH MEN. WHAT'S CUT AWAY WITH WOMEN?
AND WHY??
IT'S CLEANER.
I DON'T WANT TO IMAGINE IT AT ALL.
NORMAL ANATOMY
TYPE I: REMOVAL OF THE CLITORAL HOOD, PARTIAL REMOVAL OF THE CLITORIS.
TYPE II: REMOVAL OF THE CLITORIS AND PARTIAL OR FULL REMOVAL OF THE LABIA MINORA.
TYPE III: REMOVAL OF THE LABIA MINORA AND STITCHING-TOGETHER OF THE LABIA MAJORA OVER THE URETHRA AND VAGINA, RETAINING A SMALL OPENING FOR URINE AND MENSTRUAL BLOOD.
THAT IS HORRIBLE!

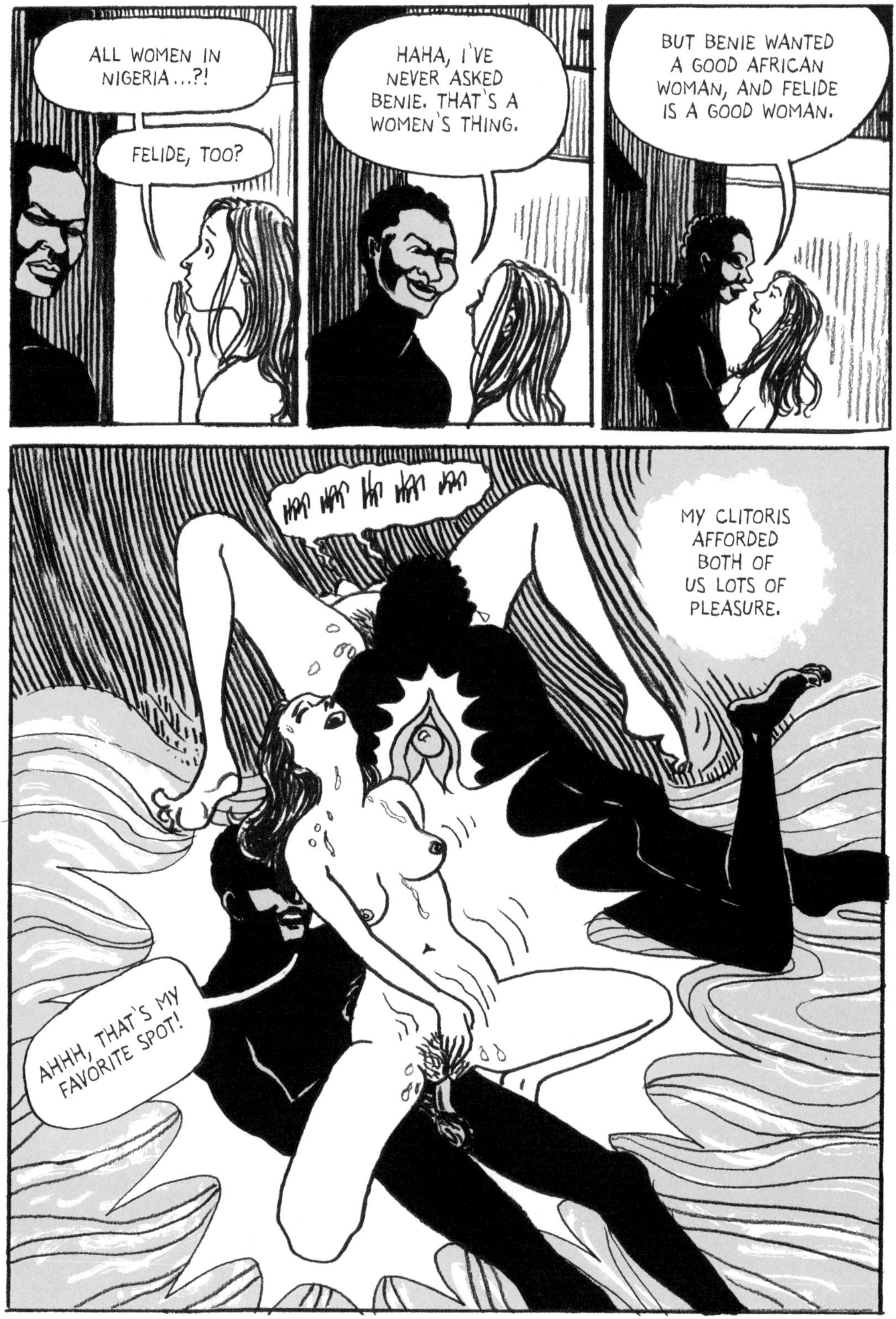
ALL WOMEN IN NIGERIA...?!
FELIDE, TOO?
HAHA, I'VE NEVER ASKED BENIE. THAT'S A WOMEN'S THING.
BUT BENIE WANTED A GOOD AFRICAN WOMAN, AND FELIDE IS A GOOD WOMAN.
MY CLITORIS AFFORDED BOTH OF US LOTS OF PLEASURE.
AHHH, THAT'S MY FAVORITE SPOT!

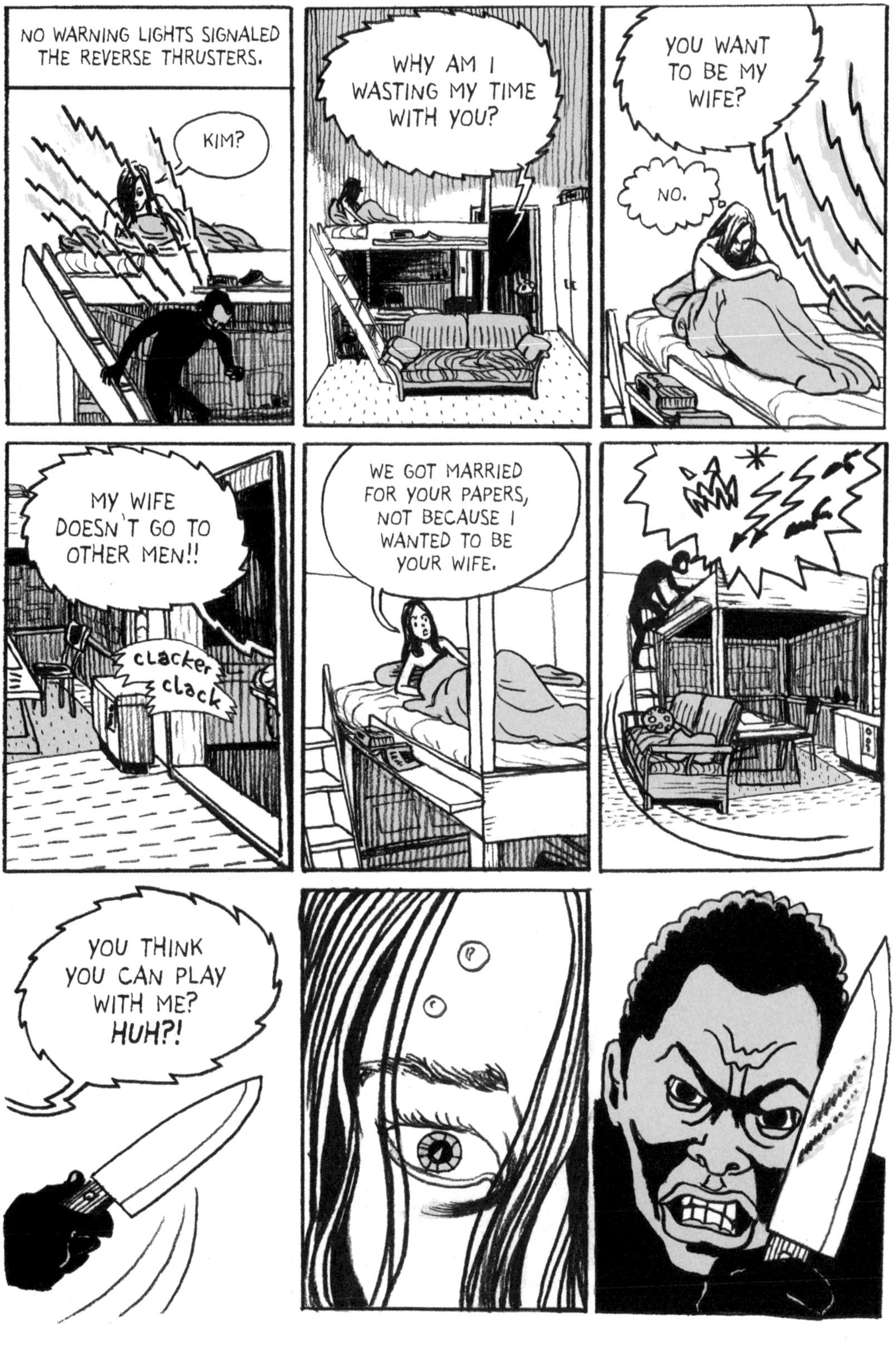
NO WARNING LIGHTS SIGNALED THE REVERSE THRUSTERS.
KIM?
WHY AM I WASTING MY TIME WITH YOU?
YOU WANT TO BE MY WIFE?
NO.
MY WIFE DOESN'T GO TO OTHER MEN!!
clacker clack
WE GOT MARRIED FOR YOUR PAPERS, NOT BECAUSE I WANTED TO BE YOUR WIFE.
YOU THINK YOU CAN PLAY WITH ME? HUH?!

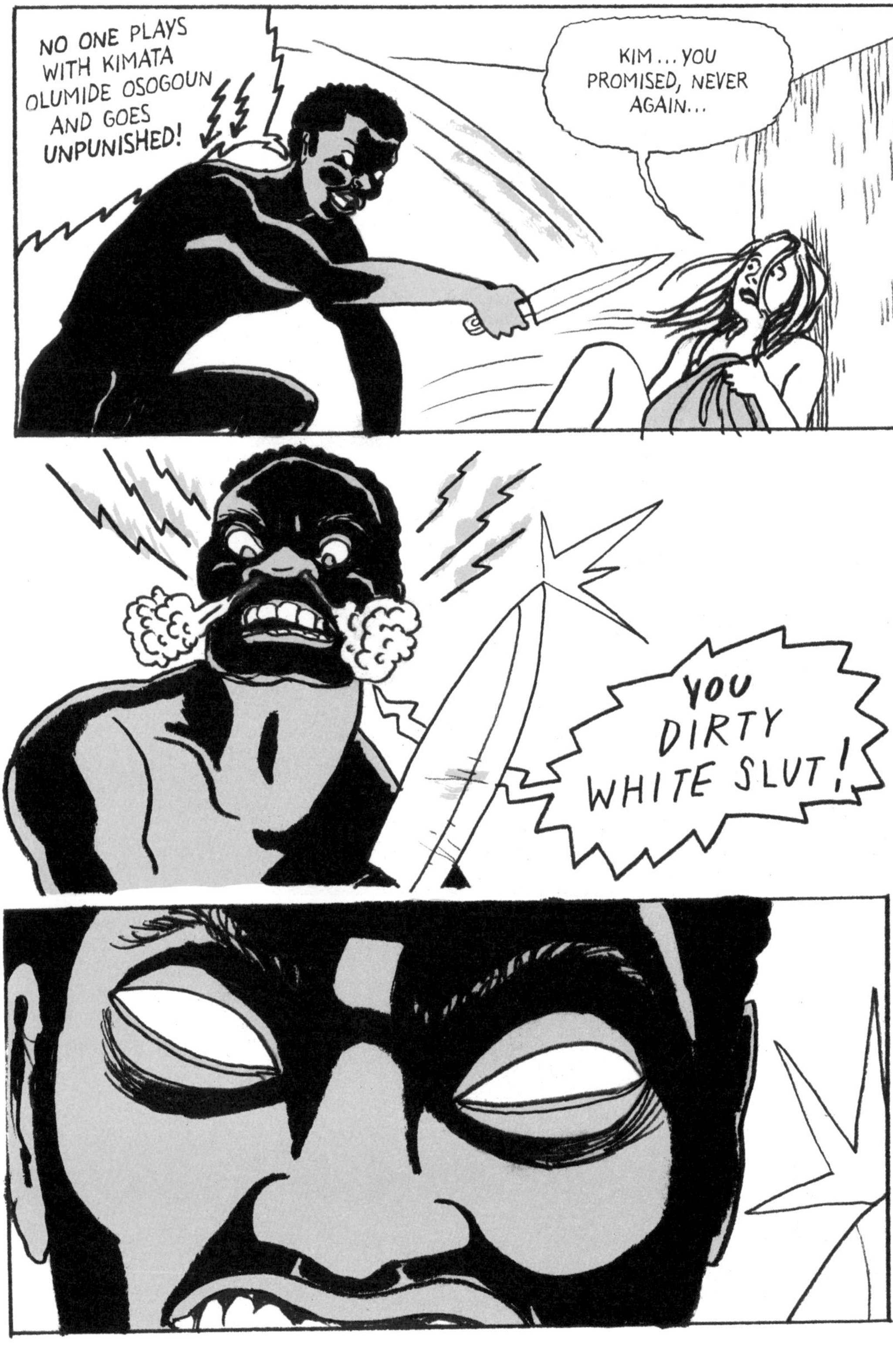
NO ONE PLAYS WITH KIMATA OLUMIDE OSOGOUN AND GOES UNPUNISHED!
KIM... YOU PROMISED, NEVER AGAIN...
YOU DIRTY WHITE SLUT!

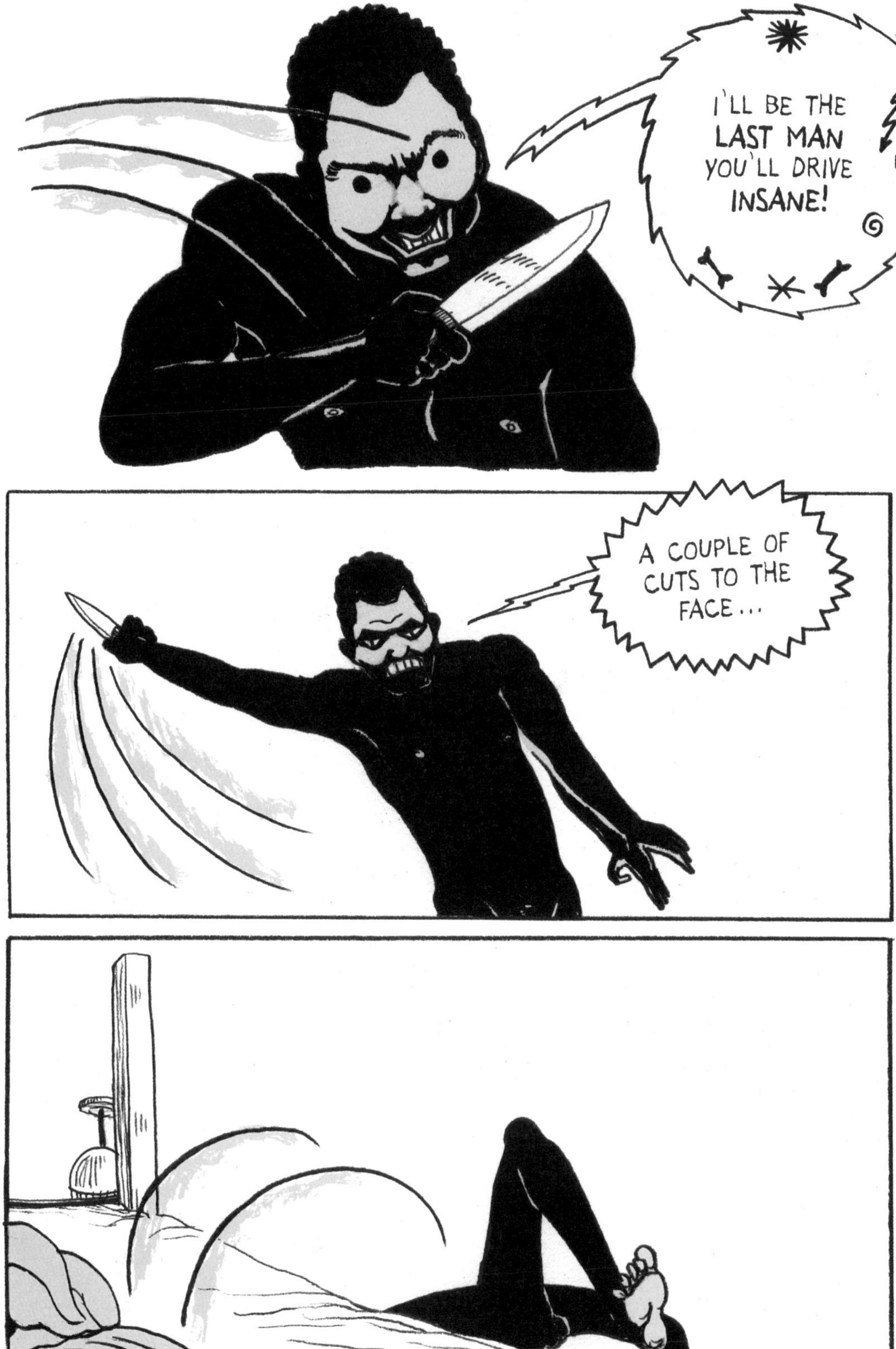
I'LL BE THE LAST MAN YOU'LL DRIVE INSANE!
A COUPLE OF CUTS TO THE FACE...

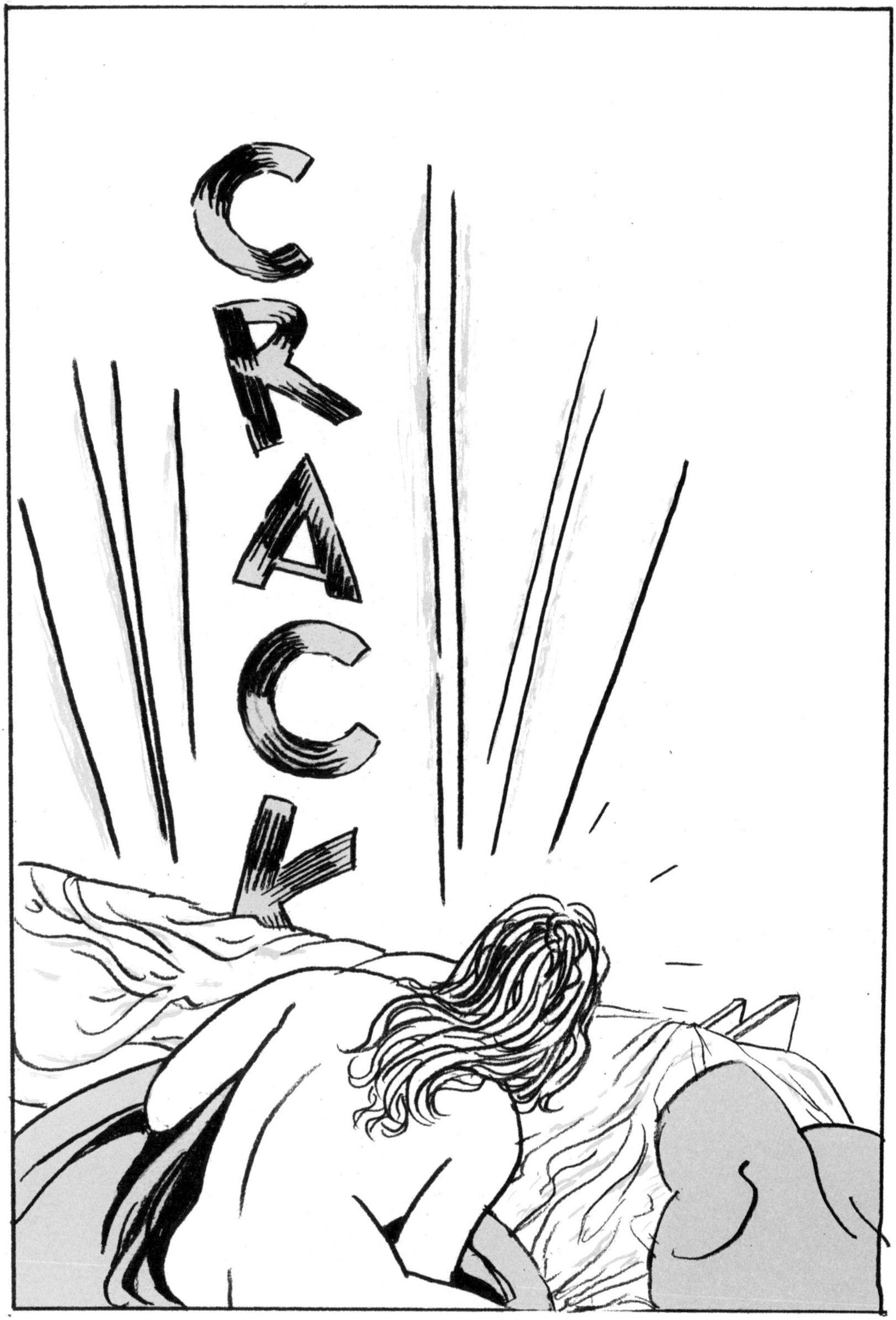
CRACK

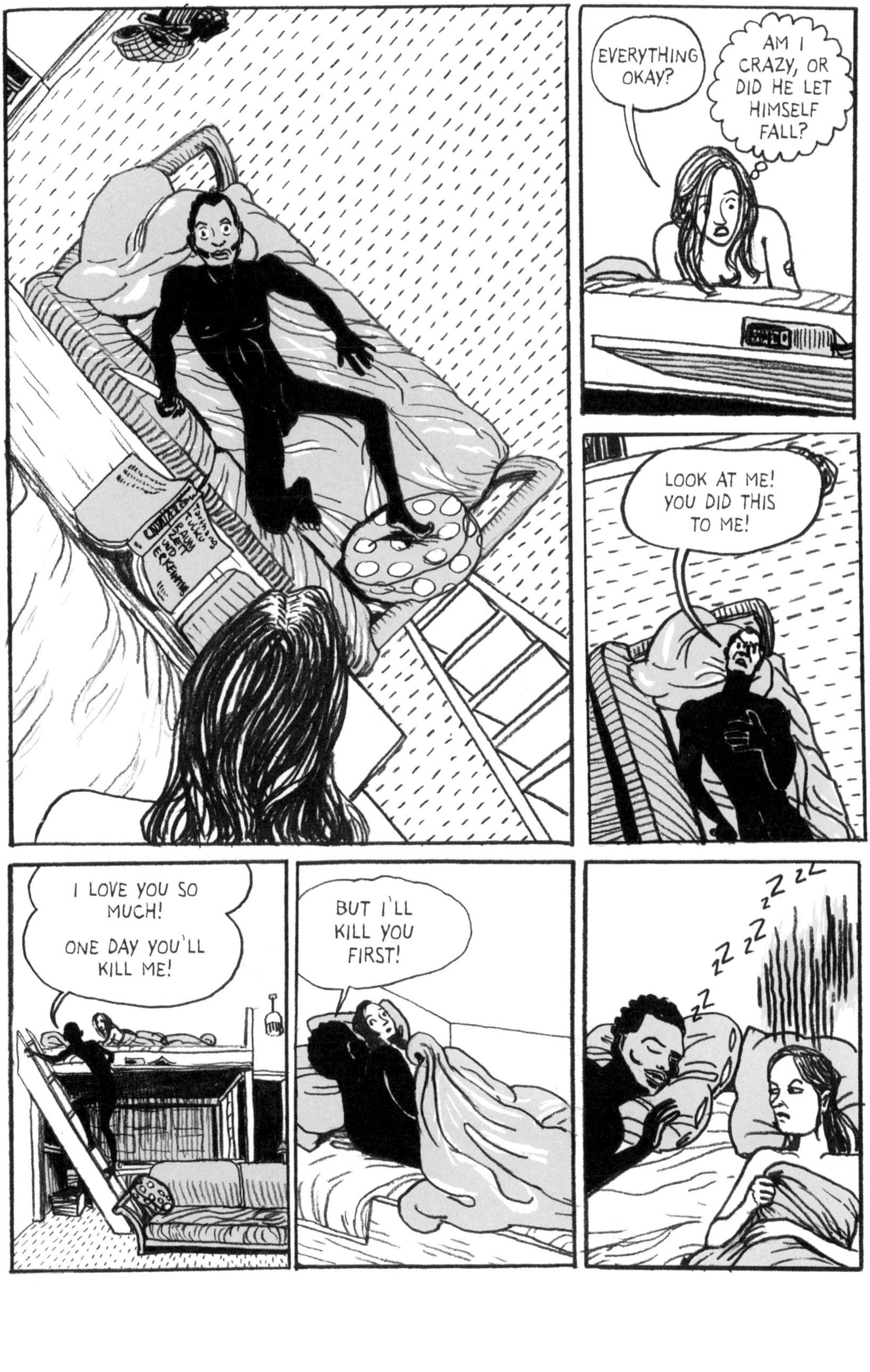
EVERYTHING OKAY?
AM I CRAZY, OR DID HE LET HIMSELF FALL?
LOOK AT ME! YOU DID THIS TO ME!
I LOVE YOU SO MUCH!
ONE DAY YOU'LL KILL ME!
BUT I'LL KILL YOU FIRST!
ZZZZZZZ

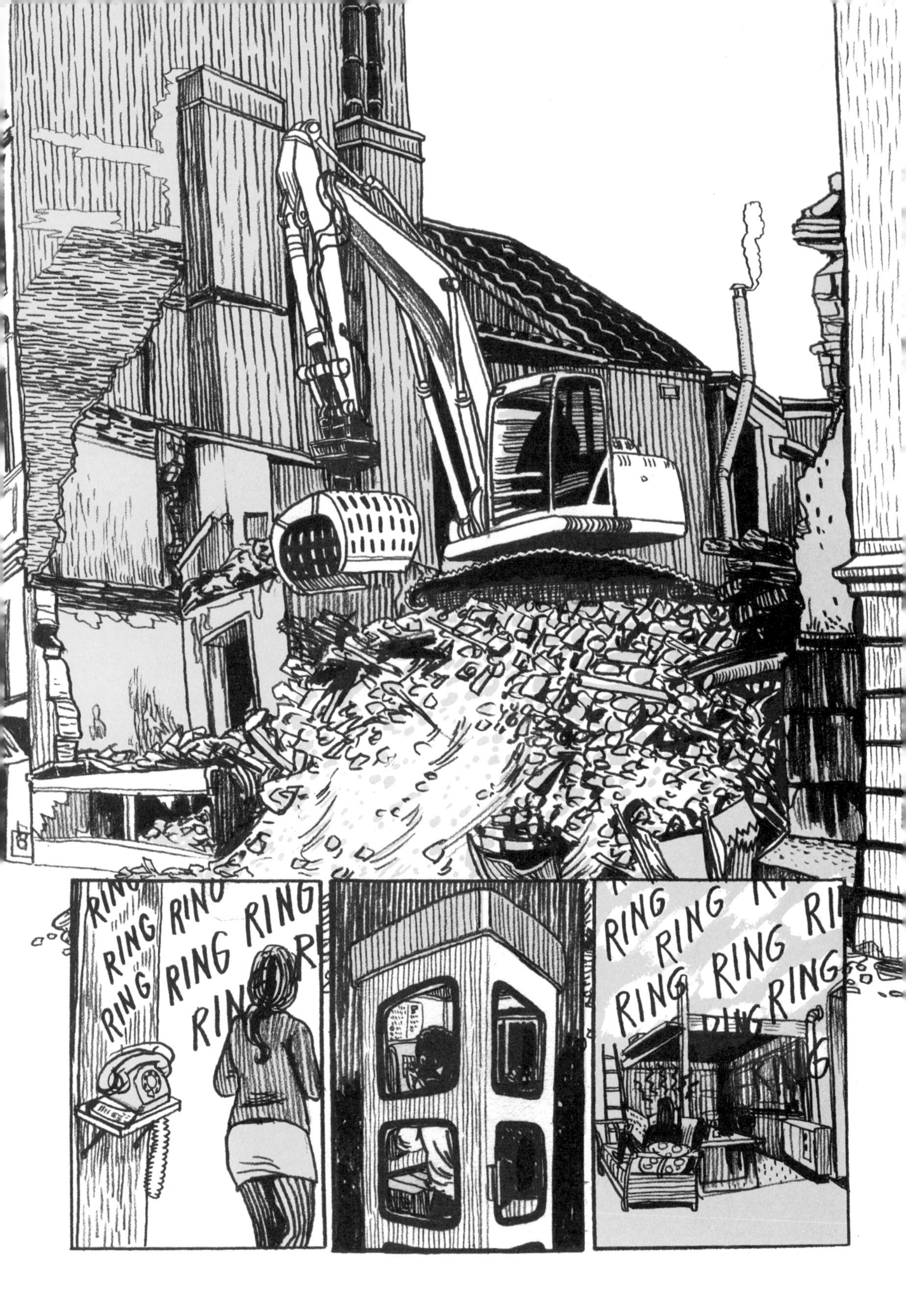
RING
RING RING
RING RING RING
RING
RING
RING RING
RING RING
RING RING

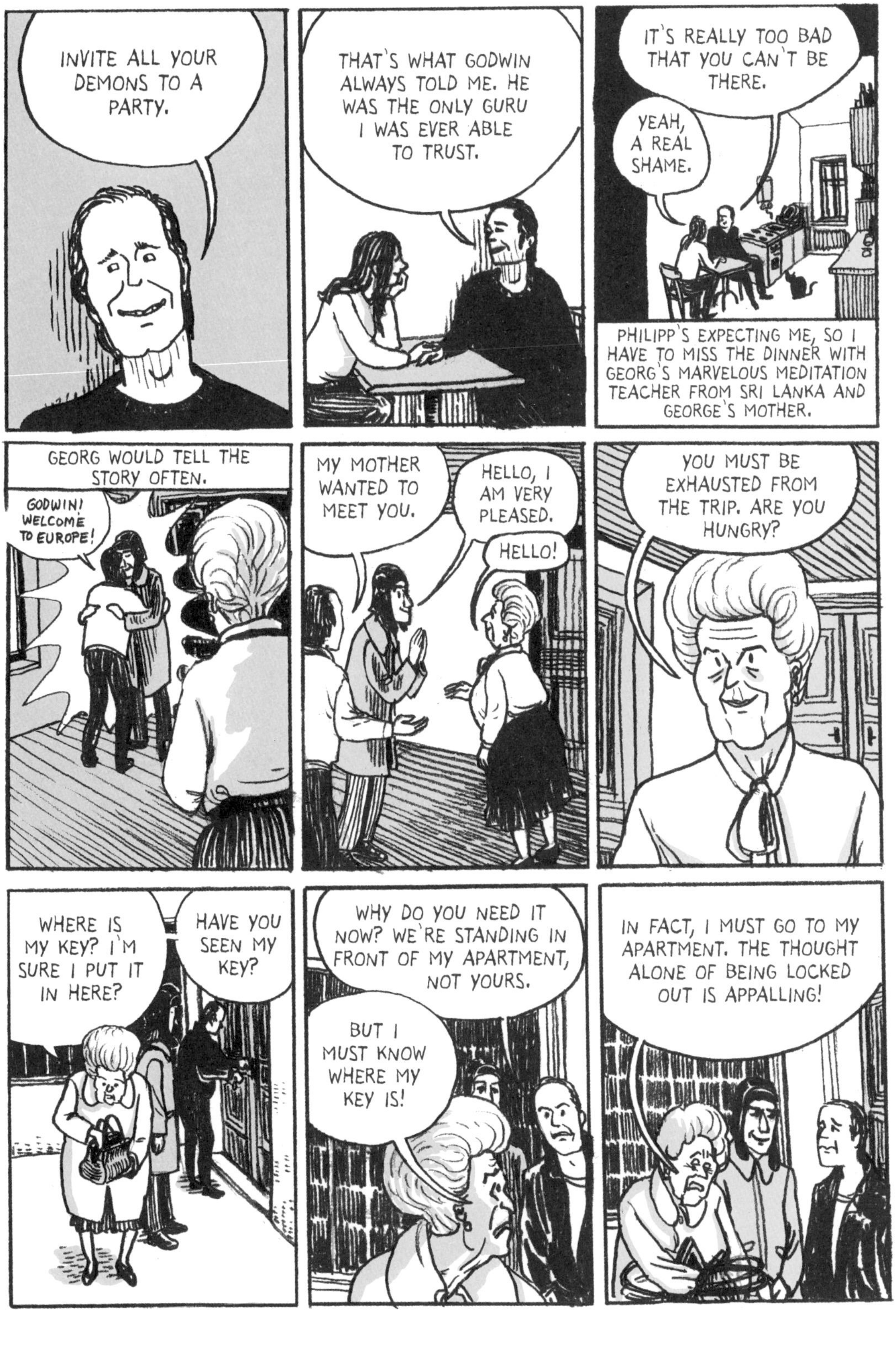
INVITE ALL YOUR DEMONS TO A PARTY.
THAT'S WHAT GODWIN ALWAYS TOLD ME. HE WAS THE ONLY GURU I WAS EVER ABLE TO TRUST.
IT'S REALLY TOO BAD THAT YOU CAN'T BE THERE.
YEAH, A REAL SHAME.
PHILIPP'S EXPECTING ME, SO I HAVE TO MISS THE DINNER WITH GEORG'S MARVELOUS MEDITATION TEACHER FROM SRI LANKA AND GEORGE'S MOTHER.
GEORG WOULD TELL THE STORY OFTEN.
GODWIN! WELCOME TO EUROPE!
MY MOTHER WANTED TO MEET YOU.
HELLO, I AM VERY PLEASED.
HELLO!
YOU MUST BE EXHAUSTED FROM THE TRIP. ARE YOU HUNGRY?
WHERE IS MY KEY? I'M SURE I PUT IT IN HERE?
HAVE YOU SEEN MY KEY?
WHY DO YOU NEED IT NOW? WE'RE STANDING IN FRONT OF MY APARTMENT, NOT YOURS.
BUT I MUST KNOW WHERE MY KEY IS!
IN FACT, I MUST GO TO MY APARTMENT. THE THOUGHT ALONE OF BEING LOCKED OUT IS APPALLING!

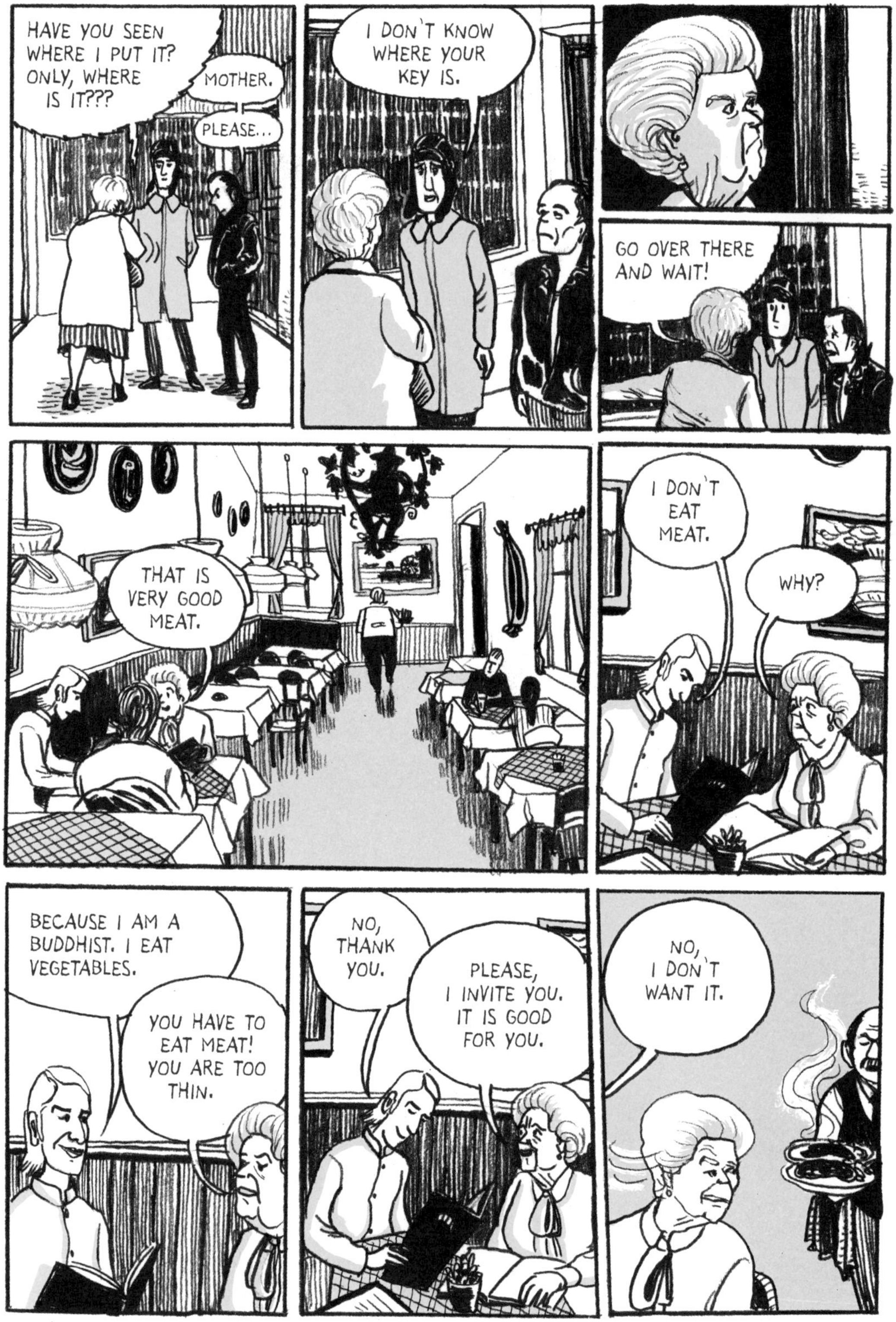
HAVE YOU SEEN WHERE I PUT IT? ONLY, WHERE IS IT???
MOTHER.
PLEASE...
I DON'T KNOW WHERE YOUR KEY IS.
GO OVER THERE AND WAIT!
THAT IS VERY GOOD MEAT.
I DON'T EAT MEAT.
WHY?
BECAUSE I AM A BUDDHIST. I EAT VEGETABLES.
YOU HAVE TO EAT MEAT! YOU ARE TOO THIN.
NO, THANK YOU.
PLEASE, I INVITE YOU. IT IS GOOD FOR YOU.
NO, I DON'T WANT IT.

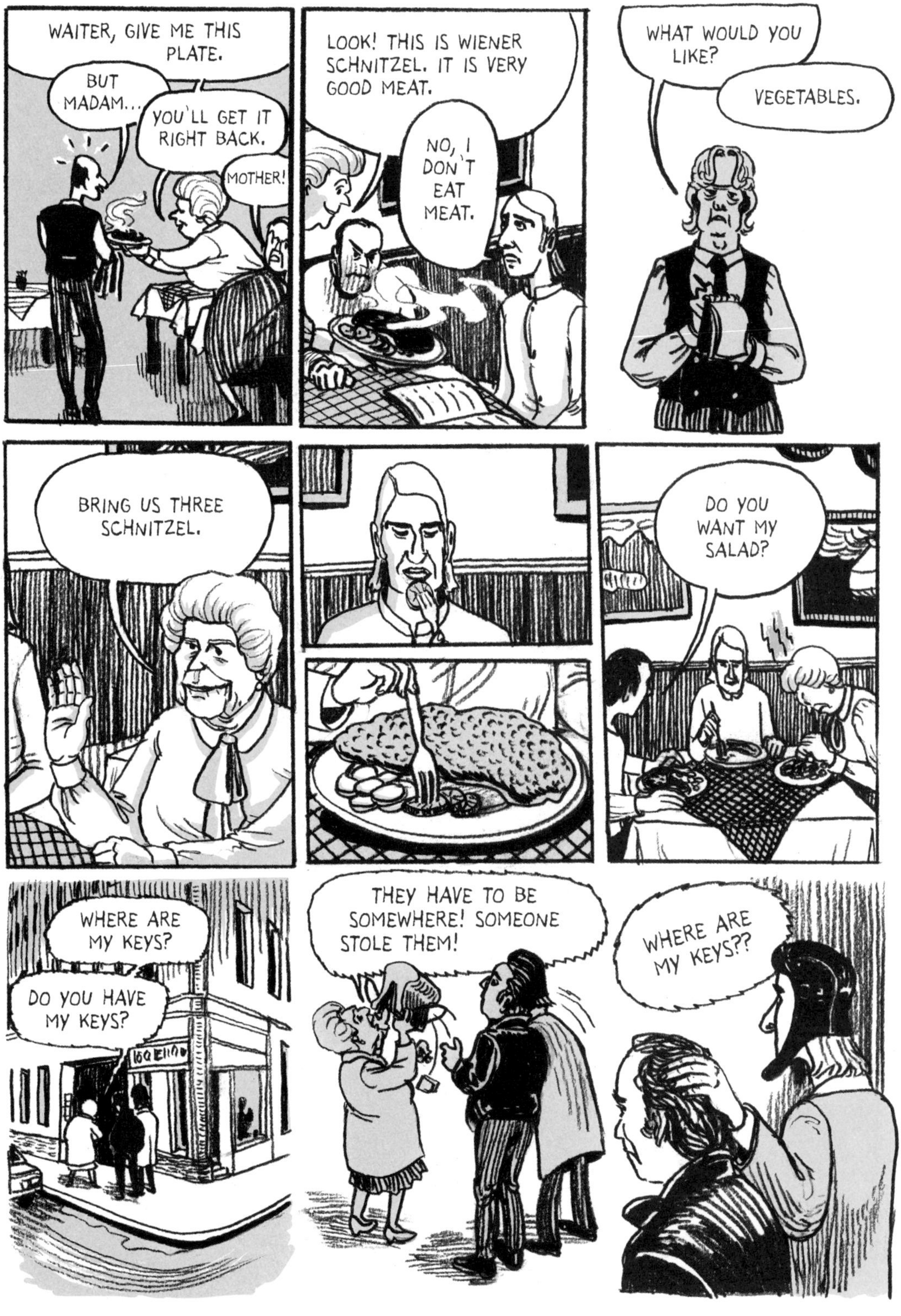
WAITER, GIVE ME THIS PLATE.
BUT MADAM...
YOU'LL GET IT RIGHT BACK.
MOTHER!
LOOK! THIS IS WIENER SCHNITZEL. IT IS VERY GOOD MEAT.
NO, I DON'T EAT MEAT.
WHAT WOULD YOU LIKE?
VEGETABLES.
BRING US THREE SCHNITZEL.
DO YOU WANT MY SALAD?
WHERE ARE MY KEYS?
DO YOU HAVE MY KEYS?
THEY HAVE TO BE SOMEWHERE! SOMEONE STOLE THEM!
WHERE ARE MY KEYS??

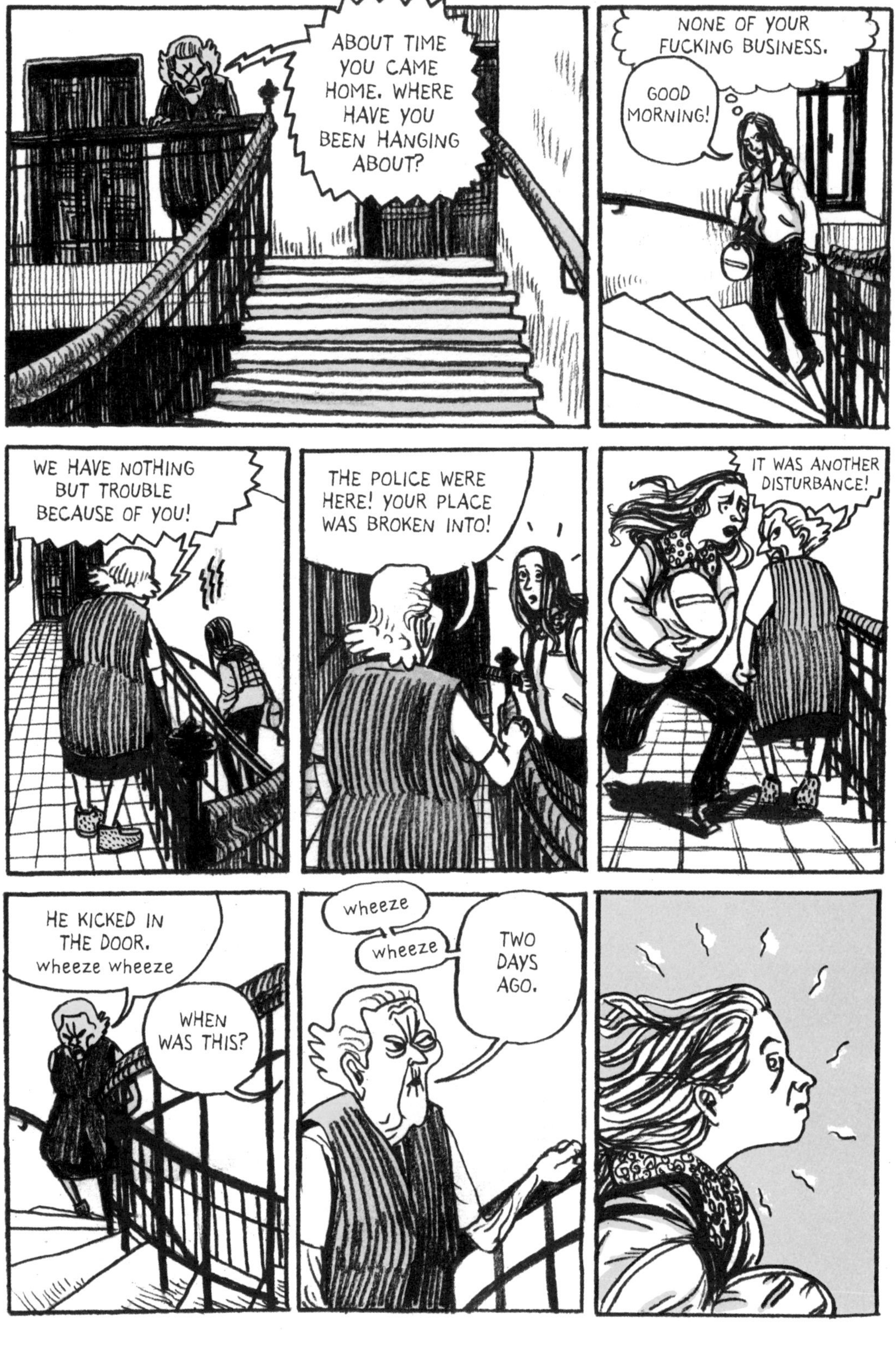
ABOUT TIME YOU CAME HOME. WHERE HAVE YOU BEEN HANGING ABOUT?
NONE OF YOUR FUCKING BUSINESS.
GOOD MORNING!
WE HAVE NOTHING BUT TROUBLE BECAUSE OF YOU!
THE POLICE WERE HERE! YOUR PLACE WAS BROKEN INTO!
IT WAS ANOTHER DISTURBANCE!
HE KICKED IN THE DOOR. wheeze wheeze
WHEN WAS THIS?
wheeze
wheeze
TWO DAYS AGO.

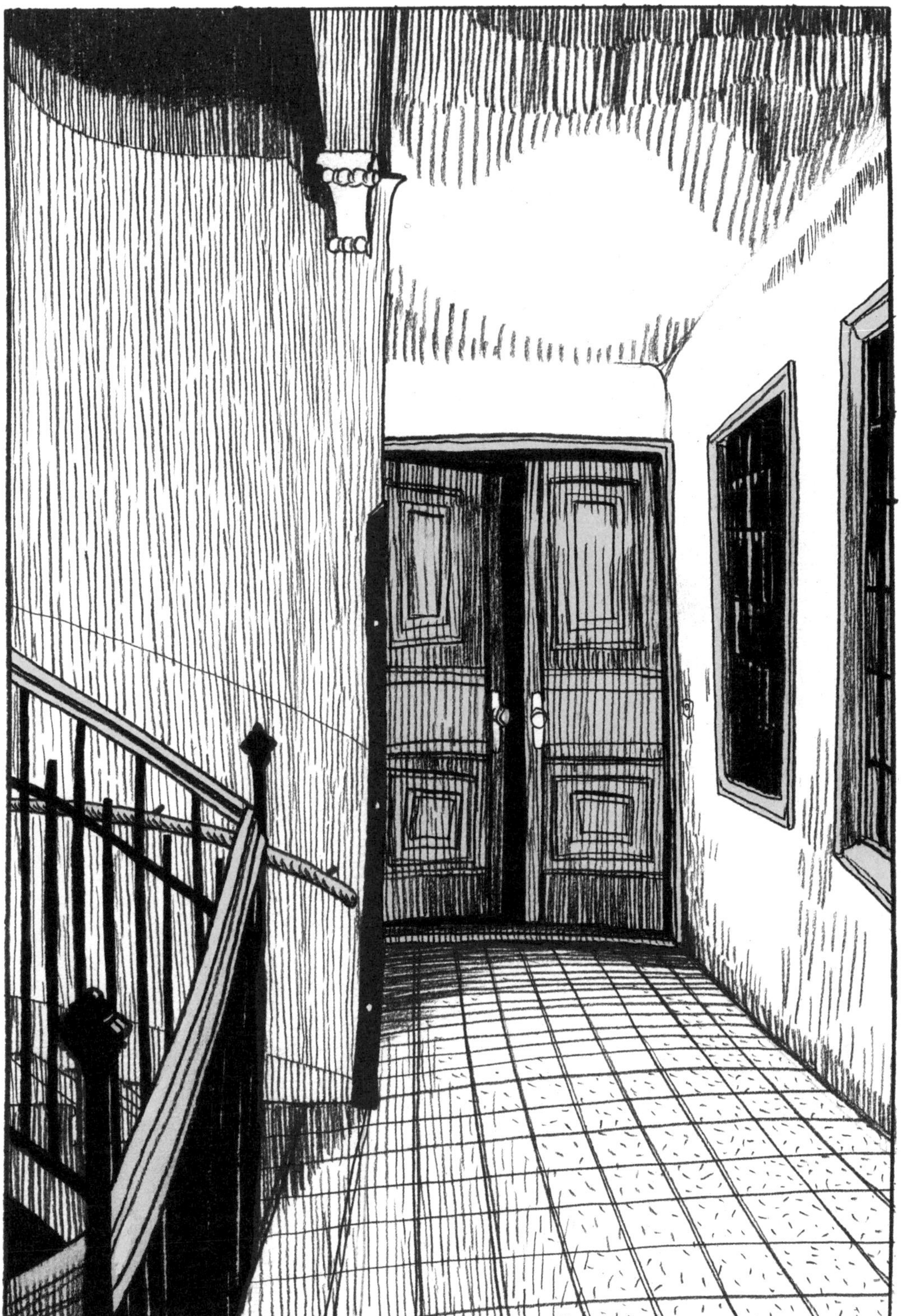

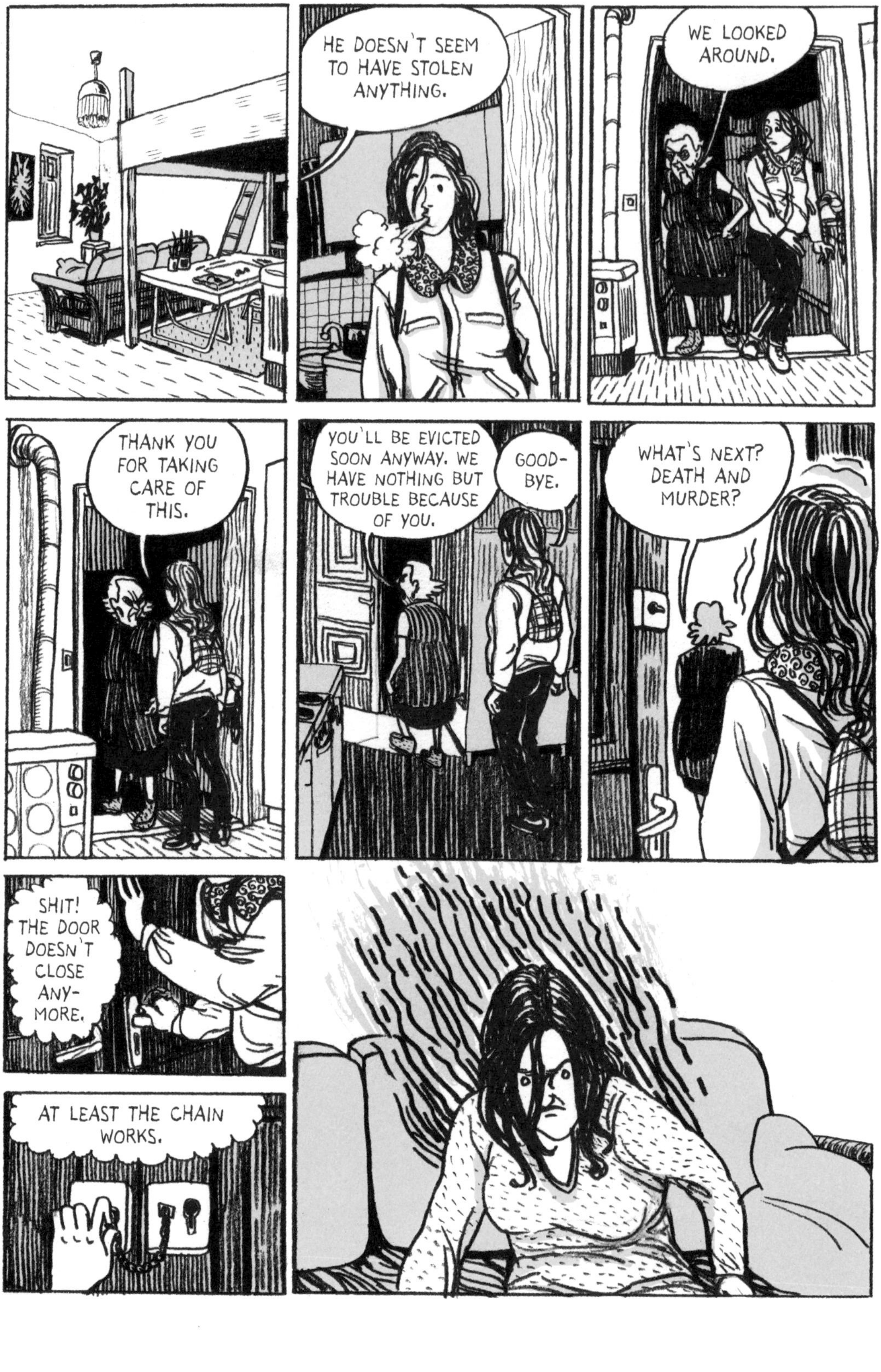
HE DOESN'T SEEM TO HAVE STOLEN ANYTHING.
WE LOOKED AROUND.
THANK YOU FOR TAKING CARE OF THIS.
YOU'LL BE EVICTED SOON ANYWAY. WE HAVE NOTHING BUT TROUBLE BECAUSE OF YOU.
GOOD-BYE.
WHAT'S NEXT? DEATH AND MURDER?
SHIT! THE DOOR DOESN'T CLOSE ANY-MORE.
AT LEAST THE CHAIN WORKS.

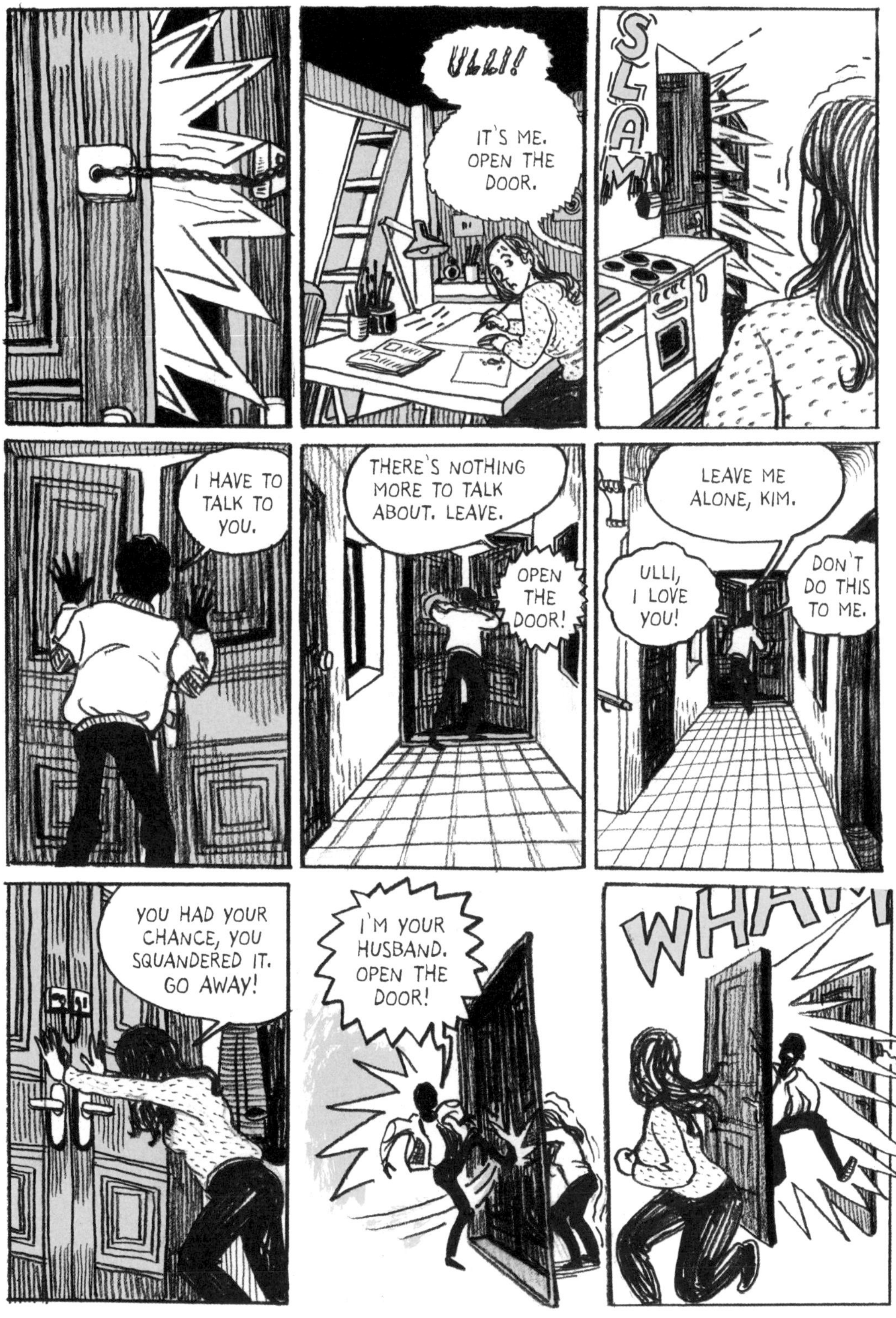
ULLI!
IT'S ME. OPEN THE DOOR.
SLAM
I HAVE TO TALK TO YOU.
THERE'S NOTHING MORE TO TALK ABOUT. LEAVE.
OPEN THE DOOR!
LEAVE ME ALONE, KIM.
ULLI, I LOVE YOU!
DON'T DO THIS TO ME.
YOU HAD YOUR CHANCE, YOU SQUANDERED IT. GO AWAY!
I'M YOUR HUSBAND. OPEN THE DOOR!
WHAM

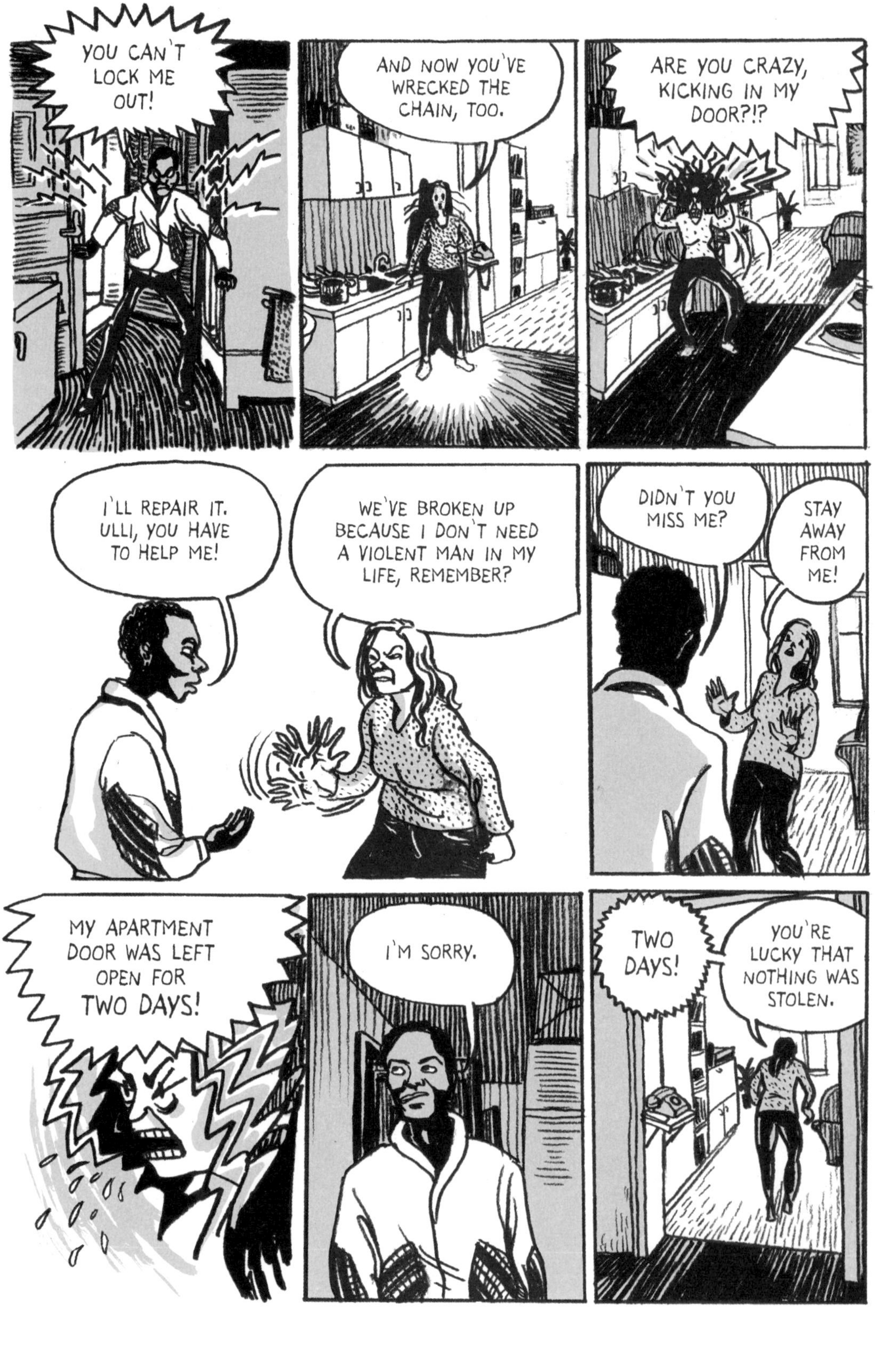
YOU CAN'T LOCK ME OUT!
AND NOW YOU'VE WRECKED THE CHAIN, TOO.
ARE YOU CRAZY, KICKING IN MY DOOR?!?
I'LL REPAIR IT. ULLI, YOU HAVE TO HELP ME!
WE'VE BROKEN UP BECAUSE I DON'T NEED A VIOLENT MAN IN MY LIFE, REMEMBER?
DIDN'T YOU MISS ME?
STAY AWAY FROM ME!
MY APARTMENT DOOR WAS LEFT OPEN FOR TWO DAYS!
I'M SORRY.
TWO DAYS!
YOU'RE LUCKY THAT NOTHING WAS STOLEN.

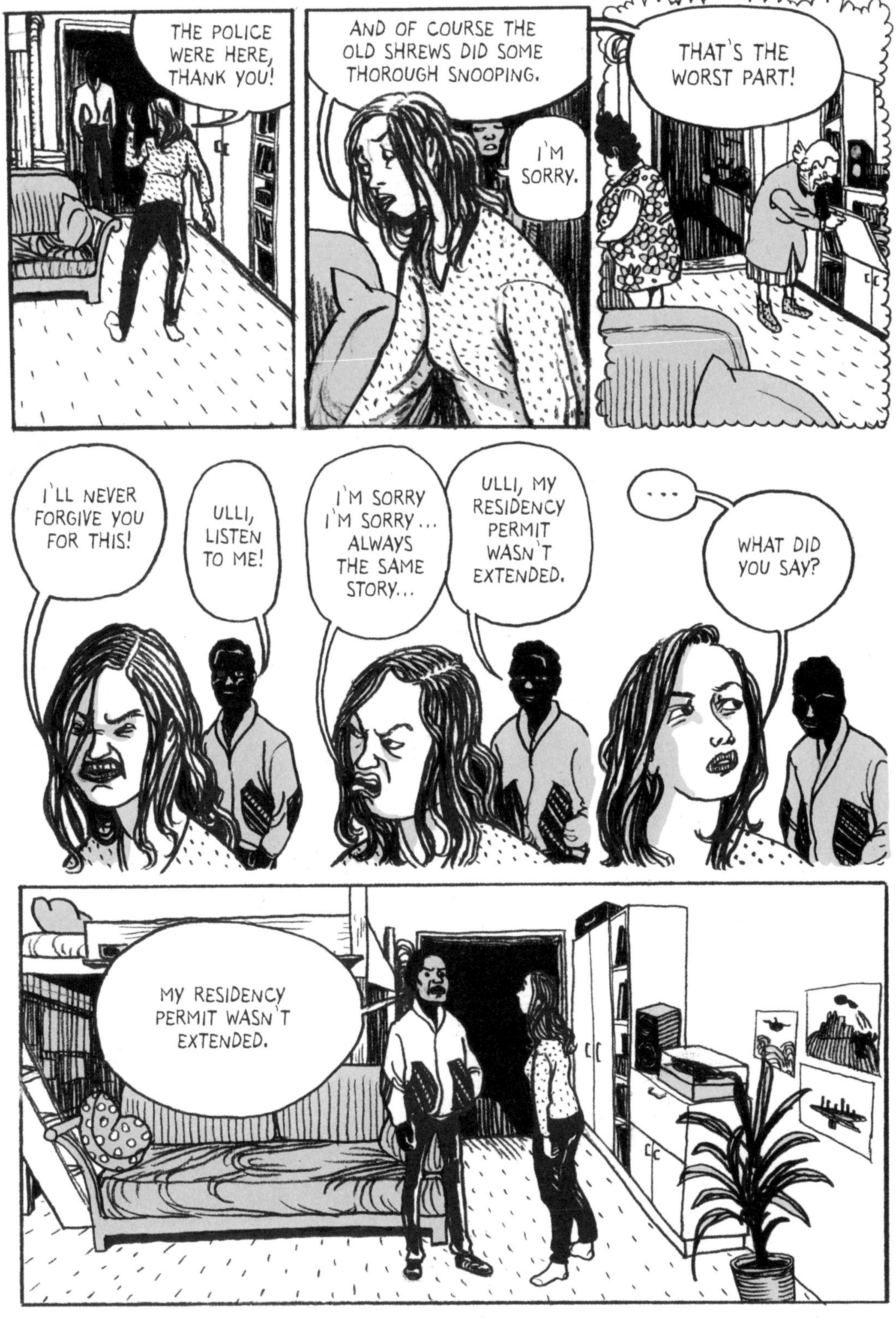
THE POLICE WERE HERE, THANK YOU!
AND OF COURSE THE OLD SHREWS DID SOME THOROUGH SNOOPING.
I'M SORRY.
THAT'S THE WORST PART!
I'LL NEVER FORGIVE YOU FOR THIS!
ULLI, LISTEN TO ME!
I'M SORRY I'M SORRY... ALWAYS THE SAME STORY...
ULLI, MY RESIDENCY PERMIT WASN'T EXTENDED.
...
WHAT DID YOU SAY?
MY RESIDENCY PERMIT WASN'T EXTENDED.

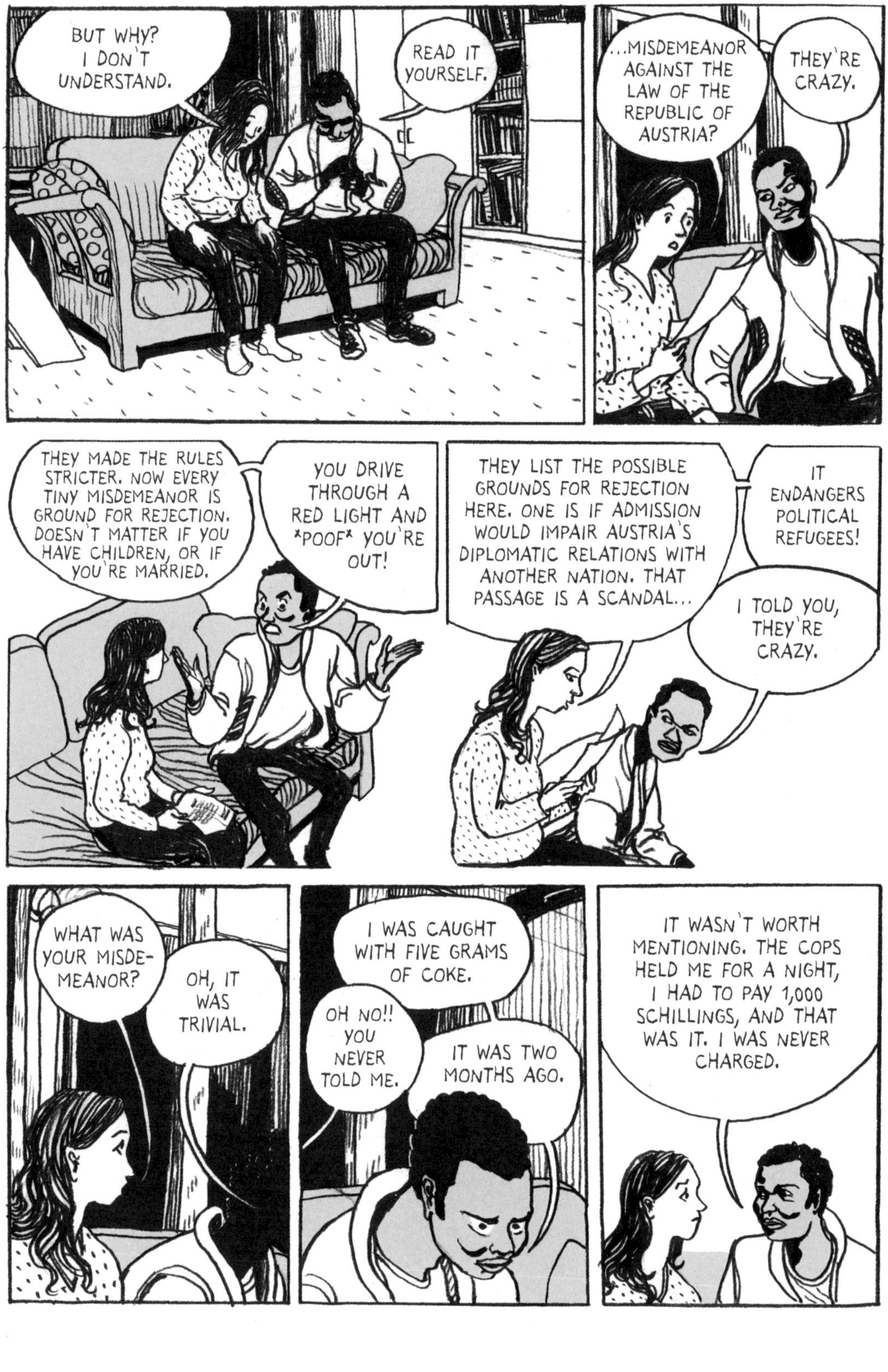
BUT WHY? I DON'T UNDERSTAND.
READ IT YOURSELF.
...MISDEMEANOR AGAINST THE LAW OF THE REPUBLIC OF AUSTRIA?
THEY'RE CRAZY.
THEY MADE THE RULES STRICTER. NOW EVERY TINY MISDEMEANOR IS GROUND FOR REJECTION. DOESN'T MATTER IF YOU HAVE CHILDREN, OR IF YOU'RE MARRIED.
YOU DRIVE THROUGH A RED LIGHT AND *POOF* YOU'RE OUT!
THEY LIST THE POSSIBLE GROUNDS FOR REJECTION HERE. ONE IS IF ADMISSION WOULD IMPAIR AUSTRIA'S DIPLOMATIC RELATIONS WITH ANOTHER NATION. THAT PASSAGE IS A SCANDAL...
IT ENDANGERS POLITICAL REFUGEES!
I TOLD YOU, THEY'RE CRAZY.
WHAT WAS YOUR MISDEMEANOR?
OH, IT WAS TRIVIAL.
I WAS CAUGHT WITH FIVE GRAMS OF COKE.
OH NO!! YOU NEVER TOLD ME.
IT WAS TWO MONTHS AGO.
IT WASN'T WORTH MENTIONING. THE COPS HELD ME FOR A NIGHT, I HAD TO PAY 1,000 SCHILLINGS, AND THAT WAS IT. I WAS NEVER CHARGED.

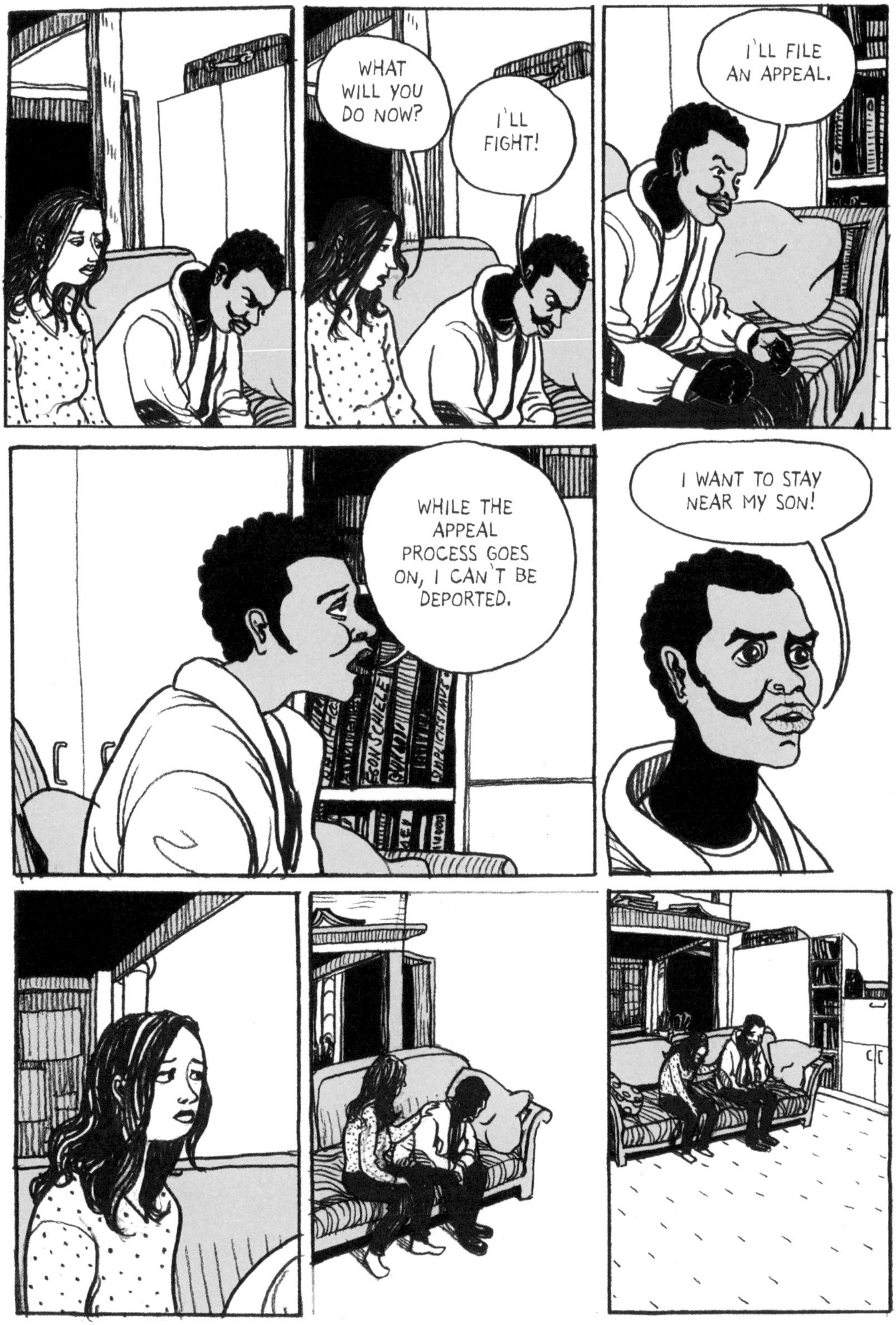
WHAT WILL YOU DO NOW?
I'LL FIGHT!
I'LL FILE AN APPEAL.
WHILE THE APPEAL PROCESS GOES ON, I CAN'T BE DEPORTED.
I WANT TO STAY NEAR MY SON!

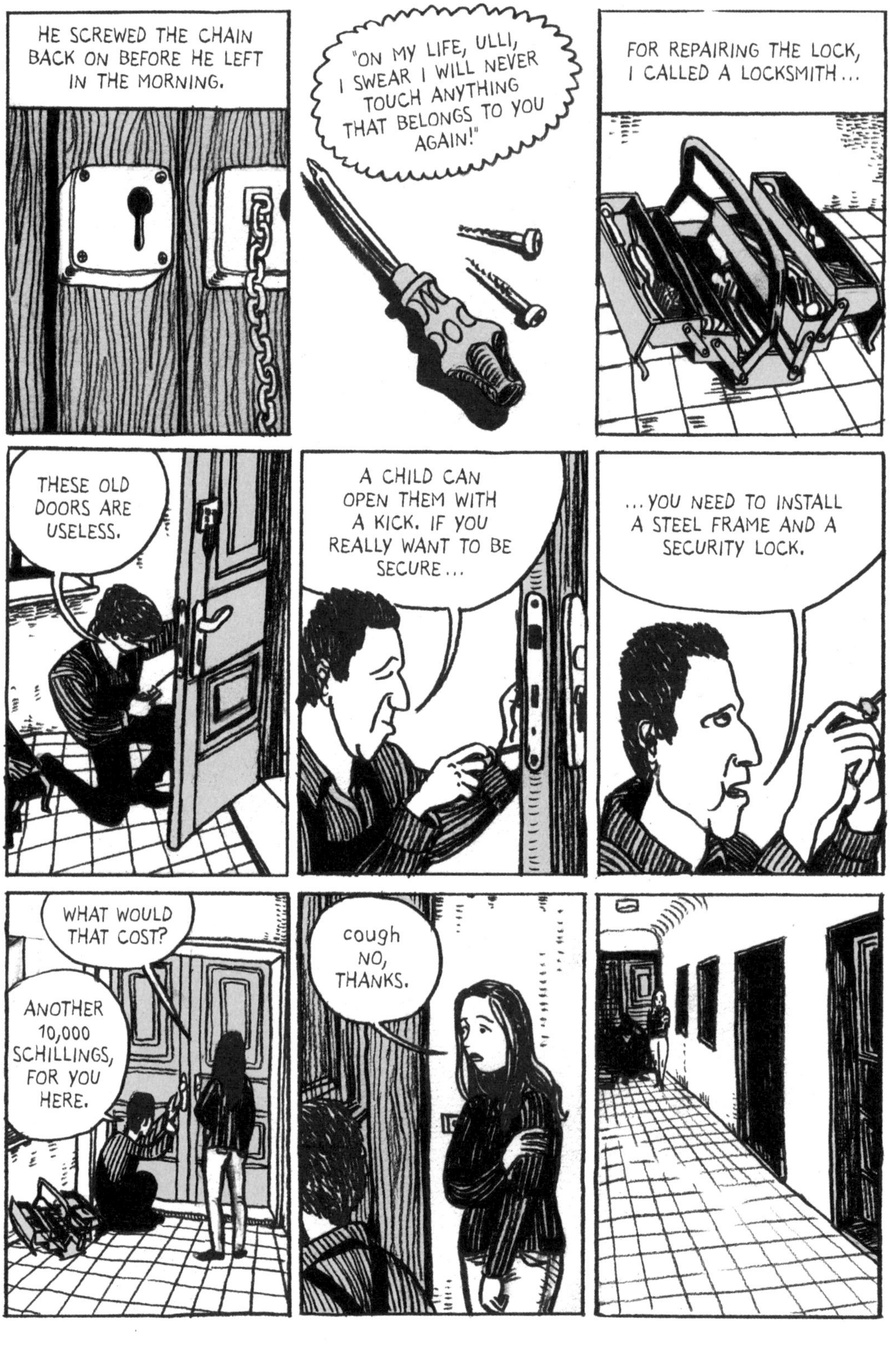
HE SCREWED THE CHAIN BACK ON BEFORE HE LEFT IN THE MORNING.
"ON MY LIFE, ULLI, I SWEAR I WILL NEVER TOUCH ANYTHING THAT BELONGS TO YOU AGAIN!"
FOR REPAIRING THE LOCK, I CALLED A LOCKSMITH...
THESE OLD DOORS ARE USELESS.
A CHILD CAN OPEN THEM WITH A KICK. IF YOU REALLY WANT TO BE SECURE...
...YOU NEED TO INSTALL A STEEL FRAME AND A SECURITY LOCK.
WHAT WOULD THAT COST?
ANOTHER 10,000 SCHILLINGS, FOR YOU HERE.
cough
NO, THANKS.

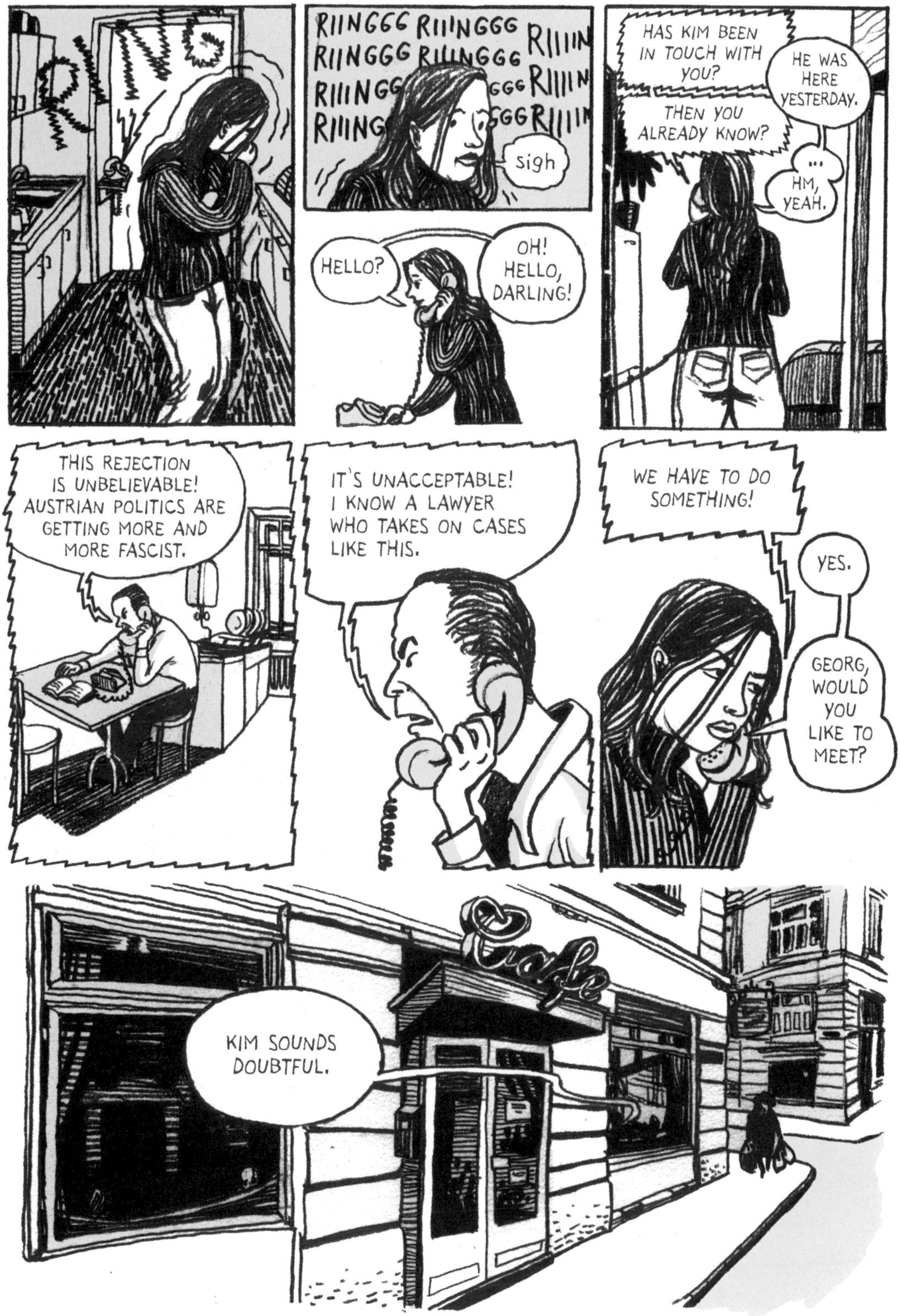
RIIIIING
RIINGGG RIIINGGG RIIIIN
RIINGGG RIIINGGG
RIIINGG GGG RIIIIN
RIIING GGG RIIIIN
sigh
HELLO?
OH! HELLO, DARLING!
HAS KIM BEEN IN TOUCH WITH YOU?
HE WAS HERE YESTERDAY.
THEN YOU ALREADY KNOW?
... HM, YEAH.
THIS REJECTION IS UNBELIEVABLE! AUSTRIAN POLITICS ARE GETTING MORE AND MORE FASCIST.
IT'S UNACCEPTABLE! I KNOW A LAWYER WHO TAKES ON CASES LIKE THIS.
WE HAVE TO DO SOMETHING!
YES.
GEORG, WOULD YOU LIKE TO MEET?
Café
KIM SOUNDS DOUBTFUL.

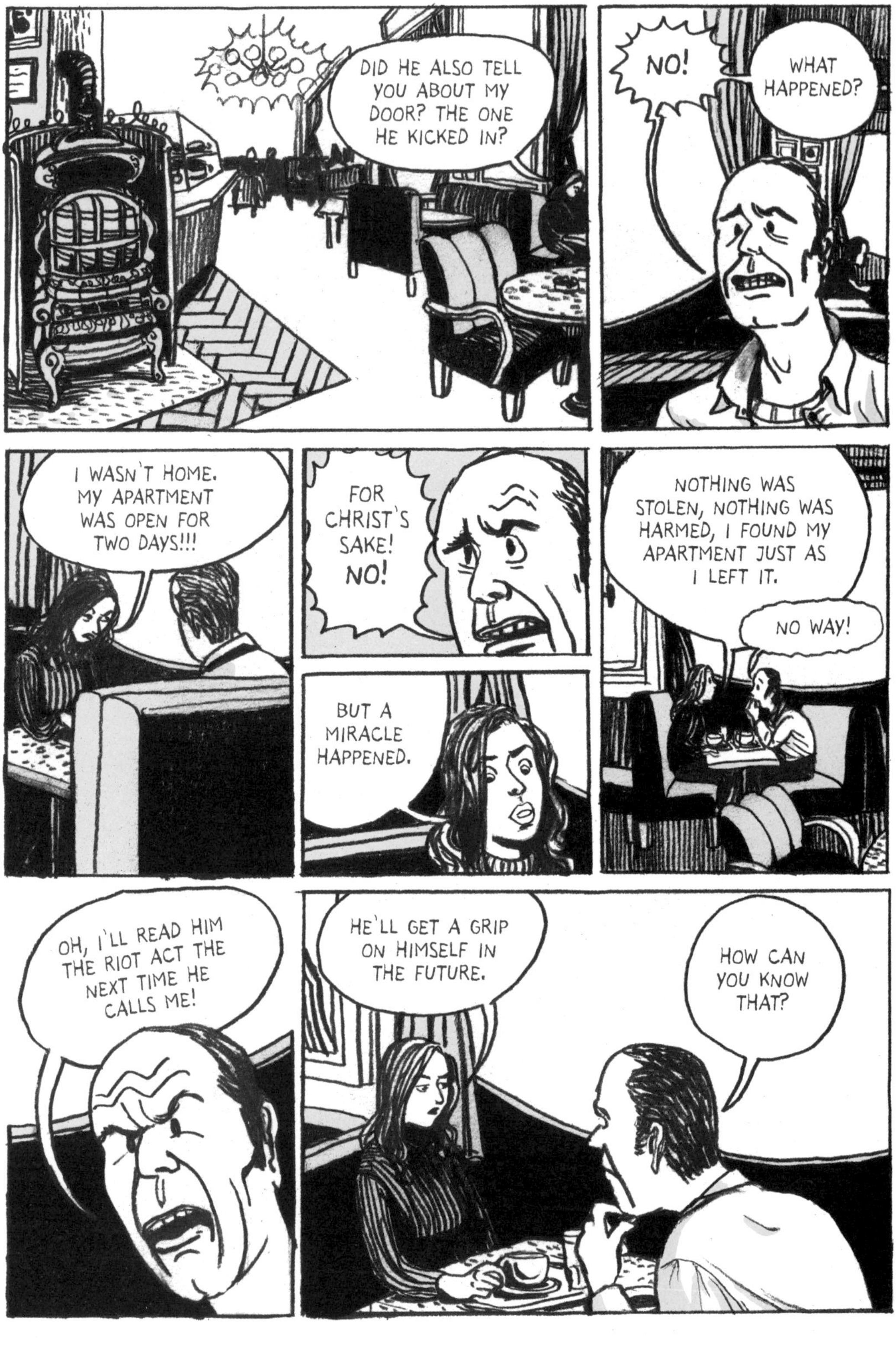
DID HE ALSO TELL YOU ABOUT MY DOOR? THE ONE HE KICKED IN?
NO!
WHAT HAPPENED?
I WASN'T HOME. MY APARTMENT WAS OPEN FOR TWO DAYS!!!
FOR CHRIST'S SAKE! NO!
BUT A MIRACLE HAPPENED.
NOTHING WAS STOLEN, NOTHING WAS HARMED, I FOUND MY APARTMENT JUST AS I LEFT IT.
NO WAY!
OH, I'LL READ HIM THE RIOT ACT THE NEXT TIME HE CALLS ME!
HE'LL GET A GRIP ON HIMSELF IN THE FUTURE.
HOW CAN YOU KNOW THAT?

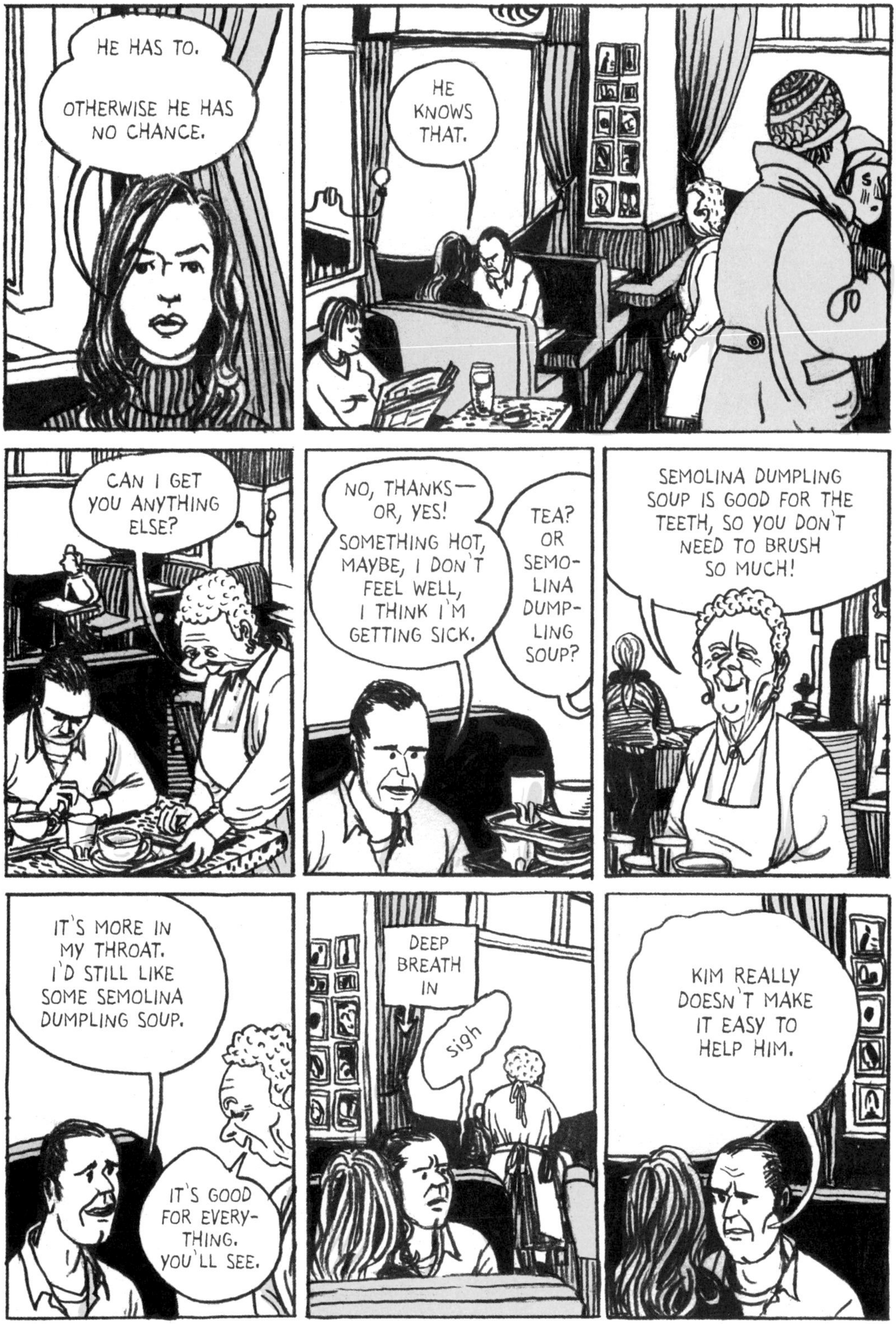
HE HAS TO.
OTHERWISE HE HAS NO CHANCE.
HE KNOWS THAT.
CAN I GET YOU ANYTHING ELSE?
NO, THANKS— OR, YES!
SOMETHING HOT, MAYBE, I DON'T FEEL WELL, I THINK I'M GETTING SICK.
TEA? OR SEMOLINA DUMPLING SOUP?
SEMOLINA DUMPLING SOUP IS GOOD FOR THE TEETH, SO YOU DON'T NEED TO BRUSH SO MUCH!
IT'S MORE IN MY THROAT. I'D STILL LIKE SOME SEMOLINA DUMPLING SOUP.
IT'S GOOD FOR EVERYTHING. YOU'LL SEE.
DEEP BREATH IN
sigh
KIM REALLY DOESN'T MAKE IT EASY TO HELP HIM.

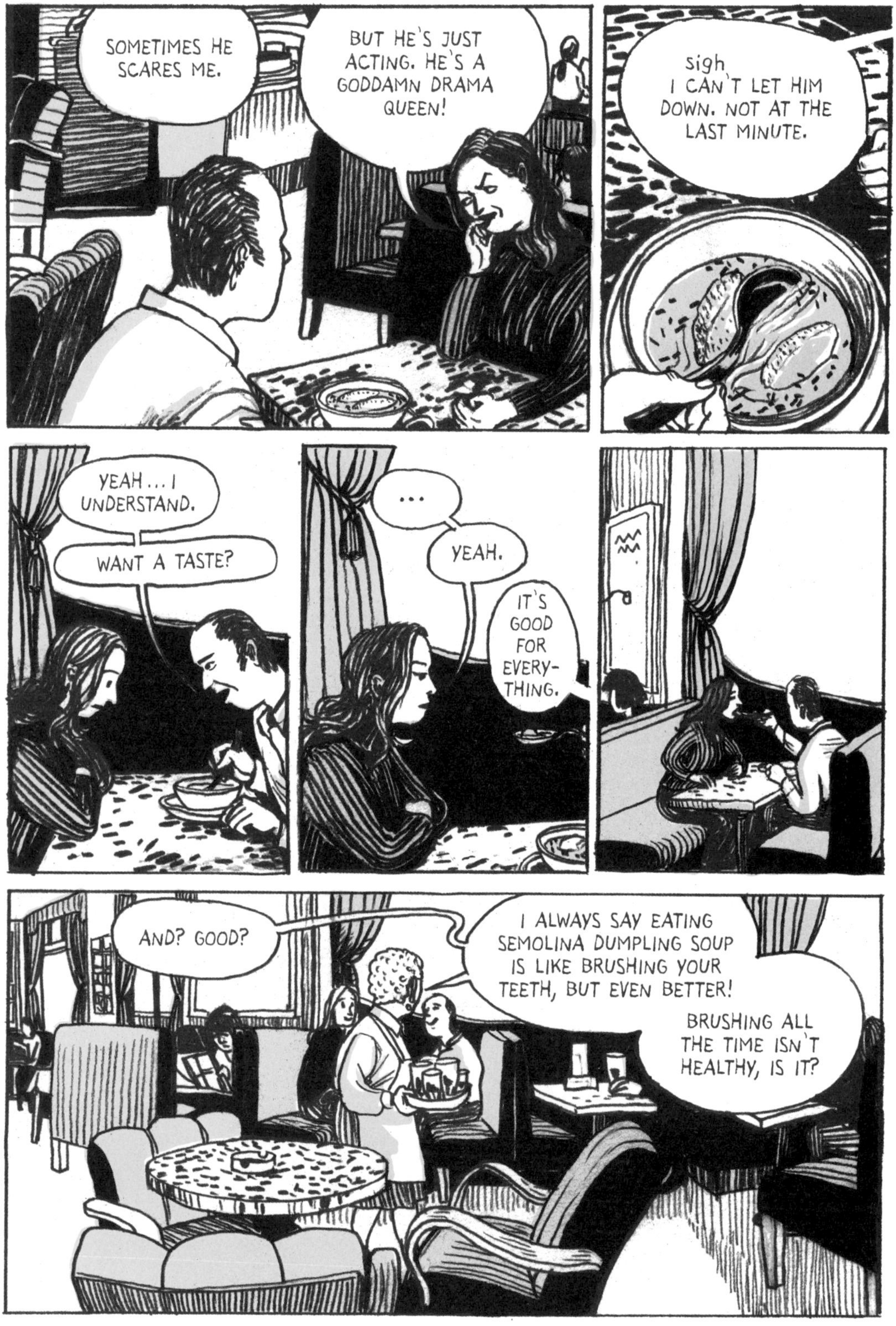
SOMETIMES HE SCARES ME.
BUT HE'S JUST ACTING. HE'S A GODDAMN DRAMA QUEEN!
sigh
I CAN'T LET HIM DOWN. NOT AT THE LAST MINUTE.
YEAH... I UNDERSTAND.
WANT A TASTE?
...
YEAH.
IT'S GOOD FOR EVERYTHING.
AND? GOOD?
I ALWAYS SAY EATING SEMOLINA DUMPLING SOUP IS LIKE BRUSHING YOUR TEETH, BUT EVEN BETTER!
BRUSHING ALL THE TIME ISN'T HEALTHY, IS IT?

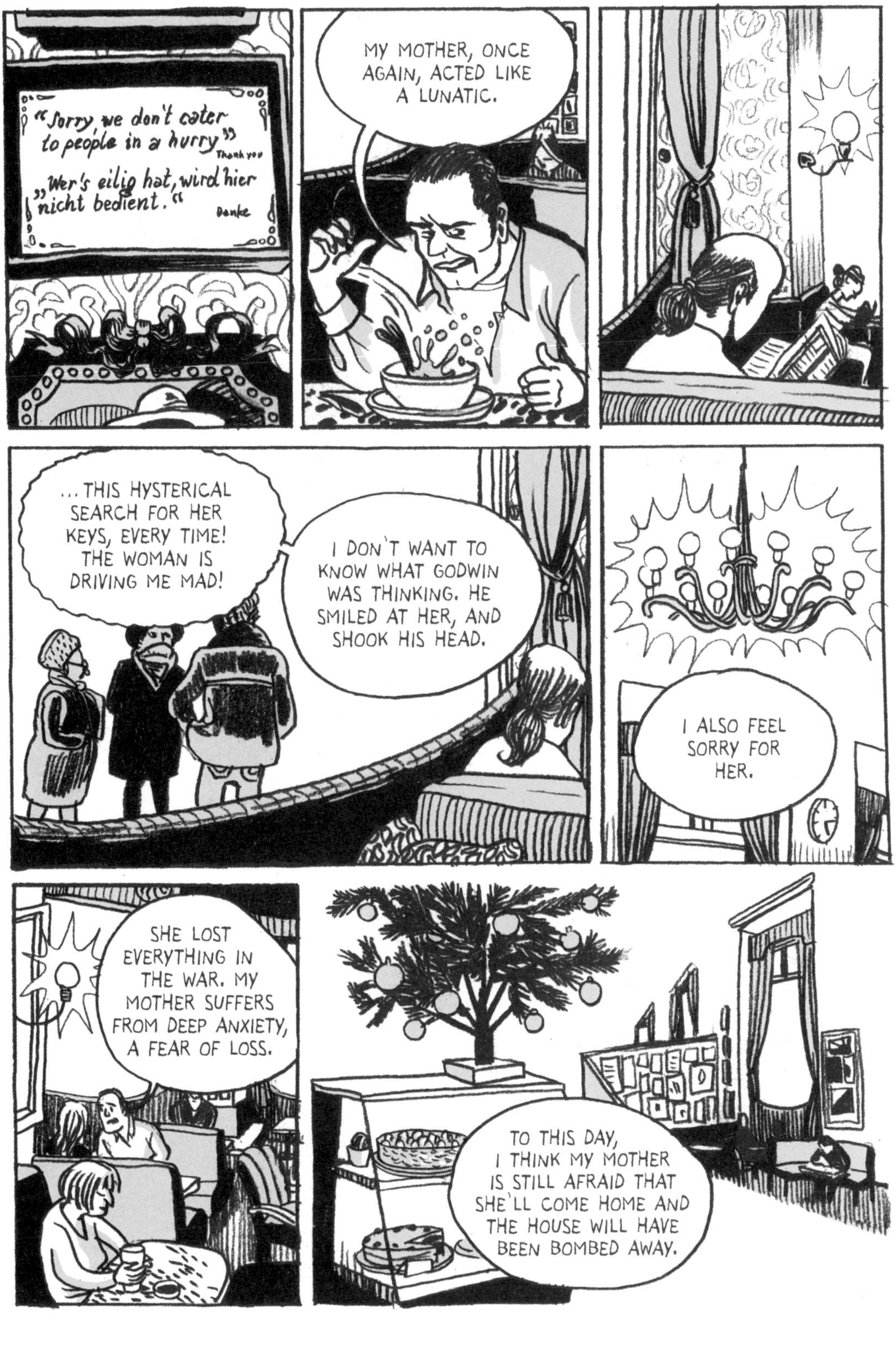
"Sorry we don't cater to people in a hurry" Thank you
„Wer's eilig hat, wird hier nicht bedient." Danke
MY MOTHER, ONCE AGAIN, ACTED LIKE A LUNATIC.
...THIS HYSTERICAL SEARCH FOR HER KEYS, EVERY TIME! THE WOMAN IS DRIVING ME MAD!
I DON'T WANT TO KNOW WHAT GODWIN WAS THINKING. HE SMILED AT HER, AND SHOOK HIS HEAD.
I ALSO FEEL SORRY FOR HER.
SHE LOST EVERYTHING IN THE WAR. MY MOTHER SUFFERS FROM DEEP ANXIETY, A FEAR OF LOSS.
TO THIS DAY, I THINK MY MOTHER IS STILL AFRAID THAT SHE'LL COME HOME AND THE HOUSE WILL HAVE BEEN BOMBED AWAY.

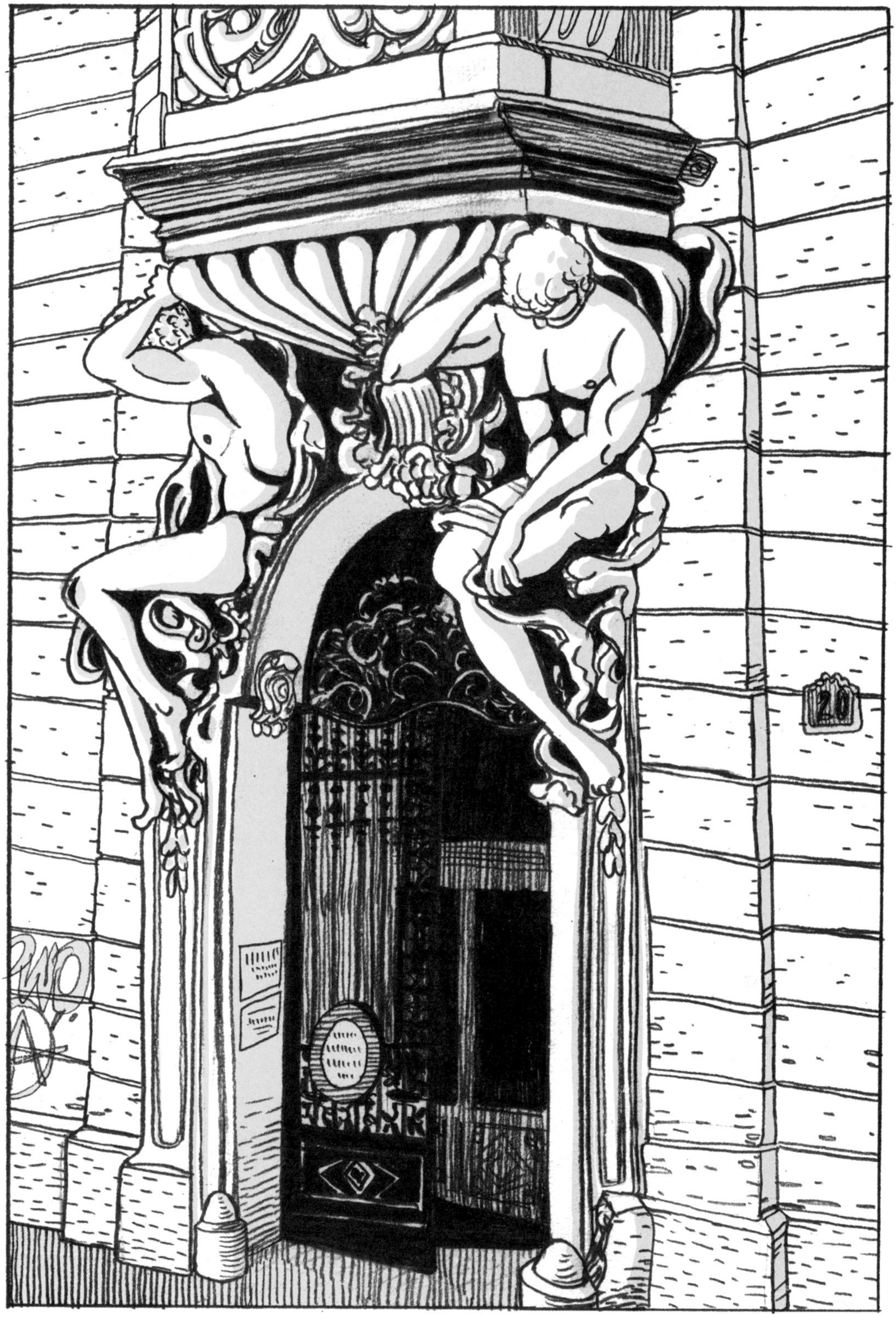
20

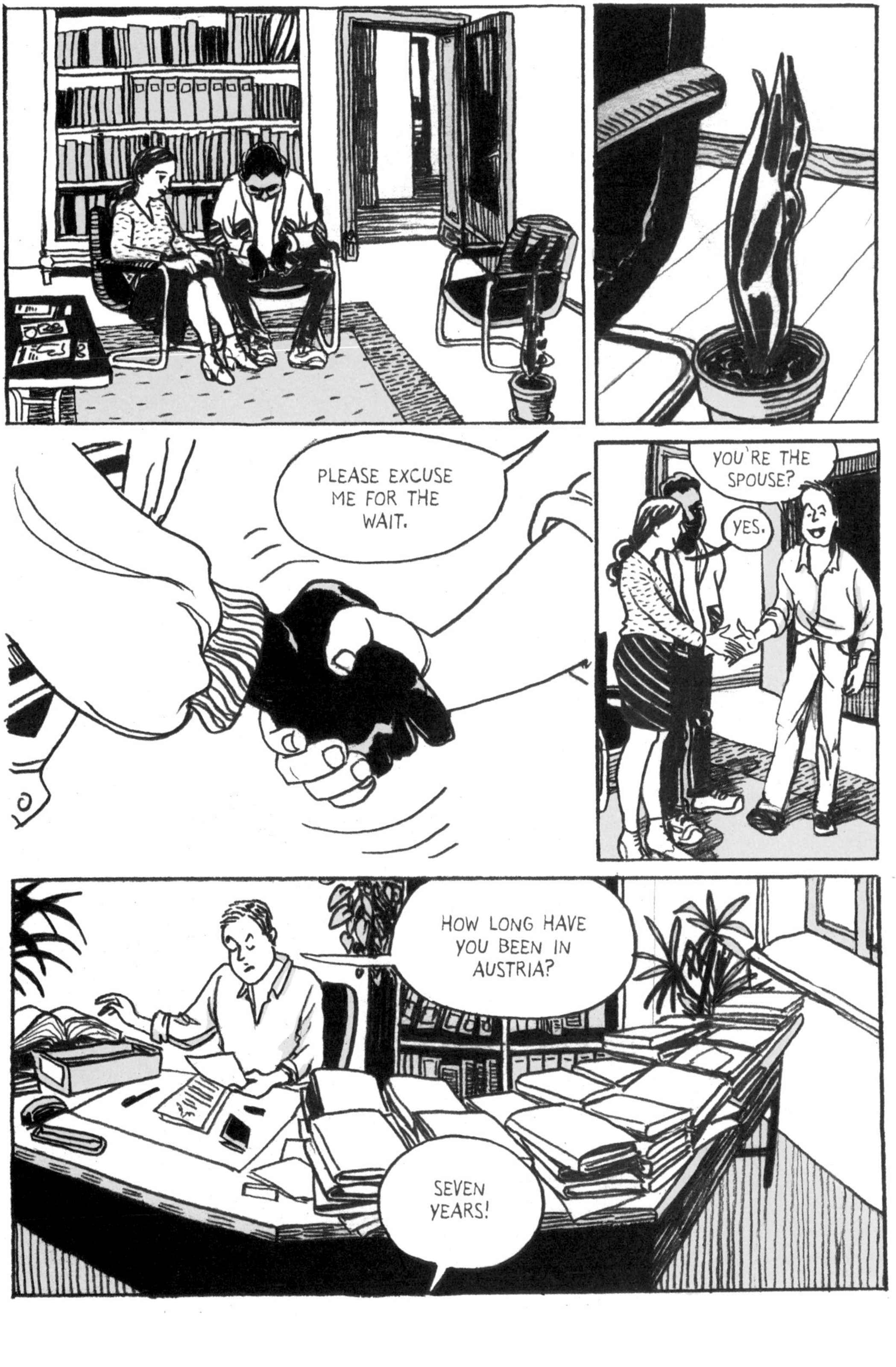
PLEASE EXCUSE ME FOR THE WAIT.
YOU'RE THE SPOUSE?
YES.
HOW LONG HAVE YOU BEEN IN AUSTRIA?
SEVEN YEARS!

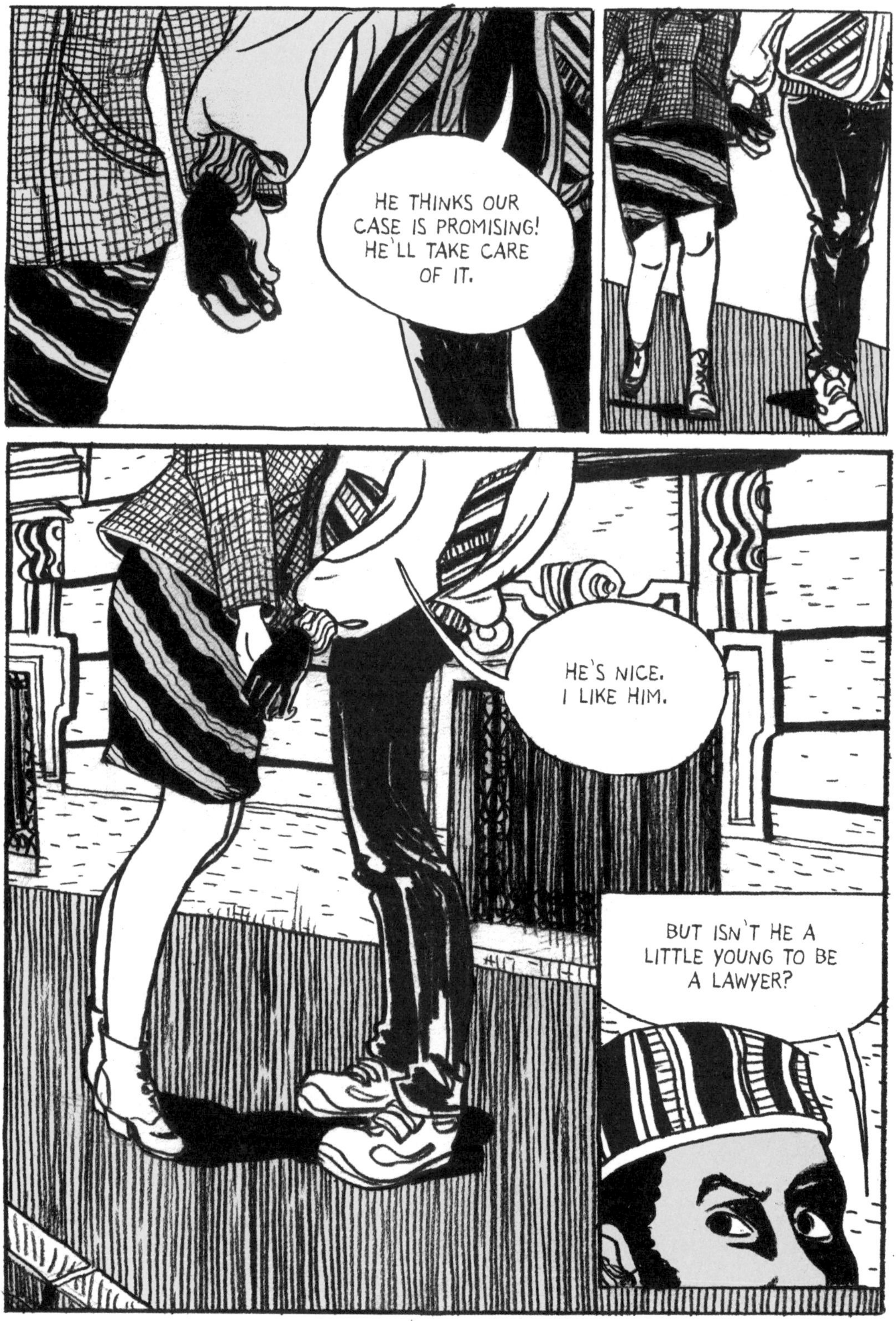
HE THINKS OUR CASE IS PROMISING! HE'LL TAKE CARE OF IT.
HE'S NICE. I LIKE HIM.
BUT ISN'T HE A LITTLE YOUNG TO BE A LAWYER?

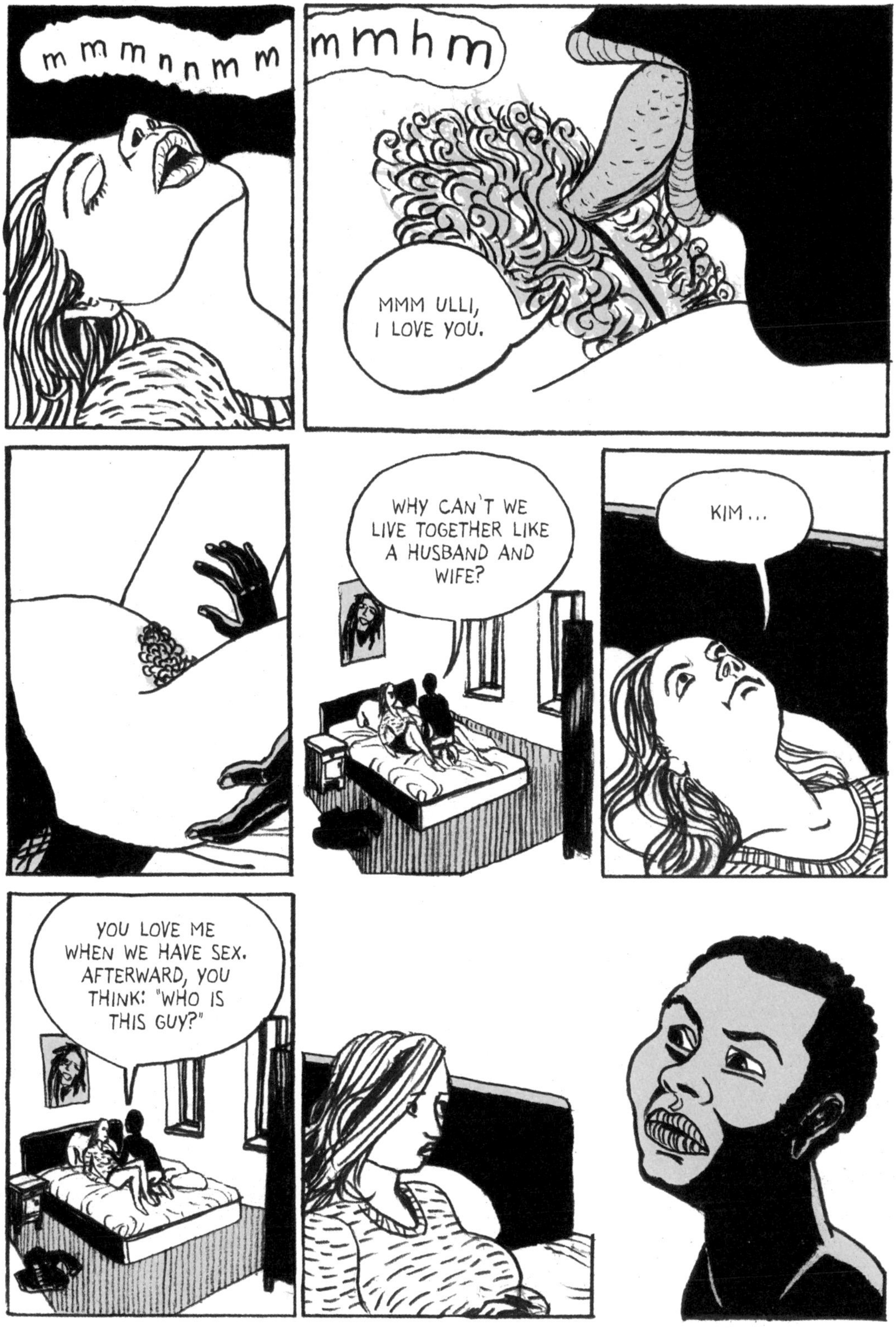
mmmnnmm
mmhm
MMM ULLI, I LOVE YOU.
WHY CAN'T WE LIVE TOGETHER LIKE A HUSBAND AND WIFE?
KIM...
YOU LOVE ME WHEN WE HAVE SEX. AFTERWARD, YOU THINK: "WHO IS THIS GUY?"

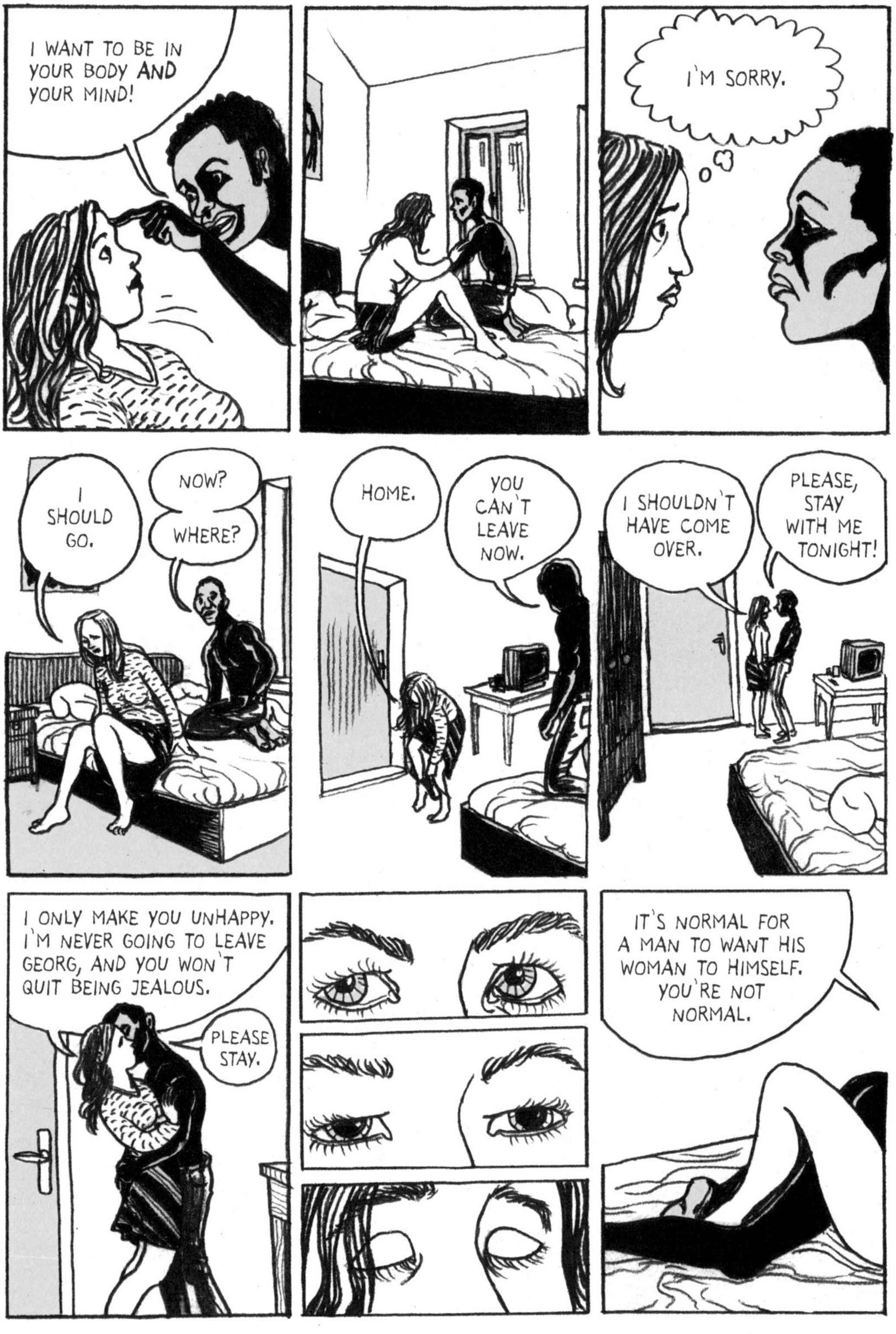
I WANT TO BE IN YOUR BODY AND YOUR MIND!
I'M SORRY.
I SHOULD GO.
NOW?
WHERE?
HOME.
YOU CAN'T LEAVE NOW.
I SHOULDN'T HAVE COME OVER.
PLEASE, STAY WITH ME TONIGHT!
I ONLY MAKE YOU UNHAPPY. I'M NEVER GOING TO LEAVE GEORG, AND YOU WON'T QUIT BEING JEALOUS.
PLEASE STAY.
IT'S NORMAL FOR A MAN TO WANT HIS WOMAN TO HIMSELF. YOU'RE NOT NORMAL.

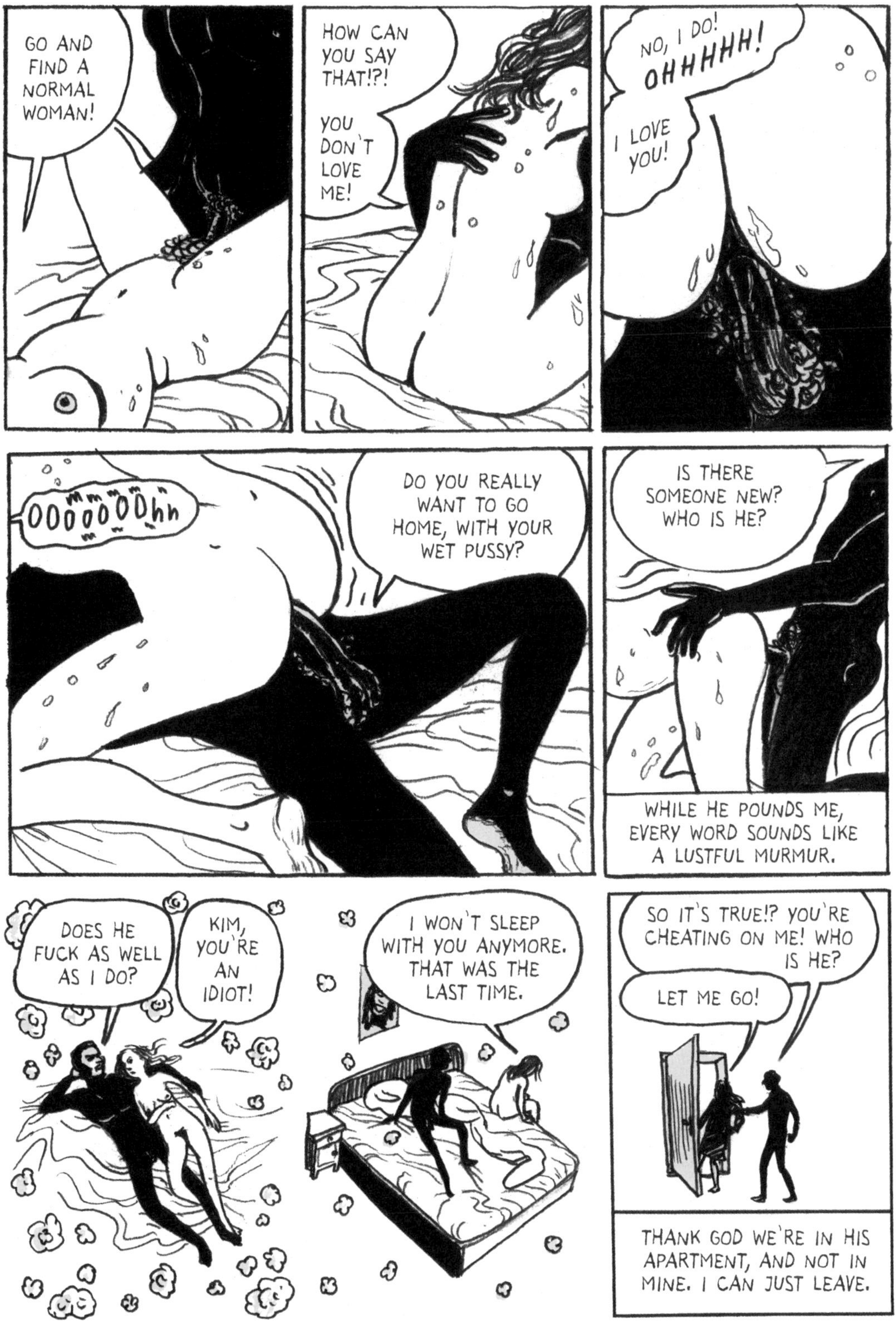
GO AND FIND A NORMAL WOMAN!
HOW CAN YOU SAY THAT!?!
YOU DON'T LOVE ME!
NO, I DO!
OHHHHH!
I LOVE YOU!
OOOOOOOhn
DO YOU REALLY WANT TO GO HOME, WITH YOUR WET PUSSY?
IS THERE SOMEONE NEW? WHO IS HE?
WHILE HE POUNDS ME, EVERY WORD SOUNDS LIKE A LUSTFUL MURMUR.
DOES HE FUCK AS WELL AS I DO?
KIM, YOU'RE AN IDIOT!
I WON'T SLEEP WITH YOU ANYMORE. THAT WAS THE LAST TIME.
SO IT'S TRUE!? YOU'RE CHEATING ON ME! WHO IS HE?
LET ME GO!
THANK GOD WE'RE IN HIS APARTMENT, AND NOT IN MINE. I CAN JUST LEAVE.

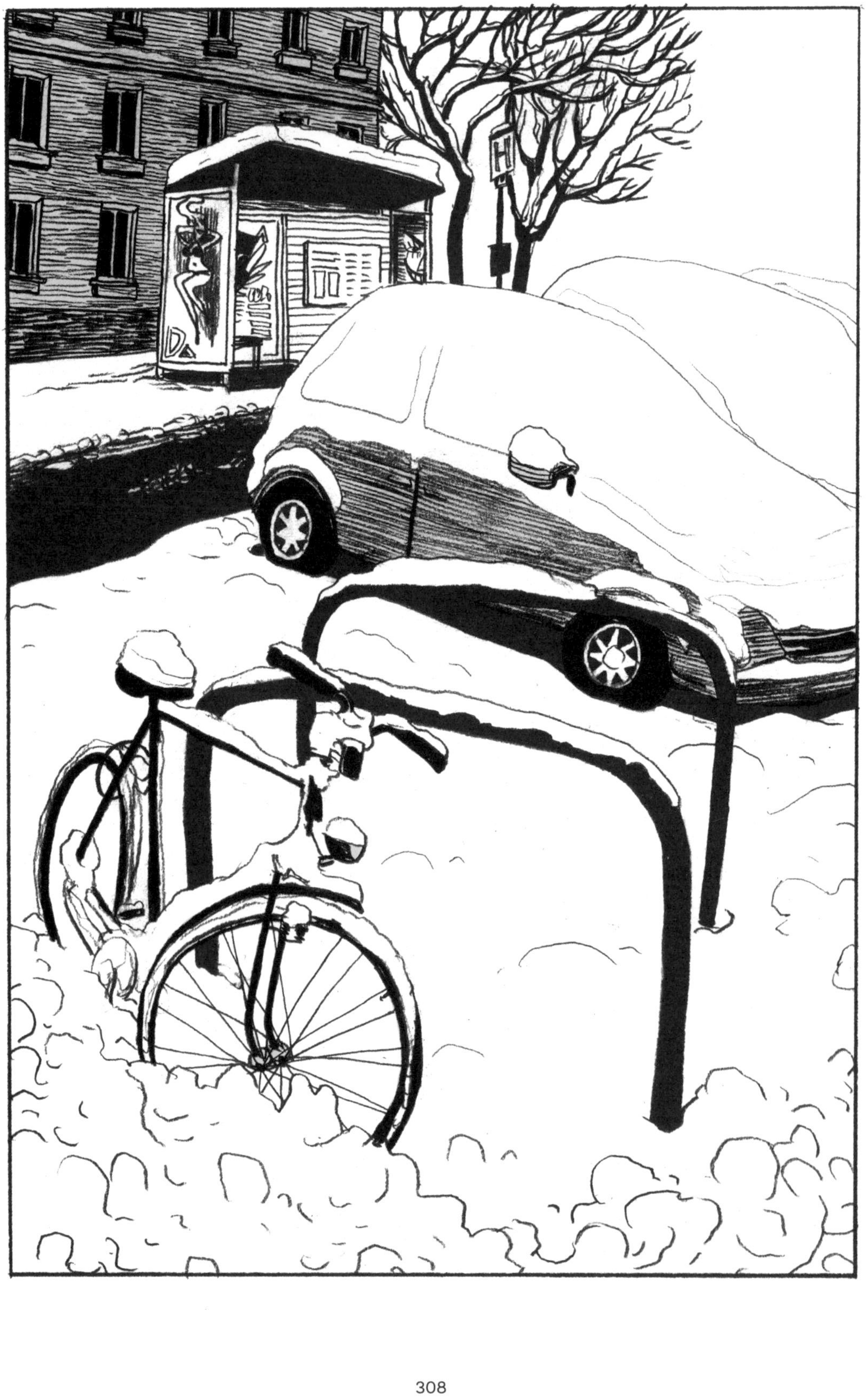

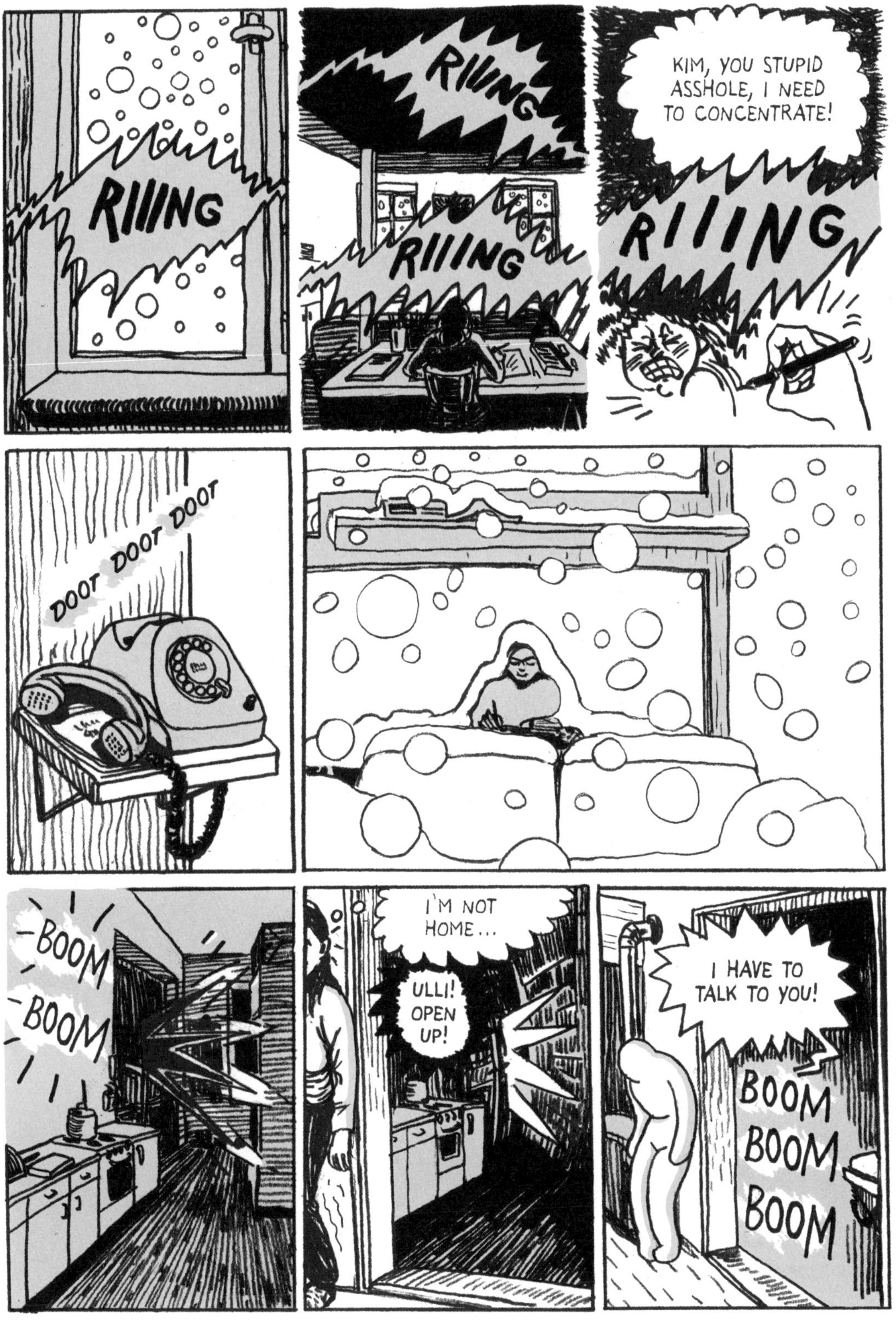
RIIING
RIIING
RIIING
KIM, YOU STUPID ASSHOLE, I NEED TO CONCENTRATE!
RIIING
DOOT DOOT DOOT
BOOM
BOOM
I'M NOT HOME...
ULLI! OPEN UP!
I HAVE TO TALK TO YOU!
BOOM
BOOM
BOOM

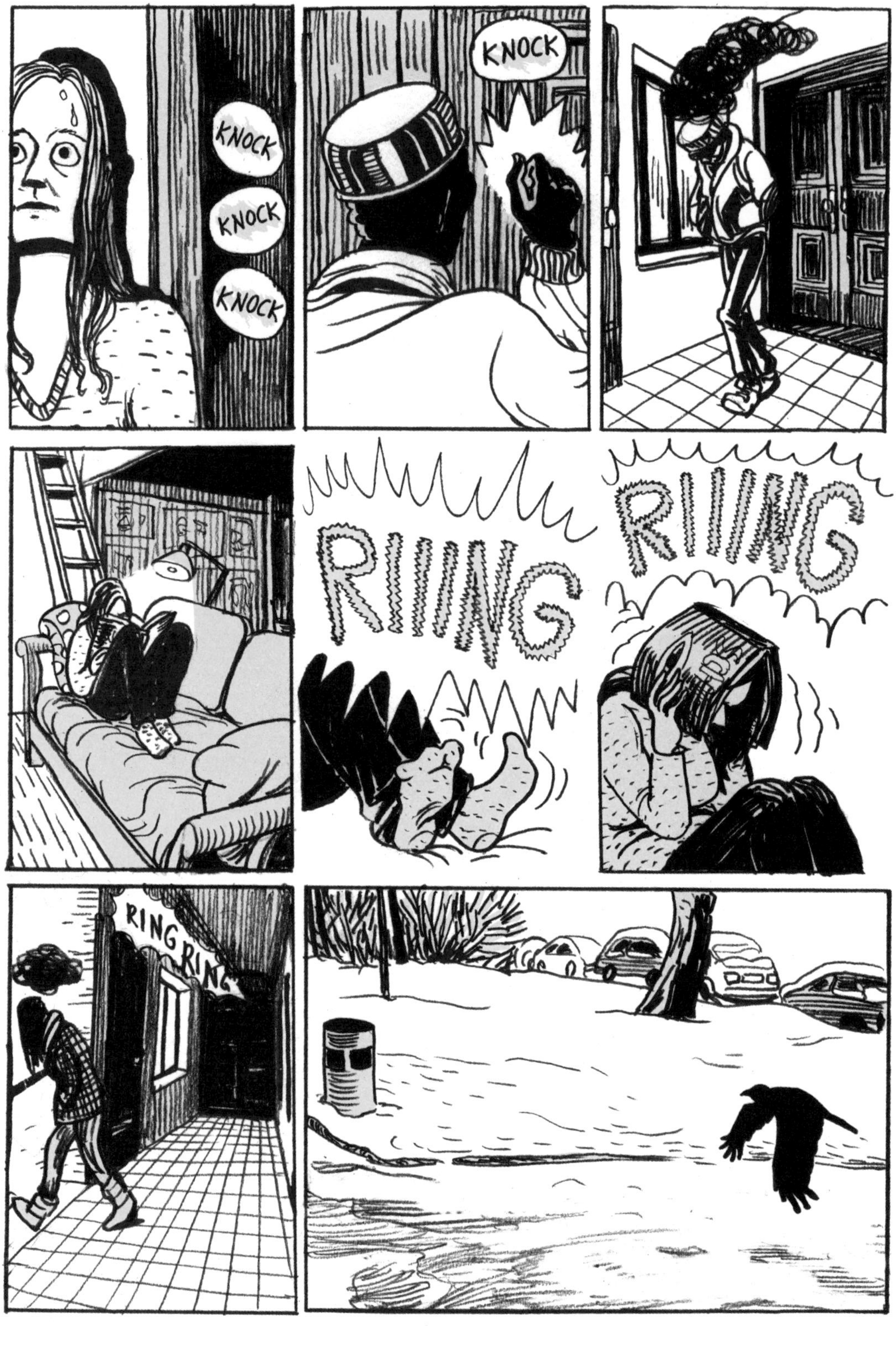
KNOCK
KNOCK
KNOCK
KNOCK
RIIING
RIIING
RING
RING
RING

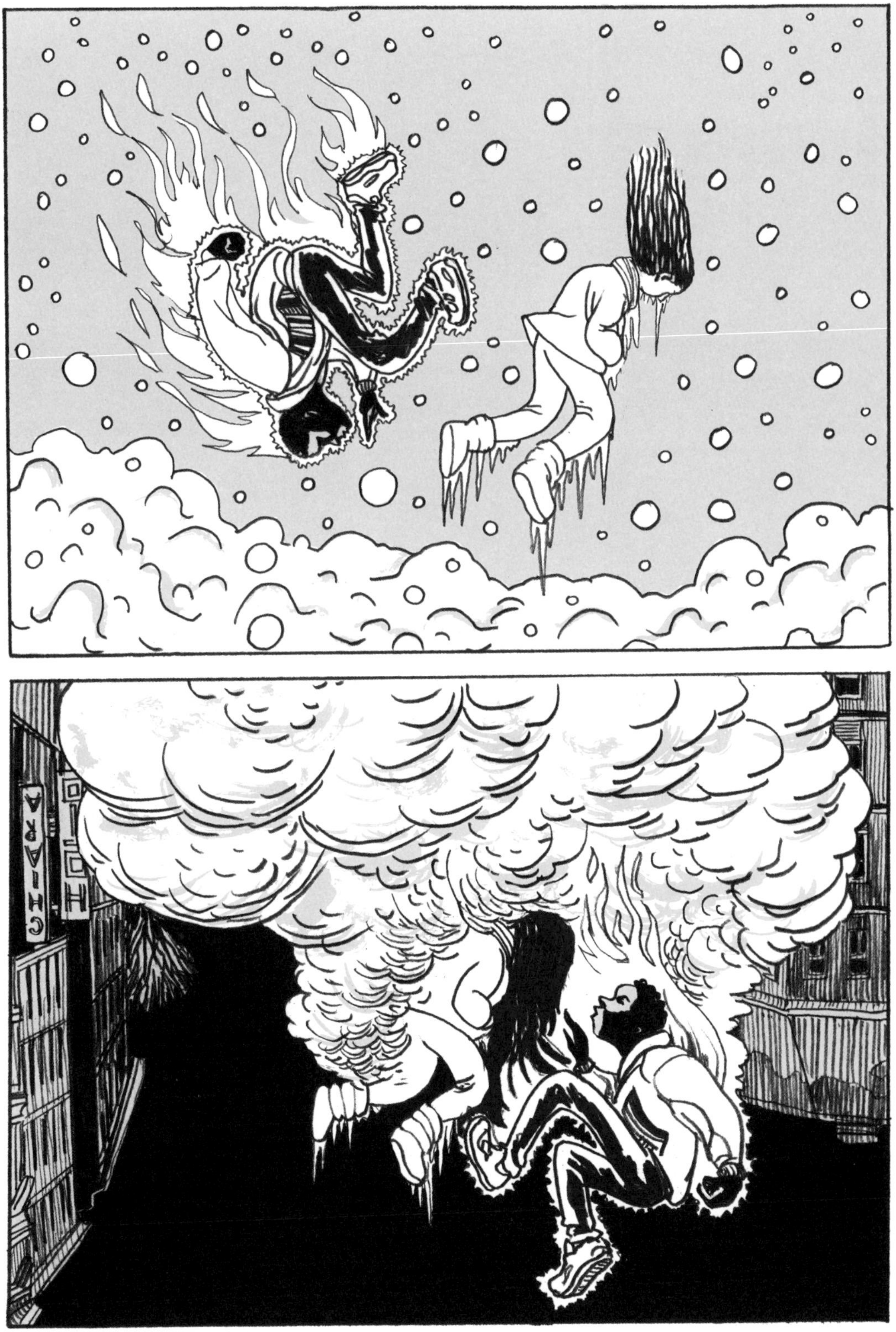

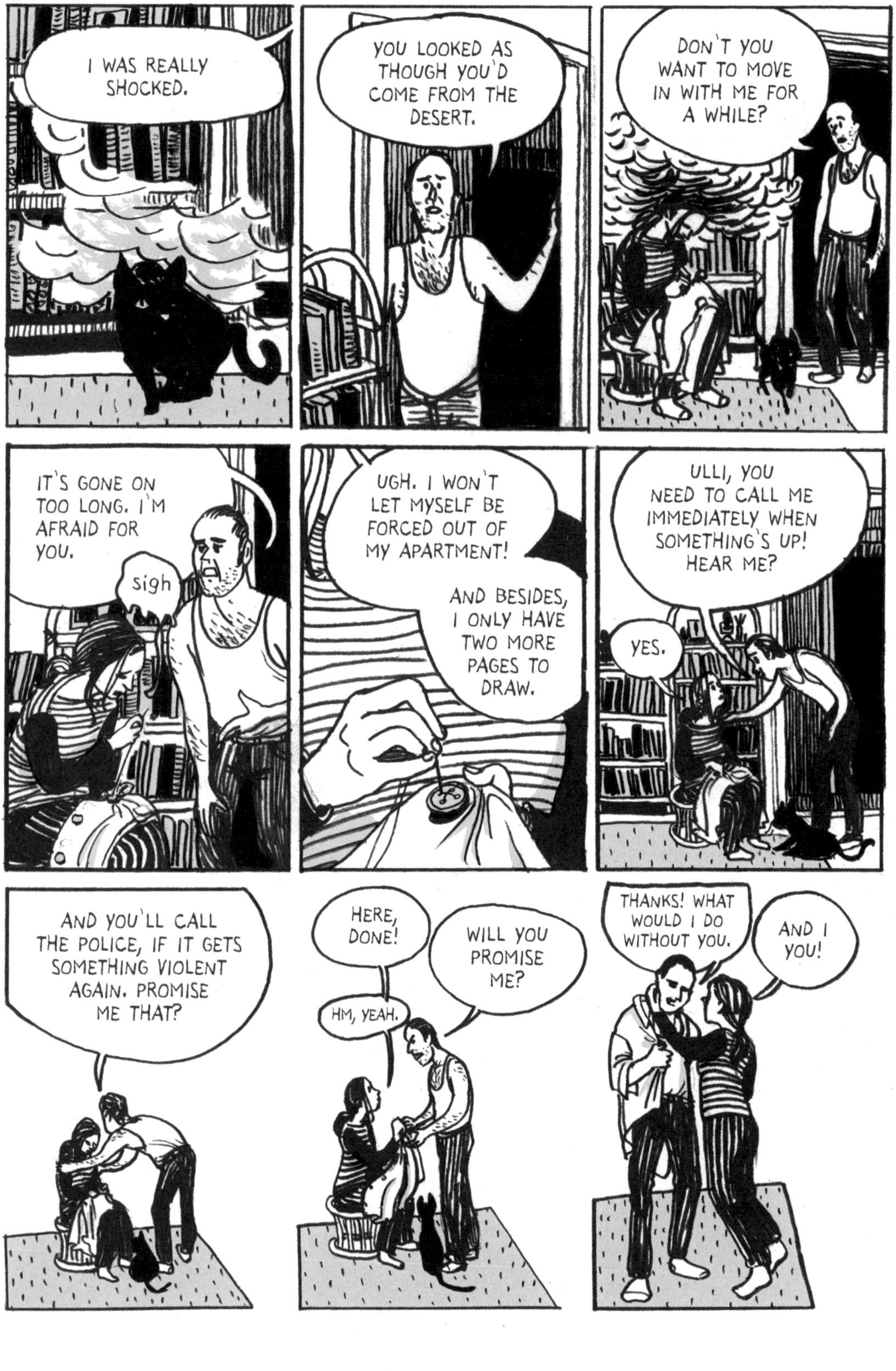
I WAS REALLY SHOCKED.
YOU LOOKED AS THOUGH YOU'D COME FROM THE DESERT.
DON'T YOU WANT TO MOVE IN WITH ME FOR A WHILE?
IT'S GONE ON TOO LONG. I'M AFRAID FOR YOU.
sigh
UGH. I WON'T LET MYSELF BE FORCED OUT OF MY APARTMENT!
AND BESIDES, I ONLY HAVE TWO MORE PAGES TO DRAW.
ULLI, YOU NEED TO CALL ME IMMEDIATELY WHEN SOMETHING'S UP! HEAR ME?
YES.
AND YOU'LL CALL THE POLICE, IF IT GETS SOMETHING VIOLENT AGAIN. PROMISE ME THAT?
HERE, DONE!
WILL YOU PROMISE ME?
HM, YEAH.
THANKS! WHAT WOULD I DO WITHOUT YOU.
AND I YOU!

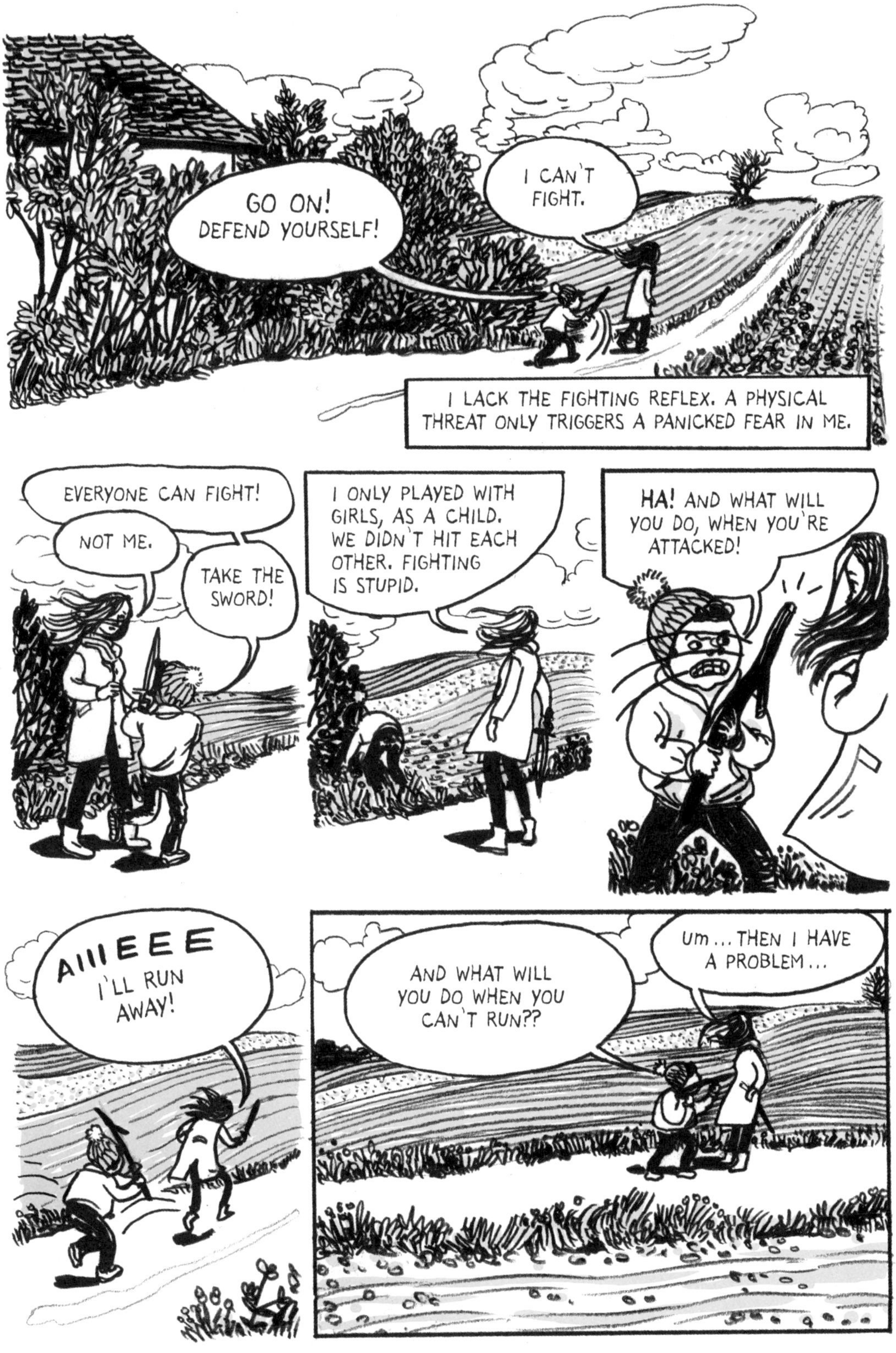
GO ON!
DEFEND YOURSELF!
I CAN'T FIGHT.
I LACK THE FIGHTING REFLEX. A PHYSICAL THREAT ONLY TRIGGERS A PANICKED FEAR IN ME.
EVERYONE CAN FIGHT!
NOT ME.
TAKE THE SWORD!
I ONLY PLAYED WITH GIRLS, AS A CHILD. WE DIDN'T HIT EACH OTHER. FIGHTING IS STUPID.
HA! AND WHAT WILL YOU DO, WHEN YOU'RE ATTACKED!
AIIIEEE
I'LL RUN AWAY!
AND WHAT WILL YOU DO WHEN YOU CAN'T RUN??
um ... THEN I HAVE A PROBLEM ...

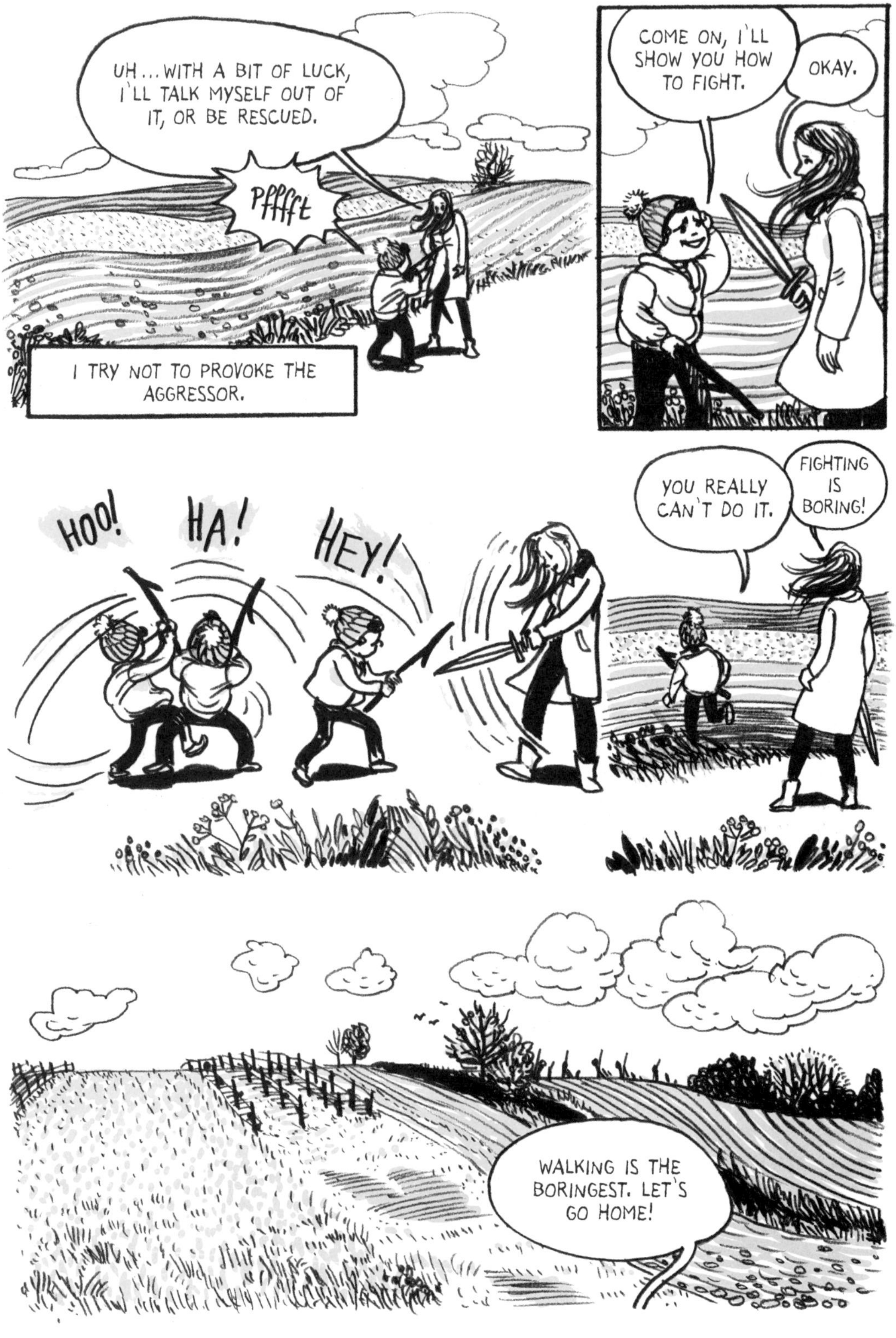
UH... WITH A BIT OF LUCK, I'LL TALK MYSELF OUT OF IT, OR BE RESCUED.
PFFFFT
I TRY NOT TO PROVOKE THE AGGRESSOR.
COME ON, I'LL SHOW YOU HOW TO FIGHT.
OKAY.
HOO!
HA!
HEY!
YOU REALLY CAN'T DO IT.
FIGHTING IS BORING!
WALKING IS THE BORINGEST. LET'S GO HOME!

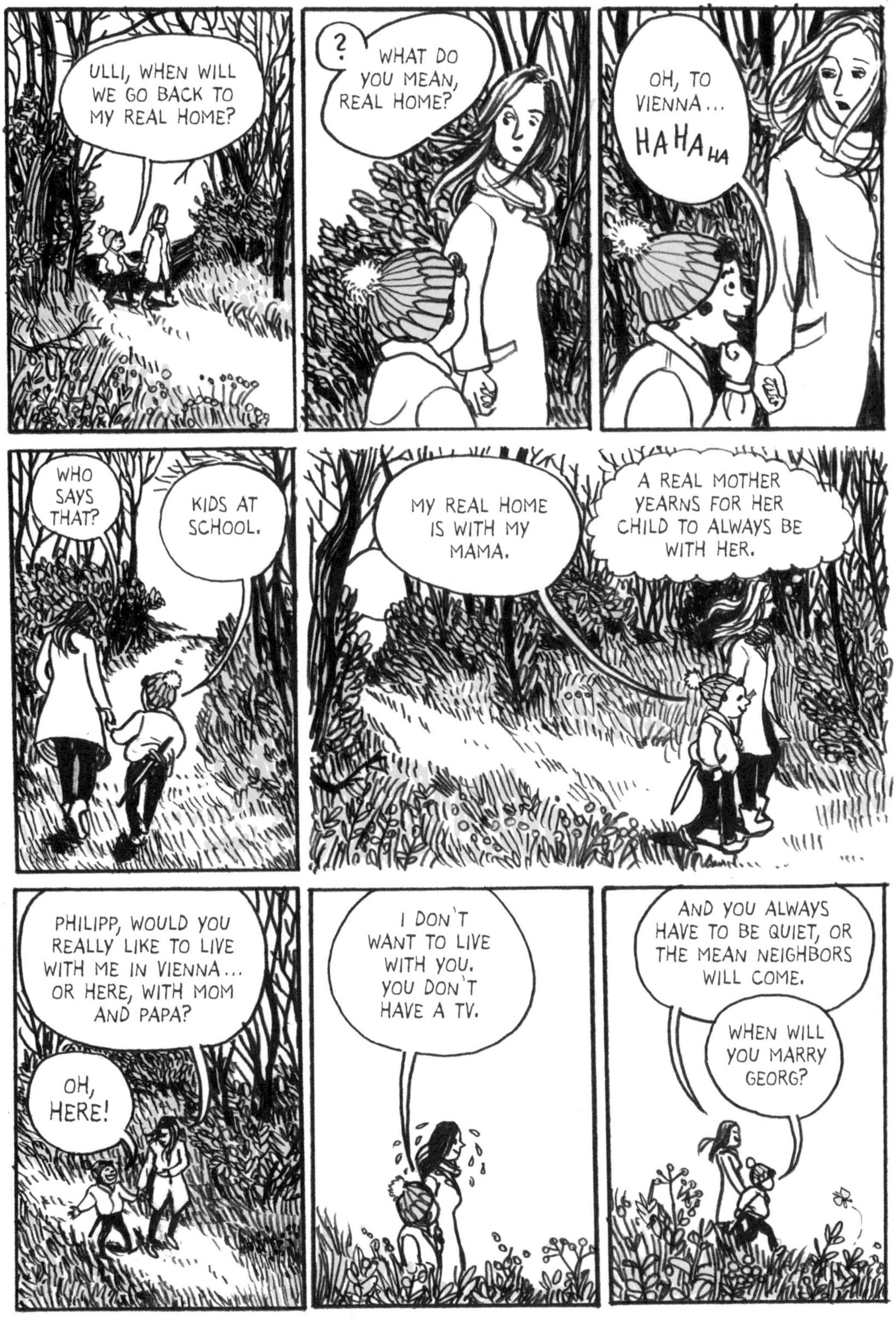
ULLI, WHEN WILL WE GO BACK TO MY REAL HOME?
?
WHAT DO YOU MEAN, REAL HOME?
OH, TO VIENNA... HAHAHA
WHO SAYS THAT?
KIDS AT SCHOOL.
MY REAL HOME IS WITH MY MAMA.
A REAL MOTHER YEARNS FOR HER CHILD TO ALWAYS BE WITH HER.
PHILIPP, WOULD YOU REALLY LIKE TO LIVE WITH ME IN VIENNA... OR HERE, WITH MOM AND PAPA?
OH, HERE!
I DON'T WANT TO LIVE WITH YOU. YOU DON'T HAVE A TV.
AND YOU ALWAYS HAVE TO BE QUIET, OR THE MEAN NEIGHBORS WILL COME.
WHEN WILL YOU MARRY GEORG?

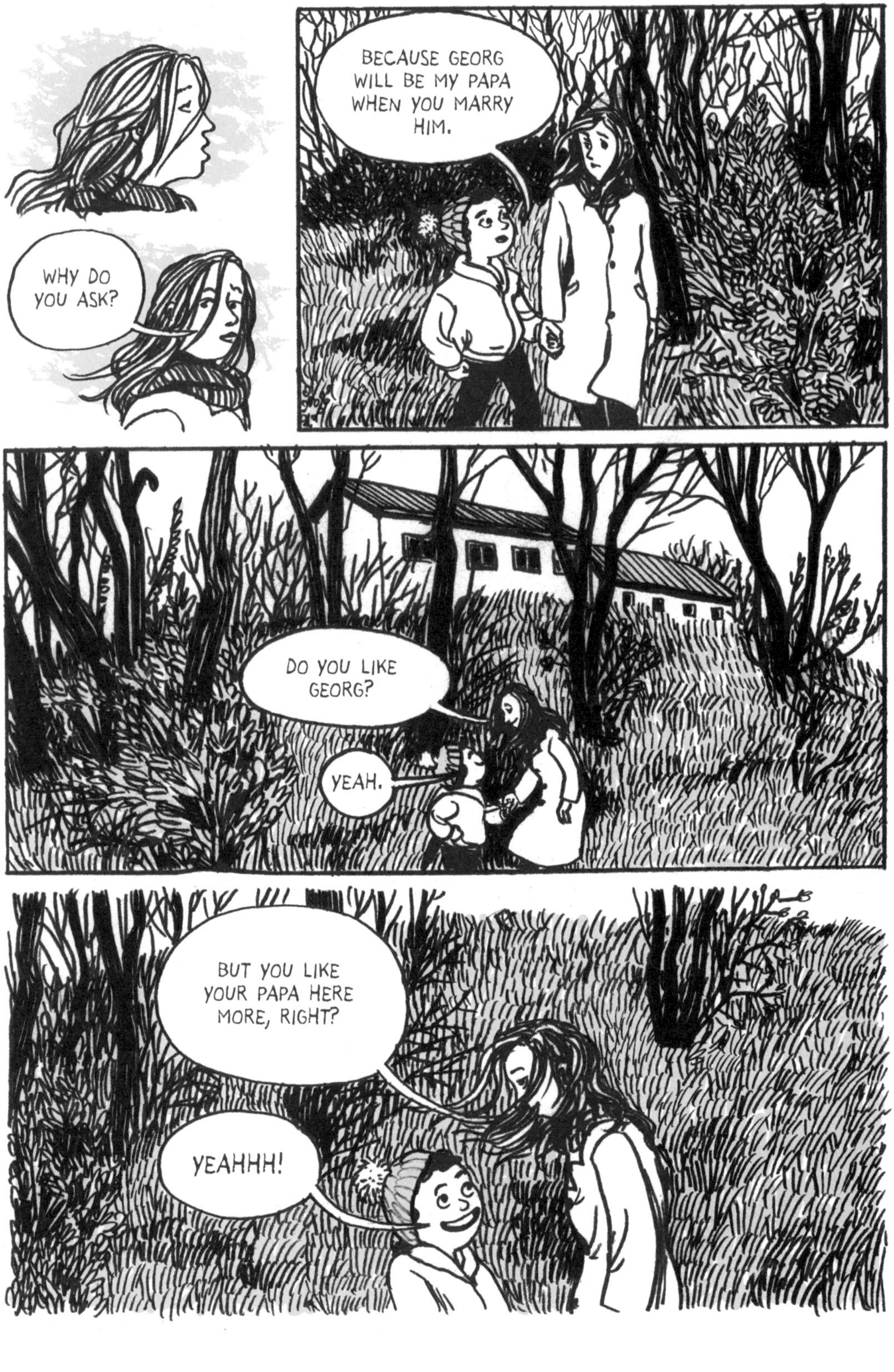
WHY DO YOU ASK?
BECAUSE GEORG WILL BE MY PAPA WHEN YOU MARRY HIM.
DO YOU LIKE GEORG?
YEAH.
BUT YOU LIKE YOUR PAPA HERE MORE, RIGHT?
YEAHHH!

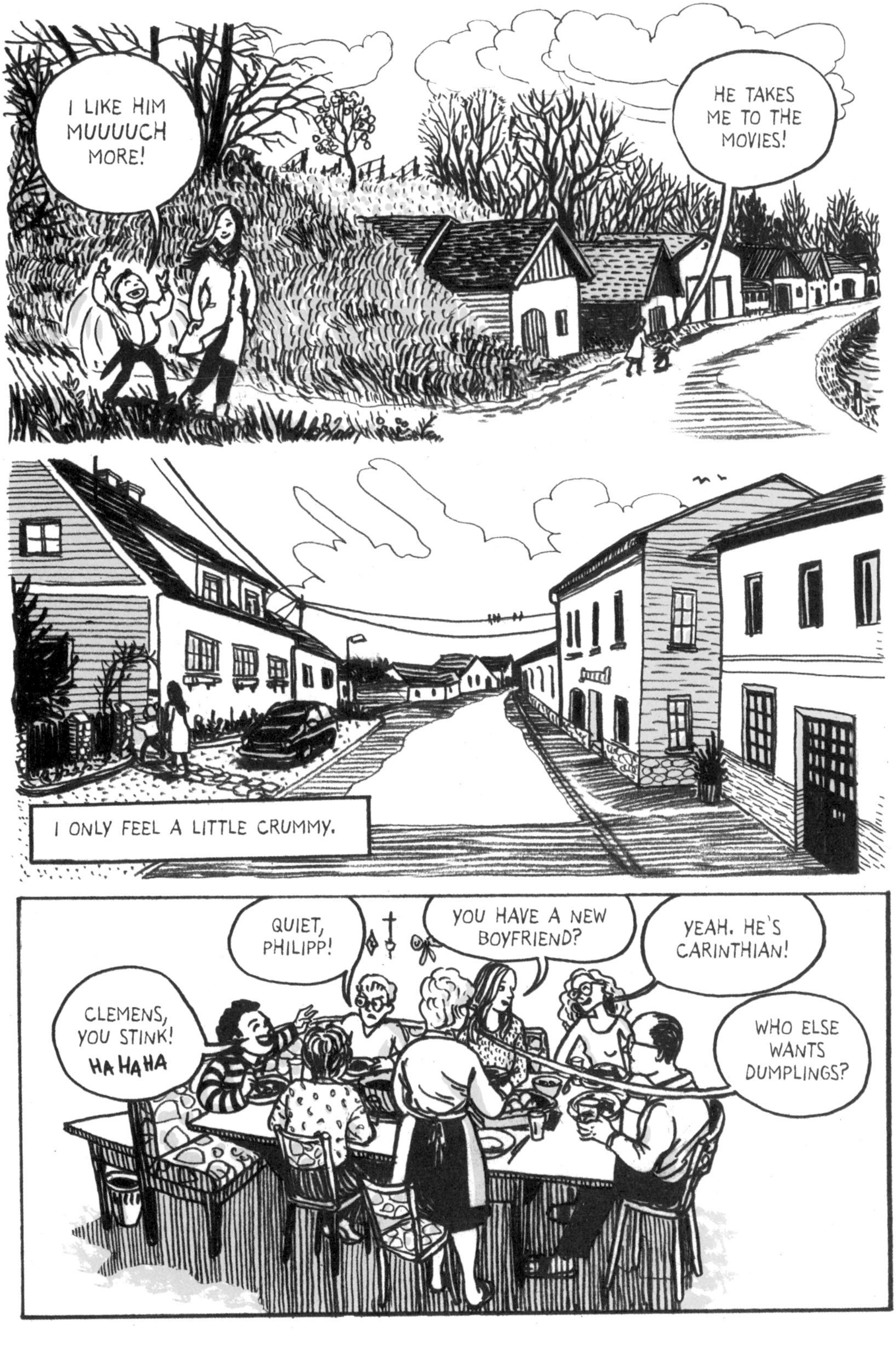
I LIKE HIM MUUUUCH MORE!
HE TAKES ME TO THE MOVIES!
I ONLY FEEL A LITTLE CRUMMY.
QUIET, PHILIPP!
YOU HAVE A NEW BOYFRIEND?
YEAH. HE'S CARINTHIAN!
CLEMENS, YOU STINK! HA HA HA
WHO ELSE WANTS DUMPLINGS?

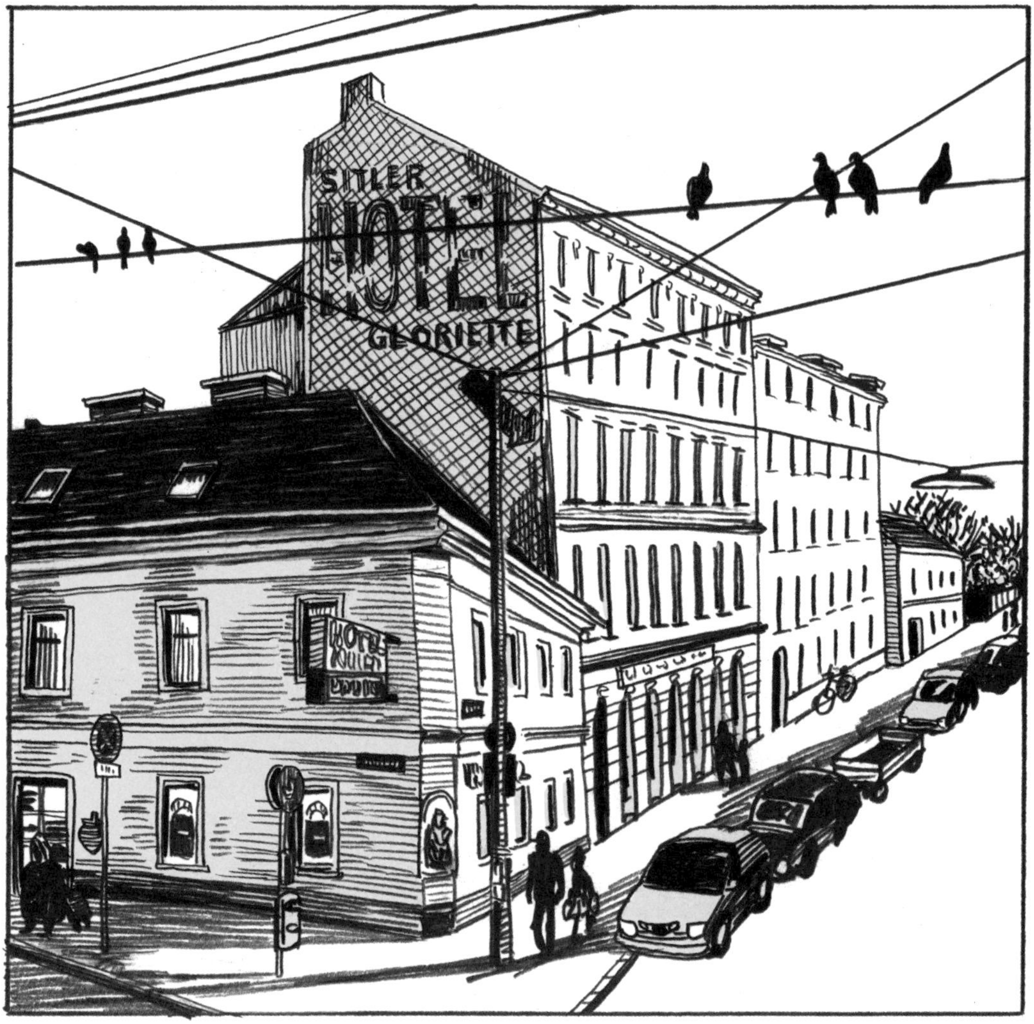
SITLER
HOTEL
GLORIETTE

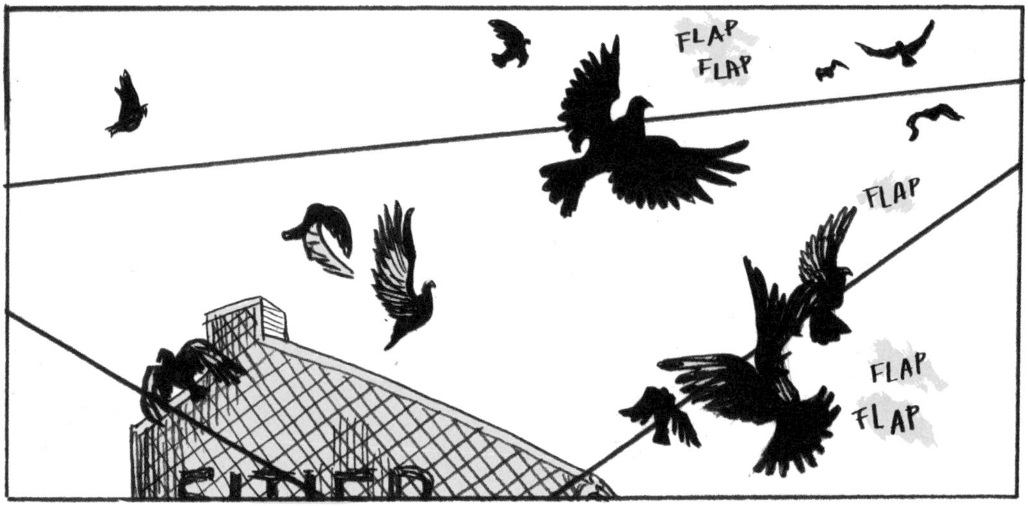
FLAP
FLAP
FLAP
FLAP
FLAP

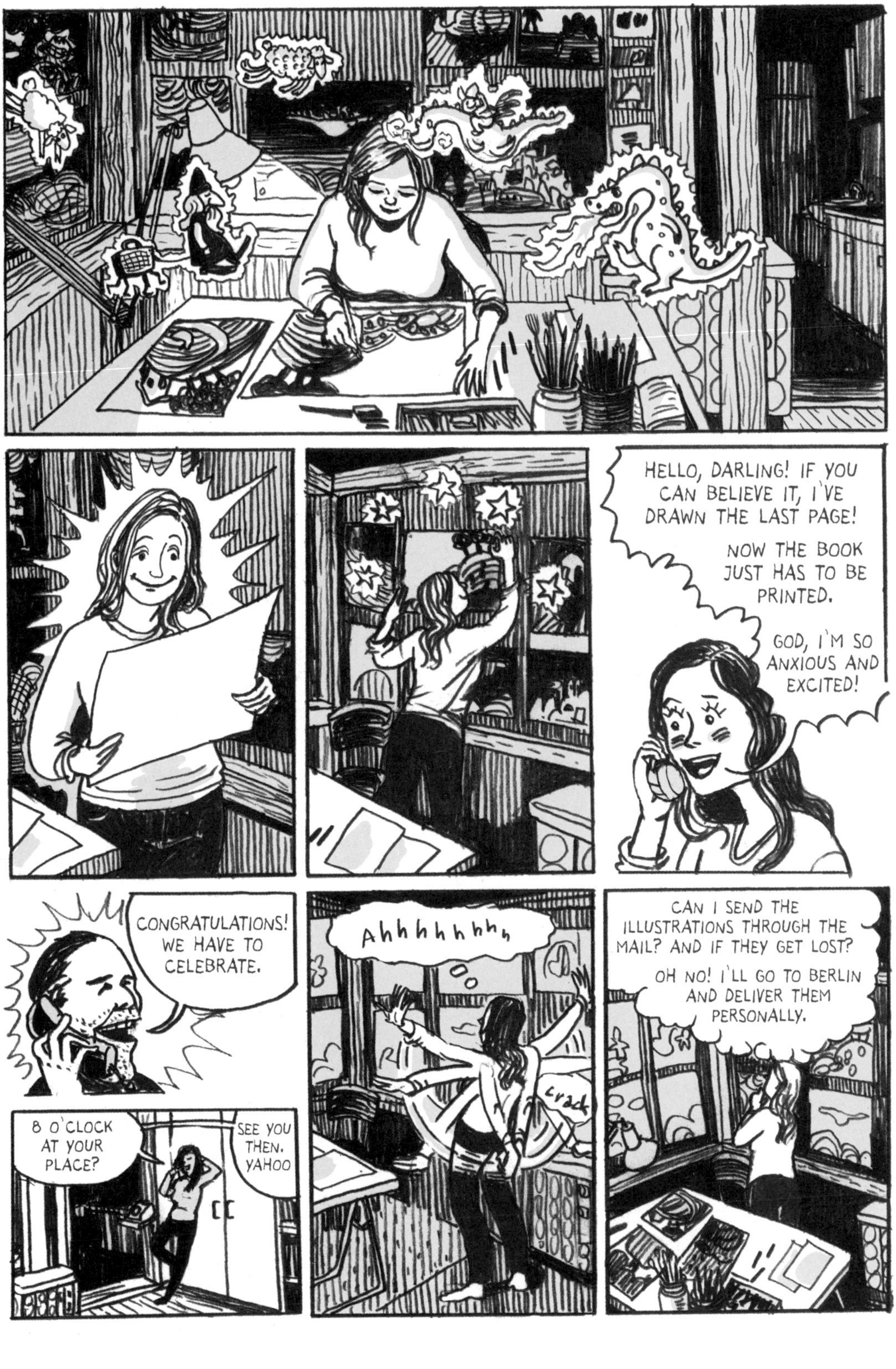
HELLO, DARLING! IF YOU CAN BELIEVE IT, I'VE DRAWN THE LAST PAGE!
NOW THE BOOK JUST HAS TO BE PRINTED.
GOD, I'M SO ANXIOUS AND EXCITED!
CONGRATULATIONS! WE HAVE TO CELEBRATE.
8 O'CLOCK AT YOUR PLACE?
SEE YOU THEN. YAHOO
Ahhhhhhhh
crack
CAN I SEND THE ILLUSTRATIONS THROUGH THE MAIL? AND IF THEY GET LOST?
OH NO! I'LL GO TO BERLIN AND DELIVER THEM PERSONALLY.

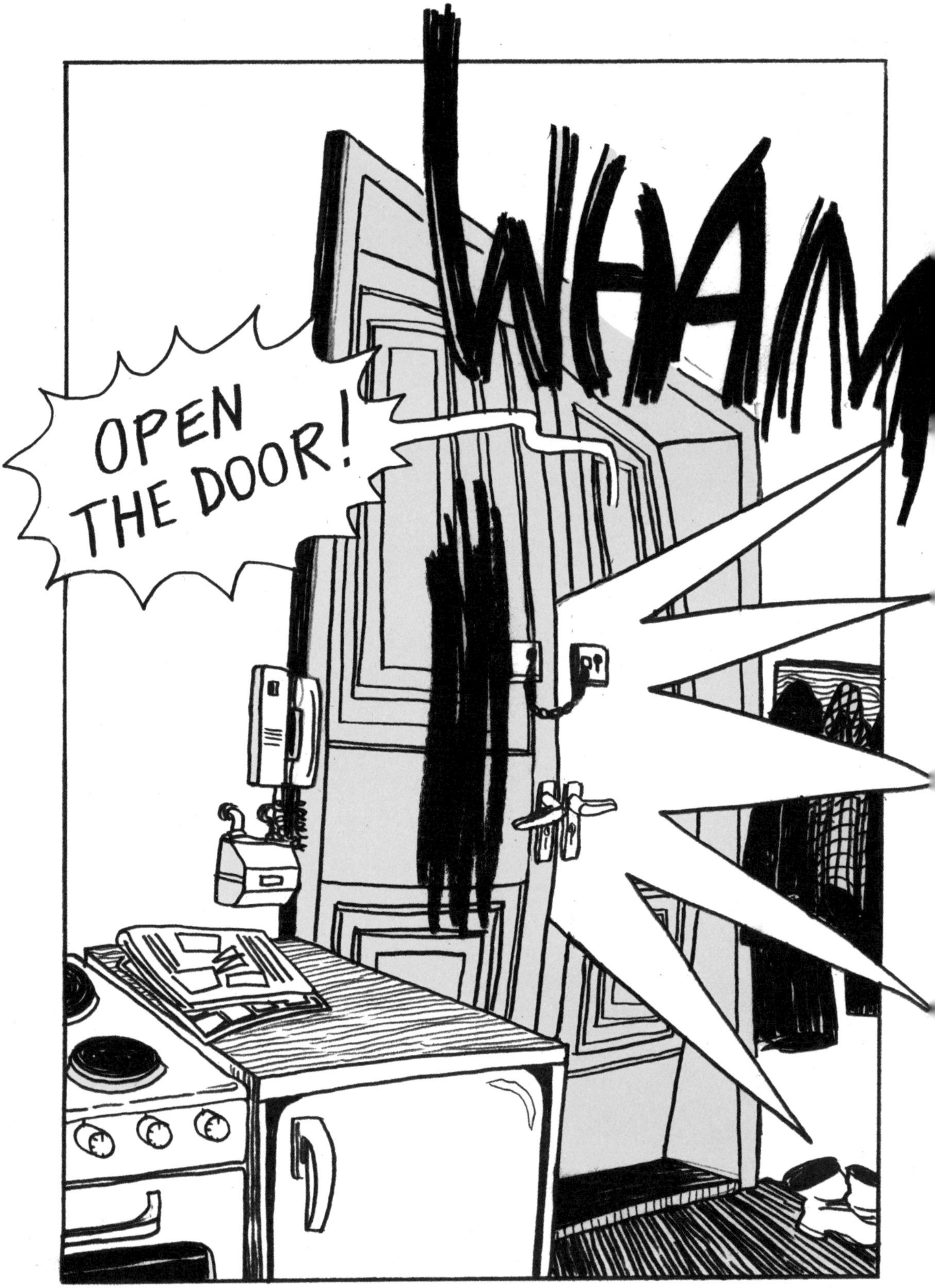
WHAM
OPEN THE DOOR!

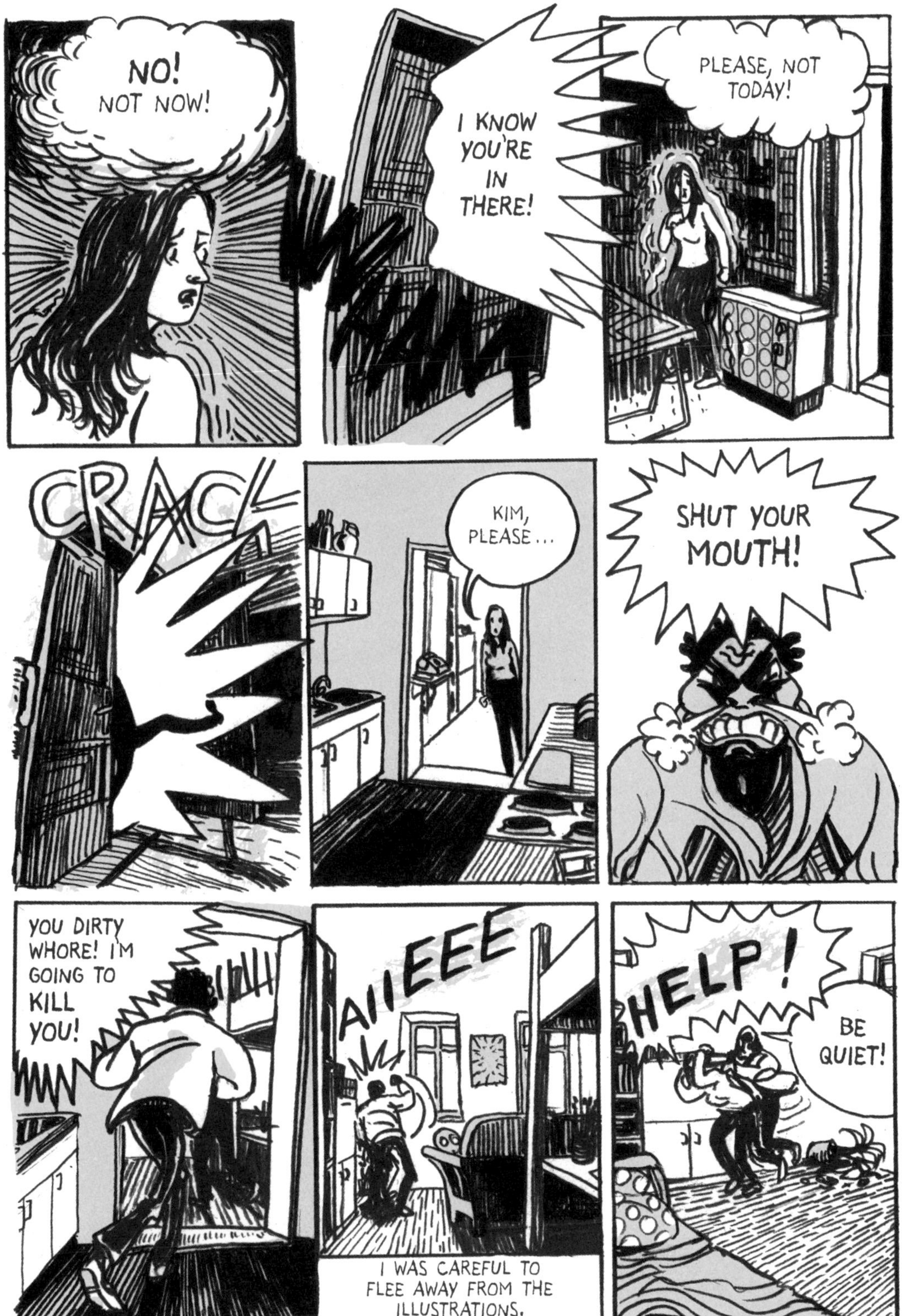
NO!
NOT NOW!
I KNOW YOU'RE IN THERE!
PLEASE, NOT TODAY!
CRACK
KIM, PLEASE...
SHUT YOUR MOUTH!
YOU DIRTY WHORE! I'M GOING TO KILL YOU!
AIIEEE
I WAS CAREFUL TO FLEE AWAY FROM THE ILLUSTRATIONS.
HELP!
BE QUIET!

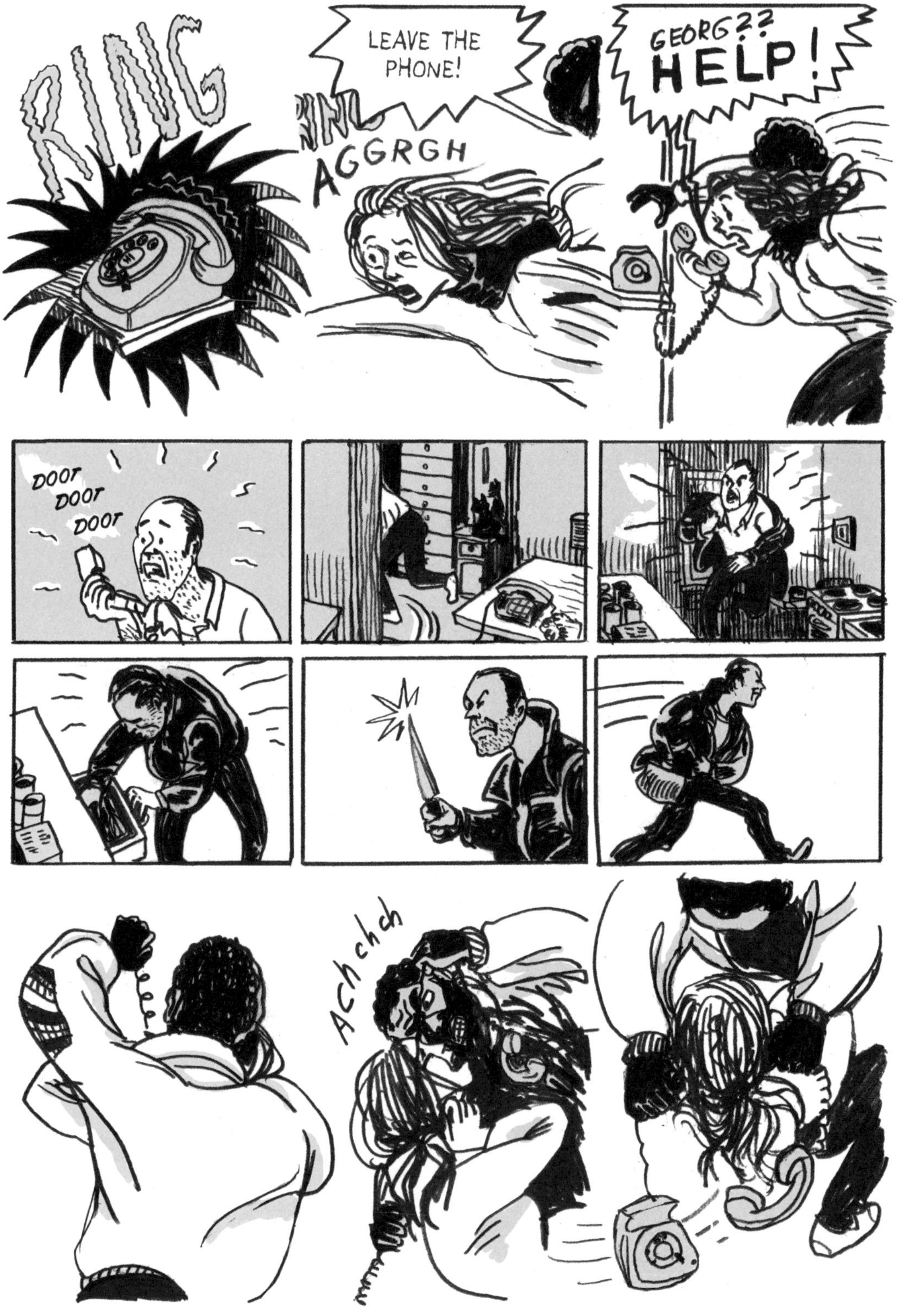
RING
LEAVE THE PHONE!
AGGRGH
GEORG??
HELP!
DOOT DOOT DOOT
Achchch

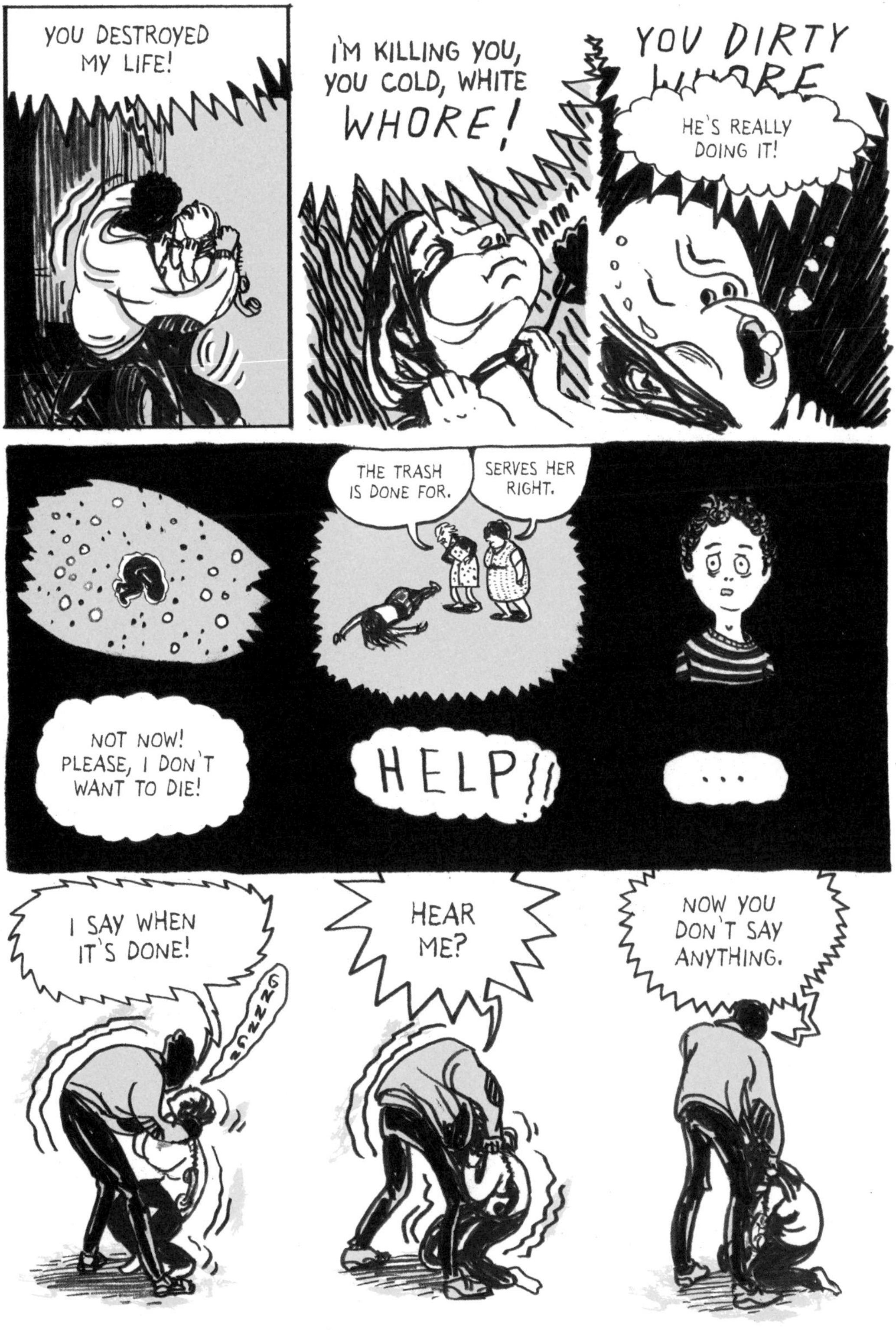
YOU DESTROYED MY LIFE!
I'M KILLING YOU, YOU COLD, WHITE WHORE!
MMM
YOU DIRTY WHORE
HE'S REALLY DOING IT!
THE TRASH IS DONE FOR.
SERVES HER RIGHT.
NOT NOW! PLEASE, I DON'T WANT TO DIE!
HELP!!
...
I SAY WHEN IT'S DONE!
HEAR ME?
NOW YOU DON'T SAY ANYTHING.

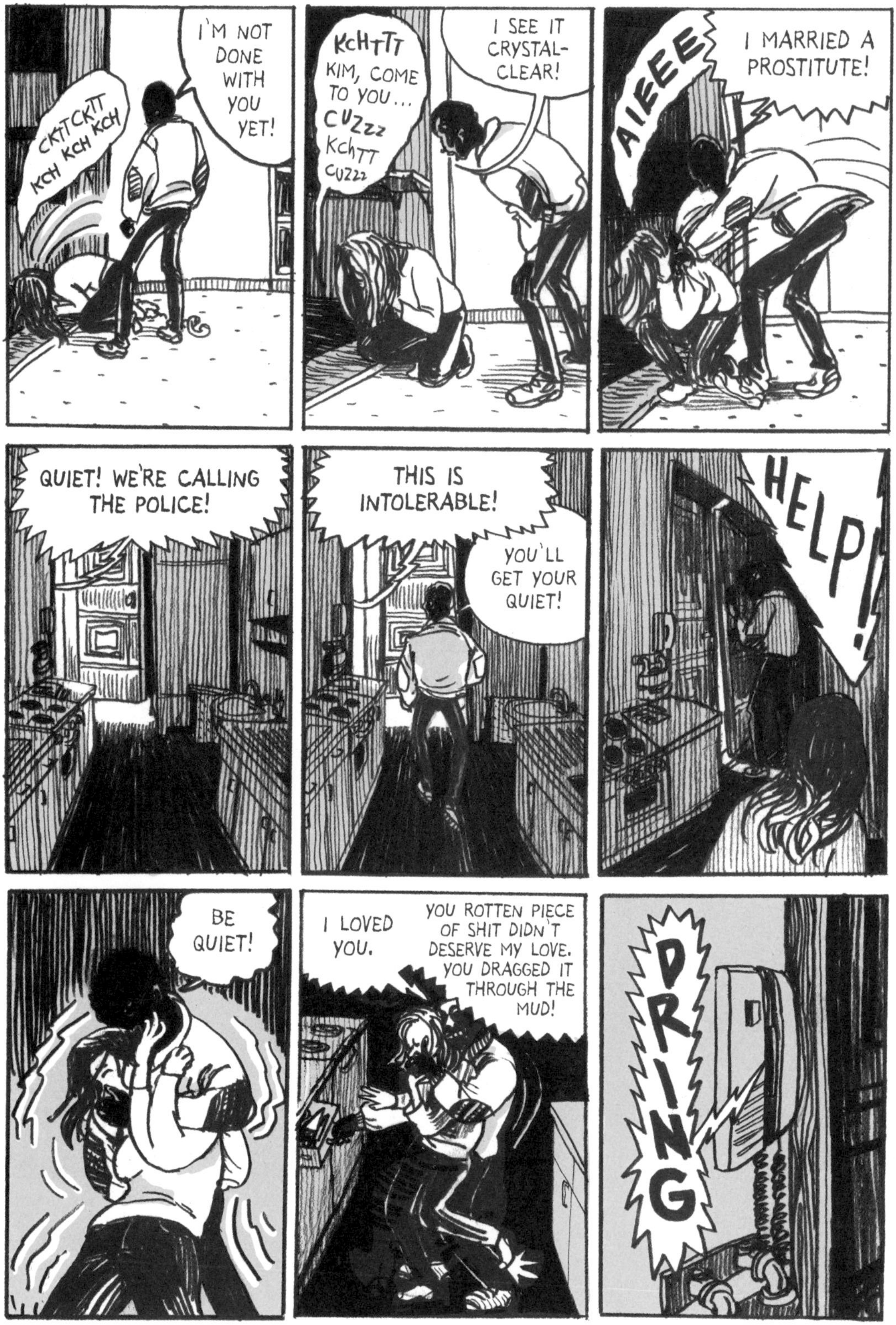
I'M NOT DONE WITH YOU YET!
CKTTCKTT KCH KCH KCH
KCHTTT KIM, COME TO YOU... CUZzz KChTT CUZzz
I SEE IT CRYSTAL-CLEAR!
AIEEE
I MARRIED A PROSTITUTE!
QUIET! WE'RE CALLING THE POLICE!
THIS IS INTOLERABLE!
YOU'LL GET YOUR QUIET!
HELP!!
BE QUIET!
I LOVED YOU.
YOU ROTTEN PIECE OF SHIT DIDN'T DESERVE MY LOVE. YOU DRAGGED IT THROUGH THE MUD!
DRING

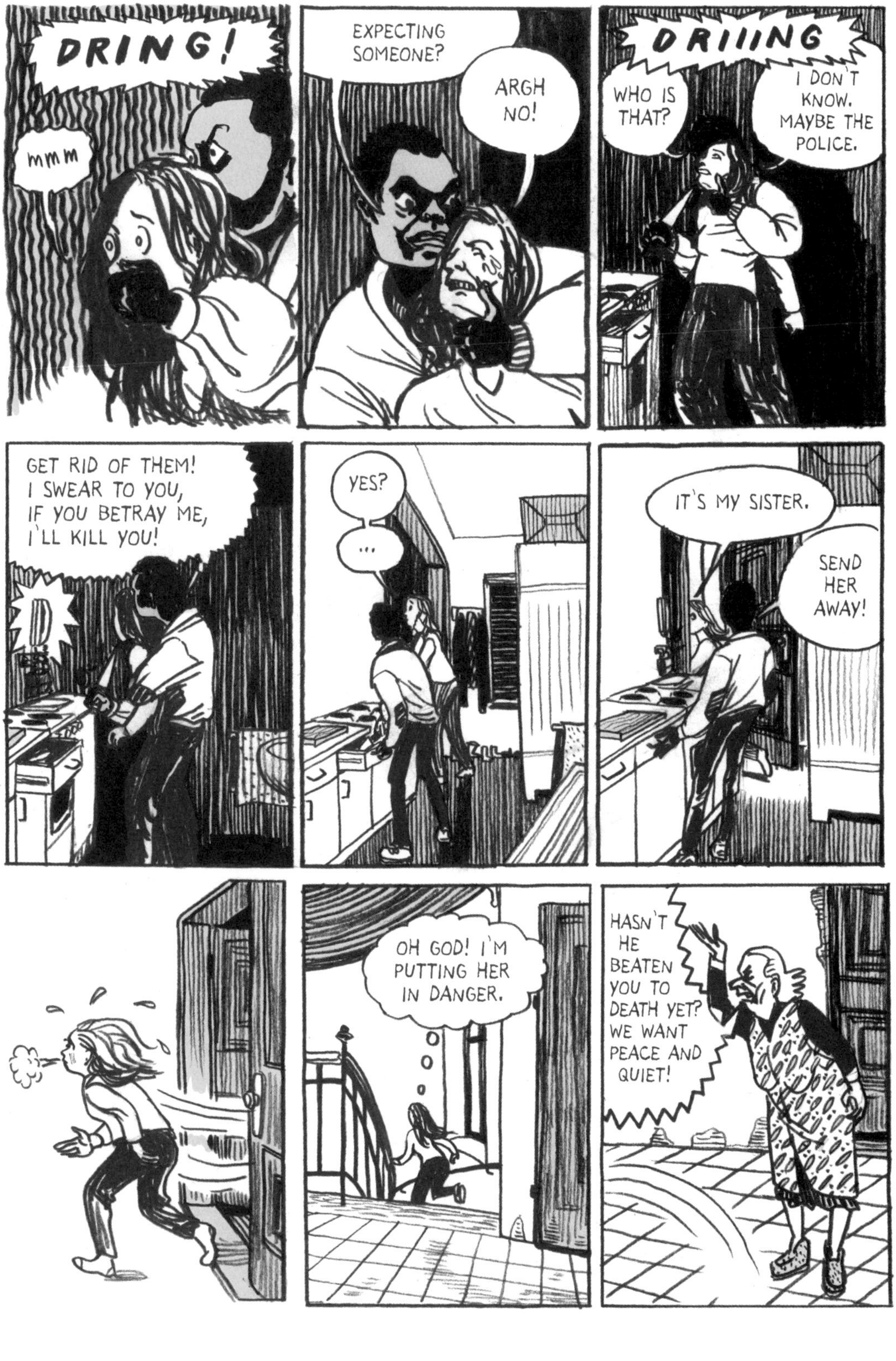
DRING!
mmm
EXPECTING SOMEONE?
ARGH NO!
DRIIING
WHO IS THAT?
I DON'T KNOW. MAYBE THE POLICE.
GET RID OF THEM! I SWEAR TO YOU, IF YOU BETRAY ME, I'LL KILL YOU!
YES?
...
IT'S MY SISTER.
SEND HER AWAY!
OH GOD! I'M PUTTING HER IN DANGER.
HASN'T HE BEATEN YOU TO DEATH YET? WE WANT PEACE AND QUIET!

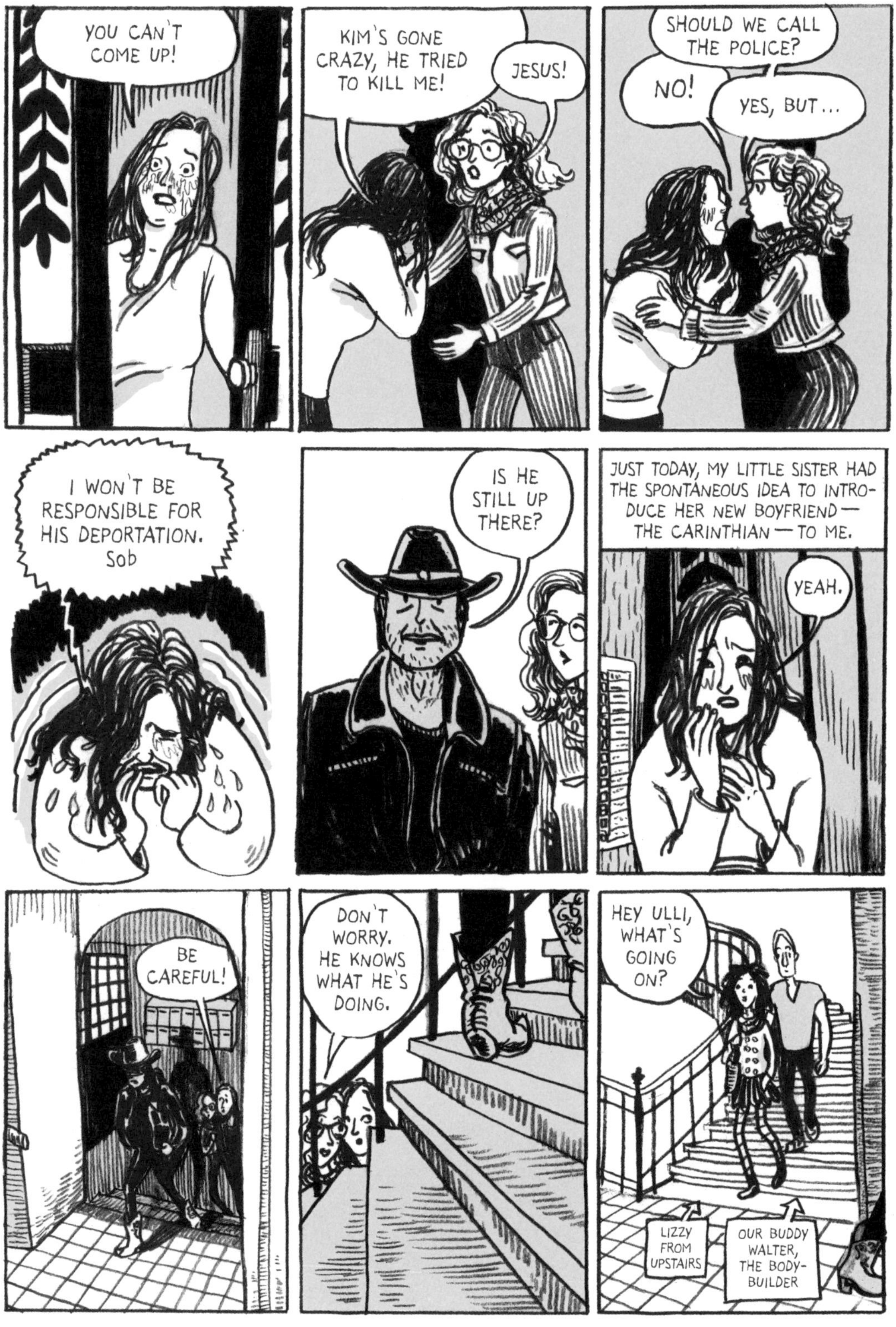
YOU CAN'T COME UP!
KIM'S GONE CRAZY, HE TRIED TO KILL ME!
JESUS!
SHOULD WE CALL THE POLICE?
NO!
YES, BUT...
I WON'T BE RESPONSIBLE FOR HIS DEPORTATION. Sob
IS HE STILL UP THERE?
JUST TODAY, MY LITTLE SISTER HAD THE SPONTANEOUS IDEA TO INTRODUCE HER NEW BOYFRIEND — THE CARINTHIAN — TO ME.
YEAH.
BE CAREFUL!
DON'T WORRY. HE KNOWS WHAT HE'S DOING.
HEY ULLI, WHAT'S GOING ON?
LIZZY FROM UPSTAIRS
OUR BUDDY WALTER, THE BODY-BUILDER

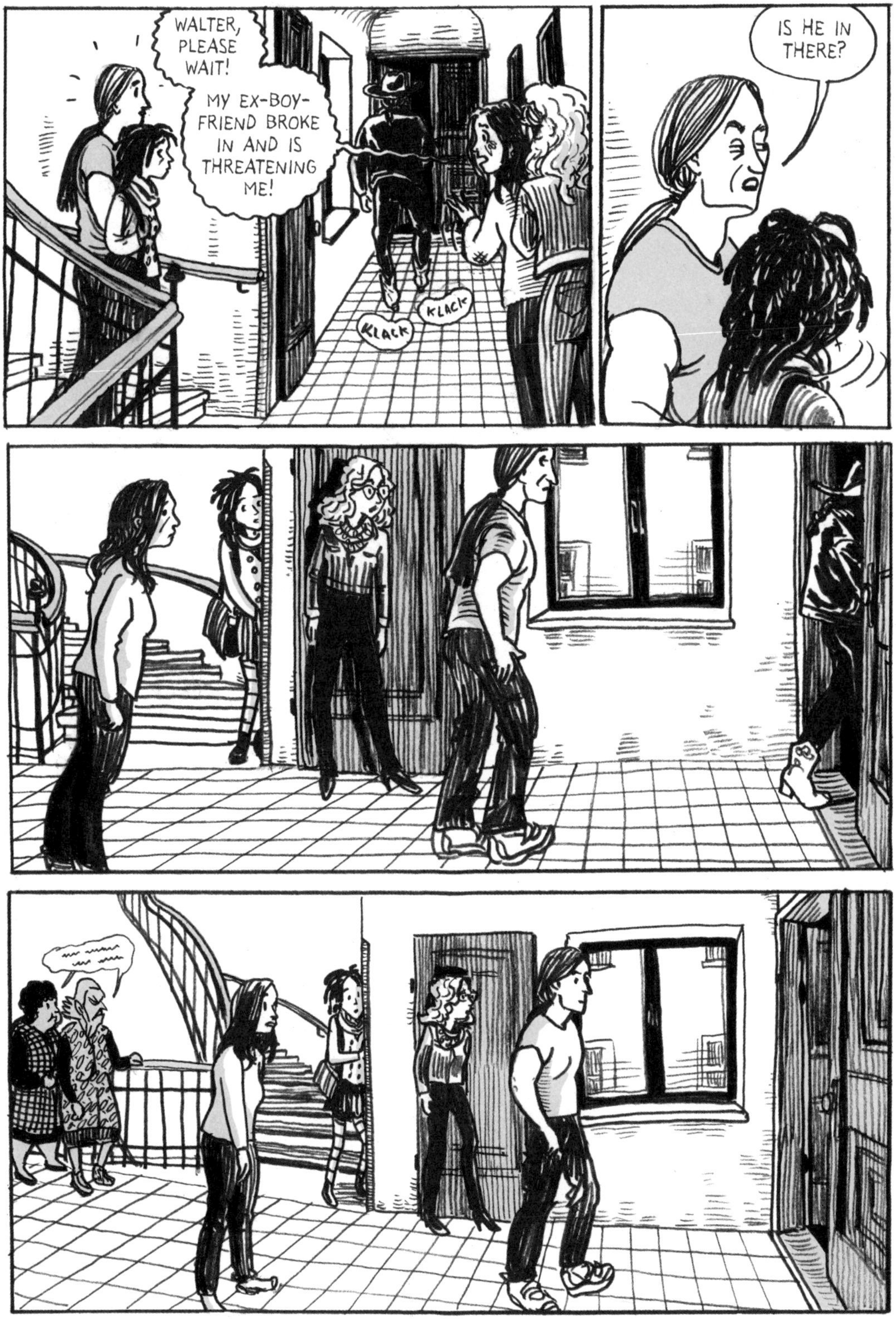
WALTER, PLEASE WAIT!
MY EX-BOYFRIEND BROKE IN AND IS THREATENING ME!
KLACK
KLACK
IS HE IN THERE?

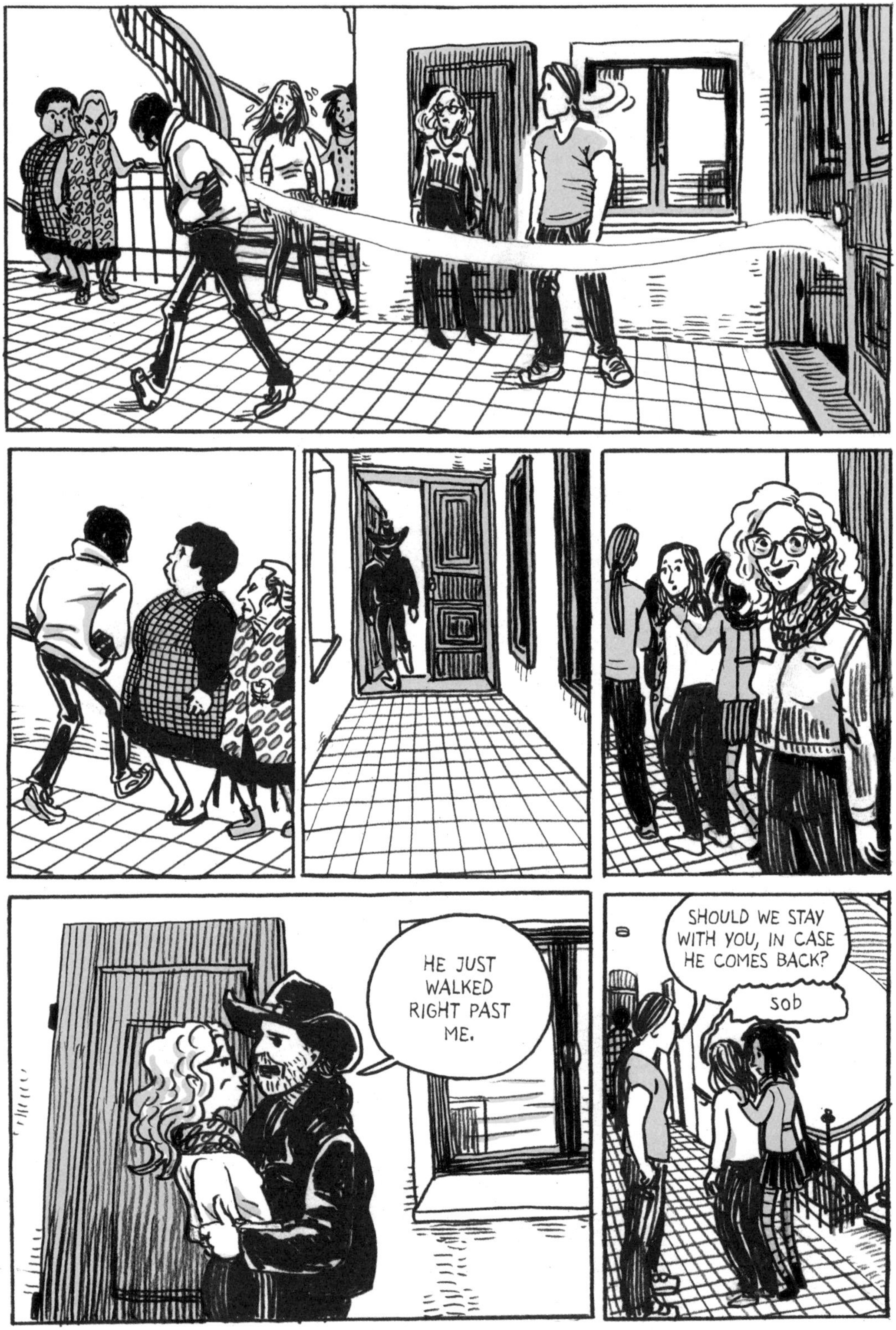
HE JUST WALKED RIGHT PAST ME.
SHOULD WE STAY WITH YOU, IN CASE HE COMES BACK?
sob

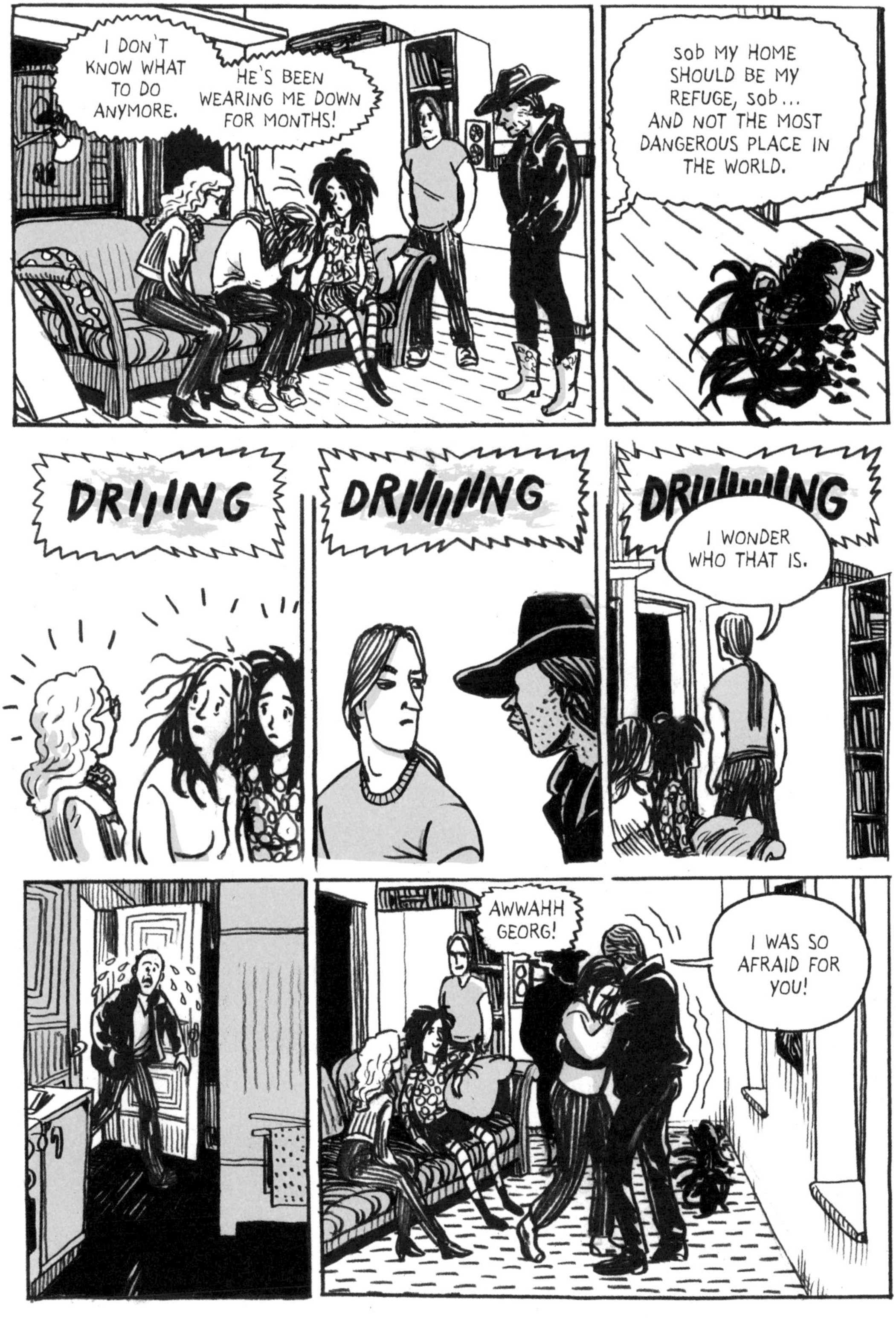
I DON'T KNOW WHAT TO DO ANYMORE.
HE'S BEEN WEARING ME DOWN FOR MONTHS!
sob MY HOME SHOULD BE MY REFUGE, sob... AND NOT THE MOST DANGEROUS PLACE IN THE WORLD.
DRIIING
DRIIIIING
DRIIIIIING
I WONDER WHO THAT IS.
AWWAHH GEORG!
I WAS SO AFRAID FOR YOU!

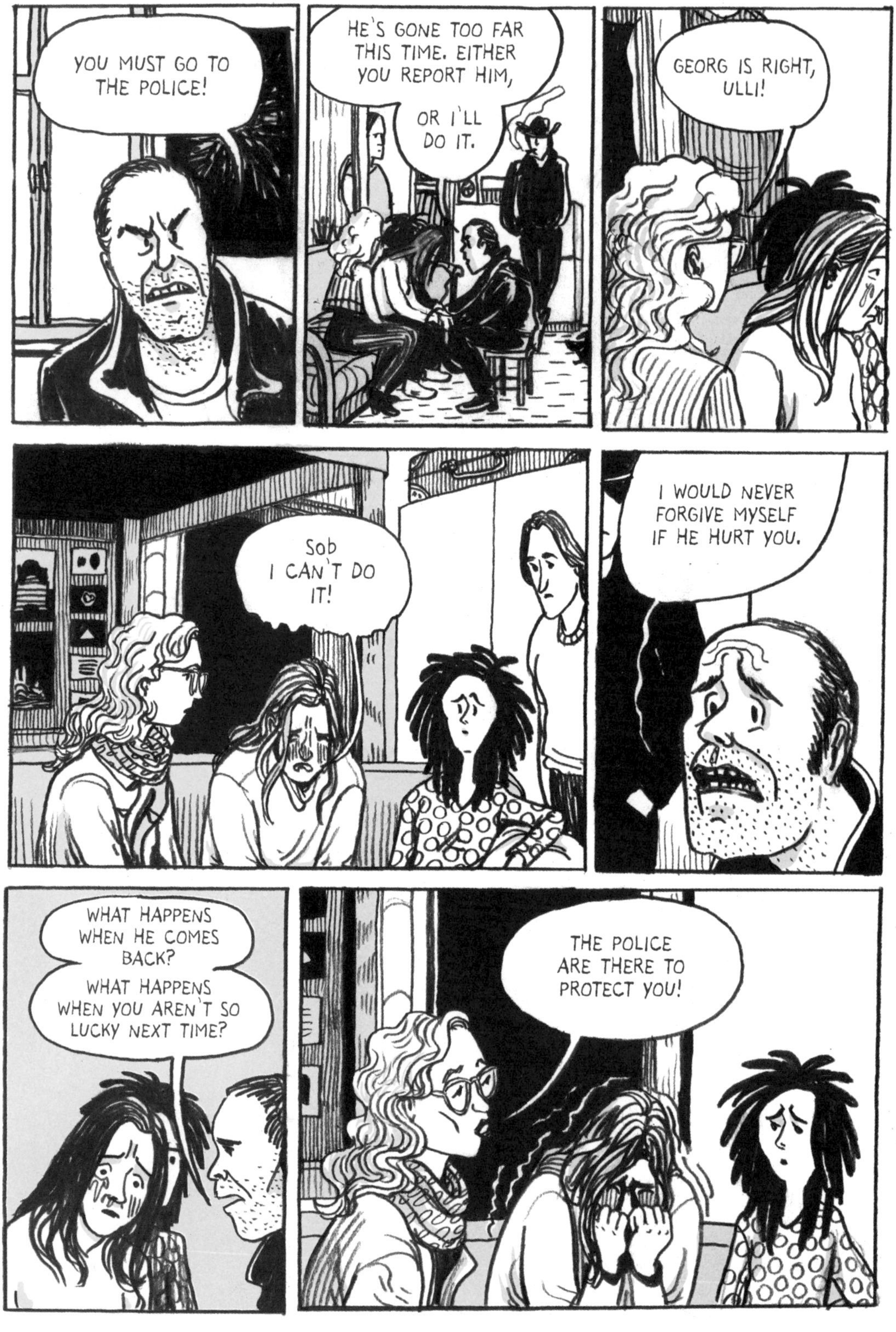
YOU MUST GO TO THE POLICE!
HE'S GONE TOO FAR THIS TIME. EITHER YOU REPORT HIM,
OR I'LL DO IT.
GEORG IS RIGHT, ULLI!
Sob
I CAN'T DO IT!
I WOULD NEVER FORGIVE MYSELF IF HE HURT YOU.
WHAT HAPPENS WHEN HE COMES BACK?
WHAT HAPPENS WHEN YOU AREN'T SO LUCKY NEXT TIME?
THE POLICE ARE THERE TO PROTECT YOU!

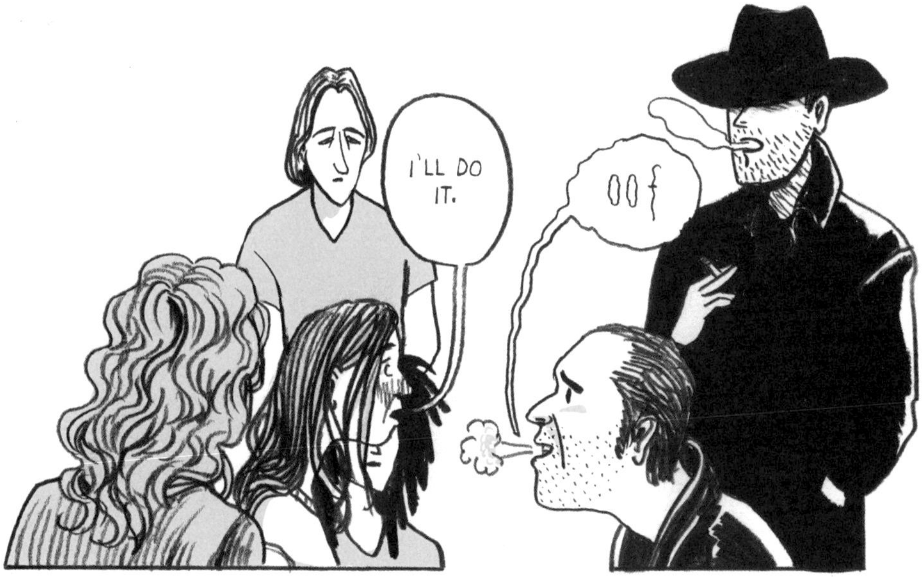
I'LL DO IT.
OOF

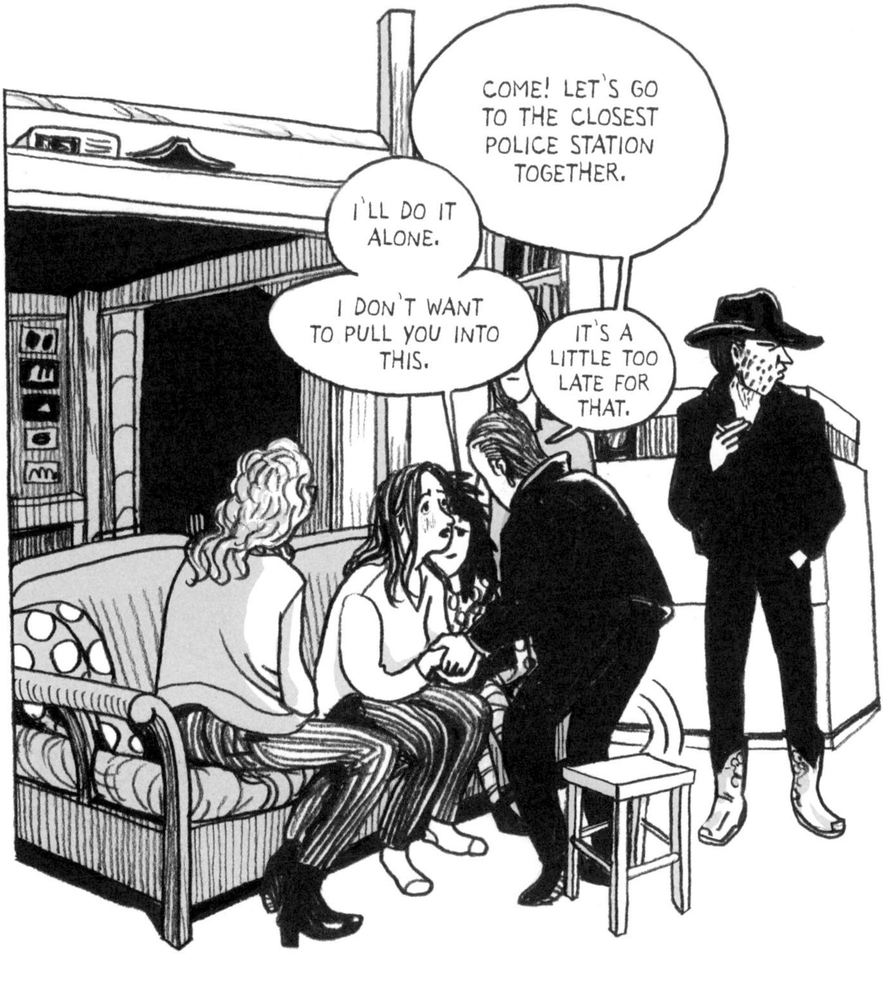
COME! LET'S GO TO THE CLOSEST POLICE STATION TOGETHER.
I'LL DO IT ALONE.
I DON'T WANT TO PULL YOU INTO THIS.
IT'S A LITTLE TOO LATE FOR THAT.

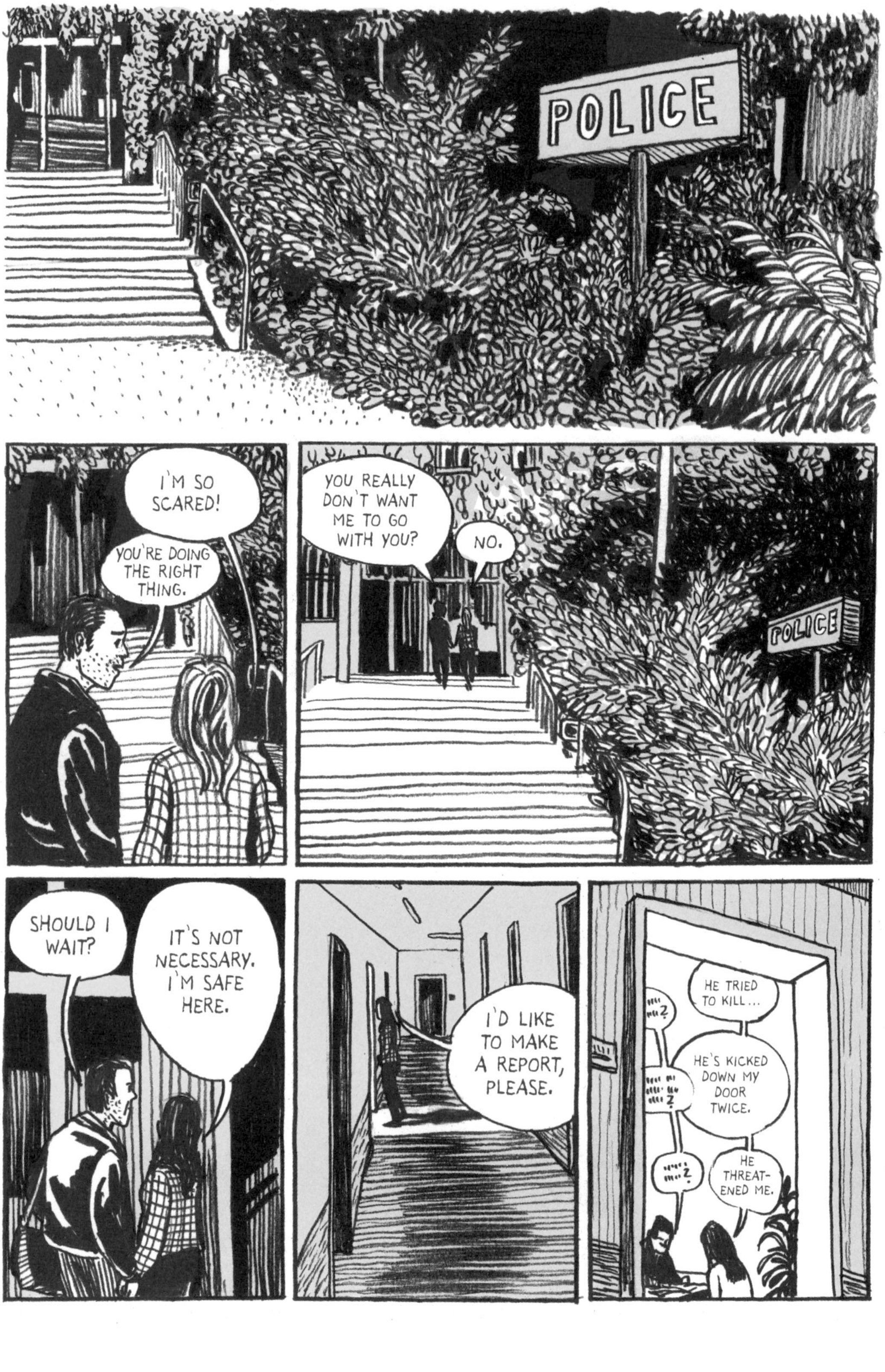
POLICE
I'M SO SCARED!
YOU'RE DOING THE RIGHT THING.
YOU REALLY DON'T WANT ME TO GO WITH YOU?
NO.
POLICE
SHOULD I WAIT?
IT'S NOT NECESSARY. I'M SAFE HERE.
I'D LIKE TO MAKE A REPORT, PLEASE.
HE TRIED TO KILL...
HE'S KICKED DOWN MY DOOR TWICE.
HE THREAT-ENED ME.

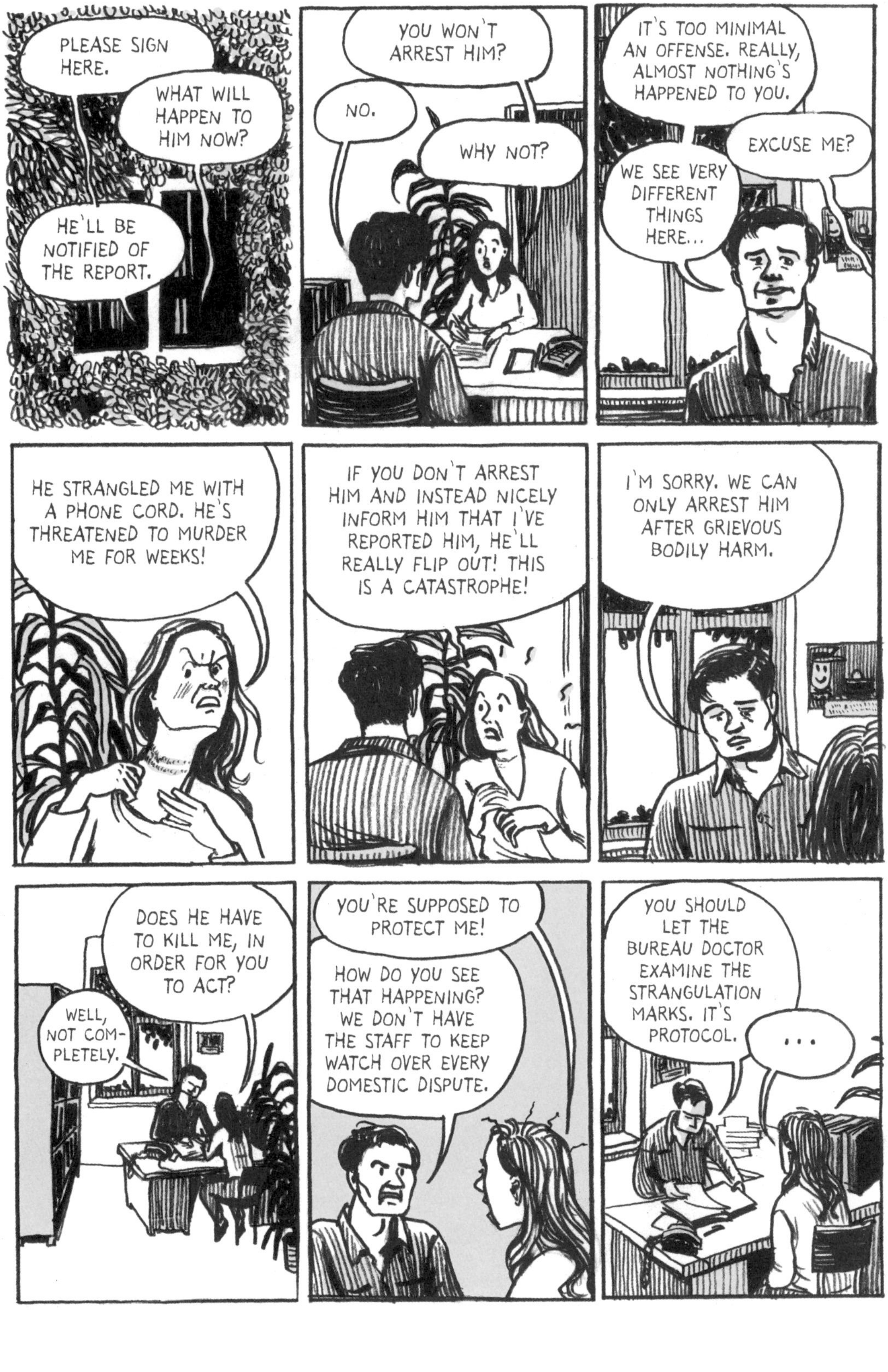
PLEASE SIGN HERE.
WHAT WILL HAPPEN TO HIM NOW?
HE'LL BE NOTIFIED OF THE REPORT.
YOU WON'T ARREST HIM?
NO.
WHY NOT?
IT'S TOO MINIMAL AN OFFENSE. REALLY, ALMOST NOTHING'S HAPPENED TO YOU.
EXCUSE ME?
WE SEE VERY DIFFERENT THINGS HERE...
HE STRANGLED ME WITH A PHONE CORD. HE'S THREATENED TO MURDER ME FOR WEEKS!
IF YOU DON'T ARREST HIM AND INSTEAD NICELY INFORM HIM THAT I'VE REPORTED HIM, HE'LL REALLY FLIP OUT! THIS IS A CATASTROPHE!
I'M SORRY. WE CAN ONLY ARREST HIM AFTER GRIEVOUS BODILY HARM.
DOES HE HAVE TO KILL ME, IN ORDER FOR YOU TO ACT?
WELL, NOT COM-PLETELY.
YOU'RE SUPPOSED TO PROTECT ME!
HOW DO YOU SEE THAT HAPPENING? WE DON'T HAVE THE STAFF TO KEEP WATCH OVER EVERY DOMESTIC DISPUTE.
YOU SHOULD LET THE BUREAU DOCTOR EXAMINE THE STRANGULATION MARKS. IT'S PROTOCOL.
...

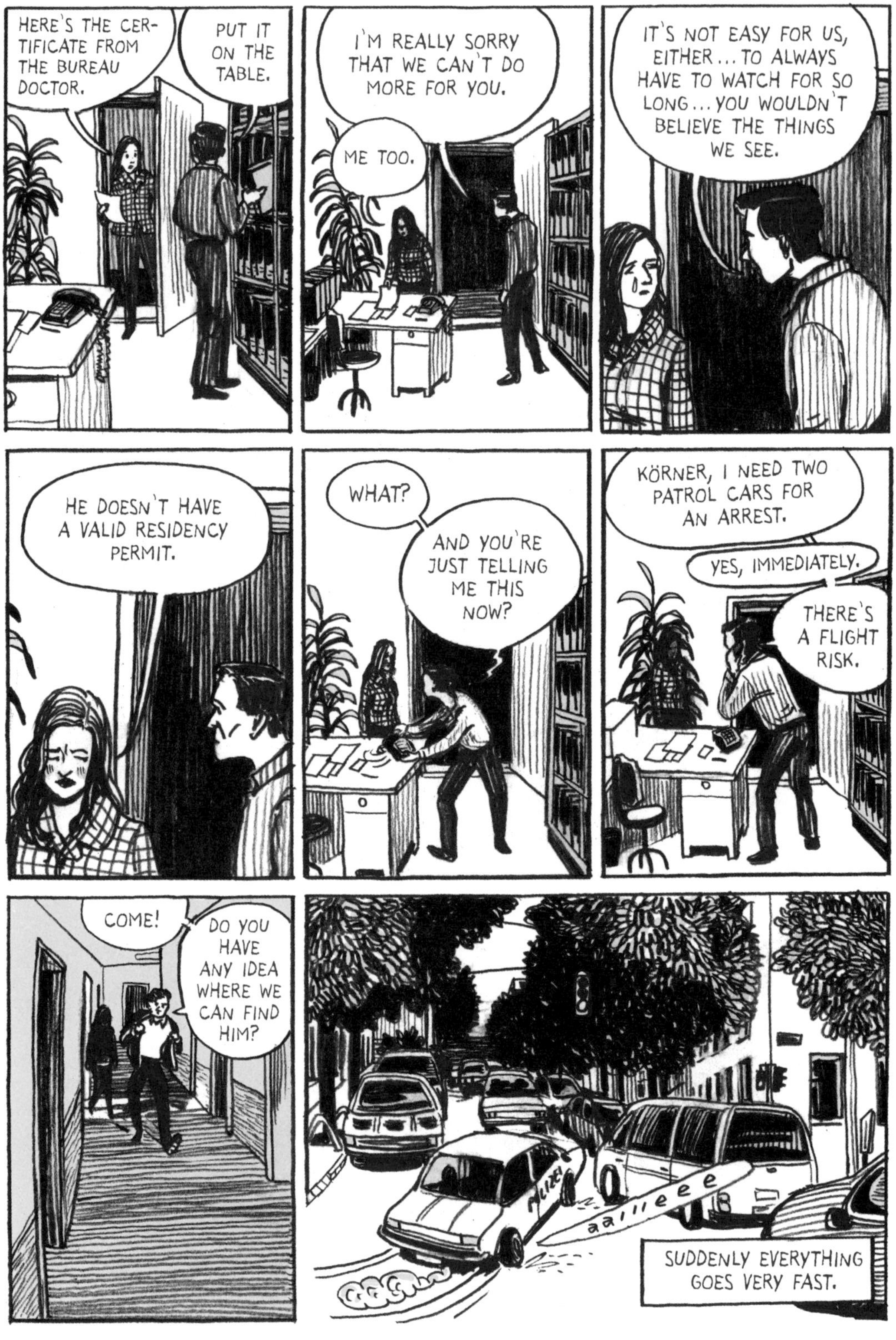
HERE'S THE CERTIFICATE FROM THE BUREAU DOCTOR.
PUT IT ON THE TABLE.
I'M REALLY SORRY THAT WE CAN'T DO MORE FOR YOU.
ME TOO.
IT'S NOT EASY FOR US, EITHER... TO ALWAYS HAVE TO WATCH FOR SO LONG... YOU WOULDN'T BELIEVE THE THINGS WE SEE.
HE DOESN'T HAVE A VALID RESIDENCY PERMIT.
WHAT?
AND YOU'RE JUST TELLING ME THIS NOW?
KÖRNER, I NEED TWO PATROL CARS FOR AN ARREST.
YES, IMMEDIATELY.
THERE'S A FLIGHT RISK.
COME!
DO YOU HAVE ANY IDEA WHERE WE CAN FIND HIM?
aallleee
SUDDENLY EVERYTHING GOES VERY FAST.

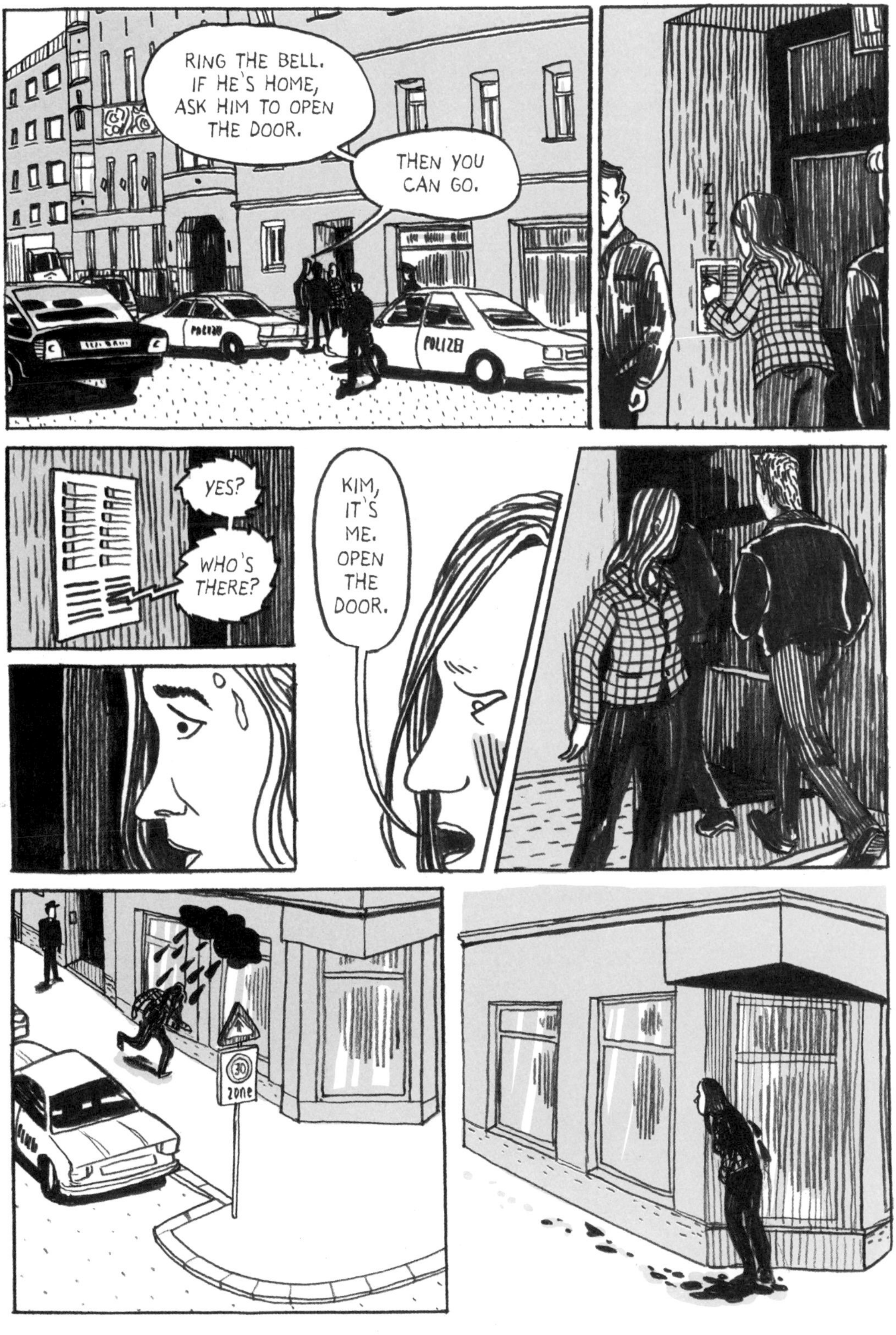
RING THE BELL. IF HE'S HOME, ASK HIM TO OPEN THE DOOR.
THEN YOU CAN GO.
POLIZEI
YES?
WHO'S THERE?
KIM, IT'S ME. OPEN THE DOOR.
30
zone

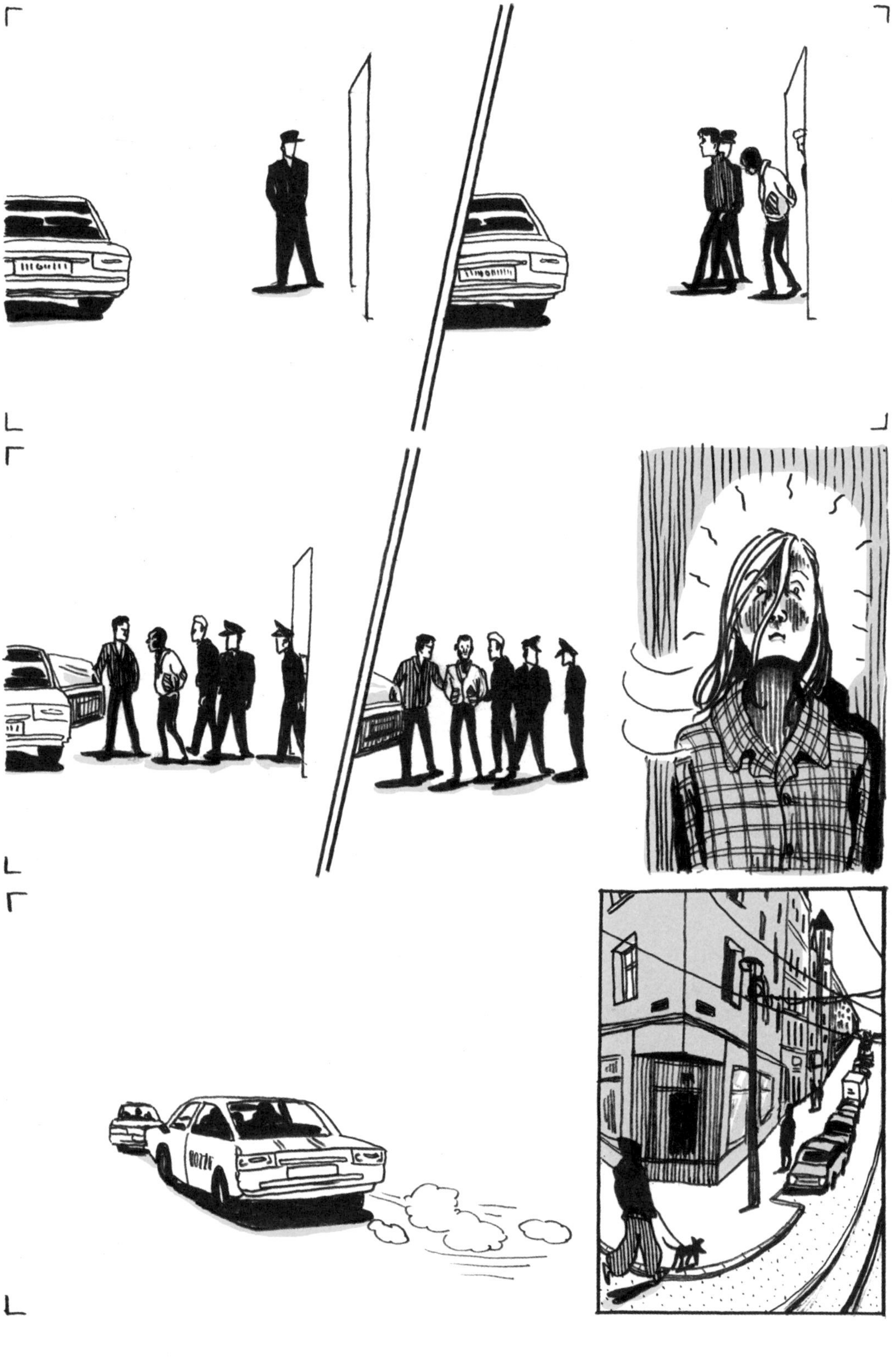

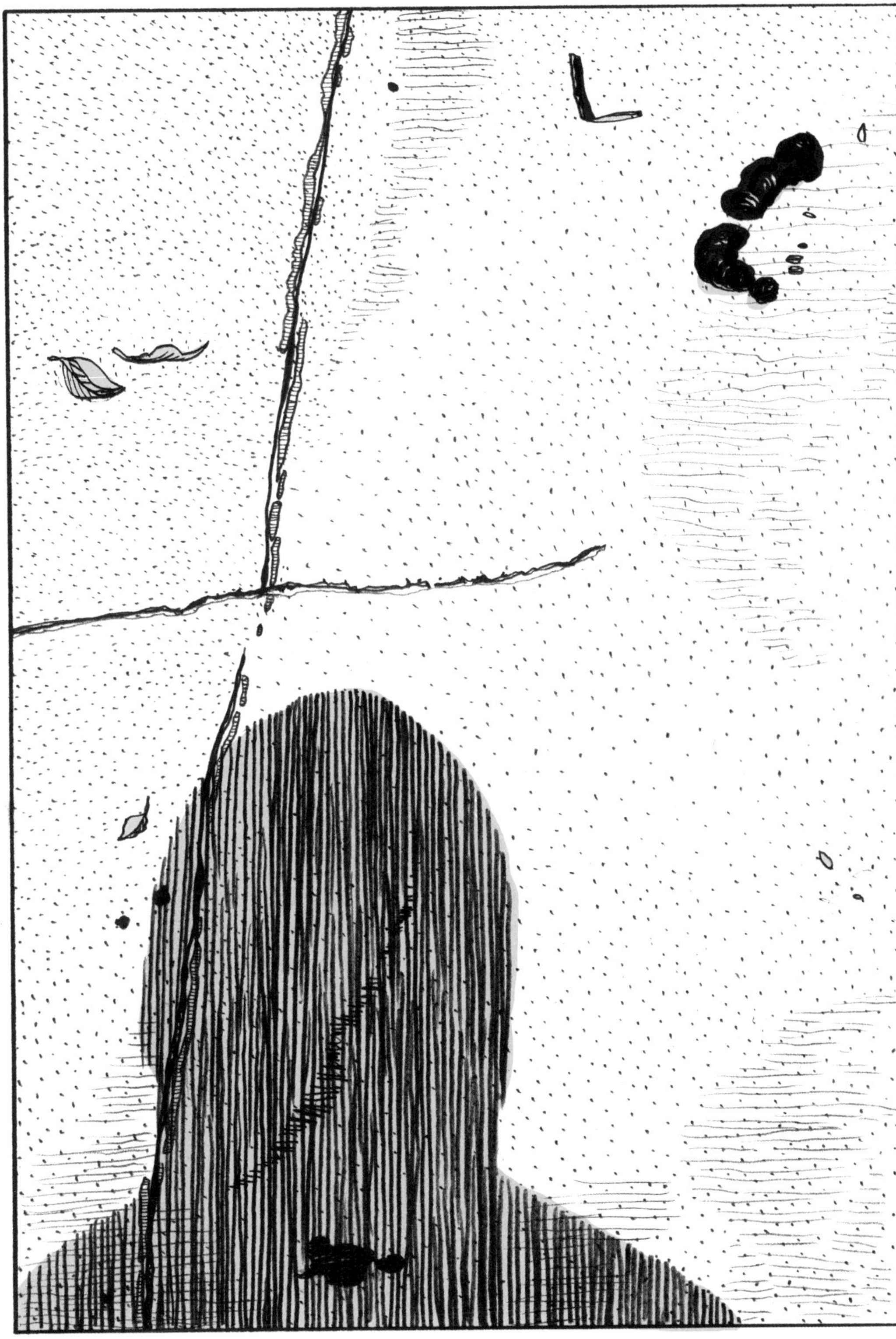

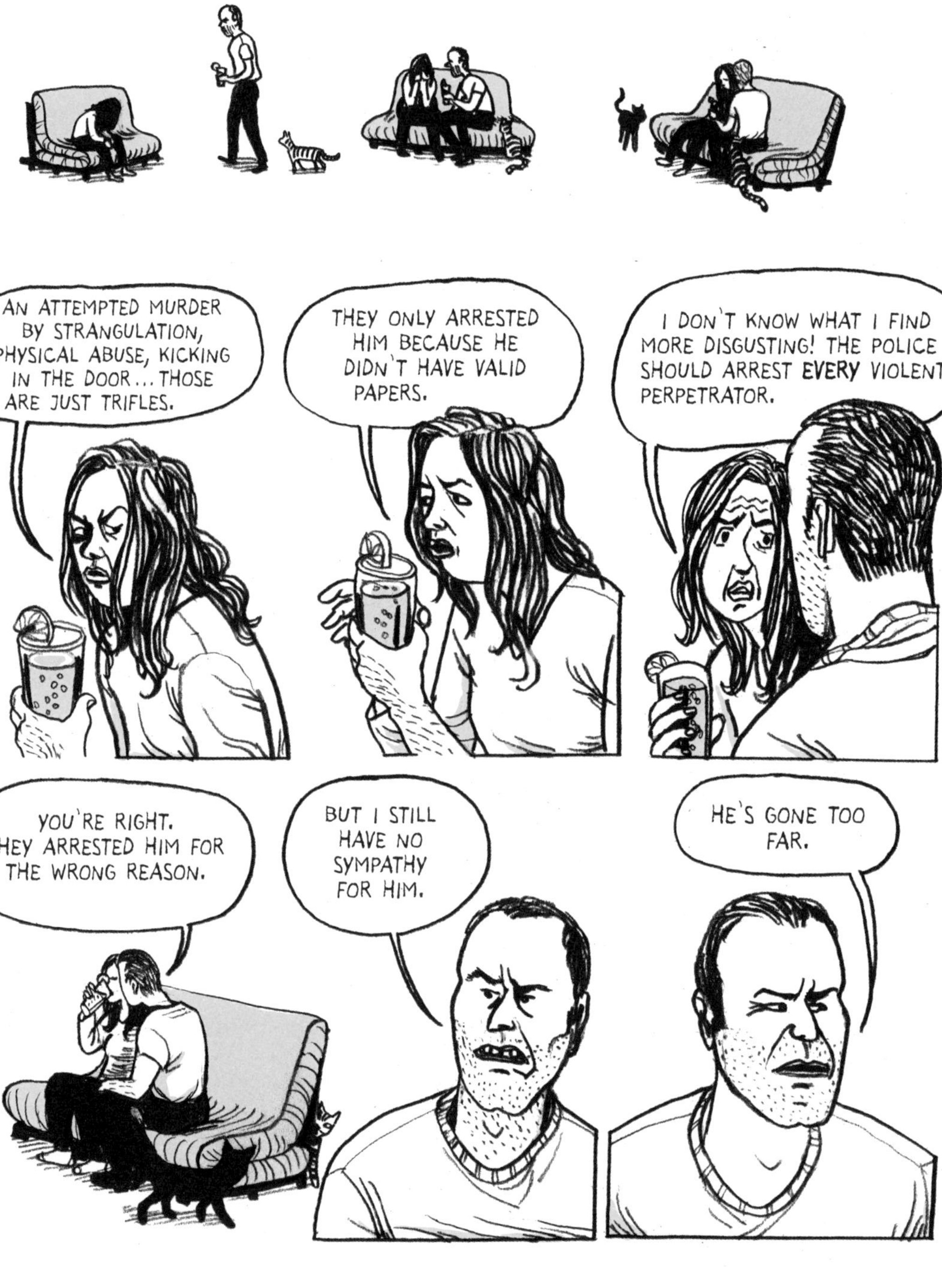
AN ATTEMPTED MURDER BY STRANGULATION, PHYSICAL ABUSE, KICKING IN THE DOOR... THOSE ARE JUST TRIFLES.
THEY ONLY ARRESTED HIM BECAUSE HE DIDN'T HAVE VALID PAPERS.
I DON'T KNOW WHAT I FIND MORE DISGUSTING! THE POLICE SHOULD ARREST **EVERY** VIOLENT PERPETRATOR.
YOU'RE RIGHT. THEY ARRESTED HIM FOR THE WRONG REASON.
BUT I STILL HAVE NO SYMPATHY FOR HIM.
HE'S GONE TOO FAR.

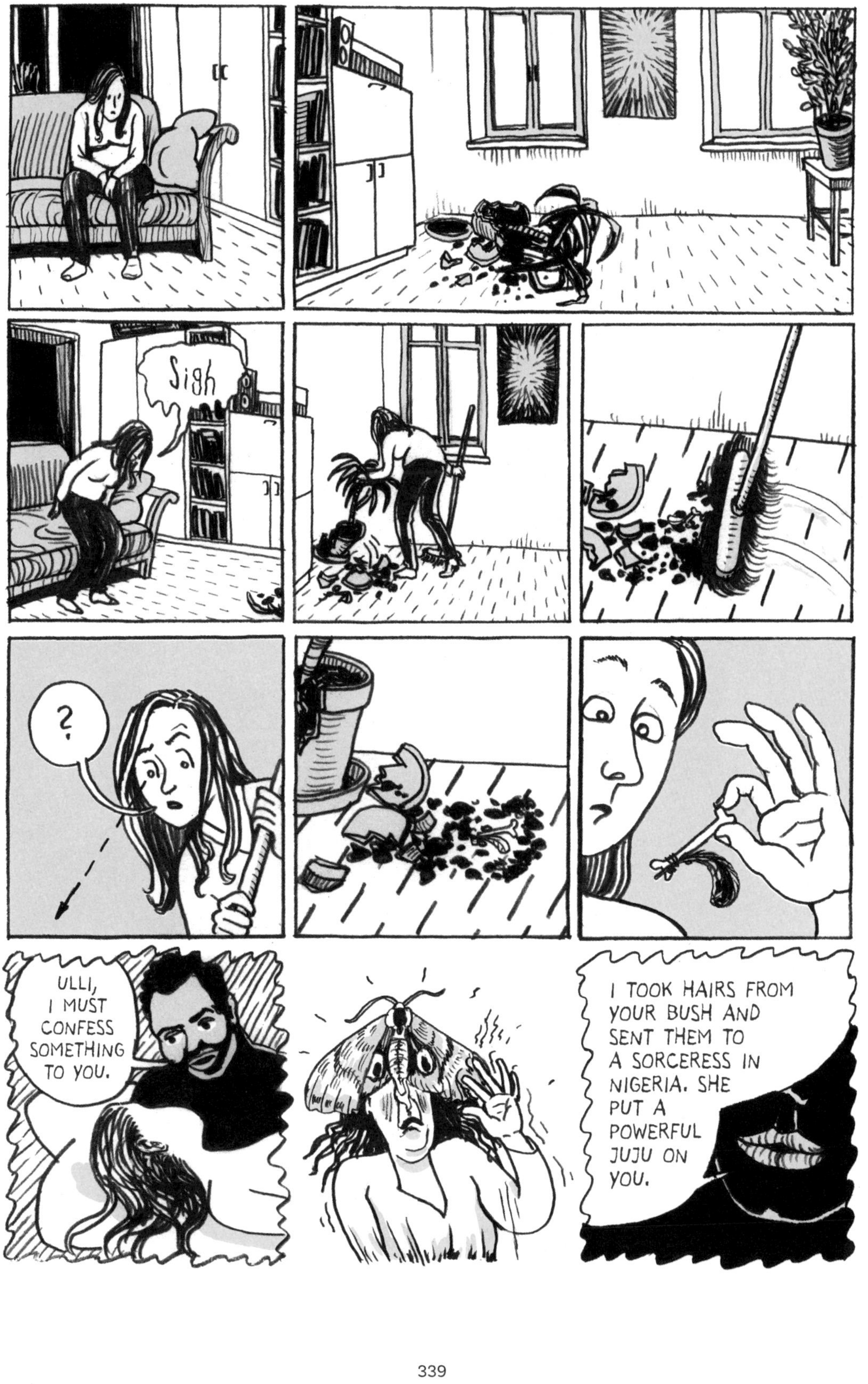
Sigh
?
ULLI, I MUST CONFESS SOMETHING TO YOU.
I TOOK HAIRS FROM YOUR BUSH AND SENT THEM TO A SORCERESS IN NIGERIA. SHE PUT A POWERFUL JUJU ON YOU.

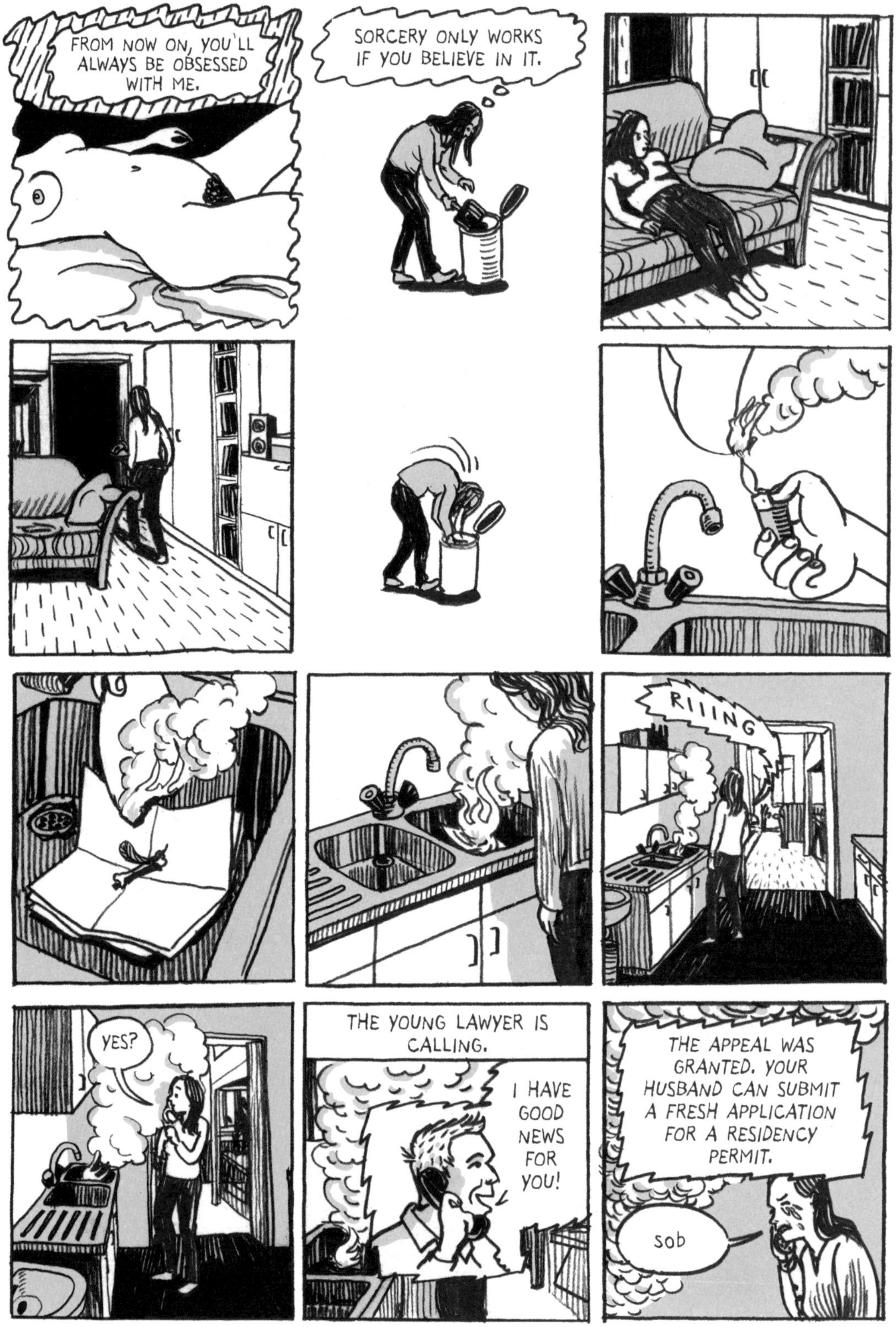
FROM NOW ON, YOU'LL ALWAYS BE OBSESSED WITH ME.
SORCERY ONLY WORKS IF YOU BELIEVE IN IT.
RIIING
YES?
THE YOUNG LAWYER IS CALLING.
I HAVE GOOD NEWS FOR YOU!
THE APPEAL WAS GRANTED. YOUR HUSBAND CAN SUBMIT A FRESH APPLICATION FOR A RESIDENCY PERMIT.
sob

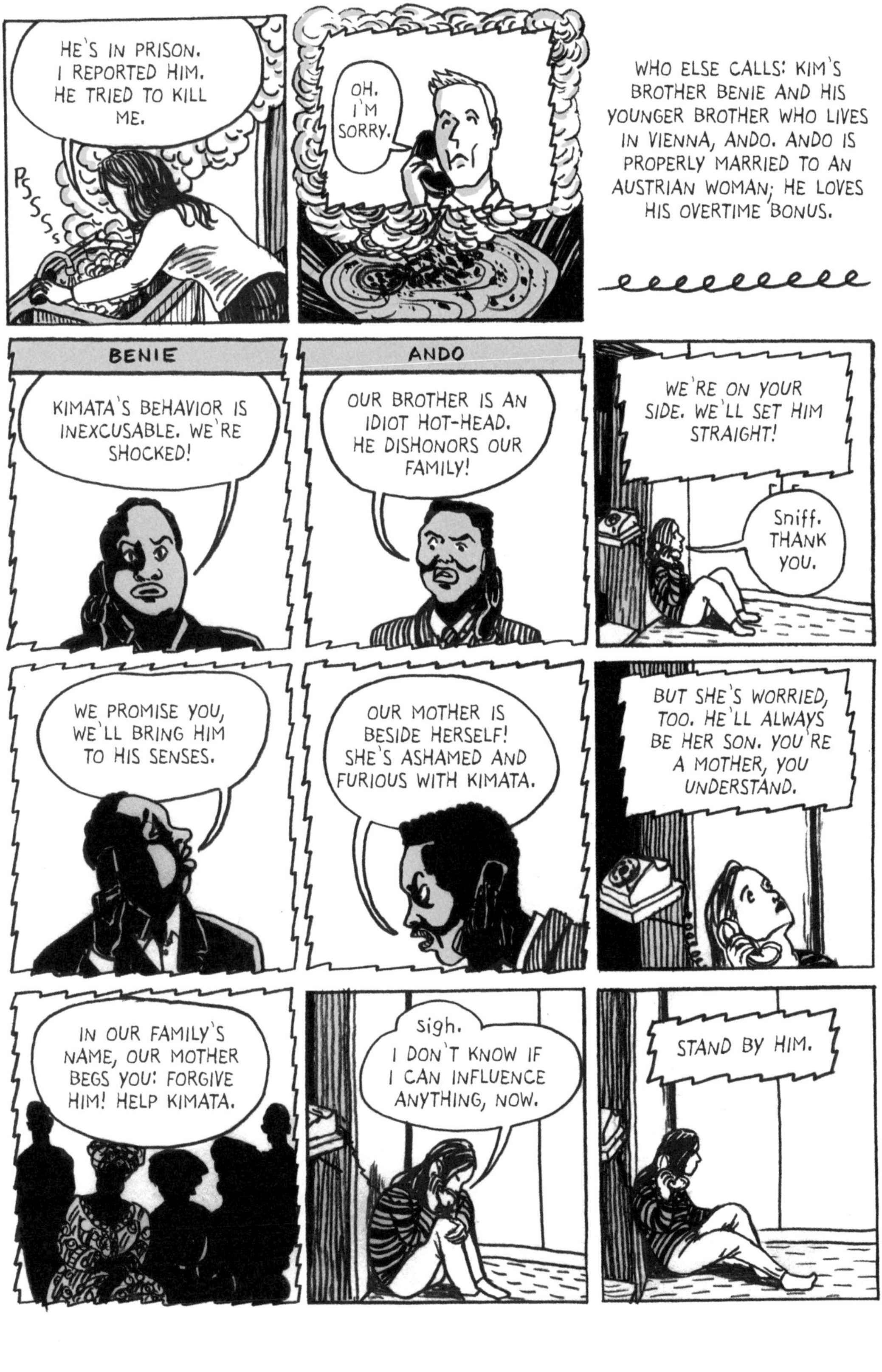
HE'S IN PRISON. I REPORTED HIM. HE TRIED TO KILL ME.
PSSSSs
OH. I'M SORRY.
WHO ELSE CALLS: KIM'S BROTHER BENIE AND HIS YOUNGER BROTHER WHO LIVES IN VIENNA, ANDO. ANDO IS PROPERLY MARRIED TO AN AUSTRIAN WOMAN; HE LOVES HIS OVERTIME BONUS.
BENIE
KIMATA'S BEHAVIOR IS INEXCUSABLE. WE'RE SHOCKED!
ANDO
OUR BROTHER IS AN IDIOT HOT-HEAD. HE DISHONORS OUR FAMILY!
WE'RE ON YOUR SIDE. WE'LL SET HIM STRAIGHT!
Sniff. THANK YOU.
WE PROMISE YOU, WE'LL BRING HIM TO HIS SENSES.
OUR MOTHER IS BESIDE HERSELF! SHE'S ASHAMED AND FURIOUS WITH KIMATA.
BUT SHE'S WORRIED, TOO. HE'LL ALWAYS BE HER SON. YOU'RE A MOTHER, YOU UNDERSTAND.
IN OUR FAMILY'S NAME, OUR MOTHER BEGS YOU: FORGIVE HIM! HELP KIMATA.
sigh. I DON'T KNOW IF I CAN INFLUENCE ANYTHING, NOW.
STAND BY HIM.

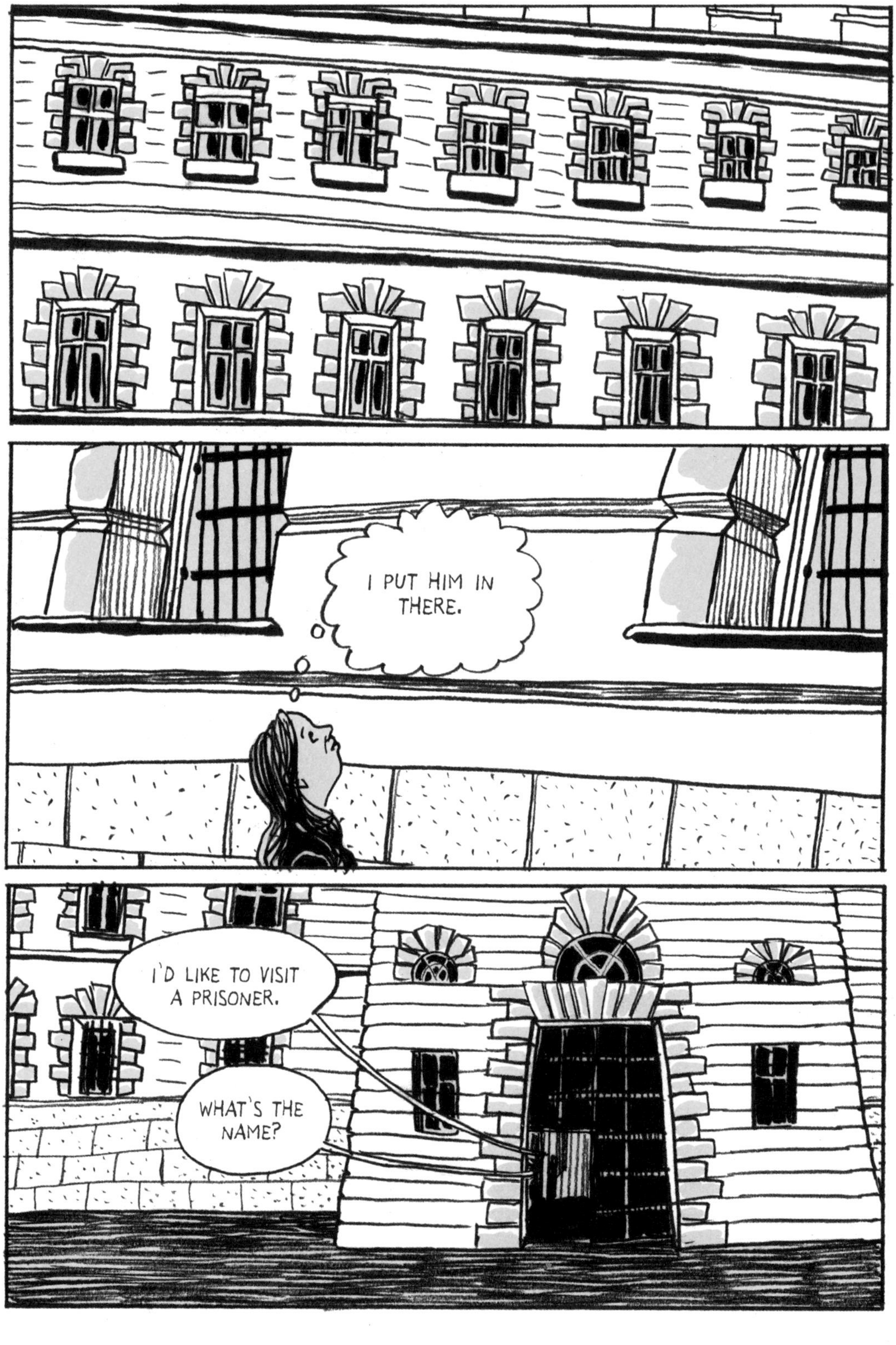
I PUT HIM IN THERE.
I'D LIKE TO VISIT A PRISONER.
WHAT'S THE NAME?

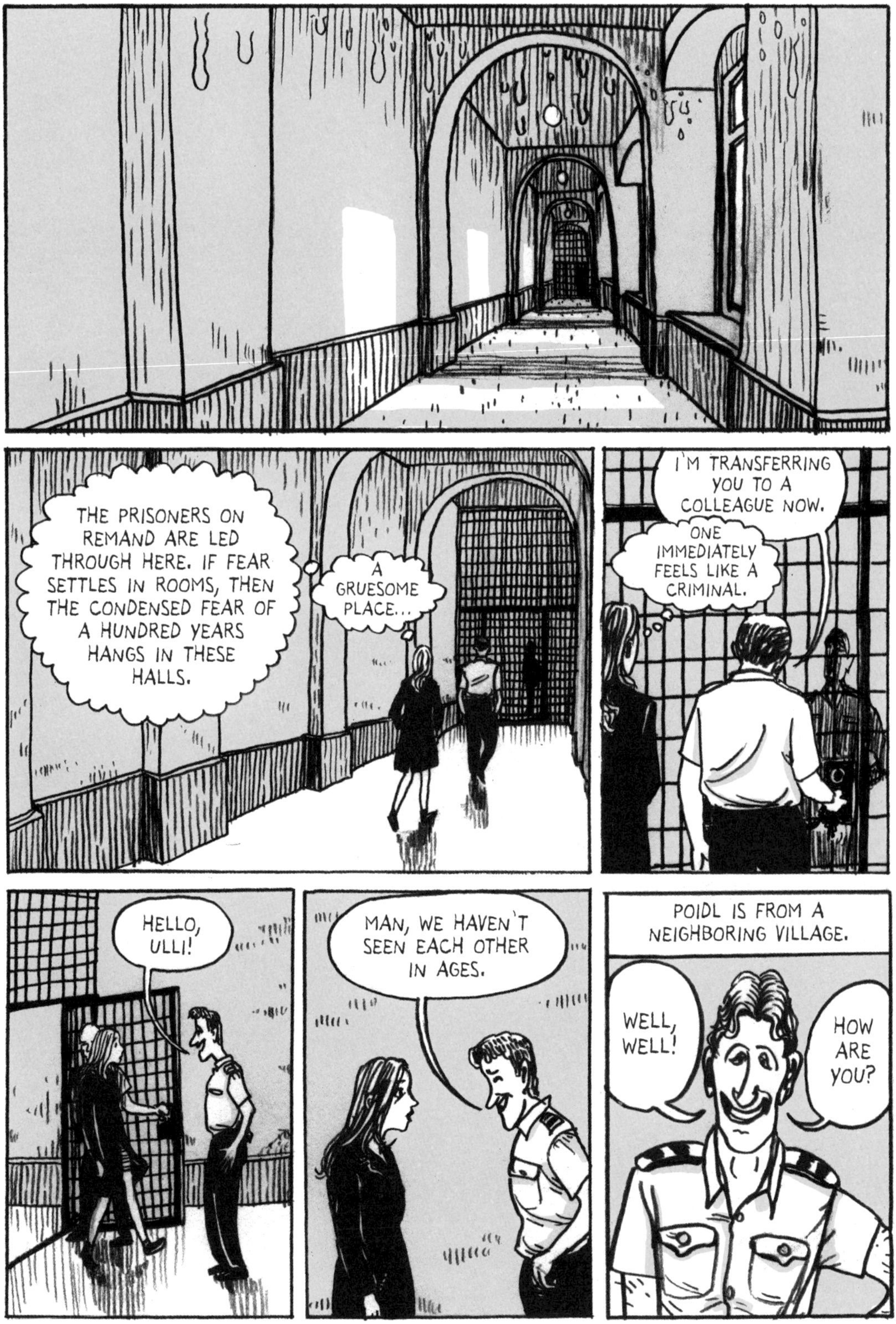
THE PRISONERS ON REMAND ARE LED THROUGH HERE. IF FEAR SETTLES IN ROOMS, THEN THE CONDENSED FEAR OF A HUNDRED YEARS HANGS IN THESE HALLS.
A GRUESOME PLACE...
I'M TRANSFERRING YOU TO A COLLEAGUE NOW.
ONE IMMEDIATELY FEELS LIKE A CRIMINAL.
HELLO, ULLI!
MAN, WE HAVEN'T SEEN EACH OTHER IN AGES.
POIDL IS FROM A NEIGHBORING VILLAGE.
WELL, WELL!
HOW ARE YOU?

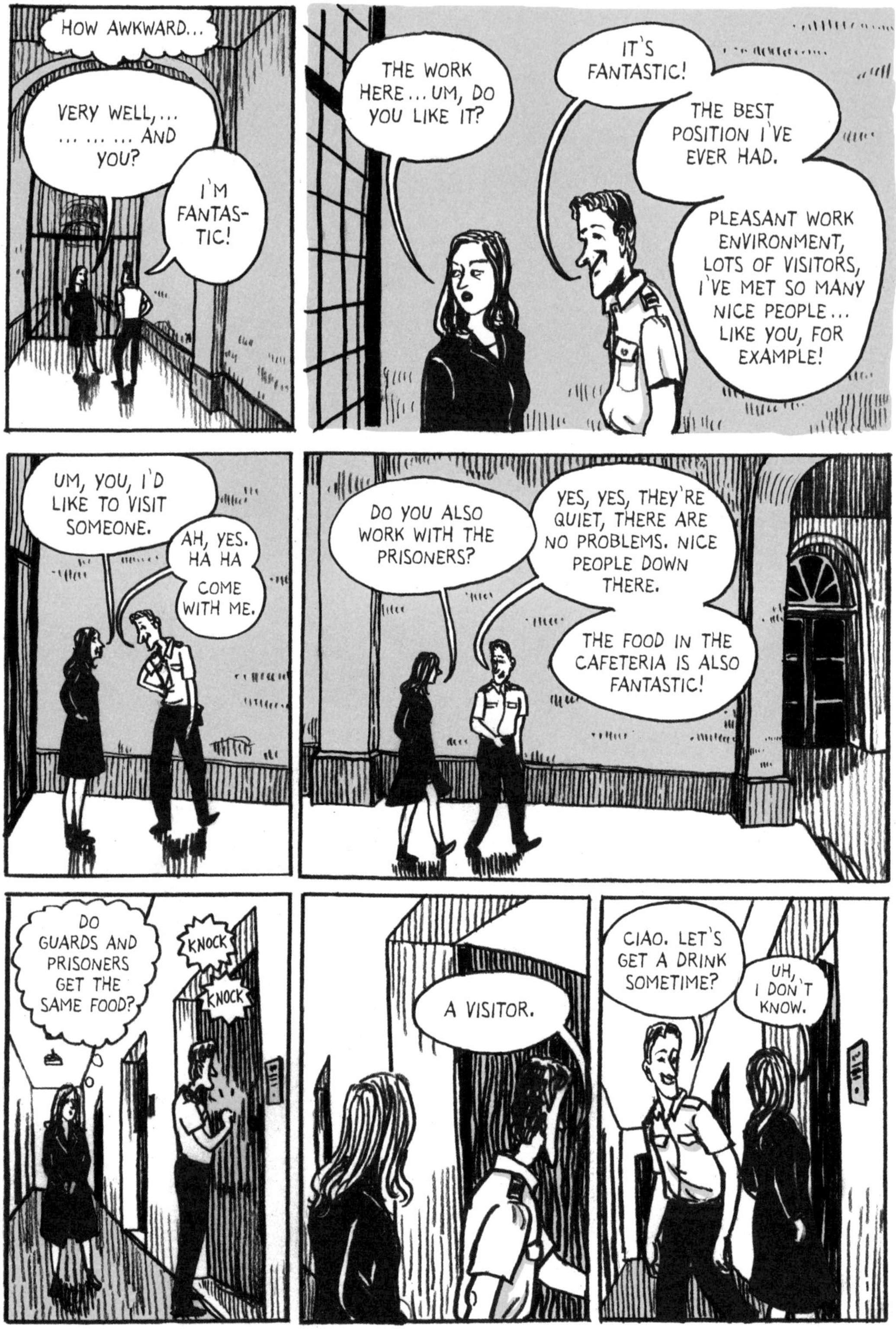
HOW AWKWARD...
VERY WELL,... ... ... AND YOU?
I'M FANTASTIC!
THE WORK HERE... UM, DO YOU LIKE IT?
IT'S FANTASTIC!
THE BEST POSITION I'VE EVER HAD.
PLEASANT WORK ENVIRONMENT, LOTS OF VISITORS, I'VE MET SO MANY NICE PEOPLE... LIKE YOU, FOR EXAMPLE!
UM, YOU, I'D LIKE TO VISIT SOMEONE.
AH, YES. HA HA
COME WITH ME.
DO YOU ALSO WORK WITH THE PRISONERS?
YES, YES, THEY'RE QUIET, THERE ARE NO PROBLEMS. NICE PEOPLE DOWN THERE.
THE FOOD IN THE CAFETERIA IS ALSO FANTASTIC!
DO GUARDS AND PRISONERS GET THE SAME FOOD?
KNOCK
KNOCK
A VISITOR.
CIAO. LET'S GET A DRINK SOMETIME?
UH, I DON'T KNOW.

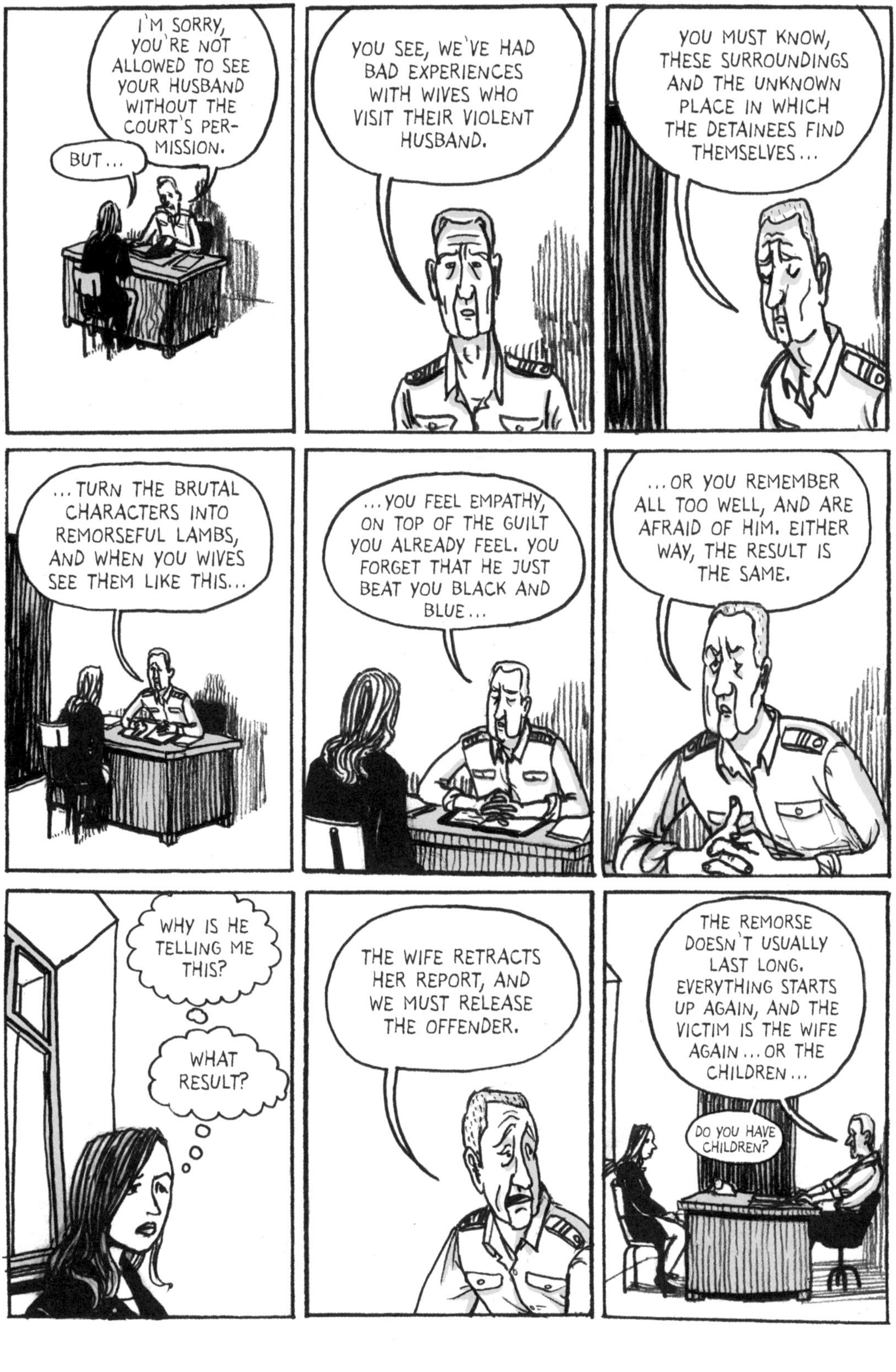
I'M SORRY, YOU'RE NOT ALLOWED TO SEE YOUR HUSBAND WITHOUT THE COURT'S PER-MISSION.
BUT...
YOU SEE, WE'VE HAD BAD EXPERIENCES WITH WIVES WHO VISIT THEIR VIOLENT HUSBAND.
YOU MUST KNOW, THESE SURROUNDINGS AND THE UNKNOWN PLACE IN WHICH THE DETAINEES FIND THEMSELVES...
...TURN THE BRUTAL CHARACTERS INTO REMORSEFUL LAMBS, AND WHEN YOU WIVES SEE THEM LIKE THIS...
...YOU FEEL EMPATHY, ON TOP OF THE GUILT YOU ALREADY FEEL. YOU FORGET THAT HE JUST BEAT YOU BLACK AND BLUE...
...OR YOU REMEMBER ALL TOO WELL, AND ARE AFRAID OF HIM. EITHER WAY, THE RESULT IS THE SAME.
WHY IS HE TELLING ME THIS?
WHAT RESULT?
THE WIFE RETRACTS HER REPORT, AND WE MUST RELEASE THE OFFENDER.
THE REMORSE DOESN'T USUALLY LAST LONG. EVERYTHING STARTS UP AGAIN, AND THE VICTIM IS THE WIFE AGAIN...OR THE CHILDREN...
DO YOU HAVE CHILDREN?

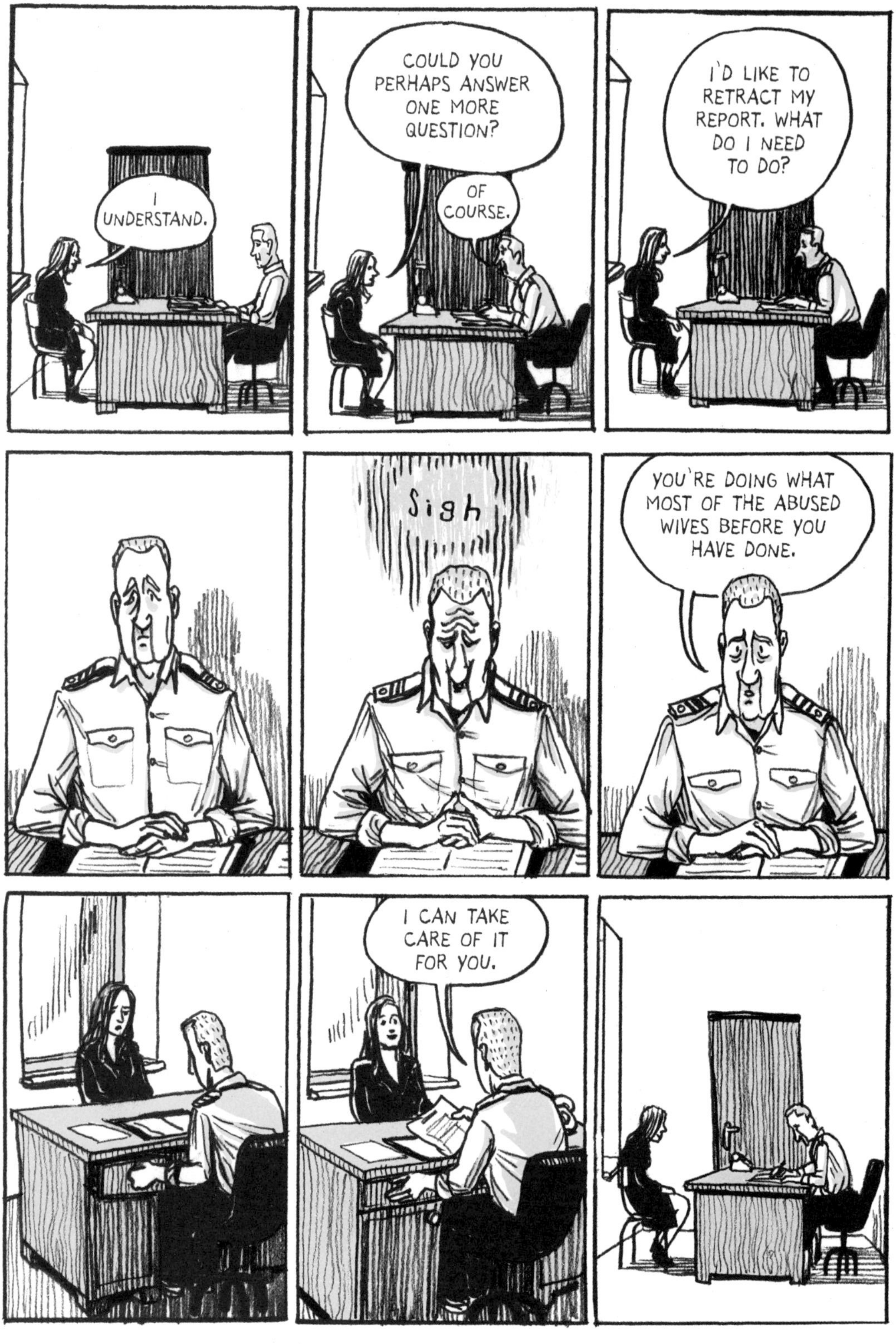
I UNDERSTAND.
COULD YOU PERHAPS ANSWER ONE MORE QUESTION?
OF COURSE.
I'D LIKE TO RETRACT MY REPORT. WHAT DO I NEED TO DO?
Sigh
YOU'RE DOING WHAT MOST OF THE ABUSED WIVES BEFORE YOU HAVE DONE.
I CAN TAKE CARE OF IT FOR YOU.

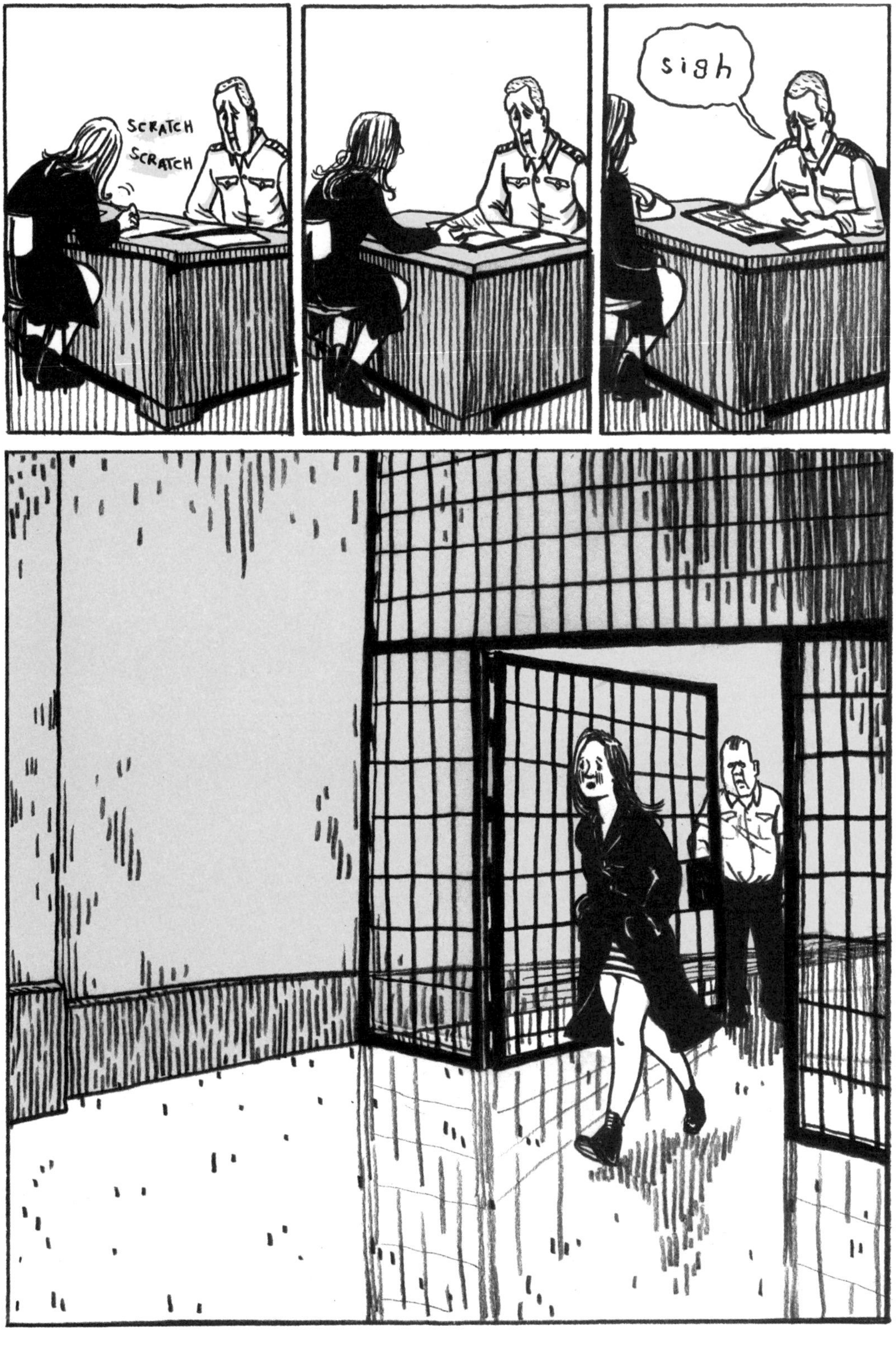
SCRATCH
SCRATCH
sigh

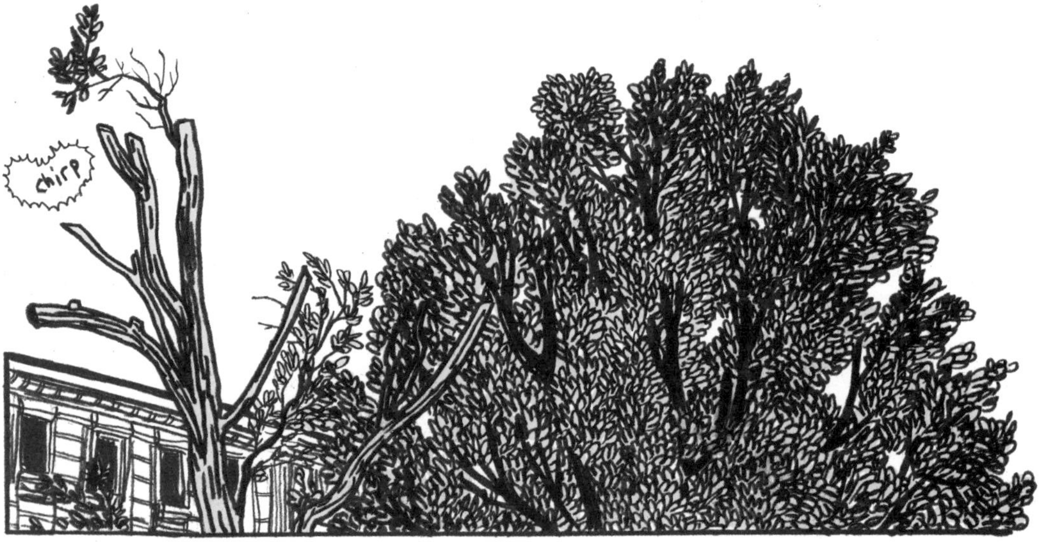
chirp

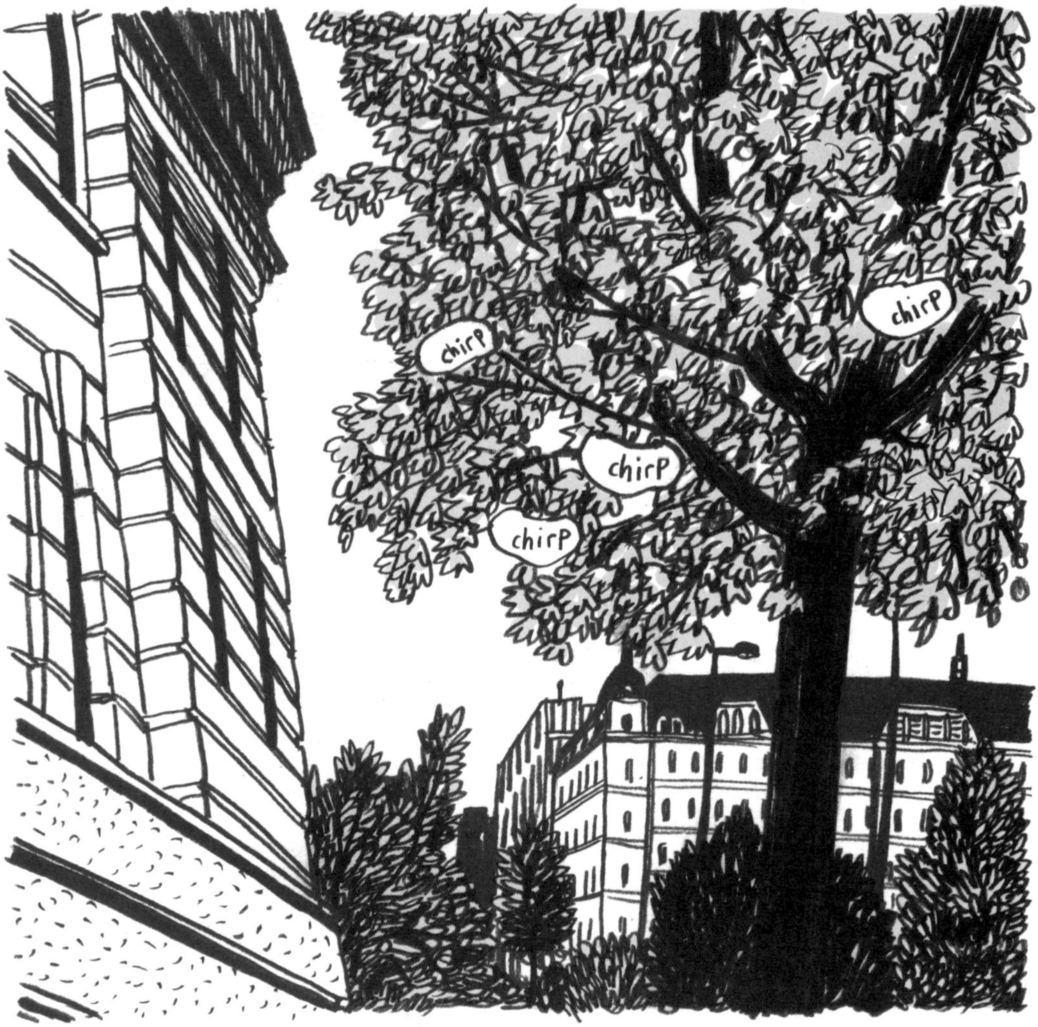
chirp
chirp
chirp
chirp

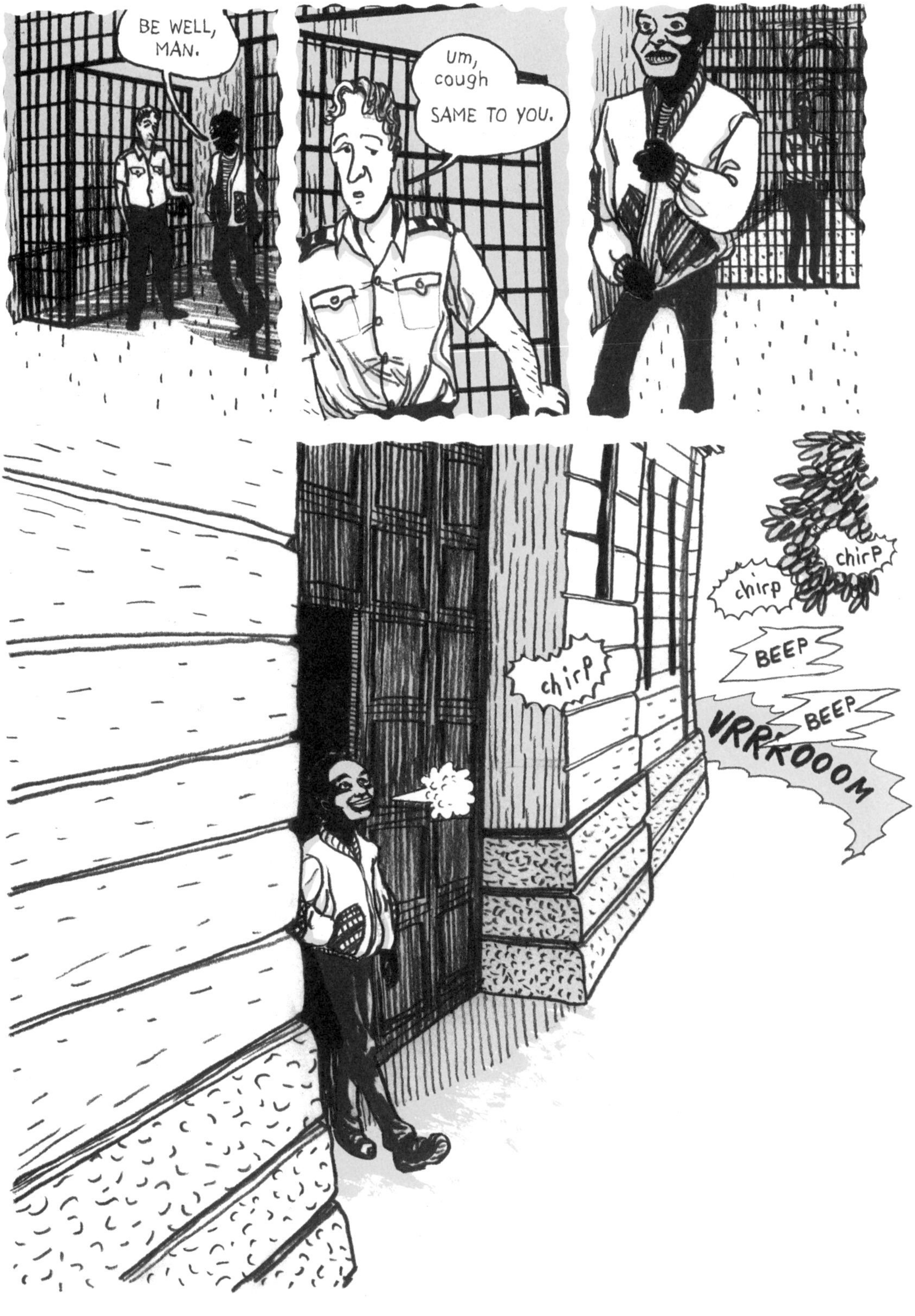
BE WELL, MAN.
um, cough
SAME TO YOU.
chirp
chirp
chirp
BEEP
BEEP
VRRRKOOOM

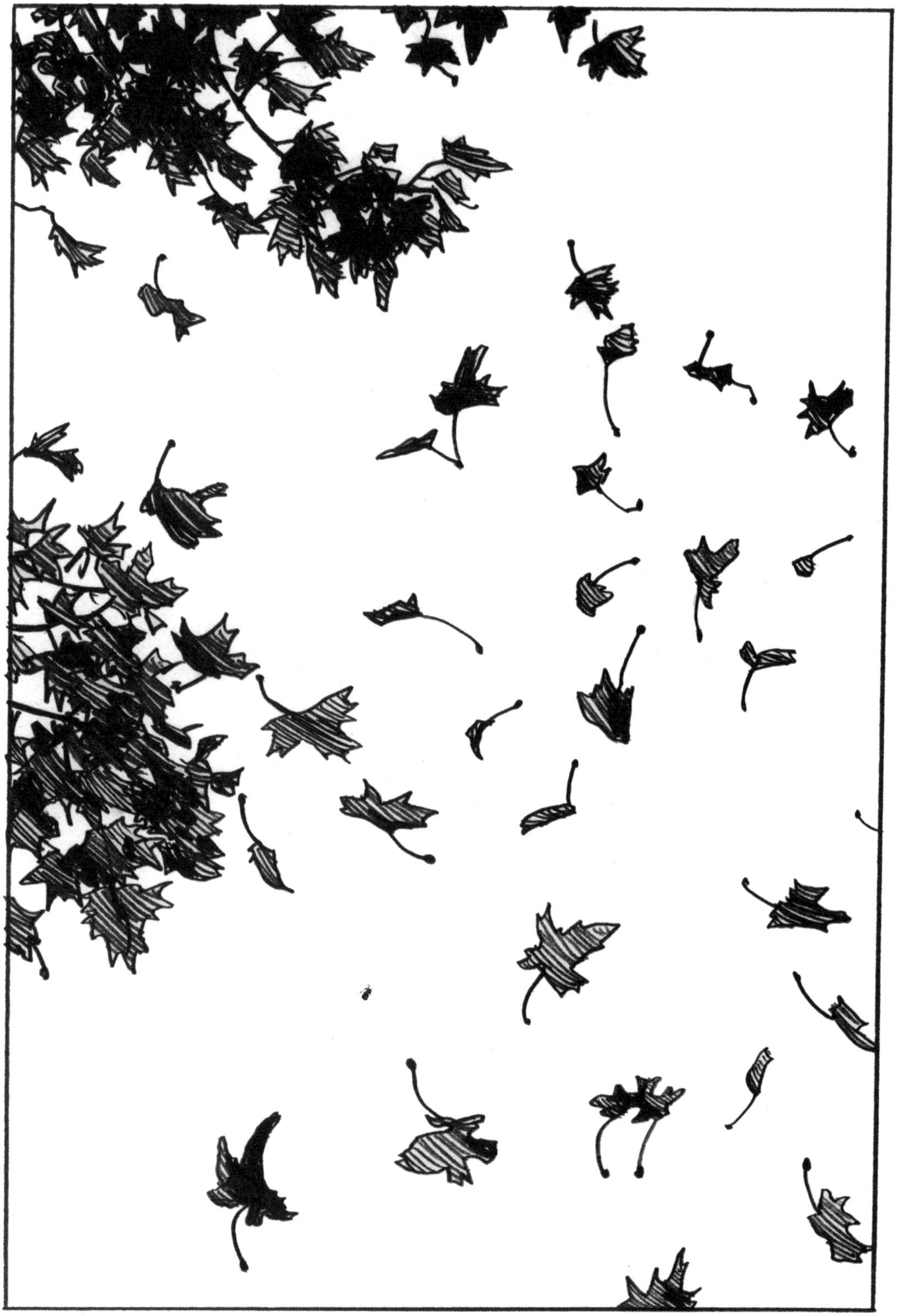

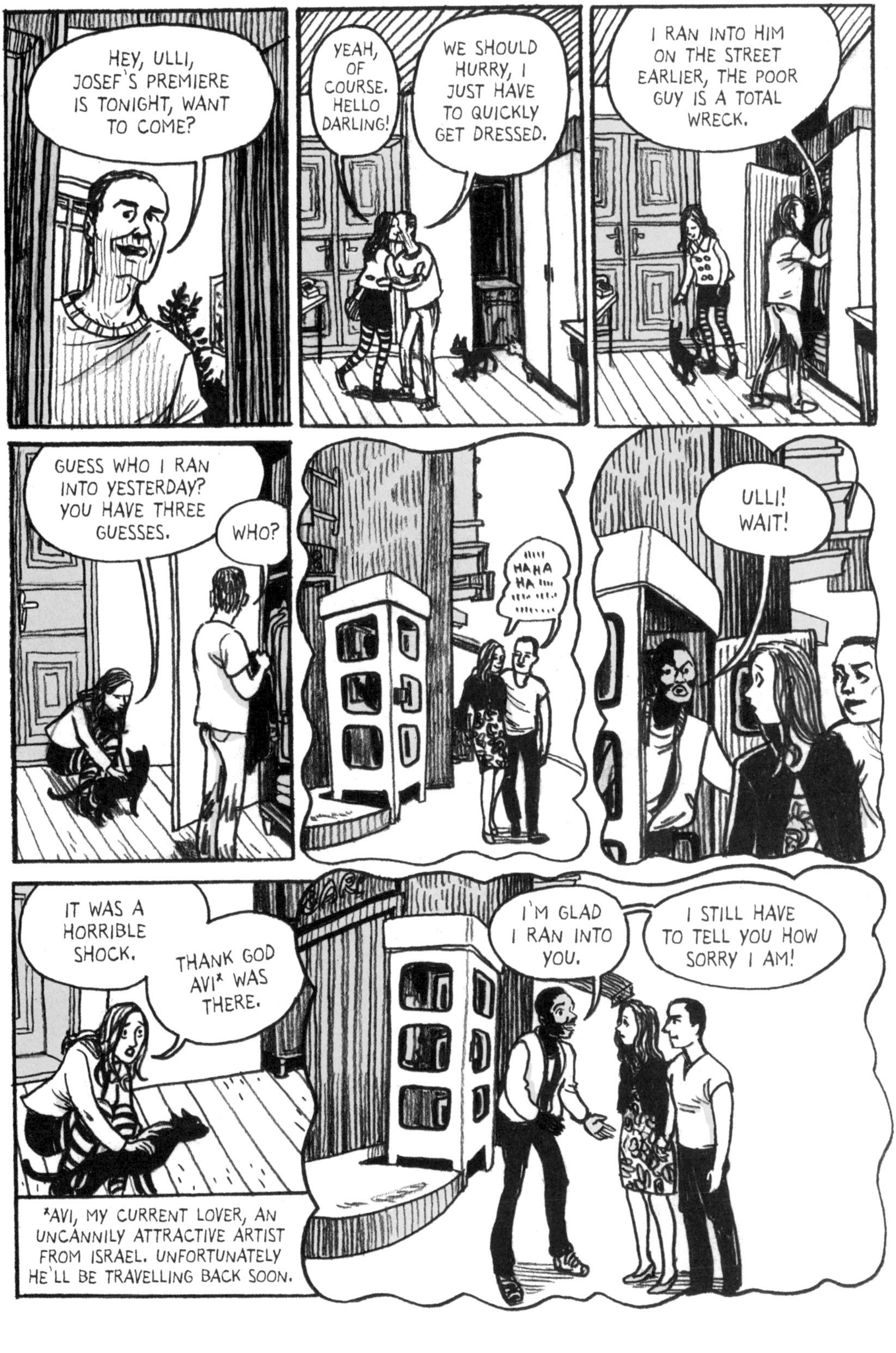
HEY, ULLI, JOSEF'S PREMIERE IS TONIGHT, WANT TO COME?
YEAH, OF COURSE. HELLO DARLING!
WE SHOULD HURRY, I JUST HAVE TO QUICKLY GET DRESSED.
I RAN INTO HIM ON THE STREET EARLIER, THE POOR GUY IS A TOTAL WRECK.
GUESS WHO I RAN INTO YESTERDAY? YOU HAVE THREE GUESSES.
WHO?
HA HA HA
ULLI! WAIT!
IT WAS A HORRIBLE SHOCK.
THANK GOD AVI* WAS THERE.
I'M GLAD I RAN INTO YOU.
I STILL HAVE TO TELL YOU HOW SORRY I AM!
*AVI, MY CURRENT LOVER, AN UNCANNILY ATTRACTIVE ARTIST FROM ISRAEL. UNFORTUNATELY HE'LL BE TRAVELLING BACK SOON.

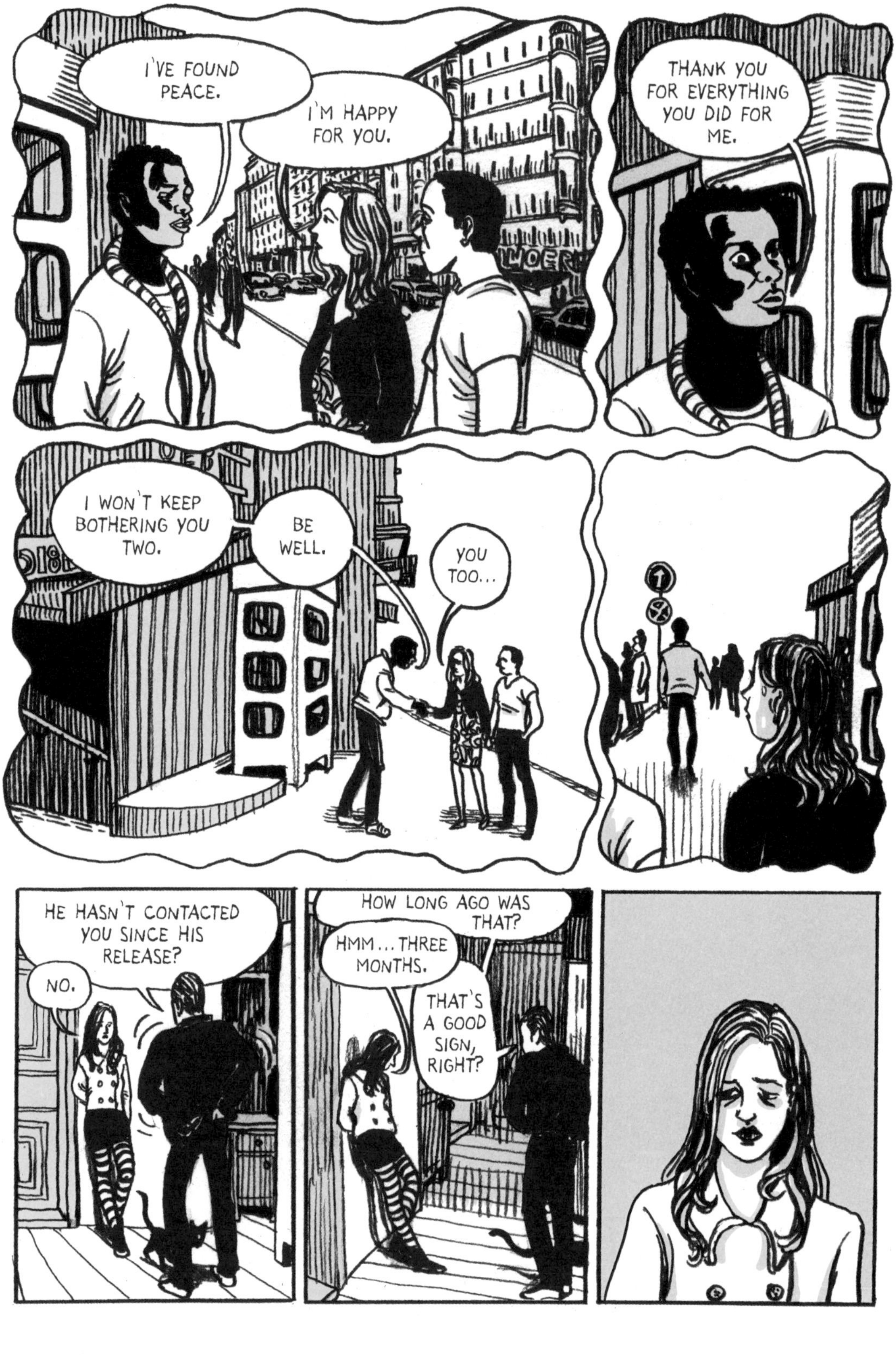
I'VE FOUND PEACE.
I'M HAPPY FOR YOU.
THANK YOU FOR EVERYTHING YOU DID FOR ME.
I WON'T KEEP BOTHERING YOU TWO.
BE WELL.
YOU TOO...
HE HASN'T CONTACTED YOU SINCE HIS RELEASE?
NO.
HOW LONG AGO WAS THAT?
HMM... THREE MONTHS.
THAT'S A GOOD SIGN, RIGHT?

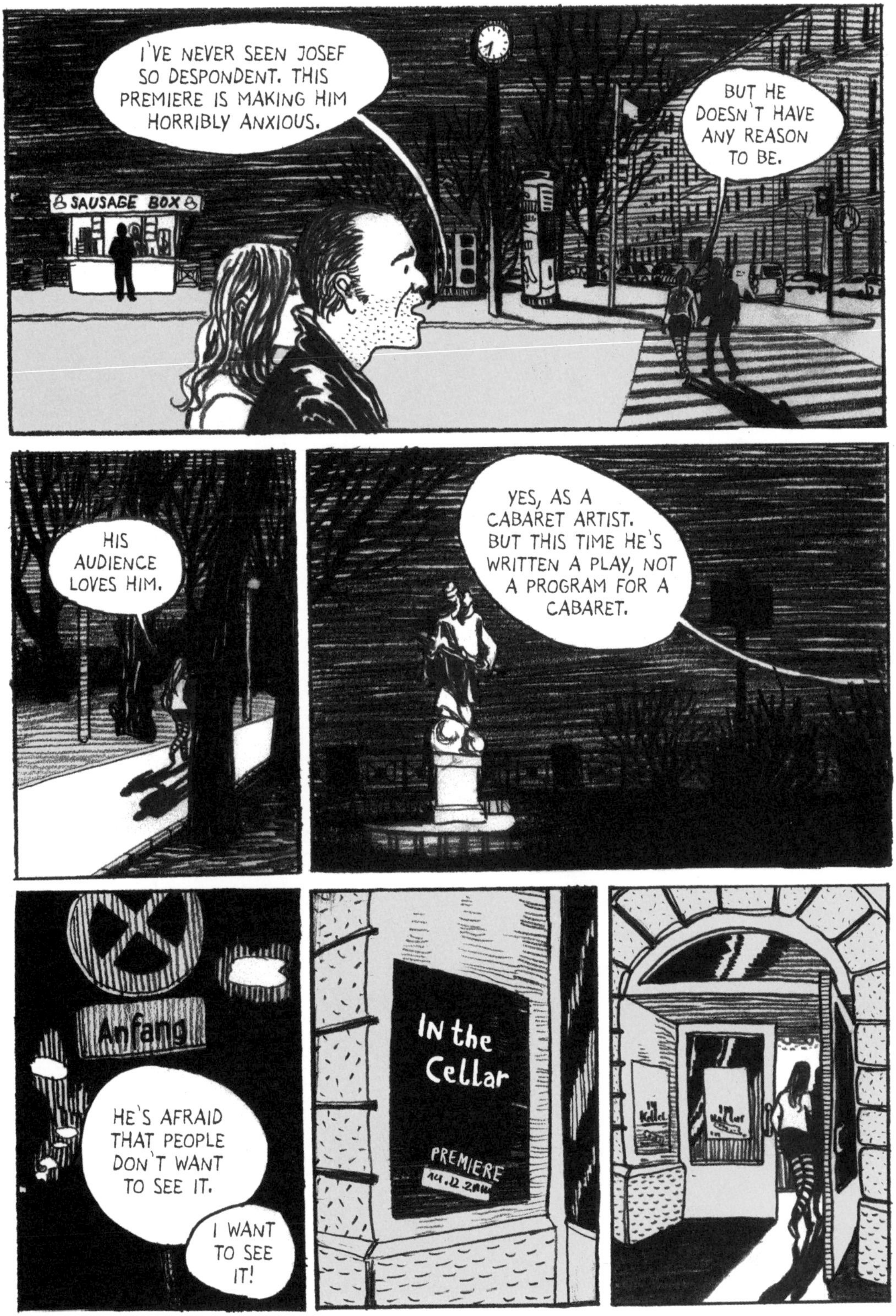
I'VE NEVER SEEN JOSEF SO DESPONDENT. THIS PREMIERE IS MAKING HIM HORRIBLY ANXIOUS.
SAUSAGE BOX
BUT HE DOESN'T HAVE ANY REASON TO BE.
HIS AUDIENCE LOVES HIM.
YES, AS A CABARET ARTIST. BUT THIS TIME HE'S WRITTEN A PLAY, NOT A PROGRAM FOR A CABARET.
Anfang
HE'S AFRAID THAT PEOPLE DON'T WANT TO SEE IT.
I WANT TO SEE IT!
In the Cellar
PREMIERE
14.12.2011

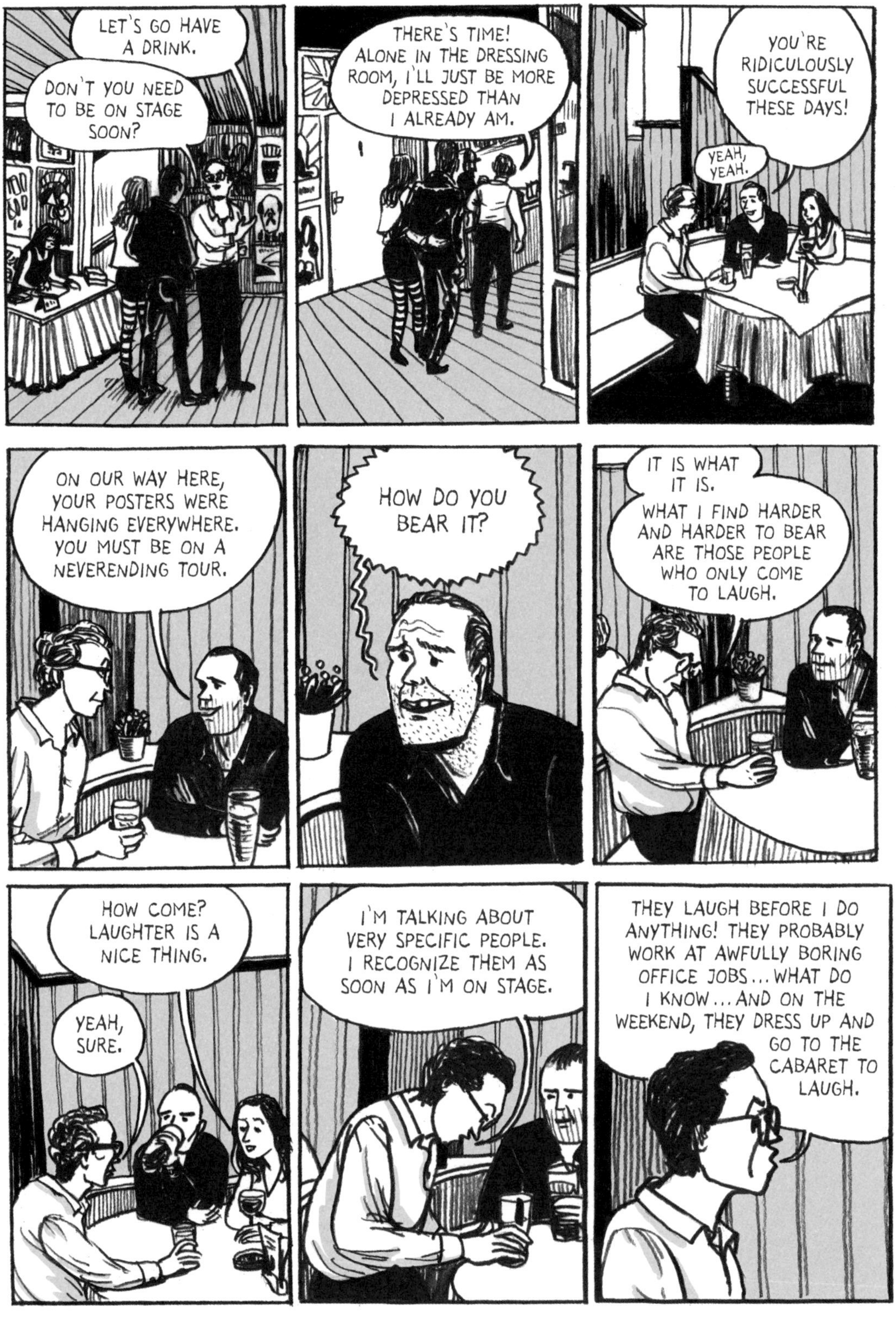
LET'S GO HAVE A DRINK.
DON'T YOU NEED TO BE ON STAGE SOON?
THERE'S TIME! ALONE IN THE DRESSING ROOM, I'LL JUST BE MORE DEPRESSED THAN I ALREADY AM.
YOU'RE RIDICULOUSLY SUCCESSFUL THESE DAYS!
YEAH, YEAH.
ON OUR WAY HERE, YOUR POSTERS WERE HANGING EVERYWHERE. YOU MUST BE ON A NEVERENDING TOUR.
HOW DO YOU BEAR IT?
IT IS WHAT IT IS.
WHAT I FIND HARDER AND HARDER TO BEAR ARE THOSE PEOPLE WHO ONLY COME TO LAUGH.
HOW COME? LAUGHTER IS A NICE THING.
YEAH, SURE.
I'M TALKING ABOUT VERY SPECIFIC PEOPLE. I RECOGNIZE THEM AS SOON AS I'M ON STAGE.
THEY LAUGH BEFORE I DO ANYTHING! THEY PROBABLY WORK AT AWFULLY BORING OFFICE JOBS... WHAT DO I KNOW... AND ON THE WEEKEND, THEY DRESS UP AND GO TO THE CABARET TO LAUGH.

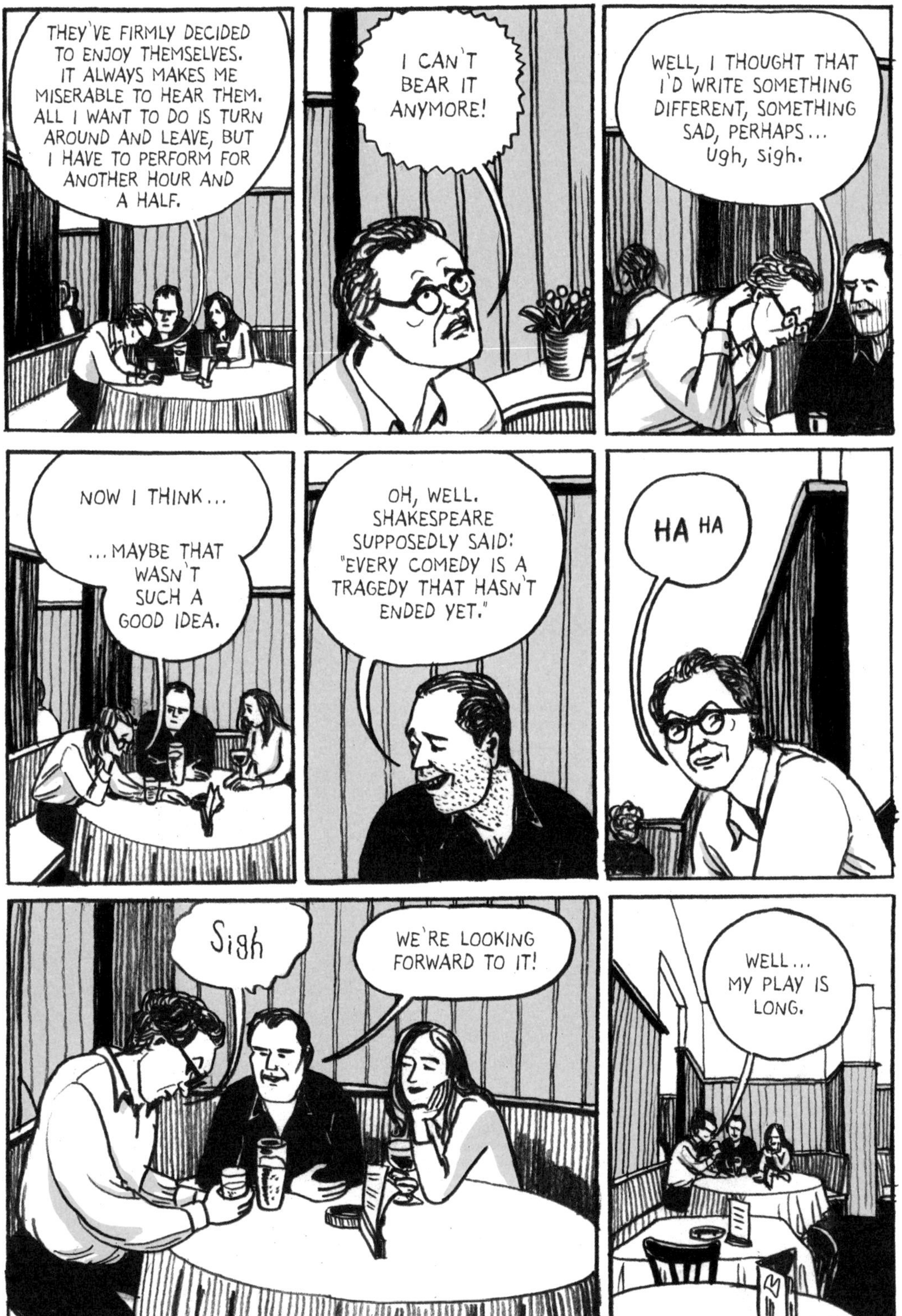
THEY'VE FIRMLY DECIDED TO ENJOY THEMSELVES. IT ALWAYS MAKES ME MISERABLE TO HEAR THEM. ALL I WANT TO DO IS TURN AROUND AND LEAVE, BUT I HAVE TO PERFORM FOR ANOTHER HOUR AND A HALF.
I CAN'T BEAR IT ANYMORE!
WELL, I THOUGHT THAT I'D WRITE SOMETHING DIFFERENT, SOMETHING SAD, PERHAPS... Ugh, sigh.
NOW I THINK...
...MAYBE THAT WASN'T SUCH A GOOD IDEA.
OH, WELL. SHAKESPEARE SUPPOSEDLY SAID: "EVERY COMEDY IS A TRAGEDY THAT HASN'T ENDED YET."
HA HA
Sigh
WE'RE LOOKING FORWARD TO IT!
WELL... MY PLAY IS LONG.

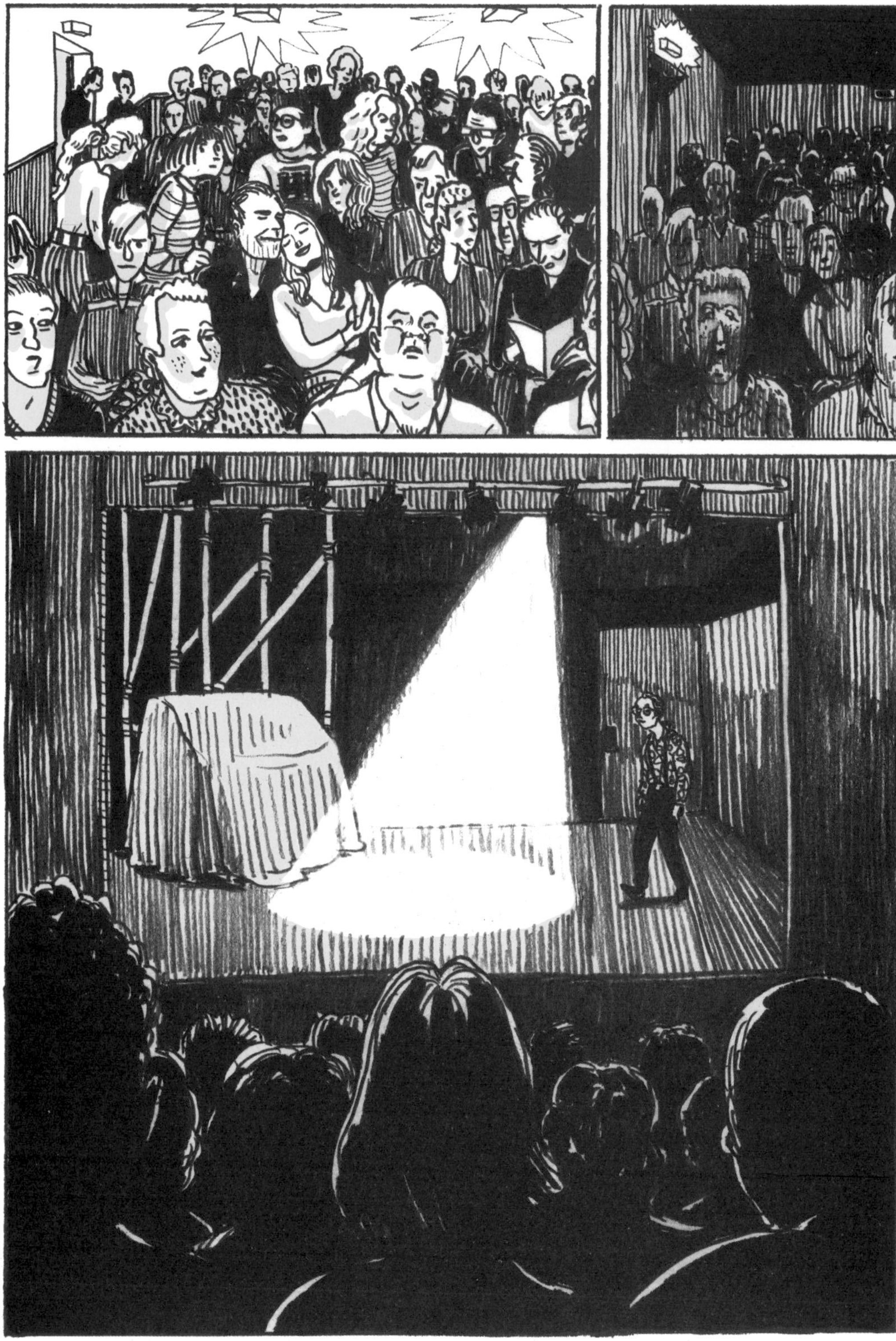

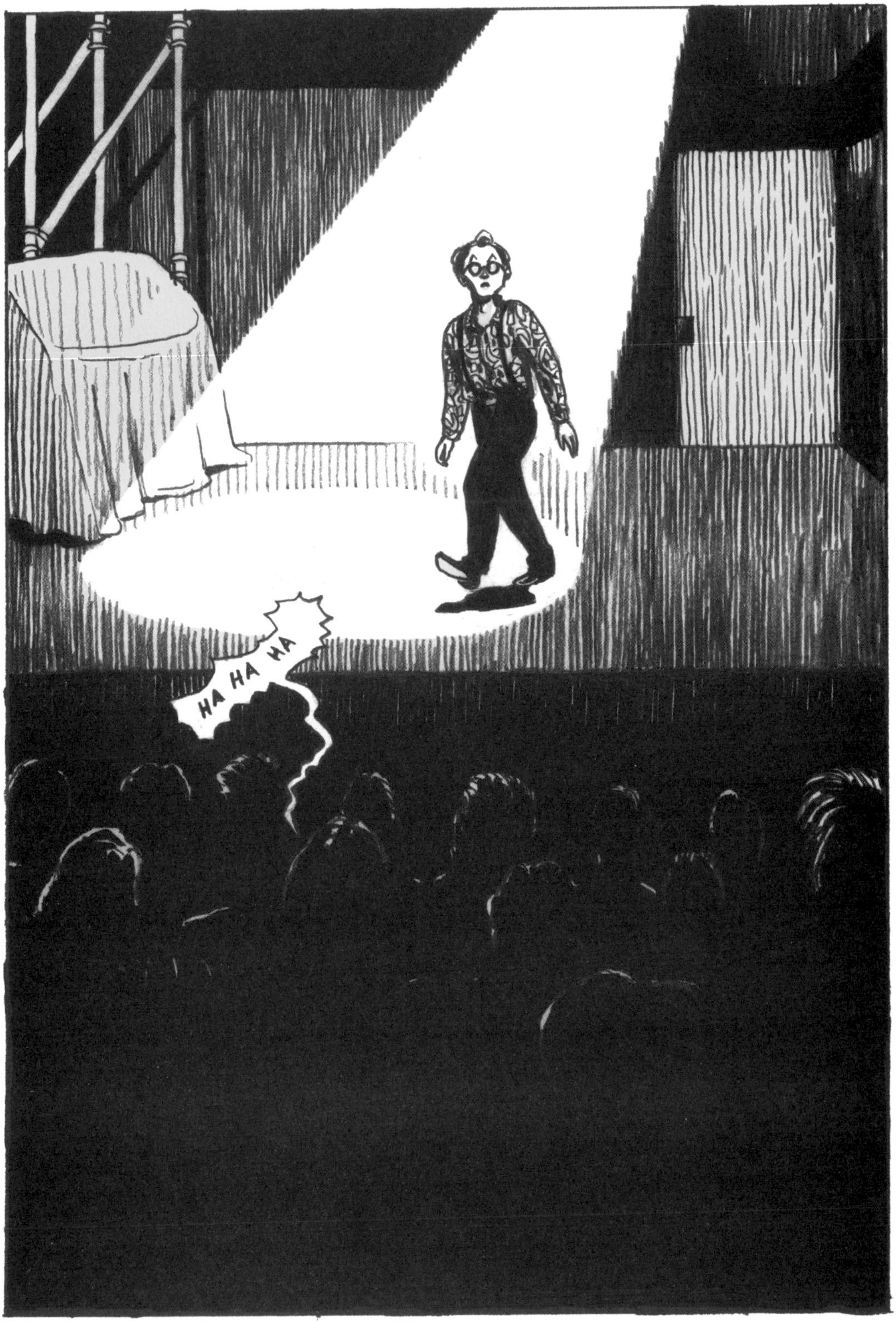
HA HA HA

KIM WAS DEPORTED TO
NIGERIA HALF A YEAR LATER.
WE NEVER SAW EACH OTHER
AGAIN. ONLY SOMETIMES,
IN VERY SPECIFIC MOMENTS,
DO I FEEL HIM.

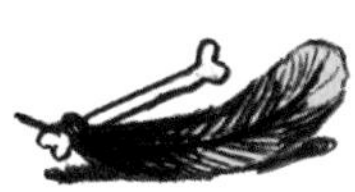

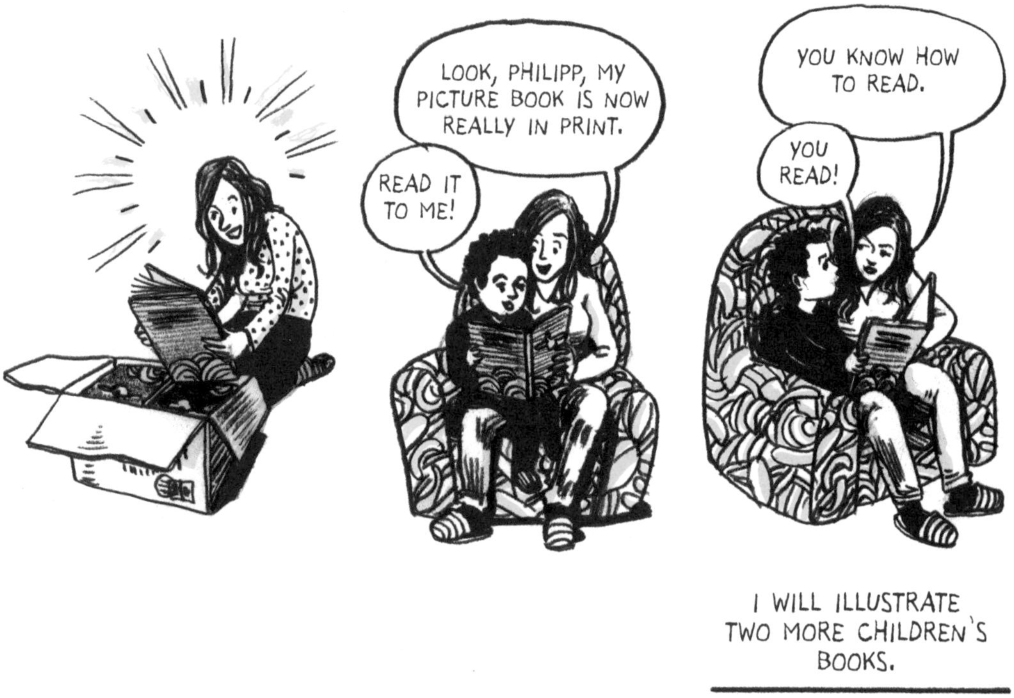
LOOK, PHILIPP, MY PICTURE BOOK IS NOW REALLY IN PRINT.
READ IT TO ME!
YOU READ!
YOU KNOW HOW TO READ.
I WILL ILLUSTRATE TWO MORE CHILDREN'S BOOKS.

GEORG WILL FALL IN LOVE WITH A WOMAN WHO DOESN'T WANT TO SHARE HIM.

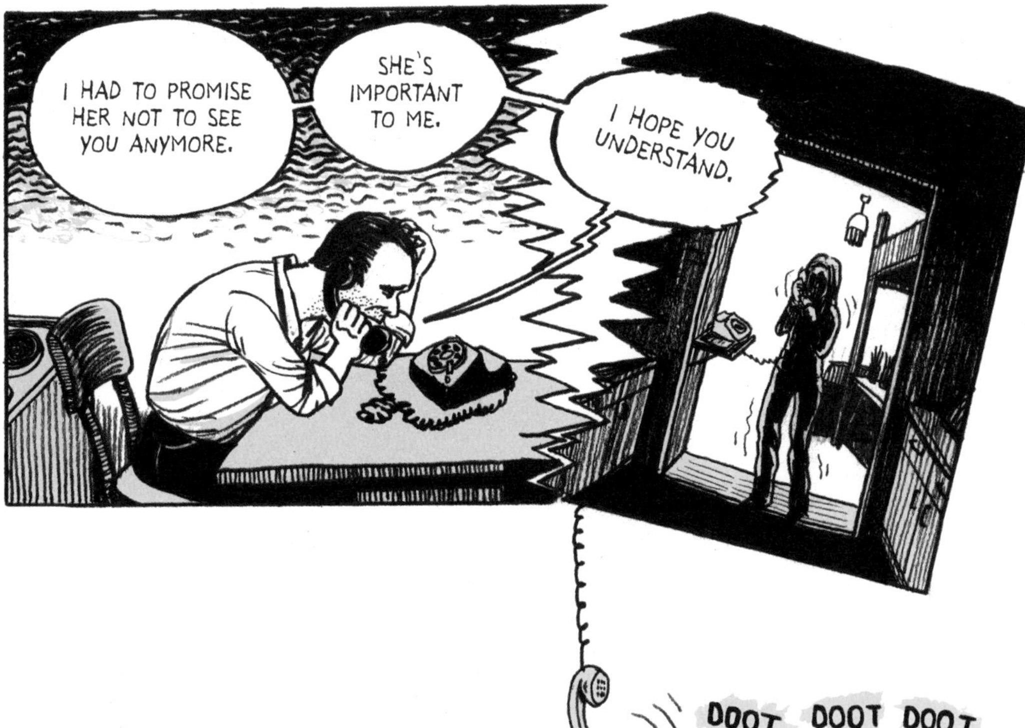
I HAD TO PROMISE HER NOT TO SEE YOU ANYMORE.
SHE'S IMPORTANT TO ME.
I HOPE YOU UNDERSTAND.
DOOT DOOT DOOT

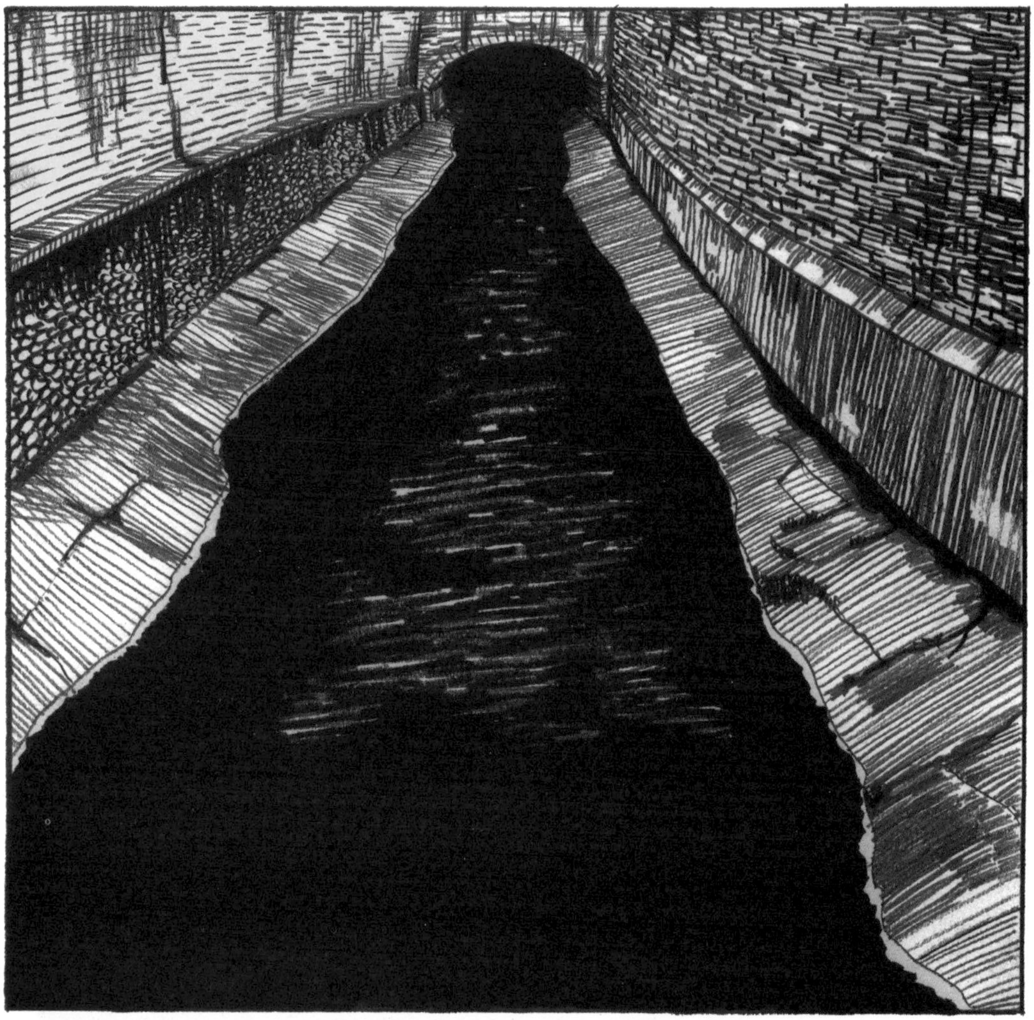

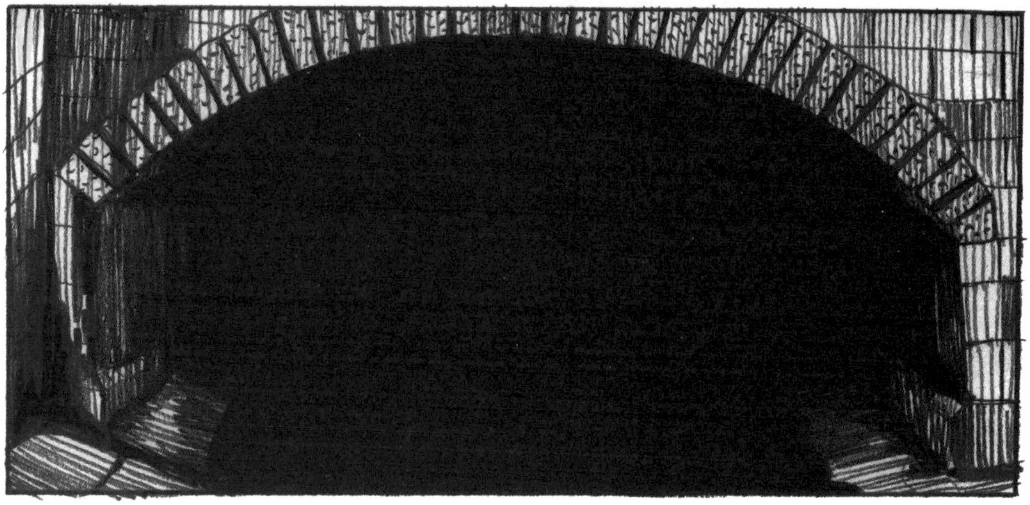

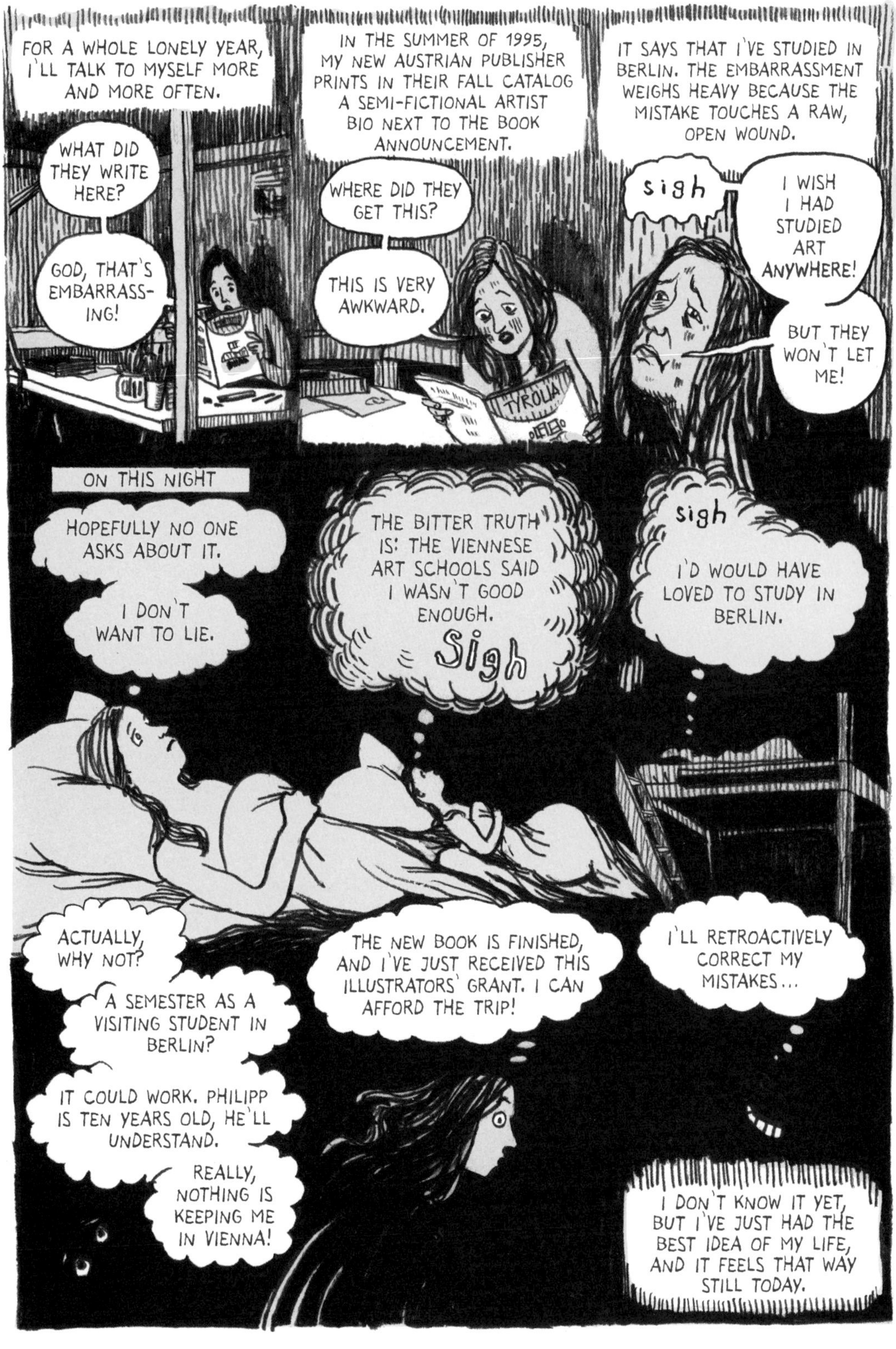

FOR A WHOLE LONELY YEAR, I'LL TALK TO MYSELF MORE AND MORE OFTEN.
WHAT DID THEY WRITE HERE?
GOD, THAT'S EMBARRASS-ING!
IN THE SUMMER OF 1995, MY NEW AUSTRIAN PUBLISHER PRINTS IN THEIR FALL CATALOG A SEMI-FICTIONAL ARTIST BIO NEXT TO THE BOOK ANNOUNCEMENT.
WHERE DID THEY GET THIS?
THIS IS VERY AWKWARD.
TYROLIA
IT SAYS THAT I'VE STUDIED IN BERLIN. THE EMBARRASSMENT WEIGHS HEAVY BECAUSE THE MISTAKE TOUCHES A RAW, OPEN WOUND.
sigh
I WISH I HAD STUDIED ART ANYWHERE!
BUT THEY WON'T LET ME!
ON THIS NIGHT
HOPEFULLY NO ONE ASKS ABOUT IT.
I DON'T WANT TO LIE.
THE BITTER TRUTH IS: THE VIENNESE ART SCHOOLS SAID I WASN'T GOOD ENOUGH.
Sigh
sigh
I'D WOULD HAVE LOVED TO STUDY IN BERLIN.
ACTUALLY, WHY NOT?
A SEMESTER AS A VISITING STUDENT IN BERLIN?
IT COULD WORK. PHILIPP IS TEN YEARS OLD, HE'LL UNDERSTAND.
REALLY, NOTHING IS KEEPING ME IN VIENNA!
THE NEW BOOK IS FINISHED, AND I'VE JUST RECEIVED THIS ILLUSTRATORS' GRANT. I CAN AFFORD THE TRIP!
I'LL RETROACTIVELY CORRECT MY MISTAKES...
I DON'T KNOW IT YET, BUT I'VE JUST HAD THE BEST IDEA OF MY LIFE, AND IT FEELS THAT WAY STILL TODAY.

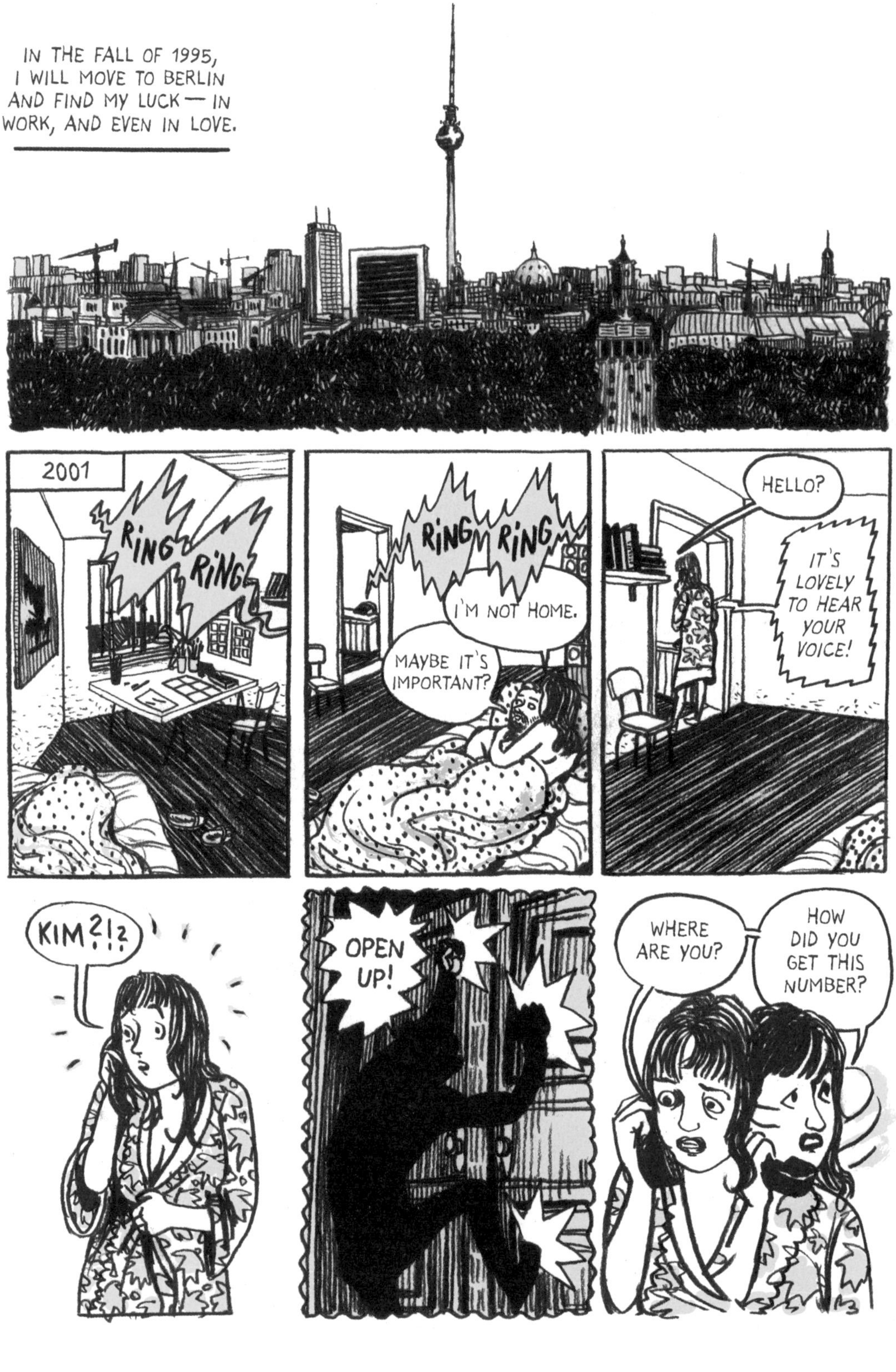
IN THE FALL OF 1995, I WILL MOVE TO BERLIN AND FIND MY LUCK — IN WORK, AND EVEN IN LOVE.
2001
RING RING
RING RING
I'M NOT HOME.
MAYBE IT'S IMPORTANT?
HELLO?
IT'S LOVELY TO HEAR YOUR VOICE!
KIM?!?
OPEN UP!
WHERE ARE YOU?
HOW DID YOU GET THIS NUMBER?

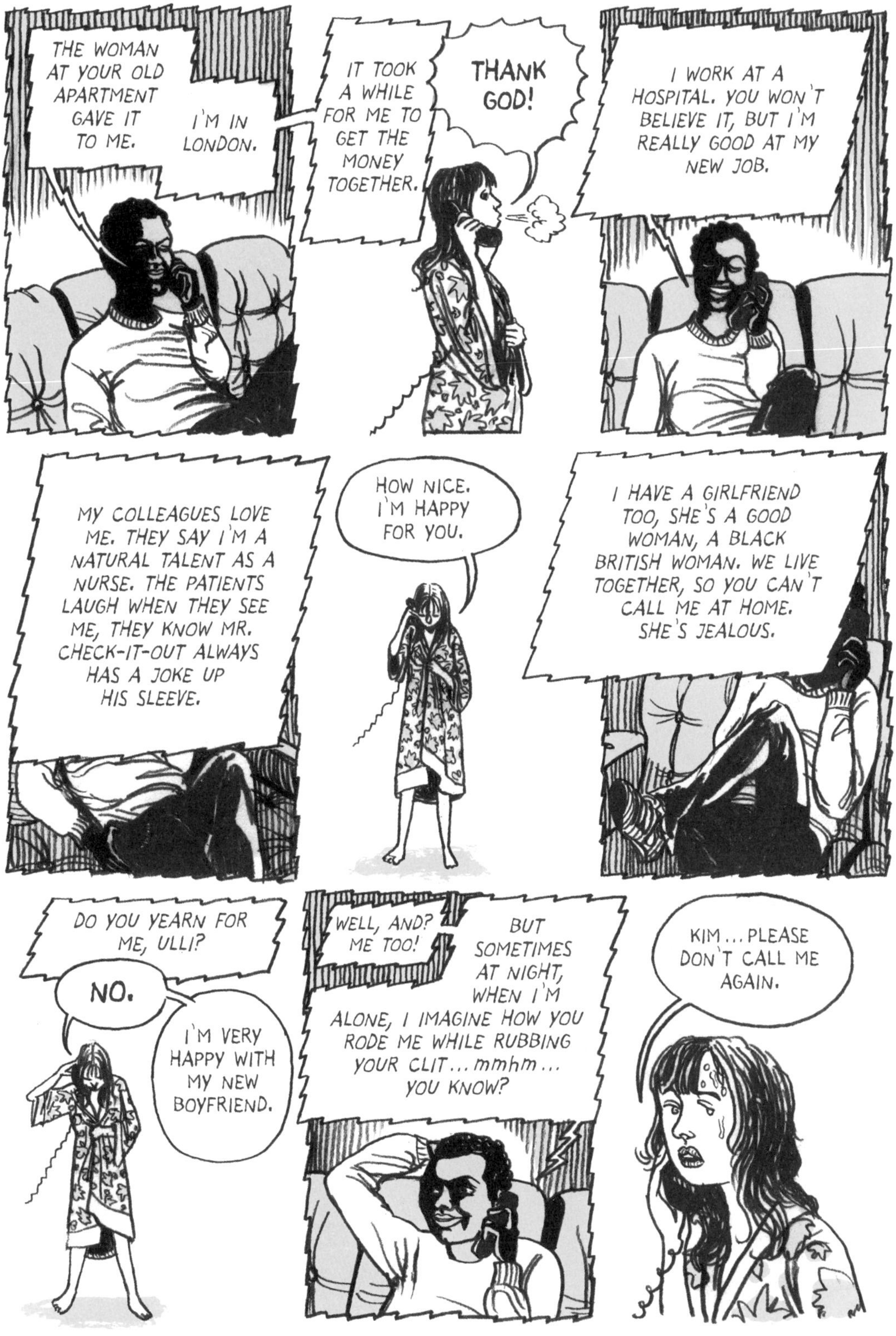
THE WOMAN AT YOUR OLD APARTMENT GAVE IT TO ME.
I'M IN LONDON.
IT TOOK A WHILE FOR ME TO GET THE MONEY TOGETHER.
THANK GOD!
I WORK AT A HOSPITAL. YOU WON'T BELIEVE IT, BUT I'M REALLY GOOD AT MY NEW JOB.
MY COLLEAGUES LOVE ME. THEY SAY I'M A NATURAL TALENT AS A NURSE. THE PATIENTS LAUGH WHEN THEY SEE ME, THEY KNOW MR. CHECK-IT-OUT ALWAYS HAS A JOKE UP HIS SLEEVE.
HOW NICE. I'M HAPPY FOR YOU.
I HAVE A GIRLFRIEND TOO, SHE'S A GOOD WOMAN, A BLACK BRITISH WOMAN. WE LIVE TOGETHER, SO YOU CAN'T CALL ME AT HOME. SHE'S JEALOUS.
DO YOU YEARN FOR ME, ULLI?
NO.
I'M VERY HAPPY WITH MY NEW BOYFRIEND.
WELL, AND? ME TOO!
BUT SOMETIMES AT NIGHT, WHEN I'M ALONE, I IMAGINE HOW YOU RODE ME WHILE RUBBING YOUR CLIT... mmhm... YOU KNOW?
KIM... PLEASE DON'T CALL ME AGAIN.

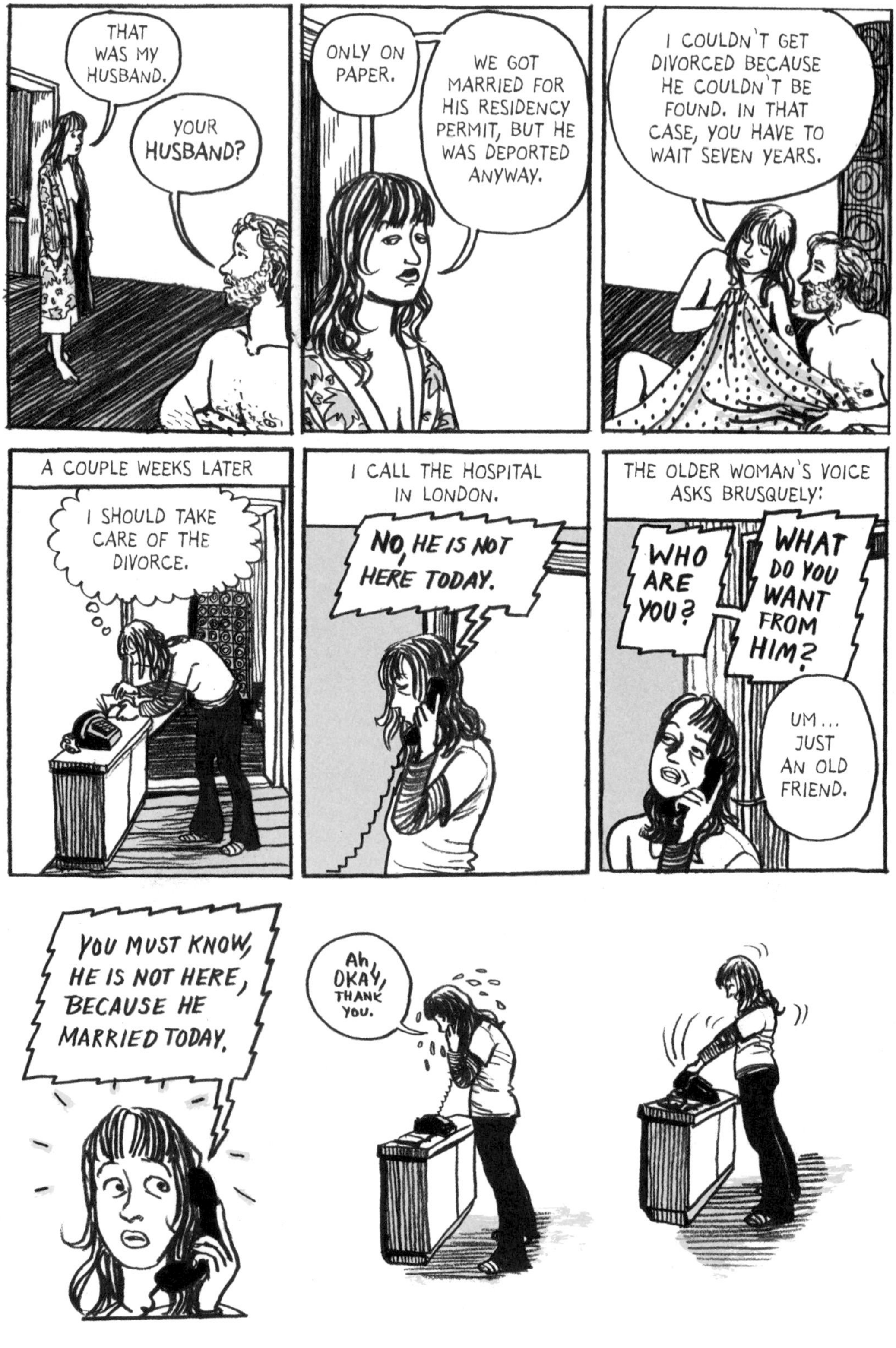
THAT WAS MY HUSBAND.
YOUR HUSBAND?
ONLY ON PAPER.
WE GOT MARRIED FOR HIS RESIDENCY PERMIT, BUT HE WAS DEPORTED ANYWAY.
I COULDN'T GET DIVORCED BECAUSE HE COULDN'T BE FOUND. IN THAT CASE, YOU HAVE TO WAIT SEVEN YEARS.
A COUPLE WEEKS LATER
I SHOULD TAKE CARE OF THE DIVORCE.
I CALL THE HOSPITAL IN LONDON.
NO, HE IS NOT HERE TODAY.
THE OLDER WOMAN'S VOICE ASKS BRUSQUELY:
WHO ARE YOU?
WHAT DO YOU WANT FROM HIM?
UM... JUST AN OLD FRIEND.
YOU MUST KNOW, HE IS NOT HERE, BECAUSE HE MARRIED TODAY.
Ah, OKAY, THANK YOU.

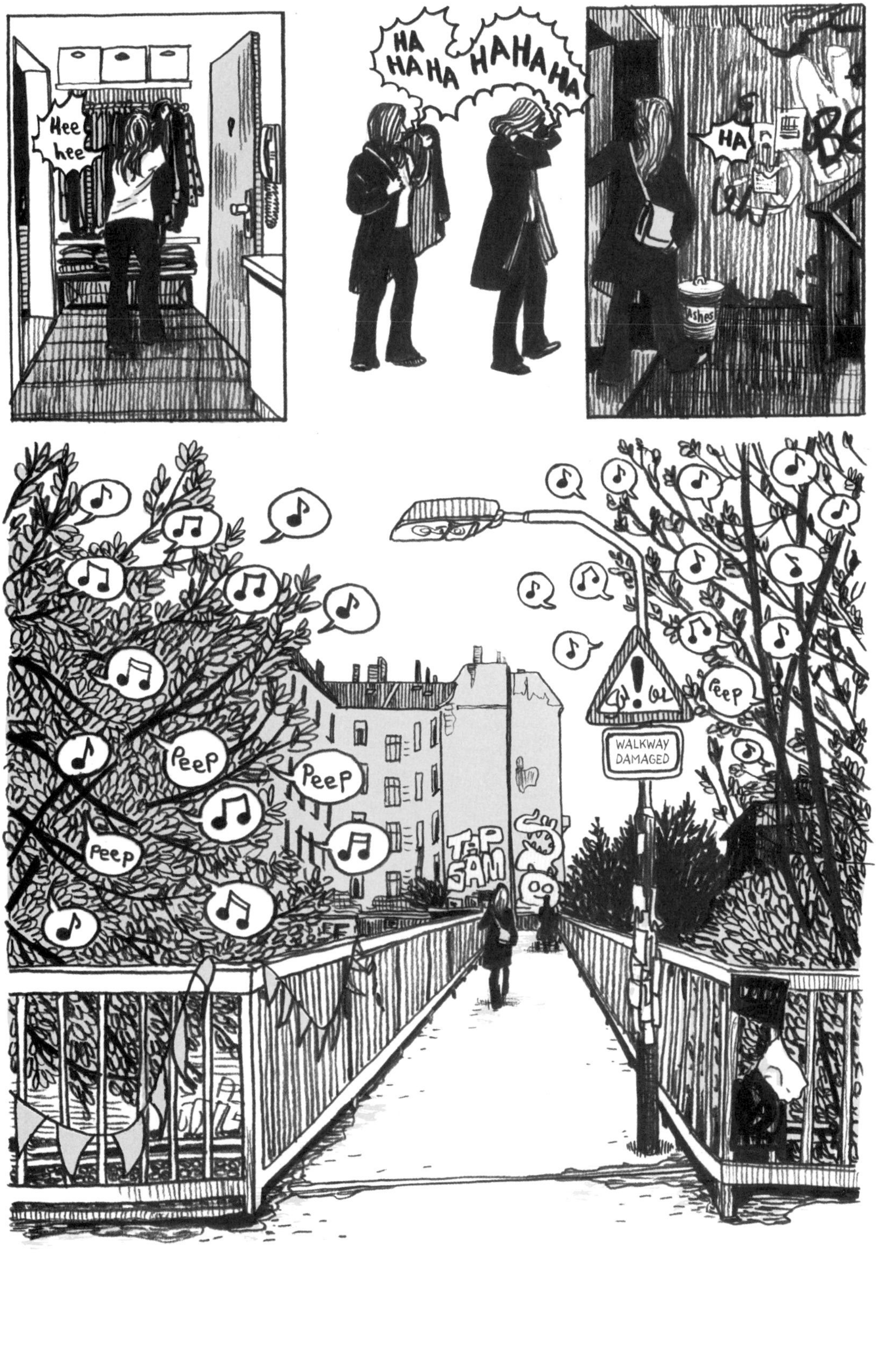
Hee hee
HA HA HA
HAHAHAHA
HA
Ashes
Peep
Peep
Peep
Peep
WALKWAY DAMAGED

FANTAGRAPHICS BOOKS INC.
7563 Lake City Way NE
Seattle, Washington, 98115 USA
www.fantagraphics.com

Translated from German by Nika Knight
Editor and Associate Publisher: Eric Reynolds
Book Design: Keeli McCarthy
Production: Paul Baresh
Editorial assistance: RJ Casey
Publisher: Gary Groth

ISBN 978-1-68396-203-8
Library of Congress Control Number 2018963704

First printing: July 2019
Printed in Korea